Praise for
Public Cowboy No. 1:
The Life and Times of Gene Autry

"A thorough, no-nonsense account of a singular life, and the prolific music writer George-Warren employs a brisk, assured style that hews to the Cowboy Code."—*The Atlantic*

"At last, in the centennial year of Gene's birth, Holly George-Warren gives us *Public Cowboy No. 1*, his first serious, full-length biography. There isn't likely to be another for a long time, so it's fortunate that Ms. George-Warren's is a good one." —*Dallas Morning News*

"The book is well researched and written with a careful eye to history and a keen appreciation of music. And it is—appropriately, I think—tinged with a bit of George-Warren's genuine appreciation of Autry the artist and star but even more of Autry the person, the one she got to know before his death in 1998. Biographers don't always meet their subjects, obviously, and if they do, the results may be disastrous—or beneficial. In George-Warren's case, it proved to be providential."—Country Music Television website (CMT.com)

"Holly George-Warren's meticulously researched, engrossing bio—she had access to Autry's personal papers and interviewed more than 100 of his intimates—takes the larger-than-life Autry down to human level. . . . *Public Cowboy No. 1* will likely stand as the definitive account of his life and work."
—*Harp Magazine*

"*Public Cowboy No. 1* increases our understanding of the American cowboy myth, perpetuated by those movies known as westerns. George-Warren creates a realistic, factual portrait of Autry, the star and the man."—*The Tennessean*

"The definitive portrait of Gene Autry."—*Commercial Appeal*

"An appealing, bittersweet success story."—*Pittsburgh Tribune-Review*

PUBLIC COWBOY no.1

THE LIFE AND TIMES OF GENE AUTRY

HOLLY GEORGE-WARREN

OXFORD

UNIVERSITY PRESS

OXFORD
UNIVERSITY PRESS

Oxford University Press, Inc., publishes works that further
Oxford University's objective of excellence
in research, scholarship, and education.

Oxford   New York
Auckland   Cape Town   Dar es Salaam   Hong Kong   Karachi
Kuala Lumpur   Madrid   Melbourne   Mexico City   Nairobi
New Delhi   Shanghai   Taipei   Toronto

With offices in
Argentina   Austria   Brazil   Chile   Czech Republic   France   Greece
Guatemala   Hungary   Italy   Japan   Poland   Portugal   Singapore
South Korea   Switzerland   Thailand   Turkey   Ukraine   Vietnam

Published by Oxford University Press, Inc.
198 Madison Avenue, New York, NY 10016

www.oup.com

First issued as an Oxford University Press paperback, 2009

Oxford is a registered trademark of Oxford University Press

Library of Congress Cataloging-in-Publication Data
George-Warren, Holly.
Public cowboy no. 1 : the life and times of Gene Autry / Holly George-Warren.
p.   cm.
Filmography: p.
Includes bibliographical references and index.
ISBN 978-0-19-537267-0 (pbk.)
1. Autry, Gene, 1907–1998.
2. Motion picture actors and actresses—United States—Biography.
3. Singers—United States—Biography.   I. Title.
PN2287.A9G46 2007
791.4302'8092—dc22
[B] 2006036369

1 3 5 7 9 8 6 4 2
Printed in the United States of America
on acid-free paper

For Robert and Jack

CONTENTS

PUBLIC COWBOY no. 1

"Me and Gene went everywhere. I was watching front row center every time Gene did anything. Anytime he sang anything. Anytime he rode Champion across the screen, I was right there with him. Me and Gene could do anything—and I think that was the deal. I felt that I could do anything Gene did—sing, ride, play guitar, and fight for the good guys. I was not only lucky enough to meet Gene Autry; we became the best of friends. My son Lucas Autry Nelson will be 18 years old this Christmas, and Gene was one of the first to hold him. Me and Gene were friends."

Willie Nelson
December 2006

INTRODUCTION

IN 1994, JOHNNY CASH, WILLIE NELSON, WAYLON JENNINGS, and Kris Kristofferson spent four days together in a Los Angeles studio making what would be their third and final album as the Highwaymen. Among their repertoire of outlaw songs and road ballads, they launched into an old favorite: Gene Autry's "Back in the Saddle Again." These four icons of country music, born during the Great Depression, had grown up with Gene Autry as their hero. He was their Public Cowboy No. 1. "I saw him in the movies when I was five years old," Johnny Cash wrote in 1977, "and haven't stopped loving him and his kind of movieland dreams. More than that, I took part of Gene Autry home with me in my heart and sang it out in the cotton fields, songs like 'Be Honest With Me,' [and 'The] Last Round-Up' . . ." Serving as a road map out of rural poverty for Cash—and for so many other future artists—Gene Autry shone as the singing cowboy star whose radio programs, recordings, and movies in the 1930s and '40s made him one of America's most celebrated entertainers.

For Highwaymen producer Don Was, a visit one day from eighty-six-year-old Gene Autry to the sessions "was very revealing." Over the course of their careers, according to Was, each of the Highwaymen had "adopted variations on the cowboy persona, and that's the guy they got it from." Captured in a 2006 documentary, *American Revolutions: The Highwaymen*, Cash, Nelson, Jennings, and Kristofferson—then in their fifties and sixties—"turned into little kids," Was related. "It was as if John Lennon came to *my* session. . . . Gene Autry is just sitting there with four of the most intimidating tough guys ever, and they're marshmallows next to him." As children, each of the Highwaymen, like so many others, had gone to Gene Autry movies on Saturday afternoons, listened to his music on the radio, and learned to play guitar on a Gene Autry Roundup Guitar ordered from the Sears catalogue. They, just like millions of other Americans who were born between the 1920s and the 1940s, bought his records and went to see him at rodeos, city auditoriums, and county fairs. Again, in the words of the Man in Black, "Reflecting upon . . . the great people I have known, as an All-American image of goodness, justice, good over bad, nothing or no one comes closer than Gene Autry."

Who was this man that exerted such an influence over Cash, his fellow Highwaymen, and countless others who experienced the Autry phenomenon from the thirties into the fifties? Born Orvon Grover Autry in 1907, he was a second-generation Texan. Both his maternal and paternal grandparents were among the frontierspeople who left the South after the Civil War and traveled west. Gene Autry embraced the tools of the twentieth century to make his way in the world—cutting phonograph records, broadcasting over the radio, appearing in motion pictures and, later, television—yet he found stardom by reinventing the saga of the cowboy and the West through his music and image. Growing up on the final vestiges of nineteenth-century pop culture—minstrel shows, dime novels, and Buffalo Bill's Wild West—he came of age during the heyday of vaudeville, whose stars Al Jolson, Gene Austin, and Will Rogers had profoundly influenced him. Gene Autry merged old sensibilities with new ideas to create a persona that bridged the gap between the two centuries. His ingenuity, ambition, and chameleonic artistry enabled him to develop further by adapting the sonics of yodeling bluesman Jimmie Rodgers and visuals of cowboy star Tom Mix.

As a recording artist, Autry evolved from a hillbilly-style Rodgers soundalike to the trend-setting crooner of cowboy songs to the progenitor of Yuletide perennial "Rudolph the Red-Nosed Reindeer" to children's balladeer. Between 1929 and the early 1960s, he made some 640 recordings, totaling sales of more than 100 million copies. Gene Autry's vocal and visual approach, with his eye-catching Western wear, shaped the sound and look of early country music and helped it grow from a regional favorite to a national sensation. After Autry's musical Westerns began screening in theaters across the country, the companion discs of songs featured in the movies became strong sellers nationwide. Eventually, the label "hillbilly music" was displaced by "country & western."

First finding local fame as the Oklahoma Yodeling Cowboy on Tulsa radio, Autry attracted a larger audience as star of Chicago's WLS *National Barn Dance*. In Hollywood, his singing cowboy character successfully made the transition to film, where Autry and Republic Pictures created the prototype of the musical B-Western genre in the mid-1930s. His reassuring presence and unassuming boyishness provided a salve to audiences struggling with the Great Depression. Beginning with *Tumbling Tumbleweeds* in 1935, Autry's movies reinvigorated the

Western with the addition of his country songcraft to action-packed morality plays. In those simpler times, good versus evil was easily delineated. He nearly always played himself—as Johnny Cash recalled, "a handsome man on a fine stallion, riding the bad trails of this land, righting wrongs, turning good for bad, smiling through with the assurance that justice will prevail."

None of the ninety-three Gene Autry pictures ever rose to the budgetary or artistic levels of a John Ford Western, yet he was more popular than John Wayne for nearly a decade. Voted the top Western star for six years straight, Autry was named the fourth most popular of all box-office stars in America by exhibitors in 1940. His movies played in every small town in the country, and he relentlessly toured the nation throughout the thirties, forties, and fifties. His Gene Autry Flying A Rodeo imbued the sport with glamour, giving it an enduring appeal and spreading its popularity eastward. His status as an entertainer brought him into the political sphere as early as the mid-1930s. He became the friend of several U.S. presidents—from Franklin Roosevelt and Lyndon Johnson to Richard Nixon and Ronald Reagan. Even John F. Kennedy invited him to the White House for "an exchange of ideas."

In 1950 Autry was the first movie star to create his own production company and play the lead in a television series, followed by a line of TV programming, including *The Range Rider*, *Death Valley Days*, and *Annie Oakley*—the first TV Western to star a woman. Following the trail blazed by his successful programs, Westerns came to monopolize the small screen in the 1950s and '60s. As a merchandising entrepreneur, he was one of the first cowboy icons to license his name and image to hundreds of products, beginning in the 1930s. During the cowboy craze of the 1950s, Autry-licensed goods ranged from comic books to bedspreads to breakfast cereal.

After Autry enlisted and served in World War II, he began to focus more on business investments and undertook a series of shrewd purchases of radio stations. By the time he retired as an entertainer in the early 1960s, his broadcast holdings had increased to include television. In 1992 he was the only entertainer-turned-businessman listed on the *Forbes 400*. The same drive and ambition that took him out of small-town Texas and Oklahoma motivated his business dealings. His final decades were spent devoted to a lifelong passion—owner of the American League baseball team the California Angels.

THE CHILD OF AN IMPOVERISHED FAMILY with an absentee father, Gene Autry consistently sought out father figures—including Jimmy Long (co-writer of his first hit), Johnny Marvin (a pop singer who helped him get his first break), and Columbia Records A&R man Art Satherley, a seminal figure in recording history. As Public Cowboy No. 1, Autry became a father figure himself to millions of children. Autry never forgot his early mentors or his loyal employees, providing many of them with lifelong jobs and/or financial aid. He in turn served as mentor to the next generation of artists, encouraging and supporting

Johnny Cash, Willie Nelson, and others who followed. Autry's audiences were black and white, male and female. His most celebrated acolytes range from Ringo Starr to Solomon Burke, Aaron Neville to James Taylor. Taylor told audiences during his 2006 tour that the inspiration behind his first hit, "Sweet Baby James," was to write a cowboy lullaby like the ones he'd heard Gene Autry sing in movies when he was a boy. Taylor's audience, though, was part of a new generation, born in the fifties and sixties, who had found other icons to worship: Elvis, Bob Dylan, and the Beatles—all with their own cowboy dreams. "I was eight years old and wanted to be a cowboy when I saw a Gene Autry movie," Ringo Starr once confessed. "I still do." Instead, Ringo and his peers became harbingers of change.

Public Cowboy No. 1 explores the world of Gene Autry, beginning with his family's nineteenth-century roots until the demise of his reign as an entertainer. The 1960s marked the end of an era—when a generation turned away from decades of infatuation with the cowboy. *Public Cowboy No. 1* is also the portrait of a man who had his darker sides, but whose legacy is as Johnny Cash once remembered it: "He made the world look better to me."

1

THE AUTRYS AND THE OZMENTS

GENE AUTRY NEVER TOOK AN INTEREST IN GENEALOGY. Being a very rich, famous man, he heard from numerous distant cousins eager to learn if he was blood kin. Gene shunned almost all of them. He chose to focus on the positive and avoid painful subjects, so family history was off limits. It brought back too many troubling memories of a childhood he wanted to forget. Before he left home at seventeen to make his way in the world, he had heard enough tragic tales to last a lifetime. Yet, Gene had much in common with his ancestors: he kept moving, he took risks, he followed his convictions. He came from a long line of traveling men and suffering women.

The first Autrys in America probably originated in France. Autry/Autrey, deriving from the French word *autre*, or "other," has twenty-seven different spelling variations in current use. Most likely, some Autrys immigrated from France to England and Ireland following the Norman Conquest of 1066. In the sixteenth century, an Autry sailed to America. According to "The Voyage Made by Sir Richard Greenville for Sir Walter Raleigh to Virginia in the Year 1585," a log detailing the seven-ship fleet's journey, "The 6th [of July], Master John Arundall was sent to the main and Manteo, with him . . . Captain Autry and Captain Boniton the same day were sent to Croatoan."[1]

Gene Autry's traceable descendents on his father's side begin with Cornelius Autry, who in 1740 settled in North Carolina, alongside Autry's Creek in Edgecombe County. A prosperous planter, Cornelius had eleven children, including James, who homesteaded in Tennessee. One of James's three children, William, married a local girl, Mary Campbell, and their son, Elijah

Henry, was Gene Autry's great-grandfather.[2] A handsome young man, Elijah was about 5' 10", with thick black hair, blue eyes, and a fair complexion. At nineteen, he married Mary "Polly" Parish.

The couple moved to Henderson County, between Nashville and Memphis. There, in 1836, Elijah, a wheelwright by trade, joined the Hopewell Baptist Church. Two years later, he was baptized and with other members of the flock organized a new church at Mount Comfort, in nearby Carroll County. Ordained in May 1840, Elijah began preaching the gospel in a building constructed of hand-hewn logs near the banks of Maple Creek. Over the years, he moved on to several small Baptist churches in the county, eventually becoming one of the region's leading Missionary Baptist pastors. In 1852, Elijah founded the Oak Grove Church, described by a parishioner as a "shelter with a dirt floor . . . covered with wheat straw. . . . Later a log house was built with a wood floor but the practice continued of putting clean wheat straw on the floor. . . . The young children were placed on quilts to sleep through the church services. In the early days, the roads were all dirt; many people walked carrying their shoes until they got in sight of the church before putting them on. Wagons and buggies driven by teams of horses and mules brought many families."[3]

Elijah was elected and served as Moderator of the Baptist Convention in his region from 1846 to 1854. In a history of Carroll County's Baptist churches, Elijah was described in depth by Elder J. P. Arnold:

> Elder Autry had only a common English education, such as could be procured in the common district school in his day. Yet, by untiring energy and industry, he acquired a very fair knowledge of the Scriptures, and was a sound Bible teacher and successful preacher. . . . Though he was compelled to work for the support of his large family, for he had twelve children, eight boys and four girls—boys all died but three, three girls living—[he spent] a large part of his time . . . preaching and building up the Redeemer's cause . . . [He] possessed of untiring energy and indomitable courage in prosecuting any enterprise that he might be engaged in, whether secular or religious, consequently he succeeded in winning many souls to Christ. . . . Our dear brother had but few enemies, though he had some, and why? Because his holy walk reproved their wicked ways.[4]

The youngest son among Elijah and Polly's offspring, Elijah William would become Gene Autry's grandfather. Born in Carroll County on December 16, 1848, he was nine years old when tragedy struck the family. On September 22, 1858, Elijah Sr. returned home after days of conducting a lengthy revival at Oak Grove Church. When he arrived at the farm, he discovered loose cattle trampling his crops. His nephew offered him a small derringer pistol to scare away the livestock. Elijah didn't want the gun, but his nephew, thinking he might need it, slipped it into his uncle's pocket. Out in the fields, Elijah noticed something in his pocket, and as he tried to get it out, the gun fired, lodging a bullet in his side. Only forty-seven years old, he died the next day. He left a forty-six-year-old wife and six children ranging in age from twenty-one to six. Elder Arnold recorded that, "Elder Autry belonged to the order of Free Masons, and was buried with Masonic honors by the order of which he had long been a worthy and consistent member."[5] His great-grandson would follow in his footsteps by becoming a Mason at age twenty-one.

"In his death, the church and community, as well as the fraternity, sustained a heavy loss," Elder Arnold reported. "His funeral . . . was attended by a very large procession. The death of E. Autry not only cast a gloom over his friends and family, but over the entire community, and especially in the association where he was so generally known and beloved."[6] Elijah left a will stating, "I want Polly to have the home tract of land for her lifetime and what the law allows her. She will need it to raise the children on. The balance of my property I want sold and equally divided."[7]

Unable to shake a severe depression, Polly died two years later.[8] Elijah's namesake, Elijah William, was eleven. He would inherit not only his father's religious calling but his good looks as well. Slightly built with pronounced cheekbones, wide-set eyes, and an impressive forehead, E. W. (as he liked to be called) also had a thick head of black hair and eventually grew a bushy mustache to complement it. On November 29, 1868, at the age of nineteen, E. W. married seventeen-year-old Mary Elizabeth "Betty" McCauley, a sturdy young woman with a broad face and deep-set eyes, one of fourteen children.[9] Betty's parents were Calvin J. and Louisa McCauley; after Calvin's death, Louisa married E. W.'s uncle Claiborne Parish, deepening family ties.

E. W. and Betty had their first two children in Tennessee. Then, like his father, E. W. took up the ministry, and with his young family journeyed west to Cooke County, Texas. About 1882, they settled in the densely wooded area known as Cross Timbers. A narrow hilly belt of oak forest dissecting vast prairies, Cross Timbers stretched from the Red River southward across North Texas. One nineteenth-century observer described the ten-mile-wide stretch of Cross Timbers as "an immense natural hedge," comprised of small post oaks and blackjack oaks.[10]

Thirty miles north, the Red River separated Texas from Indian Territory (populated by Cherokees who had survived the Trail of Tears). Cross Timbers first became settled in the early 1840s, after the construction of Fort Fitzhugh. There, in 1847, a raucous Fourth of July party attracted residents of Cooke, Grayson, Collin, and Denton Counties. Fort records stated that revelers feasted on barbecued mutton, beef, and pork, and then "danced all day and all night" to such fiddle tunes as "Injun Eat the Woodchuck," "Leather Breeches," and "Drunken Hiccups."

E. W. heeded the call at the Missionary Baptist Church, founded in 1855, in a section of Cross Timbers known as Indian Creek and populated by wild turkeys and deer. In rural Cooke County, E.W. became the congregation's sixth pastor in 1884. He preached against drunkenness and other sins in the newly constructed frame chapel on two donated acres. E. W. and Betty Autry could have populated a country church with their brood alone. In 1894 Betty gave birth to her thirteenth child, Homer Ezra, when she was forty-five years old. (One more baby would follow and die as an infant.) She had her first, Elijah Calvin, or Cal, at the age of twenty, in 1869. In between, there was Felix "Fee" Martin (1871), Elizabeth "Luda" Velulah (1873), Martha (1874), William "Will" Franklin (1876), Louise "Lula" Tryphenia (1878), Thomas "Tom" Leander (1880), Johnny Joseph (1882), Minnie Elizabeth (1883), Delbert (1886), Meda (1888), and Nora Belle (1891). Her second to youngest son, Delbert, born June 15, 1886, was the future father of Orvon Grover Autry, later known to the world as Gene Autry.

THE HISTORY OF GENE'S MATERNAL FAMILY, the Ozments, has not been as well documented. The direct lineage begins with John Jasper Ozment, born of English and French descent around 1798 in North Carolina. John Jasper was a handsome man, with a chiseled face, deep-set eyes, and thick wavy brown hair. In 1832 he married Isabelle Murchison, with whom he had two children. It is unknown what happened to Isabelle, but four years later, in Tennessee, John Jasper married Anna Mae Morgan (part Cherokee Indian), who bore three sons. The family moved south to Lafayette County, Mississippi, where Anna Mae died in 1843 while giving birth to her fourth child, Andrew Clinton, Gene's maternal grandfather. John Jasper then married his dead wife's sister, Margaret Elizabeth Morgan, with whom he had four more children. A teamster by trade, John Jasper hauled supplies from Louisiana to Texas.[11]

In the 1860s the Ozments moved to Cooke County, Texas. There, Andrew "Andy" Clinton Ozment, at twenty-six, wed a teenaged farm girl, Margaret Malinda Pierce, on January 14, 1869. She was the daughter of Irish immigrants who had traveled to the area from Jefferson City, Missouri.[12] After Andy and Malinda's marriage, he pursued his father's trade as a teamster, hauling supplies and cotton for a growing number of farmers; by 1870, Cooke County's population was 5,315. Andy and his brothers Mack, William, James, Robert, and David farmed adjacent properties, where they also raised livestock.[13] Andy and Malinda began their family right away. Their first child Martha Louisa ("Lulu") was born in 1869, followed by Mary, Isabelle ("Belle"), Elizabeth ("Sweet"), Robert MacIntosh ("Bob"), and Elnora—Gene Autry's mother—born on November 23, 1882.[14] By 1880 Andy's farm was prospering to the extent that he'd stopped carting goods for other farmers.[15] That year Malinda's father, Wesley Pierce, died, and she inherited a share of his thousand acres of land, extending the couple's grazing area for livestock.

Trail drives traditionally came through Cooke County en route to the depot in Kansas, but as the railroad moved farther west, drives were shortened. Large ranches sprang up in Cooke County, and by 1879 cowboys drove cattle to the county seat of Gainesville and its brand-new Denison and Pacific Railroad terminal. By the early 1880s Gainesville, with a population of 2,667, had become a bona fide cow town. Though not as lively as Abilene, it did boast twenty-six saloons. The number of Cooke County residents—primarily ranchers and farmers—had almost quadrupled to 20,391. Near Andy and Malinda's spread, Burns City was founded in 1881, originally as a health resort named after one George Burns, who discovered mineral springs on his property.[16]

On November 1, 1883, forty-year-old Andy Ozment drove a herd of cattle from his ranch across Wolf Creek and into Gainesville. That night, Malinda had a terrible dream: her husband was attacked and knocked from his horse, then, with his leg caught in the saddle's narrow stirrup, dragged to death. She awoke sweating and filled with dread. She calmed herself, though, remembering, "He doesn't have a narrow-stirrup saddle. I have nothing to worry about." Early the next morning, when she heard someone pounding at the door, she knew immediately something horrible had happened. Her nightmare had come true: "We found your husband's body," men from town told her when she answered the door. As Malinda's dream had forecast, Andy Ozment had been jumped, beaten over the head, then dragged to death, his boot caught in the narrow stirrup. As the story unfolded, it was discovered that after the cattle transaction, Andy had bought himself the new saddle.[17] Around dusk, he lit out for home and along the way was ambushed by unknown assailants, who attacked and robbed him. No arrests were made, but Andy's brothers suspected the culprits to be members of a prosperous family, who prevented the case from being investigated. Andy was buried in Burns City's Ozment Cemetery.

What happened next depends on who tells the story. According to some descendents, thirty-three-year-old Malinda was so distraught over her husband's murder, she had a "nervous breakdown." She galloped on horseback to her brother-in-law Robert Ozment's farm, with one-year-old Elnora under her arm. There, she dumped the crying child onto the ground, abandoning her to Robert and his Irish wife, Caroline Ellen. Elnora's older siblings were likewise dispensed among various relatives.

Elnora grew up in Robert Ozment's large two-story home near Burns City and bonded with her uncle and his wife, a good-natured woman who enjoyed jokes and music. A somber little girl, Elnora, too, found joy in music and learned to play the family's organ. She sang beautifully and accompanied herself on guitar. When Elnora was seventeen, her mother sent for her.[18] Robert escorted his niece to the Choctaw reservation in Indian Territory, where, in 1885, Malinda had remarried a widower, Mathias Reynolds, whose grandfather was one half Native American. Also residing at the Reynolds farm, located in what would become Bryan County, Oklahoma, were Elnora's sister Sweet, her brother Bob, and her sister Belle, Belle's husband William Bacon, and their young son Clinton. Elnora was no longer the youngest of Malinda's children; with Reynolds, she'd had a son named Grover in 1889. Elnora doted on her half-brother and helped around the house with the cooking and sewing skills she'd acquired at her aunt and uncle's home.

Resembling her grandfather John Jasper Ozment, Elnora was a delicate beauty, with blue eyes, long dark hair, and fine bone structure. She was a petite teenager, about 5'4" and thin. One great-niece, Phyllis Engstrom, who as a child knew Elnora, remembered her as "very affectionate with gorgeous eyes. Mother [Elnora's niece] said when Aunt Nora was young, she was very popular and had lots of beaux."[19] One of them was a young man whose name was E. A. Badgett. Soon after meeting, the pair eloped on October 17, 1903, to Denison, Texas. They set up housekeeping in Indian territory, near Colbert. In a nightmarish replay of her mother's experience, Nora's marriage ended abruptly. Around 1904, about a year after the couple's marriage, Badgett traveled to Gainesville, Texas, with a sizable cotton crop for delivery to the cotton gin. Elnora's young husband never returned home. Though presumed dead, his body, wagon, and horses were never found. Elnora was devastated.

Sometime during her period of mourning—no one is quite sure where or how—Nora Ozment Badgett met Delbert Autry.

2

CROSS TIMBERS

THE MISSIONARY BAPTIST CHURCH ANCHORED the tiny farming community of Indian Creek. There, every Sunday, E. W. Autry's fire-and-brimstone preaching terrified and elated a congregation of so-called hard shell Baptists—who got their name for sitting two hours or more on uncomfortable wooden benches. The adjacent Indian Creek Cemetery's earthen surface was kept plowed to prevent timber fires from sweeping through and engulfing the sanctuary.[1] During the blistering summer months, E. W. conducted well-attended outdoor services known as "brush arbor revivals."

A formal Autry family portrait, taken about 1899, depicts the well-dressed E. W. and Betty surrounded by their eleven surviving children, all attired in Sunday finery. With wide-set eyes, a chiseled face, and protruding ears, the gaunt thirteen-year-old Delbert resembled his father and his eldest brother Calvin, seventeen years older than he. The industrious Calvin had learned well his father's lessons of hard work and clean living, and did the lion's share of cattle raising and cotton production on the Autry farm.

The restless Delbert, on the other hand, did not take the Ten Commandments to heart. While Cal turned E. W.'s land into a prosperous homestead, Delbert lollygagged about, sampling local homebrew. His misadventures often ended badly. On one occasion, after a local dance, riding a paint pony, he tried to cause trouble for a wagon full of fellow partygoers heading home. A local man, Ross Estes, later recalled the incident: "Delbert got to ridin' around and around the wagon tryin' to make the mules run away. They was a girl in the wagon he wanted to go with, and she wouldn't go with him. So he went around the wagon several times, and I told him if he didn't stop, I was goin' to get out and take care of him. . . . We went on a little piece further, and he run the pony around the wagon again. And when he got to the back of the wagon, he jerked a gun out of his belt and was going to shoot to scare the mules, but the gun went off and he shot his pony between the ears and killed it. He got up and began to beg us to stop and help him. We just rode off and left him up there in the road with his dead horse and saddle. He hollered for us to come back. I told him to go the devil."[2]

The mischievous youth found any excuse to escape his share of chores, and began disappearing on mysterious journeys by the time he reached manhood. Meanwhile, E. W.'s other four sons—Tom, Will, Fee, and Homer—and seven daughters were more like Cal, following the straight and narrow. Gerald Autry, the grandson of Delbert's brother Will, heard family stories from his father about Delbert's wicked ways. "He was just an outlaw," according to Gerald.

> Dad said that when they all lived down at Indian Creek, his mother looked out the kitchen window early one morning and saw something moving around in the wagon. It was Delbert. He had come up through the timber the night before and had got into some kind of trouble. The law was looking for him, so he was hiding. And Daddy said his mother told him, "You get rid of him! I don't want him around my kids—he's in trouble." Another time, Delbert came running up through the timber, and his clothes were all tore up from running through the brush. He came inside and joined them at the dinner table, then they heard a car coming—back then the only one down there that had a car was the law. Delbert jumped up from the table, run out the back door through the timber, and in a few minutes the law came in looking for him. Everybody said it about Delbert—he was a rascal, a rounder.[3]

While still in his teens, Delbert began collecting wives. At seventeen, he married for the first time—to Margaret "Maggie" Patterson, who died not long after giving birth to the couple's son, Roy Wall, born on November 8, 1904.[4] A few months later, on March 21, 1905, Delbert tied the knot again, this time with Myrtle Mae Gilbert. The newlyweds settled in the Burton community, near Indian Creek. Ten months after the Cooke County Justice of the Peace officiated the ceremony, the Autrys had a daughter, Bessie, born January 8, 1906. During the baby's infancy, Myrtle filed for divorce. Mother and daughter moved to Indiana to start a new life.[5]

Soon after his divorce, Delbert met the newly widowed Elnora Ozment Badget. He was a slightly built nineteen-year-old with no visible means of support, and she was a twenty-three-year-old widow who possibly collected funds following the sale of her dead husband's property. Mrs. Nora Badget and Delbert Autry, as the couple was listed on their marriage license, wed in Cooke County on November 18, 1906.

By the time she became Delbert's third wife, Nora had already suffered a lifetime of sorrow and hardship. One cousin described her as "a sweet lady who was loving and understanding, but there was a loneliness about her." A 1904 photograph of the solemn young beauty shows a stylishly garbed woman with a thin frame, large, expressive eyes, and dark hair swept up in a chignon. A handsome young man, Delbert was long-limbed and bony, with pale blue eyes, sandy hair, and a mischievous smile. With his laid-back charm, Delbert "never met a stranger," according to relatives who remembered him as relaxed and easygoing. The couple set up housekeeping in a makeshift wooden cabin on E. W. and Betty's Indian Creek spread, a stone's throw from the church cemetery.

At Indian Creek, Elnora seemed to find the happiness that had eluded her, especially after she gave birth to her first child on September 29, 1907.[6] She delivered at home, attended by Dr. Eugene Ledbetter, who usually charged ten dollars to travel the six miles from his Tioga office—although sometimes he'd accept ten chickens in exchange. This time, the good doctor brought the baby into the world on credit, since Delbert had vanished on a ramble during her pregnancy. Elnora named the child Orvon Grover Autry; twenty-one years later, her son would call himself Gene Autry. She later told a relative she had intended to name him Orvin, but the word had been misspelled. Presumably she chose Grover after her half-brother, Grover Reynolds (who used the nickname "Bud"). Orvon grew to favor his mother and maternal grandmother, with his soft features and slight build. Five weeks after Orvon's birth, America gained its forty-sixth state when Indian Territory became Oklahoma on November 16, 1907.

On warm spring days, Elnora, suffering from cabin fever, would stroll baby Orvon in a pram the half-mile distance to the family mailbox. On the return trip, she'd visit an Autry in-law. Her only other social life took place at the Missionary Baptist Church, where she served as accompanist to the Congregationalists. The good-natured baby responded merrily when Elnora sang to him with her lilting soprano. Wrapped in blankets, he'd nestle on a church pew as she rehearsed hymns on the piano for Sunday services. E. W. and Betty became quite fond of Nora (as they called her)—she was certainly more God-fearing than their careless son. Sometimes, Delbert took his wife and baby with him on livestock-trading excursions to Oklahoma; more often, he left his family behind in Indian Creek to fend for itself. Nora had to scrimp by on Delbert's meager earnings as a part-time farmer and hapless horse trader. Before E. W. or one of Delbert's brothers headed to Tioga to buy supplies, they'd stop the wagon at Nora's little cabin to see if she needed anything. She could usually afford only five cents worth of flour or a few pennies worth of salt. Her father-in-law would sometimes treat her to more, which he would deliver on his way home. Fortunately, Nora was a good cook and could make a delicious meal out of beans and cornbread.[7]

When he was home, Delbert halfheartedly farmed his share of his father's acreage, where he also began making corn liquor. This soon turned into his most profitable pastime—since Cooke County, the adjoining Grayson County, and the whole state of Oklahoma were dry. Unfortunately, Delbert liked to sample his brew to excess. "He drank a lot, drank real bad," according to Gerald Autry.[8] Sometimes he'd ride a mule into Tioga to sell his wares or do a little trading, decide to stay on, and send the mule home riderless, its harness bearing a note stating its ownership. Often alone at Indian Creek in the evenings, Nora sat on the open porch, playing the beat-up guitar she'd had since girlhood, serenading Orvon with folk songs and hymns. By the time he was a toddler, Orvon would hum along with her. Eventually his mother showed him a few chords, and he "started fooling with the guitar," he later recalled. "I think I've been interested in music all my life."[9] When not singing, Nora read aloud scriptures and Bible stories for entertainment. Sometimes she would hitch up the wagon and take Orvon to visit Ozment relatives in Oklahoma. One cousin recalls her being "a kind of newspaper, bringing everyone up to date with what was happening in Texas."[10]

Four years after Orvon's birth, on December 14, 1911, Elnora gave birth at home to a daughter, Veda. A year and a half later, on April 14, 1913, another girl, Wilma, was also born at Indian Creek. In his 1978 memoir, *Back in the Saddle Again*, Gene Autry barely touched on his early childhood, writing that "growing up is simply one of the debts we must pay to society." He called E. W. Autry "a practical man who taught me to sing when I was five in order to use me in his church choir. He was short a soprano."[11] His grandfather didn't live to hear Orvon's voice change.

Two weeks after Wilma's birth, E. W. died at age sixty-five and was buried at Indian Creek cemetery.[12] The children divided their father's land, with some staying in the area and others selling out and moving on. Grandmother Betty lived for a while in Indian Creek, then resided with her various children until her death in 1920. Soon after his father's death, Delbert sold his share of the land and took off again. "My dad was kind of a gypsy," Gene Autry would tell an interviewer five decades later. "He was a man who traveled between Texas and Oklahoma for most of his life."[13] Six-year-old Orvon did farm chores for his Uncle Cal to help make ends meet. Cal and his family, including a son named John Ernest "Buck" two months Orvon's senior, lived in Tioga but raised livestock and grew crops on a share of the Indian Creek land. Orvon wished his father was more like his cousin Buck's. Sometimes, Nora and her children would travel by buckboard into Tioga to spend a few days at Cal's.

In the fall of 1913 Orvon briefly attended the rural one-room Burton School. A childhood friend, Ellen Kitchens Keene, remembered he'd be dressed in overalls and "had a horse he rode, and sometimes he would stop by to pick up my brother Elmer. The Autrys lived about two miles west of us. If it was raining or cold, he'd come in a buggy. [Orvon] would come in and wait, and my mother always gave him something for his lunch pail."[14] Forty years later, Gene

Autry would tell Hollywood columnist Hedda Hopper, "The kids of the present generation don't seem to understand what real work is. I'm asked how I learned the tricks of being a Western actor. I didn't have to. When I was a kid, I rode a horse five miles to school every day and learned to shoot straight to provide meat for the family."

The winter hit hard that December of 1913, and no word came from Delbert. With three small children to tend, Nora could barely keep enough wood chopped to start a fire much less find food for the table. It was too cold to travel into Tioga. There was no one to turn to, except for some kindly neighbors, the Tiptons, a mile down the road, who had a son a bit younger than Orvon. Elnora and her family crammed into the spare room at the Tipton home. The two boys would "car pool" to first grade at Burton, riding double on a mule or sharing a wagon. Mrs. Bink Tipton would often slip a bit of dried beef into Orvon's metal lunch bucket. The Tiptons didn't have much for Christmas, but they shared what food and small toys they could with the Autrys.

Eventually Nora took her children across the Red River, north to Achille, in Johnson County, Oklahoma, where her brother Bob was postmaster and ran the village grocery store. One Indian Creek resident recalled the day the family left, piled into a wagon with all their belongings, and Gene wearing a beatup, hand-me-down top hat, helping his mother with the reins. The vagabonds briefly moved in with Bob and his wife, Beulah, on Main Street, where Orvon could play hide-and-seek with his cousins Louisa and Willeen. Willeen later remembered everyone getting a laugh at a family gathering when they looked outside and saw Orvon pretending to be a cowboy, with a chamber pot on his head for a hat, galloping on a broomstick.

In an area originally settled in the 1860s by the Cherokee, the tiny village of Achille got its name from *atsila*, the Cherokee word for fire. A post office was established there in 1910, and the town experienced a minor boom in 1913 when two local oil wells became gushers. A few more buildings were constructed along the dirt main street, in addition to the livery stable and grocery store. Every fall, cattle continued to be driven right through town. Delbert eventually joined his family in Achille, and the Autrys rented a small frame house with ivy growing up one side. Unfortunately, the hamlet had begun a downward spiral, the oil already tapped out, the fields fallow by lack of rain. Twenty-five years later Gene would write, "I saw some real poverty when the country was devastated by drought. We had mighty hard scratching at times to make a living. We were so poor that my father used to drive across the country in a covered wagon with a string of horses and swap horses to make a living."[15] In his autobiography, he remembered Achille as "so small you could start a crime wave by stealing three chickens."[16]

Gene more fondly recalled the town's Dark Feather movie theater, which closed in 1919. Some Saturday afternoons the family would ante up ten cents each to watch cowboy stars Tom Mix and Harry Carey. Gene later wrote,

"When I was a young boy in Oklahoma . . . Tom Mix was my favorite actor. . . . I always envied the exciting life Tom Mix led on and off screen."[17] He recalled getting free screenings at the Dark Feather in exchange for sweeping up and pasting posters around town. In his memoir he wrote that at the Dark Feather, he learned to "thread the machine, an old Vidagraph, and how to run an arc light." He denied, however, getting any big ideas watching the courageous antics in the silent serials: "I didn't identify with those fantasy figures on the screen."[18]

PERHAPS LIFE WAS JUST TOO TOUGH FOR THAT. Delbert had stayed with the family long enough to father another son, Dudley Don, born in Achille on October 9, 1919. Dudley would grow up to favor his father, both physically and by nature. Soon after his son's birth, Delbert was off again. Gene described him this way: "My father earned good money when he felt like it, which was some of the time. Father was a livestock dealer, a horse trader, a foot-loose, aimless man who loved people and animals and the smell of the good earth. He was uneducated and a casual provider, but he had a western sense of values."[19] Gerald Autry remembers stories of Delbert camping on his sister Nora's property just outside Fort Worth. He'd arrive in a mule-drawn wagon loaded down with items for trading—anything from pots and pans to horses and mules, which he herded along. "He'd stay there a week and trade," according to Gerald. "He'd either be in the money or be broke. But he was usually broke. When he left, there'd be a big mess that my cousin Raymond [Priddy] had to clean up."[20]

Gene later recalled that he occasionally accompanied his father on these journeys. "We would ride twenty-five or thirty miles across the border into Texas, sleeping at night in our wagon," he wrote in *Back in the Saddle*. "Other times he and Uncle Homer would buy mules by the hundreds and sell them at auction to the plantation owners along the Mississippi Delta. When it came to judging stock, no one outsmarted my father. . . . I remember him talking once about his younger brother, Homer, and saying proudly, 'You know, son, that Homer is a fine man. He just won't hardly lie to you in a hoss trade.' . . . But as a business man [my father] was not very astute. Some days he would bring home five hundred dollars. Other days he would bring home only the lint in his pockets."[21]

Orvon, Veda, and Wilma attended school in Achille, while an increasingly despondent Nora cared for her new baby.[22] Of his mother, Gene Autry wrote, she was "a gentle and dainty and thoughtful lady . . . a great beauty in her day," who "always hoped I would be a professional man." Neighbors later recalled the often-hungry Autry children stopping in for buttermilk and a bite to eat. To feed the family, Nora planted a small garden and raised a few chickens— which got her into the pages of the *Achille Press*, on June 10, 1921: "Talk about freaks. Mrs. Delbert Autry had a hen setting and when she hatched [on] June 7, one chicken had two bodies, four wings, four feet, two tails and only one head. It is wonderful what nature may do."

Having her brother and his family nearby helped the Autrys make friends, and they socialized with townsfolk. Nora loved poetry and would have her children recite verses as she churned butter. Gene would strum his mother's guitar for his buddies at their gathering place by an abandoned cotton gin tank. On the Fourth of July, 1921, Veda and Wilma invited cousins and friends over for a little shindig, in which "miscellaneous games were the feature of the evening," according to a "Local Happenings" item in the *Achille Press*. "Ample portions of cake and iced lemonade were served to which the guests did justice. A good time was had by all."[23]

In September, Orvan [*sic*] was listed in "Local Happenings" as a guest at his friend James Ramsey's thirteenth birthday party, participating in "songs and recitations, and . . . several tricks."[24] Unfortunately, not all the local boys cared for the slightly built Orvon. A group of bullies began chasing him home from school every day; his sisters awaited him by the gate, and as soon as he arrived, they slammed and locked it to keep the toughs out. One day Delbert was home and became angered when he discovered the situation. "No boy of mine is going to hide behind his sisters' skirts," he bellowed. The next afternoon, when his son raced home, the thugs at his heels, Delbert would not let Orvon in the gate, demanding he face his assailants. He watched while the gang beat his son bloody.[25]

Shortly thereafter, Orvon left Achille for his Uncle Cal's home, where he remained to work on the farm and attend school. Nora and the other children stayed behind in Achille until June 1922, when the local paper noted that "Mrs. Autry and children left for Wills Point, Texas, on Monday afternoon, where they will reside with relatives."[26]

The newspaper reporter may have confused Wills Point with Pilot Point, a town a few miles from the smaller Tioga. It was there, at the Cal Autry residence, that Orvon and his family tried once again to find the stability that continued to elude them.

3

TIOGA

TIOGA, IN THE SOUTHEAST CORNER OF GRAYSON COUNTY, TEXAS, flourished in the early 1920s, some forty years after being established by the Texas & Pacific Railroad. In 1881, already populated by a few homesteaders, the hamlet took its name from the Iroquois word for "swift current" or "rushing waters." Located at the far eastern section of Cross Timbers, Tioga had a dark, sandy loam, ideal for growing cotton and grains, attracting farmers—including German and Austrian immigrants—as well as cattlemen. An expanse of prairie lay just east of town, providing acreage for grazing white-face cattle and other livestock. The workers constructing the T&P tracks had complained of the local well's bitter-tasting water, a natural resource that would become Tioga's claim to fame. In 1884 a blacksmith named Matt Rains doused his burned hand in the well water and discovered his wound healed abnormally fast. Word of the mineral water's powers spread, and locals flocked to take the water both internally and externally for a variety of ailments. To meet the demand, Rains and his brother dug another well, reportedly with an even greater mineral content, and formed the Tioga Mineral Wells Company. The brothers began marketing the water to treat "rheumatism, all female troubles, kidney disease, tape worm, colic, and dropsy," among other maladies, along with a salve for "rheumatism; acute and chronic skin diseases including tetter, cancerous or other sores; chapped hands; pains; burns; spider bites; headaches; milk leg; toothache; sprains; baldness; and neuralgia."[1]

Soon, the boom was on: the Radium Mineral Water Company came next, founded by W. F. Carroll, who called his commodity "the Well of Life No. 1," followed by W. T. Spears's Star Well Company, which produced a condensed mineral water boiled down to 2 percent of its original volume. Before long, bath houses and hotels, beginning with the Bradley Cottage located next to the Rains's wells, sprang up to accommodate out-of-towners. The town's sole black family worked for the Bradley's hotel and restaurant. By 1890 Tioga's population had increased to 200 people; twenty years later, the village received as many as 1,500 visitors annually. Tourists came from all over the country to take the waters at Tioga. In 1910 a Bradley Cottage newspaper ad offered a free chicken dinner to any tourists from Vermont, the only state not represented in the lodgings' guest book. Visiting the spa and eating fried chicken were Tioga's sole tourist attractions, according to a postcard dated August 1913 reproduced in a history of the town: "We are having a fine rest with plenty to eat—fried chicken twice a day. Tioga is the best place in Texas to save money in—there isn't even a fruit stand—This is 'Sleepy Hollow' all right. There are about fifty guests at this hotel. . . . We went to the Christian Church Sunday— the only one in which they had services."[2]

Eight years later, Tioga was bustling when Orvon moved into Cal Autry's home in 1921. With nearly eight hundred residents, Tioga had a newspaper (the weekly *Tioga Herald*), three churches, three grocers, two blacksmiths, a jeweler, a bank, a butcher shop, two dry-goods stores, two general stores, a cotton gin, a livery stable, a barbershop, and a furniture store. It also housed two real-estate offices, two doctors (including Dr. Eugene Ledbetter), a hardware store, a telephone company, a café, an undertaker, and an insurance office. One of the town's grocers, Henry G. Ball, preached at the Primitive Baptist Church where, in 1956, Brother Ball would baptize the Speaker of the U.S. House of Representatives Sam Rayburn, born in nearby Bonham. Among Tioga's prosperous citizens was Elijah Calvin "Cal" Autry, president of the Tioga School's Board of Trustees. In his memoir Gene Autry wrote, "As I grew older, I found myself drawing closer to my Uncle Calvin," whose son Ernest "Buck" was like a brother to Orvon.[3]

Soon, Orvon would become close to Tioga's prominent Gordon family, who settled in the area after the son of Georgia governor John B. Gordon fled to Texas to escape punishment for killing a carpetbagger. The Gordons' neighbors, the ranching and oil-rich Walling family, had settled in Tioga after driving cattle through the area. Children of the two clans, Eba Walling and Jeff Gordon, married; in 1915 the couple built a rambling Prairie-style home, the first in Tioga to get indoor plumbing and electric lights. Large enough for a family of nine, the house was situated on a spread three miles east of town. Orvon spent much of his boyhood there. "Back then, we knew him as Orvon, and he had a good voice," Bernice Gordon Noah later recalled of her younger sister's beau. "He constantly asked, 'Do you want me to sing?'"[4]

From the day he moved into town, Orvon Autry enjoyed performing for anyone, anytime. "We'd ask our teacher during study period if we could have

Orvon come in and sing [for our seventh-grade class]," recalled Velma Chaffin Willett. She remembered the eighth-grader holding court at recess too: "He was too poor to buy a guitar then, so he'd sing and play a Jew's [jaw] harp." The personable youngster became better acquainted with Velma when he bought her pie at a box supper, a purchase that entitled him to walk her home from church. Later, the pair spent time together at Anita Jones's birthday party. "He took me home and sang songs all the way there," Velma said eighty years later.[5] But it was her classmate Nellie Gordon "who he had his eye on," according to Bernice and the handful of their surviving Tioga schoolmates. The spring after he began sharing his cousin Buck's bedroom, Orvon met dark-eyed, raven-haired Nellie at a church picnic.[6] She was an intelligent and vivacious girl two years his junior. "He was in Mama's Sunday school class," Bernice related, "and she had lots of parties for the children." Soon Orvon and Nellie were insepara-ble, with the boy riding his bicycle three miles to the Gordon home every Sunday after church. Sometimes, pretending he was there to see Nellie's brother J. D., he spent the night on the parlor couch. Even though everyone in town knew Delbert Autry's bad reputation, the Gordons, unlike some folks, didn't hold it against Orvon—the boy was so hardworking and likable. "He was always ambitious, always trying to make a little money," Bernice recalled. "He didn't mind working—he wasn't at all lazy."[7]

In fact Orvon was usually up at dawn, doing farm chores for Uncle Cal be-fore school—milking cows and baling and stacking hay. On market day—every Saturday and on Wednesday in the summertime—Orvon rode his bike to Sam Anderson's barbershop off the town square. Mr. Sam, as he was called, kept a guitar, banjo, and fiddle on hand for any customer who wanted to play. Al-though Mr. Sam hired Orvon to sweep around the three barber chairs and run the shoeshine stand, it wasn't long before the boy picked up an instrument and began serenading patrons. One customer even constructed a homemade guitar out of a box and chicken wire for Orvon to take home. The boy's entertain-ments became so popular that his schoolmate Sam Keene (who later married Gene's Indian Creek friend Ellen Kitchens) had to handle most of the shoe-shining while Orvon sang for tips. There was room for both boys and the shoeshine stand right by the shop's front window. Mr. Sam, a short, bowlegged man with a bald pate and bushy mustache, had moved to Tioga from Kentucky at the age of thirteen. Feeling empathy for the industrious boy, he treated Orvon almost like a son, even though he had four children of his own.

Mr. Sam's daughter Kate later recalled that when Orvon first came to Tioga he didn't own a pair of shoes.[8] But things changed when he became a regular at the barbershop, and he eventually saved enough money for a gray suit and fedora. "Even as a boy I had ambition and wanted to make something of myself," he later said. He soon began to draw a crowd at his makeshift per-formances, earning enough to order a guitar from the Sears, Roebuck cata-logue. (Ten years later, aspiring musicians could order a Gene Autry Round-up

Guitar from the very same wish book for $9.75.) Orvon also learned from a magazine how to build a crystal radio set from an oatmeal container and a coiled wire. He impressed his schoolmates by tuning into a brand-new station transmitting from Dallas, just as radio began sweeping the nation. "That was the first radio I ever saw," said his classmate Jim Cook. "You had to listen to it with an earphone."[9]

Baseball became another of Orvon's passions. "We played a lot of baseball," said Cook. "I had a new glove that cost $1.98, and he didn't have one. Every time I went to bat, he'd take my glove and wouldn't give it back. He was bigger than me and we kinda fell out over that."[10] J. W. "Skeet" Smotherman, a resident of nearby Aubrey, later described the spirited games between the Tioga team, comprised of numerous Autry cousins, and his hometown club. "I remember playing Tioga on rainy days when it was too wet to plow cotton," he recalled. "I was a pitcher of sorts, but I am not sure that I ever bested the Tioga teams due principally to the Autry boys. [Orvon] was especially skilled and could have made it in professional baseball."[11]

After his mother and siblings moved to Tioga in 1922, Orvon, Veda, and Wilma began singing as a trio at church and school functions. "They just wore 'em out with singin'," remembered Jim Cook. "They sang at least once a week." Particularly memorable for Cook was the day he spent picking cotton with Veda and Wilma. "They was singin' in the cotton patch and liked to sing me to sleep. It was the prettiest thing I'd ever heard. I helped 'em with their sacks."[12] Veda was petite like her mother, while light-haired Wilma was tall and lanky like her father. Veda made a big impression on her classmate Mae Gary Richards: "Veda was a lot prettier than her brother Orvon. His hair was kinda mousy and he had those blue/gray eyes. Veda had shiny black hair, a long Roman nose, and pretty brown eyes. They were poor, but somehow Veda always had a new magazine with all the movie stars in it. She always talked that when she got grown, she was going to California and be in the movies."[13]

When Delbert eventually arrived in Tioga, he rented the family a small frame house about two blocks northwest of the school. Somehow, Delbert had managed to acquire a piano, and neighbors recalled music often wafting out from inside. A daughter of the family next door later described the Autrys in a school paper: "[Orvon] brought an old beat-up guitar to our house and sang for my great-grandmother. She never forgot it. The song he sang was 'Let the Rest of the World Go By.' . . . I've heard other tales about when they lived next door to our old home place. One of them was about their old dog Queenie, kicking over the old wood stove. There are other incidents which I dare not mention. . . . The old house has been moved long since, and the old well I remember so vividly has been burned to the ground in a prairie fire."[14]

In June 1923 Orvon auditioned on amateur night for a medicine show passing through Tioga. In the mid-1920s small-time medicine shows still rambled around Texas providing rural residents with their only entertainment.

While the focal point was selling cure-all remedies, performers primed audiences to make purchases. "They carried a dancer, a singer, and a comic—all males," Gene later recalled, "for no one in our parts would tolerate a lady traveling with a show. One of the brothers, who called himself Doctor, was the barker, and he sure was persuasive. He sold corn cure and liver pills and salve to ease the rheumatics out of aching backs."[15]

Nellie and Bernice talked their father into driving them in his big Reo automobile to the fairgrounds to watch Orvon perform. The fledgling showman's spot came late in the evening—a medicine show tradition saved locals for last. Nervous before the crowd, Orvon managed to sing with gusto. Finally, at night's end, Nellie's disgruntled father had trouble attaching Orvon's bike to the back of his car to take him home and although Mr. Gordon was put off, the whole experience exhilarated Orvon. He signed on with the Fields Brothers Medicine Show for fifteen dollars a week and left town with the troupe a few days later. "When I tell people that I paid Gene Autry his first dollar in show business, they look at each other and wink and grin—they really don't believe me," the show's "Doctor" Luke Fields later said.[16]

Along with music, medicine shows like the Fields Brothers usually featured blackface minstrelsy; Luke Fields's older brother Tod corked up as a character called Snowball. Some historians have suggested Gene Autry performed in blackface, but no photographs or other evidence support this claim: However, elements of minstrelsy and medicine show entertainment would appear in his early touring troupes and films. The press book for 1937's *Rootin' Tootin' Rhythm*, one of four Autry pictures (including his first, 1935's *Tumbling Tumbleweeds*) to feature a medicine show, includes "Pleasant Memory of Carefree Youth," detailing his days with Fields.

In his memoir Gene recalls, "I traveled with them for three months, softening up audiences with mournful ballads before the professor began pitching his wares: ointment and pills and his own product, a patent medicine called Fields' Pain Annihilator." Luke Fields recalled that young Autry had a good voice and played a cheap guitar, but suffered stage fright on his first night, fleeing the platform halfway through his opening number. In character as Snowball, Tod Fields reportedly told him, "Stay right in there, kid, and maybe some day you'll get to be a big shot like me." Eventually, he did gain confidence and some nights received several encores. By the season's end, in early September, Dr. Fields recalled, "Gene had traded his guitar for a brass-looking saxophone, and the last I saw of him after the show closed, he was sitting in a cotton wagon. He had hitched a ride toward home, and he was playing that old sax."[17]

In the fall of 1923, Orvon spent his days bent over under the beating hot sun picking cotton at Cal's farm. School didn't start until the first Monday in October, as reported by the *Tioga Herald*, "on account of so many children engaged in the cotton fields."[18] The *Herald* ran another item praising three young sisters from nearby Collinsville who'd broken a local cotton-picking record: In one day's time, "Lillian, 10, picked 355 pounds of cotton, Thelma, 9, picked 290 pounds, and Inez, 7, picked 101 pounds."[19]

In the Tioga School's ninth grade class photo, Orvon Autry looks tired, with deep-set eyes and down-turned lips. No wonder—he kept a full schedule. "I went to high school, and my cousin [Buck] . . . was probably my closest friend. He and I used to go to all the high school plays and the parties and shows and fairs and whatever they had out in that part of the country. . . . I had a cousin [Louise, Buck's older sister] who was a very good piano player. . . . She would accompany me on the piano at the different parties and functions and different clubs and entertainment that they had around Tioga." Orvon once told Bernice Gordon, who played piano with him too: "One of these nights, you'll be plunking down a quarter to see me sing." When he took her sister Nellie on a date to the picture show, his singing would pay the way; he'd perform while they changed the reels, earning free admission. "My mother and aunt and grandmother always knew he was going to be a star because of his determination and the way he kept himself," according to Nellie's daughter, Charlene Renfro Brown.[20]

On September 29, 1924—his seventeenth birthday—Orvon entered the tenth grade—the highest level available at Tioga's two-story Gothic-style schoolhouse. Delbert had vanished again, so Orvon had to work harder than ever to put food on the family's table. He'd found yet another job, helping around the Texas & Pacific depot. Never complaining, he unloaded heavy baggage and mail, along with other chores. Just as he'd impressed Mr. Sam and Uncle Cal with his diligence, he became a protégé of stationmaster J. M. Puckett, who showed him the rudiments of Morse code. Finally, in early 1925, Puckett offered him full-time employment, working the night shift for thirty-five dollars a month. With such a schedule, attending school was out of the question. Gene Autry always hid the fact that he dropped out of high school, but a few years before his death, he admitted, "I just couldn't pass the job up."[21] It was duly noted in the Tioga School's *High Flyer* yearbook that the class of 1925 had lost five of its fifteen students, including Orvon Autry, who "dropped on the wayside as they though [sic] travelling to knowledge too difficult."[22] Embarrassed by his lack of education, Gene Autry would hungrily read several newspapers a day and insist that his siblings finish school.

That spring, Delbert finally sent word for his family to join him in Ravia, Oklahoma, which they did. Orvon stuck it out at the Tioga depot a while longer. But when he heard the Frisco line was hiring relief telegraphers for $150 a month in Oklahoma, he left Tioga behind too.

4

WORKIN' ON THE RAILROAD

I WORKED FOR THE FRISCO RAILROAD for several years, and they are among the happiest of my life," Gene Autry wrote in 1986 to an old acquaintance. Although his singing career would take off during his employment by the St. Louis–San Francisco Railroad from 1925 to 1932, Orvon held tight to his job. In addition to offering financial stability, the Frisco and its close-knit world of railroad folk served as a built-in audience to the young would-be entertainer.

Soon after he arrived in Ravia, Orvon visited the local depot looking for work. His struggling family rented a small house near the train tracks.[1] Just north of the Red River, Ravia, in southern Oklahoma, was smaller than Tioga, with only a few businesses: a grocery, drugstore, livery stable, general store, cotton gin, and service station. The Johnston County village boasted no town square, no mineral waters to beckon tourists, no movie theater. Without many distractions, Orvon put his time into learning the railroad business. In addition to the guidance and lessons provided by J. M. Puckett in Tioga, Ravia's stationmaster Charles "Charlie" Webster took the boy under his wing. Orvon applied himself to the study of telegraphy and train-station procedures as he never had his schoolwork. Charlie spent long hours showing him the ropes, including Morse code lessons on a practice set at the Websters' home. Almost as important, Orvon could count on a delicious family meal with Charlie, his wife, Ella, and their sons. "Gene was just a sixteen-year-old [*sic*] kid who carried a guitar with him almost every place he went," Charlie remembered in

1941. "He wanted to learn the telegraphing business, so I taught him. . . . He always was a mighty fine boy. Just a swell kid."[2]

A devastating drought showed no signs of abating, and Ravia's farmers and ranchers struggled to raise their crops and livestock. The Great Depression, still four years away for the rest of the nation, had already encroached on the farmers of southern Oklahoma. Orvon had his heart set on getting out of Ravia; he hated the drudgery of farm work, such as helping his father chop cotton for Ravia's grocer Wade Sharrock. His parents could barely pay for groceries, so sometimes the store clerk gave Nora flour and cornmeal on credit, even slipping Veda, Wilma, and Dudley free candy sticks. The general store often gave the Autrys supplies on credit too.

The neighboring Fields family also befriended the Autrys, inviting them over for supper. Young J. E. "Red" Fields accompanied Wilma to church socials, where Gene sometimes entertained with his guitar. The family was barely scraping by, but Nora's seamstress skills kept her daughters looking their best in clothes she made for them. She taught them how to turn inexpensive ingredients such as vinegar into beauty products.

In June Orvon traveled the 154 miles northeast from Ravia to Sapulpa to apply for a job on the southwestern division of the Frisco. Sapulpa was just fourteen miles west of oil-rich Tulsa. Even though Orvon had accompanied his father on trade expeditions to Fort Worth, he had never ventured alone to a big city. On June 14, wearing his only suit, he appeared at Frisco headquarters to fill out an application. At 140 pounds and 5'7", baby-faced Orvon Autry definitely looked more a boy than a man. Since he wasn't yet eighteen—the minimum age requirement—he claimed 1906 as his birth date. He used his neatest handwriting except for the way he inscribed his middle name: "Grover" was so illegible that it turned up as "Grany" and later as "Gordon" in the Frisco railroad records. Apparently strongly disliking the name, he gradually eliminated it—it never appeared on his driver's license, passport, or even his military records. "Grover" simply ceased to exist.

Using shaky spelling and punctuation, Orvon wrote on his application that he had been unemployed since working at the Tioga depot, from which he had "resigned as helper account pay unsufficient [sic] live on." Puckett corroborated on his referral that Orvon left his employ "because pay was not enough to support him and he was soon trying for something better." After he passed his written test, Orvon visited a doctor for a required physical. The physician reported that the teenager possessed 20/20 vision, perfect hearing, and no history of disease.

On June 18 "O. G. Autry" was approved as "extra operator," for service at whichever Frisco depot needed a substitute for a vacationing or sick telegrapher. Orvon's first assignment was assistant telegraph operator in tiny Weleetka, sixty miles south of Sapulpa. His father's sister Luda and her husband, Will Ogle, lived in the neighboring village of Wetumka, so Orvon stayed for a while with his aunt and uncle. Soon after he arrived, the superintendent of telegraphy sent a notice to the Frisco's Springfield headquarters that "I am enclosing minors release furnished in favor of Orvon Grany [*sic*] Autry, employed on the Southwestern Division as telegrapher. The release has been properly executed by the boy's parents." On July 13, his employment became official. For the next several months, he traveled by train all over Oklahoma to any town that needed him for stints lasting from a day to a week. The rest of the time he worked "third trick," or the midnight to 8 AM shift, at the Weleetka station.

On days off, Orvon got to know some Autry cousins who owned a large ranch outside Weleetka. Teenaged equestrienne Callie Jane Autry, a striking brunette, became a close friend. When Orvon visited, he showed no interest in riding or other ranch activities, but would rather talk and sing. He rented a room in the home of Weleetka's Frisco section foreman, Sam White. Mr. and Mrs. White and their four daughters treated the outgoing and polite teenager as a member of the family, encouraging him to join them for dinner every night. Much to Orvon's delight, Mrs. White specialized in chocolate cream pie, his favorite dessert. In gratitude for their kindnesses, two years later Orvon bought Sam a small pocketknife.[3]

At the lonely Weleetka depot, Orvon would keep himself awake by strumming his guitar and singing. One night, he later wrote in his autobiography, his solitude was disrupted by a gun pointed at his head. "The Matt Kimes Gang hit my station," Gene recalled, and after handing over the cash box, he was locked in a refrigerated train car on the tracks outside the station. After two hours, a train pulled into the station, he related, and Orvon hollered and kicked against the door until he was rescued. An exciting story, but whether it really happened is unclear: though he may have been the victim of a robbery, there is no record of the event in published histories or newspaper accounts of the gang.[4] The Oklahoma teenage brothers and their pals did go on an eight-month bank robbery spree in 1927–28, including a Sapulpa heist in which the gang stole $42,000, at that point, the largest amount ever taken from an Oklahoma bank.

Orvon surely heard about such exciting events on the radio. By 1926, the old crystal sets with earphones were being replaced by models with speakers, suddenly so prolific that many households owned one. Radio stations were popping up everywhere, mostly transmitting live performances of local talent in fifteen-minute increments. Orvon tuned into nearby Bristow's KFRU, founded in 1925, which broadcast Otto Gray's Oklahoma Cowboy Band and Jimmie Wilson's Catfish String Band. A local sensation, KFRU was besieged by would-be singers hoping for air time, even though talent was unpaid. Station manager Roy Griffin complained to the press about "being swamped with letters by amateur and professional sopranos offering their services. 'They don't go well over the radio,'" he complained.[5]

A different story was Otto Gray—the first radio entertainer to develop a repertoire of traditional buckaroo songs like those collected by Texas-born folklorist John Lomax in the 1910 book, *Cowboy Songs and Other Frontier Ballads*. Gray and his band donned chaps, big-brimmed Stetsons, and cowboy boots. The group was originally formed by William McGinty, who had served in Teddy Roosevelt's Rough Riders and wanted to preserve the cowboy folksong tradition. In 1924 McGinty hired Gray to manage his cowboy band, whose original members were actual working trail hands recruited from Oklahoma ranches. Among the members of the Oklahoma Cowboy Band was banjo-playing comic Benjamin "Whitey" Ford, later known as the "Duke of Paducah," an early showbiz cohort of Gene Autry's. Gray and company recorded such numbers as "Cow Boy's Dream" and "Bury Me on the Lone Prairie" (in 1926), gained popularity via their radio broadcasts, then toured the vaudeville circuit to great acclaim until the group disbanded in 1936.

The jocular Jimmie Wilson's outfit of "rustics" (with such "instruments" as bones and gas pipe) made a handful of recordings for Victor in 1925 and 1929, including old parlor tunes and comical numbers like "Catfish Whiskers." Legend has it that Wilson's group "from Ole Pole Creek" was the first to ever broadcast over the Oklahoma airways; in the process, they received fan mail from as far away as Scranton, Pennsylvania: "I was getting your program fine until a loud note from your sewer pipe bass burned out my crystal detector. Before I could get it adjusted again, your program was over."[6] Renowned for playing everything from classical to novelty songs, Wilson and his bunch also experimented with humorous sound effects.[7]

Radio's dispensing of free entertainment was a real boon to struggling young music lovers like Orvon. Also gratis, his Frisco employee pass enabled him to travel where ever the rails went. On days off he hopped a train to Ravia to see his family. With Delbert usually absent, Orvon gave his mother as much money as he could spare. He had already taken on what would become a near-lifelong role—that of family provider: "As you probably know, I more or less supported my mother, Dud, and the two girls from the time I was eighteen years old," he would write to his father's fifth wife in 1956.

Taking his guitar along, Orvon would delight the doting Nora, Veda, Wilma, and Dudley—and their neighbors—with impromptu performances, showing them the new songs he was learning from the radio and his railroad buddies' 78 rpm records. He also visited Charlie and Ella Webster, who had been helping his family as much as they could. In 1959, on Charlie's death, Gene would write Ella, "I shall always remember Charlie . . . you know I considered you two as my second mother and father. I'll never forget the many nice things you did for my mother and family and also the many things Charlie did for me while I was growing up on the Frisco."[8]

Charlie had taught Orvon well. Over the next two years, he worked diligently for the railroad, becoming adept at just about every chore that needed attention at any small station where he was posted. "I not only was an operator," Gene recalled proudly in 1984. "I was an agent, because I knew how to figure freight rates and ticket rates. . . . I even worked as a yardmaster. So I knew the railroad business pretty good."[9] On August 6, 1927, he began a week's stint as the third-trick telegrapher in Claremore, the largest town on the eastern Oklahoma end of the Frisco line. Near the depot, the fancy Claremore Hotel awaited a swarm of tourists following the completion of the new cross-country highway, Route 66. Claremore was also known for one of its most famous sons, cowboy humorist, writer, and entertainer Will Rogers, who grew up in nearby Oologah and attended Indian School in Claremore (which he fondly described as "a town in physique but a city at heart").[10] Rogers still visited the area to see family, including his sister who lived in the neighboring village of Chelsea.

Just in time for his twentieth birthday, in September 1927, Orvon applied for and received a transfer to the second-trick operator position in Vinita, a hamlet just east of Claremore. Now earning $150 a month, he had become very popular with the Frisco supervisor, as well as his co-workers at his various posts. "From the time I went to work on the railroad," he would recall in 1982, "I knew everybody by their first names, and I knew their families—even my superiors. I don't know if they felt sorry for me or what, but I made it a point to be very warm to the people I worked for. I could see both sides of every story and I always tried to cooperate to the best of my ability."[11]

GENE ALSO BEGAN STUDYING FREEMASONRY. In addition to his great-grandfather Autry, several of his mother's brothers were Masons; either an Ozment uncle or a co-worker backed Orvon's petition to join. Blue Lodge #185 in nearby Catoosa accepted him as a third-degree Mason, and he began studying the Scottish rites. He would remain a lifelong dues-paying member of the Catoosa lodge, later joining lodges in California, and eventually becoming a thirty-third degree Mason, the fraternity's highest honor.

Orvon's other course of study revolved around music. When he wasn't playing it himself, he enjoyed visiting friends who owned a phonograph and 78 rpm disks. He had become a big fan of the hugely successful crooner Gene Austin, whose "My Blue Heaven" was *the* song of 1927. Orvon felt a special kinship toward Austin, who was born near Tioga in Gainesville, Texas. "In those days, Gene Austin—who, for a short time in the late twenties, was the equivalent of Elvis or the Beatles—was the yardstick by which to measure all other crooners," according to music scholar Jonathan Guyot Smith. "The Austin mode of crooning meant singing softly at the top of one's range and sliding into falsetto when appropriate . . . and blending those whimsical falsetto notes in with the solo instruments during breaks and turn-arounds."[12] Orvon did not have the vocal ability to master Austin's sophisticated style, but that didn't stop him from adding the crooner's songs to his repertoire. Another of his favorites, Al Jolson, like Austin, popularized the art of the croon: Jolson's movie hit that year, *The Jazz Singer*, ushered in the era of talking pictures. A quick study, Orvon could hear a song once and sing it. He was getting better on guitar, and with the encouragement of his co-workers, he began playing for Frisco gatherings, as well as for Rotary and Kiwanis club meetings. Sometimes on the job he would even sing over the telephone line to other operators who, like him, were working the solitary night shift.[13]

Years later, Gene Autry would say that September 1927 was when he first ventured to Chicago and New York City: "One morning when the eastbound train pulled out I was on it," he wrote in his memoir. "I was nineteen, riding free on my railroad pass, and with a hundred and fifty dollars tucked in a sock in my one suitcase. I slept in a chair car for the three days and nights it took us to reach New York. . . . Actually, I didn't take the train directly into New York. I stopped off in Chicago and saw the second Dempsey-Tunney fight on September 22, 1927, under the lights at Soldier Field."[14] But among the extensive Frisco records of his employment, there is no reference to his taking a long vacation during this time. He may have confused the trip's date with one documented in October 1928. Or, if he did use his railroad pass for such a trip, it was a quick one, perhaps just to Chicago.

In Vinita, Orvon once again made close friends; his confidence and charm, along with his sunny disposition, quickly endeared him to acquaintances. An inquisitive and natural conversationalist, he was an attractive young man, with his light blue eyes and broad smile. He'd grown two inches since being hired by the Frisco, but his soft features still gave him a boyish look. He attracted women without much trouble, and occasionally asked one for a date. His greatest romance, though, had been in Tioga, and he tried to keep in touch with Nellie Gordon, mailing her postcards and calling occasionally. Still in Tioga, she carried a torch for her erstwhile beau, but eventually dated a local boy, Otis Renfro, whom she married later that year. Constantly moving around, Orvon seemed content to play the field.

Maintaining ties to his friends from the Frisco days was important to Gene Autry. In the late 1930s, on promotional tours in the area, he would drop by old friends' homes and join them for a down-home lunch. Nearly sixty years later, he'd correspond with numerous railroad acquaintances, inquiring as to the whereabouts of various co-workers, their relatives, and friends. He enjoyed reminiscing about his days working for the Frisco. Conversely, few colleagues, friends, or relatives recall Gene Autry ever discussing his early life: "He never talked much about his childhood," according to Virginia MacPhail, who worked for Gene in various capacities from the 1930s to the 1960s and probably knew him as well as anyone. "I think he was trying to just put it all behind him and forget it."[15]

In January 1928 Orvon got a transfer to the third-trick operator spot in Sapulpa. It was a hop to Tulsa, filled with movie theaters and concert halls like the Orpheum, where vaudeville stars of the day appeared. Radio station KFRU, with the new name KVOO—for Voice Of Oklahoma—had just relocated the previous fall from Bristow to Tulsa. Neighboring Sapulpa was the location of the Frisco's southwestern division headquarters—a plumb assignment for railroad employees. Near the depot, travelers stayed at the Fred Harvey House hotel, with its accompanying dining room, part of the early hotel/restaurant chain that dotted rail stops. Orvon chose budget accommodations, though, at the Woods Hotel, where railroaders resided.

With so many employees in the Sapulpa-Tulsa area, the Frisco formed a local baseball club, part of the railway company's league. That spring, Orvon won a spot on the team. "We'd always get at least seven innings played before it got too dark," he would later recall. "Tulsa had several dozen twilight baseball leagues. I couldn't wait at times to trade a telegraph key for a ball, bat, and a glove. I could swing a pretty good bat. I was a baseball 'nut,' and if I do say so myself, I did pretty fair in the semi-pro class of ball."[16] Occasionally, scouts would check out farm teams looking for new talent. "I darn near became a Cardinal [in 1928]," he told a reporter in 1950. "But they only offered me one hundred dollars a month. I was doing pretty good with the Frisco Railroad . . . [so] the offer didn't sound good enough to go out in a Class D League and sweat it out for six months of the year."[17]

In those days, the Frisco Railroad, which spanned nine states, operated as if it were a family business. An illustrated monthly periodical, the *Frisco Employes* [sic] *Magazine*, ran news items about personnel. How-to articles, human-interest stories related to depot locations and employees' hobbies, and features for children and homemakers were included in the mix. Very soon, Orvon would find himself a topic of the magazine. Another employee perquisite, in conjunction with the International Correspondence Schools, Frisco workers could further their education and take mail-order classes at a discounted cost. "I took a course in bookkeeping and accounting and became a CPA," Gene said in 1983. "I learned . . . how to balance books. . . . I learned . . . the responsibility you had when you copied the Morse Code on telegrams. You couldn't make mistakes. In copying the stock market quotations over the telegraph wire, for instance, you had to have it right because someone could buy the stock according to what you were copying. It could mean thousands of dollars if you made one mistake."[18]

At the Sapulpa depot, Orvon became fast friends with a fellow musician named Jimmy Long. The station's dispatcher, Jimmy was a forty-year-old Arkansas native who had worked the Frisco line for two decades. The two connected over music and began harmonizing after work—and sometimes at the station—on songs they both knew. Orvon became a frequent guest at the Long dinner table, feasting on wife Jesse's sumptuous fried chicken dinners. The couple's daughter, Beverly, played piano, and Gene and Jack, the Long's son, sang to her accompaniment. Jimmy had grown up playing his native state's folk tunes, nostalgic heart songs, and hillbilly ballads, which he taught Orvon.

Soon, the Autry-Long duo was asked to entertain at various functions around town. With Jimmy's plain but kindly face and Orvon's youthful good looks, the two made a kind of father-son team. Jimmy composed songs, too, and showed Gene a few songwriting tricks. At the Long home, throughout that spring of 1928, seeds were being sown that would transform a young telegrapher into a singing star.

5

MUSICAL MENTORS

VERYTHING BEGAN WITH A MAN NAMED JIMMY LONG." So wrote Gene Autry in a 1955 magazine article recounting his rise to stardom.[1] Born in Blevins, Arkansas, in 1889, Jimmy came from a large family and, like Orvon, chose the railroad as a means to financial security. About ten years after marrying Jesse and following the birth of their two children, he joined the Frisco Railroad in 1920. As dispatcher, telegrapher, and general troubleshooter, he labored at various depots, including Okmulgee, Newberg, and Sapulpa, Oklahoma. "He was transferred about every three, four, five years," daughter Beverly, born in 1915, remembered in 2006, "so I went to about five different schools from first grade until I graduated high school. My dad wrote a lot of music, beginning about 1925. He just wrote like crazy—one time he told me that he had written about thirty songs. [Orvon] and his family didn't have much. In fact, they didn't have *anything*. So my dad took him under his wing."[2]

Orvon grew close to the Long family, spending much of his spare time with Jimmy, who schooled him in the sentimental songs and humorous folk tunes he favored. "Though he was considerably older than I, we shared an interest in . . . music, and even wrote a few songs together," Gene later remembered.[3] In 1997, he described the songwriting process as coached by Jimmy Long: "I tried to write songs—you don't just write a song right quick, you fool around and work with that song to try to get a good one. You have to keep going over and over and over it and see if you can't really write a song that means a lot."[4] With Jimmy's encouragement, Orvon became more serious about pursuing music as a career. The duo increased bookings at dances and parties around Sapulpa. Long's tenor harmonized well with Orvon's baritone, and while the younger man strummed the rhythms on his guitar, Jimmy would play workmanlike lead on his steel.

For most of the previous generation of unschooled musicians, playing music had served primarily as an amusement rather than a vocation. With the expansion of radio, the proliferation of record labels, and the popularity of songbooks, music making began to look more like a career option—even for those, like Orvon, who could not read music but instead played by ear. In addition to artists recording pop tunes at studios in urban centers, record company men had taken to the road looking for talent. Into the hinterlands, scouts like Ralph Peer and Arthur Satherley lugged heavy equipment, capturing the sounds made by rural musicians, black and white. Peer, while working for OKeh, discovered the blues artist Mamie Smith and the white rural instrumentalist Fiddlin' John Carson—the latter of whom he later boasted led to the "discovery and development of the hillbilly business."[5] Satherley recorded seminal blues singers Ma Rainey and Blind Lemon Jefferson. Termed by the record companies as "race" and "hillbilly" (also, "old time tunes" and "Native American") music, respectively, these recordings sold extremely well to a new market comprised of rural Americans. For the first time, this audience could buy their own kind of music on 78 rpm records.

Orvon began to daydream at work that maybe his music wasn't just a pastime to while away the hours on the graveyard shift—maybe he could become a singing star like the brash Al Jolson or the king of crooners Gene Austin. A household name for over fifteen years, Jolson sometimes appeared in blackface and, in the early twenties, brought "mammy songs" into vogue with "Give Me My Mammy" and "Coal Black Mammy." He scored his biggest smash of all in 1928 with the keening "Sonny Boy." Austin's huge successes that year were the sentimental heart songs "Ramona" and "Jeannine (I Dream of Lilac Time)." Orvon began to learn these songs, while keeping up with Jolson and Austin's careers. He sometimes read entertainment trade papers such as *Variety*, *Talking Machine World*, and *The Billboard* (later shortened to *Billboard*).

One day, his reading led him to discover that another popular star of the day, Johnny Marvin, "The Ukulele Ace," hailed from Butler, Oklahoma. Marvin's romantic tenor enthralled audiences on Broadway, and his "The Little White House (at the End of Honeymoon Lane)"—from a popular Broadway musical, *Honeymoon Lane*—was one of the biggest songs of 1927. He'd made his name the year before with the novelty "Breezin' Along with the Breeze," which featured his uke, yodel, croon, and vocables, in which he rendered the sound of various instruments. He'd traveled a lot of miles from tiny Butler to Broadway.[6]

"Johnny used to say he was born in a covered wagon on the Ozark Mountain Trail in 1897," according to music scholar Jonathan Guyot Smith. "He did not know whether he was actually born in Oklahoma, Missouri, Arkansas, or Kansas."[7] Hailing from Missouri, his parents had settled on a farm ten miles south of Butler. When their eldest son Johnny was seven, his brother Frankie was born "in an old dugout." At the age of twelve, Johnny left home. Frankie recalled, "We didn't hear from him for a year or two at a time, finally when we'd heard, he'd be in some little Hawaiian troupe, singing and yodeling 'Go to Sleep My Baby.' "[8] Swept up in the Hawaiian music craze, Johnny learned to play island sounds on steel guitar and ukulele, forming the Royal Hawaiians with three like-minded musicians. In the early 1920s, he traveled to New York City to audition on Broadway. "He got in *Honeymoon Lane* [in 1926] with Eddie Dowling and Kate Smith—that was her first show and his too," said Frankie. "Victor had him over to sing some of these choruses he did on the show . . . and they liked his voice so much they just signed him up." Contracted by the country's top record label, Johnny sang with orchestras led by Leonard Joy and Nat Shilkret, both powerful Victor executives.

Through the Frisco grapevine, Orvon discovered that Johnny's mother, Molly Marvin, ran a hotel and café near Butler's depot. At some point, Orvon made the trip 200 miles west from Sapulpa to Butler. According to his railroad records, he was never stationed there, so he either passed through en route to another town or purposefully ventured there to meet Mrs. Marvin. The walls of the café, located in the lobby of the hotel, were decorated with publicity photos of the owner's famous son. Orvon struck up a conversation with Molly, then sang her a few songs. He later recalled in his autobiography, "Mrs. Marvin told me to look up Johnny if I ever got to New York, and I took the precaution of getting his address and phone number."[9] In just a few months' time, this information would provide the introduction of a lifetime.

IT WAS ANOTHER INTRODUCTION that would become a crucial part of the myth behind Gene Autry's success story. By the late 1920s Will Rogers was perhaps the most celebrated man in America. He'd become a star on Broadway as a trick roper and witty raconteur in New York's Ziegfeld Follies, subsequently appearing in movies and on radio broadcasts. Newspapers in New York, Chicago, Boston, Fort Worth, Kansas City, and other cities ran his weekly column. Then, in 1926, his byline hit papers on a daily basis: Just before leaving for a European tour, Rogers met Adolph S. Ochs, publisher of the *New York Times*, who told him, "If you run across anything worthwhile, cable it to us. We'll pay the tolls." Rogers took him up on it, sending him a witty telegram about an amusing encounter with Lady Astor. The *Times* ran it on the front page on July 26; more cables followed, all published in the *Times*, to great acclaim. After Rogers's return, he continued the practice of wiring the anecdotes and observations to the *Times*. Eventually, the McNaught Newspaper Syndicate began distributing Rogers's "Daily Telegram," and by 1927, more than six hundred U.S. newspapers carried it. No matter Rogers's whereabouts, he dashed into the local telegraph office by 4 PM to cable his daily missive to New York. On May 1, 1928, he sent his telegram from the Frisco Railroad depot in Chelsea, Oklahoma.[10]

Was Orvon Autry the telegrapher on duty that day? According to Frisco records, he was stationed in Sapulpa, although it's possible he could have been sent to Chelsea for a few days as relief operator. A decade later—nearly three years after Will Rogers's tragic death in a 1935 plane crash—the *Chicago Daily News* ran a story on the meteoric rise of movie star Gene Autry:

> [Gene Autry] was busy one day when a man, just off a train, came in to send a telegram. Noting the guitar, he asked if Gene played. "Yes, sir," was the reply. "Do you know 'They Plowed the Old Trail Under?'" he asked. Gene needed no urging—he started to play and sing. While the room vibrated with the song, the singer looked at the listener and wondered where he had seen him before. Many western ballads were sung. Finally the man said, "Let me play you something 'propriate, boy." The guitar sprang to new life under the words: "All the switchmen knew by the engine's moans. That the man at the throttle was Casey Jones. . . ." The song finished, the stranger began another lively tune of the great plains country. Then the man handed him the guitar, saying, "You belong in Hollywood, boy, playing the guitar—and not that telegraph instrument. Your heart ain't in it. Well, I reckon you better take my message." "Yes, sir." The message was signed Will Rogers. The stunned boy heard the words, "Say hello to the folks for me." Then the greatest trouper of his day was gone.[11]

In 1939, the *Saturday Evening Post* featured a similar story in which Rogers advised Autry to go to New York.[12] Over the next six decades, various versions of the tale would appear in nearly every publication that profiled Gene Autry, assuming the weight of legend. Later, the story was repeated on radio and television, ranging from his own CBS program *Melody Ranch* to Ed Sullivan's *Toast of the Town* TV show to documentaries in the 1980s and '90s. Gene's own telling varied; his date for the Rogers meeting ran the spectrum from July 1925 through 1929.[13] He once told a sports columnist that Rogers would stop by the depot to check baseball scores during the World Series and that the pair would chat. His 1978 memoir opened with a similar story occurring in July 1927: "I saw Rogers several times that summer. He was visiting a sister in Chelsea, and he'd drop into the telegraph office to wire his columns."[14] During that summer, Orvon did spend a week at the Claremore depot, the stop next to Chelsea. But the May 1, 1928, "Daily Telegram" was the only column Will Rogers ever sent from Chelsea, even though, conceivably, he may have sent or received other telegrams. Or Rogers could have visited the depot to check baseball scores as they came in over the wire.

Prior to 1937, profiles of Gene Autry never mentioned the Will Rogers encounter. Instead, credit for encouraging the would-be entertainer was given to fellow Frisco employees and anonymous customers. A 1936 feature in *Screen & Radio Weekly* dramatized Gene's origins:

During the long, lonely days and nights, he improved his guitar technique, playing and singing for his own amusement as well as the unbiased approval of the few sheepherders and cowpunchers that lounged around the depot. "The job gave me free transportation on the railroad," [Gene Autry] said, "but I didn't have any place to go, until one night a cattle man from Tulsa listened to me singin' a song I'd made up myself, 'count of I'd played the old ones plumb out. 'Son,' he said to me, 'my sister's got herself a raddio, and an' some o' the singin' comes outa the thing ain't no better than that tune you're wranglin'. Why don't you git yourself up to Noow York? I hear as how they even pay folks for singin' up there.' "[15]

Gene's relatives and colleagues had their doubts about the Will Rogers story. His cousin Callie Jane asked him about it once, and Gene admitted that although Rogers had visited a depot where Gene worked, the two had not conversed except as customer and telegrapher. There had been no impromptu concert. In an unpublished manuscript, Gene's longtime guitarist Johnny Bond described meeting Gene's uncle in Tioga in 1971. "Don't take that Will Rogers stuff too seriously," the relative told Bond. "You'll note that he didn't include it in his early publicity. He tacked that on later. I think it was just a publicity man's dream." Virginia MacPhail recalled the day PR man Bev Barnett took credit for the story: "Bev Barnett used to come in the office and he used to laugh about it," she said. "He worked at Republic when Gene was there, and he used to make up stories and publicity and all that, and he told me that he made that story up [about Will Rogers], and I believe it."[16] After all, this was typical of the Hollywood system in which stars' backgrounds were invented or enhanced to make them marketable to the public.

"Will Rogers was idolized in Gene's part of the country and by Gene's potential audience," Jonathan Guyot Smith has concluded. "Countless performers claimed a personal connection to, or relationship with, Will Rogers in the years immediately following his untimely passing. Gene went to great lengths to be identified with Will Rogers. I have been told that, in bygone years, he acknowledged to family members that the details were fabricated, but that he did meet Will Rogers. I dare say he did eventually believe the story. When one tells a story that many times over a period of years, it can and does become very real. Then, too, Gene—being an expert showman—told stories which he felt his audience wanted and expected to hear."

Regardless of who advised him, Orvon Autry took his first extended leave from the railroad in August 1928. Undoubtedly, all those gigs and admiring co-workers had boosted his confidence, so he decided to go to New York City and try to make a record. Before he left, he concluded he needed a more glamorous name—one with a better ring to it than Orvon. Where better to reinvent himself than the Big Apple?

6

A NEW NAME, A NEW PROFESSION

IT IS UNCERTAIN EXACTLY WHEN AND WHY Orvon Autry took the name Gene, but Gene Austin's massive popularity in 1927–28 probably inspired the choice. The elder crooner later told his nephew (country artist Tommy Overstreet) that he had given Gene Autry his blessing to start using the name Gene. Twenty years later, when Overstreet, Austin, and Autry got together in New York, they reminisced about the acquisition of Autry's name: In the late 1920s, the fledgling singer first met the seasoned entertainer and asked if he thought "Orvon" was bland. Austin said, "Yes, you should call yourself Gene Autry . . . I'm a star—and they'll associate you with me, and that will be a good thing for you!"[1]

Gene Autry never discussed the origins of his stage name, although he once wrote of Austin: "I did not meet Gene until 1927 or 1928. That was when I first went to New York to seek my fame and fortune and, of course, he had already reached the heights as a recording artist in that era. . . . He was always a very kind person—especially to a newcomer. . . . He gave me an awful lot of good advice."[2] Others have tried to take credit for inspiring the name, including Tioga's Dr. Eugene Ledbetter, who delivered Autry, but Gene Austin is the most likely inspiration.[3] Adding to the confusion, when Gene did a 1948 radio broadcast with Bing Crosby, the two kidded one another about their real names: while Bing admitted to the name Harry Lillis Crosby, Gene confessed to being "Orvon Eugene Autry."

Still known as Orvon by the railroad, he would become Gene Autry in New York City. Beginning his two-month leave from the Frisco, on August 10,

1928, Gene used his rail pass for part of the journey from Tulsa to New York. The train stopped in Hoboken, New Jersey, where he took a ferry across the Hudson River to New York. "That was when I had my first look at the New York skyline," Gene remembered fifty years later. "It was purely a shock for someone from the flatlands of Texas and Oklahoma. I thought to myself, 'My God, if I ever get in there I wonder if I can find my way back.'" He rode a bus to Grand Central, trekked across Forty-second Street to Times Square, then checked into the rundown Riley Hall hotel on West Forty-fifth.[4] The next day, Gene recalled, he "started running up and down Broadway with a guitar."[5] He wasn't in Manhattan long before he looked up Johnny Marvin. In his memoir Gene described getting Johnny's phone number from his mother, but he later said, "I was over at Victor trying to get an audition and there was a fellow, Leonard Joy, he was the A&R director at that time, and he heard me and said, 'Where are you from?' and I told him, 'Oklahoma.' And he said, 'Well, you know Johnny Marvin . . . he's one of our top artists and he's from Oklahoma. You have that twang about your voice, you sound very much like some of those fellas,' and I said, 'I've never met Johnny, but I've met his mother.' And he said, 'Well, fine, I'll give you his number and you call him.' So I called him and he said, 'Look, my brother Frankie is living in New York at some little hotel and you two ought to get together.'"[6]

Seven years Johnny's junior, Frankie Marvin had been operating a barbershop in Butler until his brother convinced him to give show biz a whirl in mid-1927. His first job in New York was running errands for the powerful music-publishers Shapiro-Bernstein. On the side, he added comic relief to Johnny's vaudeville performances, a role he'd later play as Gene's sideman. Frankie's rubbery features made him a natural at sight gags, and his facility as a musician enabled him to pick up and learn several instruments. His Okie twang was much more pronounced than his brother's, and he put it to use singing and writing humorous novelty songs. Johnny, billed as Honey Duke and His Uke, had recorded a few rustic numbers himself in early 1927 before making it as a pop crooner for Victor. He knew the hillbilly field—and the tiny labels that recorded it. Minuscule Grey Gull, Honey Duke's label, gave Frankie a shot, and he cut his first side, "The Bully of the Town"—which he later termed "pure corn"—during the summer of 1927. Frankie made another record the following spring, but it was his June 13, 1928, recording that helped set him on his path: "Blue Yodel No. 1" was Frankie's cover of a huge hit for hillbilly music's first superstar, Mississippi-born Jimmie Rodgers.

Rodgers had turned the yodel into a sensational music trend. A bluesy echoey sound made in the glottis, it had some antecedents in vocalizations from the Swiss Alps, but the "blue yodel" had more of a haunting quality. In 1927 Rodgers and his yodel had been discovered by Ralph Peer, who'd moved to Victor Records. His second Victor recording session yielded "Blue Yodel" (also known as "T for Texas"), setting his career on fire upon its release in February

1928. Billed as America's Blue Yodeler, Rodgers recorded one best-seller after the next. Every label wanted its own Jimmie Rodgers.

"I went down to one of the companies," Frankie Marvin recalled, "and played ukulele and . . . they asked me if I could yodel, and I said, 'Sure! That's my second name, Yodeling.' They said come down and make a test record, it was 'T for Texas,' Jimmie Rodgers's blue yodel. They had one of his records there. . . . That was the old Crown company. I did it and they liked it, and then Brunswick heard about it, Columbia, Edison. . . . So that kind of got me started."[7] He recorded "Blue Yodel" for all four companies.

In those early days of the recording industry, record labels had already initiated a sort of copycat policy: If a record found success, other labels scrambled to record the song by their own artists. Sometimes, an artist would record the same song for different labels, under a variety of names. This was a boon to would-be recording artists looking for a break. Billed as "Frankie Wallace and His Guitar," Frankie Marvin became the first of a long line of artists covering Jimmie Rodgers songs. Eventually, the most prolific—and best of these— would be Gene Autry.

When Gene arrived in New York, he was less familiar with Rodgers's records than with Johnny Marvin's and Gene Austin's Victor platters. Frankie soon tipped him off to Rodgers, informing Gene that yodeling was the ticket to a recording session. When Gene and Frankie bonded, they decided to bunk together to save money. Gene moved into Frankie's room at the Manger Hotel, on Seventh Avenue at Fiftieth Street. There, he began to absorb the rudiments of the entertainment business. At the Manger, one could easily rub shoulders with professional musicians; Rodgers himself always stayed there when he came to New York to record. Most likely, the Manger (which had become the Hotel Taft by 1931) is where Gene first met Gene Austin, as well as other well-known musicians of the day, including Clayton McMichen (a sometime bandmate of Rodgers), the hugely successful pop and hillbilly singer Vernon Dalhart, Kansas-born musician and songwriter Frank Luther, and Luther's frequent partner vocalist Carson Robison.

It was Frankie Marvin, though, who became Gene's best friend and mentor. "We had a lot of fun," Gene recalled of those dues-paying days. "We'd go to some pool halls and play pool, and he knew where there were a few speakeasies around there, and we'd go up and have a bottle of beer. . . . That was before Prohibition was repealed. And we got to be very close buddies." The deep friendship would last throughout their lives. Gene never forgot Frankie's early support and kept him employed for decades in his films, recordings, radio shows, TV programs, and tours until Marvin's retirement.

Not long after Gene's arrival in New York, Frankie got him an audition at Edison, where he had just cut another version of "Blue Yodel" on June 29, and had more sessions booked for August 20 and September 18. "I took him to the old Edison company and one of the sound men there played the piano," Frankie remembered. "He tried to make a test record of [Al Jolson's] 'Sonny Boy,' and he couldn't sing 'Sonny Boy' yet!"[8] Needless to say, Gene did not pass the audition.

He persevered, however, trying to sell himself to the labels. "New York was a tough town to crash," he later remembered.[9] "[I was] an ignorant country kid . . . I got the brush-off for sure when I struck Manhattan. I don't blame them now, those busy executives whose offices I stormed. I wore my 'store' clothes, tried to seem like another Rudy Vallee, and it just didn't go over."[10] There are various versions of Gene's audition at Victor Records, beginning with a June 1931 article in the *Tulsa World*: "It was in 1928 that he first tried out . . . Gene, who admits he doesn't know one note from another, wanted a fling at recording. He found it impossible to make appointments with the musical directors of record companies, so he wormed his way into the office of a company head by sheer stubbornness. He asked a secretary if he might see the manager, saying he had an appointment. The manager insisted he had no appointment with Gene. But Gene went on with his story regardless. 'I'm from Oklahoma and I want to make records,' he said. 'I know Johnny Marvin, but he's out of town. You've got to give me a trial.' He was told to come back the next day."[11]

Johnny Marvin probably pulled strings to get him the Victor audition, even though his brother Frankie had yet to record for the label. Gene's charm undoubtedly helped as well. As Jimmy Long's daughter, Beverly, said of him, "Gene was smart, and he would talk to anybody and tell them anything. He could talk to you like crazy and sell you the moon."[12] Gene later told of persisting in the Victor lobby hoping for an audition, until the receptionist felt sorry for him and asked him to play her a song. As he was attempting "Jeannine, I Dream of Lilac Time," the song's composer, Nat Shilkret, a Victor executive and orchestra leader, walked in, heard him, and put in a good word for him. He got an appointment with Victor vice president Leonard Joy, who, as Gene later recalled, said, "I'm going to record a band tomorrow, and if you want to come in after the session is over, I'll let you do a song on the wax and we'll see what it sounds like.' In those days, they put everything on wax; that was a long time before tape."

Gene went back to the Manger and spent much of the night practicing hits by Austin and Jolson. The next day at the studio, he was feeling "nervous and scared" as he crooned "Jeannine" into a microphone. "I was no good—too stiff and self-conscious."[13] Gene recalled, "They had a committee that would listen to your test to see if they thought it was commercial or if they could do anything with it. So [Joy] played this test back to me two or three times, and said, 'You know, I think you have a good voice for recording, but I can't send this to the committee. I know that you're nervous and shaky, but they don't look at it that way. They feel that if you're going to make records, it's got to be right. I would advise you to go back to Oklahoma and get a job on radio and get some experience and then in maybe six months or a year, you come back.' "[14]

Gene stayed in New York long enough for the Marvins to invite him along to their performance at the Palace Theater in White Plains, New York, just north of the city. The venue was a favorite of Johnny's, and that night he called his green young friend to the stage. Gene debuted on the New York stage with his rendition of "Sonny Boy." After the show, the Marvin brothers "advised him to go back to Oklahoma, practice up on the guitar, and get rid of those 'Sonny Boy' type songs and learn to yodel like Jimmie Rodgers," Frankie recalled.[15] Gene told them, " 'I don't know. I never did try [yodeling].' So he tried to yodel, and he had just a very little falsetto voice, and I said, 'Well, go home and practice on your singing and yodeling and come back and I'll get you another test record.' "[16] Johnny got him a referral letter from Nat Shilkret to impress radio programmers in Oklahoma.

WITH HIS FRISCO LEAVE ABOUT TO EXPIRE, Gene needed to return to Sapulpa and his job on the railroad. Although he'd failed to make a record, he still had hope. His taste of show business and his friends' encouragement added fuel to his ambition—he could become a singing star if he just worked hard enough. As Central Park's leaves turned golden, a few days after Gene turned twenty-one—presumably celebrated at one of Frankie's favorite speakeasies—he boarded the train for home. Frankie loaned him a few dollars for the trip, and Gene swore to his friend he would see him again soon. In less than a year, Gene kept his promise.

7

THE OKLAHOMA YODELING COWBOY

AS SOON AS GENE RETURNED TO SAPULPA, he rushed over to Jimmy Long's house to describe his adventures in New York and discuss his follow-up plans. Jimmy agreed to book more shows for the duo at civic clubs, local dances, and Frisco Employes [*sic*] Club meetings. Gene later wrote in his memoir, "For the next six months, I traveled more back roads than a bootlegger, singing at Kiwanis clubs and high schools and private parties all over the state."[1] To improve his vocal technique and become microphone-worthy, Gene engaged Tulsa vocal coach Robert Boice Carson, an opera singer and impresario who promoted the first-ever Caruso concert in Tulsa. During the lessons, which Gene continued for about a month, Carson taught him breathing exercises and helped him improve his tone and enunciation. Gene also signed up for guitar lessons at Tulsa's Hawaiian School of Music, where instructor Robert Ridley taught him off and on for about sixteen months.

His next step was to secure a spot on Tulsa's KVOO. That June of 1928, the station had been purchased in full by a shareholder, wealthy Tulsa oilman W. G. Skelly. He expanded the station's facilities and programming, including an affiliation with NBC and its national broadcasts. Local talent still predominated, with fifteen-minute shows by entertainers like the Baby Grand Twins, the Industrial City Five, the Phantom Fiddler, the Oil City Hummingbirds, and Doris and Melba Harmony Girls. Staff musicians included a string trio and a Hawaiian trio. With his letter of recommendation in hand, Gene arrived at the station's East Eleventh Street office and met with station manager Harry Hutchinson, who agreed to give him a try. His vocals impressed Hutchinson enough to win a sustaining program, which meant that when KVOO didn't have a sponsored show on air, Gene could fill the time—unpaid. He also introduced Gene to Jimmy Wilson, whose Catfish String Band would sometimes back him up. Although Gene still wore his Sunday suit, bowtie, and fedora during performances, his Western twang must have inspired the KVOO announcer to create for him a new persona. "Without me knowin' about it," Gene later recalled, "the announcer introduced me as 'the original Oklahoma Yodelin' Cowboy.'"[2] He also started working up some new songs, including Jimmie Rodgers covers. On slow nights in the depot, he struggled to compose a few numbers, and on their days off he and Jimmy Long continued to collaborate.

On December 11, 1928, Gene received notice from Frisco headquarters that his application to become Sapulpa's third-shift telegrapher had been accepted. He had been serving as relief operator for the past two months. Now, before his midnight shift began, he could perform at dances and parties, as well as on the radio. Sadly for Gene, Jimmy Long also received notice that he was being transferred to Springfield, Missouri, home of Frisco's headquarters.

When the new year rolled around, Gene was on his own. The *Frisco Employes' Magazine* gave "O. G. Autry" press coverage for the first time in its January 1929 issue: "Let us remind you that he is some singer. If you should happen to be listening in on your radio some night to KVOO . . . and hear the announcer state that 'Gene Autry, the singer of popular songs, will sing for us,' just remember he is one of us." That year, KVOO became a 5,000-watt station, beaming its broadcast to a tremendous swath of the Southwest. Gene's stint at KVOO would last about nine months, during which time he grew comfortable projecting his soft vocals into the electric microphone. His weekly broadcasts also helped spread the reputation of the Oklahoma Yodeling Cowboy. KVOO would later give a boost to the careers of other country stars, including Western swing pioneer Bob Wills, in 1934. In 1949 KVOO's general manager acknowledged the status its alumnus had given the station, writing Gene in gratitude that "through the years you have never failed to mention KVOO in any article concerning your first days in radio. We sincerely appreciate your remembering us and want to thank you for that thoughtfulness." Gene responded in kind, "You can rest assured that I am always happy to give KVOO a plug, because that is really where I first started my radio career."[3]

Gene continued to win fans among his fellow workers. Frisco pals Willard Baker and Bob Brenner would cram into his tiny room at his boardinghouse and watch him practice. Afterwards, they'd all head over to the Fred Harvey House restaurant, where Willard's wife, Louise, worked. In his spare time Gene listened to all kinds of music, including hits by Rodgers and Vernon Dalhart; the latter's hugely successful "The Wreck of the Old '97" and "The Prisoner Song," particular favorites of Gene's, had ushered in the popularity of hillbilly music four years earlier in 1924.

Dreaming of the day he'd return to New York, Gene began saving as much money as he could—while still sending some home to his mother. Making seventy cents an hour, he usually netted about forty dollars a week at the depot; an occasional performance for the Lion's Club or some other group would earn him an additional fifteen dollars. Finances had not improved for the Autrys, still living in Ravia. When Gene visited, he noticed his mother getting thinner each time he saw her. Her old sparkle and energy had diminished, and she rarely sang anymore. Nursing ten-year-old Dudley back to health from pneumonia seemed to have weakened her further. Delbert rarely made appearances at home, and when he did, he and Nora bickered constantly. Veda and Wilma, who shared a room split down the middle with a quilt hanging from the ceiling to divide their quarters, had developed into attractive teenagers. Their voices harmonized perfectly when singing, and mischievous younger brother Dudley tried to warble along as best he could.

IN SAPULPA, GENE MISSED JIMMY LONG'S COMPANIONSHIP at the depot—his replacement, J. M. Smith, was no music man—so when Gene got transferred to Catoosa, only fifteen minutes east of Tulsa, he didn't really mind. Since becoming a Mason in the little town, he'd regularly returned to lodge meetings there. The brand-new Route 66 ran right through Catoosa, as it did Tulsa and Sapulpa. Sixty-one-year-old fiddler Otto Funk had recently made local news by walking and fiddling along the highway, headed to the Pacific Ocean in California. He told the *Tulsa World*, he "chose 66 for his trek to the coast . . . because it is the most advertised highway in America." In mid-February, Gene started a seven-month stint as second-shift telegrapher at the Catoosa depot. It was a quick train ride to Tulsa, so his radio broadcasts and other performances in Tulsa continued. Sometimes at the depot, Gene found it difficult to keep his mind on the mundane tasks at hand. During a shift as a substitute in Bristow, he miscalculated a customer's ticket to a town with the unlikely name of Smackover, Arkansas. A few months later, he would receive an official reprimand from Supervisor C. T. Mason: "It develops that this undercharge [of $2.59 was] caused by your misreading the Tariff. This is no good excuse for case of this kind; and for your responsibility in undercharging on this ticket am assessing your personal record with a reprimand, and trust you will read your Tariffs sufficiently hereafter to assess the correct rate."[4]

Gene quickly made new friends in Catoosa. He boarded in the home of John and Becky Paul, whose teenage son Ray and his girlfriend Helen Hamilton liked to pal around with Gene. Helen, who later married Ray, remembered those days fondly: "We had parties on Friday nights, usually at our house, and we would sing and play games. Gene played the guitar. We didn't think he sang so great, but we thought he was a great guy. He was a very nice looking young man."[5] Ray sometimes hopped a freight train to Tulsa with Gene, bound for KVOO or a dance to play. Ray and Gene frequently visited the grocery store where Helen worked behind the soda fountain—until a jealous young manager banished the boys for distracting the pretty fountain girl. Years later, a history of Catoosa reported that "many evenings [Gene] sat in the old wooden porch swing at the home of school teachers Mrs. Ross and Mrs. Mills with young people lining the porch and board walk, completely enthralled by his melodious voice."[6] One day, Helen brought along her new Brownie camera and photographed the Oklahoma Yodeling Cowboy, perched on a wall outside the depot. With the Catoosa Hotel and Frisco tracks behind him, Gene looks more like a dandy waiting for a train than a singing cowboy. Smiling and strumming the acoustic guitar in his lap, Gene is wearing his dark three-piece suit, dress shoes, polka-dot bowtie, and white shirt, with a fedora shading his eyes. "Gene always just wore basic clothes," Helen Paul recalled. It would be another year before he began donning buckaroo garb.

On Sunday, April 28, Johnny Marvin appeared at Tulsa's Ritz Theatre, on the city's vaudeville touring circuit. The *Tulsa World* heralded the show: "Johnny Marvin, Famous Victor Artist in Person—The Oklahoma lad, who took a ukulele to New York and made 'em like it to the tune of a half million dollars, returns to Oklahoma for the first time since his sensational rise to international fame and fortune." Gene must have attended at least one of the four performances—at 2:30, 4:30, 6:00, and 9:50—and may have done a song with Marvin. Helen Paul remembered going to a Tulsa concert with Gene, most probably the Johnny Marvin show. "He and a friend of his were playing there," she related, "and he invited a bunch of us kids backstage, and we thought that was really something." Later that spring, Gene probably caught one of Jimmie Rodgers's shows too. At the height of fame, with several successful records under his belt, Jimmie toured the Southwest on the Radio-Keith-Orpheum Interstate Circuit. Gene was possibly in the audience at the Orpheum Theater in Tulsa, where Jimmie headlined from May 18 to 24, before moving on to the Orpheum in Oklahoma City from May 25 to 31.

In September, Gene received notice of his transfer to the second-shift spot in Sapulpa. His last day on the job in Catoosa fell on his birthday. Gene always remembered Catoosa fondly, fifty years later calling it "a wonderful place that fills my memories." Gene promised to keep his friends posted on his whereabouts and later wrote Helen a postcard from Manhattan. He was already planning his next trip there and urged Jimmy Long to accompany him. Both Gene and Jimmy were nervous about the financial health of the railroad and the possibility of layoffs. Trucks that could now sail along paved roads like Route 66 were taking away some of the Frisco's freight-hauling business. Travelers, instead of riding passenger trains, opted to drive their automobiles or take buses on increasingly safer highways with new amenities like roadside diners and motor courts. The Frisco fought back by running advertisements boasting of its "vast transportation system embracing more than 5,800 miles of rails, and more than 25,000 alert workers." Gene was torn between hanging onto his job and striking out for the bright lights of Broadway again. "The rail-road business got kinda bad about 1929," he later related. "They were laying off a lot of employees, reducing their payroll, and it looked like I might be one of 'em." A few days after he turned twenty-two, Gene was elated to learn that Jesse and Jimmy Long would join him in the Big Apple the first week of October. With railroad pass in hand, Gene headed back to New York. Sapulpa and the Frisco would have to wait until after yet another "vacation."

Johnny and Frankie Marvin had kept their word, setting up an appointment for Gene to cut a test record at Victor on October 9. With Jimmy Long in tow, Gene and the Marvin brothers headed to Victor's Liederkranz Hall studio. At 9:30 AM, just after a session by a Greek guitar and mandolin ensemble, Gene and Jimmy stepped up to the mic to harmonize on a sentimental ballad written by Frankie, "My Dreaming of You." Gene's mellow-toned voice showed a bit of re-serve, as if he were nervously holding back any spontaneity or emotionalism. He almost seemed to be hiding behind his mentor, blending his vocals so perfectly with Jimmy's that it was hard to distinguish the two parts. Frankie contributed a boisterous yodel throughout and rhythmically strummed his guitar, while Johnny played a distinctive steel guitar riff. Frankie's yodeling kicked off the next number, Jimmy's nostalgic "My Alabama Home." Also a duet, Gene's doleful vo-cal is slightly up front in the mix, with Jimmy's harmony following his lead. The-matically a Mammy song but with an old-timey mountain-style melody, "My Alabama Home" longs for mother, home, and sweetheart. Frankie handled the guitar chores, with Johnny adding violin. By 12:15, the session was over. Victor's original recording log lists the artists as "Jimmy Long & Gene Autry vocal duet" under the category of "Native American Melodies." Accompaniment is recorded as "two Hawaiian guitars, under the direction of L. L. Watson." A handwritten note states that Johnny Marvin played violin and was "not to be paid" and that "no music" sheets had been provided for the sessions. Although not exactly off to an auspicious start, Gene Autry had officially made his first recording; but by the time Victor released the disc the following January, Gene, under several pseudo-nyms, had cut several more songs for a variety of labels.

Jimmy and Jesse headed back to Springfield a few days later, but the Okla-homa Yodeling Cowboy hungered for more recording. Rooming with Frankie at the Manger, he continued to practice his yodeling and guitar technique. Gene knew he could do better than his tryout at Victor. Frankie had been recording steadily over the past year and promised to get him another session. "We had about six, seven companies there everybody was working for," Frankie later related. "It kept me going! I was doing all the Jimmie Rodgers numbers— that was the biggest thing I had. What I could write and steal on the other side—you knew if you put one [song] on the side of [a] Jimmie Rodgers [cover], it was going to sell!"[7] Again, the Marvin brothers invited Gene to a gig at the Palace in White Plains. This time during his guest spot, Gene tried "Frankie and Johnny," an old minstrel song recently recorded as a blue yodel by Rodgers.

"They liked old Gene there, by golly!" Frankie reported about the very enthusiastic audience response.

By mid-October, when Frankie accompanied Gene to another studio, the Oklahoma Yodeling Cowboy had decided to try the Rodgers style. Gene also took a batch of original compositions to record. Located across the East River from Manhattan in Queens, New York, the studio belonged to the Starr Piano Company, an Indiana-based business that owned the Gennett record label. Starr leased the facility to the Q-R-S (Quality & Real Service) label, which primarily released "race records" made by black artists. The facilities and label were in the process of being sold to the tiny Cova Recording Company when Gene and Frankie showed up that day in October.

Ready for a new start, Gene vigorously let loose on a dozen sides, including five Autry originals. There are no session records showing specific dates, and only nine of the tracks (including two takes of one song) still exist. "Stay Away from My Chicken House," written by Frankie in the Rodgers vein, features a sly edge to Gene's vocals. Using a conversational tone, Gene's warm voice adds an intimacy to the proceedings. This time, Gene did his own yodeling with assurance; he also plucked his own guitar, with Frankie adding accents on the steel. "My Oklahoma Home," the first self-penned number of Gene's recording career, is clearly inspired by Jimmy Long's "My Alabama Home." Gene mournfully croons the nostalgic ballad, sometimes overreaching his range to hit the high notes. Both his guitar rhythms and Frankie's steel playing occasionally veer out of time with the vocals, and Frankie's ill-conceived guitar break doesn't help matters. Another Autry original, "I'll Be Thinking of You, Little Gal," merges the Rodgers and Long styles: A sentimental heart song, it finds Gene singing with more conviction and a hint of vibrato in his slightly nasal vocals. Again, Gene stretches his range a bit to hit the higher notes, but the result is compelling. Here, Frankie's steel playing sounds perfectly matched to the song, particularly Gene's lively yodeling. The second take of the song, with its slower tempo, lacks the spark of the first. Gene's very first Western-titled number, "Cowboy Yodel," is really more of a blue yodel—albeit a fine one. The song title and first line are the most "Western" aspect of the song, a kind of paean to the shiftless, happy-go-lucky life:

> I'm just a yodeling cowboy
> As happy as I can be
> Any depot or stockyard is home sweet home to me
> I have no cares like millionaires
> No grief to make me blue
> I go my way from day to day
> And paddle my own canoe.

"Why Don't You Come Back to Me," another Autry ballad, exhibits more of the Jimmy Long influence, with sentimental lyrics and crooning mixed with yodeling. Gene's lilting "No One to Call Me Darling" opens with Frankie's harmonica in tandem with Autry's guitar—his rhythmic finger-picking show-ing much improvement. A remorseful, first-person narrative about a rounder who "gambled my money away" demonstrates Gene's increasing grasp of Rodgers-style material. Marvin's humorous "Living in the Mountains" is an-other nod to the rounder songs of Rodgers, with Gene carefully enunciating lines about drinking "rock and rye," and superbly yodeling throughout. "Yo-delin' Gene," written by Arthur Fields—a twenty-year veteran who wrote hits for Vernon Dalhart, among others—is less inspired than the sessions' other blue yodels. Also recorded that day, but lost to posterity are another Fields song, "That's Why I Left the Mountains," Frankie Marvin's "Oh for the Wild and Wooly West," and Gene's first bona fide Rodgers cover, "Blue Yodel No. 6." Curiously, Rogers had not yet released the song, but somehow Gene already knew it.

On the way to New York in early October, Gene may have stopped off in Chicago and met with record executive Jack Kapp. Gene later recalled this visit as taking place variously in 1927 and 1929. "Jack Kapp was the vice president and A&R for OKeh [a division of the Columbia Phonograph Company]," Gene told broadcaster Mike Oatman in 1983, "and he said, 'Gene, if you're going to New York, you go on over to OKeh. There's a friend of mine there, Tommy Rockwell, and I think he can give you some good advice . . . and you tell him that I sent you in there.' So I said, 'I'll do that.' So I talked to Tommy Rockwell, and he said, 'I think that where you ought to go is over at Velvet Tone,' . . . so I went over there, and I got a test with them and they recorded me. A fellow by the name of Herman Rose was in charge there, and that's where I first met Vernon Dalhart and . . . Kate Smith and Rudy Vallee . . . all of them, because they were all in and out of there recording at the same time I was. So I met them and the first record I did [there] was 'Left My Gal in the Mountains.' They called it hillbilly music at that time."[8]

THE VELVET TONE LABEL was among a family of budget labels, including Diva and Harmony owned by Columbia, which often used these less expensive lower-grade pressings to release popular songs rerecorded by unknown, new artists. The three labels would release the exact same recordings but distribute them through different chain stores at varying discount prices; Diva, for exam-ple, was sold exclusively through the W. T. Grant dime stores. Velvet Tone and Harmony specialized in issuing pseudonymously released songs recorded by stars such as Dalhart and Vallee.

On October 24 a self-assured Gene Autry, with guitar in hand, strolled into Columbia's studios in the Gotham National Bank Building, at Columbus Circle and Broadway, in Manhattan. Gene later wrote of this session, "I walked into the studio with nothing but my guitar and my own courage. Our equip-ment consisted of two old-fashioned horns. I sang into one and the engineer, an old-timer named Clyde Emerson, placed the other on the chair in front of my guitar. We had no arrangements. I just kept singing until Clyde Emerson was satisfied, and that was it."[9]

By 1929 most companies had switched from acoustical recording, in which musicians played and sang into horns, to electrical, using microphones; budget labels, however, like Velvet Tone were among the last to make the transition. Electric microphones also changed live performance. Prior to its development, big-voiced tenors like Al Jolson used a megaphone to belt even louder. As microphones were perfected, a whole new style and era of softer singing was ushered in, benefiting such vocalists as Gene and his peer Bing Crosby. As Crosby biographer Gary Giddins points out: "According to an old theatrical shibboleth, an entertainer who could not project to the balcony's last row was not ready for the big time; Jolson exemplified the leather-lunged belter of songs. With the arrival of the microphone—and instant exit of the preposterous megaphone—a new and more intimate kind of singing for larger audiences was made possible. Technology changed music. Ironically, mechanics led to a more human and honest transition between singers and listeners."[10]

By this time, Gene had made enough recordings to feel comfortable in the studio, and adhering to the budget-label marketing strategy, he chose two popular covers to record for his Columbia test. Carson Robison's narrative song about a jailbird, "Left My Gal in the Mountains," had been a hit the previous spring for Robison and his duet partner Frank Luther. Gene's plaintive version is warm and personable, with a strong vocal delivery and superb yodeling. His other selection, Jimmie Rodgers's month-old smash, "Blue Yodel No. 5," is a near-perfect imitation of the original. Gene had clearly studied the record to the point of copying Rodgers's intonations, pauses, and pronunciation. This is the first hint of the precision with which Gene would develop his blue yodel covers over the next two years.

The day Gene made his breakthrough recordings at Columbia went down in history as Black Thursday—nearly 13 million shares of stock were traded at a loss of six billion dollars. The economic crisis that had ravaged rural Texas and Oklahoma for five years soon swallowed the country whole. For Gene Autry, though, the next few months would see him become a recording star.

8

HILLBILLY RECORDING ARTIST

YOU CAN NEVER TELL WHEN THAT BREAK COMES ALONG," Gene
Autry once said, "and when it does, you have to be prepared for it,
and you have to work hard for it after you get it."[1] That philosophy, voiced in
1991, probably dates from the autumn of 1929. Gene had labored to improve
his singing and guitar playing to succeed at his first shot at recording. Now,
with several sessions under his belt, Gene could not guess the fate of the songs
he had cut—even whether or not they would actually be released on disc. He
was obligated, nonetheless, to resume his telegrapher duties on the Frisco in
Sapulpa. Once again, he said goodbye to the Marvin brothers and took the
train home to Oklahoma.

Soon after his return, he received word that six of the recordings made at
the Gennett studios had been pressed and released by Cova on Q-R-S. The
three discs, issued in very small quantities, included "I'll Be Thinking of You,
Little Gal" coupled with "Living in the Mountains," "Oh for the Wild and
Wooly West" backed by "Blue Yodel No. 6" and "That's Why I Left the Mountains" with the flipside "Yodelin' Gene." The 78-rpm platters' bright red label
listed the artist as Gene Autry, but so few were issued that decades later record
collectors gave Q-R-S the nickname "Quite Rarely Seen."

Even better news came on November 15: a wire from Columbia informed
Gene that his recordings would be issued on Velvet Tone under the name
"Gene Autry, the Yodeling Cowboy" and that he should hurry back to New
York to record more. Although Gene's name was unknown to record buyers, the
songs he cut were in demand, and upon release in January his Velvet Tone 78

took off. Those who couldn't afford to pay seventy-five cents for "Left My Gal in the Mountains" by Robison and Luther on OKeh could scrape together the twenty-five cents to purchase it on Velvet Tone. Other buyers would purchase Gene's budget disc for his version of "Blue Yodel No. 5," which had cost seventy-five cents on Victor. Thus began a pattern for Gene's early success, beginning with his first Columbia release: He would cover hit records on inexpensive, budget labels, building a name for himself in the process. When he began recording for pricier imprints, he used a pseudonym—the opposite approach of such singers as Vernon Dalhart, who made discount releases under an alias. While the Depression (and radio) ate into the record business, limiting the sales of higher-priced records, the budget 78s—of poorer quality, using less shellac—continued to sell. They could be found at dime stores and via mail-order catalogues, which delivered the goods to rural areas where retail outlets were limited and radios scarce.

As copies of "Blue Yodel No. 5" backed with "Left My Gal in the Mountains" were headed to record bins and catalogues nationwide, Gene climbed aboard the Frisco, en route to New York City. Although he'd briefly held down his position at Sapulpa, as soon as he received the wire, he'd requested and received a sixty-day leave "to visit the folks." Why didn't he confess that he was returning to Manhattan to make more records? His Frisco supervisors and co-workers had been supportive of the budding entertainer's music career, but Gene probably did not want to push his luck.

On December 1 Frankie Marvin welcomed him back to the Manger, where he began practicing for his next Columbia sessions. Over three days, Gene would record sixteen sides: During the first session on Tuesday, December 3, Gene accompanied himself on guitar, as on the October 24 session. The six songs he cut that day included his own compositions, the plaintive "Why Don't You Come Back to Me" and waltz-tempo "No One to Call Me Darling," both of which he'd recorded in October for Cova but were still unreleased. His new versions were greatly improved, with stronger singing and guitar picking.

Gene had learned the value of releasing songs for which he owned the copyright. In addition to the glory of being considered a songwriter, the disc, sheet music, and songbook sales yielded additional earnings for the material's composers. It was common practice in those days for artists such as Jimmie Rodgers to purchase a song's copyright from its writer, particularly if the composer was an unknown—or broke. Depending on the situation, a song's author would sometimes not only give up its copyright (partially or wholly) but his or her name as composer, too. Thus, it can be hard to discern the true author of a song—as is the case for many of the early compositions credited to Gene. He later admitted to buying from the composers all rights to some of these early songs. In any case, his knack for choosing good material became evident early on—whether he actually wrote the number, or bought and transformed it, making it his own.

With Gene's growing popularity, Jimmy Long was more than happy to permit his protégé to share credit on songs—whether or not Gene penned a lyric or hummed a chorus. One of those credited as a Long-Autry composition, "Hobo Yodel," was their version of Rodgers's "Yodeling Hobo." For the first time in the studio, Gene included a spoken aside and an a capella yodel. Another high point of this session was Gene's personable and spirited reading of the catchy Frankie Marvin number "Dust Pan Blues." Gene also recorded the Rodgers hit he had performed so successfully onstage with the Marvins in White Plains, a confident "Frankie and Johnnie," which sounded as though Gene had been doing nothing but yodeling since October.

Two days later, on Thursday, he returned to the studio with Frankie. The buddies' camaraderie is documented by their lively reading of Gene's rerecording of "Stay Away from My Chicken House." This time, Frankie added some hilarious barnyard sound effects to further animate the song. Frankie is probably responsible, too, for the soaring train whistle in Gene's admirable version of the Rodgers smash "Waiting for a Train." Other songs attempted that day were Rodgers's ballad "Lullaby Yodel," Carson Robison's rambling-man narrative "Railroad Boomer," Frankie's novelty number "Slue-Foot Lue," and an improved redo of Gene's first-ever recording, "My Dreaming of You"—demonstrating Gene's vocal development since the Victor session.

Gene returned alone for the final day's session, again, ably handling three Rodgers selections, "California Blues (Blue Yodel No. 4)," "I'm Sorry We Met," and "Daddy and Home." Between 1929 and 1931 Autry would record twenty-eight different Rodgers songs, repeating several, totaling thirty-eight sides. Gene's versions were more sparely recorded than the Rodgers originals, which sometimes included small jazz bands and other instrumentation. Except for the occasional steel or banjo, Gene's usually featured only vocals and guitar. Gene eventually covered four of Rodgers's blue yodels, with the rest of the covers culled from the Singing Brakeman's repertoire of sentimental ballads and narrative story songs. Gene showed a real flair for the material, sometimes personalizing the songs with his own spoken asides. His version of "Waiting for a Train," for instance, starts with Gene, unaccompanied, speaking into the mic: "Oh lawd, I left dear old Frisco for my home down in Dixieland. But here I am all stranded down by the Rio Grande. I'm looking for a handout now. As I go on my weary way, the stars are my only blanket. I do my traveling by day." A train whistle blows, the guitar strum kicks in, and Gene emotes the familiar opening line of Rodgers's signature song. In the middle break, Gene again breaks into his verbal drawl, which ends with his wishing "for a good ole bowl of chili."

In addition to the financial motivation to cover Rodgers's work, Gene developed a special affinity for the Blue Yodeler and his songs. Music scholars have argued whether or not Gene ever met the doomed Rodgers, who tragically died of tuberculosis in 1933. Gene once told country singer Eddy Arnold that he'd been introduced to Rodgers in New York by none other than Gene Austin. Arnold later recalled, "Gene Autry . . . told me of how he was foolin' round in New York in the late twenties; he hadn't happened yet and was trying to get a record deal. . . . He got a call from Austin saying he wanted him to come to his office [at the Knickerbocker Hotel]. So he went, and when he arrived, he found Jimmie Rodgers sitting there. That's how Gene Autry met Jimmie, because of Gene Austin—which [Gene Autry] said was the biggest thrill in his life."[2] Gene told a similar story in 1983 to broadcaster Mike Oatman: "When I first met Jimmie, we had a lot in common because I was a railroad man and so was he. He was a brakeman, and I was, of course, a telegraph operator and . . . a train dispatcher. . . . He had made some records for Victor, and Ralph Peer at that time was his manager. . . . I met him in a hotel in New York. I forget who told me that Jimmie was in town . . . so I gave him a call, and he said, 'Fine, come by and we'll have a drink,' and I went over and I introduced myself to him and we got together, and he was a lot of fun. I always liked him. I met him several times on several occasions after that. . . . Later on, I'd run into him, and he traveled with a tent show for quite a long time, and he drew big crowds everywhere he went."[3]

When Oatman asked Gene about his Rodgers-style records, Gene responded, "I've had a lot of people who said that I did sound like Jimmie Rodgers, and not intentionally I did. . . . but I can see now where it would be very easy to fall into a pattern such as Jimmie Rodgers or even probably Vernon Dalhart when he would sing some of those songs . . . I think especially if you learned them off of a record, it would be very very easy to fall into that pattern. I can see that." In other interviews over the years, Gene became defensive or even dismissive about his Rodgers soundalikes—perhaps because Gene's later musical innovations yielded its own share of imitators: "Being the first of the singing cowboys," he related, "whoever followed [me] had to be probably ten times better than I was or they would always be [considered] a copy."[4]

AFTER GENE COMPLETED HIS THREE JIMMIE RODGERS SONGS at his last Columbia session, he was ready for socializing. Frankie Marvin liked to tell a story about some celebrating that went on at their hotel.

> Gene and me, we roomed together a lot. At the Manger, we had adjoining rooms with one bath. We could leave the door open and visit back and forth. And we drank a little. It was easy to get, and we would sit by the window and look out into the [air shaft], as opposed to overlooking the street. We could see the other boarders through the windows and every now and then we'd see somebody throw an empty bottle out the window. It would crash below and make a lot of fuss and, naturally, somebody complained. So, what the heck . . . after a few drinks, we too, would throw a "dead soldier" out the window, then we'd duck down so nobody could tell where the bottle was coming from. Anyway, after two or three more bottles were thrown out, the

house dick figured it might be us and came up and knocked on the door. I guess he
could tell that we were the culprits and he chewed us out real good and said that if
we didn't stop it he'd have us kicked out of the hotel. I was a pretty good talker . . .
and I talked him out of it promising that it wouldn't happen again. With that, the
house detective left.

After a while I noticed that the incident had upset Gene a little for he walked
over to the telephone and said, 'Let me talk to the house detective.' Even though I
tried to get him to lay off, he got the officer on the phone and chewed him out
something fierce. "You've got a lotta gall!" Gene shouted into the receiver. "Comin'
up here and insulting us like that. Why, I'll have you know that I work for the
Frisco Railroad. What's more, my buddy here, Frankie Marvin, he's one of the
biggest . . . selling stars on records. Who'n the hell do you think you are threatening to kick us out of our room?"

Well, that fixed that. The next thing we knew, both Gene and me, we were
walking the streets with our suitcases in our hands. "I wasn't going to let him get
away with that," said Gene, as we looked for another place to stay that night.[5]

Chances are that Gene and Frankie easily found a nearby watering hole to
drown their sorrows after the hotel fiasco. By late 1929, with an estimated
32,000 speakeasies flourishing in New York City, local police were barely en-
forcing the Volstead Act.[6] Frankie "was making plenty of money . . . run[ning]
around, single, we didn't care what happened," Marvin later remembered.
Occasionally, the two buddies would find a couple of gals to step out with them
too. Frankie had become quite popular as a recording artist over the past year.
Among his numerous discs on a variety of labels, his biggest success was the
self-penned "Oklahoma Blues." "Used to get seventy-five or one hundred and
fifty dollars for making a number," Frankie remembered, "and then you get
royalties too. Like the 'Oklahoma Blues.' I wrote it . . . and finally I made the
doggone thing. I made it for the old Crown label, and the first [royalty] statement on it, I think it was a three-months statement, it sold 41,000 records.
That's pretty good in those days!" Marvin went on to record the song for prestigious imprints like OKeh and Brunswick. "Between my royalties and everything, I was doing pretty good," he remembered, "probably fifteen, eighteen
thousand a year, or something like that. Then that Crash came."

As banks began to fail, Marvin eventually numbered among those whose
investments vanished, including a farm he'd bought in Oklahoma, but he considered himself fortunate compared to some. "Boy, a lot of those guys in the
stock market—some musicians—killed themselves!" he related. "Guys were
making big money. Old Andy Snell used to play saxophone—he got five hundred dollars for every time he played a solo on that sax in a theater. And those
guys, they lost their shirt in the stock market!"[7]

There were many lessons Gene had learned in New York as the year came
to a close. When he returned to Sapulpa, he discovered his "secret" was out, and
that his boss at the Frisco knew he'd been in New York making records while on
leave. He could hardly keep it quiet, of course, when Velvet Tone released two

more Gene Autry 78s on January 7: "Dust Pan Blues"/"Hobo Yodel" and "Slue-Foot Lou"/"Waiting for a Train." Rather than receive a reprimand, however, Gene had become the talk of the railroad—garnering his very first feature in the February 1930 *Frisco Employes Magazine*: The half-page article, titled "He Makes Records: Gene Autry of Sapulpa Scores as Recording Artist," included a photo of the grinning telegrapher, dressed in suit and tie and playing guitar.

"Many Frisco employes [*sic*] who own Victrolas have purchased the records of Mr. Gene Autry," the article began, "however, few of them know that this highly talented boy is an employe of the Frisco Lines." The story then gives a synopsis of Gene's trials and tribulations in New York, his determination to succeed, the help given him by the Marvin brothers, and his successful December sessions. "And one of the nicest parts of the recording was the check for approximately $1,000 which he received," the story concluded. "It seems that this musical genius has a bright future. With a bit more experience and publicity there is a chance that he might get on the Orpheum circuit, the Velvetone [*sic*] Company promising to furnish him financial backing when he has acquired the experience and publicity and when his records have become more popular. Meanwhile one finds him hard at work as a telegrapher in the Frisco offices at Sapulpa, and working hard on his repertoire, and when his chance comes, it will find him ready to take it."[8]

As the new decade began, Gene Autry would indeed get plenty of chances, and he would be ready.

9

MIDWESTERN BUCKAROO

GENE'S NEXT LEAVE FROM THE FRISCO, spanning February 14 to April 15, 1930, gave him sixty days to make more records. His first stop: Velvet Tone's Manhattan studio, where he'd had such great success in December. On Monday, March 3, with Frankie Marvin on steel guitar, he cut stronger versions of "Cowboy Yodel" and "That's Why I Left the Mountains," than his previous Cova and Victor efforts. Gene returned to the studio alone two days later, polishing off a remake of his "I'll Be Thinking of You, Little Gal" and a spirited version of a Jimmie Rodgers rounder number, "My Rough and Rowdy Ways." Later that afternoon, he shuttled over to the Gennett studio in Queens. His tired voice failed him as he tried yet another version of "I'll Be Thinking . . ." as well as "Cowboy Yodel," and the label rejected his attempts. Returning to Columbia on Saturday, March 8, Gene attempted both numbers again—this time successfully, except for the occasional flubbed note or off-kilter timing on his guitar. The pairing would be released on OKeh—its higher priced label—under the name Johnny Dodds so as not to compete with Gene's versions of the songs on the budget labels Velvet Tone, Diva, and Clarion.

These February recording sessions were to be the first of eleven that would occur in 1930, during which he would cut more than forty songs. He was gaining a reputation as a big seller among the budget labels, under his own name as well as through various pseudonymous releases. Victor had limited success with the Autry record it released in January, but Columbia continued to issue his records to strong sales. Although the Depression was bankrupting some companies, including Q-R-S/Cova, Gene's records sold well. Q-R-S went back to its original business—the manufacture of piano rolls—and Cova's unreleased Autry masters were purchased in April by the Boston-based label Grey Gull. It used the pseudonym Sam Hill to issue "My Oklahoma Home"/"Stay Away from My Chicken House" on its budget imprints Radiex, Van Dyke, and Grey Gull—bottom-of-the-barrel records, costing only ten or fifteen cents each. "John Hardy" and "Tom Long" were the artist names that appeared on Gene's other Grey Gull 78s of "I'll Be Thinking of You, Little Gal," "Cowboy Yodel," "Why Don't You Come Back to Me," and "No One to Call Me Darling." Soon after these records hit discount bins, Grey Gull folded.

Another victim of the Depression and radio, vaudeville houses were closing, too, limiting lucrative venues for Johnny Marvin's shows. But when he did have bookings, Johnny occasionally invited Gene to join him and his brother at performances in the New York City area and as far afield as Elmira, in upstate New York. As usual, Gene roomed with Frankie, who continued to record for a host of labels—billed on his Victor recordings as "Oklahoma's Blue Yodeler." Gene also attempted to make inroads at New York radio stations, and may have appeared on WPCH, WOR, and WMCA around this time. He continued to meet and mingle with other hillbilly artists, including A. P. Carter of the Carter Family, and Frank Luther.

When April rolled around, Gene returned to Oklahoma, only to discover that his shift in Sapulpa had been reassigned. With the Depression adding to the railroads' losing battle against the highways, positions were being eliminated and employment schedules shortened. For the rest of his residency with the Frisco, Gene would find himself "on call," filling in where needed rather than steadily employed. He bounced from depot to depot along the Frisco line across Oklahoma and into Missouri, working sporadically. With several shiny black 78s as calling cards, he wrote to the Gennett Records headquarters in Richmond, Indiana, seeking more recording opportunities. Fred Wiggins, Gennett's A&R man, had heard Gene on KVOO and been impressed enough to book him into the Richmond studio for June 5 and 6.[1]

On the road during April and May was Gene's role model, Jimmie Rodgers. He headlined the Swain's Hollywood Follies tent show, playing one-nighters throughout Texas and Oklahoma, on a bill with blues singer Eva Thomas, comedian Jimmy Vann, and Freita's Hawaiian Revue. Gene probably saw the show in Ada on May 28 or in Wetumka the following night, chatting before showtime with the Singing Brakeman. Jimmie, whose debilitating tuberculosis caused him to miss some performances, confided in his yodeling colleague that he was quitting the tour. He suggested Gene might audition for the gig. In a 1971 letter to Gene, railroader Grover T. O'Dell recalled Jimmie's last Swain's show, on May 31, and Rodgers's encouragement to Gene: "One night I was working 2nd trick at Holdenville," O'Dell wrote.

Swain's Hollywood Follies were playing in a big tent show just across the tracks from the depot, along about 8 PM a well-dressed fellow came to the ticket window and said he wanted to send a Western Union telegram and I immediately shoved a blank to him and told him to write it out. His signature was Jimmie Rodgers, whom I had recognized right instantly. Before I went off shift at Holdenville, I received a message from Chief Dispatcher at Sapulpa to report to Tulsa next AM to relieve at East Tulsa. . . . You met me at the depot, saying "Let's go over and have breakfast," which we did, and I recall you ate four fried eggs for breakfast and you did not drink nor smoke. I marveled at this! Then you showed me a telegram from the great Jimmie Rodgers which I had sent the very night before, reading, "I am leaving Swain's Hollywood Follies tomorrow and I understand he is going to run a friek [*sic*] yodeler in my place, would you be willing . . ." And I laughed as I had sent that wire the night before. You said, "Help me on the train and I'll show you my first recording," which we did."[2]

Although Gene appreciated Jimmie's tip for the tent-show gig, he had already made exciting plans for more recording sessions, with an imminent departure from Oklahoma.

TO PREPARE FOR HIS NEXT SERIES OF DISCS, Gene had been practicing several new numbers: a Rodgers morality tale "Whisper Your Mother's Name," the old standard "The Tie That Binds," the sentimental parlor ballad "In the Shadow of the Pines," and a recently composed song, "They Cut Down the Old Pine Tree." The sheet music credited "Pine Tree" to Edward Eliscu, Willie Raskin, and George Brown; the latter turned out to be the pseudonym for Billy Hill, then an unknown composer whose "The Last Round-Up" would be a major hit for Gene in 1933.

Perhaps stopping in Springfield to visit the Longs and work on his repertoire with Jimmy, Gene headed into the heartland to make more records. Gennett Records had developed out of the nineteenth-century Starr Piano Company, founded in Richmond, a small Quaker town about forty miles from Indianapolis, alongside the Whitewater River. In 1921 the feisty upstart (operated by the Gennett family) had won a legal battle against Victor's control of the lateral-cut recording technique. Beginning in the early 1920s, Gennett made seminal recordings with jazz pioneers King Oliver, Jelly Roll Morton, Louis Armstrong, and Bix Beiderbecke. The original "Stardust" was cut there in 1928 by its composer Hoagy Carmichael, who later recalled, "The studio was primitive, the room wasn't soundproof, and just outside was a railroad spur with switch engines puffing away noisily. Yet this obscure recording studio in a small Indiana city saw a history-making parade of musicians. They made the name of the Hoosier Gennetts one of the greatest names in recorded music."[3]

It is unknown if Gene was familiar with any of Gennett's jazz recordings, but he had probably seen the company's glossy 1928 catalog of hillbilly music: "New Electrobeam Gennett Records of Old Time Tunes." The name

Electrobeam emphasized Gennett's switch to electric recordings in late 1927. In addition to the Gennett label, the company specialized in manufacturing discs for budget chains and mail-order businesses, including Sears, Roebuck's labels (Conqueror, Silvertone, Challenge, and Supertone) from 1924 to 1929. (The Sears labels would play a large part in Gene's career—after they were no longer manufactured by Gennett.) Recalled recording engineer Joe Geier to author Rick Kennedy, "All the Gennetts were interested in was hillbilly music. That's where they made their money because the Gennett discs catered to Sears, and Sears catered to the hillbillies." Gennett produced its own budget lines Champion and Superior, and later manufactured discs for such labels as Paramount, including legendary recordings by country bluesmen Charley Patton and Blind Lemon Jefferson. Angering many of its German Catholic employees, Gennett also manufactured custom recordings for the Ku Klux Klan. Since Indiana had more KKK members than any other state at that time, it was a highly profitable venture for the company.

Gene ventured alone into his first Gennett session on Thursday with only his acoustic guitar. Crossing the Whitewater River bridge into Starr Valley, or "Banjo Valley," as nicknamed by the locals, Gene felt at home as he entered the single-story, gray wooden studio located fifty yards from the Chesapeake and Ohio (C&O) tracks. The railroad "produced noise and vibration at the most unpredictable times," according to Rick Kennedy.

> Some collectors of vintage records are convinced that a couple of Gennett discs contain the faint sound of chugging trains in the background. . . . The Richmond studio, about 125 by 30 feet, adjoined a control room where the engineer oversaw the recording session through a double pane of glass. Sawdust between the interior and exterior walls was a feeble attempt at soundproofing. . . . The Richmond studio's location in the bottom of a humid river gorge made recording during summer months unpleasant enough. But in order to keep the wax discs soft during recording, the unventilated studio had to be kept uncomfortably hot throughout the year. . . . In photographs taken in the Richmond studio, the musicians appear as if they had been performing in a sauna.[4]

Even for a native Texan accustomed to the heat of the Lone Star state and Oklahoma, cutting ten songs over the course of two days' must have been sweltering. The best of the six recorded on day one were "Cowboy Yodel" and "I'll Be Thinking of You, Little Gal" (in which Gene coyly added the spoken line, "It's *true*, honey!"). This marked the fifth recording of each in a year's time—practice *did* make perfect. Rodgers's "Whisper Your Mother's Name" had just been released by Victor in April, and Gene demonstrated he had learned it well. The next afternoon, Gene tried four new selections with varying degrees of success—"They Cut Down the Old Pine Tree," the strongest.

After recording ended, the "studio staffers took the fragile wax master discs . . . to the plating department in another building in the Starr factory," according to Kennedy. "Copper-plated master discs were then made from the wax masters. . . . From the copper master a few test pressings and a 'mother' disc were produced. The mother disc, from which final record pressings were derived, was made from very highly durable shellac-based materials. The test pressings went to the Starr Piano administrative building, where Gennett family members, company managers, studio engineers, or anyone who was available, played them on a phonograph to determine which selections would be pressed into finished records." Seven of Gene's numbers made the cut, eventually released by the company on Gennett, Champion, Superior, Supertone, and Montgomery Ward. Gennett paid between fifteen and fifty dollars per session, and Gene possibly signed an agreement to receive royalties of one-half cent per side on the budget labels and a penny a side for the Gennett releases. Pleased with the results, Fred Wiggins invited Gene back to record again.

"They Cut Down the Old Pine Tree," originally paired with "In the Shadow of a Pine" on the Gennett and Champion labels, became popular and well known at baseball games, thanks to Chattanooga Lookouts announcer Arch McDonald. Soon after its 1930 release, McDonald played it over the P.A. system during the Lookouts' seventh-inning stretch. He continued the tradition when he moved to the Washington Senators in 1934. As announcer for the New York Yankees and the New York Giants, McDonald maintained the custom until his retirement in 1957, popularizing "Pine Tree" among legions of baseball fans.[5]

Baseball possibly lured Gene to Chicago to see the Cubs after he completed his recordings. The Windy City was only 250 miles away, and Gene may have planned to visit the always-helpful Dave Kapp. His brother, Jack, was now program director of up-and-coming WJJD, which beamed its hillbilly music into Chicago and environs from Aurora, Illinois. By 1930 Illinois residents were among those Americans most likely to own radios—along with New Yorkers and Californians.[6] The Kapp brothers liked Gene's new Velvet Tone platters, so much so that Jack offered him a spot on WJJD—twelve programs a week, at 6 AM and 6 PM, for fifty dollars a week.[7] Exactly when Gene's stint started is unclear, but since his Frisco assignments had become irregular, he might have begun immediately and worked throughout the summer. WJJD had studios located in Mooseheart, an area north of Aurora owned by the Moose Club; broadcasts also originated from Aurora's upscale Leland Hotel's penthouse Sky Club. On his fifteen-minute program, Gene accompanied himself on guitar and crooned his own songs and hits of the day.

A town of about 40,000, located forty miles west of Chicago, Aurora was a friendly place. Gene met other hillbilly musicians at the station and joined a group called the Buckle Busters, formed by two Native American brothers with the last name of Doolittle. No recordings exist of the group, but its repertoire probably consisted of Jimmie Rodgers, Vernon Dalhart, and Carson Robison covers, along with a few originals. An undated, early Buckle

Busters advertisement depicts five members, including Gene, all dressed in cowboy hats and western-accented clothing. Billed in the ad as GENE AUTREY [*sic*] AND THE INTERNATIONAL BUCKLE BUSTERS, the members played guitar, banjo, mandolin, and fiddle. On WJJD the combo broadcast from the Sky Club mornings from 7:00 to 7:30, and Monday, Wednesday, and Friday nights from 8:30 to 9:00 PM, sponsored by the International Oil Heating Company of St. Louis. In his spare time, Gene attended square dances with Leland Hotel employees, sometimes traveling to nearby Oswego for hoedowns held above a hardware store on Main Street. One fellow reveler, Bob Renton, recalled the night Gene dared him to ask a "rather heavyset lady" to dance, promising to give him a dollar if he did it. Bob went through with the dance, but Gene reneged on the bet. Other nights, the chums would gather in the basement of a friend's home on South Lincoln Avenue, where Gene would entertain everyone with his guitar.[8]

According to local legend, Gene bought himself a new three-piece suit on credit at the Leland Hotel's swanky Anderson and Duy Men's Shop. "When Gene Autry was just getting started in show business and needed a suit for a show in Aurora, Adam [Duy] helped him out," remembered Roger Haag, an old buddy of the haberdasher. "Autry took the suit, did the show, and took the suit with him. He never paid Adam for the suit."[9] Once he became successful in Hollywood, Gene infrequently referred to his Aurora days at WJJD—even though he worked and lived there, off and on, from 1930 until 1932 or so. Locals were a bit miffed at the slight: "Gene never answered any of the Aurora friends' letters," complained Aurora *Beacon-News* columnist Betty Barr in 1991. "When he was featured on *This Is Your Life*, he failed to mention the time he was in Aurora. He may have been afraid Bob [Renton] would be after him for the buck."[10] Gene did confirm his WJJD stint in one 1968 letter: "I . . . start[ed] a program for WJJD which was owned by the Moose Lodge and the program originated in Aurora. Dave Kapp was the agent and had the package."[11]

Two months after his initial Indiana recordings, Gene traveled the nearly 300 miles from Aurora to make more. To return to WJJD as soon as possible, he tried to cut eight songs in a single, long, hot Monday. Entering the studio on August 4, he brought along a repertoire of seven Jimmie Rodgers songs plus Frankie Marvin's "Dust Pan Blues"—one of the three rejected by Gennett in June. Performing all summer on the radio had paid off for Gene; his guitar picking had improved measurably, and he added personality and verve to Marvin's song, as well as his renditions of "Train Whistle Blues," "Hobo Bill's Last Ride," "My Carolina Sunshine Girl," and "Texas Blues"—in which he raved about Dallas's virtues over Chicago and Memphis. His bluesy delivery on "Texas Blues" and "Hobo Bill's Last Ride," in particular, could have fooled listeners that the singer was a black man from the Delta, rather than Oklahoma's Yodeling Cowboy. Curiously, "Hobo Bill" had only just been issued on 78, so

Gene must have learned the song by hearing Jimmie do it live or by some other means. Overall, Fred Wiggins was pleased with the recordings, and Gene agreed to return for another session in three months' time. Gennett released six of the songs on a plethora of budget labels.

IN EARLY SEPTEMBER Gene was called back by the Frisco to fill in as acting agent in Snyder, Oklahoma. Whether he gave his notice at WJJD or asked for a leave is unknown, but clearly he told Jack Kapp he'd be back. After all, he had a November recording session already booked in Richmond. In Snyder, Gene boarded with the Sharp family, to whom he presented a handful of discs. His railroad buddies welcomed him home, and he was happy to see them. But a month later, on October 9, when the Frisco offered him the permanent position of third-trick telegrapher at the Snyder depot, a more confident Gene turned it down. In addition to the WJJD job and the Gennett session, he had big plans for New York, coming after the Indiana trip by less than two weeks. The newly organized American Record Corporation (ARC) had booked him for some sessions on November 18, 20, and 24.

On October 26 his replacement arrived at the Snyder depot, and Gene took his leave for the Midwest. After stopping at WJJD for a few days of performances, he arrived on Thursday, November 6, at Gennett. To his chagrin, the session did not go as well as the previous one. He retried two of the Rodgers songs that had flopped last time; again, they failed to pass muster with Gennett. Another Rodgers tune, "Any Old Time," was also rejected. Only two numbers made the grade but received only limited release: Gene's guitar was out of tune on "In the Jailhouse Now No. 2," one of Rodgers' newest and best hits, but "Anniversary Blue Yodel (Blue Yodel No. 7)" came across better, with Gene personalizing the line, "I rode the Frisco, I rode the L&M" with a spoken ad lib, *"Yes, I have!"*

The next day Gene set out for the Big Apple. He was eager to see the Marvins, and he wanted to rehearse for his upcoming sessions. Frankie and Johnny had told him that ARC's A&R man, Art Satherley, was a force to be reckoned with. Indeed, Gene was about to meet the man who would propel his career forward with more momentum than ever before. And the work they would create together would change the course of American popular music.

10

UNCLE ART

TO THE ONE PAL WHO 'MADE ME'—best wishes to the greatest of them all Art Satherley," Gene inscribed on a photograph depicting the pair in the 1940s. Both are dressed to the nines, but what a contrast in styles: Gene in a Western-cut ensemble with Stetson and cowboy boots, Satherley in an elegant double-breasted tweed suit and tie, his white hair combed back. Although their attire differed greatly, the two formed a symbiotic bond from the beginning, in 1930. Over the years Gene would come to trust Satherley's judgment implicitly; Satherley had recognized in Gene a raw earthy talent that he would help to polish into twenty-four-karat gold, and Gene responded almost intuitively to his profession of faith.

Gene was the first of several country music giants discovered by Satherley; Roy Acuff, Bob Wills, and Bill Monroe, among others, followed. Satherley's background made him an unlikely candidate as one of the pivotal figures in the development of commercial country music. Born on October 19, 1889, the son of a clergyman in Bristol, England, Arthur Edward Satherley's peripatetic lifestyle began soon after he left Queen Elizabeth College, when he took a job road-testing motorcycle tires, traveling throughout England, Scotland, Wales, and Ireland. "In search of cowboys and Indians," he later recalled, he boarded a steamer to the States in 1913. He disembarked in Canada, then traveled to Milwaukee, eventually taking a job at the Wisconsin Chair Company. Employed originally to grade lumber in Port Washington, Wisconsin, Satherley transferred to the bookkeeping department at the firm's Grafton and New London locations. When Thomas Edison bought the New London facility, which built the High Boy cabinets for his phonograph machines, Art became his assistant secretary. There, he began to learn the rudiments of the newfangled record business. Meanwhile, Wisconsin Chair started its own record label, Paramount, at its Grafton plant. In 1918 Satherley rejoined the company, at the increased salary of sixty dollars a week.[1] His first job was overseeing the manufacture of discs, in which he perfected a compound of shellac, lamp black, white clay, cotton flock, and gum arabic.[2] Thanks to his beguiling English accent and Old World charm, he became Paramount's field representative. Traveling the South, selling discs to rural outlets, he began moonlighting as a talent scout. He was initially drawn to such blues artists as Ma Rainey and Blind Lemon Jefferson, whose recordings he supervised, along with a few pop acts, at Paramount's New York and Chicago studios. A vain man, he left prospective recording artists with an 8 × 10 photo of himself, his contact information printed on the back. Encouraging his artists to think of him as their benefactor, he encouraged them to call him Uncle Art.

By 1927, when most companies were switching to electrical recordings, Paramount declined to spend the money to modernize its techniques. Art resigned in a huff. (Before leaving Paramount, he leased the more advanced Gennett's facilities to make some recordings.) Satherley briefly worked for Q-R-S around 1928, but the fledgling label's shaky financial situation resulted in his moving on to Plaza Records. In July 1929 Plaza merged with several businesses, including the Regal and Cameo labels, as well as the Scranton Button Company (which pressed records), to form the holding company American Record Corporation (ARC). Then, in October 1930, ARC was purchased by Herbert J. Yates, owner of Consolidated Film Industries, which processed motion pictures for several Hollywood studios. This series of events would prove fortuitous for Satherley—and for Gene Autry.[3]

"Mr. Gene Autry was introduced to me by a gentleman by the name of Johnny Marvin," Satherley later recalled. "I remember vividly Johnny saying to me, 'This is Gene Autry.' Gene then asked me if I could do something for him, as he was singing, and he had some songs, and I said, 'Well, I'd like to hear you.' . . . This was around . . . the beginning of 1930." Satherley set up a meeting. With his formal speech, impeccable manners, and debonair appearance, Art surely dazzled Gene. Like Jimmy Long and Johnny Marvin, Uncle Art would serve as mentor and role model to the eager, still-maturing entertainer.

"I was then employed by the American Record [Corporation]," Art related about the company that billed itself the "World's Largest Manufacturer of Popular Priced Records." "I was there to build a country catalogue for Mr. Yates who had recently purchased the Plaza Music Company with all their masters. [Plaza had been] at a very low ebb and weren't making any money." When Gene showed up for his appointment, Satherley recalled, "He had nothing but an ordinary suit on . . . and a guitar in a case. He looked like the devil in an ordinary suit." For his audition, Gene played and sang some hillbilly numbers, including an old folk song called "The Preacher and the Bear." "He sang the regular country songs," according to Art. "The word 'cowboy' meant nothing, wasn't even mentioned—that came later on. The first two recordings [we did together] had none of that at all. Gene came to me, he was a hillbilly . . . Gene said to me, 'I got to make some records.' "[4]

After he became a singing cowboy movie star, Gene downplayed many aspects of his early recording career, including his pseudonymous releases and Rodgersesque vocals: "They called it hillbilly music at that time," Gene later told an interviewer in one of his few detailed remembrances of those days, "but in my opinion it was not real country music. [When] I met Art Satherley, . . . I had three or four records with Velvet Tone and by that time, I was getting pretty well established. . . . I had eight or ten records [in total]. And Victor wanted to listen to me. I made some records . . . for a company called Gennett Record Company and they had a label called Champion Records and Conqueror [which] they made for Sears, Roebuck . . . [Art] had heard a couple of those, and he was very interested in me. He said to me, 'I just came to this company to build a hillbilly catalogue for them. You would be the first artist that I have.' "[5]

Satherley met Gene in the studio for the first sessions in November. Accompanying himself on guitar, Gene attempted Rodgers's "He's in the Jailhouse Now," which he'd cut for Gennett two weeks earlier, followed by five original songs: "Cowboy Yodel" (for the sixth time), along with new numbers, "The Yodeling Hobo," "Pictures of My Mother," "Blue Days," and "Dad in the Hills." As in his sessions for other labels, Gene mixed sentimental ballads with rambunctious rounder songs. Even though Gene's guitar veered out of tune, his spirited yodeling impressed Satherley. Partially deaf in one ear, Art always stood up next to the mic while his artists recorded. Satherley released all six sides from the sessions on various ARC labels, including Oriole, Perfect, Banner, Jewel, Broadway, Romeo, and Regal. Each sold for about twenty-five cents, available at dime stores and through mail order catalogues.

A few days later, Gene returned to Gennett's New York studio and again cut "Yodeling Hobo" and "I'll be Thinking of You, Little Gal," along with Rodgers's maudlin "Whisper Your Mother's Name" and frisky "High Powered Mama" ("When they start steppin', it ain't no use / cause a triflin' mama's got a good excuse / . . . I was a good man and you had a good home / But you just couldn't leave other daddies alone"). "Yodeling Hobo," a superb Rodgers imitation both sonically and lyrically ("I hear a Frisco freight train and it's calling me / And when the sun sinks in the West in that dark blue sky / Just say that I'm a hobo and will be 'til I die"), was the session's real standout. All but "Little Gal" were selected for release by Gennett staffers in Indiana; Gene had become one of the label's most popular and frequently recorded hillbilly artists.

Gene spent the waning weeks of 1930 back in Oklahoma, visiting his mother, whose health had continued to deteriorate. Drought conditions had not subsided, the harvest had been disastrous, and sometimes the Autrys had nothing to eat. His mother gave what little food they had to her children, and she subsided almost entirely on cornbread. Only in her mid forties, Nora had become gaunt and frail. Gene continued to turn over as much money as he could, but it never went far enough. Popular Wilma and Veda had numerous friends, but Dudley was more of a loner. Delbert was often on the run from creditors (including grocer Wade Sharrock, for writing bad checks) as well as the law, mainly for petty theft and bootlegging. No one blamed Nora for her shiftless husband's delinquency, and neighbors and relatives shared what food they could spare. The clerk at Sharrock's Grocery continued to extend credit to the family, sometimes giving Veda and Wilma a fifty-cent piece for the picture show in neighboring Tishomingo. Bob and Beulah Ozment also lent money from time to time. Nora's only happiness came from her oldest son's newfound success as a recording artist. She proudly showed off his 78s—though the family could not afford a phonograph to play them on.

GENE TOOK A TEMPORARY ASSIGNMENT at the Bristow depot, where he worked sporadically until May 1931. By now, his discs were selling well enough that he'd become a hot property at Gennett, Columbia, Victor, and ARC, each of which booked sessions with him for early 1931.

Just after the new year, Gene traveled back to Richmond for a long day of recording on January 29. This time, he was accompanied by a mandolin player. Gene repeated a pair of compositions from the previous ARC sessions in November, but also tried a couple of new Jimmie Rodgers numbers: "Blue Yodel No. 8" and "Mean Mama Blues," both of which had not yet been released by Victor. Either Gene had learned the songs by watching Jimmie perform them live, or someone—perhaps a Victor employee—had slipped him a test pressing of the recordings before they were available to the public. Thus, Gene's versions of the songs were released on Gennett's budget labels just days after Victor issued Rodgers's originals.

Gene spent much of February traveling between various recording studios; bouncing from depot to depot had been good training for his hectic recording schedule. He first returned to Indiana, where on February 9 he successfully cut his cover of Rodgers's "Any Old Time." Among Gene's originals, "Money Ain't No Use Anyway" features lyrics that would prove ironic in light of his budding business acumen: "Money don't mean everything/It only makes life gay/I didn't bring it in this world/And I won't take it away."

Eight days later, on February 17, Gene entered Columbia's New York studio to cut another intriguing original, "The Gangster's Warning." (It would be issued under his own name on budget imprints Velvet Tone and Clarion but on the premium Columbia label as Overton Hatfield.) A sort of morality tale, it was doubtless inspired by the era's most famous hoodlums, Al Capone and Pretty Boy Floyd: "It seems there's no hope for a gangster / Not a moment of peace to be found / . . . Once when you join with the gangsters / It's a game you must play to the end." A pair of humorous songs "That's How I Got My Start" and "True Blue Bill" lightened up the proceedings.

The following day, for the first time since his debut recording in October 1929, Gene returned to Victor's studio. The Depression had hit the label hard, with disc sales plummeting from an all-time high of 24 million in 1927—to a low of 1.6 million in 1933. The company didn't even release its annual catalogue in 1931–32.[6] Looking for fresh talent, A&R man Eli Oberstein had expressed interest in the young Oklahoman who sounded so much like Ralph Peer's discovery. A rivalry between Peer and Oberstein had been brewing at Victor over which man would eventually head the race and hillbilly divisions. Believing he'd found the new Jimmie Rodgers, Oberstein eagerly supervised Gene's recording session.

Beginning at 10 AM, in Victor's Studio #2, Gene cut an entire set of Rodgers-style, rather risqué originals, including those he'd just waxed at Gennett and a pair of colorful new ones: "Bear Cat Papa Blues" (co-credited to Frankie) and "Do Right Daddy Blues"—all featuring loose women and their lotharios:

> You can cheat on me once
> you can cheat on me twice
> but you must keep your daddy warm at night . . .
> I don't want ya mama,
> if you don't want me
> There's too many mamas will sit on my knee
> I'm a do-right daddy
> and I don't have to stay with you.

Frankie, playing harmonica on one song, added steel guitar to two others. (Curiously, Victor's recording ledger noted: "F. Marvin not to appear on label per Mr. Oberstein.") Pleased with the results of the three-hour session, Oberstein and the company's Loren Watson discussed the possibility of Gene's signing an exclusive contract with Victor. The company would release four sides and produce one of Gene's first-ever promotional cards, depicting him nattily dressed in a business suit, guitar in hand, a sultry expression on his face.

A week later, on February 25, Frankie Marvin, again toting his steel guitar, accompanied Gene to his ARC session with Art Satherley. In addition to repeating some of the songs he had just cut for Victor, Gene recorded the original "I'll Always Be a Rambler" and W. C. Callaway's topical number, "The Death of Mother Jones." The latter told the story of Mary Harris Jones, the radical labor activist who had just died in November at age one hundred:

She fought for right and justice
She took a noble stand . . .
The hard-working miners
They miss her guiding hand
May the miners all work together
To carry out her plan
and bring back better conditions
for every laboring man.

Satherley was becoming more convinced of Gene's potential and made his own first overtures toward the Oklahoma Yodeling Cowboy to sign exclusively with ARC. "I said, 'We can use you,' but he said, 'I've got another deal—what can you give me?' I said, 'Well, I'll give you a deal. We're going into this thing with a lot of money and a lot of chain stores back of us, and if you care to come with us, that's up to you, Mr. Autry, and if you don't, I have someone that I'm sure will come.' He didn't tell me he'd made a couple of records for Victor." Wanting to consider his options, Gene tried to put Art off for a while and not commit himself. At this point, he liked getting paid for each side he recorded, and he reasoned that he could record more sessions as a free agent, cutting sides for a variety of labels. "In those days, I was paid about $100 for each side that I made," Gene later recalled. "I got a half-cent royalty at that period." ARC would release eight of Gene's nine recordings, on ten different labels under his own name, as well as Gene Autry (the Yodling [sic] Cowboy), Bob Clayton, and Hank Bennett.

One name he was rarely called anymore was Orvon. In its March issue, the *Frisco Employes Magazine* ran the item: "Gene Autry, who has entertained often at Frisco Employe's Club meetings with his songs and yarns, spent a few weeks in New York City; and while there recorded for the Victor, Columbia, and OKeh Phonograph people. 'Gene' is known as the 'Yodeling Cowboy.' He plays his own guitar accompaniment and makes a very pleasing rendition." The following issue pointed out that "extra operator A. N. Graves is relieving Operator Gene Autry at Sapulpa while Autry is on vacation."

His "vacation" consisted of several more busy days of recording: twenty cuts on March 31 and April 1 for Victor, plus a duet session of eight with Frankie Marvin; three ARC sessions on April 10, 13, and 14; then a quick getaway to Richmond for an April 16 session—forty-five sides altogether.

Victor had just started its own budget imprint, Timely Tunes, so sides were needed for it as well as the Victor label. Among the compositions Gene waxed on March 31 was another pair of Rodgers songs not yet on the market, and both were exceedingly autobiographical: "TB Blues" and "Jimmie the Kid" had just been recorded by Rodgers. It's almost certain that Oberstein took Rodgers's test pressings so Gene could learn and record them for Timely Tunes—thereby scooping the Rodgers originals on Victor. Employees of Southern Music, Ralph Peer's publishing firm, later said that Gene would stop in for advance copies of Rodgers sheet music, which could explain his knowledge of the lyrics. Since Gene didn't read music, he couldn't have learned the melodies from sheet music; he had to *hear* the songs to sing and play them. His cover of "TB Blues" became Timely Tunes' debut release, followed by five other Rodgers covers, all under the name Gene Johnson (so as to not compete with his own Gene Autry 78s released simultaneously on Victor, and to not infuriate his buddy Jimmie Rodgers).[7] On the April Fool's Day session, Frankie Marvin played harmonica, jaw harp, and steel guitar; most of these songs also appeared on Timely Tunes, this time under the name Jimmie Smith—the alias Gene used in his Frankie Marvin duets as well. Two of the more off-color numbers, "Bear Cat Mama from Horner's Corners" and "She's a Hum Dum Dinger," were credited to a Louisiana-born hillbilly singer named Jimmie Davis, who would later become Louisiana's governor. Also a Rodgers imitator, Davis became best-known for his composition "You Are My Sunshine," a future hit for his longtime friend Gene Autry.

Art Satherley was not willing to lose his Yodeling Cowboy to Victor, and during Gene's three sessions in April, Art made a case for his label over its chief competitor. Satherley could see that Victor was trying to turn Gene into its new Blue Yodeler, and he strategized with a plan of his own to keep Gene recording for the host of ARC labels. "I challenged him," according to Satherley. "I said, 'If you want to go with Victor, please yourself. But you're trying to yodel and you're trying to imitate Jimmie Rodgers. That's their star—and they're not looking for a young fellow that's not known. Jimmie Rodgers is known. They have a star there in Jimmie Rodgers, and they're going to throw you in the basket. But if you want to go with us, we expect you to stay with us.'" He explained to Gene that at ARC he would get preferential treatment and a vast number of labels on which to appear, in outlets that Victor didn't have, but again Gene said he'd have to think it over.

For the April sessions, Gene handled one alone, with Frankie Marvin playing harmonica and steel guitar on the other two. They stuck mainly to the repertoire just completed at Victor. Gene did bring a few more of his Rodgers "answer songs": "Jail House Blues" and "Dallas County Jail Blues," the latter a co-write with the author of "The Death of Mother Jones." Pleased with the new selections, Satherley recommended that Gene bring him more of his original numbers. When Gene told Art about his former songwriting and singing partner Jimmy Long, Art encouraged Gene to invite him to the next session. They agreed on a date six months hence, in October, 1931.

After his quick trip from New York to Richmond for one more session, Gene spent much of the late spring and summer in Oklahoma. He primarily shuttled between the Davenport and Schulter depots, with festive interludes at his cousin Callie Jane's in nearby Weleetka. She confided in her handsome cousin about her beaux and introduced him to her friends—who enjoyed listening to the budding recording star try out his new songs.

Gene later wrote one of the pals, Homer Shurley, saying, "I guess you have heard the record 'Bear Cat Daddy Blues' it's a good hot song and is selling very fast would like for you to go hear it. . . ."[8] Occasionally, Gene returned to WJJD in Aurora, Illinois, stopping en route at the Long home in Springfield. His busy schedule resulted in his falling asleep on the job, and on June 1 a report issued from the Frisco's headquarters in Springfield pointed out that train delays in Davenport on May 19 and 20 were caused by "an extra operator [Gene] . . . You will note that he has been criticized and I believe his service will be better hereafter. . . . He was told to call relay office for business before closing at night and immediately after opening in the morning." A more auspicious occasion occurred when his first big write-up appeared in the *Tulsa World*. On June 21, accompanied by the Victor promotional photo, page 12 of the paper's first section ran the headline: "Former Tulsa 'Brass Pounder' Sings Way to Fame Via Records: Gene Autrey [*sic*] Crashed the Gates as an Artist Two Years Ago." The un-bylined article colorfully described Gene's ascension as an entertainer:

> The click of telegraph keys can hardly be likened to melody, but that is how one of the country's leading recording artists got his start. He is Gene Autrey [*sic*], who plays a guitar and sings to make phonograph records. Gene is a native of Oklahoma and claims Tulsa as his home. He made his first record in 1929 after trying a year before to 'crash' the record companies and failing to register. . . . He returned to New York City in October 1929. . . . This time he passed the test. . . . Things began to break and the other record companies asked for his services. Since that time Gene has made nearly 50 records and only recently returned from a trip when he made eight.

This would not be the final occasion that Gene appeared in an Oklahoma newspaper, but it was the last in which he could be called a resident of the state. In October, Gene Autry returned to New York for a rendezvous with Jimmy Long. The result of their October 29 ARC recording session, as later described by Art Satherley, would "set the world on fire."

11

FROM "HIGH STEPPIN' MAMA" TO "SILVER HAIRED DADDY"

BY THE FALL OF 1931, numerous twenty-five-cent labels, including Victor's Timely Tunes and ARC's Banner, Perfect, Jewel, and the appropriately named Romeo, had released Gene's lusty blue yodels. They sold particularly well on Conqueror, the Sears, Roebuck imprint now manufactured by ARC. The handsome twenty-four-year-old's self-penned repertoire of off-color compositions, such as "High Steppin' Mama" and "She Wouldn't Do It," rivaled those of Frankie Marvin, Jimmy Davis, and Jimmie Rodgers:

"High Steppin' Mama"

She's the kind shakes and shimmies
She's wild as she can be
She shoots dice and gambles
She drinks corn whisky and smokes
She throws wild parties
And this ain't no joke
She's a high-steppin' Mama
She works like a Chevrolet
she does the hula hula
but it's in a different way.

"She Wouldn't Do It"

We went out in my car
It sure is some swell hack
You can find it parked anytime in the dark

the girls swingin' round my neck . . .
Just the other night
she said I was pettin' the women
She said I could see you
play with that gal's knee
the night we went in a-swimmin' . . .

Oberstein at Victor and Satherley at ARC were both pleased with their latest yodeling artist and awaited Gene's return to their respective studios in October. Gene invited Jimmy Long to join him at each session. It had been two years since they'd recorded together. Long, still employed by the Frisco, had waxed a few sides himself the previous year. On Gene's recommendation, he'd tried out as a solo artist at the Gennett studios in New York and Indiana, but the label rejected his efforts. He'd successfully cut one record for Velvet Tone, but he had had better luck harmonizing on duets, with his daughter, Beverly, or fellow Springfield Frisco employee Cliff Keiser. In December Long and Keiser had cut a song that Gene and Jimmy worked up back in Sapulpa, "That Silver Haired Daddy of Mine," which Gennett issued on its Champion label. Jimmy and Beverly had returned to Richmond, spending the first two days of June in the studio. For the most part, Jimmy steered clear of the type of rounder material Gene had perfected, preferring sentimental parlor songs that hearkened back to the nineteenth century. He and his daughter also recorded hymns, some of which Gennett marketed to mortuary directors.

Before leaving Oklahoma, Gene continued to spend time, between Frisco shifts, with the vivacious Callie Jane and her friends in Weleetka. Monsoon rains had finally hit Oklahoma, partially alleviating the ongoing drought. He'd planned one last Weleetka visit for a double-date with Callie Jane, her beau from Shawnee, and a pretty girl friend, but the heavy cloudbursts prevented him from making the journey. He used his train pass for a quick trip to Springfield, spent a few days with the Longs, then moved on to New York.

Gene arrived in Manhattan in a chilly mid-October, rooming with Frankie, and socializing with his friends before the Victor and ARC sessions. Feeling lonely one night, Gene tried telephoning his teenage flame Nellie Gordon in Tioga, but instead reached her sister, who informed him Nell was now married with a new baby. Still a bit homesick, he sent cards to friends back in Oklahoma.[1] Using fairly good penmanship, he wrote a letter on Hotel Taft stationary to Callie Jane, dated October 20. He opened his correspondence by apologizing for missing a final rendezvous ("but the way it rained, I just couldn't make it"). Although there is no documentation showing that Gene had done any recording in October prior to the 29th, he informed his cousin that "I've had a good time so far since I came up here. We are doing a lot of recording and having a lot of fun. Wish you were here with us. We would stage a good one. How are you and your friend from Shawnee getting along by now are you still fighting or not. [sic] Well anyway give him my best regards. I like it up here only its cold as H. and my blood is plenty thin and no foolin but I almost freeze every time I get out side. . . . Well Callie I don't know a thing to write that is interesting so will ring off for this time so write me real soon. With love, Your Cuz—? Gene" At the bottom of the page, he scrawled "If you see any one I know tell them helo [*sic*]. Make a special call to tell Mr. Wilcox."[2] Wilcox was probably a Frisco employee, one of many with whom Gene had bonded.

His closest Frisco pal, Jimmy Long, arrived right before the ARC sessions. They had just enough time for a few run-throughs before meeting Art Satherley in the recording studio on Thursday, October 29. Joining them on steel guitar were Frankie Marvin *and* Roy Smeck—who also brought his banjo. A highly talented instrumentalist, Smeck was deemed a "wizard" among musicians, according to Satherley, who extravagantly described him as "fantastic with his fabulous fingers on the strings." The self-taught Pennsylvania native had hit it off with Marvin; since January they had collaborated on various records, as a duo, as part of the Roy Smeck Trio, and as the Roy Smeck Hawaiian Orchestra.

The ARC session was evenly split between Gene's "stepping out" numbers and Jimmy's old-timey tunes. Gene wanted to try a pair of new originals, the catchy, banjo-driven "Atlanta Bound" and "Rheumatism Blues"—his spin on Rodgers's "TB Blues," which was probably inspired by the "jakeleg" epidemic of 1930. A form of paralysis caused by toxic chemicals added to a bootlegged concoction called Jamaican ginger, jakeleg resulted in impotence as well as the loss of the use of its victims' legs—possibly referred to by the lyrics' "broke backbone." In his 1978 memoir, Gene recalled that he and future baseball star Dizzy Dean would play poker at an Oklahoma City bootlegger's shack where Jamaican ginger booze was sold.

Sounding confident, Gene sang his numbers solo, backed by Smeck. For their duets, the duo turned to Long's songs: "My Alabama Home," which he and Gene had cut for Victor at their first-ever session; the chestnut "Missouri I'm Calling," complete with percussive railroad noises and a train whistle simulated by steel guitar; and the clincher, "That Silver Haired Daddy of Mine," which opened with a striking steel-guitar riff. Throughout, Jimmy's tenor blended well with Gene's dulcet tones; Gene sounded just as convincing as a grieving prodigal son as he did a good-time Charlie. But "That Silver Haired Daddy" was the standout. Struck by the sincerity Gene conveyed with his voice, Uncle Art pegged "Silver Haired Daddy" a winner: "It's what the people wanted to hear at that time," he later recalled of the nostalgic narrative about a wayward son's regret following his father's demise.[3] On the opposite end of the spectrum from "Do Right Daddy Blues," the ballad oozed nostalgia and sweet sentimentality.

Although "Silver Haired Daddy" was credited as an Autry/Long composition on the various ARC releases and later on sheet music, it previously had been credited solely to Jimmy. Satherley always referred to it as a Long composition, and chances are that Long did write the song, with minimal—if any—help from Gene, who throughout his life took partial credit for it.[4] This would remain common practice well into the 1950s, with such artists as Elvis Presley putting their names on songs as coauthor.

In those years, publishers hired song pluggers to pitch their copyrighted material to established singers or bandleaders, and often a songwriter could only get a publishing deal if a popular singer would sign it up with his or her publisher. Likewise, some A&R men like Ralph Peer started their own publishing companies to capitalize on their artists' material, which as a matter of course they published, then shopped to singers on other labels.[5] It is impossible to discern just how many of the eventual 327 songs credited or co-credited to Gene Autry were actually written by the Singing Cowboy. Many of the songwriters who shared credit with Jimmie Rodgers also pitched songs to Gene, including Waldo O'Neal ("Pistol Packin' Papa") and prison inmate Raymond Hall ("Moonlight and Skies"). On his early recordings, Gene shared songwriting credits on several songs with Jimmy Long, Frankie Marvin, W. C. Callaway, and an unknown, George Rainey. Decades later, Gene admitted his contributions usually amounted to the idea for a song, a title, or a line or two. Even as a fledgling recording artist Gene became savvy as to potential earnings from song copyrights, and in 1939 Gene formed his own publishing company, purchasing the rights to numerous songs.

Arthur Satherley knew he had a big seller with "That Silver Haired Daddy of Mine," which he planned to release immediately as the A-side to "Mississippi Valley Blues." He continued to urge Gene to sign with ARC, and booked him for another session the following afternoon. Although Gene had an appointment at Victor that morning, he figured he could squeeze in both. On Friday at 9:30 AM, things got under way at Victor's Studio One on Twenty-fourth Street in Manhattan. Jimmy (on steel guitar) and Gene (on standard guitar) were joined by Frankie Marvin, who brought along his kazoo. For the Long-Autry duets, Eli Oberstein helped them choose the pseudonym the Long Brothers on the Victor releases. Over the next two hours, Jimmy and Gene harmonized on several of the previous days' ballads—excluding "Silver Haired Daddy." Apparently, Satherley had convinced them not to cut the song elsewhere. The Long Brothers also recut "My Dreaming of You," from their debut Victor session in 1929, as well as a few other heart songs and the humorous mountain ballad, "Cross-Eyed Gal That Lived Across the Hill." At 11:30 AM, Gene put on his blue yodeler cap and took the reins solo, performing his Rodgers-style originals. A new one featuring Marvin on kazoo, "Wild Cat Mama," was a sequel to his popular Victor 78 "Bear Cat Papa," which warned: "Listen here wild cat mama / I'm gonna make both eyes black . . . / There never was a bear cat papa / That could live with a wild cat mama."

After finishing at 12:45 PM, they dashed uptown with Frankie to Broadway and Fifty-seventh Street to meet Roy Smeck for the ARC session. Together they waxed "Cross-Eyed Girl" [*sic*] and the two Long songs they'd just cut that morning on Twenty-fourth Street—soon to be released on ARC's labels under their real names (with Long's first name spelled Jimmie).

After the session, Jimmy headed home on his pass to Springfield. Art booked Gene for two more sessions in November, continuing his campaign to woo him. "I said, 'Gene, this is going to be a big organization, we've already got the outlet for hundreds and hundreds of stores," Uncle Art later recalled. Behind the scenes, Satherley had been working a new angle at promoting his discovery. "I'd been dealing with Sears, Roebuck . . . ," he recalled, "and the buyer . . . was Jeff Shay. He was a short Irishman, in charge of a mighty department—all music, all classes of instruments." Previously, the Chicago-based Shay and Satherley had added to the Sears catalogue a two-page spread advertising Conqueror's hillbilly 78s, moving a lot of product in the process. "Immediately the orders came in!" Satherley exhorted. Art rushed a test pressing of "Silver Haired Daddy" to Shay, who agreed with Satherley on its commercial potential. Shay recommended WLS radio as the next step: "Art, this Autry guy is big," he told Satherley. "We have a program here [at WLS]. . . . We'd like to have [Gene] on [a] half hour in the mornings. We have quite a program, but we [can't] pay him any money. But if you can afford to keep him in there, I'm sure it will be big for us all."

Satherley took the idea to Gene, who, from his time at WJJD, knew how powerful WLS was. In addition to reaching millions of listeners with its 50,000 watts, its popular Saturday broadcast, the WLS *Barn Dance*, was a hotbed of hillbilly music. "Gene, I haven't got much money to spend," Uncle Art told him, "but if you'd like to spend a few months in Chicago, I'll give you thirty dollars a week out of our petty cash, with which you can get a room and a bed at the YMCA . . . for one dollar a night. . . . The rest [will go] for wine, women, and song. Gene, if you will do this, I'll guarantee that within the first year, you'll be getting a thousand or fifteen hundred or seventeen hundred and fifty dollars a week!"[6] They finally agreed on thirty-five dollars a week beginning December 1.

Brimming over with excitement during his November 11 ARC session, Gene received simpatico backing from Smeck and Marvin; the trio cut a pair of Rodgers-style numbers and a ballad. Two days later, on Friday, November 13, he was listed for the first time in the *New York Times* in that day's radio programming guide: "WPCH, 4:30 PM Gene Autry, yodeler" announced his fifteen-minute slot. On Monday he returned to the ARC studio and waxed another version of "Wild Cat Mama" and three ballads, with Smeck on steel and banjo.

Gene was eager to take the WLS job but still indecisive about signing exclusively with the unproven ARC. "I told [Art] that I had talked to Victor and there was a fellow by the name of Eli Oberstein over there," Gene later recalled.

> Art said, "Gene, Victor is a big company and they've got a couple of country singers over there right now—they've got Jimmie Rodgers and naturally they're concentrating on him. But over here, if you want to come along with American Records, I'll guarantee that we'll put everything behind you." And I said, "Alright, then, I'll let you know. I've got to see Mr. [Loren] Watson. I promised that I would go back and see him . . . after I talk to him, I'll let you know." So I went down to Victor and I talked to Watson then, and he wouldn't guarantee me any records or anything like that, so I started thinking about it and thought that if Art Satherley would guarantee me some records, I'd go over there. So I went back the next morning to see Art Satherley. And I said, "Mr. Satherley, I've talked to Mr. Watson . . . how many records can you guarantee me?" And he said, "I'll guarantee you eight records a year." And I said, "Well, if you'll guarantee me eight records a year, then I've decided then that I'm going with you."[7]

Gene also turned to the Marvin brothers to help make his decision: "Johnny had been through the ranks and he knew pretty well what was going on," said Gene. "Frankie Marvin also."[8] Years later, Frankie recalled that his own footloose-fancy-free lifestyle prevented him from getting such a deal: "When Art took over [at ARC], I was out of town and I shouldn't have been. I was supposed to make two numbers a month for them, and Art signed Gene up and took my contract, cause I had a $5,000-a-year guarantee, and $150 a side making them, and here I was on the road with Johnny and we were down in Kentucky and when I got back I didn't have any contract." He harbored no ill will toward Gene, however, and would eventually follow him to Chicago, then Hollywood, once his own recording career dried up.

Satherley and Shay decided that Gene's cowboy persona would be the right image to project on his WLS program. Gene was not so sure, and asked Johnny Marvin for his opinion of buckaroo-styled singers. Johnny referred Gene to a buddy who'd been a member of Otto Gray and His Oklahoma Cowboys. A banjo picker with a comic flair, Benjamin F. "Whitey" Ford had performed with Gray's outfit at WLS. Fifty years later, Ford, who later became known as the Duke of Paducah, recalled his first meeting with Gene: "I was in New York City playing vaudeville with Bob Vann, and we were working a lot with Johnny Marvin," he said.

> One day, Johnny called me and he said, "I got a friend in town, and I'd like for you to come down and meet him." I had to ride the subway to get to where he was . . . at a little cheap hotel. . . . So we went in there, and Gene was a little old skinny boy sitting on the bed, and he called me "Benny." He said, "Benny, I'm sure glad to know you. . . . I recorded . . . for Art Satherley, and I'm going to go to Chicago, and I'm going to go to work at WLS. Now, I understand that you worked at WLS." I said, "Yes, I worked there with Otto Gray's Oklahoma Cowboys. We did an early morning program, and then we went out and played all those towns around there."

He said, "Well, did you wear cowboy clothes?" I said, "Well, Otto Gray's group just wore hats and boots, and he required that if you wore a hat, it had to look decent and clean, and you never wore your boots outside of your pants. Your pants was always down over your boots, because he said that was the real Western style."

He said, "Well . . . I've ordered some clothes from Hollywood and they're Western style, or at least the fellows told me they were, like the cowboys are wearing in the movies and stuff. I'm just going to walk around Chicago a couple of weeks with them on, so I get used to them before I go out to WLS. Then I'm going to go on the air for them, and Sears, Roebuck is going to sponsor me. . . . Then, after I get built up, well, I'm going to go on the road."[9]

Gene had just enough time to rush back to Oklahoma, put in a few shifts at the Henryetta depot, and pack his bags for Chicago. He was beginning to see that his days at the Frisco were numbered. He wrote Homer Shurley that he'd lost a job he bid on, but "I dident [sic] much care anyway because I have been laying off so much that I can get relieved easier if I am on the extra board than I can if I have a regular job."

Satherley's unwavering belief in him, and his promise of big things to come, gave Gene the confidence to take the plunge in Chicago. He wouldn't be allowed to miss his slots at WLS as he had at WJJD. He'd spent nearly seven years on the railroad, and as much as he hated to give up the Frisco's extended family, he'd grown to love the life of an entertainer—the status, the money, and the attention. He enjoyed rubbing shoulders with established artists like Jimmie Rodgers and Carson Robison, and flirting with beautiful women who asked him for his autograph. Although his spot on WLS paid nothing compared to the Frisco, he figured it would be a stepping-stone to something big. "One day I came across this Ralph Waldo Emerson quotation," Gene later wrote. " 'This time, like all times, is a very good one, if we but know what to do with it.' I believe if you take good stock of yourself, examine all your possibilities, then try your best, you can discover what to do to make *this* time of your life 'a very good one.' " In Chicago, Gene did exactly that.[10]

12

SWEET HOME CHICAGO

WHEN GENE DISCUSSED HIS MOVE to Chicago and WLS in his autobiography, he wrote, "Sometimes you can yank on one stitch and an entire sweater will unravel. Well, this was my stitch. Hit records, a movie career, a happy marriage, goodies and groceries all came to pass."[1] "That Silver Haired Daddy of Mine," Gene's first hit record, sold a then-phenomenal 30,000 copies during the first month of its release, eventually selling 500,000 copies. The other items on Gene's list would come gradually over the next four years.

In Chicago, Gene found a new family to replace his co-workers on the Frisco: the staff and musicians who worked for WLS. From the beginning, the station had built the reputation as a friend to farmers and former country folk now living in the city. The station was founded in 1924 by Illinois-based Sears, Roebuck and Company's Agricultural Foundation, "dedicated to serve the people on the farms of America" as its mandate. Programming was directed to listeners likely to order their goods from the Sears, Roebuck catalogue, or World's Largest Store, from which WLS got its call letters. The "Grand Opening" broadcast featured "celebrity radio speakers," including arguably the first great silent Western film star, William S. Hart. The solemn theater-trained actor gave "a spell-binding reading of *Invictus*," while fellow speaker Ethel Barrymore "froze at the mike and had to be coaxed back to it."[2] Following farm reports and other informational programs, chanteuse Grace "The Bring-Home-the-Bacon Girl" Wilson[3] and other vocalists sang pop hits of the day.

WLS's greatest innovation was its weekly *Barn Dance* program, originated during the station's first week of programming on Saturday, April 19. Following the ringing of a cowbell, the announcer read WLS program director (and former agriculture publicist) Edgar L. Bill's directive: "This program is to be sincere, friendly and informal—planned to remind you folks of the good fun and fellowship of the barn warmings, the husking bees, and the square dances in our farm communities of yesteryear and even today." Early acts included Tommy Dandurand's Fiddle Band, banjo player Chubby Parker, "The Kentucky Wonder Bean" on guitar and harmonica, square-dance caller Tom Owen, animal-imitator Tom Corwin, and Kentucky transplant Bradley Kincaid, who specialized in nineteenth-century English folksongs and sang his way into radio stardom. Popular from the start, the *WLS Barn Dance* became the model for similar radio programs around the South and Midwest that helped disseminate country music. One of the most famous, the Grand Ole Opry, debuted in Nashville a year later in 1925, with an early WLS emcee, George D. Hay (a.k.a. "the Solemn Old Judge") at the helm.

By 1928, WLS had secured as its listeners 59 percent of the Midwest farm families who owned radios. That year, Sears sold WLS to Prairie Farmer, a Chicago publishing company with a similar demographic to Sears'. *Prairie Farmer* was distributed throughout Illinois, Indiana, and Wisconsin, and its publisher, Burridge Butler, "believed that radio was the daily link that would fill in between the publication dates of his paper," according to Stephen Cisler, an early announcer at WLS. "Butler's philosophy was a broad daily practical service to the small towns and the farmers. . . . He opened the station up to more of the country flavor." Sears continued to own 49 percent of the station until Prairie Farmer paid off its note, and was entitled to free programming (whereas regular sponsors had to pay a fee to back a particular show). One of these was the 9:20 AM *Conqueror Record Time*, where the Oklahoma Yodeling Cowboy would begin his trial run in December.

A few days beforehand, Gene arrived in the Windy City to get settled. Karl Davis was one of the first WLS artists with whom he became acquainted. A mandolin player, songwriter, and singer, Davis had traveled to Chicago in 1930 with duet partner Harty Taylor at the behest of their hometown friend Bradley Kincaid. "Several of us were doing the early morning program called *Smile-a-While Time* when we noticed a young man looking in from the reception room," Davis recalled forty-five years later. "When the program ended, we greeted him at the studio door. He was nicely dressed in a regular suit—not Western—and had a guitar with him. He asked about a good place to get a room, said he had . . . been to New York, had recorded while there and that he was . . . to get a job on WLS. The name of our handsome young visitor was Gene Autry." Eventually, "Gene and I moved into a double room at the old Union Park Hotel near WLS rather than pay a dollar or two more for two singles," according to Davis.[4]

Once Gene paid his $104 membership fee to join the Chicago Federation of Musicians, he was ready to go on the air. His easy smile, sincerity, and warmth soon won him the support of another important WLS staffer, Anne Williams. A striking brunette seven years Gene's senior, she had taught high school after graduating from the University of Illinois. Her next job was secretary to Sears, Roebuck executive Robert E. Woods, who determined that the well-spoken young woman would do well on WLS. She took over *The Homemaker's Hour*, featuring practical tips and music, on Monday and Wednesday afternoons. "Anne is a specialist in women's styles and makes trips to New York twice a year to get acquainted with the newest fashions," related the *WLS Family Album*, the annual publication introducing the station's personnel to its listeners. With cohost Sue Roberts, Anne also broadcast every Monday morning *Tower Topics*, billed as "the only household program for men on the air in the Middle West."[5]

Gene most likely appeared on Anne's programs before she was tapped to emcee Gene's *Conqueror Record Time* show. In her on-air chatter, she lavished colorful descriptions of his arrival to the studio via horseback, oohing and aahing over the appearance and feats of the fetching buckaroo. Uncle Art later gave an account of the show: "Sue Roberts and Anne Williams did a fabulous job for Gene Autry. The two girls brought Gene on every morning . . . [They] would say, 'Here he comes; he's fence riding—I see he's got a break. He's repairing a fence right there. Now he's got that done, and he's very fast on his horse, and just as fresh as a daisy early in the morning. He's our Gene Autry and he's going to sing for us, I'm sure!' And, Gene, of course, had probably just rolled out of bed!"[6] Gene would perform mostly Western songs, such old favorites as "Home on the Range," along with the more nostalgic of his recordings, including "That Silver Haired Daddy of Mine."

Anne Williams and her husband Eugene Heinz (she used her maiden name on air) befriended Gene, helping him ease into his new life in Chicago. "Anne was vivacious, stylish, and above all enthusiastic and interested in the people and activities around her," recalled her niece Eleanor Chapin. "Anne and her husband took this 'young boy' Gene under their wings, and Gene Autry and Anne's husband spent some of their free time together. The WLS group was very much like a family. As a child, I remember visiting in Chicago and meeting the staff and performers. It was very pleasant and we heard stories of their parties and casual gatherings."[7]

Gene later counted Anne, following Johnny Marvin and Uncle Art, as "the third influence in the creation of the singing cowboy." He described her role in the article "Three Pals," for *Country Song Round-up* magazine: "Anne was the announcer for my broadcasts, which plugged the sale of my phonograph records. I sang cowboy songs, not because I felt the listeners liked 'em better, but because Arthur [Satherley] insisted upon it. Anne began to build up my Oklahoma-Texas background and sprinkled the program with talk of sagebrush and tumbleweeds. That sort of stuff didn't sound very glamorous to me, as my recollections of ranch life included aching muscles and endless days in the sun and dust. . . . But there was Anne Williams bringing the West back East with bright talk of the wind-swept plains, of coyote howls in the moon-light, and cowboys on galloping horses."[8]

To look the part, Gene began wearing his new Western duds, including a recently purchased white Stetson hat and some fancy boots. He also sent out his 1927 Martin 00-42 guitar to the Pennsylvania-based company to get it cus-tomized. Founded in 1833, the C. F. Martin Guitar Company took the occa-sional order from entertainers for "special ornamentation." In 1927 Jimmie Rodgers had commissioned an 0-42 Martin with his name placed in stylized lettering along the fingerboard, and now Gene had to have one too. He care-fully drew his signature on a piece of paper and sent it to Martin, so it could be inscribed in mother-of-pearl on the neck where Jimmie put his. At the same time, he had Martin add pearl tuner buttons, a peghead decal and binding, and a new bridge and pick guard.[9]

Gene's thirty-five-dollar-a-week WLS salary wouldn't go very far with ex-penses like these, so to make extra money he reacquainted himself with WJJD's program director Dave Kapp. Kapp gave him the 6 AM early-bird slot again and offered to refer the Oklahoma Yodeling Cowboy to brother Jack's label, Brunswick, where big-band singer Bing Crosby had recently signed on as a solo artist. Eventually Brunwick would become a subsidiary of ARC, and Kapp and Crosby would move to Decca Records.

With daily exposure on the radio, along with the success of "Silver Haired Daddy," Gene found he could get bookings all over the Midwest. "That record kind of put me on the road," he later said.[10] He hoped to be invited onto the *Barn Dance* program on Saturday nights, but until he did, he lined up weekend performances around the area, often at a movie house before the screening of a film. "From 1931 to 1934, I played every theater in Chicago and throughout the Midwest," Gene once reminisced. "I didn't have a business manager at that time, so I would perform on the stage, and then I would go up to the box office and figure up my take."[11] Again, his correspondence course in accounting was paying off.

WLS listeners took to Gene immediately. "The fans loved him, lots of mail came in, and the Singing Cowboy was a big star," said Karl Davis. "He soon started making personal appearances and the listeners flocked out to see him." Gene rarely sang his blue yodels on the air, sticking to "Silver Haired Daddy," cowboy folksongs, and the sentimental ballads Jimmie Long had taught him. This pleased WLS's conservative owner Burridge Butler, although program di-rector George Biggar later admitted to tiring of "Daddy." "He sang it on every program, we got sick and tired of it, but he sold over a million of them," said Biggar, who knew his hillbilly and cowboy music. Biggar had earlier worked with local musicians on Sears radio affiliates in Dallas, including early cow-boy balladeer Carl T. Sprague, and in Atlanta, where he brought on the seminal hillbilly group, Gid Tanner and the Skillet Lickers, featuring Riley Puckett and Clayton McMichen (before he backed Jimmie Rodgers). Biggar's more recent discovery, Arkie the Arkansas Woodchopper (the former Luther Ossenbrink of Knob Noster, Missouri) became the longest-running star of the *WLS Barn Dance*, singing, fiddling, and calling square dances from 1928 to 1960.

Gene was invited to continue his WLS broadcasts for 1932. To commute between his Aurora and Chicago radio shows, as well as drive the countryside for his performances, the "range rider" needed a car. He located a used Buick through a friend back in Oklahoma and triumphantly traveled home by rail to make the purchase. While there, he managed to pull a few shifts at the Henryetta depot, still wishing to hold onto his rail pass, and he visited his family in Ravia. Even though much of his earnings had gone to the new guitar, clothes, and car, he had some left over to give his mother. Her health had not improved, and he urged her to see a doctor. Early the following year, a disintegrating Nora would describe her condition in a letter on Hotel Taft stationery (which she received from Gene). Scrawled in pencil in a messy jumble, she wrote to her sister-in-law Beulah Ozment, who had moved from Oklahoma to Cookville, Texas:

> I guess you thought I was never going to write but I have been sick. The rest is all well. It sure is cold. Last night was the coldest we have had this winter. Bulah [*sic*] I don't know any news to write. I had a letter from Orvon today and he had lost Bobs letter and wanted me to send your address to him. He said for me to tell you all that he would let you have it [money] in a few days. For you all to watch for it. Well Bulah, how are you getting along. I was sorry you was sick. Bulah the way I am I feel like I am drunk and everything is flying. That is the way the words . . . on this paper if I walk to the toilet I walk like a drunk man running back. . . . Well Bulah the same old neighbors are here and still complaining with bad blood and Bob was here the other day he is awful poorly has a carbuncle on his leg when he came after you had gone tears run out of his eyes said he knew someone told him something as he would not have gone off without coming back Well beaut (?) I must close tell kids and Bob hello Tell Bob that Orvon may be kind of slow about sending it he is ours same time we get on starveation [*sic*] before he sends it. . . . Goodby sugar Pie from your sis Nora Autry. Delbert is here now.[12]

AS HE HEADED EAST ON ROUTE 66 toward Illinois for a stopover in Springfield, in December, Gene's spirits lifted. The thought of Jesse Long's home cooking always cheered him up. He also wanted to ask Jimmy to accompany him at some of his upcoming performances. When he pulled into the Longs' driveway, for the first time in a car of his own, what awaited him made Jesse's fried chicken pale in comparison. The Longs had a houseguest, Ina Mae Spivey, the twenty-year-old daughter of Jesse's sister, Lilly, and her husband, Barney Spivey, who worked for the Rock Island Railroad in Duncan, Oklahoma. "A coed with blue eyes and skin like rose petals" is how Gene described the lovely freshman studying at Springfield's Teachers College.

"The reason Ina was at our house," recalled her cousin Beverly Long Moss, five years her junior, "is that her dad was a telegrapher down in Oklahoma and they didn't have much—they had a living but that was about it. And so my mother had told Ina when she got out of high school, if she wanted to come up to our house and go to the college there, that my dad would pay for the college. Ina was so good looking and wore the best clothes. Aunt Lilly was an excellent seamstress. She just made up everything. Ina and her sister Anita always had the best looking clothes because Aunt Lilly could make them. So Ina started in the college and Gene . . . maybe a month or six weeks later . . . came through on his way to Chicago, and he met her and he stayed there a couple of days. Gene didn't have a dime to his name at that time, but he told my dad, 'I'm going to marry her.' My dad was stunned."[13]

In addition to the immediate physical attraction between them, Gene and Ina found they had much in common, beginning with their family backgrounds. Texan Barney Spivey was a troubled man who sometimes drank up his railroad paycheck. "Because her father was an alcoholic, Ina learned at an early age the pitfalls [of addiction] and its effect on a person's livelihood and productivity," Ina's niece once observed.[14] Born in 1887, Barney had married twenty-two-year-old Lilly Hubbard, a Kentucky native. They had two daughters: Anita, born in 1909, and Ina Mae, born in Francis, Oklahoma, April 19, 1911. The Spiveys lived in a rural area near Marlow, Oklahoma, until Barney got a job on the Rock Island Line. They moved into a modest home in Duncan at 517 Ash Street, and in 1920 they had another child, a son named John. Since Lilly Spivey and Jesse Long were both married to railroad men, the sisters used their free rail passes to visit back and forth or go on little train trips together.

Only one year apart in high school, Ina and Anita could nearly pass for twins, with their bobbed auburn hair, similar height, and high cheekbones. Ina had an unusual double pupil in her left eye, an anomaly that did not affect her vision. The sisters sang together in Duncan High School's all-female glee club, which won first place in a statewide competition in 1926; as part of a quartet, they earned a gold medal at the State Fair. Ina played piano and read music, too. Outgoing, popular, and studious, she acted in school plays—just as Gene had in Tioga. An athletic young woman, the 5' 5" Ina had a well-proportioned figure, with long shapely legs. She played forward on the high school basketball team where she "was a large contributor to the team's scoring," according to the 1927 Duncan high school yearbook, *Treasure Chest*: "Although light, she is fast and a hard fighter."[15]

Ina and Anita studied Morse code so they could get jobs at the local Western Union office. After graduating from high school in May 1928, Ina went to work as a full-time telegrapher. She later wrote, "My life . . . was that of an average girl in a small city. Social life was simple. It consisted of any evening spent at a friend's home, a church supper, or an occasional dance or often just an hour or so with the family around the parlor piano." Since the Spiveys didn't own a piano, she may have been referring to her family's visits at the Longs' home. After three years as a telegrapher, Ina took the six-hour train ride to Springfield and enrolled at Southwest Missouri State Teachers College, starting in the winter semester on November 30, 1931.[16] She had been taking classes for a few weeks when Gene walked through the Longs' front door.

Ina had heard so much about Gene from her aunt and uncle that she was smitten from the start and hung onto his every word as they chatted. Jimmy had once told her, "There are people who just sit, and people who give out. Now you take Autry, he gives out."[17] She was also impressed that he seemed genuinely interested in what she had to say. As for Gene, "I knew I'd found my girl right away," he told a fan magazine years later. "It wasn't just that she was so vivacious and pretty—though . . . she was the loveliest girl I'd ever seen. It was a lot more. She seemed so lacking in self-consciousness, so free of conceit, and so *interested* in everything. Just being with her made me feel good. I knew I wanted to be with her a lot."[18]

Doubtless, music was a part of that first visit. Jimmy, Beverly, and Ina, who planned to become a music teacher, had been working up some songs together, with Ina and her cousin taking turns on the piano. Gene and Jimmy harmonized on "Silver Haired Daddy," "My Old Pal of Yesteryear," and "My Alabama Home." Later in the evening, Gene serenaded Ina with his guitar. As he played, she noticed his attractive hands with long slender fingers. He seemed worldly but at the same time down to earth, polite, and soft-spoken. His sunny disposition, broad grin, and blue-gray eyes also made an impression. To Ina, Gene was already a star.

At one point, Gene sat down with Jimmy to discuss his career: Had he written any more songs that Gene could sing? He hoped to find a Chicago music publisher to release a Gene Autry songbook, and he would like to include Jimmy's compositions. He was lining up shows not too far from Springfield. Would Jimmy be interested in performing with him? Jimmy, who was growing more worried about his job security, eagerly agreed to participate as much as he could in Gene's plans. He warned Gene that the Frisco was losing so much business that more cutbacks seemed inevitable.

When Gene had to leave for Chicago, he and Ina found it hard to say goodbye. They agreed to write one another, and Gene "promised he would dedicate his next radio song to me," Ina remembered nearly twenty years later.[19] In just four months' time, Ina Mae Spivey would become Mrs. Gene Autry.

13

"THE SINGING AND YODELING MARVEL"

S 1932 ARRIVED, GENE SETTLED INTO HIS ROLE as WLS radio entertainer, enjoying his enhanced status as a best-selling recording
artist. Uncle Art had started an advertising campaign for his records, calling
Gene "The Singing and Yodeling Marvel." Gene met with Maury Cole,
founder of Chicago's largest songbook publisher, M. M. Cole, and the two
inked a deal to release a folio in the ensuing months. Gene now had enough
songwriting and co-writing credits that music publishers released Gene Autry
sheet music as well. On evenings and weekends, Gene booked numerous appearances primarily at movie theaters before film screenings. He specifically
looked for bookings near Springfield, Missouri. He was eager to see "Miss Ina
Mae Spivey," as he called her, again.

On January 2, after his daily program, he typed a note to C. F. Martin Guitars on Prairie Farmer Radio Station WLS letterhead. Martin had notified
Gene that his 1931 correspondence had never arrived, so his custom guitar order had been delayed. Gene hurriedly typed:

> Go ahead with the job and have the name put on the Guitar have it script written
> on the Fingerboard and if you cant put the regular keys on the guitar put the new
> ones on as you mentioned in your letter but of course I like the regular ones bet-
> ter. When you have the instrument about ready write me and I will write you
> where to send it to if I am not in Chicago I will write you where to sent it to.

He gave his address as the Union Park Hotel, Washington and Warren Blvd.,
Chicago.[1]

Gene felt at home at WLS and enjoyed meeting the station's other new-comers. Several hailed from Kentucky's Renfro Valley and had been encour-aged to travel to WLS by their fellow Kentuckian, folk-song collector, and manager John Lair. Lair, who played the jug, had formed an old-timey string band, the Cumberland Ridge Runners, which had become a popular compo-nent of the *Barn Dance*. Karl and Harty (also known as the Renfro Valley Boys) played in the group as did another recent transplant to Chicago, Clyde Julian "Red" Foley. Three years younger than Gene, Red sang and played bass in the Ridge Runners, and began writing songs as well. After bunking briefly with Karl, Gene moved in with Red, sharing inexpensive quarters at the Union Park, with Murphy beds that flipped down from the wall.

"I knew Red very well," Gene later related. "He and I were very close friends, and I admired him very much. I always thought that Red Foley, at that time, had one of the greatest voices of any country singer I'd ever heard. He could do all types of things. He could do a hymn, a song with a beat . . . he was just very versatile. If Red Foley had not been lazy, there's no telling. . . . I'd be in the room when they would call him [for] a program, *Smile-a-While*, early in the morning about 5:30 or 6:00. The phone would ring and if he was sleeping, he'd just take it off the hook and drop it on the floor and go back to sleep. He was easygoing and he didn't care. It didn't make a bit of difference to him. But he had a voice. I don't think anybody could sing like him. He was a good-looking fellow . . . he had red hair . . . a likable man. I was very fond of him. If he'd have come to Hollywood and made pictures, if he'd had a little get-up about him, and really got out and hustled, then he could have given me a run for my money in the picture business."[2]

Never lazy, Gene dashed from one early-bird radio show to another. Sometimes, he appeared on WLS's *The Farm and Home Hour*. Other mornings, between programs, he met with arranger Nick Manoloff, who wrote the arrangements for Gene's songs for the M. M. Cole folio. Years later, Manoloff's niece recalled Gene's visits. Violet Petranoff wrote Gene:

> I was a teenager going to high school when you used to come to our house to work with my uncle on your songbook. You came early in the morning before going to WLS to sing. My uncle made the arrangements for the book as you sang your songs to him. On my sixteenth birthday, I remember you were in the living room with my uncle, and my mother had me treat you with some cookies and lemonade on a tray and you wished me "happy birthday." One morning when you had come for another work session and were waiting in the living room for my uncle to re-turn from the engravers, you had come into the kitchen asking Mother if she would mind if you watched her bathe my baby brother and you reminisced to her about your mom and your childhood in Oklahoma.[3]

With his grueling schedule and ambition for the future, Gene didn't have much time for nostalgia. He rented a room in Aurora so that some nights he

Elijah William Autry family portrait, ca. 1899, Cooke County, Texas. Top row (left to right): Delbert (Gene's father), Minnie, Tom, Meda, Will, Luda, Lula. Bottom row (left to right): Felix, Cal, Betty, Nora, Homer, Elijah.

Ozment family portrait, ca. 1900, Bryan County, Oklahoma. Top row (left to right): Nora Ozment (Gene's mother), "Sweet" Ozment Tipton, "Belle" Ozment Bacon. Middle row (left to right): Dera Tipton; Nora's mother, Malinda Ozment Reynolds; Daniel Tipton; Geneva Tipton; Sidney Tipton; Bill Bacon; Jesse Bacon. Bottom row (left to right): Marie Tipton, Frances "Frankie" Bacon, Clinton Bacon.

Inset, young Nora Ozment (detail of Ozment family portrait), ca. 1900.

The Missionary Baptist Church, Indian Creek, Texas, where Gene's grandfather preached, 2001. The church has since been restored. (Photo by Holly George-Warren)

Wilma, Veda, and Orvon Autry, exact date and location unknown.

Class Organization

First Term

President .... Velma Reynolds
Vice-President .... Tom Wheat

Second Term

President .... Yewel Brooks
Vice-President .... Ernest Fuson
Vice-President .... Essie Miller
Secretary .... Lula Turner
Sergeant Arms .... John Fries
Social Committee .... Edith Cook, Mary Eva Isbell, Hurbert Cargile
Motto .... Excelsior
Colors .... Pink and Green
Flower .... Pink Carnation

JOHN ERNEST AUTRY
EIDTH ETHEL COOK
ORVON GROVER AUTRY

Home of Cal Autry in Tioga, Texas, where Gene spent some of the happier moments of his childhood, 2001. In 2007, the house was scheduled for demolition. (Photo by Holly George-Warren)

Gene's page in the 1925 High Flyer Yearbook, Tioga, Texas, perhaps the only instance in which
his birth name, Orvon Grover Autry, was published. Gene is at right and his cousin "Buck"
is at left.

Gene, photographed ca. 1928 in a Frisco engine, spent seven years working for the St. Louis–San Francisco Railroad.

Gene's earliest publicity photo, taken in Sapulpa, Oklahoma, ca. 1929.

Gene's first New York City publicity shot, ca. 1930.

Early mentor Jimmy Long, the uncle of Ina Mae Spivey and author of Gene's first hit, "That Silver Haired Daddy of Mine," listens to his protégé.

Johnny Marvin was known for his tenor and his ukelele in 1920s vaudeville.

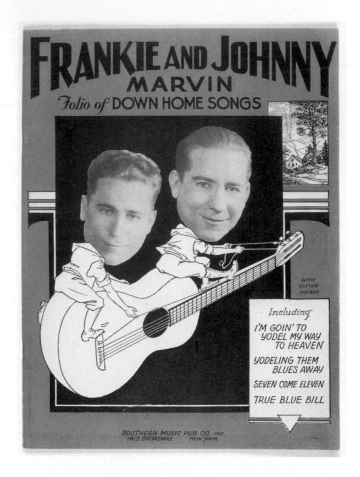

A 1932 Frankie and Johnny Marvin songbook; the Marvin brothers helped Gene tremendously during his early visits to New York. (Courtesy of the Autry National Center's Museum of the American West, Los Angeles)

Early promotional ad for one of Gene's first combos, based in Illinois, ca. 1931. Gene is at left in the back row. (Holly George-Warren Collection)

Gene sent Ina Mae Spivey this autographed picture of himself not long before the two married in
  1932. The inscription reads: "To Ina Mae, You are one of the sweetest girls I ever met, Sincerely,
  Gene Autry."
WLS announcer Anne Williams helped to promote Gene's image as a singing cowboy
  beginning in 1932.

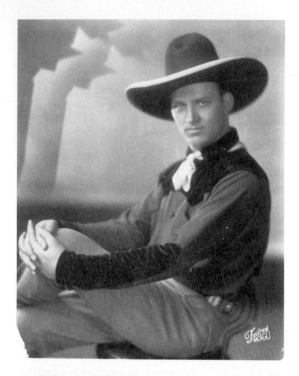

The cowboy look surfaces in this early Chicago publicity photo, ca. 1932.

Gene (standing, at left) with fellow *WLS Barn Dance* members, including Patsy Montana (standing, fourth from right) and the Prairie Ramblers; Millie and Dolly, the Girls of the Golden West; and Smiley Burnette (seated, center), 1934.

Ina Mae Autry, ca. 1934, ready for a swim.
Jimmy Long, Gene Autry, and Smiley Burnette (left to right) on the road, ca. 1934.

The Oklahoma Yodeling Cowboy in Chicago, ca. 1934.
Gene Autry and one of his early baseball buddies, Chicago Cubs pitcher Guy Bush, ca. 1932.

Stopping on one of his many jaunts through the Midwest, ca. 1933.

Gene Autry never smoked, but he did pose with a cigarette for this striking publicity shot made in Chicago, ca. 1934.

Gene Autry and Frankie Marvin worked together from 1928 to 1955; this publicity shot was taken in Chicago, ca. 1934.
Smiley Burnette and Gene Autry in Chicago, ca. 1934. (Stanley Rojo Collection)

Gene bought Ina a fur coat soon after his success in Hollywood in 1935.
Delbert Autry and his fifth wife, Ruby, soon after their 1937 marriage. (Stanley Rojo Collection)

Gene Autry visits his Aunt Etta and Uncle Cal Autry in Tioga, Texas, 1941.
Recording industry pioneer Art Satherley always considered Gene Autry his greatest discovery.

Some of Ina and Gene's first friends in Hollywood were the professional boxer Dude Chick and his wife, Ruth, ca. 1935.

Gene debuted as a leading man in the Mascot serial *The Phantom Empire*; Murania's robots had previously starred in a Joan Crawford film and would be seen again in a 1951 sci-fi thriller.

Gene Autry's first feature film starring as himself, 1935's *Tumbling Tumbleweeds*, included his friends Frankie Marvin and Smiley Burnette in the cast.

Beginning in 1935, Gene tirelessly traveled America, making personal appearances with Champion in tow.

could stay there before doing his 6 AM WJJD program. On Hotel Aurora stationery, he typed a letter to his Uncle Bob, enclosing money to repay a loan from Ozment to his mother:

> I got your letter a few days ago and lost it so I dident [*sic*] have your address then I had to write Mama to get your address again so I hope that you get this letter in time and it will do you some good.
>
> Things are awful tuff down there now I guess well they are awful tuff up in this country also and I don't see much chance for them to get any better but all any one can do is hope for the best.
>
> Be sure and write me and let me know if you get this letter and let me know if you got the money I am sorry that I never got to mail it sooner than I have but I didn't so that is all there is to it.
>
> Well I will stop for this time so write me some time and if you all are up this way be sure and stop in and see me. Will expect an answer from you soon.
> Your Nephew
> Orvon

Although Gene used hotel letterhead, the envelope was customized, touting his pre-ARC labels:

GENE AUTRY
The Sunny South's Blue Yodeler
Recording Artist
Victor, Velvet Tone, Champion and OKeh[4]

To EARN AS MUCH AS HE COULD, Gene performed all over Illinois when not broadcasting. "I worked out of Chicago because I was on WLS about five days a week," Gene later explained. "I would play around there where that I could get in time to do my show of a morning, and then from there, you could drive most anyplace you'd want to. Then on Friday a lot of times, you'd take a longer trip because you'd have a Friday night, then Saturday, and Sunday. You'd always have to take those things into consideration."[5] Sometimes Jimmy Long would join him for performances, singing duets and playing guitar.

A typical show for Gene occurred on Sunday, January 21, when he appeared at the Gabyle Theatre, in North Judson, Indiana, before the screening of Preston Sturges's debut film, *Strictly Dishonorable*. Its subject—a singing star who falls for a Southern Belle—surely must have brought thoughts of Ina to Gene's mind. The handbill, which Gene had printed up, advertised him as "Oklahoma's Yodeling Cow Boy, Famous Radio Recording Artist from WLS Chicago . . . You hear him every morning at 9:20 AM on the radio—Now for a real treat, see and hear him on the stage playing and singing your favorite songs." Gene later recalled, "Most everybody who worked on WLS did personal appearances because that was the only way they really made any money."[6] Karl Davis said of the earnings yielded from Karl and Harty's similar bookings:

"We'd make a personal appearance in a place like Ishpeming, Michigan, and we would get $25."[7] But the theater owners would often treat Gene and other performers like family, inviting them home for dinner before the night's festivities. Eventually, Gene's own movies would headline in the very same small-town theaters.

These early years of building Gene's fan base paid off in the decades ahead. Gene's rural fans, who would flock to his pictures, listen to his radio show, and watch him on TV, would remember these appearances. Fifty-two years later, Gene recalled one such theater, the Scenic, on Main Street in tiny Lexington, Illinois, where movies were shown four nights a week. WLS artists often performed before the screening, but would first go to a 6 PM dinner at the home of the owners, Tilden and Helen Patton. On February 27, 1932, Gene and Jimmy Long did the show, joining the Pattons for supper, after which Gene played the family a few songs on their piano. In 1984 Gene wrote Helen Patton, "I remember very well back in 1932 when I appeared with Jimmy Long at the theater-stage which you and your husband owned, and also when we visited you in your home. . . . I still recall many of the early acquaintances that I made during the four years I put in at WLS. They are memories which I shall always treasure."[8]

Such appearances also helped Gene's record sales. "That Silver Haired Daddy" continued to sell briskly on ARC's various labels: Conqueror and Silvertone, through the Sears catalog and the few Sears stores then open; Perfect at McClellan dime stores; Banner at W. T. Grant five-and-dimes; Romeo at S. S. Kresge dime stores (the predecessor to K-Mart)—for about twenty-five cents each. "We had all the chain stores of America—we had about twenty labels," related Uncle Art. "I was sitting on top of the world with all those companies taking our records."[9] Soon, Gene began to see some ARC royalty checks: even at a half-penny per side, by the end of 1932 Gene would gross close to $2,200 from ARC, more than any of his other record company affiliations. Victor brought him only $1.56 for the entire year, Columbia $3.87, and Gennett $15. Uncle Art let Gene know that he expected a financial "reward" for the help he bestowed upon his protégé. In 1932, with a handshake agreement, Gene began paying Satherley a 25 percent "commission" on his ARC royalties, totaling $566.20 the first year. In addition to covering all of Jimmy Long's travel expenses for their performances, Gene began paying him a percentage of the publishing income he received from songs Jimmy had written, which amounted to $1,727.05 in 1932.

As Gene's theater dates increased (in January, he earned $25.50 from engagements; February $104, and March $224.50), he realized he needed a better car. On March 10 he bought his first-ever spanking new Buick roadster for $1,200. He hoped to increase the size of his traveling ensemble, so the larger vehicle was mandatory. But as a result of these expenses, the pressure was on to get more lucrative bookings in larger theaters. Sometimes, though, the Oklahoma Yodeling Cowboy simply could not draw large numbers of paying customers.

Such was the case at the 340-seat Tivoli Theater, on Main Street, in Danville, Illinois, where Gene had booked a two-night stand for March 19 and 20. Jimmy met him there, just after a recording session at Gennett in Indiana. Years later, in a fan magazine, Gene recalled the wintry night as "the low point in my life." "It was the middle of the Depression," he wrote "and the theater was nearly empty. I was so discouraged that I printed in big letters on my dressing room door: GENE AUTRY AMERICA'S BIGGEST FLOP."[10] After Gene became a Hollywood star, the theater management framed the door and displayed it under glass in the lobby.

Gene's spirits were certainly lifted with the release of his first songbook, *Gene Autry's Sensational Collection of Famous Original Cowboy Songs and Mountain Ballads.* Uncle Art had promised Gene before he embarked for Chicago, "You'll be making a thousand to fifteen hundred dollars a week," with the sales of songbooks and personal appearances. When Gene held in his hands the glossy blue-and-orange 8×12 book with his name emblazoned next to his likeness on the cover, he could almost believe him. Eventually, Harry Shay, who advertised Gene's folio in the Sears catalogue, reported to Satherley, "We're selling two thousand Gene Autry songbooks a day." At seventy-five cents, the songbook sold well at Gene's performances too.

His *Sensational Collection* featured thirty-two recent Autry recordings, including "Silver Haired Daddy" and his Jimmie Rodgers–style material. In his preface to the book, Gene's tone was grateful and sincere:

> To My Radio Friends: This book is my answer to the thousands of letters received asking for my songs. Most of the numbers are my own compositions. They have never before been published. Each song was inspired by some happening, pleasant, comic or tragic, in my life and travels. Many of them are about people whose life stories were unusual, interesting. These songs are your songs now. I hope that you will find as much pleasure in singing them as I have had in getting them ready for you. . . . To each and every one, who loves these cowboy and native American ballads, I dedicate this book. To you folks who have made this book possible, to Station WLS for its earnest cooperation, and to Anne Williams, who has worked with me on this book, and announces me on Conqueror Record Time—a hearty "thank you."

"Native American ballads" was actually the category given his songs by Victor Records in their recording ledger; other labels called the style "folk," "mountain ballads," or "old-time tunes." As a musical description, "hillbilly" was only beginning to be used widely in print, primarily by trade publications, followed by the mainstream press, and then the labels' advertising.

Although Gene still played more hillbilly than cowboy songs, Anne Williams, in her introduction to the folio, made no bones about Gene's dramatic new buckaroo image:

A figure on horseback silhouetted against the hazy moonlight that floods the cattle country with silver haze! The quiet plunking of a tuneful guitar, accompanied by a low, clear voice, broken only by the fretful stirring of a restless steer. A cowboy riding herd through the still watches of a Texas night—a lone herder thrumming and humming the Requiem of the Range. That is the background of Gene Autry—with the great outdoors for his theater—his audience a herd of steers. No "drug store" cowboy, this lad. No synthetic crooner made cowboy overnight through the acquisitions of a ten gallon hat and a pair of woolly chaps. Born to the saddle, a hard ridin', straight shootin', carefree cowboy singing the songs as he learned them on the range around the campfire; and at the bunk house on wintry nights when a Norther swooped down from the Panhandle and sent the steers huddling in the lee of the storm with their heads together and their tails to the wind. All this Gene Autry brings us in his voice and his songs. A sincere reflection of that great, friendly country and this chap who is a first rate cowboy, a "knock-out" radio personality, and a much loved recording artist.

GENE WAS ALSO MAKING A NAME FOR HIMSELF AS A SONGWRITER. In addition to his M. M. Cole songbook, sheet music offered such Autry songs as "The Gang-ster's Warning." Gene's composition, "Bear Cat Papa Blues," was featured in another 1932 publication: *Frankie and Johnny Marvin Folio of Down Home Songs*, published by Southern Music (the publishing company formed by Victor's Ralph Peer).

Gene could hardly wait to show his new songbook to Jimmy and Jesse Long, but most of all to Ina Mae. He had showered her with phone calls and notes, and sent her his autographed publicity photo. In one letter he wrote, "I made my first personal appearance today at Rockford, Illinois. I made thirty dollars. I think that's pretty good, don't you?" Gene and Ina Mae had only had one brief visit since December, and he took her to the movies. "I remember af-ter my second meeting with Gene," Ina recalled years later, "a girl friend asked me to tell her about him. I said he had a good face and nice blue eyes and sang very pleasantly. She thought these were excellent reasons for liking a man."[11] On March 2 Ina finished her first semester of college, and during the break ac-companied her uncle and cousin to Richmond, Indiana, for their two-day ses-sion at Gennett. The recordings, under the name of the Long Family, yielded a handful of hymns that were distributed on the Chapel label to funeral par-lors. Although her participation was minimal, Ina enjoyed the experience, mainly because it gave her a taste of her new beau's professional life.

Gene finally booked a concert date in St. Louis, only a couple hours from Springfield, and asked Jimmy to join him. He also invited Ina and Jesse, who agreed to come on Saturday. Jimmy and Gene performed at a theater on Friday night, March 31, and the women arrived by train the next day. When Gene and Ina met again, they could not take their eyes off one another. "She looked so pretty and sweet that people in the street turned around to take a second look at her," he later said. After months of anticipation, they wanted to spend as much time as they could alone together and decided to go for a drive. "It seemed to me I had never been so happy," Gene recalled. "Just to have my arm around Ina and feel her soft hair blowing against my cheek was pure delight." Gene had something on his mind to discuss with her. Ina's sister, Anita Karns, remembered, "Ina had no idea that Gene was going to propose to her the second or third time they met. It was a complete surprise to her."[12]

"I went off with Ina," Gene later wrote in his autobiography, "and we agreed to meet the Longs for dinner in a little café on the city's south side. We arrived early. As we sat there, I suddenly blurted out, 'Honey, let's get married.' The next thing I knew, we had rushed off to get a license and find a wedding chapel or a justice of the peace."[13] Ina later recalled feeling embarrassed that she had discovered a rip in what was to be her wedding dress. Gene stopped in a dime store to purchase an imitation gold ring. Pastor Richard Jesse, of the Mount Calvary Lutheran Church, did not know that "Orvon Autry," the name on the marriage license, was a recording and radio artist when he married the couple. "His wife, who had already gone to bed . . . put on a bathrobe over her night dress and witnessed the ceremony," according to Gene. On the marriage documents, Ina and Gene both listed their residence as Springfield; Ina was just shy of her twenty-first birthday, the legally required age to wed in Missouri (but somehow this little detail slipped through the cracks).[14]

The newlyweds eventually made it back to the restaurant to meet the Longs, who were "really mad at Ina and Gene . . . because they were gone for hours," said Anita. Gene remembered, "Ina said, 'Uncle Jim, Gene and I got married.' Jimmy said, 'I don't believe it. Gene would have told me. I know he would.' He looked at me sharply. I sort of ducked my head. Then Jesse said, 'Jimmy Long, today is April Fool's Day. Don't you know a joke when you hear one?'" But it was no joke, and the Longs initially were quite disturbed, especially when Ina said she wasn't going back to school but planned to move immediately to Chicago with her new husband. Eventually, they accepted the couple's elopement.

There was not enough time or money for a honeymoon; the couple had to be back for Gene's radio show on WJJD Monday morning. Gene sped home to Aurora, frightening Ina with his fast driving, and she begged him to slow down. They also discovered that while Gene was a morning person, Ina was not. "I was grumpy in the morning," Ina later related. "Gene was unaware of it and went about preparing for the day by chatting, laughing, and bubbling with the joy of living. Gradually I changed. How could I help it? The melody of 'That Silver Haired Daddy' . . . being boomed from the shower every morning is a mighty fine tonic."[15]

Ina quickly tried to adjust to Gene's frantic pace, she later recalled:

At the beginning, Gene was living in Aurora . . . where he was singing on a morning program, and also making radio appearances in Chicago at WLS, and personal theater appearances in any town he could get to and return from in time for his

Aurora broadcast. Gene was so wrapped up in his work and in such a hustle generally in those early days that he sometimes would go all day without even thinking
of eating. . . . At first I was such a diffident little bride that I would never think of
speaking up even though I was famished. Still, one afternoon when we were getting a train out of Chicago for Aurora, after a long day without lunch, he made a
mistake. If he had done nothing about it, I would have said nothing. But he
stopped at a fruit display and bought a bag of apples, which he offered to me. Even
as I reached for one, I burst into tears. "What's wrong?" he asked in alarm. "I'm
hungry!" I bawled. "I want to eat. Not those—*food!*" Never since that little out-
burst of independence has Gene ever skipped a mealtime without doing something
about it, as least when I'm along.[16]

A week later, the couple decided to travel back to Oklahoma to meet each
other's parents. Duncan was very close to Henryetta, where Gene, still trying
to hold onto his railroad credentials, had been asked to work at the depot on
April 9. He was eager for Ina to meet his mother, too. This time, the newlyweds spent the night in a hotel along the way. That evening, Gene emptied his
wallet of $1,500 and spread the bills out on the bed for Ina Mae to see. "That's
all the money I have in the world," he told her, "and I want you to know that it's
yours as much as mine." Over the next forty-eight years, that would be a
moment Ina would never forget.[17]

14

MOTHERLESS SON

NORA'S HEALTH HAD DETERIORATED DRAMATICALLY by the time Gene and Ina Mae arrived in Ravia. Bedridden, his mother looked like a tiny bird in a nest of coverlets and sheets, her skin pulled taut over her bones, her cheeks and eyes sunken. A rough, dark rash covered much of her face and arms, as if she had a bad sunburn. A country doctor, Dr. Cummings, had just left her side, but Veda and Wilma were unable to give Gene a clear explanation of his diagnosis. Nora seemed confused, somewhat delirious. Seeing her favorite child, though, helped immensely; her face brightened when Gene walked into the room. Soon, Nora was sitting up in bed, making more sense, and when Gene introduced her to his bride she showed genuine happiness. She was thrilled to hold in her long, bony hands the fancy new songbook with her son's name on front. He showed her the book's first page with a paragraph about his family. Gene discussed his career, telling her he was soon to appear on the *WLS Barn Dance* and that his publisher already wanted to issue a second book. Having just completed a monotonous shift in Henryetta, he had finally decided to quit the Frisco. He was too busy with his radio programs in Chicago to travel up and down the Frisco line as a relief operator.

Gene later described this troubling visit in his autobiography: "She had been ill quite a long time and suffered terribly with stomach pains," he wrote.

> No one ever heard her complain, but her health was never very robust. She didn't weigh much over one hundred pounds. . . . She had gone years without proper medical care. We didn't know about clinics and specialists . . . and couldn't

afford them if we had. The family had no savings . . . I was able to send part of my pay home, but not enough to help Mother. The last time I saw her, my first records had been released and were attracting notice. I was on my way to Chicago . . . If Mother knew she was dying, she didn't let on. I talked about postponing my trip. She insisted I leave. "You go to Chicago, Gene," she said. "There might not be a next time." The last question she asked me, was I *sure* I ought to give up my job with the railroad?[1]

Gene believed his mother had cancer, although he related that his family never discussed the nature of her illness. Nora Autry actually suffered from pellagra, a scourge during the Depression among impoverished Americans whose diet consisted primarily of corn. Pellagra raged in epidemic proportions in the South and Southwest in the 1930s. The disease occurs when a person does not get enough niacin (B3) or tryptophan (an amino acid) in the diet. It can also occur if the body fails to absorb these nutrients. Pellagra is characterized by red, scaly skin sores (dermatitis), diarrhea, inflamed mucous membranes, and mental confusion and delusions. Early stages of pellagra often exhibit as malaise, apathy, weakness, and lassitude. The final phase of the illness is dementia, which can become so severe it mimics schizophrenia, including delusions, hallucinations, and stupor. Then comes organ failure and death. According to epidemiological data collected during the U.S. pellagra epidemic in the 1930s, women, children, and the elderly of both sexes were most commonly stricken with pellagra while infants, adolescents, and working young males were affected least frequently. Medical professionals theorized that the disparity in prevalence resulted from an unbalanced distribution of food within households. In 1932 many rural doctors didn't realize that altering the diet to include meats, dairy products, and green vegetables could relieve the symptoms of pellagra, even stop its progression. It was not learned until 1937 that administering niacin to the patient could cure the disease.

Nora had well-meaning neighbors and relatives who told Gene they would help Veda and Wilma care for his mother. After having his sisters promise to call him if Nora's condition worsened, Gene did as his mother asked: He and Ina Mae returned to Chicago. Deeply troubled, he wrote Nora before traveling the next weekend to play more bookings.

Soon after their return to illinois, the newlyweds rented their first home in a newly constructed large yellow-brick building. Located at 4501 Malden Street on the north side of Chicago, it was in a pleasant neighborhood with leafy trees and tiny parks scattered about. Several musicians and WLS artists lived in their building, and residents often spent time together socializing. Ina set to work decorating their fourth-floor, two-bedroom apartment, turning it into a place where their new friends would feel welcome.

These were exciting days: George Biggar had begun booking Gene onto the *WLS Barn Dance*, "not every week, but enough to get exposure," Gene later recalled.[2] On March 19, 1932, the *Barn Dance* had moved from a studio in the Prairie Farmer building, at 1230 Washington Boulevard, to the 1,200-seat Eighth Street Theatre on Wabash and Eighth Street, behind the Stevens Hotel. Folks who had bought a fifty-cent ticket lined up every Saturday for either the early or late show, each of which ran about two hours. "Few seats were empty," according to WLS historian James F. Evans. "Crowds even filled the orchestra pit, and tickets were sold out five to eight weeks in advance." Between 50 and 60 percent of the audience traveled from outside Chicago to attend.[3] Around the time Gene began on the *Barn Dance*, the show was picked up by NBC to air regionally on its affiliated stations; then on September 30, 1933, it went national, with thirty stations carrying the Alka-Seltzer-sponsored portion of the program from coast to coast. At that juncture, the show became better known as the *National Barn Dance*.

With a backdrop and set constructed to look like the hayloft on a midwestern farm, the *Barn Dance* presented its entertainers as an ensemble sitting along the stage periphery, some perched on hay bales, taking turns appearing on center stage. The varying performance lineup included pop and hillbilly vocalists, novelty acts, string bands, and square dancing exhibitions. In 1932, when Gene started, regulars included Arkie the Arkansas Woodchopper; the Cumberland Ridge Runners; the Maple City Four, a slapstick-comedy-meets-barbershop-quartet from LaPorte, Indiana; singing duos Mac and Bob, who were blind; and the Log Cabin Boys, who lived in Gene's apartment building. Joking and pranks during performances were not uncommon: while Arkie warbled a tune, for example, members of the zany Maple City Four might crawl around on all fours, snorting like pigs.

When he first appeared on the *Barn Dance*, Gene was paid fifteen dollars per show. He was thrilled to be part of the program and requested autographed publicity photos from his fellow artists, a collection he had started back in New York with stars like Carson Robison. From WLS banjoist Jesse Doolittle ("to a real pal, Gene Autry") to announcer Jack Holden ("with a deep appreciation of a lasting friendship") to the Hayloft Dancers ("to a good fellow and swell showman"), he accumulated quite a batch of glossies. After the evening's performances ended at midnight, cast members would head over to a Greek restaurant for food and revelry. Off hours, WLS artists would play golf or take in Chicago Cubs games together. Gene began working on new songs with other *Barn Dance* cast members, including Hugh Cross of the Cumberland Ridge Runners.

The WLS management was involved in other aspects of the performers' schedules. WLS Artists Inc. agents Earl Kurtze and George Ferguson booked package shows of *Barn Dance* performers at state and county fairs and other venues. Program director "George [Biggar] was one of the greatest forces in guiding some of these WLS people into prominence," said former WLS executive Stephen Cisler. "George was very soft-spoken, with a very dry wit, and was one of these contemplative Buddha types and would devote himself to the personal interests of talent, and they warmed up to him, would bring their troubles to him, and he would try to solve them. He just had a knack for doing the right thing for these people, and they loved him for it."[4]

Soon, Gene would be needing that kind of support. The second week in May, he received a letter in an envelope he'd given his mother, from Claremore's Hotel Will Rogers, where he and Ina had spent the night on their recent visit. In pencil, Nora had marked through the hotel's return address and scrawled her name. She addressed it to Mr. Gene Autry, Radio Statioin [sic] WLS, 502 Superior Street, Aurora Ill—which may explain why it took a while to reach him, though postmarked May 8, 1932. Nora had written it the previous day in pencil; sometimes in nearly indecipherable handwriting, it was a poignant, stream-of-consciousness missive to her son. Gene would keep the last letter his mother ever wrote him in a safety box for five decades.

Dear son
We received your sweet letter sure was glad to hear from you and know you and Ina May was well the first we had heard from you 7 days son I am better but still in bed I don't know when I will ever be out I am so week Bulah wrote they was starting to Michigan last Monday I sure hated for them to leave the girls said they sure was good to all of us and we needed them so bad but they told the girls they had to go to work I am sure lonely for you son Delbert is in the can for 60 days I guess he will cause us a lot of trouble when he gets back son I want you to tell them you sold out and going to make another book and when you compose a song put it in another book and when you use the things that is in the first book say you are imitating then they can't hurt you maby. leave off the ranch don't you mention it to anyone unless Jimmy Long I dreamed your announcer said to you to always say that you was imitating things you put in your book only what you and others compose and I dreamed that they arrested you and I dreamed they mistreated you and I thought you came by to tell us goodbye and Willma [sic] would not let me let on that you was there and you played your records for me and then I told nothing and you left and I seen you no more [?] dreamed you was having a trial and some one said they sure hated to tell about the old *Barn Dance* so I would fix it without mentioning to anyone unless it be to Jimmie Long maybe he will help you can announce over the radio you had sold [?] started a new band and still sing and advertise son pay others their royalty on their song for I feel like you will soon have trouble all okay [?] but if anything happens don't leave without you come and kiss me unless I am dead I wish you could come I would tell you a lot more but your dad or a lot of his dirty company is liable to turn you in so I would die son I got so I did not know a thing after you left they said the Dr. had to put two needles in my arm they all had to hold me so Bulah caught your papa in the other room laughing at me son write soon and after ward [?] I feel so lonesome so tear this letter up just as soon as you get it so no one can read it address our letters to Veda
    so goodby sweet heart from mother Nora Autry tell Ina May we sure would love to see her and appreciated her coming I am in bed yet[5]

After Gene read his mother's disconcerting letter, he began making plans to return to Ravia. But it was too late: On May 29, he received word that his mother had gone into a coma and died at home at 11:30 the night before. Alongside Veda and Wilma, Dr. Cummings and a nurse had been at her bedside and signed the death certificate, giving "palagria," a variant spelling of pellagra, as the cause of death. Nora Autry was forty-nine years old, but when she died, she looked close to seventy. "I always regarded the death of our mother as a tragedy," Gene later wrote, "because I was on the verge of making the kind of money that might have prolonged her life or made her last days more bearable. The money came too late." As an Ozment cousin helped ready Nora's body for burial, she found under her dressing gown a small photograph of Gene "carefully laid upon her chest close to her heart," she later recalled.[6]

THE FIRST THING GENE DID UPON HIS ARRIVAL IN OKLAHOMA for his mother's funeral was to find out which jail Delbert was in and request his temporary release to attend the services. The Autrys had offered a burial plot for Nora at Indian Creek Cemetery, a stone's throw from where Gene was born less than twenty-five years before. There, on June 2, she would be laid to rest near Gene's grandparents. The funeral was held in Tioga at the Baptist Church. Friends and relatives from Texas and Oklahoma attended, then the funeral procession traveled Cross Timbers from Tioga to Nora Autry's final resting place. Gene paid all the costs of his mother's funeral, and over the next five decades, he would send money to his cousin Buck Autry and family for cemetery upkeep and flowers for his mother's grave.

It was clear that Delbert would not provide for his children, so Veda, Wilma, and Dudley piled into their big brother's new Buick and traveled to Chicago to live with Gene and Ina. Up until 1961 Gene occasionally would hear from Ravia merchants still trying to collect the unpaid bills his family left behind. Back in Chicago, Gene spent his time racing around entertaining on radio and performing on theater stages, while Ina Mae suddenly became a pseudo mother/big sister to a pair of teenage girls and a ten-year-old boy. Just three weeks after his mother's funeral, Gene returned to New York City to make his first new recordings in seven months. Between June 24 and 30 he spent nearly an entire week in both ARC and Victor studios. Even though Gene was in discussion with Uncle Art about an exclusive contract, he was still a free agent.

He met Jimmy Long on Friday, June 24 at the ARC studio to do more songs in the nostalgic vein of "Silver Haired Daddy." Perhaps his mother's recent death influenced his choice of material, too, which weighed heavily on the bittersweet and sentimental. Gene co-wrote a pair of songs for the first session with Hugh Cross, who played banjo and guitar in the Cumberland Ridge Runners. With an uncredited guitarist—probably Roy Smeck—Gene sang solo on a lovely "That Ramshackle Shack"; he harmonized with Jimmy on "Back to Old Smoky

Mountain." After the weekend, on Monday, June 27, again with Smeck, Gene cut the similar-sounding ballad, "Back Home in the Blue Ridge Mountains." Unlike the previous Friday's songs, this one was embellished with yodels. The next day Gene and Jimmy harmonized on the jailbird weeper, "The Crime I Didn't Do," punctuated by Roy Smeck's emotive Hawaiian guitar; Gene took a solo turn on another sorrowful ballad, "Kentucky Lullaby," ("one summer day she went away / and left me with sad memories"), then was rejoined by Jimmy singing a falsetto harmony on "Alone with My Sorrows," a new tune the pair had written. On Wednesday, June 29, Gene and Jimmy tried a slightly revised, newly titled version of an old number: "I'm Always Dreaming of You." Gene's revisit of Jimmie Rodgers's "Moonlight and Skies," written by convict Raymond Hall, had a real poignancy to it, and "Returning to my Cabin Home" was a lively up-tempo number.

Gene's last day of recording that year began on Thursday morning. He started the day cutting a pair of wistful duets with Jimmy Long at ARC. Smeck accompanied them on his steel guitar, and he added banjo to Gene's solo number, "In the Hills of Carolina." That afternoon, Jimmy and Gene dashed over to Victor, where they would take turns doing individual sessions. Gene started from 1:30 to 3:00, then Jimmy had an hour's turn at 3: 00, with Gene again for forty minutes at 4:00, ending with Jimmy from 4:40 to 5:15. Why did they split it up this way? Perhaps it was Gene's session, which he shared with Jimmy, while he rested his voice. Jimmy performed solo versions of his own songs; Gene redid several of the mountain ballads he'd waxed over the previous week at ARC. He sang a couple of his original blue yodels, including the tried and true "Gangster's Warning." Most striking about these renditions was Gene's greatly improved guitar playing. He upped the tempo on one brand-new number, the delightfully naughty "Black Bottom Blues": "When you go down in Black Bottom / This is what you will see / a redheaded mama with her dress to her knees / Listen, redheaded mama, your daddy's got the black bottom blues / The women in Black Bottom all wear their high heel shoes / They smoke cigarettes and they drink home brew / Listen mama, your daddy has got the Black Bottom blues."

Nineteen sides would be released from the week's recordings. Those on the various ARC budget labels, including Conqueror, Banner, Oriole, Perfect, Romeo, and Vocalion, sold briskly. Those released on Victor at seventy-five cents each (the budget imprint Timely Tunes had been discontinued) did not fare as well. Several of Gene's new songs were issued on sheet music by Calumet, including "Ramshackle Shack," "The Crime I Didn't Do," and "Alone with My Sorrows."

A new kind of Gene Autry product was also released that fall: the Gene Autry Round-Up guitar, featured in the Sears, Roebuck catalogue and stores. Produced by the Harmony guitar company, the beginner model was the standard size, with a spruce top and mahogany sides and neck. It marked the first time a guitar featured stencil-painted designs on the headstock and top. These all emphasized the singing cowboy and his favorite past-time—the round-up. Pictures on the headstock depicted a cowboy on horseback swinging his lariat, accented with the word Round-Up. The guitar's top featured a Western scene, with a trail drive, a buckaroo at work, and Gene's autograph. The first of many Gene Autry guitars that varied slightly over the years, this one would be the template for a style ubiquitous among kids' Western guitars. The price— $9.75—was even less than Gene paid for his first guitar when he was twelve years old. Over the years, the Gene Autry guitar would become the first guitar played by a number of young fledgling guitarists, including such future country stars as George Jones.

The 1932 Sears fall catalogue page, featuring a picture of Gene holding the guitar, painted him as a role model:

> Gene Autry, the smiling Oklahoma Yodeling Cowboy, is one of Radio's outstanding entertainers of the day. With his large number of yodeling cowboy songs he has attracted to him thousands of "Autry fans." So popular has he become that his public has demanded a reproduction of his famous "Round-Up" Guitar and here it is at a popular price. Two years ago, Gene Autry was unknown. Today his fame is countrywide. A noted radio artist, a famous stage star and the well known Conqueror Record Artist. Simply because he learned to play the guitar while on the ranch and became a singer of cowboy songs. Tomorrow, next year, and every year new stars will develop. Maybe one will be you. Even if you never reach the fame of Autry—a boy or girl who plays the guitar is always welcome where ever young folks gather.[7]

The logic of the Sears advertisement would serve as the basis for hundreds of licensed Gene Autry products that would be merchandised over the next twenty-five years.

Gene received his copy of the Sears, Roebuck catalogue in the mail in October, around the same time he got a letter from Frisco Railroad headquarters. Dated October 7, 1932, the letter from Superintendent C. T. Mason in Tulsa informed him that since six months has passed since he last reported to duty in Henryetta, his seniority on the southwestern division had expired. He was required to return his annual rail pass immediately.

On October 14, Gene typed a heartfelt letter in reply. On his new letterhead reading "GENE AUTRY, RADIO AND RECORDING ARTISTE, VICTOR AND AMERICAN RECORD CORPS., YODELING THE BLUES AND OLD TIME SINGING, he wrote:

> It is with much regret that I leave the service of the company that I have worked for, for eight years, but as railroad business has been so hard hit that it was necessary to reduce forces I felt that I could do better in some other line of business. However, I will always feel more at home in a railroad office than any other place.

I want to take this opportunity to thank you, Mr. Rudd, and Mr. Hale for all the favors and courtesies you have shown me while in your employment, and I want to say here that I believe you have the best set of officials to be found any place, this also includes your train dispatchers and, in fact, your entire force, and should business ever permit, and you are in need of men I would be very glad to return to work, should I be out of work.

Mr. Mason, I would appreciate a service letter from you covering my services on the Frisco, for my files.

I wish you and all the gang all the luck and success in the world, and kindest personal regards, I am,

Yours very truly,

Gene Autry

It must have been with both relief and sadness that Gene received the Frisco's reply two weeks later: "Very much appreciate your kind words respecting Frisco officials and employes [*sic*] and can assure you it is with deep regret that your service with this company is terminated." With the Frisco job and his mother's death behind him and his family and wife now with him in Chicago, the Oklahoma Yodeling Cowboy was on the verge of becoming a national singing star. Gene Autry's new life had begun.

15

WLS RADIO STAR

ENE LINED UP MORE THEATER BOOKINGS for the autumn of 1932 than ever before. He decided to add to his stage show, patterning it after the combined comedy and music proven successful by the *Barn Dance*. In addition to Jimmy Long, he invited Frankie Marvin to perform with them, making a trio. Frankie and Jimmy also would serve as an opening act, doing a comic routine similar to the one Frankie had perfected with Johnny in vaudeville. To look like bumpkins, they donned tight-fitting plaid or hounds-tooth suits and silly hats, while Gene continued to embellish his buckaroo persona. He invested quite a bit of money in his new Western wardrobe, purchasing three pair of trousers and six shirts, all in the cowboy style; five pairs of custommade cowboy boots; four Stetson hats; and a fancy belt buckle, totaling $384.50. He wore a flowing scarf knotted around his neck; he usually tucked his pants legs into his ornate boots; and he alternated between a black and white Stetson.

Gene also had to spring for a new automobile and guitar after his Buick— with his Martin inside—was stolen on October 15 from a Chicago street. On November 1, he paid close to $2,000 for an upgraded model. Driving his new Buick, he could comfortably carry his musicians, their instruments—and occasionally Uncle Art. "Frankie Marvin and Jimmy Long used to travel around with Gene out of Chicago," Art Satherley remembered of the period. "They made a trio. They were being booked in little theaters, and there was no place for them to undress, really—just a place behind the curtain. Jimmy Long . . . had one of those pencils that ladies used . . . for their lips and hair, and he used it all over his face to make him a freckled boy. I would sit down in a seat, so they wouldn't think I was with them."[1]

Although Art found the act embarrassing, Frankie recalled that it went over well and that "four or five nights a week we'd play theaters around there. [Gene] didn't have a regular band, just Gene and I would work together, and Jimmy Long worked once in a while with him."[2] Eventually, Frankie also got radio work, broadcasting on WJJD as the Lone Star Yodeler, and on WLS as the Singing Cotton Planter. In late 1932, Jimmy's appearances with Gene became more regular, after he and his family moved to Chicago, following his layoff from the Frisco in October.[3]

"My dad, after about forty years, was out of a job," Beverly Long Moss related. "So he called Gene and Gene said, 'Come on out and we'll work out something.' So he did, and they had an act. My dad was a good comedian—the second banana—and Gene would give the lines, and [my dad] would get the fun part, and the audience laughed." Jimmy would later be billed "The Country Cut Up." Gene got the Longs an apartment on the third floor of the building where he and Ina had set up housekeeping. "I went to my senior year in Chicago," said Beverly, "and my brother, Jack, was two years younger, and he went, too, and I graduated high school there in Chicago in 1933. Gene and my dad would go out usually on Friday afternoons, and they'd be gone most every weekend, and sometimes during the week, playing places around there. And then Ina and my mother and I and Jack, after school and on Saturdays especially, we would go on the El downtown and just bum around down there."[4]

In addition to driving his trio to "almost every town in Illinois with a population of more than a couple thousand," as Gene later recalled, he handled the local advertising, saw to the distribution of window cards and handbills, checked the box office receipts, and supervised all the other business details. Gene perceived this as his real education regarding the business side of entertainment—knowledge that would help him greatly in the years to come. "I picked up a lot of business ideas," he recalled.[5] Gene did well financially with these appearances, netting $466 in September, $460 in October, and a whopping $692 in November.

The national press began to trumpet the increasing popularity of the type of music Gene was playing. The December 4–10, 1932, issue of *Radio and Amusement Guide: The National Weekly of Programs and Personalities* (published in New York City, and available on newsstands for a nickel) heralded the news on its cover: HILLBILLY CRAZE SWEEPS BROADWAY. Below the headline were photos of Gene and a fetching new *Barn Dance* vocal trio, the Three Little Maids.

"America once again jigs to the folk songs of its fathers—commonly called Hillbilly songs—and it likes it," the article declared.

If two years ago, you had told the broadcasting moguls of New York that they'd be sending hillbilly songs into the air instead of jazz they'd have snickered. "Hillbilly songs will become popular when we sell Manhattan back to the Indians," they might have said. They didn't pay any particular attention when some of the larger independent stations, notably WLS in Chicago, began to devote much of their time to hillbilly tunes. . . . From Greenwich Village's country nightclub, the Village Barn, to the newest hayseed ginnery in hottest Harlem, New York is being swept by a countrified craze. . . . In Chicago, WLS, the station which has consistently plugged the hillbilly motif, is sitting on top of the world. It has under contract a group of the best known folk song singers, including Gene Autry, Linda Parker, the Three Little Maids, and the Cumberland Ridge Runners. Every Saturday night WLS holds a barn dance in a theater in the heart of Chicago. They send it over the air for hours. . . . Before the doors open, a line has formed in front of the theater which is often three blocks long and packs to the sidewalk from building line to curb. There are sophisticates in evening clothes, college boys, business men with their wives, and a great group of visitors from Iowa and Nebraska, anxious to see in person, the stars they have heard on the air.

But it took Rudy Vallee to place officially the stamp of approval on radio's 'back to the soil' movement. For weeks Rudy brought Broadway and Hollywood notables before the microphone in his famed *Fleishmann Hour* . . . Then the other day Rudy staged a barn dance! Hillbilly tunes, hillbilly singers! When the radio audience recovered from its surprise it began to flood the studios with telephone calls and telegrams. It wrote letters by the thousands. Rudy Vallee's barn dance was acclaimed the hit program of the season.

At one time Gene wanted to be Rudy Vallee, and now Vallee was broadcasting the Oklahoma Yodeling Cowboy's sound! The perfect ending to the year, Gene clinched a prestigious booking at Chicago's lovely Roseland State Theatre. For four days, December 30 through January 2 (the latter, a matinee and evening show), audiences could "see and hear him sing and yodel your favorite songs" before the screening of the John Ford movie, *Air Mail*. The future director of America's greatest Westerns had just made a film about a daredevil pilot, played by Pat O'Brien. As Gene (accompanied at some showings by Ina) watched the daring aces on the big screen, he couldn't help but daydream about learning to fly himself one day.

While planning his future, he also took stock of what 1932 had brought him. For the first time, Gene filed an income tax return. He had earned more money than he thought possible: $3,454 in royalties from various record labels and publishing companies; $950 from radio station WJJD; $1,110 from WLS (paid by ARC); $750 in flat fees for his recording sessions; and $3,330 from theater bookings. (He didn't bother to include his negligible Frisco pay.) When he compared his royalties from ARC—$2,199.02—to those from Victor—$56—he was glad he'd chosen to sign an exclusive deal with ARC—even though he had already promised Eli Oberstein that he would do one more session for Victor in January before going exclusive with Satherley's company. Of Gene's $8,594.56 total earnings, he netted $6,140, after paying a percentage of his earnings to Jimmy Long, Uncle Art, and Dave Kapp, and deducting his business expenses. In addition to his stage wear, his expenses included $153 for advertising costs, $48 to Chicago Theatrical photographers for publicity pictures, $750 for automobile travel costs, $72 for hotels ("hotel bill for JW Long and I . . . 24 at $3," he noted), and $172.50 for "meals and eats while on road—$1.50 per day, 115 days." Also listed as an expense was $240 for five prints of an "action trailer"; Gene probably commissioned a film short of himself playing and singing to be shown at theaters where he had upcoming bookings. Although he didn't declare it as an expense, he also noted in his ledger the cost of "Mother's Funeral—$300."

Gene declared three dependents for the year, excluding his wife; he later wrote of his decision to bring his siblings to Chicago: "My two sisters and my brother were still in school, and I, as their big brother, felt that they would be better off living in a bigger city, where the educational advantages were better. I was very anxious to have the kids live with us, but I felt that would be unfair to Ina. You can judge that lady's character when I tell you she urged me to get the children. . . . And from then on until all the kids were fully grown up, they lived with us." Ina had to learn to cook in a hurry in order to feed Gene's family. And since sometimes Veda, Wilma, and Dudley misbehaved, the twenty-one-year-old had to learn to discipline them. "Poor Ina, she was the one who had to take care of them," related Virginia MacPhail, who met Gene and Ina in 1932. "They were a handful, those three. Veda was sort of ornery—she liked to cause a little trouble. Wilma was a little bit better. And they had to look out for Dudley from 'day one.'"[6] Veda had already finished school, but Dudley and Wilma continued their studies in Chicago. "My mother was a little older than her classmates," according to Wilma's daughter Kirsten Gleissner, "but Gene wanted her to have a high-school diploma, so she continued with school in Chicago and graduated in 1933." In the beginning, Wilma had trouble adapting to the fast pace—and style of speaking—at her Chicago school. "By the time she could answer the question with her slow Western drawl," said, Kirsten, "the teacher had already moved on to someone else." Occasionally, Gene would invite Wilma and Veda to harmonize on his radio show, and once they made a test record for the fun of it.[7]

Gene concocted his own system of discipline, which had a positive side effect, he later stated: "I developed a peculiar talent as a result of our enlarged family. I can name every state in the Union, every large city, every river of any decent size, etc. How did I get that way? When the kids were naughty, I imposed punishment on them, which usually took the form of writing down the name of every state in the Union, every large city, very big river, etc. And since they transgressed often and I had to correct their lists, I got to memorizing them."[8]

Gene began nurturing another new family as well—his fans. "Long after other members of the *Barn Dance* cast were home in bed," *Radio Guide* commented, "Gene would still be signing autograph books." M. M. Cole planned to release another songbook later in the year, but in the meantime, Gene decided to work with Eddie Brown, founder of E. H. Brown Advertising Agency, and Sears, Roebuck public relations man Eddie Condon, on a product that could be sold to fans through mail-order. They named their business Frontier Publishers.

Their digest-size, thirty-page book was titled *Rhymes of the Range* by Gene Autry. Available for seventy-five cents, the slim collection of cowboy folk songs featured mostly public domain material. The "Publisher's Note" proclaimed: "In reviving the popularity of the long forgotten music of the cow country and the frontier, the author of this little book has made a distinct contribution to American music. The songs he writes and sings are as fresh and clean as the open prairie from which they spring. They bring to a work-a-day world a glimpse of the romance and the adventure that was once part of our everyday lives. If the spirit of that day can be restored in any small degree the effort has been justified." Autry's bylined introduction was accompanied by a new photo of the Oklahoma Yodeling Cowboy, wearing a large white Stetson, a lengthy dark scarf nattily knotted at the side of his neck, and a vest appliquéd with diamonds, clubs, hearts, and spades. Autry's text advises his readers:

> If you are a real American, either by decision or descent, whose heart throbs quicken to anything that smacks of the good Old West that is fast disappearing, I think you'll like [these songs]. If you prefer originality to mimicry, honesty to commercialism, sincerity to sham, I cannot but feel that you will enjoy them fully as much as I do.

GENE AUTRY'S COWBOY IMAGE was becoming firmly established. Among his new portraits commissioned from Chicago Theatrical Studios, one depicted his handsome sandy-haired profile, eyes shut, sensually blowing smoke from his lips. The evocative shot captures another, moody side of Gene Autry; although he never actually took up smoking, in this photo, he held a lit match in one hand and a hand-rolled cigarette in the other. Another, earlier series of shots also featured a lit cigarette, perched, smoke wisping overhead, on a fence behind Gene. Most likely, it was a prop, along with a little stuffed dog (perhaps a WLS mascot), intended to convey the idea that Gene Autry was a *real* Oklahoma cowpuncher, with his smoke and his "dogie."

Gene needed a plethora of photographs to advertise his numerous activities. As the just-elected President Franklin D. Roosevelt launched his multifaceted New Deal to conquer the Depression, Gene worked to build a successful career through his various ventures. An Illinois Theatre advertisement featuring his new photo announced: "Gene Autry 'Oklahoma's Yodeling Cowboy' in Person—Direct from WLS—with movie showing also: *Rockabye* with Constance Bennett & Joel McCrae—To celebrate inauguration of President Roosevelt, prices 10 & 35 cents."[9]

Still featured on WLS's *Tower Topic Time*, Mondays through Fridays, from 8:50 to 9:10 AM, Gene continued to broadcast from the Sears Tower studio, rather than the Prairie Farmer building where most programming originated. Beginning in 1933, he was announced solely by Sue Roberts, after Anne Williams was transferred to New York to become the buyer of women's fashions for the Sears catalogue. Gene was sorry to see Anne go. The year before, he had given her his promo picture, autographed, "Best wishes to a sweet girl. Oh boy, if you were only single." In addition to working together on the broadcasts and his songbook, he sometimes participated in fashion shows she directed at Chicago theaters. Anne's niece Eleanor Lang Chapin recalled one such event: "Anne was the mistress of ceremony and described the models' clothes sold in the Sears catalogue and in the new retail store. Gene Autry played and sang for these shows. When I was about five years old, Anne put a Sears dress on me and I paraded on the stage with the other models. Needless to say, I was thrilled and remember Gene being so very nice to me." After her departure to Manhattan, Anne and Gene stayed in touch, however, and at one point he asked her to consider becoming his manager. She demurred, remaining with Sears, Roebuck, where she had her own line of women's fashions featured in the catalogue.[10] Gene later wrote of her, "Anne Williams was a dear friend and a tremendous support to me as a performer. She was responsible for my success in the early years of my career on radio and later in the movies. She never missed an opportunity to give me encouragement both on the air and off. Anne was one of the finest women I have ever had the privilege of knowing."[11]

Through friends like Anne and musician pals like Roy Smeck, Gene had developed a real sense for recognizing quality merchandise, from handmade Nocona boots to custom Martin guitars. Soon after the beginning of the year, Gene began discussions with Martin for a new model. He even visited with Fred Martin at the company's Nazareth, Pennsylvania, factory. He wanted a guitar similar to the Martin that was stolen, but with a larger body and a booming bass resonance. His earlier 0-42, like Jimmie Rodgers's, was a smaller instrument (then standard), with a clear treble sound. Martin was in the process of developing a line of Dreadnoughts, or D-size, guitars. Its sound was perfect for backing up vocals and for playing hillbilly music with fiddle and banjo, particularly when there was no upright bass.

That spring, Martin created for Gene its most famous guitar, the D-45, #53177; like his previous Martin, his name in pearl script decorated the fret board. As on all early Dreadnoughts, Gene's D-45 had an elongated body and a twelve-fret neck. The body of the guitar was ringed in iridescent greenheart abalone pearl. Gene's guitar was unique from Martin's future D-45s (ninety-one were produced in total) in that its peg head had a torch inlay pattern—rather than the C. F. Martin logo, standard on its D-45 models that became available to the public in 1938. According to Martin's records, the guitar cost $200, but Gene recorded its expense as $300.[12] The *Wall Street Journal* once called Gene's Martin D-45 "the holy grail of acoustic guitars,"[13] and guitar historians George Gruhn and Walter Carter labeled it "the most valuable American guitar ever made."

Gene's new Martin wasn't ready in time, unfortunately, for Gene's final Victor session with Eli Oberstein. The label had a Chicago studio located in the Daily News building at 400 West Madison, and Gene headed there on Friday morning, January 27, after finishing the *Tower Topics* program. At 11 AM, he recorded his first-ever straight Western song, "Cowboy's Heaven," a Frankie Marvin composition that Frankie had recorded himself in June 1931. Gene's version transformed the song; his increasingly warm, smooth vocals gave it much more of a mainstream feel than the hillbilly version Frankie had waxed. Gene's name was now added to the songwriting credit, too. Accompanying himself (with his guitar a bit out of tune), Gene kicked off the number with a buckaroo yodel before crooning lyrics about the travails of a "tired weary cowboy": "I've been in the saddle all day / searching the hills and the valleys / for cattle that strayed away."

Another Western ballad, with a similar melody to "Cowboy's Heaven," "The Little Ranch House on the Old Circle B" was credited to Gene and one Volney Blanchard: "Travel on little pony / Back to Texas to stay." Soon to become a cowboy classic, "The Yellow Rose of Texas" was actually a mid-nineteenth-century minstrel song about "the sweetest rose of color." Gene could have learned it as far back as the Fields Brothers Medicine Show. Another old number that Gene appropriated, "Your Voice Is Ringing" was derived from "Silver Bell," a song composed by Percy Wenrich in the early 1900s. It had been a childhood favorite of Gene's, and his Victor adaptation featured an unknown fiddler playing the delightful melody. "It was still under copyright [to Wenrich] when Gene recorded his version," according to music historian Jonathan Guyot Smith. "Some years earlier, Jimmie Rodgers had responded to Ralph Peer's demand for original compositions by dusting off some half-forgotten pop songs and presenting them as new, copyrightable material. 'Mother was a Lady,' a hit from the 1890s, was recorded by Rodgers as an 'original' piece called 'If Brother Jack Were Here,' but horrified copyright holders threatened a lawsuit. Whether or not Wenrich's publishers complained about Gene's recording of 'Silver Bell' as 'Your Voice Is Ringing' [is unknown but], it is a splendid record."[14] The Victor ledger for the session stated that the song was arranged by Gene Autry, and that the copyrights for all the selections were in his name. (Wenrich's name was later added to the composition credit.)

Gene's last cut for Victor was the nostalgic ballad "Louisiana Moon," with guitar and fiddle accompaniment complementing Gene's dulcet vocals.[15] All five sides would be released on the Victor label, with "Your Voice Is Ringing" as his final Victor issue in July 1933. None of the records sold very well, probably due to lack of advertising and the seventy-five-cent price tag. Gene would rerecord all the songs—excluding "Your Voice Is Ringing"—in March for ARC. Soon after, Victor discontinued releasing hillbilly music on its seventy-five-cent label, eventually establishing the Bluebird imprint to release the "rural" sound at budget prices.

Gene's vocal style and material had matured since the recordings he made the previous year. As he signed exclusively with ARC, he would continue to move away from the Jimmie Rodgers approach. With Uncle Art's encouragement—and because of his success on Chicago radio—Gene had begun to formulate a unique sound of his own.

16

COWBOY BALLADEER

BY THE TIME GENE STARTED RECORDING COWBOY SONGS, he had three decades of buckaroo ballads to draw from. Whether real cowboys ever sang to their dogies remains a point of contention. In his cowpunching memoir, *The Old-Time Cowhand*, Texan Ramon Adams recalls, "Away back at the beginnin' of the cow business, it didn't take the cowman long to savvy that the human voice gave cattle confidence and kept 'em from junin' 'round. I reckon it started when the herder got to hummin' a tune to keep 'imself from getting' as lonesome as a preacher on paynight. The practice got to be so common that night herdin' was spoken of as singin' to 'em." Other cowboy memoirists, including Teddy "Blue" Abbott and Charles Siringo, wrote similar accounts. Some folklorists and song collectors disagreed. Jack Thorpe, one of the genre's pioneering songwriters ("Little Joe the Wrangler," 1898) and collectors (the seminal 1908 booklet *Songs of the Cowboys*), said, "I stood my share of night watches in fifty years, and I seldom heard singing of any kind."

A number of early cowboy songs at least partially originated on the trail, however: cattle-punching lyrics found their way into the melodies of antique English folk songs, resulting in "The Old Chisholm Trail," possibly based on "A Dainty Duck," and "The Cowboy's Lament" derived from "The Unfortunate Rake." "Oh Bury Me Not on the Lone Prairie" was likely inspired by the 1839 poem "The Ocean-Buried." Abbott said of "Bury Me Not": "They sung it to death. It was a saying on the range that even the horses nickered it and the coyotes howled it; it got so they'd throw you in the creek if you sang it. I first heard it long about '81 or '83, and by '85 it was prohibited." The song

"Whoopee Ti Yi Yo, Git Along Little Dogies" was first mentioned in the 1903 book, *Log of a Cowboy*, by drover Andy Adams. In 1910 John Lomax issued his first gathering of folk songs, *Cowboy Songs and Other Frontier Ballads*. Soon, Americans in all parts of the country knew the words to "Home on the Range," itself the subject of years of copyright litigation. The popularity of such books as Owen Wister's *The Virginian* (1902) and Zane Grey's *Riders of the Purple Sage* (1913) also spurred interest in cowboy-themed pop songs. To meet the demand, Tin Pan Alley tunesmiths who had never ventured West composed sagebrush melodies, including 1905's "Cheyenne (Shy Anne)" and the 1912 hit, "Ragtime Cowboy Joe." The latter has been described by Western music historian Douglas B. Green as "neither ragtime nor cowboy, [but] it still struck a national nerve, combining the thrill, danger, and nostalgia of the Old West with the exciting modern music that presaged the jazz age. It was a formula that would work again and again in coming years."[1]

Such was the case when Gene first started recording: in 1925, native Texan Carl T. Sprague had waxed for Victor "When the Work's All Done This Fall," considered "the first recorded cowboy music hit."[2] Gene was a fan of Carson Robison's and Vernon Dalhart's buckaroo ballads, too. Even Jimmie Rodgers cut cowboys songs: "Yodeling Cowboy," "Land of My Boyhood Dreams," and "I've Ranged, I've Roamed, and I've Travelled" in 1929, followed by "When the Cactus Is in Bloom" in 1931. In 1933 Gene didn't have to look much farther than Frankie Marvin for his first bona fide Western number, "Cowboy's Heaven." Most of the songs he included in his *Rhymes of the Range* booklet were folk tunes from the Lomax collection.

For his last ARC session before becoming exclusively contracted to the company, Gene revisited the Western ballads and heart songs he'd cut solo in January for Victor. On Wednesday, March 1, in New York City, he had his duet partner, Jimmy Long, plus other accompanists to fill out the sound. By then Uncle Art had thoroughly convinced Gene to sing in his own natural voice rather than imitate Jimmie Rodgers. Over the course of fourteen ARC recording sessions in 1933, the bluesy vocal style would cease to exist. When later questioned about his Rodgers period, Gene answered, "I don't think that I copied Jimmie Rodgers . . . and I think that it's a very bad trait for anyone to try and copy anyone else. If they have a style of their own, they have a far better chance, I think, of hooking on, than they would if they tried to copy someone else, because if you're going to do that, why buy the copy—buy the original. I think to a certain extent that I had a style of my own. He had more of a Southern accent like they have in New Orleans or Mississippi, Alabama . . . and I had more or less a western-type of a twang to my voice that they had out in Texas and Oklahoma."[3]

Backed by piano, celesta, and fiddle, Gene and Jimmy's new versions of the Victor songs were cut over the first two days in March. The nostalgia quotient was high, with "Silver Haired Daddy" sentiment prevailing throughout. Their more polished "Yellow Rose of Texas" became a hit, with President Roosevelt later citing it as a favorite Gene Autry song. Throughout FDR's presidency, Gene would sing it for him at several presidential Birthday Ball radio broadcasts benefiting the March of Dimes. "If I Could Bring Back My Buddy" was a new Autry number, its maudlin message harmonized sweetly by Jimmy and Gene. Jimmy's "Gosh! I Miss You All the Time" ("I miss our little spoonin'") and the chestnuts "Old Folks at Home" and "When It's Lamplightin' Time in the Valley" were also in this vein. Gene later said of such pop balladry, "In that era . . . a recording artist probably was good for, at the most, ten years. But I always thought that if you would sing good standard songs, that they would last longer." Gene would later "Westernize" one of the numbers, "Louisiana Moon," by changing the title and chorus to "Nevada Moon" on his February 9, 1941, *Melody Ranch* radio program. Gene finished his March 2 session, accompanied by haunting fiddle, with the somber "Don't Take Me Back to the Chain Gang" ("where they torture before they kill"), his own composition (with Ed Condon).

Gene's songwriting techniques became the subject of another venture with Frontier Publishing. *The Art of Writing Songs and How to Play a Guitar* by Gene Autry also became available in 1933 for seventy-five cents. In it, Gene described the inspiration behind his compositions, including ballads and "humorous songs," such as "True Blue Bill": "I wrote it in conjunction with a couple of friends of mine [Frankie Marvin and George Rainey]. We were feeling particularly jovial and the conversation turned to a story about accomplished liars. One word led to another, one joke led to another, and the result was 'True Blue Bill.' Of course, [the lyrics] didn't sound so well when we first put them down but somehow, if you keep at a verse or a lyric long enough, it will work itself out." In the how-to section, Gene explained that, "Many of the most popular song hits of recent years have been the product of two people—one to write the lyric and the other the music. You may be surprised to know that a great many of the outstanding songwriters of the past two decades could scarcely tell one note from the other."

To give hope to beginners, Gene pointed out, "I guess I wrote a hundred [songs] before I had one which was worth writing home about." Reproduced in the pages were purportedly two of Gene's original manuscripts, changes and corrections included, for "That Silver Haired Daddy of Mine" (with Jimmy's credit omitted) and "The Gangster's Warning." Of "Gangster's Warning," he wrote, "When I started to write that song, I had a completely different song in mind. It was to have been a comedy song called 'Lem Burkett's Wedding,' and it wasn't until I had the first two lines written that I decided to change the whole idea."

The booklet also pointed to Gene's departure from blue yodels: "The racy, risqué song just doesn't last. Regardless of what kind of a song you write, keep it clean and wholesome. . . . Nine out of ten requests that I receive both on radio and on the stage are for the simple wholesome type of songs. I'll go that one better. I'll make it ninety-nine out of a hundred." The guitar-instruction section included elemental chords, practical advice, and a few public domain compositions. Gene's partner Eddie Brown crafted a full-page magazine advertisement for the previous *Rhymes of the Range* and *The Art of Writing Songs* (both available for one dollar), by "The Yodeling Cowboy, Famous Radio and Stage Star," which promised "with these books you receive a great big original photo of Gene Autry in his cowboy regalia, taken out on the Western plains." Years later, Brown reminded Gene, "Those were happy days when you, Ed Condon, and I would meet at our agency office at 140 Dearborn and, after deducting printing expenses and postage, would stack the [dollar] bills in three equal parts for distribution. I remember many times you asked for a check for your share, which you then endorsed and mailed to your father. Between your WLS radio plug and our magazine ad, we sold thousands."[4]

Gene's WLS audience included children as well as adults. For the former, his radio program initiated a "Junior Round-Up broadcasting club." Listeners were encouraged to write in and choose a name for the club, which became "Harmony Ranch"; their motto: "No Room for Rustlers—Just Honest Hustlers." To join the club, listeners were required to submit an original song about Harmony Ranch. According to Gene, "there were thousands of . . . Harmony Ranch songs."[5] One particular WLS artist was the age of a typical Harmony Ranch member: George Gobel was only eleven when he was discovered singing in a Chicago Episcopal church choir by WLS talent scouts. At twelve, billed as "The Little Cowboy," the young soprano joined the *Barn Dance*. "It was the same thing as a kid who grows up two blocks from Yankee Stadium someday finding out he's going to get to play in Yankee Stadium," recalled Gobel, who would later become a comedian and TV star. "You could walk down the street on summer Saturday nights . . . and all the windows were open, and the *Barn Dance* was coming out of every window."[6] Gene was among the WLS artists who befriended the youngster, and on April 12 he provided guitar accompaniment on four songs for Gobel's first-ever recording session with Art Satherley. Uncle Art also recorded the Cumberland Ridge Runners, and Karl and Harty. "Gene took us over to the Sherman Hotel and introduced us to Art Satherley," Karl Davis remembered. "Then we went to recording after that."

Newcomers on the *Barn Dance* kept the show fresh and helped expand its audience. Particularly popular were such female performers as the Three Little Maids, whose Eva Overstake married Red Foley that year; Linda Parker, who sang with the Cumberland Ridge Runners; and Lulu Belle (Myrtle Eleanor Cooper), a pioneering comedienne who teamed first with Red, then with singer-songwriter "Scotty" Wiseman. In addition to their *Barn Dance* duties, they headlined WLS touring revues. Gene, too, was looking to stretch his bookings farther afield. Enter booking agent J. L. Frank, later known as the "Flo Ziegfeld of Country Music Show Business." Just as Art Satherley had pioneered the recording of rural artists, so did Joe Frank set the standard for promoting early country music package tours. The Alabama-born Frank, who was seven years older than Gene, became another mentor to him and a key to his success. Years later, when he was inducted into the Country Music Hall of Fame, it was noted that Frank "took performances out of the little schoolhouse and put them into auditoriums and coliseums."

A thin man, whose jaunty fedora complemented his pencil-thin black mustache and wolfish grin, Frank had moved from Tennessee to Chicago, where he met and married Marie Winkler, a widow with five children, in 1925. Her late husband had been a concert pianist at the Edgewater Beach Hotel, where Frank worked as a bellhop. Many of Marie's friends were radio entertainers who became her second husband's first clients, including radio stars Fibber McGee and Molly. Joe also began booking *Barn Dance* performers, including Karl and Harty's one-time trio-mate Doc Hopkins. "Joe would go out in his car and drive over in Michigan or up in Wisconsin to these theaters and book Doc in there," Karl Davis recalled. "Then he'd drive him out to the booking. He was so honest and fair and square with everyone." Pee Wee King, who would soon play with Gene, said of Joe Frank, "He took a personal interest in his people that he managed and booked. . . . He studied people."[7]

Gene signed with Frank in 1933, and soon he and Marie became close friends of Gene and Ina and their extended family. Gene's bookings increased, and Joe's 25 percent booking fee for the year amounted to $1,250. An ad for an early Autry-Long show Frank promoted read: "Two famous radio artists Gene Autry and Jimmy Long from radio station WLS will appear in person at the Plumb Theatre on Sat. April 22 one day only. . . . . The stage performances will be at 3, 5:10, 7:35, and 9:50 PM. Admission prices, adults 40 cents and children 10 cents. Gene Autry, better known to the radio audience as the Oklahoma Yodeling Cowboy, the Idol of Radio Land, and his partner Jimmy Long will render a number of their famous songs."[8] Among Gene's increasingly high-profile bookings that year was a performance at the World's Championship Rodeo at the Chicago World's Fair.

Advising Gene to create a strong touring revue, Frank reintroduced him to Benny "Whitey" Ford: "Joe helped get Gene started, [and was] a great, great help," Ford recalled. "That's how I got with Gene, because Joe Frank knew me . . . I got a call from him and he said, 'You know Gene Autry, don't you?' And I said, 'Yeah.' He said, 'Well, he's been working here and he's doing real good on the air, but he really needs a show around him. Now I can get Frankie Marvin, who does good comedy to do the part that Owen Gray did for you with the Oklahoma Cowboys. You two could rehearse an act, and you'll do a pretty good job with Gene.'"[9]

Ford established a comic partnership with Frankie, re-creating his and Gray's "Ralph and Elmer" vaudeville routine. Pee Wee King remembered the act: "They'd come on with their crazy suits and play musical instruments and tell jokes."[10] Benny Ford described the Gene Autry Revue: "Autry sang, I did comedy and MC'd and played banjo in the band. We had a four-piece band. We were playing all those same little towns I played with Otto Gray. Autry was on the air as much as he possibly could be, plus the Saturday night *Barn Dance*, and he was an automatic draw. He was just born to be that way." The comedy and musical aspects of Gene's early shows would become elements of his personal appearance tours for the next twenty-five years. "He learned many, many things from me on the stage," according to Ford. "I don't say this egotistically, because he said so himself."[11]

GENE'S CONSTANT TRAVELING IN THOSE DAYS, usually minus Ina, would be a staple of his career for decades to come. "When I worked with Gene, he drove Buick cars and I rode with him most of the time," Ford recalled. "We played theaters . . . four shows a day. We carried a P.A. system because very few theaters had one. They always had a movie—that's what ran out the vaudeville, the talkie movie. They came in droves to see us. He called me 'Country.' I got $7.50 a day, and he paid my hotel bill. In those days, there were no motels . . . just little rooming houses and small hotels. And his room rent, if it cost him over $2.50, he'd holler."[12] Gene would usually ask Benny to check out the accommodations, and if the price was too high, the two would share a room.

With the Depression still raging, Gene had every reason to be fiscally cautious. He and Ina had lost some of their savings in an earlier bank failure. Uncle Art recalled an occasion when Gene jumped into action to prevent another such loss. "Gene was in the studio with Perry Botkin, who became the great guitarist on Bing Crosby recordings. We're working away and all of a sudden Gene says, 'I've got a telephone call,' then he comes back and sits there for a moment. We finished that number and then all of a sudden I was getting ready for the next number, and the only one there was Perry Botkin. In about a half hour, Perry said, 'Look, I've got another date tonight, Art. We'd better get going!' [Then] I get this telephone call . . . 'Art, this is Gene.' I said, 'Where the hell are you?' He said, 'I'm in Jersey! I got a telephone call that Roosevelt's going to close the banks in the next twenty-four hours—I've got to get in that bank before it closes and they screw me out of all my money!' I said, 'Who the hell told you?' He said, 'Never mind—I'm gone!' So I went back in and said, 'This is all for the day. That guy is on his way to Chicago. . . . Sorry . . . he couldn't help it, had to go.' They made a nonstop, I think, that was faster than the train to Chicago . . . . There was two or three guys that took the wheel . . . all they did was fill up and run, fill up and run, and they got back there in time. He'd gotten a message from Sears, Roebuck, some friend there . . . and he got there and cleaned [out] his bank before they shut down on them."[13]

In the studio on April 17, this time in Chicago and billed as Gene Autry and His Trio, Gene waxed for Uncle Art another ballad, "In the Valley of the Moon." Some discographers erroneously have reported that Smiley Burnette was part of the group, but Gene had not yet met his future sidekick. It is unknown who provided the harmonies, but the trio probably included musicians then playing on the road with Gene: guitarist Don Weston and fiddler Pete Canova.[14] The trio also cut "When the Mailman Says No Mail Today," which was not released. Gene handled "When the Humming Birds Are Humming" as a solo number with a fine yodeling finale. The next day, on the April 18, Gene's two-year contract with ARC commenced. It stipulated that he would be recording a minimum of twenty-four sides per year, earning a flat fee of $250 for six sides, payable upon the sides' release. Gene would also receive a penny per side in royalties "on his own selections." For the year, his gross earnings from ARC would be $4,500 in royalties, $1,000 in recording fees, and $900 for his radio broadcasts.

Gene's first session as an exclusive ARC recording artist (listed in the label's hillbilly category) was in New York on June 20. Roy Smeck joined him on two more sentimental ballads: Gene's self-penned sequel to "Silver Haired Daddy," "That Mother and Daddy of Mine" and "Roll Around Kentucky Moon." The next day Gene may have popped into the studio to play guitar on a recording by Frank Luther, then returned on June 22 with Smeck for a very productive session. Among the seven tracks they waxed were a pair of delightful new cowboy ballads, Gene's catchy " 'Way Out West in Texas" and a narrative co-credited to Frankie, "The Dying Cowgirl." Each would become a Western classic.

Less than a month earlier, on May 26, Jimmie Rodgers had tragically succumbed to tuberculosis; songwriter Bob Miller quickly memorialized the Singing Brakeman with two compositions: "The Death of Jimmie Rodgers" and "The Life of Jimmie Rodgers." Uncle Art rushed them to Gene to capitalize on poor Jimmie's demise. "I used to make all those death songs, like 'The Sinking of the Titanic,' " Uncle Art later bragged. "I got up the idea and called Gene and said, 'We've got a song called "The Death of Jimmie Rodgers." You go today and get a photograph made of yourself with your hat in your hand . . . as if you're looking at a departed person, a grave.' So I had Len Snyder [do] a fabulous job on drawing the grave and the tombstone [superimposed with Gene's photo]. . . . We must have had 20,000 of those [printed handbills for the song] . . . given away to people in the country just to put . . . in their living rooms." Gene sang both narratives empathetically.

The next day Gene was backed for the first time by piano, possibly played by composer Bob Miller, on the swinging "That Old Feather Bed on the Farm." The upbeat number was followed by another death ballad, Gene and Frankie's "There's an Empty Cot in the Bunkhouse Tonight," which told the tragic tale of heroic ranch hand Limpy who sacrificed his life rescuing a stray.

At some point in the New York ARC studio, maybe as early as the November 1931 sessions, as a private joke, Gene and Roy Smeck (whom Gene nicknamed "Prick Smack") recorded an explicit version of "Frankie and Johnny" and the X-rated "Bye-Bye Boyfriend" (to the tune of "Bye-Bye Blackbird"): "Push your ass against the wall / Here I come balls and all / Bye-bye cherry / I ain't got a hell of a lot / But what I've got is gonna tickle your twat." The raunchy number was well known among musicians, according to Atlantic Records' Jerry Wexler. Hokum songs, with graphic lyrics about sexual escapades, had been popular among blues artists for years, and hillbilly singers had also joined in the fun; one of the most prominent artists to record such smutty numbers was future Louisiana governor Jimmie Davis. Apparently, Uncle Art (who Gene had started calling "the Chinese Hillbilly") encouraged his artists to make some of these numbers for release under fictitious names. In 1935 he cut several with the Prairie Ramblers, under the name the Sweet Violet Boys. Gene's saucy recordings, which ran completely contrary to his admonition against risqué tunes in his songwriting booklet, were never released during his lifetime.[15]

The rest of Gene's recordings that year took place in Chicago, wedged in between personal appearances and radio broadcasts. Gene didn't have much time for songwriting and on September 8 wrote a letter soliciting compositions from Raymond Hall, a Texas inmate who had penned hits for Jimmie Rodgers. Typed at the head of the letter "Enroute Marquette, Michigan," Gene thanked Hall for songs he'd already sent and asked for more:

> I am returning them all to you with the exceptions of "Sweetheart of the Cimarron" and I want to hold it a few days as I think I can use it. . . . Clayton [McMichen] told me about you saying something about a song "Life's Weary Ways" I am just wondering what you ever did with it and if you would send it to me as it seams [sic] to be a very good tital [sic] and might be my type of song. Also I wish you would write me some stuff such as "Mississippi River Blues" or something of a good old southern ballad. . . . Yes I will be only too glad to do anything I can to help you out while you are in there . . . if wrighting [sic] a letter for you will help I will do it. . . . Write me at your convenience and send me anything you have but if possible I want all the best songs I can get as I want to make good records.[16]

With the *National Barn Dance* now heard across the nation, Gene's audiences continued to grow. In October, perhaps due to his busy performance schedule—always heaviest in the fall—Gene's WLS radio schedule was shortened to Tuesday, Thursday, and Saturdays at 8:30 AM.[17] On October 4, he waxed a song by his neighbors Freddie Owen and Frankie More of the Log Cabin Boys, the rollicking "A Hill-Billy Wedding in June," featured Gene's touring unit: Don Weston on guitar, Pete Canova on fiddle, Benny Ford on banjo, and Frankie Marvin on bass.

Then on October 9—the fourth anniversary of his first recording—Gene recorded what would become a landmark hit as well as a signature song for the Singing Cowboy: "The Last Round-Up" by Tin Pan Alley composer Billy Hill. The song had appeared in *Ziegfeld Follies of 1933*, but Gene's enthralling version elevated it to the buckaroo national anthem. Backed simply by guitar, with fiddle accents on the chorus, Gene's voice sounds absolutely stunning—with just the right amount of vibrato added to his natural, intimate phrasing.

Gene's last session of the year, on November 1, included two more songs bidding farewell to the Blue Yodeler: "When Jimmie Rodgers Said Good-bye" ("He left a yodel for the cowboy") and Gene's self-penned "Good Luck, Old Pal ('Til We Meet Bye and Bye)." As if to compensate for the crass commercialism of the earlier tribute releases, Gene's vocals sound honest and sincere in their emotion. "Good Luck, Old Pal," in particular, also serves as a swan song to Gene's previous style. For the final time on record, Gene relapses into Rodgers mode, delivering his bluesiest vocal and yodels: "You've left me ole pal / I'll never see your happy smile no more."

17

SMILEY, PATSY, AND PEE WEE

DURING THE LAST MONTH OF 1933, Gene would make a new discovery that would bring to him a whole wealth of material. He would keep Gene laughing, too. His name was Lester "Smiley" Burnette.

"I've always said that Smiley certainly was responsible for a lot of my success," Gene told documentary filmmaker Len Morris in 1983.[1] Looking for a substitute accordion player, Gene instead found a man whose many talents would make him an invaluable part of Gene's life and career for more than twenty years.

Lester Alvin Burnette grew up in rural Illinois, not far from the town where Gene discovered him in December 1933. He was born March 18, 1911, in Summum, to Almira Hezlep and George Washington Burnette, both Presbyterian ministers "who got the calling," according to Smiley's son Stephen.[2] The family moved every two years from one impoverished congregation to the next. Having been a farmer, George preferred agricultural communities, and the Burnettes' parishioners frequently paid their tithes in produce. While living in Astoria, Illinois, the Burnette family was befriended by musical neighbors: an orchestra conductor, Bill Baird and his wife, Maude, recognized Smiley's natural talent when the eight-year-old sat down and started playing their piano. They encouraged his precocity with a few lessons and the loan of some of their instruments.

By the next year, the boy—then nicknamed Buzz—had earned his first payment as a musician: three dollars for a musical-saw performance at the local YMCA. Although he could soon play ten instruments, Smiley never learned to read music. He had to quit school before finishing ninth grade to help augment the family's income with a series of odd jobs. The friendly, jocular teenager convinced one of his employers, a furniture company, to let him to do its advertising spot on radio station WDZ in nearby Tuscola. The tiny station's owners, James and Edith "Mommy" Bush, immediately took to the industrious teen when they heard him enthusiastically play the piano. The childless couple offered him a job at the 100-watt station, which broadcast from dawn until dusk. He did everything from sweep the floors to play harmonica on air to lock up at night. By 1931 the Bushes promoted Smiley to staff announcer, and soon he was singing and playing piano, vibraphone, guitar, accordion, and other instruments on various programs. "I did about ten shows a day," Smiley recalled in a 1965 press release, "usin' a different name on each one so folks'd think they were listenin' to different people." On an early morning show, to perform hits by the Mills Brothers and other popular acts, he formed the WDZ Trio with a couple of friends (including Denver Darling, who later became a popular country artist and co-wrote "Choo Choo Ch'Boogie").

One of his WDZ programs was a children's show, for which he took the name Mr. Smiley, borrowed from Mark Twain's "The Jumping Frog of Calaveras County." It was soon shortened to Smiley, which suited his chubby, beaming face to perfection. In addition to playing numerous instruments, Smiley could do funny things with his voice, including the ability to drop his vocal register in an instant from a falsetto to the deep *ribbit* of a frog. Smiley's increasingly popular reputation in the farm belt eventually reached Gene.

"I was playing in Champaign-Urbana, Illinois, and I had a guitar and a bass fiddle and a violin with me, but the accordion player was ill," Gene remembered fifty-one years later. "So I asked the manager of the theater, 'Do you know of anyone down here?'"

"In Tuscola, there's a guy that works on a radio station WDZ, and he can play anything—he can play an accordion, plays the guitar, sings, and he might be the guy you want," the promoter told him. "His name is Smiley Burnette."

Gene promptly got on the phone: "Smiley Burnette, I'm Gene Autry."

"Oh, Gene Autry, from WLS in Chicago—what can I do for you?"

"I'm short a man in my band, and they tell me that you play accordion."

"Yeah, I play a little bit."

"How much money are you making down there?"

"I'm making about fifteen dollars a week and my gasoline—the guy over here on the corner has a service station and I give him a few announcements and he gives me my gasoline."

"I'll tell you what I'll do. I'll give you thirty-five dollars a week and your expenses while you're traveling with me. You think it over and let me know."

"Well, I've thought it over—Mr. Autry, you just hired yourself a man!"[3]

J. L. Frank, acting as Gene's manager, then stepped in. "Joe said, 'Listen, you've hired a guy and you've never heard him—you don't know whether he can play that damned accordion or not,' " Gene related. "Why don't you go down there and talk to him?" It was about fifteen or twenty miles, and I said, 'Sure, I'll drive down there.' So I called him back and I said, 'Smiley, maybe we ought to get together and talk a little bit. I'll drive down there to see you,' and he said, 'Fine.' So I went down and I met Smiley. I went out to his house. He lived with his mother and father at that time. He was a great big kid, he could sing, and he could harmonize with me. He played the guitar and he played the accordion and he'd bug his eyes out and sing in that froggy voice. So he said, 'Well, do you think I'll do?' and I said, 'Hell, yes, you'll do, come on!'

"So he went with me and he didn't even have a suit. I took him over to Sears, Roebuck and bought him a suit."[4] Smiley's first appearance backing Gene on the *National Barn Dance* was on December 24. "He hadn't had very much experience on the stage, but he was real funny and funny to look at," Gene said. "He played all those theaters with me, in Wisconsin, Illinois, Iowa, Missouri, Indiana, Michigan."[5]

Gene was now headlining a larger touring troupe, the WLS *Round-Up*, which included many of his *Barn Dance* co-stars. Included on the bill were the blind duo from Kentucky, Bob and Mac; the Girls of the Golden West, featuring Millie and Dolly Good; and Patsy Montana and the Prairie Ramblers. Patsy had recently been signed by WLS to sing with the Ramblers, who, as the Kentucky Ramblers had dressed in overalls and sang mountain ballads on the *Barn Dance*. Because Gene's Western music had become such a sensation, WLS program director George Biggar had suggested the Ramblers change their image, dressing as cowboys and backing up the station's new "singing cowgirl." Patsy, who was born Ruby Blevins, in Hope, Arkansas, had already adopted her Western image and name while performing in California with Monty Montana. The petite brunette wore cowgirl outfits, a large-brimmed Stetson, and cowboy boots—unless WLS owner Burridge Butler was in attendance. The conservative Prairie Farmer honcho frowned on the unladylike appearance of such footwear and insisted that female *Barn Dance* performers wear high heels.

Gene and Patsy began working together on the *Round-Up* just after she arrived in Chicago. "To me, he was the first big star I ever met," Patsy recalled in 1985. "I remember shaking hands with him. I put out my hand to shake hands, and I had to hold on to his hand. I've kidded him since then. My first thought was, 'You ain't no cowboy!' His hand was sorta weak, a weak handshake. I remember one number he did . . . It was 'The Last Round-Up' . . . Gene would say, 'Get along little doggie,' and I'd want to scream, 'Don't say "daw-gee," it's "doa-gee." But he learned that after he went to Hollywood. He began to say 'doa-gee.' " Their first WLS *Round-Up* performance together was at Chicago's impressive State and Lake Theater. "Gene Autry was the headliner," Patsy related. "There [was] about fifteen, twenty people on the show. . . . All of us sat on the stage on bales of hay . . . just like a big happy family thing. . . . Gene was always fun to work with."[6]

With Smiley's versatility as a musician and his comic flair, Gene moved him around to different spots in the group. Patsy recalled the first time she performed with the rotund showman: "I remember Smiley walking out on the stage that night, [he] liked to knock the scenery over, to start with, and we thought that was funny. We all laughed. . . . [I] learned years later, like it broke his heart. He thought we was laughing *at* him. . . . We felt Smiley was *supposed* to be funny, because we knew Gene wanted a comedian. . . . Smiley, you know, was never slender."

Realizing Smiley also had the makings of a good songwriter, Gene encouraged him in that direction. "He can do so many things," Gene would tell anyone who would listen. On March 26, 1934, Gene recorded his first Smiley Burnette composition, "The Round-Up in Cheyenne," in which he used the pronunciation "doa-gee," contrary to Patsy's assertion. Credited to Smiley and Gene, the soon-to-be cowboy classic "Dear Old Western Skies" was waxed the next day. Gene eventually introduced Smiley to Uncle Art, who agreed to record him, beginning in May. "Smiley told me, 'Mister, I can play any instrument, I play them all,'" Art recalled. "'If you give me a chance, I'll try and make good!'"[7] Backed by Roy Smeck, Smiley mostly cut novelties, with only a few songs released by various ARC labels. His most successful was his first, "Mama Don't Like Music." Based on a rural black folk song, the energetic number capitalized on Smiley's facility on different instruments and his various vocalization techniques.

In the meantime, Jimmy Long was tiring of life on the road, although he continued to harmonize with Gene during several of his March recording sessions. He had kept in touch with his Frisco supervisor, to remind him that he would take his job back should things improve. Jimmy missed the steady income, even though his entertainment earnings were not bad in 1933—he netted 50 percent of Gene's songbook royalties, amounting to $300; his share of Gene's recording income totaled $800; and his personal appearance salary came to $1,000. But he longed for the stability of life with his family back in Springfield and started hinting to Jesse that a move could be imminent. Patsy Montana numbered among many who had become fond of Jimmy. "He was just the sweetest guy, Jimmy Long—the most beautiful person I ever met," she recalled. "He wasn't good-looking, but you looked through that. He was just a sweet person inside. For some reason or other, he wanted to quit." Jimmy would last a few more months, but by the following year, he and his family would return to Missouri, where he remained the rest of his life.

GENE HAD NO REASON TO WANT TO SLOW DOWN. He did quite well in 1933, but his expenses had increased: He paid out $750 that year to Jimmie Dale and his Oklahoma Cowboys, who accompanied him on some dates and backed him in the studio.[8] Gene also listed on his ledger a payment of $290 to guitarist "Ray" [Don] Weston. And not only did he continue to pay Art Satherley a share of his royalties—$1,200 that year—but he also gave $187.50 to Sears, Roebuck's Jeff Shay, presumably for his prominent placement in the Sears catalogue. Having put 40,000 miles on his Buick for appearances, Gene spent $1,200 on car expenses, $414 on hotels, and $310 on meals for his touring unit. Additional expenses that year included $302 for his Western garb (his Nocona boots cost $100), $150 for photographs, and $150 for advertising. His theater and radio taxes amounted to $215. But his fame was spreading, and he could see that 1934 would be an even better year for him.

Gene stayed busy the early part of the year on the road; his original WLS *Round-Up* salary was fifty dollars a day, from which he paid his musicians' salaries (five dollars per man, per day) and their road expenses. His fees gradually increased so that he grossed that year close to five thousand dollars from the WLS Artists Bureau. Of that, he paid 10 percent to Joe Frank, who was serving more as manager than booking agent. "I was making maybe $75 to $150—sometimes as much as $250—a day for personal appearances in theaters," Gene later related. "And I was working damn near every night somewhere."[9] Prairie Rambler Tex Atchison recalled that Gene had no qualms about playing the smaller places: "Gene would say to the guys, 'If you think you're so good, play Boone, Iowa! There was nobody in the house there but the ushers.' Gene was always pulling jokes on everybody, then laughing himself half to death."[10]

In March, Gene performed before 4,000 prisoners at the Joliet penitentiary. "The WLS *Round-Up* show played to one of its most enthusiastic audiences in its career," declared an item in the *Tulsa World*: "Gene Autry, Oklahoma Cowboy, who is master of ceremonies for the road show, said he never had heard more gratifying applause. He also learned that the better seats in the auditorium were at a premium. Prisoners who arrived first auctioned off seats near the stage for prices ranging from a plug of tobacco or a handful of cigarets [*sic*] up to as high as 25 cents. Autry said he recognized Martin Durkin, Chicagoan, convicted on murder charges, on the front row."[11]

Gene enjoyed the footloose lifestyle, occasionally "forgetting" he was married when temptations came his way. One of his troupe later remarked of Gene in those days that "only two things in the world he was interested in, was women and money."[12] Tex Atchison claimed that Gene and Dolly Good (Tex's future wife) had a fling on the road, and other musicians spoke of Gene's trysts with amorous fans. "We used to go out about every night after the shows," Tex recalled. Gene "liked to go out nightclubbing. . . . Generally would wind up in a fight due to his big ten-gallon hat and cowboy clothes and women after him. Boyfriends would get jealous, including husbands. . . . He would meet the sheriff in every county we played and would some way be made a deputy sheriff. I believe that would help protect him from any bad publicity if it should come up."[13]

Gene became acquainted with several people during this period who would later play a large role in his career. Tin Pan Alley tunesmith Fred Rose lived in Chicago then and became acquainted with Gene through mutual friends. A few years later, Gene would bring him to Hollywood, where he would write several of his biggest hits and a number of his movie songs. As Gene recalled in his memoir: "In the 1930s I was constantly looking for musical talent. Anyone who ever tried to keep a group together knows that it is like traveling with gypsies. You wake up in the morning and someone else has left, gone into business for himself."[14]

That spring, traveling through southern Wisconsin, Gene's Buick was involved in a car accident, slightly injuring three band members. While Gene and Joe Frank waited at a gas station in Racine for the car to be repaired, they happened to hear a local polka group, the King's Jesters, on the radio. Joe called the station and spoke to the accordionist and band leader, Frankie King (born Frank Kuczynski), to see if he and some members could fill in for the ailing musicians that night. The answer was an excited yes, and Frankie, who got the nickname Pee Wee, because "there were too many Franks in the band," stayed on the tour for two weeks. "Gene was a likable guy," King remembered. "He . . . taught me a lot about business and showmanship. . . . 'Memorize people's names,' he said, 'especially the names of booking agents and show managers.' They are the ones who can give you an audience, and without an audience you can never be a star.' He knew where he wanted to go. When I left Gene and his band, I realized I had been working with a very talented and versatile performer, [but] I didn't realize that I had just had the big break of my life."[15] King, who would eventually marry J. L. Frank's daughter, Lydia, and become a Grand Ole Opry star, collaborated with Gene several times over the next few years. "That spring of '34," said Pee Wee, Gene "knew where he wanted to go. And he knew what it took to get there."[16]

Indeed, Gene was beginning to set his sights on bigger and better things—moving pictures. And he'd developed the connections in that direction: ARC's owner, Herbert Yates's other business concern, Consolidated Film Laboratories, provided financing to several Hollywood studios whose film they developed. One of these was Nat Levine's Mascot Pictures, which came up in a conversation between Yates and Art Satherley, who pitched Gene's acting potential to his boss:

"I took Gene's records to Yates's penthouse at 1776 Broadway [in New York]," according to Art, "and he listened, and he said, 'Is this the fellow you wanted in pictures?' I said, 'Yes,' and he said, 'I've never heard anything so lousy,' and I said, 'I'm your vice president, [but] if you don't want him for pictures, I can take him and put him in Paramount Pictures tomorrow.' . . . Two or three days passed, he said, 'I've heard something about this Autry fellow, and I want to hear him again. Where is he?' I said, 'In Chicago, on the air every morning heard by many, many people in many states, and many, many people want Gene Autry.' He said, 'I have a friend [coming to] Chicago, Nat Levine, he's in the picture business. Get Autry to meet Nat Levine.' I said [to Gene],

'Dress up, comb your hair, and go meet this fellow . . . and you have a chance to go to Hollywood to make pictures."[17]

Gene recalled getting the news from Uncle Art: "I got a call from Art Satherley, and he said that Nat Levine would be in Chicago on a certain date and he said, 'He would like to talk to you about working in a picture.' At that time, Nat Levine was one of the biggest independent producers. . . . Nat Levine decided that he would make a picture with [cowboy star] Ken Maynard, and he went to New York to get the financing from Herbert J. Yates, and somewhere in this conversation, Mr. Yates and Mo Siegel, who was president of American Records, said, 'Why don't you think about a singing cowboy? Gene Autry records for us and he's the biggest star we have.' "

Gene nervously arrived at the Blackstone Hotel to meet the bespectacled Levine, a native New Yorker dressed in a three-piece suit and tie. Levine thought the attractive young man with the Texas drawl and big smile could prove photogenic—though he couldn't imagine him a brawny cowboy actor. "They told me back in New York that you're selling a lot of records and you've had a lot of exposure on radio," Levine said to Gene. "I'm going to make a picture with Ken Maynard, and I don't know how you would fit in the picture, but we would try to write in a sequence where you can sing a few songs. It could be a good screen test for you, and yet it will give you some exposure on the screen. I wouldn't pay you very much for coming out—probably your expenses, about $500." Gene answered in a heartbeat, "Well, that part's alright."[18]

Gene rushed home to tell Ina Mae the exciting news, and they began making plans for the trip. Smiley happened to stop by the apartment, and on a whim, they invited him along too. The more time he'd spent with Smiley, the more potential he thought he had, and Gene had begun acting as his manager. On the Fourth of July, Gene, Ina, and Smiley began their journey west.

18

CELLULOID COWBOY

IN JULY OF 1934, SPEEDING WEST ON ROUTE 66, Gene dreamed of becoming part of an entertainment phenomenon that had developed just a few years before his birth. Western movies became a staple of the film industry beginning with 1903's *The Great Train Robbery*. In 1910 the first cowboy hero had emerged—Broncho Billy Anderson—and every few years, a new action star would come along. Between 1910 and 1919 William S. Hart, a solemn believer in presenting the "real" West, became the first screen cowboy to put his horse in the spotlight, appearing with his pinto Fritz in every outing. Hart's place was usurped in the 1920s by showman Tom Mix, who flamboyantly depicted a clean-cut buckaroo with a steed named Tony. His sharp shooting, daredevil escapades, and amazing riding skills elevated the action to new heights. Other cowboy stars including Harry Carey, Tim McCoy, Hoot Gibson, Buck Jones, and Ken Maynard built their own enthusiastic followings, starring in "series Westerns," or "programmers," made on a shoestring by such studios as Universal, Monogram, and Fox.

Broncho Billy, Bill Hart, and Tom Mix movies established a template, followed to a degree by subsequent pictures: Typically opening with a fistfight or gunplay, the plot usually involved the hero's unraveling a crime—be it rustling, robbery, murder, or kidnapping—with at least one horseback chase scene and a dramatic shootout or showdown as the final denouement. Frequently, the character's first name would be the same as the actor's (only the surname would change from picture to picture), and the lead's basic personality would remain consistent over the course of seven or eight programmers a year.

By 1929 audiences were tiring of the homogeny of so-called oaters. *Photo-play* magazine declared, "Lindbergh has put the cowboy into the discard heap . . . the Western novel and motion picture heroes have slunk away into the brush, never to return. The cow ponies are retired to the pasture . . . Tom Mix, Hoot Gibson, and Ken Maynard must swap horses for airplanes or go to the old actors' home." Maynard, for one, resolved to come up with something new. Sound had arrived to Western pictures that year, beginning with *In Old Arizona*, featuring the Cisco Kid, played by Warner Baxter. Around the same time, the strapping Maynard insisted on singing in *Sons of the Saddle*, released in 1930. An amateur fiddler and fan of Western songs, the raspy-voiced Maynard warbled two tunes, "Trail Herd Song" and "Down the Home Trail with You." He had previously wowed audiences with his fearless horsemanship astride his horse Tarzan; now he wanted to serenade them. He recorded a few cowboy songs for Columbia, which opted to release two sides. In 1933 he sang in *The Fiddlin' Buckaroo* and *The Strawberry Roan*, the latter based on the Curley Fletcher narrative poem about an untamable mustang.

Gene had met both Tom Mix and Ken Maynard before his trip to Holly-wood. While on the road in Harrisburg, Illinois, he discovered that Mix, tour-ing with a circus, was playing a local theater. "I went around to see him and he seemed glad to meet me," Gene later related. "He had heard some of my cow-boy records, he told me, and liked them. I had just had [the] offer from Mascot Pictures to come to Hollywood, and I asked Tom what he thought about them. He told me they were a good outfit and advised me to go to work for them."[1] Pee Wee King also recalled a 1934 meeting with Mix on a stop in Madison, Wisconsin, when he was a member of Gene's backup group, the Range Riders. "[Gene] thought Tom Mix was a great performer and he loved Tom Mix," ac-cording to Pee Wee. "I'll always remember the time . . . at the Park Theater, and Tom Mix was up a couple miles from us in a tent show, and we all wanted to go see Tom Mix in between shows, and [backstage] Gene says, 'Don't go, he'll be here.' . . . And he did! Tom Mix knocked on the door and said, 'Which dressing room is Gene Autry in?' and I said, 'Right down there.' God almighty, everybody worshipped Tom Mix! He was America's top movie cowboy, with that beautiful cowboy suit of his."[2]

Gene first met Ken Maynard at a show in Chicago. Maynard's valet, Johnny Brousseau, who would eventually work for Gene, reminisced about the circumstances of their early acquaintance:

I first seen the man [Gene] in a dressing room of the Chicago Theater . . . I was then in the employ of Ken Maynard. . . . He was playing one-night stands from Montgomery, Alabama, north to a closing week at the Chicago house. One of the hawkers following the show sold sheet music of popular songs. He told me he had a big seller, handing me a copy of "That Silver Haired Daddy of Mine" by Gene Autry. I had never heard the name. He told me he was a popular singer on radio. One afternoon, the stage doorman called the dressing room to say that Gene

Autry was there wanting to see Ken. After hearing that name, the answer was "Send him up, let's see what that character looks like."

He was a medium size man, light complexion, and a boyish smile that made him look younger than his age, wearing just a white shirt, gray slacks, and fancy cowboy boots. On a second visit, Ken told him he heard his radio show that morning: "I'm going back to the Coast to make two pictures. . . . One has a big barn dance. If you want to try pictures, I'll try to get the studio to use you and your boys."[3]

Levine planned to star Maynard in both a serial, *Mystery Mountain*, and *In Old Santa Fe*, one of the first in a series of new Mascot features. In the September 17, 1934, issue of the *Los Angeles Times*, an item ran: "Maynard Returns for New Picture." It noted that "Ken Maynard's return to Hollywood has caused Nat Levine to place 'In Old Santa Fe' in immediate production. Levine has signed George Hayes, veteran character actor, to enact an important part in the Maynard film. Gene Autry, singing cowboy, is the only other member of the cast signed."[4]

En route to California, Gene, Ina Mae, and Smiley stopped along the way at various relatives of Gene's to spend the night. Gene and Smiley serenaded their hosts and Ina with the songs they had recorded in May and June. Other selections were brand new; Smiley had written some while sitting at the Autrys' kitchen table before leaving Chicago, and he continued to compose in the Buick's backseat. Smiley recalled:

> Gene had been getting up a book of songs, and he had all the songs that he needed for it, but I kind of got in a habit of collecting a little money. I said to him as he was driving, "Hey, how would you like to buy a song?" Gene inquired, "What's the name of it?" I admitted, "I don't know—I ain't wrote it yet." Gene wondered, "How much is it?" I exclaimed, "This is a bargain day! I'll take five dollars for it." Gene said: "I don't know—I might buy a pig in a poke." I responded, "No, it's bound to be a good song for five dollars!"

Smiley looked out his open window at the gorgeous Southwestern scenery of New Mexico, inspired by what he saw: "Cactus plants are bloomin' sagebrush eve'ry where / Granite spires are standin' all around / I tell you folks it's heaven / To be riding' down the trail / When the desert sun goes down." "I wrote the words on a magazine and put the music to it," he recalled of the genesis of the gorgeous Western song, "Ridin' Down the Canyon (When the Desert Sun Goes Down)." "You listen to the words, and you'll know what I was looking at."[5] Gene's five-spot yielded what would become one of his most popular numbers.

When the travelers finally arrived in "the glamour spot of the world," they checked into the Hollywood Hotel on the corner of Hollywood and Highland—"one of those California gothic places with a portico and a dimly lighted lobby."[6] Eventually, they moved into the Riviera Apartments on a hilltop off Franklin, with a great view of Hollywood. Five-year-old Spanky McFarland of the *Our Gang* series lived in the building with his family. The first friends Gene made were earthy Westerners—the cowboy artist Fred Harman, who created the Red Ryder comic strip; cowboy poet Curley Fletcher (author of "The Strawberry Roan"); saddle maker Jim Davis; and professional boxer Dude Chick.

Gene took Smiley along to a gathering at Mascot president Nat Levine's home to meet his production staff; Smiley's sense of humor kept Gene's nerves in check, and he also hoped to find a part for his protégé in the movies. His jovial pal made a good impression, and it was agreed that Smiley could join Gene in the pictures. Levine had bought the rights to the title song, "Down in Old Santa Fe," which he gave Gene to learn, and they discussed additional music to be included. Gene's lack of acting experience had everyone worried, though.

"I knew very little about pictures," Gene later related. "I was really green. In fact, I had never been around a studio—I didn't know anything about a camera."[7] Levine concurred, later saying, "Gene was completely raw material, knew nothing about acting, lacked poise, and was awkward. . . . The next day my associates questioned my judgment putting him under contract. They thought I was slipping."[8]

Gene, of course, had plenty of experience singing, playing guitar, and calling a square dance—his duties for *In Old Santa Fe*. Nonetheless, director David Howard spent extra time preparing him for working before a camera lens. "For the first four months, he went through a learning period," Levine related. "We had at that time in our employ, a professional dramatic and voice teacher, and Autry became one of her pupils." The producers liked Gene's smooth singing, but did not care for Ken Maynard's rasp. For the film's opening sequence, featuring Maynard's character Kentucky riding Tarzan and singing, "As Long as I've Got My Dog," Ken's voice was replaced by that of vocalist/songwriter Bob Nolan, of the harmonizing group Sons of the Pioneers.[9]

In Old Santa Fe, like several of Maynard's Westerns, takes place in a contemporary setting, rather than the Old West. George Hayes, later known as "Gabby," plays Kentucky's sidekick Cactus. He and Kentucky are cheated at a horse race by crooks planning to fleece the owner of a dude ranch. During filming, Gene intently watched the black-clad Maynard interacting with his flirtatious leading lady, Evalyn Knapp. And Smiley picked up a few pointers observing Hayes, an experienced thespian, winning laughs as the rubber-faced Cactus. Hayes's beat-up felt hat, brim pushed up and pinned to the crown, helped to add to Cactus's comical appearance. The affect would inspire Smiley's own future floppy black hat.

The square-dance scene opens with a close-up of a moonfaced Gene, grinning widely and looking self-conscious, clapping his large hands and calling out, "Doe-si-doe, your partner!" When the revelers (dressed as if at a nightclub rather than a barn dance) request a song, Gene responds by crooning a waltz, "Someday in Wyoming." He is backed by a cowboy band, featuring

Smiley on accordion. A natural on camera, Smiley looks relaxed—as if he were having the time of his life. After asking Gene for a turn, he grabs one instrument after the next. He plays, sings, and croaks his delightfully comic "Mama Don't Like Music." Their moment in the spotlight closes with Gene, looking a bit more comfortable, on the ballad "Down in Old Santa Fe." He visibly relaxes when he's joined by the exuberant Smiley, harmonizing on the last verse. Smiley and Gene were uncredited on the title card; but, the GENE AUTRY emblazoned on his Martin guitar's neck advertised his identity.

"After the barn dance sequence, Maynard told the brass, 'This feller is going to make it!'" Johnny Brousseau recalled. Film editor Joe Kane, who was promoted by Levine to help direct the film (uncredited) when Howard's contract expired, enjoyed working with Gene but had a nasty run-in with Maynard. Gene managed to calm down the hot-headed leading man, who pulled a loaded gun on Kane. "I always got along fine with Ken," Gene later said. In fact, Gene would never forget Maynard's supportive attitude toward him; years later when the troubled former cowboy star was living on public assistance in a trailer park, Gene sent him a check every month.

After the completion of *In Old Santa Fe*, Levine gave Gene and Smiley bit parts in the Maynard action serial, *Mystery Mountain*. This did not go well, according to Brousseau. "They put Gene in a scene that would be hard for veteran riders—Maynard sitting on his horse, waiting for three riders to ride to him at a gallop, and line up facing him. Gene is one of them, on a new horse with a strange saddle, and not knowing camera angles, it was anything but good. Disgusted of his showing on the horse, he told [supervising producer] Mandy [Armand] Schaefer, 'This picture business is not for me. I'm going back to radio!' Mandy, also disgusted for having a singing cowboy in Western pictures, agreed that it was the best thing he could do—go back to radio."[10]

Levine concurred that Gene "wasn't much of a horseman," and hired top stuntmen Yakima Canutt and Tracy Layne to teach him to ride. Gene was relegated to a small part, primarily in chapter six of the twelve-part *Mystery Mountain*. He is seated next to Smiley, driving a wagon in pursuit of Maynard's character, Ken "Williams," who has been framed by the villain, the Rattler. Gene shoots Maynard off his horse, and speaks a few angry lines in his pronounced Texas drawl.

Gene was horrified when he viewed the rushes for both films. "I moved like my parts needed oiling, and I didn't like the way I looked or sounded," he later wrote.[11] He wanted to immediately pack up and return to Chicago: "I don't think I'll ever be worth a damn in pictures," he told Ina Mae. "I don't think I'm the type."[12] In the meantime, the temperamental Maynard, who was earning ten thousand dollars a week, had infuriated Levine with his Wild-West behavior and drinking binges. As soon as *Mystery Mountain* was finished, Maynard left Mascot. Another twelve-part serial in preproduction and intended for Maynard now needed a leading man.

Levine called Gene to his office on the Mascot lot, located at the old Mack Sennett movie studios on Radford Avenue, off Ventura Boulevard, in the San Fernando Valley. "Look, Gene, I would like to star you in a serial," he told him. Gene, who had felt Levine's previous disdain for his abilities, found his change of heart hard to believe. And as much as he had wanted to be a movie star, he'd lost confidence in himself. "I don't know if I want to do that or not—I don't think I'm ready to be a star in a picture yet," he told the studio boss. "Well, let me worry about that part of it," Levine answered. "I'm going to take a shot with you." Uncertain, Gene walked back to the car, where Ina Mae was waiting for him, and told her about the conversation. "Gene, I don't think you were as bad as you thought you were in those pictures," she insisted. " I think if you can do the job, and Nat Levine wants you for the lead, then you ought to do it!"[13]

Gene's starring vehicle turned out to be the most unusual Western serial ever made. Blending the cowboy genre with science fiction, *The Phantom Empire* features the ancient yet advanced civilization of Murania, located far beneath the earth and powered by radium. Its ruler, Queen Tika, uses a television screen to tune in to the comings and goings of the "surface people," and primitive robots lurch along doing her bidding. "Had there been no *Phantom Empire*, it is doubtful if there would have been a *Flash Gordon* from Universal in 1936, or a *Buck Rogers* (Universal, 1939) . . . nor would science fiction have become so much a staple of serial production for the next ten years."[14] Above ground stands the Baxter family's Radio Ranch, which attracts guests who want to see and hear radio star Gene Autry broadcast there every afternoon. The Baxter children, Frankie (Frankie Darro) and Betsy (Betsy King Ross, a pre-teen rodeo champ), form a Junior Thunder Riders club to help Gene solve the murder of their father. Gene was framed for Baxter Sr.'s shooting death by evil scientists wanting to bankrupt the dude ranch, so they can mine the property's radium deposits.

Over the course of twelve chapters, and through plot devices including an airplane, tear gas, laser guns, and thrilling horseback riding, Gene, Frankie, and Betsy are captured by Muranians and become involved in an underground revolution, while Gene somehow manages to broadcast his radio show on time. A humorous rescue attempt is made by the bumbling Oscar (Smiley) and his blundering buddy, Pete (character actor William Moore). Not every episode includes a musical interlude, but the opening chapter, "The Singing Cowboy," features Gene backed by a buckaroo band singing "That Silver Haired Daddy" and another whimsical song by Smiley, "Uncle Noah's Ark." Enunciating stiffly, Gene looks somewhat more relaxed in front of the camera. His riding has improved a bit, and he successfully pulls off the cowboy hero staple, the running mount. The film was directed by Otto Brower and Breezy Eason, who also directed *Mystery Mountain*, and continuity was again handled by Armand Schaefer. Still unconvinced of Gene's potential, Schaeffer would turn out to be one of Gene's most trusted collaborators.

The screenplay, written by Wallace McDonald, Gerald Geraghty, and Hy Freedman, was inspired in equal parts by a 1931 book called *The Lost Continent of Mu* and the Carlsbad Caverns tourist attraction. McDonald claimed the idea originated while he was under the influence of laughing gas at the dentist. When Gene came on board, they revised the script to take advantage of his reputation as a radio star. "Gene was chosen because his records were selling sensationally and Nat Levine was canny enough to capitalize on that," remarked Maurice Geraghty, who with his brother Gerald later refashioned the serial into a 1940 feature. "Nobody, even Levine, expected Gene to make another picture, although he had a hold [option] on Gene, just in case. [But] the picture hit big and opened up a whole new era in Westerns—the singing, musical Western."[15]

For his work in *The Phantom Empire*, Levine offered Gene a four-week exclusive contract with Mascot for December 1934 and January 1935, stipulating that he would be paid one hundred dollars per week, "no compensation for any time not used as an actor." The agreement included an option clause, which raised his weekly pay by fifty dollars after one year, and, if the option were renewed, would continue to do so at six-month intervals capping at $550 per week (after five years). It also stated that Mascot was entitled to 50 percent of Gene's revenue from endorsement advertising and 15 percent "of all radio activities (not to conflict with production)." Another draconian clause required him to make personal appearances on behalf of the films, for which he would earn "50 percent revenue over direct expenses." And if any of his discs earned an amount greater than his then-standard royalties, he was required to turn over to Mascot 50 percent of the monies.[16]

GENE WAS HOPEFUL ABOUT HIS FUTURE IN HOLLYWOOD but ready to go back to the life he knew as a recording and radio artist. He was committed to promoting the pictures with public appearances, J. L. Frank had booked a tour and lined up a new radio show, and Uncle Art had reserved studio time for him to record Smiley's new compositions. Before leaving town, Gene looked up Tom Mix, back in Hollywood preparing to shoot his own Mascot serial, *The Miracle Rider*, directed by Mandy Schaefer. "We started going around together and I got to know Tom very well," Gene remembered. "I asked his advice as to whether I should stick to Westerns or try becoming a singing star in regular pictures."

"Gene," Tom told him, "the life of an ordinary star may only be five years, but a Western star can go on forever—it's like life insurance."[17] Gene listened carefully and never looked back.

19

NEGOTIATIONS BY POST

NE OF THE BEST WESTERNS I'VE EVER RUN . . . Good story, plenty of thrills, comedy, and some good music and singing by Gene Autry and his band. This is the kind of Western that pleases my patrons."[1]

A rural Alabama theater owner's comment published in *Motion Picture Herald* exemplified the response to *In Old Santa Fe*, Gene's screen debut. Not long after the film's November 15 release, exhibitors and small-town audiences became intrigued by the singing cowboy featured in the barn dance scene.

Others in show business took note of Gene as well. While in New York for a week in early January recording for ARC, Gene was scouted by 20th Century Fox. Alexander Leftwich, a veteran musical-comedy theater director, best known for 1930's *Strike Up the Band*, came to see Gene during a session. Impressed, Leftwich called his friend Cole Porter to get his opinion on Gene. Porter and Leftwich returned together to 1776 Broadway to hear Gene sing, backed by the Prairie Ramblers. The composer of "Don't Fence Me In" agreed with Leftwich, and the two recommended Gene to Fox for a film in preproduction.[2] (Porter may have had more on his mind than Gene's acting potential.) On January 21, Gene typed a letter in his usual run-on style to Nat Levine to report these exciting developments and seek his permission to test at Fox:

> Alexander Leftwich came to the Studio where I was working after he heard me work he called Cole Porter and I did some numbers for them after that he ask me what experience I had in the way of screen work and I told him what I had done and was under option to you then he immediately called a Mr. Pincos of Fox Films and told him that I was the one he wanted to play the part in 'Adios Argentina'

then I was taken to the Fox companys office in New York and had a talk with them and Cole Porter told them he would like very much to have me in the picture and they made arrangements to make some tests of me. However, after I told Mr. Pincos I could not take any tests until I had informed you it was called off until I had heard from you. They wanted me to see if I could obtain a release from you for the picture then let them know and they would make tests. . . . Then I was called upon the following day by a fellow named Sidney Winters of Edward W. Schewing Inc. 570 Lexington Ave. N.Y.C. and wanted to sign me up exclusively for pictures said he could get me a deal with Fox. However, I told him the whole thing was up to Mascot as to where they want me for the future or not.

I understand the picture is to be quite a big picture and Leftwich said he would see that I had a leading role in the picture. Cole Porter also said he would see someone at Fox in Hollywood this week.

Mr. Levine I do not want to do anything to hurt myself and do not desire to go to another place to work unless it would be entirely satisfactory with you as I know you gave me the breaks and I appreciate it very much and I would like very much to do a series of westerns for you. However, if you do not see your way to do so I would like and believe this would be a great break for me to work in this picture.

Gene enclosed a newspaper advertisement for *In Old Santa Fe*, featuring his name in bold type. He wrote, "I also understand Great States and Warners have booked this picture 100 percent on account of my name in this country I am also getting the Serial lined up and think it will get a great booking." Indeed, many theaters began listing Gene's name above Maynard's in their advertising for the movie.

Levine, however, was apparently stalling until after the release of *The Phantom Empire* before giving Gene an answer: In his correspondence Gene referred to having already sent Levine a telegram and letter "regarding a picture with another concern." These had gone unanswered from Mascot. Decades later Levine said, "I received a dozen letters from Autry during 1933, asking for an opportunity to work for me in anything I would suggest in pictures. . . . On one of my trips east, I stopped off in Chicago, not to meet Autry, but for business I had with my distributor. But I did get to meet Autry and he virtually begged me for an opportunity to come to Hollywood and work in pictures."

After Gene received national attention in 1933 for his hit record "The Last Round-Up," perhaps he was indeed motivated to get into pictures and contacted Mascot. Or Levine could have confused the dates of Gene's letters, mistakenly thinking those from 1935 had been written earlier. By the time Levine recalled the 1933 letters in interviews, he was a broken man. In 1959, then relegated to managing a movie theater, the former mogul wrote Gene: "In going over my past papers, came across your letters to me—imploring me to give you an opportunity—and if I did, you would be ever grateful and beholden and never forget it. . . . The tide has turned—and today I need an opportunity to make a come back." He wrote Gene again in 1960: "Am having a mighty difficult time trying to get started again. Folks figure a man who dissipates a fortune must be a fool—and I certainly am getting my come-uppance, deserving or not . . . I have a lot of thoughts on how to get started again. . . . Your seeing me is no obligation on your part—nor am I thinking of important money." Although Levine's plans apparently never materialized, Gene replied at one point: "It was awfully nice to hear from you, and the next time you're down around our office drop in to see us." As late as 1983, Gene contacted Levine at his residence at the Motion Picture Home: "I have been giving a few of my friends some financial assistance over the last couple of years and as you were one of the great contributors responsible for me being in pictures and you are certainly responsible for my coming to Hollywood and, perhaps launching my career as the first singing cowboy, I am enclosing a small token of my appreciation." (The amount of Gene's gift is unknown, but Frankie Marvin and Art Satherley were among the other recipients.)

Although Gene's *In Old Santa Fe* cameo was getting a good response from audiences, Levine and Mascot associates were still uncertain about Gene's potential. According to Levine, "He was nice looking, [but] it seemed to me he lacked the commodity necessary to become a Western star—virility!"[3] Most likely, Mascot wanted to gauge the public reaction to Gene's starring role in *Phantom Empire* before taking up his option. The initial chapter of *Phantom* reached some theaters on February 23, 1935. Even Gene didn't think the serial would amount to much, but rural audiences loved it. After the first two episodes received positive reactions from exhibitors, Mascot producer Jack Fier wrote Gene on March 9:

> We have been giving serious consideration to our investment in you and still feel today as we did when we first got together and that is, that there are definite possibilities for you in the motion picture field. . . . There is still a considerable proving stage period to go through with you, but nevertheless, because of our confidence in the future possibilities we would like to follow through with our contract arrangements, except instead of taking up the option immediately, we would like the contract to commence as of June 1.
>
> However, another problem presents itself at the moment and that is that while we have almost definitely decided to go through with the series of pictures as per our arrangement, this decision has only been made in the last day or two, which naturally places us in the position of not having our material ready to be able to start production at once. It will take approximately three months or so to get our story material etc. lined up.
>
> While dictating this letter, another thought comes to me and that is your closeness and interest in Smiley and it is my thought that it would be advantageous for both of you to sort of work together in the pictures, etc., and it would be advisable to work out an arrangement whereby Smiley would also have a contract with us. However, whereas I appreciate the thoughts outlined by you in your letter to Gordon Molson, I feel that these thoughts were expressed by you without analyzing them, because, if you would consider what you wrote, you would appreciate the gamble that Nat Levine is taking in bringing you boys to the motion picture public's eye and at the expiration of any arrangements between you and Mascot

you would be the possessor of the background and ability, while Mascot will have no further hold on you and will have had to give up something that it had worked hard to create. In view of the above thought, I know that you will appreciate that Smiley would have to consider a reasonable figure."[4]

Gene spent the next few days in Chicago meeting with various advisors, including Joe Frank, Art Satherley, and WLS announcer and writer Joe Kelly, deliberating whether to accept Mascot's proposal. His salary while making pictures would be one hundred dollars a week (he'd been paid five hundred dollars from Mascot the previous year); he often earned three or four times that amount performing. In 1934, for six months of touring, he had grossed nearly $5,000 from the WLS Artists Bureau. And Frank had just lined up a new radio program for him at another 50,000-watt station, WHAS in Louisville, Kentucky. "I recall when I left WLS in Chicago I was making in the neighborhood of $350 a week and I went to Hollywood at $100 a week," Gene later wrote Kelly. "I realized it was much less than what I was making, but I thought that the future held much more for me to learn than it would have been to remain where I was in Chicago."[5]

On March 16 Gene wrote Fier that "it will be satisfactory with me to have the contract begin June first, as stated in your letter." He also elaborated on other concerns:

Regarding Smilie [*sic*] Burnette, I will bring him to California with me and I am sure we will get together without any trouble when I talk to you. In my previous letter to Gordon Molson, my reason for not wanting him to sign up with you, was that in case you did not renew my option, I would have to get some one else to work with me. As you know I have spent quite a sum of money on Smilie in placing him with the American Record Company, bringing him to California, and also by plugging him on all of my radio programs. I do not feel that after I have discovered a fellow like this, spent my time and money on him, that I should turn him over to someone without receiving something for my work. However when I get to California I want to talk this over personally with you, and I know we will have no trouble in getting together.

By then, Gene was paying Smiley fifty dollars a week when touring, twenty-five while on break.[6] In New York in January, Gene tried to sell Smiley's contract to the Prairie Ramblers, according to the group's fiddler Tex Atchison. The talented string band, which also included bassist Jack Taylor, guitarist/harmonica player Salty Holmes, and banjo player Chick Hurt, had left WLS for a radio program on Manhattan's prestigious WOR. They also did numerous sessions for various ARC labels—making their own records, backing up Patsy Montana (who sang with them on WOR), and accompanying Gene. They declined to purchase Smiley's contract.[7]

Gene had other ideas for Smiley—pairing him in the movies with Frankie Marvin: "I have working with me," he wrote in the letter of the sixteenth, a fellow who is very much on the type of Harpo Marx, and I believe he and Smilie would make an excellent comedy team such as Laurel and Hardy. He is much smaller than Smilie, also sings and plays, and has been working in vaudeville for ten years. He is a brother of Johnny Marvin, the Lonesome Singer of the Air, who broadcasts over NBC from New York. He also has been broadcasting and making records for several years, and has recently played the Roxy Theatre in New York. He is really the best 'Mugger' of any comedian I have ever seen on the stage. If I did not think he had talent and personality enough for the screen, I would not take up your time, but I really think he would make a good comedian. If you are interested, I will bring him out.

Frankie, Smiley, and Benny Ford remained part of Gene's spring touring revue, listed in a full-page advertisement J. L. Frank placed in March issues of the weekly trade, *Billboard*. Under the headline "Back From Hollywood Gene Autry the Original Yodeling Cowboy," there he was, smiling and decked out in buckaroo garb, holding his fancy guitar, his foot in a Nocono boot propped up on a post.

Radio Records Stage Screen—Now making a personal appearance tour of the country with his own show the greatest of its kind in the country—Starring in Mascot's Serial "The Phantom Empire."

Gene mentioned the ad in a letter to Fier and described his latest radio venture: "Next Monday March 18, I open on a commercial program for the Texas Crystal Company on Station WHAS in Louisville, Ky. I have a very nice set-up there with my band, consisting of six people on this station together with my show which is booking out of WHAS. Due to this arrangement, I would like to stay in this territory until about the 1st or 15th of May, however, if this will not be satisfactory, I will come to California a little earlier."

Gene's next missive to Fier came from Louisville, on March 30: "It is satisfactory with me to have the contract start six weeks after I arrive in Hollywood. I also thank you very much for the privilege staying here a little longer as I have a very good thing here and want to get all I can before I leave here for the coast. You see I am selling my song book on the Air have a commercial program and making personal appearances so I wanted to get all I could while the opporunity [*sic*] was here." Gene told Fier that he planned to arrive in Hollywood on May 4 and would be bringing Frankie and Smiley. Of the latter, he emphasized "I want to talk with you on the contract as I feel that should he ever get any place I would certainly be entitled to a share of it as I was the one who picked him up and gave him the breaks."

Gene enjoyed his five weeks at WHAS, which featured several talented musicians. There, the singing cowboy renewed his acquaintance with fiddler Clayton McMichen and also became lifelong pals of McMichen's bandmates in the Georgia Wildcats, brothers Slim and Loppy Bryant. Kentucky-born siblings Bob and Ted Atcher bonded with Gene, and Bob's duet partner Bonnie

Blue Eyes would be featured vocalist on Gene's *Melody Ranch* radio show in 1940. Another new friend was fledgling chanteuse Dale Evans, who many years later would become "Queen of the West"—and recount how handsome Gene looked when he first arrived in Louisville. Dressed to the nines in his Western gear, he made quite an impression on her. For Gene's 7 AM program, which ran until April 25, his announcer was Foster Brooks, who later gained fame as the "Lovable Lush" and also remained Gene's buddy.

Gene and his backup band the Range Riders always traveled with gloves, bat, and ball for a quick pickup game of baseball between engagements. Among his musical troupe were his old neighbors the Log Cabin Boys, Chicago guitarist Don Weston, Frankie, Smiley, and Benny, the latter of whom remembered, "We could be on every morning at seven o'clock, and we could reach almost any town in Kentucky in time for a matinee."[8]

Notably missing was Jimmy Long. In January he and Gene had recorded five duets and three songs as a trio with Smiley (with whom Gene also cut four duets). Earlier in the month, they had traveled to Springfield, Missouri, where they visited Jimmy's former duet partner Cliff Keiser, which resulted in an item in the *Frisco Employes* magazine: "C. S. Keiser, night roundhouse foreman, had as his guests recently, 'Jimmie' Long and Gene Autry, stage radio and record stars. 'Jimmie,' who was dispatcher here for many years, is destined it seems to climb high in the entertainment world, his song hits, 'That Silver Haired Daddy of Mine,' being one of the greatest songs to come out in a decade . . . . Mr. Autry . . . recently appeared in talking pictures and was very successful in his role. After their visit with Mr. Keiser both boys left for New York to make a number of victrola [*sic*] records. Following that work they will return to Chicago where they will engage again in radio broadcasting."

Once back in the Windy City, Jimmy, at age forty-five, knew his position with Gene gradually was being usurped by Smiley, who constantly wrote songs and sold them to Gene for five dollars each. Still, M. M. Cole was planning to release a Jimmy Long–Gene Autry songbook, which would add to the royalties Jimmy continued to earn: That year he would receive 25 percent of Gene's ARC royalties ($799.74, the same amount Gene paid Uncle Art) and 50 percent of the M. M. Cole income ($571.60) from Gene's previous songbooks. Their visit at the Frisco depot had rekindled his desire for the comfort of his old life. Soon, Jimmy got his wish: the Frisco, which had become solvent, offered him his job back, and soon he and his family returned to Springfield for good.

Gene's family packed their bags too: Dudley, Veda, and Wilma rode with Frankie Marvin and his wife, Mary, to California. Gene, Ina, and Smiley drove out in Gene's brand-new Buick. The Autrys had found a spacious, two-story Craftsman-style home at 6824 Whitley Terrace on a winding road with breathtaking views of the Hollywood hills. Built in 1915, the house was located in a chic enclave known as Whitley Heights, filled with Mediterranean-style mansions that had belonged at one time to such stars as Rudolph Valentino, Carole Lombard, and Charlie Chaplin. Residents of Whitley Terrace included Maurice Chevalier and Rosalind Russell. On a hilly lot populated with eucalyptus and pine trees, the wood-shingled home's three bedrooms could comfortably accommodate Ina, Gene, and his siblings. Ina immediately jumped into furnishing and decorating the rental property.

Gene had his own work to do: Unable to secure an agent to negotiate on his behalf, he signed on May 17 a one-page document with Mascot, extending his September 4, 1934, contract and stating that his option would commence on July 1. A clause was included stipulating that Gene would "hold myself available from day hereof until the commencement of the said term in order that I might secure proper training from you and your representatives in such manner as you, in your discretion, might deem advisable in cultivating, teaching, training and/or developing me for use in motion pictures; and I further agree to devote such period to such study and development as you determine." Although the contract was completely favorable to Mascot, Fier promised its terms would improve toward Gene once he proved himself.

A Mascot interoffice memo, dated May 21, from contracts attorney Al Levoy to Armand Schaefer outlined Nat Levine's strategy to turn Gene into a celluloid cowboy:

> You are to try and buy Western stories at $100 each. If the story is particularly good, you may go as high as $150. The pictures are to cost $12,000 apiece, no more.
>
> Follow thru with Gene Autry to the end of having him improve his acting. . . . Before starting the "Phantom Empire" serial, Gene took up a preliminary course in acting but it has evidently been wasted. THIS IS IMPORTANT.
>
> Also get in touch with the Westmore Makeup Salon and have them give Autry several types of makeup that would give him the appearance of a Western star. During "Phantom Empire," we had him use quite a dark makeup. However, he could go even darker—anything that will give him the appearance of virility.

Indeed, Gene had a much softer look than the rugged masculine cowboys who had come before him. Hart, Mix, and Maynard were large, well-built men with angular faces and strong jaws. Gene emitted a vulnerability that was just as alluring to women, bringing out maternal and sisterly instincts in some. He would go on to play role after role as a diplomatic, gentle warrior—winning the fight through his music and wits more often than fisticuffs and gunplay. Gene exuded sincerity and warmth. Moreover, his attractiveness on screen wasn't threatening to his female fans—because he seemed attainable, it was comforting. During such uncertain times as the Depression, the public needed an unassuming hero like Gene. Being a "non-actor," he appeared to be simply playing himself—the boy next door—to whom movie-goers could relate. His would be a new more feminine hero archetype, which would reverberate in future generations of well-dressed singing stars who also transitioned into acting, including Frank Sinatra and Elvis Presley. As Gene aged out of the sex-symbol role, his appeal remained; as a father figure, he served as a role model and security blanket to boys and girls who needed moral support and affection as they watched—and felt—his reassuring presence on screen.

Gene Autry film and music scholar Jonathan Guyot Smith recalled the effect Gene had on him when he became a fan as a young boy and the reasons why audiences judged Gene more as a personality than as an actor.

> He had a tremendous charisma. Gene was appealing to the people. You saw him—and it didn't really matter what he did—you liked him. And it was at a time in history, during the Depression, when people wanted to be soothed. He could walk into a room and be the peacemaker—calm everybody, just by his presence—and I think that came across onstage too. He was very likable. The audience, if they like you, are going to meet you more than half-way in whatever it is that you do.

And so a massive audience would—over the next twenty years—for Gene Autry.

20

REPUBLIC PICTURES STAR

AS GENE STRUGGLED TO LEARN THE CRAFT OF ACTING, Mascot executives worked to prepare scripts for his first few films. The studio had been successfully making serials since 1927, and recycling was part of the low-budget production house's modus operandi. In the May 21, 1935, memo outlining Nat Levine's plan for Gene, Al Levoy advised Armand Schaefer: "Inasmuch as we have quite a period of preparation, you should take advantage of it by lining up several stories in final continuity form before shooting our first one. Check our files for all of our old Western stories, also a Western story that John Rathmell wrote called 'Skeleton Town.' Consider some of our old serial stories to the end of making modern Western pictures out of them. Just as soon as you have arrived at a definite outline, we could consider Sherman Lowe, Gerald Geharty [sic], Ed Parsons—however, definitely making sure that the entire story cost does not exceed $400.00 which includes the purchase and the final continuity." Rathmell co-authored the story behind *In Old Santa Fe*, and Geraghty co-wrote the screenplay of *The Phantom Empire*; Lowe would pen the script for Gene's second Republic feature.

While plans jelled for Gene's first pictures, Levine was involved in negotiations with former American Tobacco Company executive Herbert J. Yates. Yates had expanded the record labels under his ARC banner, acquiring Columbia and Brunswick in 1934, and now he was transforming Consolidated Film Industries to include a movie-making operation. Yates's lucrative film development company was processing movies for several financially troubled independents, as well as funding some of the companies' productions. In March Yates agreed to merge with two of his clients, the independent studios Monogram and Majestic, forming a new conglomerate called Republic Pictures. Monogram executives Way Ray Johnston was named Republic's president and Trem Carr its production head. Monogram's *Westward Ho*, in preproduction and starring its leading contract player John Wayne, would be Republic's first film, with a start date of May 19. Republic stipulated that all its screenplays were to be given approval by the Motion Picture Producers and Distributors of America—better known as the Hays Office, which enforced an increasingly strict moral code in Hollywood movies. Complaints had been lodged by religious leaders about provocative "flaming youth pictures," and Westerns provided a conservative, clean-cut alternative. Those in development as Gene Autry vehicles would be embraced by the Hays office for Gene's virtuous heroics.

Throughout the spring of 1935 Yates had been wooing Nat Levine, who initially resisted his bid to add Mascot to the Republic stable. In fact, Levine ran a trade-publication ad in early May stating "You Must Ignore Rumors! . . . Mascot Remains Independent and Will Continue Its Expansion" . . . Mascot Is Not 'Taking Over' Nor 'Affiliating With' Any New or Established Producer-Distributor Organization." In the meantime, Republic absorbed two more studios, Chesterfield and Liberty. Finally, on June 11, Levine, succumbing to financial pressures, signed papers merging Mascot with Republic. It was determined that Mascot's first two Gene Autry pictures, by then in pre-production, would be released by Republic as a "Nat Levine Mascot Production."

On July 6, after weeks of training and rehearsal, Gene started work on his debut feature, *Tumbling Tumbleweeds*. Joe Kane, who had replaced David Howard uncredited *In Old Santa Fe*, was the director, while Schaefer again handled the production's supervision. The standard Western plot of ranchers versus nesters is upended with the twist that a powerful cattleman's son is a musician who opposes the violent altercations between the two factions. The film opens with Gene, looking young and innocent, strumming his guitar and singing "Yodeling My Troubles Away." After being disowned by his father for not battling the nesters, he hits the road with his guitar. When he returns five years later with a medicine show, his father has been murdered and his best friend accused of the crime, so Gene sets out to find the real killer. For the dangerous riding sequences, Ken Cooper doubles for Gene, but the star handles the fight scenes himself, pleasing Schaefer with his improvement. Mascot had hired the best stuntman in the business, Yakima Canutt, to teach Gene how to brawl.

As in *Phantom*, his character's name is Gene Autry. Even more than before, the songs propel the plot forward, with nine musical interludes in the hour-long picture. The film is named for Gene's hit record issued that February, the evocative "Tumbling Tumbleweeds," written by Bob Nolan and recorded on January 11, 1935, by Gene with the Prairie Ramblers, Smiley, and Jimmy Long. Pointing the way to music videos of the future, Gene's movies would cross-promote his record releases, while his well-known songs gave name recognition to his new films.[1] Gene's first smash, "That Silver Haired Daddy," is featured in a poignant scene in which Gene has just discovered his father's death. The song, as originally recorded with Jimmy Long, would be reissued on Vocalion to tie in with the movie and find a whole new audience.

The medicine show extravert—whose character's name is Smiley Burnette—gets two humorous musical spotlights. Traditional action segments of horse chases, fistfights, and gunplay coexist with the humor and music, and the setting mixes the contemporary with the past, thus establishing the basic blueprint of the Gene Autry musical Western, which would be refined and tweaked over the next few films.

Much is made in *Tumbleweeds* of Gene's musicianship; he's considered a pacifist weakling by his father and his violent ranch hands, and is called "a lavender cowboy" by thugs who taunt him when he performs onstage with the medicine show. Courageous Gene demonstrates that he can use his fists when necessary, but it is his music and wits that serve him best. Gene is re-teamed with George Hayes, who uses a stentorian voice as the worldly medicine show "doctor." Also among the troupe are Frankie Marvin, who has a few lines but mostly plays music, and Eugene Jackson, whose tap-dancing "Eightball" character is derived from the "Step 'n Fetchit" minstrel tradition. Gene's acting has improved somewhat, but it is his singing sequences that remain most compelling. One device used often to solve a problem in future Autry films is an Autry 78-rpm record (in this case "Ridin' Down the Canyon") being played on a phonograph. This also helps to hammer home the point that Gene is simply playing himself—that's why he's a little awkward and not much of an actor. Throughout his career, Autry movie press books, distributed to exhibitors by the studio and filled with stories (often embellished or just plain fiction) to promote the current release, would falsely claim that he had never studied acting—and why should he since he's simply playing himself. This did not prevent one film critic from lambasting him that his only means of displaying emotion is by changing his clothes.

Tumbling Tumbleweeds took one week to make and cost $18,801. While the film was in production, another studio, Warner Brothers, motivated by the success of *In Old Santa Fe*, tried to capitalize on the nascent musical Western trend. Starring an operatic tenor, Dick Foran, *Moonlight on the Prairie* was released close to *Tumbleweed*'s September 5 debut. Most audiences and exhibitors, however, preferred the Autry film. Whereas Foran was more of a pop crooner, Gene's twangy yet intimate singing seemed natural, not contrived. His likable, more authentic style easily translated to the screen. Soon, studios would be scrambling to find real country boys to compete with Gene Autry and star in their attempts to make musical Westerns.

Tumbleweeds wrapped and Hollywood stardom beckoned, but Gene didn't forgo his bread-and-butter career. He wanted to assure this important source of income would continue as well. He wrote to publisher Maury Cole on July 18 about his forthcoming songbook with Jimmy Long, mentioning his Republic debut in terms of its promotional value:

> I mailed you 25 songs for the Jimmie [*sic*] Long and Gene Autry Book they are all good songs and should make a good book. You will find some of these songs have already been arranged and I believe you told me that the piano arrangements I had already made up you would pay me for them so I am listing the ones below that have already been arranged for piano.
>
> I just completed "Tumbling Tumbleweeds" and should be a good picture as it has a lot of action and songs in it. I will have the lead sent you in a few days on the songs. I am also sending you a few of the stills from the picture if you want to use some of them in the new book but be sure to take care of the photos and return them to me as I cannot get duplicate copies of these photos and I want to keep them.

GENE WAS AWARE ALREADY OF REPUBLIC'S STINGINESS with promotional materials—a holdover from Levine's policies at Mascot.

As with his recordings, Gene's songbooks directly helped to promote his movies and vice versa. M. M. Cole had contacted Gene about his songs in the serial: "Regarding the picture songs from the 'Phantom Empire,' with exception of the 'Silver Haired Daddy' song, we would suggest that we put the songs in the Calumet [sheet music] Edition. This would give the picture a great deal of publicity, as the songs would be on the counters all over the country and in the smallest towns. They would retail for 5 cents per copy. The 30 cents and 35 cents sheet music, today, is not selling, only the top songs are selling a little. For this reason, we are enclosing 3 contracts and we would suggest that you have the Mascot Film Co. and yourself, sign same, which would give us the privilege of putting them in the Calumet Edition."

To capitalize on the film, M. M. Cole would re-release "That Silver Haired Daddy" sheet music, using the stills Gene sent him and the tagline, "From the Republic Picture 'Tumbling Tumbleweeds,' Starring Gene Autry. Released late in the year, *Gene Autry–Jimmy Long Cowboy Songs Mountain Ballads* included more country than Western numbers but did feature "Someday in Wyoming," promoted as being from *In Old Santa Fe*. Also included was a song, "If I Had You," with the credit "Words by Jimmy Long, Music by Ina Mae Spivey." Illustrating the book were publicity shots of Gene and Jimmy, plus stills from Gene's first two Republic Pictures, the second of which, *Melody Trail*, got underway on August 21.

The lighthearted *Melody Trail* developed further the template of the singing cowboy picture. Inspired by Smiley's signature croak, story authors Sherman Lowe and Betty Burbridge named the Autry sidekick "Frog Millhouse," his moniker for the duration of his tenure at Republic. Smiley used his croaky voice more often, and his comic pratfalls, only glimpsed before, became a running gag in *Melody Trail*. Rather than one of a crew of comical characters as in

Tumbleweeds, he became Gene's foil, establishing the sidekick role to a degree never before seen in Westerns. The duo would become inseparable on film for the next seven years.

Also in *Melody Trail*, Gene's dark sorrel horse received billing for the first time in the title credits. During Gene's initial summer in Los Angeles, a year earlier, he had purchased a pair of horses for $425, and hired trainer and stunt rider Tracy Layne to work with them.[2] One was a sorrel with three white stockings, a dark foreleg, and a distinctive T-shaped blaze, which Gene named Champion. The horse may have been used for the first time in *Phantom Empire*. Since Gene's riding was still shaky (especially compared with that of his co-star, the young trick rider Betsy Ross King), there are not many close-ups of him on horseback. Both of Gene's mounts may have been used in *Phantom* to determine which photographed and handled the best. Regardless, beginning with *Tumbleweeds*, Gene rides only Champion.[3] In an early scene in *Melody Trail*, Champ gets his first close-up, when admired by a gypsy. Over the next thirty years, Gene would own six different horses named Champion, three of which would variously star in his movies and TV shows, with the others trained for personal appearance tours and rodeo performances.

Melody Trail opens with a documentary-style rodeo scene with real-life rodeo announcer Abe Lefton, who would become a lifelong friend and eventual employee of Gene's. Smiley begins the film in a comic disguise—another frequent element in Autry pictures. As the rodeo clown, he offers comic relief to Gene's earnest singing cowboy. An exciting horse bucking event, with Ken Cooper or Cliff Lyons doubling for Gene, substitutes for the typical horse-chase scene. *Melody Trail* co-stars ingénue Ann Rutherford as Gene's love interest (Millicent Thomas). The fifteen-year-old brunette had already performed in radio dramas and starred in Mascot's 1934 film, *Waterfront Lady*, and the 1935 serial, *The Fighting Marines*. Her vivid description of shooting the latter, directed by Breezy Eason, is probably similar to Gene's experience on *Phantom Empire*: "The directors were far more interested in keeping the action going than dialogue. . . . There were virtually no rehearsals except you sort of walk through in a hurry for the cameraman so he'll know what he's aiming at. We lined up for the cameras and tried not to blow our lines or be out of camera range. . . . The big banner cry was 'Fighting light.' That meant hurry up, for God's sake, the sun's gonna go down and we can't shoot anything. Sometimes people would get klieg eyes—red, sore eyes from those big klieg lights. They'd put cold raw potatoes over their eyes. The prop man carried the potatoes around. We would start in at first light in the morning."[4]

More a ranch romance than a shoot 'em up, *Melody Trail* gave Gene his first stab at a love scene (only hinted at in *Tumbleweeds*). Fifty years later, Rutherford remembered how thrilling it was for a young girl to be smooching with an older man. The sparkling Ann and shy Gene worked well together and had good onscreen chemistry—the first of four film collaborations. "Here was this dear, unprepossessing man," she related. "He was just as happy as he could be. He had been on the radio, but being in pictures was really pay dirt.[5] Gene was a lovely man, but he was one cowboy who couldn't ride a horse!"[6]

Rutherford earned fifty dollars a week more than Gene—whose Mascot contract had been transferred to Republic with the original terms intact. Gene had backed down regarding a studio contract with Smiley, who had signed a Mascot/Republic agreement with the same terms as Gene's, but earning just thirty-five dollars a week. Gene's only compensation as his former manager was that once Smiley's salary increased to fifty dollars a week (in two years time with option renewals), Smiley would pay him a commission of fifteen dollars a week—an amount that would escalate at five-dollar increments upon option renewals.

Smiley had taken bit parts in other films beginning in 1934, including *Waterfront Lady*, during which he got to know Rutherford, who became extremely fond of him. "Smiley Burnette was the most talented young man, musically, I ever met, with the possible exception of Mickey Rooney [with whom she would co-star in the successful Andy Hardy series]," she later said. "I can see him now with his accordion—what he called his Stomach Steinway—and his guitar, or 'git-fiddle.' There wasn't an instrument he couldn't make music of."[7]

Melody Trail's plot twist surrounds the recruitment by the Thomas ranch of a bevy of cowgirls—ranging from a short-haired butch "foreman" to a platinum Kewpie doll named Cuddles who falls for Frog. One of several musical numbers features the cowgirls providing Gene's chorus on "Western Lullaby." All the characters share screen time with Buck the Wonder Dog, recent star of *Call of the Wild*, the latest installment in a fad that began with *Rin Tin Tin* in the 1920s. Co-author of *Melody Trail's* story, Betty Burbridge would contribute to numerous Autry films, as would several other women writers, creating spunky female characters and the ranch romance style that particularly appealed to Gene's growing audience of women. Gene's third film, *The Sagebrush Troubadour*, written by Oliver Drake, introduced another frequent component of Autry films: the feisty female lead (in *Sagebrush*, vivacious Barbara Pepper) who spars with Gene until she finally falls under his spell.

Tumbling Tumbleweeds and *Melody Trail* were released five weeks apart, on September 9 and October 14, 1935. Gene readily agreed to travel to promote the films at theaters, establishing a precedent of personal appearance touring that would become a Republic standard. Ina Mae, along with Gene's cousin Callie Jane, had been handling Gene's fan correspondence, developing a system to nurture a national following. Ann Rutherford recalled:

> When we were doing the last day of our shoot on *Melody Trail*, Ina came on the set and their car was piled high with boxes . . . Ina said they all contained Gene's fan mail from people who liked the serial. She said, "After he finishes here, we're going to get Champion in a trailer and we're going to play [at theaters] . . . Gene's

been answering his fan mail and signing pictures, but I set up a filing system where, for instance, if we go to Button Willow . . . I have the cards from all the kids there who write to him. We'll get the local phone books when we get there and Gene will call them." . . . Gene and Ina took such care with his fan mail and they followed through. . . . She hung onto the addresses and had them cross-indexed and, believe me, that sort of thing is the foundation of his fortune.[8]

Gene hired Jimmy Long's son, Jack, to help drive the horse trailer, and they set out for Texas and Oklahoma, to capitalize on his name being known in those states. Over the years, Gene frequently employed old friends and relatives to fill positions in his organization. Jack's wife, Virginia, worked for Gene sporadically over the next three decades, remaining loyal long after she and Jack divorced. Gene was enthusiastically welcomed home by Oklahomans with movie ads proclaiming, "This is the first picture of Gene Autry that this theatre has ever shown. Gene, in this picture, reminds you who know him, of the days he spent in this county."[9] After completing Sagebrush, he returned in November to the Sooner State to perform at the Convention of Theaters Owners of Oklahoma, in Oklahoma City. His wooing of theater exhibitors would continue on a national scale until 1953.

Back in Hollywood, the initial trade reviews were quite favorable. The Hollywood Reporter said of Gene's role in Tumbleweeds, "He handles a horse and a guitar with equal ease, and most of his natural awkwardness in action and dialogue was of the sort that fits the part," and of Melody Trail, "The ingredients are stirred together with the irresponsible verve of a vaudeville show on the loose. . . . Gene Autry stars as cowboy and radio singer and he is handsome and likeable."[10] Gene also received mention in a Los Angeles Times item on the formation of Republic Pictures: "Six features to be made with increased budgets are being prepared for production by [Nat] Levine, as well as several serials and John Wayne and Gene Autry westerns."[11] And two months later, the Los Angeles Times reported that, "Probably the largest percentage of fan mail that enters Hollywood is received by western stars, even though they might make only a few pictures each year. Their products gross large returns. Gene Autrey [sic], while somewhat of a newcomer to the western ranks, is already among the topnotchers, mainly for the reason that he brings to the screen an important part of the range that was heretofore missing—he combines a pleasing singing voice along with his ability as a western actor—and singing westerns have been scarce."[12]

Soon, because of Gene Autry, the musical Western was the new Hollywood standard and even ushered big-budget Westerns back to the major studios.

21

BATTLES—ON SCREEN AND OFF

WHILE MAKING APPEARANCES IN TEXAS during the fall of 1935, Gene stopped at a makeshift recording studio in a Dallas hotel. This was his longest stretch without recording, and Uncle Art met him there on September 22—as did Jimmy Long, Frankie Marvin, and another pair of musicians. At a local radio station, Gene had met guitarist Bill Boyd and his twenty-one-year-old fiddler, Oathar "Art" Davis, a member of Boyd's Cowboy Ramblers. Davis had also played in seminal Western swing bands, such as the Light Crust Doughboys and Milton Brown and His Musical Brownies. Boyd and Davis played on several cuts, backing Jimmy and Gene's duets; the session's one hit, however, was Jimmie Davis's mournful "Nobody's Darling But Mine," featuring only Gene's vocals and Frankie Marvin on steel.

Gene liked the strapping Art Davis and offered him sixty-five dollars a week to play fiddle at his personal appearances and for the occasional movie spot; the studio wanted Gene to put together a band that could back him on screen. "I was getting $14.50 a week," Art recalled, "playing on the radio. I said, 'You just hired a fiddle player!' " Soon after Art joined, they did some shows in Chicago, and Gene put his new employee—whom he nicknamed "Goon"—to the test.

"Goon, come in and get your money," Gene said.

"I went in there," remembered Art, "and he counted out ones, but instead of giving me sixty-five dollars, he gave me sixty six."

"Count that, Goon, and see if that's right," Gene told him.

"Yes sir," Art answered. "I came back in my room, and Frankie's sitting there, and Smiley. So I count that money. I needed that money because I had a date that night and I wanted a bottle. I counted it five times. Finally, I told them—and they was watching me—I said, 'Frankie, he give me sixty-six dollars.' Smiley and Frankie are winking at each other—they'd done been through this. I went back in there, and I said, 'Gene, you paid me too much!'"

Gene said, "Thanks!"

Frankie and Smiley said to Art, 'You're in, *now!*"

Goon wondered, "What the hell are you talking about?"

"He done the same damned thing to us," they answered. "Wants to find out if you're honest!"[1]

Art Davis would debut on screen, along with Frankie and guitarist Charles Sargent, in *Sagebrush Troubadour*, providing the music at a masquerade party. Gene's final and fourth film of 1935, *The Singing Vagabond*, began production on November 16. One of the few period pieces Gene made for Republic, the film reunited him with both Ann Rutherford and Barbara Pepper. Gene had long been a Stephen Foster fan, and *Vagabond* opens with stock footage from Mascot's *Harmony Lane*, a Foster bio-pic that features an uncredited William Frawley in blackface performing "De Camptown Races" (actually sung by Robinson Neeman). In the mid-1930s, minstrelsy and blackface had not yet been shunned by the general public or Hollywood. Minstrel-style characters recurred in Gene's early Republic films, and Smiley appears in blackface in 1937's *Round-Up Time in Texas* (and in Charles Starrett movies in the mid-1940s). No characters of this type populate Gene's later work, where he had more control over his scripts. Whether this shift is a sign of Gene's own sensitivity toward such racist imagery, or just the changing times of the 1950s, is not clear. From the beginning, though, Gene's films appealed to both black and white audiences and were popular in segregated "black only" theaters in the South. In fact, the artists Lead Belly (Huddie Ledbetter), B. B. King, Solomon Burke, and Aaron Neville all have said they were inspired musically by Gene Autry.

Another aspect of *Singing Vagabond* that became increasingly rare in Autry pictures—eventually disappearing completely—was the sustained embrace and lusty kiss between Gene and his female lead, in this case, Ann Rutherford. Once Gene's audiences grew to include vociferous young boys who detested the clinch, such romantic gestures were kept to a minimum. "The films have to please women and young boys—so no hanky-panky but altercations between Gene Autry and the lead, which indicates the beginning of a relationship to gals and putting girls in their place to boys," screenwriter Gerald Geraghty explained in 1939. "Gene pleases his sub-adolescent audience—boys—when he is girl-shy. It strikes a sympathetic chord in them."[2] Later, fan magazines would capitalize on the kiss question, publishing articles on the topic and soliciting fans to vote whether or not Gene should be allowed to smooch. The joke carried over to radio and eventually television, with Gene frequently the butt of jokes about kissing his horse and only his horse.

The day he finished *Vagabond*, on November 29, 1935, Gene signed an addendum to his Republic contract, which gave him a month off to do performances and permitted him to keep the proceeds without giving the studio a percentage (as his original contract mandated). Undoubtedly, as his movies proved successful at the box office, he was beginning to regret signing such an inequitable contract.

His return to Chicago began with another trip to the studio, on December 5. Accompanied by Smiley, Goon, Frankie, and guitarist Charles Sargent, Gene waxed three wonderfully melodic cowboy songs, two of which he co-wrote and one written by Smiley. Gene's preference, though, was an original sentimental ballad, "You're the Only Star (in My Blue Heaven)," inspired by an obsessive fan letter. Also an homage to his mentor Gene Austin's biggest hit, "My Blue Heaven," the composition remained a favorite of his throughout his life.[3]

In his memoir, Gene described the song's genesis, "I found myself receiving love letters from a lady in Iowa. . . . She had developed the notion that I was singing to her, just to her, and the letters, reeking with Gypsy Rose perfume, would begin: 'Gene, darling, I heard the song you sang to me last night and I *understood.*' . . . In the last one I received, she described being alone that night. After hearing me sing she walked outside, stood on the porch, and gazed at the evening sky. 'I looked at the stars in the heavens,' she wrote. 'I saw millions of them. But you are the only star in my blue heaven.'" In the next passage, Gene added, "Music has been the better part of my career. Movies are wonderful fun and they give you a famous face. But how the words and melody are joined, how they come together out of air and enter the mind, this is art. Songs are forever."[4]

Gene spent Christmas Eve recording the gorgeous waltz "Mexicali Rose," at the Chicago studio with Frankie, Art, and Charles. (Three years later Bing Crosby would cover the song.) He performed throughout December, billed as Gene Autry and His Hollywood Gang, including Smiley, Frankie, Benny Ford, and WLS *Barn Dance* cast members. The revue took them into Wisconsin and Illinois through New Year's Day. "I'll tell you a funny experience in working with Gene," Benny later said.

> There were two blind boys at WLS, Mac and Bob. They played mandolin and guitar and they sang . . . Gene put them in our show . . . but always, when you got ready to do the show, you couldn't find Mac and Bob. They'd be down the street in the saloon, playing the slot machine. Nickel slot machines were everywhere then. Gene had bought a one-ton panel truck, and he carried all this stuff with him. . . . He'd bought a fine saddle . . . and had it on display in the lobby. In Chicago, Gene bought two nickel slot machines and put them in the truck. He had them set at a reasonable payoff, and he took them to the next theater we played. He put the slot machines in our dressing room, and he bought a pint of whiskey.
>
> He got Mac and Bob, and he said, "Alright Bob, that one's yours, and Mac, this is yours. Now, I don't want you to leave the theater. I don't want to have to go and hunt you when we start the matinee. You going to play the slot machines today?"

Mac and Bob answered, "Yes, sir!"

"All right," Gene said, "Here's ten dollars worth of nickels. Give me ten dollars." And they gave him the money. And he said, "Now, here's a pint of whiskey that I donate. You can take a little nip along, but don't get drunk." They never did get drunk. They just liked to have a little nip once in a while. They'd stand right there and pull that lever on them doggone machines until somebody would say, "Alright, you guys, get your mandolin and guitar ready to go!"

Benny and other revue members would hawk Gene's songbooks to audiences, earning a quarter for each one they sold. Smiley spent most of his spare time writing songs, Benny recalled, and onstage he performed solo with his accordion and did a one-man comedy routine.

Although he was becoming a movie star, music was still more lucrative for Gene. In 1935 he'd grossed $3,200 from ARC; $2,500 in earnings from songbooks and other music-related endeavors; and $1,679 in performance fees (before expenses). His total earnings from Republic, however, amounted to only $2,300, after starring in the serial and four features. He was slated to make eight pictures in 1936, beginning with *Red River Valley*, which started production on January 21. As he prepared to leave for location in Yuma, Arizona, he knew he'd made a big mistake signing the Mascot/Republic contract without consulting a lawyer. Back in June he had been so excited about his forthcoming film roles, and his mind had been on other business. For example, he had sent a telegram to M. M. Cole asking about usage fees for the composition "Red River Valley," which the company had published in a songbook. At the studio's request, Gene inquired: "We are interested in the song Red River Valley as a picture title and for song useages [*sic*] in picture. Please wire immediately quoting lowest price." As it turned out, the song was considered public domain, and Republic did not have to pay a cent.

In fact, *Red River Valley*, a fast-paced action film, featured only two musical numbers by Gene, although Smiley also did a pair. The picture did, however, use symphonic incidental music throughout (including a Beethoven piece), which heightened the movie's intensity and gave it a modern, more polished feel. Directed by Breezy Eason, *Red River Valley* was written by the talented McGowan brothers, Dorrell and Stuart, who would write some of Gene's best movies. Many of their ideas, Dorrell later said, came from topical stories they read in the newspaper. A drama with only minimal comedy (from Smiley), *Red River Valley* centers on the building of a dam (inspired by the Hoover Dam, constructed in the 1930s), which is sabotaged. Gene later recalled *Red River Valley* as the "toughest" film he ever made. "We were right out in the desert," he related. "We shot a lot of it along the Colorado River, and I did a big fight on the dam [with veteran heavy George Chesebro], and the dam was very slippery. It had kind of a moss over the spillway, and I darned near drowned in that thing too. When I went over the spillway, why, it was in the wintertime and I

Gene and Ina Autry's first Melody Ranch off Balboa Avenue, in the San Fernando Valley, California. (Stanley Rojo Collection)

Gene later recalled nearly drowning while making 1936's *Red River Valley*, one of the most exciting of his early features.

Gene spent lavishly on his vast custom Western wardrobe, tailored primarily by Rodeo Ben, Turk, and later Nudie, but paid only $425 for his first Champion.

Gene attended to business in his office located in the backyard of his North Hollywood home. He decorated the walls with photos of those he admired, such as Rudy Vallee.

Gene became known as Public Cowboy No. 1 in headlines and on marquees, following the 1937 release of this, his seventeenth starring feature.

In *Public Cowboy No. 1*, Gene serenades co-star Ann Rutherford, one of his early leading ladies, who appeared in five Autry films, including his second, *Melody Trail*.

Round-Up Time in Texas, 1937, actually takes place in Africa (popularized at the time through the success of Tarzan movies), with Smiley Burnette disguised as a tribal medicine man in order to save the day; the African American vocal group The Cabin Kids was also prominently featured in the film.

Ina never got tired of listening to the Singing Cowboy, pictured here at their new North Hollywood home, ca. 1938.

Gene (shirtless and hatless) and Republic Pictures crew on location in the Mojave Desert, ca. 1938 (Stanley Rojo Collection).

Gene Autry and songwriter Walter G. Samuels, co-writer of "Take Me Back to My Boots and Saddle." (Stanley Rojo Collection)

Gene Autry, performing on Champion, at an early rodeo. (Stanley Rojo Collection)

Gene constantly included his buddies from Chicago radio station WLS in his pictures. Former touring mate Patsy Montana, author of "I Want to Be a Cowboy's Sweetheart," sang her hit in 1939's *Colorado Sunset*.

Just before their departure to England in 1939, Gene and Ina attend Gene Autry Day, among the festivities at the New York World's Fair.

Gene faces a line of photographers while fans surround him outside London's Savoy Hotel, where he appeared with Champion, 1939.

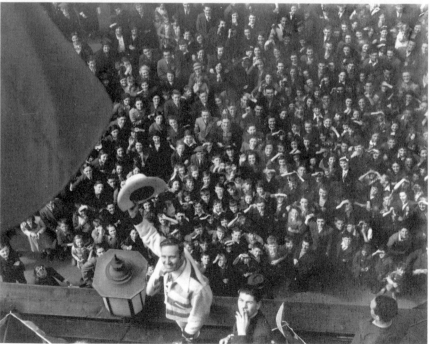

When Gene traveled to Ireland in 1939, he was feted by thousands of Dubliners, here hoisting a sign reading "Ceád Míle Fáilte" (a hundred thousand welcomes).

As Gene paraded through the streets of Dublin in August 1939, approximately 250,000 people turned out. He also discovered "South of the Border" while there.

Mexicali Rose, from 1939, was one of several Latin-themed Autry pictures; here, Gene wins over the banditos, including the ringleader played by Noah Beery, thanks to their love of his Western balladry.

Named for his successful radio show, 1940's *Melody Ranch* featured such A-players as dancer Ann Miller (pictured here with Gene) and comedian Jimmy Durante. Miller reportedly had quite a crush on her co-star.

Ride, Tenderfoot, Ride, 1940, features an astounding cast of women, including frequent co-stars June Storey and Mary Lee (seated, left to right), plus Texan Cindy Walker (standing, second from left), who would become the most successful female songwriter in country music.

In 1940, in New York City, Gene was included in a prestigious tribute to American music, among such composers as Irving Berlin, Richard Rodgers, and Jerome Kern (pictured here, left to right), as well as early blues pioneer W. C. Handy.

Gene Autry, *Melody Ranch Radio Show*, CBS Studios, Hollywood, 1940. Left to right: Frank Nelson, Horace Murphy, Mary Lee, Gene Autry, Jimmy Wakely, Dick Reinhart (standing), and Johnny Bond, with Lou Bring and his orchestra in the background (Holly George-Warren Collection)

Beginning in 1946, Gene's radio show was augmented by Ione, Beulah, and Eunice Kettle—The Pinafores. (Stanley Rojo Collection)

Ina and Gene Autry at a Hollywood gala with Herb Yates (far right), Vera Ralston (blonde in fur coat), and George "Gabby" Hayes (far left). (Stanley Rojo Collection)

Genc Autry and "Shorty Long" (actor Horace Murphy) on Gene Autry's *Melody Ranch Radio Show*, ca. 1940. (Stanley Rojo Collection)

Gene Autry, June Storey, and Rudy Vallee, ca. 1940. (Stanley Rojo Collection)
Gene Autry and June Storey on a personal appearance tour, ca. 1940. (Stanley Rojo Collection).

Gene Autry and Oklahoma natives the Jimmy Wakely Trio—Jimmy, Johnny Bond, and Dick
Reinhart (from left) on the *Melody Ranch* program, 1940. (Stanley Rojo Collection)

The sultry Fay McKenzie became Gene's frequent co-star following June Storey; here the Irish
actor plays a senorita in *Down Mexico Way*, 1941.

Gene always loved baseball and played pickup games while touring in the early 1930s and later on location for his movies, including *The Singing Hill*, in 1941.

Dancer Carol Adams co-starred in *Ridin' on a Rainbow* (1941): "He was a quiet man," she remembered in 2006. "The only time he flirted with me was when we took the publicity pictures in the 'still gallery.' He wanted to put his arms around me and get his face up next to mine. None of those pictures made it onto the lobby cards, though."

Gene's Flying A Ranch in Berwyn (later Gene Autry), Oklahoma, was constructed of Arbuckle stone with his Flying A logo decorating the stable walls. The walls still remained in 2001. (Photo by Holly George-Warren)

On November 16, 1941, Berwyn, Oklahoma, officially became Gene Autry, an event attended by state officials and broadcast on Gene's *Melody Ranch Radio Show*.

couldn't get my breath, and I had kind of a tough time there. . . . When you go over a spillway in a dam, there's a great pressure there and you really have to swim to get out of it."[5]

Frankie Marvin played one of Chesebro's henchmen: "I did the fall off one of the gates . . . forty two feet into the water," he remembered. "They had a [stunt] guy supposed to do it and he got cold feet, I guess, and old Mandy Shaefer was the producer, and he was tight as the devil, so I said, 'What was you going to give him?' Said, 'A hundred dollars.' I said, 'Hell, I'll do it for a hundred dollars!' So he said, 'You've got a part in the picture!' So I did it, I fell off and when I got almost to the water I dived in. They picked me up in this river—it was ice cold—and old Mandy, he says, 'Marvin, I'll give you a dime to jump back in,' and I said, 'A dime from you is like a thousand dollars from anybody else!' so I dived right back into that cold water out of the boat."[6]

Such pranks did not make it into the papers, but Gene's name had begun popping up in various celebrity columns in the *Los Angeles Times*. The year before, Gene had run into former *Tulsa World* reporter, George Goodale, who had moved to Los Angeles to work at the *Examiner*. Goodale had just lost his job when he saw Gene at the Brass Rail watering hole. Gene hired him on the spot as his press agent, and Goodale got his client on the invitation list for high-profile social events, as well as mentions in movie-news columns. Another longtime loyalist, the good-humored Goodale, who always bragged of being one-quarter Cherokee, would stay on Gene's payroll for decades, eventually as a publicist for the California Angels.[7]

In February Gene finally signed with an agent, Harry Wurtzel—introduced to him by Goodale. Wurtzel set to work negotiating a better contract with the studio. On February 24, 1936, a "Demand for Cancellation of Agreement" between Gene and Mascot Pictures was drawn up, to the attention of Nat Levine, stating: "that said contract is unfair, inequitable, one-sided and unconscionable in that the benefits flowing therefore are solely for the benefit of and advantage to the 'Producer' and is highly technical and complicated in nature, and my consent thereto was given by mistake in that the same was signed by me without the independent advice of counsel, and the full import and legal effect of said agreement was not fully understood by me, nor was same explained to me prior to my said signing thereof."[8]

It is unclear as to the effect of the document because Gene began work on a new picture three days later, followed by two more. After completing the third one, the appropriately titled *Guns and Guitars*, on May 9, Gene left Hollywood. Ten days later, a flurry of telegrams indicated the battle had begun. Nat Levine fired the first shot:

AMAZED THAT YOU LEFT LOS ANGELES WITHOUT OBTAINING OUR CONSENT AND WITH THE KNOWLEDGE THAT WE ARE GOING INTO PRODUCTION IMMEDI-ATELY ON *OH SUSANNAH* IN WHICH YOU ARE FEATURED. . . . UNLESS YOU

REPORT AT THE STUDIO NO LATER THAN FRIDAY MORNING MAY 22 AT 9 AM
WE SHALL IMMEDIATELY SUSPEND YOUR CONTRACT AND COMMENCE DUE LE-
GAL PROCEEDINGS TO RESTRAIN YOU FROM RENDERING SERVICES TO ANYONE
ELSE AND FURTHERMORE HOLD YOU PERSONALLY RESPONSIBLE FOR ALL DAM-
AGE SUFFERED BY US THRU LOSS OF PRODUCTION OR OTHERWISE.[9]

Levine finally addressed Gene's February demand, in a telegram the same day
to Moe Siegel, Yates's deputy in New York.

AUTRY DESIRES TO BREAK CONTRACT AS HIS CONTENTION IS THAT IT IS EN-
TIRELY ONE SIDED.

He asked Republic's New York attorney to read the agreement and advise as to
"whether he feels that it is unilateral . . . Gordon Levoy definitely feels the
contract is not unilateral."

Gene had returned to Texas, stopping in Tioga and making a surprise
gratis performance at the local school where his cousin Buck's fiancée taught.
Trying to forget his worries, he visited with his relatives and old friends, and
played the guitar at Sam's Barbershop. Republic's Dallas district manager, G.
Underwood, tracked Gene down on the nineteenth, though, and delivered
Levine's telegram. Underwood reported back,

URGED HIM TO RETURN AND ALL WOULD BE FORGIVEN AND I FELT THAT IF HE
DID HIS BEST THAT UNDOUBTEDLY HE WOULD GET CONSIDERATION. HE
STATED HE WANTED YOU TO SUSPEND CONTRACT. . . . FINALLY PROMISED TO
CALL YOU OR HIS AGENT TONIGHT.

The next day, Gene wired Republic from Tioga:

BE ADVISED THAT MY PRODUCTION OF EIGHTH PICTURE COMPLIES WITH THE
CONTRACT FOR THIS YEAR. UNLESS SUPPLEMENTAL CONTRACT AGREEABLE
TO ME AND MY MANAGER HARRY WURTZEL IS OFFERED AM NOT RETURNING
UNTIL JULY FIRST. REMAINDER OF TIME IS MY OWN. ANY INTERFERENCE
THEREWITH BY YOU WILL BE ACCOUNTABLE IN DAMAGES.

Gene then left for Kansas, where he'd booked several performances for his trio
(with Frankie and Goon). A formal letter from Republic on the twenty-first
notified him that "the statements contained in your telegram are absolutely
baseless and without foundation. In as much as our contract with you calls for
your exclusive services, regardless of any series, we are entitled to all of your
time, fifty-two weeks a year." The letter threatened legal action to prevent
Gene from performing elsewhere and a suit filed against him for damages. The
studio then contacted the Department of Motor Vehicles to track down his

license plate numbers; and after determining the location of Gene's bookings, wired the theaters that

GENE AUTRY UNDER EXCLUSIVE CONTRACT TO US AND ANY SUCH PERSONAL APPEARANCE IS NOT AUTHORIZED AND WE SHALL INDEAVOR [*SIC*] TO PREVENT SAME BY RESTRAINING ORDER AND OTHER PROCEEDINGS.

Republic meant business, but so did Gene, who wired back two days later:

AM READY TO LEAVE FOR HOLLYWOOD PROVIDING YOU WILL TALK TO ME ON ADJUSTING MY CONTRACT ON MY ARRIVAL. WILL MEET YOU HALF WAY ON ANY FAIR DEAL.

Blowing his top, Levine charged:

YOU APPARENTLY ARE STILL WORKING UNDER THE DELUSION THAT YOU ARE DOING BUSINESS WITH CHILDREN, AND THAT YOU FEEL THAT YOU HAVE THE PRIVILEGE OF WALKING OUT ON US AND DOING ANYTHING YOU DESIRE EVEN THO [*SIC*] IT DOES NOT MEET WITH OUR APPROVAL. . . . WE CERTAINLY ARE NOT GOING TO BE COERCED INTO MAKING ANY ADJUSTMENT ON OUR CONTRACT. . . . OUR CONTRACT WITH YOU IS FAIR AND REASONABLE TAKING EVERYTHING INTO CONSIDERATION. IF YOU DON'T AGREE YOU HAVE THE PRIVILEGE OF DISCUSSING IT PERSONALLY WITH ME.

Republic then filed injunctions preventing Gene's Kansas performances, and he returned to Hollywood, where the standoff and the correspondence continued: Republic sent its standard option renewals to both Gene and Smiley; demanded reimbursement for various petty expenses; and charged Gene $14,325.60 as reimbursement for "damage suffered by us to date hereof due to your failure, refusal and neglect to perform your required services." Gene's letter in response stated: "I beg to state that I am not indebted to your company in any amount of money whatever . . . on the contrary, you and/or Mascot Pictures Corporation have breached its contract with me and is indebted to me in the sum of $900 for salary due under contract up to June 30, 1936; $22.45 for royalties on sale of music from M. M. Cole Publishing Company; and damages for your wrongful interference with my personal appearance tour at the rate of approximately $1,000 per week, from the twenty-third day of May, 1926, together with advertising fees in connection therewith in the approximate sum of $180."

These very personal attacks and recriminations would continue to play out, resurfacing every few years (with new players) until Gene finally left Republic in 1947. Gene soon discovered that Herb Yates would be even "tougher" to deal with than a dam in Arizona or the vindictiveness of Nat Levine—who would depart Republic (a million dollars' richer) in 1937, following his own disputes with Yates. Levine's position as president would be taken by Yates's man in New York, Moe Siegel.[10]

Finally, on July 8, 1936, Gene signed a new contract with Republic, requiring solely his services as an "artist" (and no longer stipulated to provide songs for his movies). Republic's signatory was producer Jack Fier, who would resign in 1937 and be replaced by Moe's brother, Sol. The previous lawsuit and injunctions against Gene and his countersuits were dropped and his back pay tendered. Most important, he was guaranteed a new salary of two thousand dollars per picture, eventually escalating, by 1942, to ten thousand dollars with six-month option renewals. The terms were improved throughout, with clauses stipulating that Gene could pursue music and performance ventures outside his movie making (a minimum of eight pictures per year) and that all income from such outside ventures was his to keep. Four days later, *Oh, Susannah!* would finally start production under the terms of the new contract.

With Republic capitulating rather than risk losing its number-one star, Gene had won this match—at least round one.

22

THE SINGING COWBOY

GENE'S FAME WAS SPREADING FASTER THAN A PRAIRIE FIRE, as Republic released one new musical Western each month, in January, March, April, and May of 1936. The title of the picture issued on May 11, *The Singing Cowboy*, clearly identified the national trend Gene had initiated. In the comic ranch romance mode, *The Singing Cowboy* features plenty of musical interludes, with Gene performing hits spanning his career and styles—from "True Blue Bill" to "When the Bunkhouse Is Empty Tonight" to "I'll Be Thinking of You, Little Gal." Its plot centers on Gene's attempt to raise money to save an injured young cowgirl and solve the murder of her father, using modernistic television transmissions to broadcast his music and catch the killer (played by Lon Chaney Jr. in his screen debut).

Winning the contract battle with Republic had increased Gene's confidence, but it also reminded him of how quickly the rug could be pulled out from under him. No longer worried about financial solvency, he now worked toward accruing wealth and establishing an unassailable multifaceted career. Due to his box-office success, Republic began increasing the budgets to elevate the production values of Gene's Westerns. After completing another period piece, *Ride, Ranger, Ride* in mid-August, he would embark on a large-scale tour of Texas. It would culminate in an appearance at Dallas's Texas Centennial, which would be filmed on location as the centerpiece of *The Big Show*, billed as Republic's first Gene Autry "Special."

While Gene kept busy making movies and traveling, his family had adjusted to Hollywood life. Gene and Ina Mae encouraged Veda and Wilma (whom Gene nicknamed "Bill") to learn a trade, so they attended a nearby beauty school. There, the strong-willed Veda, a 5' 3" brunette, met a dashing Sicilian immigrant seven years her senior: Bartolomeo "Benny" Coppola had been Rudolph Valentino's double in silent pictures but had switched professions since "talkies" came in. The two married later that year, and Benny opened his own beauty shop. "Bill," tall and lanky with tinted auburn hair, began dating Erik Gleissner, born in Copenhagen in 1903. An entrepreneur, he had migrated first to Canada, then California. Wilma and Erik would marry in 1937, with the ceremony presided over by Smiley's parents, now relocated to the San Fernando Valley. "Ina was so relieved," when Veda and Wilma left the nest, recalled Virginia (Long) MacPhail "because she had to feed them, and when they'd come home, she'd have something fixed for dinner, but they'd get into the refrigerator and eat it all up before she could serve it."[1]

Tall and thin like his father and sister Wilma, fifteen-year-old Dudley had grown into a sweet but aimless teenager who idled away his time, dreaming of becoming a star like his brother. Gene demanded that he pull his own weight, which became public news when the May 28 "Around and About in Hollywood" column of the *Los Angeles Times* ran an item stating "Gene Autry insists that his small brother Dudley earn his own spending money and that is why the youngster is selling papers in front of a Hollywood theater."[2] The itinerant Delbert, in and out of jail, still wandered Texas and Oklahoma. His crimes ranged from writing bad checks to theft to assault (he apparently stabbed his brother-in-law, who, Delbert believed, was abusing his wife—Delbert's sister). At some point, he remarried, but when that brief marriage dissolved, he moved on to Clovis, New Mexico, to work for his brother Homer. There, he met Ruby Estelle Lane, a pretty young woman the same age as his daughter Wilma.

"I just happened to be around—actually in person—when Gene was telling his dad off," Virginia MacPhail remembered. "Ruby was in the picture, and he was going to get married, and Gene told him that if he did, he was on his own. He had taken care of one of his families, and that was all he was going to do. He was so mad at him, and he told him he was not going to raise another family. And of course, that's what they did right away—they had kids. Gene and Ina tried their best to talk Ruby out of marrying him, but she went ahead and did it, and she was kind of sorry later on." Ruby and Delbert wed in 1937, and the couple had the first of three daughters in 1938 (the last in 1956). Needing Gene's help, they eventually relocated to California, where the good son sent Delbert money every month.

Gene and Ina Mae received frequent visitors from home: The Spiveys, the Longs, and Ina's sister Anita and her husband, Russ Karns. Ina liked spending time with fellow transplants such as Virginia and Jack Long, Frankie and Mary Marvin, and Gene's cousin Callie Jane, who worked at a Western magazine owned by Gene's friends Fred Harman and Curley Fletcher. Ina enjoyed dressing up in glamorous gowns, but she felt intimidated by the Hollywood so-phisticates she met at celebrity functions.

"Ina was just down-to-earth, nothing put on about her," remembered Dorothy Phillips Bowman, who became Gene's first secretary.[3] Ina needed help with Gene's fan mail and correspondence, and Dorothy, who was a ste-nographer at Republic, took the job. A willowy brunette, Dorothy started her seven-year tenure with Gene at twenty dollars a week. They agreed that as his salary increased, so would hers. He rented an office at 6305 Yucca Street, in the Postal Life Building near the Knickerbocker Hotel. There, in a room on the second floor, the cheery stenographer assisted Gene and Ina with their busi-ness affairs, and also handed bookkeeping and general clerical duties. Dorothy soon became a good friend to them both. That summer Gene got a new "client," Max Terhune, a talented ventriloquist, cardsharp, magician, and mimic. He had worked with Max on the WLS *Barn Dance* and recommended him for a part in *Ride, Ranger, Ride*. Impressed, the studio had signed Terhune, renowned for mimicking "anything from a mosquito to a train." On August 21 Gene, as his manager, signed an agreement with the studio to receive 10 percent of Max's earnings. The card-trick specialist, who didn't sing, acted in several of Gene's films with his dummy "Elmer," and eventually starred as one of the Three Mesquiteers, protagonists of a popular Republic Western series that at one time included John Wayne and Bob Steele. As Gene's income increased, he set up a separate bank account for Ina, in which was deposited half of his earn-ings. Beginning with his 1936 tax returns, Gene would split his income equally with Ina, which that year totaled almost $24,000 (before expenses). This served both as a tax benefit because of community property regulations, but also as a sign of appreciation for Ina's support and council.

In his position of Hollywood cowboy star, Gene continued to improve and add to his buckaroo trappings. At the beginning of the year in Chicago, he had bought a 1936 Buick Club Sedan, trading in his two-year-old model. When he first came to Hollywood, he had purchased a 200-acre ranch off Balboa Av-enue near Chatsworth in the San Fernando Valley. He kept his horses there, and he'd since spent $2,000 building a barn and outbuildings, and $1,200 for a frame ranch house adjoined by an indoor riding arena. Now, he added a $1,000 stallion to the herd and bought a supply of custom, hand-tooled leather saddles and tack. For Champion he ordered a custom bit decorated with miniature guns and a bridle with green onyx handles. His fanciest saddle, for which he'd paid $815 in 1934, featured intricate leather carvings of Western scenes and sterling silver embellishment. For his upcoming tours, he bought a $2,000 horse trailer with air conditioning, leather-padded walls, and a cork-lined floor to protect the horse's hooves.

Gene also invested in his wardrobe, spending $500 on custom cowboy ap-parel, an amount that would more than triple over the next two years. He had vowed to always dress Western in public ever since first meeting cowboy star

Hoot Gibson, attired in a loud sports shirt and two-toned shoes, looking nothing like a buckaroo. The Colonel W. T. Johnson Rodeo, in Dallas, which required its bronc busters to wear bright-colored cowboy shirts, had impressed Gene and inspired him to choose flashy designs for his personal appearances. Rodeo Ben, based in Philadelphia, worked with Gene on designing imaginatively detailed shirts, with unique piping and, in a few years, lavish embroidery. Together, Rodeo Ben and Gene even devised a special lacing that resembled railroad tracks to decorate his shirts. In the San Fernando Valley, he found Nathan Turk, on Ventura Boulevard, who tailored exquisite Western-accented suits, reminiscent of the sartorial splendor of Tom Mix. After receiving a pair of custom boots as a gift from the governor of Texas, Gene began ordering his fancy, pictorial boots from the Lucchese Boot Company in San Antonio.

Dressed in his best gear and backed by Frankie, Goon, and Smiley, Gene spent two weeks in July touring the tiny towns of Oklahoma, appearing at places like the Rook Theatre in Watonga, and the Crystal in Okemah. Virginia MacPhail, who occasionally accompanied them, remembered what those road trips were like. "They'd drive all day, take turns, and drive all night straight through," she related.

> One time, we left Tulsa, at 10:00 at night on Saturday and drove into Los Angeles and arrived on Monday morning at about 1:00 AM. It was less than a day and a half. They went fast, and when we stopped for gas, if you wanted anything to eat, you ran in and grabbed whatever you could get your hands on while they were gassing up, and that's all! Gene had a lot of energy, and he liked his work. In the early days when they were going back and forth by car, he was performing at the littlest towns you can imagine and he loved it.[4]

Gene, in fact, would never stop touring. He continued to do personal appearances until 1963, and even after his career as an entertainer ended, he traveled constantly with his baseball team.

The return trip from Oklahoma caused a delay in the production of *Ride, Ranger, Ride*. Gene's car overturned near Roswell, New Mexico, and was totaled. Miraculously, he escaped with only a few cuts and bruises. After completing *Ride, Ranger, Ride*, Gene and his troupe hit the road again for a three-week tour of Texas, beginning in Fort Worth. Gene took with him what the *New York Evening Journal* later described as "the most expensive set ever built for a vaudeville act—a running waterfall before which he stood to sing." "In the history of the Lone Star State, there has been no tour more triumphant," Whitney Williams crowed in *Screen Book*. "Where ever he went vast crowds turned out to see and hail the cowboy star as the state's own, and he was fortunate to escape, literally, with a whole skin. So enthusiastic was the reception accorded him everywhere that even Champion, his trained horse, emerged minus much of its tail and mane."[5] In an illustrated feature in *Screen and Radio Weekly*, the reporter declared "Crosbys and Vallees may come and go. But from where we're sitting, it looks like hillbillies are going on forever." The Singing Cowboy's down-home image was solidified by a biographical profile released by George Goodale to newspapers and magazines: "Gene Autry has the distinction of being top man in the first musical Western movie to hit the silver screen. . . . We asked him how he liked the movie racket. 'It's all right,' he said placidly. 'Long as I can sing and play my guitar, it's real fun. Feel kinda foolish, though, makin' love to some girl I just met up with a little while before.' Gene Autry is real people. He can't figure out the husky young leading men who have valets and such to 'do' for them. 'Shucks!' he declared. 'When I get to the place where I can't take my own boots off, by gosh, I'll have to be in a wheel-chair.' "[6]

GENE AND SMILEY MET THE REPUBLIC CREW IN DALLAS to begin filming *The Big Show*, in which Gene plays a double role—a petulant cowboy star named Tom Ford and the stuntman who eventually replaces him. Republic's press book for the film raved "Never before has a musical Western film contained as many notable names in the cast. Aside from the twenty-one Hollywood players and five noted orchestras, Republic spent several weeks at the Texas Centennial . . . photographing the exposition and as many notables as the director could obtain . . . [including] Governor Scholtz of Florida; Leonard Pack, Captain of the Texas Rangers; the mayor of Dallas; Sally Rand, star fan dancer; Lady Godiva; and the thousand and one stars of circus, vaudeville and legitimate theaters, who were appearing at the Fair." Gene had first met the legendary burlesque star Sally Rand when they both appeared at the Chicago World's Fair in 1933. The two remained friends for decades, and she sometimes appeared in Gene's rodeos. For his two previous films, a different regional hillbilly band had been featured—a Republic ploy to drive the guest group's fans to the theater. Here, there would be three such groups, including the Sons of the Pioneers (with Leonard Slye, a.k.a. Dick Weston, still unbilled at this point), the Beverly Hill Billies, and the Light Crust Doughboys.

With such deluxe productions as *The Big Show*, Republic managed to stay ahead of the pack, as other B-Western studios tried to cash in on the trend. Dick Foran made a dozen for Warners, but "they caused no wave of excitement as Autry's series had," according to *Singing in the Saddle* author Douglas Green.[7] The equally smooth-voiced Fred Scott also fizzled at the tiny Spectrum studio. More in direct competition with Gene was another native Texan, former law school student Tex Ritter. He had starred on Broadway in *Green Grow the Lilacs*, which inspired the musical *Oklahoma!* in the 1940s. (Gene always rued the fact that he could have bought the film rights to *Green Grow the Lilacs* in 1939 but didn't want to spend the $15,000.) Ritter's deep baritone attracted Uncle Art, who recorded him unsuccessfully for ARC. Tex's movies, beginning with *Song of the Gringo* in 1936, for "Poverty Row" studio Grand National could not compete with the more accomplished Republic pictures. In the late 1930s, the press wrote that there was a rivalry between Gene and Tex, but the two remained chummy over the years.

Many now-forgotten singing cowboys came and went, including Smith Ballew and Bob Baker; a year before Gene's debut, in 1933, John Wayne starred as Singin' Sandy Sanders, with his vocalizing dubbed in. Republic's two top leading men would frequently kid each other about this in years to come: "Just think, Gene, if I hadn't quit singin', you wouldn't have happened!" Wayne joked. "Well, Duke, it wasn't my singing that made me a star," Gene snapped back. "It was my *acting*!"[8]

Another personality not usually associated with singing cowboys, Bing Crosby made the big-budget *Rhythm on the Range* in 1936 for Paramount. His wry version of "Home on the Range" was already a staple on radio's *The Hit Parade*. The fact that Paramount jumped into musical Westerns demonstrated the impact Republic's Autry films were making in Hollywood. "Although Crosby attracted an audience entirely different from Autry's, both singers contributed enormously to the interest in cowboys, the West, and western music that permeated the country in the middle 1930s," Green points out.[9] Quite collegial, Gene and Bing would eventually share a backing band, the Cass County Boys, in the 1940s and in 1948 co-host a star-studded Christmas radio special on CBS.

Gene's final release of 1936, *The Old Corral*, also features Sons of the Pioneers and includes an amusing fight sequence in which Gene pummels Dick Weston and forces him to sing. The following year, renamed Roy Rogers, the fledgling actor would assume Gene's role in a picture amid another Autry versus Republic battle: In Roy Rogers, Republic would create the only other singing cowboy star of Gene's stature.

In November Gene shot his ninth picture of the year, *Round-Up Time in Texas*, which gave Smiley as much screen time as Gene. Set in South Africa, the film includes a wacky sequence with Smiley disguised as a medicine man ordered to cure the tribal chief's son. A youthful black vocal group, the Cabin Kids, play the Zulu chieftain's children. This was Smiley's first film as a married man. The previous year, he had met a columnist for the *Hollywood Citizen News* at a party in Griffith Park. Also an Illinois native, Dallas MacDonnell was twelve years Smiley's senior. Immediately smitten, she wrote about him in her next column: "Gene plays leads and Smiley is the comedy relief, and both boys have been getting some fine notices for their work. Smiley has just bought a ranch in San Fernando Valley and resides there with his equally nice father and mother. He came out here only a year ago and his progress in films has been exceptionally rapid. One of these days, a major film concern is bound to realize what a gold mine this talented lad is."[10]

The couple fell in love, and Smiley worked extra jobs such as providing the voice for Columbia's "Barney Google" cartoons to save money for marriage. They finally tied the knot on October 25 after an arduous journey to Santa Ana that included a flat tire and a taxi to the church. "Smiley was always telling jokes when he came into the office," Dorothy Phillips Bowman remembered decades later, "and he'd have something new to spring on us. One day he came in and sprung this on us: He was in Dallas last night—of course, that happened to be her name!"

A family atmosphere prevailed around the Autry office—with Virginia MacPhail sometimes stopping by to help with typing, George Goodale pulling pranks, and Gene humming a tune as he signed correspondence. Similarly, Gene remembered his Republic shoots as

> a big country picnic actually. It was a very close-knit family. . . . I had a wonderful crew that I worked with. I was always very close to the crew. . . . When we'd go on location to shoot my films, we used to sit around after the day's work and we'd have maybe a drink or two and then we'd play cards. I used to like to play poker, because I'd sit around and relax. And we'd play poker sometimes until twelve o'clock . . . you get five hours of sleep and get right up and start working the next morning by six-thirty. You think nothing about it . . . long days. There were no unions at first, and we would shoot twelve hours a lot of times, from the time the sun came up until it went down.[11]

GENE AND INA HAD BECOME FRIENDLY with producer Mandy Schaefer and his wife, Audrey. Although Mandy had been a skeptic when he first worked with Gene at Mascot, he was won over the first time he saw him perform for a large audience at a rodeo. The crowd had been ecstatic. The box-office success of the Autry films, of course, convinced him further. Schaefer and Gene would eventually form their own Flying A Productions in 1948.

Occasionally, Ina stopped by the Republic lot, but she never went on location with Gene. From his touring days in Chicago, she was used to staying behind. She and Gene were anxious to have children, but to their great disappointment discovered that they were unable to conceive. Upon being tested, Gene was found to be sterile, possibly from a childhood case of the mumps. Ina threw herself into furthering his career and devoting herself to being his helpmate. "She loved everything she did for Gene," Dorothy said. "He didn't realize how much she loved him, I don't think. She told me how they got married on the quick, and that she had a tear in her dress, but they got married anyway. Afterward, she picked out what she wanted in a wedding ring . . . she got a nice one. They didn't mix with the movie crowd in Hollywood much at all. They never put on any high-falutin' stuff."[12]

As they celebrated the end of Gene's first full year in Hollywood, Gene and Ina had no way of knowing that his fame was only just beginning.

23

PUBLIC COWBOY NO. 1

GENE BEGAN 1937 TOURING NONSTOP THROUGHOUT OKLAHOMA. During the third week of January, he took Champion with him to appear on Oklahoma City radio station WKY. The host of the program featuring Gene was his old friend Johnny Marvin, billed as "The Lonesome Singer of the Air." Once his pop hits had fizzled, Marvin had recorded a few hillbilly sessions with Frankie, then left New York and joined WKY the previous April. Captioned "A Whinny Goes on the Air," a photograph of Johnny, Gene, and Champ appeared in the local paper, noting that this "was believed to be the first time a horse has participated in a studio broadcast." More fortuitous for Gene was the reunion with his early mentor: Gene needed Johnny's assistance with songs and arrangements for his upcoming pictures and recordings. In September, Johnny would join him in Hollywood, and together they would caress Gene's music into a smoother, more lush Western sound. Also, Johnny would introduce Gene to his WKY protégé, Jimmy Wakely—soon to form a Western trio including guitarist Johnny Bond. They, too, would move to California and there become Gene's primary backing group on radio and recordings for several years; Bond would be his collaborator for nearly two decades.

In Texas that spring, Gene built another new relationship that would benefit him in many ways in years to come. This friendship began with Gene giving his support to a man who would become a powerful ally. In March, Lyndon Baines Johnson—at twenty-eight, two years younger than Gene—was running for his first seat in Congress, to represent the tenth district of Texas. He had found a mentor in Congressman Sam Rayburn, who had started his formidable political career in 1912 in tiny Bonham, Texas, spitting distance from Tioga. "Mr. Sam," as he was known, was the local hero whom Gene and many other rural Texans hailed and revered. Rayburn had never forgotten his roots or the impoverished farmers who were his constituents. In 1931 he had become chairman of the Committee on Interstate and Foreign Commerce and would play a critical role in passing much of FDR's New Deal legislation. The fifty-four-year-old Rayburn kept abreast of the achievements of former local boys like Gene.

"Back in 1937," Gene remembered, "Mr. Sam Rayburn, who was my congressman from my district in Texas, called and said there was a young man down there from Austin runnin' for Congress and could use a little help. Mr. Rayburn asked if I'd go down and help. So I went down with my guitar and a couple of musicians and we stayed with young Lyndon maybe two weeks."[1]

Lyndon and his wife, Lady Bird, put the trio up at their Austin home, and Gene and his act accompanied the candidate to various campaign rallies, performing rousing numbers on the back of a flatbed truck. The appearance of the Singing Cowboy enticed numerous voters to the gatherings as did the free beer and barbecue. On April 10, Lyndon B. Johnson won the election. Once LBJ was entrenched in Washington, it was only a matter of time before he and Mr. Sam introduced Gene to President Roosevelt.[2]

Gene's stature in Hollywood had continued to rise. "Hail the western star! . . . Give him the least opportunity in the way of good production or good stories, and he will bring in a larger revenue proportionately than that of the majority of greater and more pretentious personalities," the *Los Angeles Times* pronounced. "One of the fan magazines recently reported, for example, that Gene Autry, a relative newcomer, receives as many mentions in incoming missives as Jeanette MacDonald and Bob Taylor . . . Autry has scored a skyrocket hit. Evidently he is the Taylor and Tyrone Power of the horse operas. . . . His singing has apparently endeared him to the women folk." Another paper later reported that "in one recent month Autry received 2,728 fan letters, topping his closet rival Tyrone Power by more than a thousand."[3]

Gene hadn't cut many records the year before, with only two Los Angeles sessions, totaling six songs, in all of 1936: Among the highlights were *Guns and Guitars'* title tune (credited to Gene and Republic screenwriter Oliver Drake) and "Ridin' All Day," by Smiley, who also contributed the delightful cowpoke yodeler, "I'll Go Ridin' Down That Old Texas Trail." Gene and Smiley's poignant "Mother, Here's a Bouquet for You," perhaps inspired by Nora Autry ("how we've missed you since you've gone above"), was not released.

In 1937 Gene made up for lost time, booking nine studio sessions, beginning in Los Angeles on March 22. As on the previous year's outings, he used his trio—Frankie on steel guitar, Art Davis on fiddle, and Charles Sargent on guitar. A bluesy "The Convict's Dream" ("your dad is locked up in the death house") featured Frankie for the first time on electric steel guitar. Two months later, while in Chicago, Gene spent two days in the studio, cutting ten songs.

The nostalgic Western ballads came from a variety of sources. Among them were Pee Wee King and J. L. Frank, Gene's former manager now King's father-in-law, who contributed "End of My Round-Up Days." Frankie's electric steel guitar predominated, at times overpowering Art's fiddle. Jimmy Long joined Gene on five tunes, three of which ARC released: the Western duets "With a Song in My Heart" and "I Hate to Say Goodbye to the Prairie," and the sentimental "When the Golden Leaves Are Falling." The latter, waxed on June 2, marks Jimmy's last known recording with Gene.

By June Gene had completed three more films, and his agent Harry Wurtzel began negotiations for improved terms for his option renewal with Republic. Big plans were under way for his next picture, *Public Cowboy No. 1*, which would reunite him with Ann Rutherford, who had signed with MGM and was on loan. Nat Levine had left Republic the previous year, but his frequent director Joe Kane was on board. The film's budget would be the biggest so far of Gene's career: $40,000. *Public Cowboy No. 1* combines the typical Western plot of cattle rustling with a new angle: the rustlers use short-wave radio, refrigerator trucks, a high-powered sedan, a truck filled with saddled horses, and a monoplane to carry out their scheme. The victimized ranchers' cattle seem to vanish into thin air. The theme of Old West versus new-fangled modernism is extended in that the sheriff (played by silent cowboy star William Farnum) is criticized by uppity newspaper reporter Helen Morgan (Ann Rutherford) as being too old and out of touch to solve the crime. To counter her, Gene sings "The West Ain't What It Used to Be," custom-written for the picture by Fleming Allen, a friend from WLS. Urban detectives with police cars are called in to replace Sheriff Doniphan. Gene proves that, combined with a little contemporary know-how (his radio broadcast, *Dragnet* style, recruits assistance, "Calling all cowboys, calling all cowboys"), old-school methods still prevail—he and Champion join the sheriff on horseback and catch the rustlers (while the cops end up in overturned vehicles).

Rutherford detected more assurance in Gene's acting since their last picture together, *Comin' 'Round the Mountain*, in February of '36, and noticed his horsemanship had improved as well. "He was getting acquainted with the fine points of riding," she later remarked, "and he got real good at it. He looked wonderful in the saddle. . . . You know, up to that time, many of the cowboys looked grubby—but Gene was in the white hat, and he also sang so pretty . . . Gene had what my mother used to call a real 'come out of the kitchen' voice. When he sang on radio, if you were out in the kitchen and you heard him, you knew right away who it was!"[4] This would be the last pairing of Gene and Ann, who went on to play one of Scarlet O'Hara's sisters in *Gone With the Wind*.

By *Public Cowboy*'s completion on June 28, Wurtzel had negotiated Gene's pay increase to $5,000 per film, with "$250 paid per picture for the use of his wardrobe, horses and trailer, and for any and all publicity for which he is personally responsible," according to an interoffice memo at Republic. By year's end, this extra fee would add $1,267.50 to his Republic salary of $29,590.42, making him the studio's highest-paid contract player. Among the top-earning Hollywood stars of 1937, Fredric March earned $484,687, Greta Garbo $472,499, Marlene Dietrich $370,000, and Joan Crawford $351,538. In comparison, Gene's fan-mail rival Tyrone Power was paid $88,691; child superstar Shirley Temple grossed $110,256; and crooner-turned-actor Al Jolson made $85,424.[5]

The first film after Gene's salary increase, *Boots and Saddles*, began production on July 29 at the foot of Mount Whitney, near Lone Pine, California. Gene made numerous pictures at the location over the years, and he often spoke fondly of the area. *Boots and Saddles* ran over budget, from the planned $42,179 to $43,483. Shortly after it wrapped on August 9, Wurtzel ruffled Republic's feathers with the request that Gene be given a month's leave in September to make a picture for Paramount. The studio's reply, in no uncertain terms, was: "Our contract with Gene Autry definitely provides that he may not render services for anyone other than ourselves in connection with motion pictures." Over the next few months, a flurry of rumors ran in the *Times* and elsewhere: Gene's new salary "was $7,500 per picture"; "there was no truth to the rumor that he was leaving Republic for Paramount"; "Darryl Zanuck is reputed to have offered Republic $500,000 for Autry's contract," "Gene Autry . . . denies he is leaving Republic"; "Herbert Yates . . . sends out wires to all his exchanges [exhibitors] to deny that Paramount had signed his singing cowboy star Gene Autry."[6] Gene's growing fame also resulted in his winning a guest spot on NBC's high-profile radio program, "Rudy Vallee's Variations," hosted by his longtime idol, on July 22. (Gene returned to the show on October 21, earning $1,648.50 for the two appearances.)

Republic's concession to Gene's pursuit of outside film projects was to offer him a cameo in its top feature, categorized by the studio as an "anniversary special": *Manhattan Merry-Go-Round*, starring Phil Regan and Leo Carrillo. Other cameos included Cab Calloway, Louis Prima, and Joe DiMaggio—the latter doing a monologue, which thrilled Gene, who mingled with as many baseball players as possible. Gene's contribution was a most modern "It's Round-Up Time in Reno," with humorous lyrics about soon-to-be-divorced cowgirls. In a scene where Regan, duded up in furry chaps, joins Gene's band for a solo, the contrast between authentic cowboy singer and overblown pop crooner is striking. (Regan and Gene would remain friends, with Gene coming to Regan's aid in the 1960s when the crooner hit bottom, winding up in prison.)

On November 5, *Boots and Saddles* became the first Autry picture to play a Broadway movie house. In the *New York Times* review (another first for an Autry film), snooty critic Bosley Crowther skewered it:

It may be that we shall all eventually rue the day when the horse opera first became vocal. At any rate, a picture which has a marked resemblance to a signpost pointed grimly toward an era in which leather breeches will invariably denote leather lungs has just arrived at the Globe Theatre, under the premonitory title of *Boots and Saddles*. Its star is that personable and pleasant-voiced singing cowboy, Gene Autry, who is said to have one of the most formidable fan followings in the nation, but its supporting musical interludes, full of Latin-American hip swinging, range from indifferent to bad, and its story, involving Gene's effort to sell horses to the army, in order to save the old "rawnch" for its youthful English owner, is one of the least justifiable of the year, especially as a libretto for livestock.

Regardless of Crowther's negative critique, it was clear Gene had arrived—and his popularity was expanding from rural to urban areas. Chicago had embraced him early on, thanks to his history at WLS and his many return visits to perform in the area. His personal appearance fees at risen to a $350-a-day flat fee, or a $250 guarantee with a 50/50 split of the daily gross. In May he had headlined the prestigious Chicago Theater, and the *Chicago Daily News* had reported that Brunswick (now an ARC subsidiary, issuing Gene's discs on its Vocalion imprint) sold "more of his records of western ballads than the platter of any other singers. One tune, when recorded, hit 50,000 sales in the first month." (Another paper reported "That Silver Haired Daddy" had reached a half-million in sales.)[7] On November 21 Gene got his first major feature in the *Chicago Sunday Tribune*, illustrated with three large photos of the singing cowboy. It was the first of hundreds of articles to come that included the fictitious story of Will Rogers's discovery of Gene.

The article's author, Rosalind Shaffer, gave a detailed description of her subject: "We accepted luncheon with him one noon recently," she wrote,

and we were surprised when a mild-mannered, medium-sized, brown-haired chap with gray-blue eyes quietly appeared in the doorway. . . . Gene is a westerner all right even if his Lone Star drawl has been somewhat smoothed by several years of urban living. He's proud of his cowhand background and off screen wears specially cut western suits, distinctive rather than ostentatious, cut along the lines of equestrian clothing. Gene does not own a civilian suit to his name except for a tuxedo he bought when he wanted to escort a young lady to a nightclub. His suit that day was a quiet-toned gray from which specially made high-heeled lether [*sic*] boots protruded. A gray shirt striped in black, and set off by a conservative bandana, peeked out from the vest. The star's only concession to wild-west flamboyancy was a distinctive white low-crown sombrero. . . . Autry is looking ahead to the time when westerns will show in the big cities instead of being confined to smaller towns and side street theaters, as they are now. . . . He thinks pictures with rich natural settings will bring into the cramped life of metropolitan dwellers a greater appreciation of the open prairie and create in them the urge to get closer to the grandeur of the west.[8]

GENE'S SOUND HAD SUDDENLY ATTAINED MORE GRANDEUR—documented that fall by some of the most exquisitely rendered recordings of his career to date. In Los Angeles, on October 11, he delved into the Hawaiian music craze, using his rich romantic baritone with a hint of vibrato: "The One Rose (That's Left in My Heart)," which Gene had attempted in Chicago in May, here comes across nuanced, emotive, and intimate. Its subtle instrumental backing cushions Gene's voice rather than competes with it (as in the previous rendition). The other lush island ode, "Blue Hawaii," had been the primary number in Bing Crosby's recent hit film, *Waikiki Wedding*.[9] Gene's artistic phrasing indicates he had been listening closely to Der Bingle's records.

Johnny Marvin, by then ensconced in Hollywood, helped Gene make the transition into a more sophisticated style that maintained Gene's vocal warmth. Serving as musical contractor, he selected musicians, wrote arrangements, and composed songs (with Gene usually credited as co-writer). Johnny carefully merged his pop sensibility with Gene's Western style, resulting in a sound pleasing to Gene's rural fans but also to mainstream America. Marvin's masterful songwriting would provide Gene with a slew of hits, including the Autry co-write "Dust," another highlight of the October 11 session. Instantly memorable with its compelling melody and sing-along lyrics, "Dust" features the expressive, sprightly violin of Carl Cotner. A twenty-one-year-old prodigy from Indiana, Cotner had first crossed paths with Gene during a midwestern tour in 1935. The buoyant Marvin-Autry number "Listen to the Rhythm of the Range" also features Cotner's spirited violin and Autry and Marvin's lighthearted lyrics. The instrumental breakdown, prefaced by Gene's "Play it, boys," gives a nod to the increasingly popular Western swing sound pioneered in Texas by Bob Wills, the Light Crust Doughboys, and Milton Brown. An ear-pleasing, toe-tapping anomaly, Marvin's "Down in the Land of Zulu" showcases Heinie Gunkler's jazzy clarinet. The minor-key, klezmer-style number was sung by Smiley in the just completed *Springtime in the Rockies*. Also prominently featuring Gunkler and Cotner on record are the tongue-in-cheek "It's Round-Up Time in Reno" and the pop ballad, "Were You Sincere?"—where Gene employs his "Bingest" croon.

The crew, minus Gunkler, returned a week later to record theme songs of Gene's two recent pictures: "Take Me Back to My Boots and Saddle" and "Springtime in the Rockies" both come alive with rousing choruses provided by the Marvins and other uncredited vocalists. On November 24 Gene spent one more day in the studio for his final session of the year, again singing with dulcet tones, backed by a vocal group and strings. The result was a double-sided hit, "Sail Along, Silv'ry Moon" backed with "There's a Gold Mine in the Sky"— the future title song for a 1938 picture featuring a cameo by Pee Wee King. Its New York–based composers, Charles and Nick Kenny, would provide numerous hits for Gene into the 1950s. Gene's last recording of the year was the nostalgic "At the Old Barn Dance," the title of his feature, which was to start production in three days.

It had been two months since Gene wrapped *Springtime in the Rockies*, which was released on November 15. Gene's co-star, the seductive Polly Rowles, had made quite an impression on her leading man, according to Art

Davis, who plays a bit part in the picture. "Gene had a little crush on her," he remembered, "but she was a head taller than him, and [instead] we had a thing going." The affair ended badly, though, with Art getting beaten up by another suitor "who looked like a wrestler." Gene got the last laugh, however, said Art. "I had two black eyes from where he hit me . . . Gene found out about it, and do you think there's anything that's going to make him happier!" As a joke, Gene hired an artist (probably Till Goodan, who designed his annual cowboy Christmas cards) to re-create the fight in a drawing, which was printed on cards and mailed to Art's friends. "We had our teeth capped in those days," said Art, "and in the picture [on the card], Polly is standing over me and this guy's hitting me in the mouth, and she's saying, 'Oh, please, don't knock his caps off!' "[10]

Springtime received a rave from the New York *Daily News*, when it played a second-run theater in the Big Apple. Calling it "the brightest Gene Autry picture this observer can remember," the reviewer added, "that's saying something because these Autry hoss operas come along as often as New York parades."[11] Gene's follow-up, *The Old Barn Dance*, includes a parade of musical guests, Walter Shrum and His Colorado Hillbillies, the Maple City Four (from WLS), and Dick Weston of Sons of the Pioneers. It would be Gene's last picture for nearly six months. After it wrapped, Gene told Joe Kane, who had just directed his fourteenth Autry film, "Don't break your neck getting ready for the next picture, because I won't be there."[12] Even before filming started, Republic had been battling Wurtzel over Gene's refusal to commit to making two more pictures in December and January, a period he always reserved for personal appearance tours. In fact, according to the *Los Angeles Times*, "Gene Autry, who has a large fan following in South America, will leave for a ten weeks' tour of that continent right after the first of the year."[13] The studio, meantime, had announced that Gene's next film would be its biggest special yet: *Washington Cowboy*, with a budget of $175,000.

Soon after finishing *The Old Barn Dance*, Gene headed east, leaving behind a flurry of angry demands from Republic to report to the studio. It is unclear exactly where he was when the news came. On December 21, announced in nearly every newspaper in the land, it became official: Gene Autry was, in effect, Public Cowboy No. 1. Every year, trade publications *Motion Picture Herald* and *Box Office* conducted a nationwide poll rating the most popular film stars, by surveying "independent theatre owners, motion picture editors, civic organizations and other interested groups," according to the *New York Times*. For 1937, in the action melodrama category of the poll, Gene Autry, who the year before had trailed Buck Jones and George O'Brien, was voted first place.[14] Overnight, the stakes were higher than ever before.

24

STRIKE!

ENE'S LIFE IN THE OPENING DAYS OF 1938 seemed like something out of, well, a Gene Autry movie. Both he and Republic notified the press that he had gone on strike. As he made his way to bookings across the country, a posse on his trail sought to prevent his shows with injunctions filed by Republic Pictures. It was a repeat performance of 1936, but this time Gene was hot property and he knew it. "They chased him all over the South—he was very big in the South," Joe Kane remembered. "Process servers tried to catch him. He was so popular in these small towns, the people would just surround those process servers and gently walk them out of town. They never did catch him."[1]

Gene wanted another salary increase, but Herb Yates refused to budge and suspended him for not reporting to work in December. Gene was further angered over a Republic practice called "block booking": in order to rent the latest Autry picture, an exhibitor had to pay for a package including other, less popular Republic films. On January 27 Gene's complaints were aired in the *Los Angeles Times*: "From Nashville, Tenn., Gene Autry opened fire with his trusty six-shooter on Republic, declaring that his pictures are being used as leverage in selling other output of that organization. The Autry challenge (wired) says:

> My effort to get a salary raise has met with the statement from the studio that my films don't get much money in the exhibition field, despite the fact that the box-office reports have proved them to be leaders among westerns. It is known that my pictures are being used as a blackjack to force exhibitors into buying other Republic productions and on this tour I've found out exhibitors are greatly discontented because of this procedure.[2]

The process servers caught up with Gene in Nashville, and on February 4, Chancellor R. B. C. Howell issued a temporary restraining order in Chancery Court that prohibited him from doing performances for anyone other than Republic. Following the ruling, Gene, who bore no ill will toward Judge Howell over his predicament, dined with the chancellor at the Belle Meade Country Club.[3] He had learned the benefits of rubbing shoulders with members of local law enforcement and the judicial system, as well as congressmen, governors, and—soon—U.S. presidents.

Gene did not want to cancel his three, sold-out performances at Nashville's 2,000-seat theater, the Paramount. "I took [a] look at the summons," Gene wrote in his memoir,

> and I said, well, the law is very clear, and you don't mess with the law unless you have your own army, so I won't go on the stage. And I didn't. What I did was put Champion up there, and Smiley Burnette, and whatever group we had with us, and I . . . sat in the front row . . . and put Champ through his paces. So the show went on. It had been announced to the crowd, of course, that I had been served and could not perform. But people enjoy being a part of events that are out of the ordinary pattern, and they reacted warmly to everything we did.[4]

Gene "paid his admission like any other patron," the *New York Times* reported that week, "and held receptions for the customers in the foyer. The system was not overly successful, for theatre managers felt uneasy in their realization that they were outwitting a Federal Court."[5]

The battle continued to be waged in the press. The *Chicago Daily News* reported that "Sol Siegel, top hand at Republic, insisted that [Autry's $5,000 salary] was plenty. The picture which Autry should be starring in now is entitled 'Washington Cowboy.' Seigel has found another cowhand who can croon named Roy Rogers who will take Autry's part. Siegel said the movies make the cowboys, not vice versa, and that Roy Rogers would be as big a star in a year as Autry. . . . Autry claims that nearly all the other movie cowhands earn more money than he does. Buck Jones, for instance, draws $16,500 for each picture."[6] Gene announced he planned to return to Hollywood, cancel his contract, and sign with another studio. Elsewhere it was reported he would be touring South America for five thousand dollars a week. A Republic spokesman told the *Los Angeles Times* that the studio had been grooming Rogers, its twenty-five-year-old "discovery" purportedly from Cody, Wyoming, for four months.

Roy Rogers, of course, was none other than Ohio-born Leonard Slye, aka Dick Weston, who had played bit parts in Gene's films as a member of Sons of the Pioneers and, in *The Old Barn Dance*, on his own. He had been signed as a contract player to Republic on October 13 for seventy-five dollars a week. Even before Gene's strike, Republic had held a casting call for a new singing cowboy because "Gene's contract was up for renewal and the word around town was that he was going to go to the mat to fight for the great raise he thought he deserved," according to Roy. "To put the pressure on Gene to keep his contract demands in line, Republic had set up these auditions."[7] Roy heard about the tryouts and dashed over to the studio where he'd worked as an extra. "I had no agent . . . I just went out there and tried to get in and the security guy wouldn't let me in," he remembered:

> so I waited until the guys started coming back from lunch, and I just walked in with the crowd—I think Smiley was in that group. A hand fell on my shoulder, and I thought, Oh my God, it's the security guard! I turned around and it was Sol Siegel, the producer of all westerns, and I told him I was trying to get in because I knew they were looking for another cowboy . . . and he said, "We are, and we've tested quite a few, and you never once entered my mind until you walked in the door, and that's why I stopped you."[8]

In January, Yates and Siegel began grooming him to replace Gene, dropping "Dick Weston," which they considered too bland, for "Roy Rogers" (after Will).[9] They teamed Roy with Smiley in *Washington Cowboy*, which they re-named *Under Western Stars* for release in April. The film, which predated the similarly plotted *Mr. Smith Goes to Washington* (starring Jimmy Stewart), was about a cowpoke who becomes a congressman to help Dust Bowl farmers and ranchers. The script's key song, "Dust," had already been recorded by Gene for ARC and was copyrighted in his and Johnny Marvin's names. Before negotiations were resolved on Gene's contract, Republic began wrangling for the rights to use the song. The *Los Angeles Times* reported on February 25, "Maybe it's preliminary to making up at Republic, but anyway Gene Autry has sold a song which will be used by Roy Rogers in a picture. . . . Understanding is that things are being ironed out."[10]

Such was not the case—neither party would budge on the contract. Yates, who was notoriously tightfisted, thought cutting off Gene's income would force him to buckle. Gene had, in fact, borrowed two thousand dollars from Republic the previous year to help with his mounting expenses. He had purchased property on Bluffside Drive in North Hollywood, where he and Ina were building their dream house. He also paid $2,281 for his first Cadillac and $3,258 for new trucks and horse trailers. Gene continued to make improvements to his Chatsworth ranch and bought five more horses, bringing his herd to eight. He had hired Tom Mix's old trainer, Johnny Agee—known to be the best in the business—to work with them. Gene bought, for $1,250, a Tennessee Walking Horse named Lindy that Mix had ridden while touring in a circus; the horse was born on May 20, 1927, the day Charles Lindbergh flew from New York to Paris, thus the name. Agee, who had been Barnum and Bailey's horse trainer before joining Mix, had trained the horse specifically for stage and rodeo appearances. Lindy, who looked like Mix's movie steed Tony, became Gene's touring horse. "Johnny went to work for me taking care of all my horses," Gene later said. "He worked the original Champion, too, as to certain tricks he had to do in pictures. When I went on rodeos, I used Lindy because he looked like Champion. He had four stockings and a bald [blaze on his] face."[11] "He was truly one of the finest animals I ever owned and perhaps the most talented and easiest to train of all my Champions. I used him primarily for my stage appearances and in parades because he was even-tempered and well behaved."[12]

With such expenses, the studio hoped to squeeze Gene financially. "They didn't know it, but Autry had a nice nest egg," said Joe Kane. "They thought he was broke. But he was far from broke. Autry was never broke." In addition to his Republic paycheck, Gene had earned $5,000 the previous year from his record and publishing companies, and had his best year yet in personal appearance fees, grossing $17,588. In addition, Gene's star stature had resulted in numerous merchandising and endorsement offers.

In December he had been contacted by Mitchell J. Hamilburg, an agent who handled licensing deals for Edgar Bergen and Deanna Durbin, regarding an offer from the Kenton Hardware Company to manufacture a Gene Autry cap pistol.[13] On December 14 Gene signed a management contract with Hamilburg (who would receive 25 percent of Gene's licensing royalties) and an agreement with Kenton Hardware. The Ohio-based company, founded in the 1890s as a maker of cast-iron banks, had been hard hit by the Depression. As the main employer in Kenton, a town of 7,000, it had cut back to two production days a week. Willard R. Bixler, the founder's son, had devised a plan to save the company. "The idea involved the manufacture of a deluxe cap pistol capable of selling at twice as much as any ordinary cap pistol . . . collecting half a dollar each," according to Bixler. "Why not design the toy after the gun used by some famous movie star?"[14]

Gene would receive 5 percent of the wholesale price for each cap pistol sold. In return he "sent to Kenton the very same pearl-handled gun he uses in his rip-rarin' sagas of the West," said Bixler. "Patterns and molds were made from the weapon and after the expenditure of nearly $10,000, the first cap pistol was ready for market."[15] Gene's signature was emblazoned below the cast-iron gun barrel. Available in February, the cap pistol, advertised as "patterned after the original six shooter of Public Cowboy No. 1," flew off toy store shelves. By August a million cap pistols had been manufactured, with Kenton's plant doubling its work force, operating twenty-four hours a day, to keep up with the demand. During the first year of sales, Gene netted $15,458 in royalties and became a hero to the residents of Kenton, Ohio. On August 8 he visited the town, toured the factory, dined at the Bixlers' home, and played five performances to 4,500 people at the local theater.[16] In 2004 a mural honoring Gene was painted on a wall adjacent to the town square and unveiled during the town's annual Gene Autry Days.

Sears, Roebuck had also expanded its line of Gene Autry guitars to include different sizes and styles, as well as an "Old Santa Fe" arch-top guitar, with

Gene's signature across the front. It became country singer George Jones's favorite instrument growing up: "It was a brand new Gene Autry guitar with a horse and lariat on the front. I took it home and it hardly ever left my hands . . . I've owned countless expensive guitars in my life, but none of them ever meant any more to me than that little Gene Autry model."[17]

M. M. Cole was at work creating a one-hundred-page, deluxe Gene Autry songbook, illustrated with two hundred photographs, including film stills and shots of Gene with celebrities, and including eighty-five compositions. "This book will be one of the [most] outstanding books ever published," Maury Cole wrote Gene in February, "and for this reason we need a great many more songs. . . . Kindly send us every possible song you have on hand. . . . We hope that you have gotten together with the picture people to your satisfaction because we really think you deserve everything."

A line of Gene Autry comics also had been introduced by Dell. And for men there were the Gene Autry Brushless Shaving Cream and Gene Autry Hair Tonic, each of which came with a song booklet. Another company sold Gene Autry cowboy hats. This was just the beginning of hundreds of products, known as "tie-ups," that would become available with the Gene Autry "brand" over the next twenty years.

GENE CONTINUED TO BUILD A LOYAL and very active fan base. Columnist Sheilah Graham wrote that his pictures were shown in ten thousand theaters a week, and the *Los Angeles Times* reported he received forty thousand letters a month.[18] Republic refused to cover the expense of answering fan mail, so Gene hired assistants to help his secretary respond to letters and send out autographed photos. (When Roy Rogers asked the studio for help with his fan mail, Herb Yates advised him to just throw it away.) One avid Autry fan was a young hairdresser in Gary, Indiana, named Dorothy "Dot" Pinnick, who requested permission to form a fan club. In February the Gene Autry Friendship Club was founded with thirty members, each of whom received a quarterly newsletter featuring reports on Gene's latest activities. The well-organized, energetic Dot contacted all the magazines that listed fan clubs, and by the following year the group had grown to four hundred. A decade later, there were regional branches and more than five thousand active members.[19]

On April 4, 1938, Gene returned to chancery court in Nashville and the injunction against his performances was ruled permanent by the judge. En route, he had performed in California, New Mexico, and Texas—tailed by Republic's minions gathering signed affidavits documenting his "illegal" shows. Republic's lawyers presented them to the judge as evidence for citations of contempt of court. A trial date was set. Exactly a month later, in Hollywood, at the annual convention of Republic's distributors, on May 4, sales representatives "climbed all over Yates," Gene wrote in his memoir.

It was going on six months since an Autry movie had been released. . . . Many of them had gone along with the block booking to the extent that they would buy a package of twenty, my eight [pictures per season] plus twelve others. . . . Now they demanded some assurance I would be working for Republic next year. Otherwise, they warned Yates, their theaters would be in trouble. At that point, Yates called. While our attorneys got together and worked out a compromise, we went off to play golf. In a curious way, there were no hard feelings.[20]

Charges were dropped in Nashville, and the case was dismissed. "They finally had to settle with Autry because he wouldn't come back, except on his terms," Joe Kane pointed out. "They paid him what he wanted because they wanted him back."

Herb Yates and Gene Autry arrived "arm in arm" at the convention, followed by Gene wiring Republic's regional salesmen:

I want to convey some real good news to all my friends. Republic has rewritten my contract and for the first time I want to say that I am very happy to be a member of the Republic family. I will work day and night to catch up with the two remaining pictures of last year's program and will work continuously to get the 1938–39 program off with a big bang. Republic is moving ahead so rapidly that it is only a question of time when this bunch will be eating from the same table as the big shots in the business. The Republic organization is young, businesslike, aggressive and no one can keep such a gang of two fisted fighters from progressing rapidly. Republic is going to spend much more money than they have in the past and if you want my quality pictures to continue to improve you must get higher rentals and wider distribution. I know I can depend on you to help me fulfill this desire.

No mention was made of the dissolution of block booking, but Gene got everything else he wanted in his new contract.[21] After completing the two films from the previous season at $6,000 each, his increased salary would be $10,000 per picture, which would escalate every six months. He was guaranteed to have December and January free for his personal appearances, and every six months he could make a picture for another studio.

By May 21 Gene was on location east of Los Angeles at the mountainous Big Bear with Kane, shooting *Gold Mine in the Sky*. From Nashville, J. L. Frank's Golden West Cowboys, featuring Pee Wee King, came out to join him in the picture. Gene had spent time with them during his legal problems and selected the group as the film's featured musical act. "He hired bands like mine from cities that had 50,000-watt radio stations," Pee Wee explained about Republic's use of regionally popular entertainers. "The local bands were good tie-ins to the movies when they were released. Fans of every musical group wanted to see the movies they were in. It increased the audience for each movie."[22]

A novice at movie making, Pee Wee studied Gene on the set. "Gene wanted to do his own stunts," he remembered, "but he knew what he was doing.

He was an excellent horseman. He did his own riding and took his own falls and did his own fighting. He loved the fight scenes and got a big kick out of all the action. Gene did have one accident while we were shooting the movie. . . . He was supposed to jump off his horse onto another guy and they would tumble down a hill. . . . When he was jumping out of his stirrups, he got his legs crossed and fell to the ground on his knees. He had to be taken to the hospital in Hollywood and didn't get back for two days.[23]

The mishap cost the film a few days' time. The Autry films' increased budgets permitted a slightly longer shooting schedule: about fourteen days—rather than the previous length of one week. *Gold Mine*, which wrapped on June 9, was the most expensive Autry feature to date—costing close to sixty thousand dollars. As fences were mended between Republic and its top star, Rogers's films continued to be made, but were quite different than Gene's. Modeled on the Autry template (singing cowboy, comical sidekick, smart horse), the early ones were low-budget period pieces, with Roy playing characters like Billy the Kid or Buffalo Bill. Smiley returned to the Autry films, and in 1939 George "Gabby" Hayes, who had been Hopalong Cassidy's sidekick Windy Halliday, took over as Roy's longtime co-star.

True to his word, Gene knocked out six movies in as many months. In between, he continued to get press, including, in June, his first feature in a Hedda Hopper gossip column: "Gene Autry . . . has that indefinable thing called charm" opened a glowing profile that included her inquiring "if he trained women as he did his horses." His ambiguous answer: "Don't know anything about women—been married seven [*sic*] years and still happy!" She concluded, "When you meet Gene Autry, you've met a real guy."[24] Hopper would become one of Gene's staunchest, most loyal cheerleaders. In another column, she quoted him on the advantages of his movies' appeal to children: "If the kids of today like me, they may continue to do so when they are parents of tomorrow."

Seeking longevity in a profession known for short-term careers, Gene would find his prediction borne out.

25

AT HOME AND ABROAD

ENE AND INA MAE SETTLED INTO THEIR SPACIOUS NEW HOME at 10985 Bluffside in North Hollywood. Completed in 1937, it was conveniently situated near the Republic Studio lot and not far from the Chatsworth ranch. Located on a small rise above the Los Angeles River, the house looked out onto a manicured lawn with flowerbeds and a towering eucalyptus tree, a favorite of Gene's. Near the corner of Vineland, the pleasant, shady street was homey rather than glamorous. With the Chatsworth ranch reflecting Gene's taste in its rustic architecture and furnishings, the Bluffside home's interior design became Ina's domain.

In contrast to the ranch's white pine walls and wagon-wheel furniture, the Autrys' new home was decorated in English country style. Ina chose cabbage-rose wallpaper for the dining room, and the living room, with its large white brick fireplace, was furnished in chintz upholstery and drapes. Throughout most of the house, rose-beige wall-to-wall carpeting covered the floors. The dining room was decorated with Ina's antique glass and china collection. "I had to keep track of the money that came in and gave Ina so much to furnish the new home with," Gene's secretary Dorothy Phillips Bowman recalled. "She had a separate bank account and wrote her own checks and paid for everything. And when she ran out of money she came and asked me if I'd put some more money in her account. I told Gene, and he said, 'You give her anything she wants—don't question her. Just give it to her.'"[1]

In her column, Hedda Hopper described Gene's "pretty, brown-haired wife" as having the master bedroom "done in peach color, soft and feminine with beds covered with peach satin. But it was her idea, not his—he'd rather have a bed in his harness room than take the kidding that goes with the satin."[2] Indeed, Gene's favorite room in the house was the den, with an oversized stone fireplace, hardwood floors covered with a large hook rug, and Western-style furniture. In 1938, Gene commissioned the construction of a cozy office building down the hill from the house, reached by a set of brick steps, surrounded by trees. The two acres that fanned out around the office had brick walkways, timber fencing, and an abundance of eucalyptus. Two years later, the Autrys would put in a swimming pool near Gene's office, and a barbecue party celebrating its completion would make the papers.[3] For the cottage office, Gene bought Dorothy a new $86 typewriter; a large framed photograph of her boss hung over her desk. His own office's wainscoted walls were sprinkled with autographed 8×10s of such celebrities as Rudy Vallee. "It was a beautiful place," Dorothy remembered.

The Autry home could easily accommodate guests. The previous year, eighteen-year-old Dudley had moved out after Gene helped get him a job in the wardrobe department at Republic. Ina's fifty-year-old mother, Lilly, had taken his place; she had been visiting her daughter and son-in-law when Barney Spivey died suddenly in Oklahoma. At loose ends, she moved in with the Autrys, except for occasional visits to her other daughter in Tulsa.

Gene and Ina's social circle had widened to include more newcomers: Johnny and Gloria Marvin, Fred and Lorene Rose, and Ray and Kay Whitley. Most of Ina's friends were the women married to the men in Gene's world. Fred and Lorene had just relocated from Nashville and were staying with the Whitley's until they got settled. A successful pop songwriter in the 1920s, Fred Rose had worked at Chicago radio stations in the early thirties, when he first met Gene. Alcoholism took its toll on his career and his personal life. But, in 1935, things began to turn around for him: he successfully quit drinking after adhering to the tenets of Mary Baker Eddy's Christian Science. The following year, Rose scored his first cowboy hit, when his composition "We'll Rest at the End of the Trail" was recorded by both Bing Crosby and Tex Ritter.

While Gene was in Nashville fighting his court battle in February and April of 1938, he had gotten reacquainted with Fred and invited him to Hollywood to write songs for his pictures. Fred and Johnny Marvin immediately began collaborating to provide numbers for *Gold Mine in the Sky* and for Gene's records. It was a good fit. Both schooled in pop, they also had a sensibility for the Western sound. "Rose was a classic journeyman songwriter who carried on the Tin Pan Alley tradition of producing on demand," according to John Rumble, senior historian at the Country Music Foundation Hall of Fame and Museum and author of a dissertation on Rose. "Throughout his extensive writing experience with vaudeville stars, jazz bands, and country singers . . . , he [could] tailor his compositions to suit almost any performer."[4] For Gene, Fred Rose merged sophisticated wordplay with simple, catchy melodies.

As with his Johnny Marvin "collaborations," Gene would get a composition credit for facilitating the assignment, making the song famous, and occasionally brainstorming lyrics or musical ideas. Of course, his unique phrasing also added to the song's final sound. "In those days I would get the script first from Republic Pictures and would get together with Fred and we would come up with the ideas for the songs," Gene once explained in a letter to Fred's wife. "Many of them Fred cared nothing about because they were simply picture songs and I bought them outright from him. Many of them were on a royalty basis. Also at that time [in the 1940s], the most that was paid for a song by the picture companies was around $350 per song. I never kept any of this money because I knew Fred was having it rough, so I turned all of the money received from Republic for the songs directly over to him."[5] In 1939 Gene formed his own music publishing company, Western Music.[6] Previously, he had published his compositions (and those he had purchased) primarily with M. M. Cole. With his own ASCAP-registered concern, he could actively exploit his increasing number of copyrights (including those of Rose and Marvin) for various commercial outlets, including songbooks and recordings by other artists; in 1940, Johnny Marvin would become his partner in the business.

On June 22, 1938, Gene waxed his first Rose composition, "I Don't Belong in Your World," a mournful ballad unissued on 78 but eventually featured in an Autry picture. A pair of Marvin-Rose-Autry efforts, the urbane "Dude Ranch Cowhands" and witty "As Long as I Have My Horse," were selected by Republic for *Gold Mine*. The new songwriting team's "Good-Bye Pinto" and "The Old Trail," as well as the *Gold Mine* numbers, were all released on 78. In December, Herb Yates would sell ARC to William Paley's Columbia Broadcasting System. Renamed Columbia Recording Company, it would eliminate the dime-store labels, issuing Gene's releases primarily on Conqueror, Vocalion, OKeh, and eventually solely on Columbia.

The musical backing on the June 22–23 sessions featured, for the first time, violinist Hugh Farr and his guitar-playing brother Karl, both members of Sons of the Pioneers. That group's manager, Ray Whitley, also came to play a key role in Gene's creative and personal life. The Alabama-raised Whitley held the distinction as being the first Western singer to perform at the prestigious Madison Square Garden Rodeo, in 1935. The next year, he moved to Hollywood after starring on a New York City radio show, where he sang and played his own Western tunes. A gregarious man, Whitley had met Tom Mix, who recommended him for a bit part in pictures. Whitley eventually became the musical sidekick to the nonsinging cowboy star George O'Brien in a series of oaters. Fiddler Art Davis, who first met Whitley during an earlier sojourn in Dallas, introduced him to Gene, and the two became good friends.

"We used to get together so often," Whitley later recalled. "The way [Gene] invited you to dinner was to say, 'Well, come over and let's have some beans!' Ina was always anxious to have company and was a wonderful hostess, and we'd go over to their house and she'd have a wonderful dinner, but to be sure, she'd have beans because there's nothing that Gene likes better than beans in any form—baked beans, string beans, or anything beans. And cornbread, and buttermilk, and turnip greens, or mustard greens, or anything like that."[7] The Roses and Marvins, who lived around the corner on Vineland, were also frequent dinner guests.

Like Fred Rose, Johnny and Gloria Marvin had become Christian Scientists, and the conversation frequently turned to its philosophies. Ina Mae became intrigued by Eddy's teachings of healing through prayer. After she read Eddy's 1934 book, *Science and Health with Key to the Scriptures*, she, too, joined the Thirty-sixth Church of Christ, Scientist, located nearby. Ina shared what she had learned with her sister, Anita, whose family converted as well. For Ina, the Christian Science teachings would remain a strong presence in her life, sustaining her through the difficulties that lay ahead.

Smiley Burnette became a Christian Scientist, too, through his wife, Dallas, whose mother had been a member of Eddy's original congregation in Boston. "My dad got thrown from a horse, and he had backaches for two years," according to the couple's son Stephen Burnette. "He'd be taking Epsom salt baths and going out onstage on one-nighters and doing his show. And [the pain] was very bad, and he called up Dallas one night and said he would do anything to get rid of this. And she said, 'Will you try me calling a [Christian Science healing] practitioner for you?' And he said, 'Anything.' And so he woke up the next morning and he didn't have a backache. That night, it started coming back, so he called her again. She called a practitioner again, and he never had any more backache from that day forward."[8]

Gene showed no particular interest in Christian Science, but continued his activities as a Mason, joining the Al Malaikah Shrine in Los Angeles, which included members Clark Gable, Dick Powell, Buck Jones, and Harold Lloyd, and the Scottish Rite Consistory temple, in Long Beach, in 1936.[9] In 1938 Gene became a member of the Benevolent Protective Order of the Elks in Burbank. During the holidays that year, Gene participated in the Al Malaikah Shrine charity ball, as well as a star-studded benefit in the San Joaquin Valley for 2,500 children who were refugees from the Dust Bowl.[10] "The youngsters were asked what star they most wanted to see," reported the *New York Times*, "and the big majority voted for Mr. Autry, the 'cowboy.' "[11] The *Los Angeles Times* called Gene "the Tom Mix of the talking films," pointing out that "Gene neither drinks nor smokes" just as "Mix . . . would not smoke or drink in a film because he felt it would have a bad influence on his best patrons, the youngsters."[12]

Gene's popularity showed no signs of abating, with the *Motion Picture Herald* survey again placing him as top Western star of 1938. Republic announced that his new leading lady would be twenty-year-old June Storey, a cherub-faced blonde born in Toronto. She had acted in films at MGM and Fox before Sol Siegel signed her to Republic in 1938. In December she and Gene began work on *Home on the Prairie*, the first of ten films they would make together. She frequently played a feisty female rancher or business owner won over by the older, wiser Gene. June's comic timing brought out the best in Gene, and made a big impression on Smiley. Gene called June—who would accompany him on personal appearance tours—"my favorite rein holder" in his memoir:

> June was Smiley's favorite audience. He had a conviction . . . that your feet were the key to your physical and mental health. Whenever people looked tired, Smiley would bathe and massage their feet. He carried a pail around with him on the set. June thought it was a very generous thing for Smiley to do and took frequent advantage of the service. . . . June was one of those people who wanted to nominate you for a prize anytime you did a good deed. I found a tiny kitten once, I'm not sure where, just abandoned on the street . . . I brought it to the shooting that day in a sock . . . and held it in my lap between scenes. June loved to tell people about that."[13]

June and Gene remained in touch even after June quit the entertainment business and became a nurse. In 1975 she wrote to Gene, "Your life story should have a thread woven thru—how you directly or indirectly helped small people—didn't you?"[14]

THE POPULARITY OF GENE'S FILMS definitely helped the previously ailing Western genre—reflected in the *Los Angeles Times* headline: HORSE-OPERA VOGUE REVIVED: SINGING COWBOY HAS REVOLUTIONIZED WESTERN PICTURES.[15] For years the major studios had abandoned "outdoor features" as money-losers, but in 1939 a number of big-budget pictures brought back the Wild West to the screen, including John Ford's breakthrough, *Stagecoach* (starring John Wayne on loan from Republic) and Cecil B. DeMille's *Union Pacific*. Matinee idols such as Tyrone Power were starring in Westerns (*Jesse James*); even James Cagney traded a Tommy gun for a six-shooter in *The Oklahoma Kid*. The timing was right for classic good versus evil plotlines: Nazi Germany's encroachment in Europe had polarized the country; isolationists demanded the United States remain neutral, while Roosevelt and his cabinet tried to mobilize American opinion against Hitler—asking studio heads to help convey the right message with their output. "While the [movie] industry is busy with propaganda pictures designed to create a national consciousness, the Western is employed as the logical medium in which to expound the American philosophy and to show that right thinking, clean living, and a devotion to duty are the ingredients necessary to success," opined *New York Times*'s commentator Douglas Churchill. "That some of the outdoor pictures will make no attempt to conceal the propaganda goes without saying: most, however, will strive for adroitness and preach in general terms and by inference."[16]

Who better to convey that message in person to America's British cousins than Gene Autry? His recordings had been available on UK labels since the early 1930s, and his pictures, distributed there beginning in 1936 by British Lion, had created Gene Autry mania among children. Talks had been under way for Gene to make a personal appearance tour in the British Isles to promote his pictures and—perhaps—to serve as ambassador of American support and strength as war clouds gathered. Gene and Ina had dined at the White House that year with the Roosevelts, who undoubtedly approved of such a venture. Originally planned for April, Gene's UK tour was postponed "because of unsettled European conditions."[17] Finally, an August itinerary was set for England, Ireland, Scotland, and Wales. Ina would accompany Gene, as would Republic PR man Bill Saal and Mr. and Mrs. Herb Yates—along with an $18,000 horse trailer and two steeds, Lindy-Champion and a new golden palomino, Pal, purchased for $1,500 in 1938.

Premiering in the UK would be Gene's just-released film, *Colorado Sunset*, featuring June Storey, Barbara Pepper, and a delightful cameo from WLS pal Patsy Montana, as a café waitress singing "I Want to Be a Cowboy's Sweetheart." The song had become popular after she recorded it for Art Satherley in 1934, but following its spotlight in *Colorado Sunset*, it sold even greater numbers, becoming the first country record by a female artist to sell a million copies. The film "introduced a nationwide audience to my song and to me," Patsy later wrote, and her record "settled into the top ten pop chart." Patsy's husband Paul Rose shot home-movie footage on the movie set in Lone Pine: "The camera scans the real movie being made," according to Patsy. "Gene rides fast and hard on the back of his horse, Champion . . . and does some very dangerous stunts. And then our little camera pans to a hammock tied between two trees and a napping Gene Autry. His 'double' sure was working hard, even if Gene was not."[18]

Patsy probably did not realize that Gene had to start another picture, *In Old Monterey*, just four days after *Colorado Sunset* wrapped. Republic wanted to release one Autry picture per month, and time was of the essence since Gene's touring would occupy July, August, and half of September. Plans were already in the works for Gene Autry Day at the New York City World's Fair on Saturday July 22. During his few days in New York, he kept up a pace equal to that of his movie-making—which climaxed with his being feted as "King of the Cowboys." Even the *New York Times*'s notoriously cranky Bosley Crowther, who devoted an entire feature to profiling "A Cowboy Without a Lament," seemed in awe: "Gene was around the other day before embarking on that European jaunt. If you missed him, it was only because you weren't at City Hall when Mayor LaGuardia received him, or you weren't at any one of ten Loews theatres in which he made personal appearances all in one day, or you weren't at the Yankee Stadium when the kids swept him up in a stampede." Crowther went on to recount his own meeting with Gene at his hotel: "It was Gene all right—a medium height, sandy-haired, pink-cheeked, blue-eyed, baby-faced fellow with a slow smile and an easy drawl. . . . It was quickly obvious that . . . his really artistic inclination is along the line of song. . . . The moments when his soul comes out are those nicely spaced interludes when he picks up his old guitar and plucks forth a cowboy ballad."[19]

His day at the fair included a parade and an appearance at the World's Fair Wild West Show and Rodeo, where his coronation was conducted by Ruth Mix, daughter of the former king—Gene's hero Tom, who would be killed the following year in a car accident.[20] Gene's besiegement by fans would be a practice run for what was to come in the British Isles.

The *Manhattan* set sail from New York Harbor on July 26. Herb Yates covered all the trip's expenses, a reported fifty thousand dollars. Earlier in the year, the *New York Times* had reported on the production of the studio's first A feature, *Man of Conquest*, starring Richard Dix. Yates would be promoting that film in Britain, as well as Gene Autry, his top money-maker. "Republic has the reputation of making more profit per invested dollar than any studio in the business," according to the *Times*.[21] Yates had finally determined to lavishly spend some of those earnings on publicizing his product overseas.

When Gene landed on British shores, the hysteria was equivalent to the Beatles' first trip to America three decades later. The snooty Savoy Hotel even permitted Champ (aka Lindy) to accompany Gene into the dining room. A near mob scene took place in the streets of London, after Gene's appearance at the Paramount Theatre. "I never saw so many people in my life," Gene recalled.

> The whole front of the theater and the streets were all blocked and people every-where. Well, Bill Saal was quite a PR guy, and he had a lot of cameramen with him. He had a cameraman on the right side, a cameraman on the left side and he was in the middle setting up on a car. He'd said, "I want you to jump off the stage and just walk up the middle of the aisle because I want to get your picture outside with all of that crowd." Well, that's exactly what I did. I went outside . . . but I couldn't get out of that mob, so finally Bill yelled, "Come on up here," and I got up on top of this small Austin convertible car . . . and this bobby came up to Bill Saal and said, "Is this your car?" and Bill said, "Hell, yes, get away from it and don't bother me!" I often wondered what the owner of that automobile thought when he came back and saw the condition of it![22]

The UK press followed his every move, most journalists noting that he was accompanied by his "very pretty wife." Headlines roared: ACTOR MOBBED IN GLASGOW, 50,000 WELCOME COWBOY GENE, COWBOY STAR MOBBED IN BELFAST.[23] With the threat of war hovering, people seemed to feel that Gene Autry was the conquering hero, come to save them. This outpouring of adulation af-fected Gene as never before. It was an experience he would talk about for the rest of his life. An estimated 250,000 people turned out in Dublin to see him ride in a parade astride Champion. Especially meaningful to him was his last night in the Irish capital, when a reported 10,000 people surrounded the Theatre

Royal following his performance. As he emerged onto the fire escape outside his dressing room to wave to the crowds below, the Irish people broke into song, with a spontaneous "Come Back to Erin." Fifty-eight years later, Gene still described that moment with wonder, and how those voices in unison had brought tears to his eyes.[24]

While in Dublin, he met for the first time the songwriter Michael Carr, who, with Joseph Hamilton Kennedy, wrote one of his favorite numbers, "Ole Faithful." Carr, along with Kennedy's brother Jimmy Kennedy, had done it again: they presented their new composition "South of the Border" to Gene. He loved it on first listen and would record it as soon as he returned to the States.

Most shocking for Gene was seeing his own headlines juxtaposed with those of Hitler's. According to a Birmingham reporter, "Then [Gene] picked up a newspaper and looked suddenly serious. 'You fellows must be close in on this Danzig business. What's going to happen? So you don't know either. Well, if it comes to a showdown, I don't see how America could keep out.' "[25] While Gene was in Liverpool, Hitler mobilized German forces to begin the invasion of the free city of Danzig, followed by Poland. France and England warned that such an action would result in their declaration of war—which it did. The UK tour was cut short, as foreign visitors scrambled to escape the war-torn continent, and ocean liners filled to capacity. On August 25, a transatlantic cable arrived instructing the Republic group to "book passage on first available American-owned ship."[26] Douglas Fairbanks Sr. asked Gene if he and his wife could share their berth home—but found other means of travel at the last minute.

Safely aboard the *Manhattan*, the Autrys, Yates and his wife, and Saal sailed for New York, arriving on September 3. In just over two year's time, Gene's words to the Birmingham reporter would come to pass, and his life—like millions of others—would be forever changed.

26

MELODY RANCH

GENE RECEIVED A HERO'S WELCOME HOME with his first-ever glossy magazine spread: "Tenor on Horseback," illustrated with a commissioned color portrait of Gene and Champ, filled four pages of the *Saturday Evening Post*. Journalist Alva Johnston described Gene's movie persona as "a combination of Sherlock Holmes in a ten-gallon hat, Don Quixote with common sense, and Bing Crosby on horseback."

Johnston's detailed recounting of the Will Rogers discovery tale placed it permanently in the Autry hagiography. He also highlighted the popularity of Gene Autry merchandise, ranging from sweatshirts (the previous market leader was Babe Ruth) to the Kenton cap pistol, now at two million in sales—but noted that Gene had turned down a three-thousand-dollar cigarette endorsement deal. As for his screen appeal: "The fact that [Autry] couldn't act was at first considered a negligible flaw, and later an asset," Johnston wrote. "Like Gary Cooper and Jimmy Stewart, Autry has the kind of awkwardness and embarrassment that audiences like." An estimated forty million people had flocked to Autry movies, he noted, and "about seventy-five Autry records are on the market, and in total sales they have outsold Bing Crosby's."[1]

Gene had scored numerous hit records that year. On April 13–14, he had returned to the studio with a batch of Rose and Marvin pop ballads. Still under the sway of Bing, Gene gave them a smooth reading while retaining the sincerity in his voice. His careful enunciation would influence future artists such as soul legend Solomon Burke, who recalled in 2006, "I always loved Gene Autry . . . just because I liked to listen to the stories. But my grandmother was always saying, 'Listen to the pronunciation of the words. . . . Think about what the words are, what they mean; listen to how it's being phrased."[2] A full instrumentation filled out the sound on both April sessions, including two violins, electric steel guitar, ukulele, bass, and supplementary guitars. Many of the numbers got the Hawaiian treatment, with the Autry-Rose number "Paradise in the Moonlight" and a rerecording of Gene's "You're the Only Star" particularly benefiting from the style. Bosley Crowther singled out these releases in his August *Times* profile. Predominantly a selection of romantic pop balladry, the sessions' only Western output were the rollicking "Rhythm of the Hoofbeats" and "'Neath Blue Montana Skies," the title song of the Autry movie about to be released.

One of the violinists prominently featured on the recordings was Carl Cotner, who had contributed to Gene's October 1937 sessions. Described by Gene as "a young fellow with a kind of kewpie face and dark blond hair,"[3] Carl first learned violin at age five. Born in Indiana in 1916, he had traveled with his father, Elmer, a professional musician on the local circuit, and eventually studied at the Cincinnati College-Conservatory of Music. Carl's career had included membership in Clayton McMichen's Georgia Wildcats and stints on WHAS, WSM (the Grand Ole Opry's home station), and since 1937, the 50,000-watt WLW in Cincinnati. Following their first session together, Gene had wired Carl at WLW inviting him to be a part of his regular group. The station employee who received it—not wanting to lose the talented musician—withheld the cable, so it was eighteen months before Gene and Carl reconnected. The versatile Cotner could read music and was adept at jazz, pop, Western, and hillbilly styles. When he first arrived in Hollywood, he stayed with Ina and Gene until he found his own place. Forming a lifelong bond with Gene, Carl participated on nearly every Autry session and tour and later became his arranger, orchestra leader, and musical director—all on a handshake. The two never signed a contract.

It was Carl's violin that kicked off the song that would become Gene's signature and one of the top cowboy numbers of all time. Recorded on April 18, 1939, "Back in the Saddle Again" engages the listener immediately with its catchy lyrics and memorable tune. Ray Whitley wrote it for the 1938 George O'Brien picture *Border G-Man*, and originally recorded it for Decca. When Gene decided to do it, Whitley permitted him to add his name to the credit. "The song would have been just another song without the help of my friend and co-writer Gene Autry," the songwriter later explained when asked about sharing credit.[4] Gene's warm vocal style did indeed transform the song, as did the lively violins, chugging accordion, and echoing steel guitar.

Ray Whitley also introduced Gene to a new, top-of-the-line guitar, the Gibson SJ-200. Ray had met with the guitar manufacturer in 1937 to advise the company on crafting a jumbo "cowboy-style" acoustic with a bass-heavy sound. The following year, the company made twelve of the SJ-200 model, specifically for Ray's friends, including Gene, who bought two at the discounted price of

$150. After the purchase, his showy new Gibson frequently turned up in Gene's publicity pictures and movies. Second only to his Martin D-45 in value, the guitar was embellished with a two-tone mother of pearl border; horses and bucking broncos inlaid with pearl; and his name writ large alongside horseshoes inset on the fingerboard. Sounding impressive onstage, the guitar traveled with Gene on his UK tour.

Soon after his ship's arrival from Britain in New York Harbor in September 1939, Gene took a flight to Chicago to meet his musicians in the studio. On Monday the eleventh, he cut Kennedy and Carr's "South of the Border (Down Mexico Way)." Its melody was not unique; in fact, it sounded very much like "Red Sails in the Sunset," another Kennedy (with Will Grosz) hit from 1935. But its fanciful lyrics about senoritas and old Spanish lace, and its narrative's tragic denouement, were perfect for the times—Latin culture and music were beginning to supplant Hawaiian sounds as a trend. Republic quickly bought movie rights to the song from which the MacGowan brothers would concoct a story, and Betty Burbridge and Gerald Geraghty would craft a screenplay. "Down Mexico Way," too, became a Gene Autry picture title in 1941.

After the recording, Gene flew back to California to start work on back-to-back movies. *Rovin' Tumbleweeds* features a plot very similar to *Under Western Stars* (the retitled *Washington Cowboy*, in which Gene was replaced by Roy Rogers). Although the film is more of a populist social drama than a Western, it includes an exciting rodeo sequence—when Congressman Gene Autry goes to Washington and needs a dose of bronco-bustin'. "Back in the Saddle Again," the picture's featured song, had just been issued by Columbia to great success in September. Upon the film's November release, sales of the 78s were propelled even farther (and in fourteen months would provide yet another movie title for Gene).

Rovin' Tumbleweeds, with its focus on corrupt politicians' ties to big business, contrasted with Gene's previous effort, *In Old Monterey*, which had hit screens in August. Gene's most expensive feature to date, *Monterey* cost nearly $99,000, with a cast including Smiley and June, plus Gabby Hayes and WLS musical guests the wacky Hoosier Hotshots and the Grand Ole Opry female duo Sarie and Sallie. In light of recent events in Europe, its plot was quite timely, with a message preaching patriotism and wartime preparedness. Gene plays an undercover doughboy who must convince resistant ranchers to sell their land to Uncle Sam for bomb testing. *In Old Monterey* was to be Gene's last effort with director Joe Kane, whom *Variety* praised: "In handling a heavily manned and mounted finale, he has accomplished an outstanding piece of work."[5] Kane would go on to direct a string of Roy Rogers releases.

South of the Border, like *Rovin' Tumbleweeds* directed by George Sherman, has a topical plot. As incognito federal agents, Gene and Smiley uncover a scheme to capture Mexican oil fields by foreign spies manning a secret submarine base. Just like the song that inspired it, the film comes to a tragic end when Gene's love interest Delores (Lupita Tovar), sister of a revolutionary aiding the spies (Duncan Renaldo), joins a convent. The film introduced fifteen-year-old Mary Lee, a petite brunette with a big voice who would play the mischievous "Patsy" (frequently the little sister of Storey's character) in nine Autry films.

Born Mary Lee Wooters in 1924, she began singing at the age of six in a hillbilly group with her father, a small-town barber, and her older sister, Vera. Living in Illinois, the family had been fans of Gene's WLS show and actually met him and Smiley after a performance in 1935. When she was thirteen, Mary Lee's preternaturally mature vocals got her an audition with the Ted Weems Orchestra. Not quite five feet tall, she became the band's female vocalist, belting out pop songs over the next two years. Gene caught a performance in California, and, impressed, arranged with Weems for her to audition for Republic. Although she'd never studied acting, she'd played a bit part the year before in a Nancy Drew film and cinched the tryout.

"Mother and I flew out to Hollywood," Mary Lee remembered, "and our plane was about four hours late, arriving at four in the morning. Mr. and Mrs. Autry were at the airport themselves to meet us, and they took us to their home to spend the remainder of the night. Two days later I reported at the studio."[6] Gene and Ina took the struggling Wooters family under their wing. They relocated from Illinois to a Hollywood bungalow, with Vera getting a secretarial job at Gene's office, assisting Dorothy with the new Western Music Publishing company. Increasing the films' musical quotient, Mary Lee's songs became featured numbers, as both solos and in duets with Gene, Smiley, or June. A natural in front of the camera, the vivacious Mary Lee became a popular addition to the films, and Republic began grooming her toward starring in her own pictures.

Another young brunette clamored to play opposite Gene—the spirited Jane Withers (today most remembered for her Josephine the Plumber persona). Two years younger than Mary Lee, Withers had become a successful child star at age six. At thirteen, she was calling the shots at 20th Century Fox, and she wanted Gene. For months, the *L.A. Times* had been running items that the two would work together in a remake of a Will Rogers film. Republic agreed to the loan-out and Gene earned $25,000 (compared to the $71,000 Republic paid him for the entire year). *Shooting High* was not much different from a Republic picture, with Gene playing his usual character—but named Will Carson—and getting second billing to Withers.

As 1939 drew to a close, Gene's schedule had been relentless, remarked upon earlier by Hollywood columnist Jimmy Fidler: "Next time you hear some star moan about 'too much work,' cite the case of Gene Autry. Thanks to that prolonged European tour and his contract to play in a 20th Century super, he must finish three Westerns for Republic between now and Nov. 15."[7]

All that hard work paid off, however: For the third straight year, Gene was voted top Western moneymaker in the exhibitors poll. In December, one newspaper called him "the most popular film actor in the world because of the great circulation of his pictures in every town and hamlet throughout the nation." He'd also been a guest on numerous national radio programs throughout the year (earning $5,500 in appearance fees), and now was making plans to host his own show. Chewing-gum magnate Philip K. Wrigley had been in Dublin for an international equestrienne event in August and had witnessed the tremendous reception Gene had received. Returning to Chicago, he discussed with his advertising agency, J. Walter Thompson, a Gene Autry weekly radio show sponsored by Wrigley's Doublemint gum. Gene got the call on the set of *Shooting High*, and plans were finalized for his *Melody Ranch* show to debut on the Columbia Broadcasting System in January.

On December 21, 1939, Republic sent a congenial letter of agreement to Gene stating "we shall be very glad to lend you our fullest cooperation to the end that the series of broadcasts will be a success," provided that Wrigley would permit "Republic Productions Inc. [to] be given credit on the broadcasts, we shall not call upon you to render services to us between the hours of 6:00 PM Saturdays to 7:00 AM Mondays," the period when Gene would be rehearsing and broadcasting the program, presented live before an audience. A fifteen-minute introductory pilot was produced specifically for Doublemint gum merchants, available on December 31. It included a dramatization of Gene's first meeting with Will Rogers at an Oklahoma depot and featured Gene singing two songs, including "Back in the Saddle Again," soon to become the *Melody Ranch* theme.

Gene's friendly Texas-accented voice and southern pronunciations contrasted greatly with the studied elocution of most urbane radio hosts on national radio programs. But since FDR had initiated his comforting "Fireside Chat" broadcasts early in his presidency, the public had shown support for homey, intimate-sounding radio. And Gene's "everyman" screen persona and mellifluous voice easily translated to the airwaves. "When I went on the radio for the Wrigley company back in 1939 . . . I remember having a conversation with Mr. Phil Wrigley in which I stated that I was not sure of the rating I would get," Gene later said. "His reply was that he would prefer I had a 1. minus rating and sell chewing gum, rather than have a 50. plus rating and no sales."[8] Gene also remarked that Wrigley actually approved when cast members flubbed lines, since it made the characters seem more "real."

On January 7 the *New York Times* announced "Gene Autry, 'Public Cowboy No. 1,' and singing star of the films, headlines a new Western series from the 'Double M Ranch,' which will join WABC's Sunday round-up tonight at 6:30."[9] Walter Winchell plugged the show in his *New York Mirror* column, for which Gene dashed off a note of personal thanks:

> I want you to know I appreciate everything you give me. Of course the radio show I am doing is not a sophisticated program and probably a lot of the boys in the city won't enjoy it, but the thing I am trying to do more than anything else is to keep

the program down to earth, and especially so the kids will like it. I want to concentrate on trying to point out the value of Americanism and what America should mean to everyone in these days where there is so much communism and other isms going so strong in this country. I feel we cannot go too strong on preaching this to the people, and I think the best way to do this is playing particularly to the kids and teaching them Americanism while they are young.[10]

The show's original format, with a few personnel changes, would endure for the first two years of its existence. The thirty-minute program featured Gene's musical selections, as well as those from singer/actress Nancy Mason (called "Miss Nancy" by the cast), and a cowboy drama conveying a moral lesson, featuring Gene and his sidekick, Shorty Long. Played by the talented character actor Horace Murphy, who had co-starred in several Tex Ritter films, Shorty was a cross between Gabby Hayes and Smiley Burnette. Murphy had previously worked with Gene on *Rovin' Tumbleweeds*. Interspersed throughout the program were several hard-sell Doublemint gum pitches by Gene and announcer Wendell Niles, as well as plugs for Gene's movies. Johnny Marvin and Lou Bring conducted the orchestra, and Gene was backed by a harmonizing vocal group called the Texas Rangers.

On January 28, *Melody Ranch* departed dramatically from its usual format. Gene had been invited to Washington, DC, along with such movie stars as Olivia de Havilland, Mickey Rooney, and Tyrone Power to participate in celebration of FDR's birthday, an annual fund-raising event. All proceeds from related festivities, held nationwide, went to the National Foundation of Infantile Paralysis. Roosevelt's fifty-eighth birthday featured ten days of star-studded events, including a White House luncheon, glamorous balls, and the live broadcast of Gene's radio program from the Press Club Auditorium. Gene, joined by Eleanor Roosevelt, hosted a patriotic tribute to diverse American music and sang his cowboy songs. A gospel performance from Elder Michaux and the Church of God choir was introduced by Gene, in his Texas accent, as a presentation of "nigra spirituals," a southern pronunciation of "negro" for which Lyndon Johnson would be criticized in the 1960s. Other regional music included remote broadcasts from Pappy Cheshire[11] and his "Ozark hillbillies" in St. Louis, the hymns of the Franco-American Octet from Fall River, Massachusetts, and a big band from Chicago doing *Hit Parade* selections. A local barbershop quartet appeared onstage with Gene and the First Lady, who conversed about horses. Gene sounded uncharacteristically nervous and ill at ease, while Eleanor chatted merrily about "dashing young things."

Photos from the birthday events were later featured in the "photogravure" sections of the New York and Los Angeles *Times*, as well as *Life* magazine. At the January 30, 1940, luncheon for Hollywood stars, Gene stands out in his gleaming white Western-cut suit with scarf tie, in contrast to the male celebrities (including Bill Boyd, aka Hopalong Cassidy) attired in dark business suits. (Cassidy would later complain bitterly that Gene had stolen his thunder.) At the luncheon, Gene presented the president and First Lady with a pair of Stetsons, and was the sole guest to make a speech.

Two other photos of the birthday events depict Gene in a cozy tête-à-tête with "socialite horsewoman Mrs. John Hay [Liz] Whitney," and Gene dancing with Whitney, alongside Franklin Roosevelt Jr. and Dorothy Lamour. Gene and Liz had met in Dublin, according to Hedda Hopper, who reported, "Gene Autry . . . gave me a giggle about his trip to Ireland. Landing there during horse-show week, he and his entourage took up practically an entire floor in the best hotel. Along came Liz Whitney, who, being unable to get a room and hearing that Autry had most of 'em, decided to introduce herself. 'I'm Mrs. Jock Whitney,' she said after knocking on his door, 'you've got so many rooms, how about subleasing one to me? Cowboy—I'm moving in!' " Whitney's marriage to her wealthy blue-blooded husband, who had been linked to Tallulah Bankhead and others, ended later that year. (After their divorce, Jock Whitney would marry FDR's niece.) Gene later confided to his cousin Callie Jane that the smitten Liz had promised him that if he married her, "he'd never have to work another day in his life." Liz and Gene would remain lifelong friends.

BACK IN CALIFORNIA, Gene's celebrity resulted in his being named honorary mayor of North Hollywood, putting him in the same company as his old idol Al Jolson. In February, Republic for the first time hosted at a Hollywood theater a gala premiere for an Autry film: *South of the Border*. The film went on to earn "millions," as reported by the *Los Angeles Times*.[12] Gene's title song, released by Columbia the previous October, was already a hit record, and the picture's featured duet by Gene and Mary Lee, "Goodbye, Little Darlin', Goodbye," followed it onto *The Hit Parade* after Gene recorded it in March. Johnny Marvin and Fred Rose continued to supply Gene with outstanding compositions, and five musically sophisticated sessions that year would yield some of his most enduring hits, including the Autry co-write "Be Honest With Me," nominated for an Oscar in 1942 (for its use in 1941's *Ridin' on a Rainbow*).

Between February and December, Gene made another six movies, all the while continuing the radio show every weekend. His stardom had not affected the down-to-earth quality he displayed on the set. Producer Gordon Kay, hired by Republic in 1939 as third assistant producer, a "lowly position," later recalled that Gene "was one of the nicest guys to work with. Gene always called me Gordon, politely asked for something. He was a gentleman."[13] Jimmie Fidler spent half a column raving about Gene's altruism:

> I've had letters from theater managers, school superintendents, civic officials, and just plain fans. They all tell the same story—Autry has been there and proven himself a regular. These p.a. jaunts of his are undertaken, primarily, as good-will investments. He always visits schools, orphanages, and hospitals. Because he believes that he should be an example of clean living to his millions of kid fans, he never smokes or drinks. He's accessible to anyone who wants to talk with him and I doubt

that he's ever refused any demand on his time if he could possibly meet it. . . . We need more stars with the same friend-making ability. . . . Gene Autry is doing Hollywood a favor and rates a great big hand.[14]

Director Frank McDonald had taken over the reins on Gene's films, beginning with *Rancho Grande*, his first picture of 1940. Beforehand, Republic's Moe Siegel gave him two Autry pictures to watch, saying, "Now don't expect to see a great actor. Gene is what he is, and whatever he's doing, that's what they're buying. It's what they like, so don't change a thing and don't try to direct him. Direct everybody else; have everybody else do what you want them to do, but Gene does what he does and that's all he can do and that's what they like." Gene himself told McDonald one day over lunch, "I know I'm no great actor, and I'm not a great rider, and I'm not a great singer, but whatever it is I'm doing, they like it. So I'm going to keep doing it as long as I can."[15]

Gene also continued to give fledgling entertainers a break. While promoting *Rancho Grande* in Oklahoma that spring, he asked the Jimmy Wakely Trio (Johnny Marvin's protégés) to back him for some performances. Afterward, he gave the guys his number to look him up if they ever came to California. The hopefuls—Wakely, Dick Reinhart, and tall, thin Johnny Bond—took him at his word, gave notice at WKY, and arrived in Hollywood near summer's end. They auditioned for Gene with a Bond original, the evocative "Cimarron," and were hired as his new backing group for *Melody Ranch*, in September. Bond, who gradually took on a sidekick role in the show, recalled early rehearsals:

> We would gather in one of CBS's small studios at Columbia Square, Sunset and Gower Streets in Hollywood . . . to read the script and make possible changes. Sitting around in an informal circle . . . we waited for our Star to make his entrance, almost always on time. He would stop in the doorway of the studio and speak to the entire cast. . . . Then he would take his seat within the circle. . . . His first reading was usually a bit on the rough side, leading us to wonder if he was going to be able to handle it or not. After a couple of times through, he fell into it pretty good, although he was never completely relaxed on the subsequent sixteen years that the show remained on the air. He took direction well, hardly ever making any changes or suggestions on his own. . . . While Autry was the quiet, easy-going sort, director Tony Stanford was just the opposite. He drove everyone pretty hard, so much so that we newcomers were often shaking in our boots.[16]

Soon after the Wakely trio joined the program, Mary Lee became a cast member, and June Storey and other co-stars stopped by and participated in the dramas. Gene and Ina invited the trio and their wives, Carl and Kitty Cotner, and Mary Lee and her family, to join the usual guests at the Autrys' home for parties. "Refreshments most likely included coffee, tea, soda pop, cakes, cookies, sandwiches, ice cream and the like," Johnny Bond recalled. "There were no alcoholic beverages served at this time. That came a few years later. . . . After about an hour of visiting and chatting, Gene would likely wind up seated in a corner with several of us gathered about him popping questions, after which the musical instruments would start coming out of their cases, and playing and singing would then begin and last until midnight. We learned that Autry loved to sing whether onstage or off."[17]

Gene's radio show proved so popular that Republic decided to make a film called *Melody Ranch*—Gene's most expensive prewar feature, budgeted at $181,275. Going outside the "stock" members, Republic hired famed composer Jule Styne to collaborate on the music, as well as such A-list cast members as tap dancer Ann Miller and comedians Vera Vague and Jimmy Durante, along with Mary Lee and Gabby Hayes. With all its veneer, the film did not possess the warmth of Gene's usual productions. The *Los Angeles Times* called it "chop suey, with the story hardly ever jelling and much of the comedy dragged in by the heels and strained." This didn't prevent public enthusiasm, however, and the film was exhibited in more urban cinemas than any Autry film to date. Gene enjoyed being around the crotchety Durante (who some critics derided for "slumming it" in an Autry picture) and for years would regale audiences with his Durante imitation. A talented mimic, Gene sometimes "did" FDR at his 1940 performances to great audience acclaim.

Melody Ranch was released a month after Gene made a triumphant return to New York to star in the sold-out fifteenth annual Madison Square Garden Championship Rodeo. The nineteen-day-long spectacle, beginning on October 9, kicked off with a parade to City Hall featuring Gene as the star of two hundred featured cowboys and cowgirls. New York's annual rodeo was the climax of the season, the year's top contestants winning cash and trophy buckles, including All-American Cowboy Champion. Garnering headlines and newsreel coverage, Gene flew with Champion/Lindy—the first horse to make a transcontinental flight cross-country—on a specially outfitted TWA plane to co-star with him at the Garden. A press release from *Melody Ranch*'s network reported, "Miss Esther Benefiel, chief hostess of TWA . . . fed Champ carrots at take-off and landing on route, to protect the horse's eardrums as the pressure suddenly changed. She fed Autry his air sponsor's chewing gum for the same purpose."[18] He also took the Jimmy Wakely trio as his backup group, along with Carl Cotner, Frankie Marvin, and his talented new accordionist Paul Sells.

Unfortunately, Gene's Grand Entry at the rodeo was marred by an embarrassing accident—Champion reared, and Gene tumbled from the saddle. The next day, newspapers reported that "the movie cowboy" couldn't stay on a horse. A darker rumor circulated that intoxication had caused the spill. One particularly spiteful sports columnist, Bill Slocum, described it this way in "The Day Gene Autry Fell Off His Horse": "Ol' Gene came a-ridin' into the ring, all spotlighted up, and grinnin' away. He pulled his horse up on its hind legs in salute to the throng. Ol' Gene ain't much of a singer, perhaps, but he's a worse rider. He fell right off that horse on his backside. You just can't get entertainment like that anymore."

Gene blamed the incident on a sterling saddle horn and slippery gloves, later writing:

> It became an unforgettable night in my career and a number of creative stories have since grown up about it. So I will tell you now exactly how it happened. I had a saddle that was made of silver. . . . It was so slick that if you wore regular cotton gloves you'd slide right off. I rubbed rosin on the gloves to make sure I wouldn't slip. But this night I planned to introduce a new song, and because I was a little unsure of the lyrics, I wrote them in ink on the palm of my glove, and I skipped the rosin. That night, as I rode into the center of the ring, I raised one hand to wave to the crowd and in an instant of splendid ill timing, I lost my grip and went tumbling to the good earth. Luckily, the microphone was only a few feet away. I stood up, dusted myself off, and said, "I've got to find an easier way to get off that horse."[19]

Gene recovered enough to perform songs with his group, as well as do tricks with Champion. One day, the entire rodeo paraded to Bellevue Hospital for a benefit show for patients, with Gene visiting bedridden invalids afterwards.

The *New York Times* toasted Gene in a feature, "Youth's Model 1940." George A. Mooney applauded Gene for being "conscious of his obligations to his followers, especially in times like these." Gene told the reporter that though he didn't include politics in his radio programs, he strove to present "Americanism." He explained, "If I can show our youth what it is like to be a real American, then I'm doing a good job. I want to show them that in this country everybody has a chance—just like I did. . . . In the programs we try to keep everything strictly American and down to earth. That's the sort of thing that will do more to knock any Communist, Nazi, or other such ideas out of their heads than anything else." Gene went on to say he equally enjoyed his radio shows and filmmaking and that doing both "keeps one from getting stale in either," but for "Americanism" work, he preferred radio. "In a single broadcast one can reach more people faster with the American doctrines."[20]

BOTH RADIO AND RODEO would loom large in Gene's future, with his successful stint at the Garden leading to future investments in the latter. By year's end, it became clear that Gene Autry's cinematic presence had won over the nation. On December 27, when the annual box-office survey results were announced, Gene not only topped the Western list of stars for the fourth year in a row but came in fourth place in the list of the ten most popular all-around stars, following Mickey Rooney, Spencer Tracy, and Clark Gable. "Autry thus becomes the first cowboy star to achieve that distinction since the late Will Rogers outdistanced all other rivals in 1934," the *New York Times* pointed out.[21] There could have been no more fitting comparison to describe the zenith of Gene Autry's hard-won conquest of all areas of American entertainment.

27

A TOWN CALLED GENE AUTRY

FOLLOWING HIS TREMENDOUS SUCCESS AT RODEOS, Gene began 1941 by looking into investing in his own show. His net income the previous year had risen to nearly $205,000, up from $131,000 in 1939.[1] For the previous two years, his investments mainly had been directed toward his music publishing company, his Chatsworth ranch, and a share in businesses reflecting his personal interests—Hollywood Silversmiths and the Hollywood Baseball Club. Gene firmly believed in investing profits back into his career and advised his friends to do the same. "Gene Autry always told me I was silly not to put something back in," Ray Whitley once related. "[Gene said], 'Ray Whitley is just like an automobile or a farm, or any other enterprise, you've got to grease it and put something back into it in order to make it function.' "[2]

In addition to headlining 1940's Madison Square Garden and Boston Garden rodeos, both produced by Dublin, Texas-based Everett Colborn, Gene also had played sold-out shows at rodeos in Pittsburgh, Washington, DC, and other cities. With Gene as headliner, attendance soared, and in some locations extra shows were added to meet the demand. Rodeo arenas held many more people than the theaters housing his previous shows, so the payoff increased greatly. But why earn just a performance fee, when he could reap the financial rewards of being rodeo owner?

One of his many associates in Oklahoma—Ardmore oilman and rancher Hardy Murphy—told him about a twelve-hundred-acre spread available near the hamlet of Berwyn's Santa Fe railroad depot. Located in southern Oklahoma's Carter County, the expanse of prairie unfolded near the base of the Arbuckle

Mountains. Gene purchased the property, which he soon began populating with rodeo stock, setting up headquarters for his Flying A Ranch Rodeo. Although his father had barely scraped by as a livestock dealer in nearby Achille and Ravia, Gene set out to prove he could create a lucrative business from such an endeavor. "I watched them build the ranch," recalled Les Gilliam, who grew up nearby.

> I remember going into those two barns and I can still recall the smell of fresh pine on the inside. And there was a man wood-burning the name "Champion" on the first stall on the left. The two barns were connected by a corral fence, and that's where they had Sunday afternoon rodeos so they could try out the rodeo stock. People came from all over and sat up on the corral fence and watched. They would bring in the bucking horses and bulls on railroad trains, unload all the rodeo stock, and then take them up the back trail there to the ranch.[3]

The outside of the barns and stables was constructed of colorful Arbuckle stone, each graced with the ranch's logo: a winged letter A made of eye-catching red rock.

The Flying A employed many locals as ranch hands, including former rodeo champ Lonnie Rooney as foreman. Word got out that Gene had even grander plans for the property. "At one point, Gene said, 'This would be an ideal place to make cowboy movies,'" according to Gilliam. "And that was part of Mr. Autry's plan, to set up a movie location in Oklahoma—I guess not only for himself, but maybe to lease out to others."[4]

Five years earlier, in 1936, a Republic PR man had proposed a similar idea to the hamlet of Tioga, which had gone into decline during the Depression. The aggressive press agent informed town fathers that Republic might make a picture there, and Gene would possibly build a new hotel and spa in town if they changed the hamlet's name to Autry Springs. Assuming the town would not refuse, Republic sent out a premature press release about the newly named town of Autry Springs. But the proposal turned embarrassing for Gene when Dr. Eugene Ledbetter led a contingent opposed to the name change; the physician even posted his unpaid bill for Gene's birth in his office window to show why the name "Autry" was unsuitable. The *Tioga Herald* published an anti-name-change editorial and a letter from Ledbetter arguing that rather than proclaim himself a Texan, Gene had started his career as the Oklahoma Yodeling Cowboy. When a special referendum was held on January 6, 1937, Tioga's citizens voted down the change. "All the young people here were for it," according to Gene's old flame Nellie Gordon Renfro. "But it didn't matter. . . . One doctor in town was against it, and that's all that mattered." Fifty years later, Tioga's tiny main street was renamed Gene Autry Drive, and in 2001, it began hosting an annual festival in its native son's honor.[5]

Tioga's folly did not dissuade Berwyn citizens, excited about the Flying A Ranch Rodeo, from circulating a petition to change their village's name to Gene Autry. This time, Gene had the top citizens' support, spearheaded by prosperous rancher Cecil Crosby, and plans got underway for the event to coincide with Oklahoma's thirty-fourth anniversary of statehood.

Gene's frenetic schedule in 1941 included eight recording sessions, seven pictures, and his weekly radio show. The year's first two films featured Mary Lee, but co-starred new leading ladies. June Storey, who the previous year had joined Gene on promotional tours, had moved on after her Republic contract expired. Gene and June wrapped their last film together in July 1940 (*Ride, Tenderfoot, Ride*). Almost a year later, Republic moved Mary Lee into starring roles, so she departed Gene's radio show and films after *The Singing Hill*'s completion in March. Her radio replacement was Ella Sutton, who recorded for Art Satherley, followed by Bonnie Blue Eyes, whom Gene knew from WHAS in Louisville, then South Carolinian Virginia Vass, a former member of a family group popular on WLS.

Gene's recording sessions also featured new musical contributors, including guitarist Johnny Bond, who joined him in the studio on June 18, 1941. Born Cyrus Whitfield Bond in 1915, Johnny would become Gene's faithful, longtime accompanist. He had been a fan since attending an Autry performance and screening of *Tumbling Tumbleweeds* in Oklahoma City in September 1935. A wry, articulate man, Bond was 6' 2", beanpole thin, with large liquid brown eyes and black hair. After joining Jimmy Wakely's trio in late 1937, he wrote the group's most well-known song, "Cimarron."

In addition to performing with the trio on *Melody Ranch* and playing on Autry recordings, Bond accompanied Gene on the road for performances. On March 27, in Washington, DC, he attended a luncheon given in Gene's honor by Oklahoma senators and congressmen. On the way to the Capitol, Gene showed his new guitarist his favorite historic sites. "Never been to Washington, DC, before?" Gene asked Johnny. "Well, I hope you don't do like I did the first time I came here. . . . I sat down on the Capitol steps and killed a fifth."

On that spring day, with the cherry blossoms in bloom, Gene and Johnny discussed their draft registrations and the possibility of America entering the war in Europe. "Gene was very much interested in politics," Bond remembered, "and on each subsequent visit thereafter he always placed the Capitol or White House on his itinerary."[6]

Johnny's 1941 Columbia sessions with Gene led to Uncle Art's signing Bond as a solo artist to the label. Bond later described working in the Hollywood studio with Satherley, to whom Gene continued to pay an annual "commission" ($3,500 in 1939 and $4,500 in both 1940 and '41). "Talk about your ego," said Johnny. "The first time I saw [Art] and worked for him on a session, he came in and he . . . looked around for a little box [to stand on]. He could easily command attention, and he says, 'Gentlemen . . . we're in Hollywood, but I don't record Hollywood music. I record country boys. If you play Hollywood music, you can leave now!' He looked straight at me, for the first time and said, 'Now, where are you from?' I said, 'Oklahoma.' 'Okay, you stay!' "[7]

Regardless of Art's mandate to play "country style," Gene's music veered more and more toward pop themes and sounds. Fred Rose kept providing songs in this vein, and Gene's success in the mainstream pop field motivated him to further pursue that course. In 1940 Gene had earned six thousand dollars in record royalties, with the songs' exposure on his radio show and movies helping to fuel sales. His first big hit of 1941, soon to become a standard, was written by old pal Jimmie Davis: "You Are My Sunshine" had been recorded by Davis and others, but Gene's reading became the definitive version. A two-sided hit, it was backed with Davis's "It Makes No Difference Now," which Gene had performed in 1939's *Mountain Rhythm.*

Gene's embrace of "Americanism" was also evident in his waxing of the World War I–era "Don't Bite the Hand That's Feeding You" and Rose's patriotic "God Must Have Loved America." A pair of Western songs made it into the mix: "Purple Sage in the Twilight" and "Keep Rollin' Lazy Longhorns" (including the prescient lyrics "rockin', rollin' "). Gene continued to cut Latin-tinged records, including his new film's title song, "Under Fiesta Stars." It featured for the first time a muted trumpet, played by Don Linder, who became a frequent contributor to Autry sessions. Hispanic-flavored numbers included "Spend a Night in Argentina," "Maria Elena," and "Amapola," with the latter (recorded in September) featuring a vocal trio on the chorus.

As in the previous two years, Gene's pictures still included Latin themes and/or settings. Early in his administration, FDR had implemented a "Good Neighbor policy," emphasizing unity between North and South America. "President Roosevelt's main concern was economic," according to Michael Duchemin, curator of the Museum of the American West, who has examined and written about the symbiotic relationship between the federal government and the film industry. "Germany was edging U.S. business interests out of Latin American markets. German trade with Brazil grew substantially between 1933 and 1938, with exports climbing from 12 percent to 25 percent and imports rising from 8 percent to nearly 20 percent. In Mexico, President Lázaro Cárdenas nationalized the oil industry in 1938, causing real anxiety when Mexican trade with Germany jumped by 12 percent in the first quarter alone. The economic strategy of the Third Reich was designed to gain access to raw materials while simultaneously weakening the trade relations of Great Britain and the United States. The prospect of a Nazi invasion in Latin America startled most Americans. President Roosevelt used this threat to frighten isolationists in Congress and get them to support Great Britain in the war against Germany."[8]

With Gene's popularity in Latin America dating to 1936, he was the perfect emissary to convey a friendly message of strength and support from the United States to Mexico and South America—beginning with 1939's high-profile *South of the Border*, followed by 1940's *Gaucho Serenade* (again with Duncan Renaldo), and 1941's *Down Mexico Way*. Mexican stereotypes were banned from Autry's 1941 picture; African American stereotypes, by contrast, continued with Uncle Tom characters in the 1940's *Carolina Moon*.

"In these days of hemispheric solidarity, it turns out the movies have got to be mighty careful about stepping on nationalistic toes," according to a 1941 news report titled "No Mexican Bandits, Says Hays Office." The reporter pointed out that the script for *Down Mexico Way* could not include Mexican outlaws—or Nazi villains because it would imply that Mexico was in cahoots with Germany. The screenplay was therefore rewritten to feature a reformed bandit, and the bad guys became phony movie producers. "The censors warned Republic Studios to be mighty careful about this lily-pure ex-bandit and under no circumstances to let him look silly."[9] The article also pointed out that *Down Mexico Way*'s Joseph Santley also directed *South of the Border*, which "grossed a fortune"—in some cities selling more tickets than 1939's *Gone With the Wind*. Gene and an audio excerpt from the film were featured in October on the national radio program hosted by columnist Louella Parsons, who introduced *Down Mexico Way* by saying, "We're doing our part for Pan American relations."

Another Republic "special," seventy-eight minutes long and costing $133,520, *Down Mexico Way* features the musical Herrara Sisters in picturesque production numbers sung in Spanish. Opposite Gene is Fay McKenzie, with hair and skin darkened to look the part of senorita Maria Elena Alvarado. The daughter of actor parents, McKenzie had been in pictures since childhood, but *Down Mexico Way* marks her first co-starring role and the first of five films with Gene: "I was just starting to do grown-up parts at the time, and Gene was the biggest star in the world," she later related. "Nobody was a bigger star. I was in awe just to be the in room where he was."

WHEN NOT TOURING, in the studio, or on a set, Gene could be found in his cozy home office—the setting that year for a couple of interviews with journalists. A *Chicago Tribune* feature writer reported that the star and his wife "live in jumbled comfort in a sizable but unpretentious house" and that his cottage office out back housed his two secretaries, who "work in a small outer room," while Gene "works in a small inner room which is a fascinating litter of souvenirs and guitars. On a sofa is a small rug into which is woven a likeness of Gene and Champ, done by a Colorado convict who wanted and got fifteen dollars for it. Just below the ceiling is a row of framed song sheets, including those Gene Autry has coauthored—work he has all but abandoned now—and a number which he picked up in London and made famous, 'South of the Border.'" Also decorating the wall were framed photos of celebrities, including self-help pioneer Dale Carnegie, who had become friendly with Gene. The reporter observed "on a mantel a clutter of pistols—some real antiques, some carved from wood—and steer horns." Giving the writer a tour, Gene explained, "The playroom [adjacent to the pool] hasn't been straightened out yet," with the journalist noting that "the pool table is covered and everything is tacked around any old way. On the floor is a buffalo head; on the table are several old music boxes, including a wine jug that plays 'How Dry I Am.'"[10] For the past few years, Gene had been collecting antique firearms, spurs, and music boxes, some of which he displayed at his ranch and others he exhibited in his office.

In July, at the Bluffside office, Gene met with *Los Angeles Times* sports writer Tom Treanor, who was covering Gene's forthcoming rodeo. "Mr. Autry allowed that more people go to see rodeos each year than any other sports except football and baseball," he reported. "He had just begun buying up a whole rodeo to appear at Madison Square Garden and other points in the East." Gene showed Treanor innovative fluorescent fabrics from which glow-in-the-dark flags and costumes would be created for "spectacular effects." "The Autry rodeo will need about 150 horses and 500 head of livestock," Treanor continued. "[A] tough problem is finding old-time Texas longhorn steers. They're almost extinct. I asked him what was the toughest problem an actor had when he got into the money. 'People selling you things you don't need,' he said." Treanor followed up: "How about doing a lot of foolish things and going broke?" "Listen," Gene told him, "some of the smartest people on Wall Street have jumped from windows because they lost their money. Why do people ever expect a poor dumb actor to keep his money?"[11] Gene would demonstrate that inside this "dumb actor," was the mind of a brilliant businessman.

Before debuting the Flying A Rodeo, Gene was booked to star once again at the Madison Square Garden and Boston Garden rodeos in the fall. (While on the road, Gene broadcast the *Melody Ranch* show from a local studio or theater.) The nineteen-day run in New York began on October 8. A devastating fire, horribly, would forever mar Gene's memory of his 1941 Boston Garden appearance. On November 8 he and Ina, who was with him at the rodeo, received the news that their Bluffside dream house had been destroyed. The company Ina had hired to clean the carpeting and draperies had set the house ablaze with its flammable solvents. "The flames spread so rapidly that before aid could be summoned to bring the fire under control, the [living] room exploded," stated one press account. Firefighters "were able only to save three shirts belonging to Autry and the shell of the two-stories [*sic*] house because of the fierce nature of the blaze."[12] Damage estimates ranged from $50,000 to $250,000. Fortunately, the fire was contained to the house and did not destroy Gene's office.

Nonetheless, just one week later, Gene traveled from Boston to Berwyn, Oklahoma, for a public ceremony celebrating the town's name change to Gene Autry. The event was broadcast live on Sunday, November 16, on *Melody Ranch* (with Wrigley forgoing its usual bombardment of commercials). A stage was set up on a flatbed rail car perched on the tracks near the depot. Governor Leon Phillips spoke on Gene's behalf, as did a Santa Fe representative, who touted his former telegraphy career. Gene and the usual *Melody Ranch* cast provided entertainment, including "Don't Bite the Hand," "You Are My Sunshine," and "Tumbling Tumbleweeds." The community's 227 residents had purchased war bonds and stamps in Gene's honor, and a telegram of commendation from Washington was read aloud.

An estimated crowd of thirty-five thousand visitors overwhelmed the village. "I remember a train coming in from Dallas and people were actually sitting on top of it, there were so many people on that train," related Les Gilliam. "There were chartered trains coming in, and buses from south and north, east and west. . . . People parked everywhere . . . two or three miles away and walking in, because everywhere was covered with people . . . shoulder to shoulder. They were going to have a parade, but they called it off . . . it couldn't go down the street."[13]

On the balmy eighty-degree day, townsfolk sold buffalo burgers, and young women handed out free Doublemint gum. Years later Gene recalled, "It seems to me that not only everyone from Carter County attended but everyone in the State of Oklahoma and North Texas was there. I remember they completely ran out of toilet facilities and there was no drinking water. The shortage of water was no problem since they were all drinking [bootleg] Choctaw beer and corn whiskey."[14]

Sadly, Ina missed her husband's big day—reportedly the first time a town had been named for a movie star. She had flown from Boston to Hollywood to deal with the repercussions of the fire and set up housekeeping at the Chatsworth ranch. Before flying back to California, Gene visited with Charlie Webster's family and the old depot in Ravia, then drove to Tioga to see Uncle Cal, his cousin Buck, and Sam Anderson. Gene dreaded facing the destruction of his beloved Hollywood home, but even that would pale in comparison to what happened three weeks later, on December 7, 1941.

28

WAR!

EVERY YEAR BEGINS ON JANUARY 1—EXCEPT 1942. That one started December 7, 1941. And on that saddest day in our history, Hollywood started a new regime which included not only its living but its thinking."[1] So began Hedda Hopper's 1941 year-end column published in newspapers across America.

On the day Japan bombed Pearl Harbor, Gene, his cast, and audience had assembled in Hollywood for their live Sunday afternoon presentation of the *Melody Ranch* radio show. Just before airtime, a special report from CBS's New York newsroom was transmitted through the theater's loudspeakers. Audience and cast members alike sat in stunned silence as the newscaster told of the devastating Japanese attack on the U.S. Pacific Fleet. Immediately afterward, Gene and company went on with the show, singing the songs and reading the lines in the script they had rehearsed. Later calling the program "one of the most awkward of my life," Gene remembered getting through it on "reflex and instinct." *Melody Ranch*, which recently had been increased from thirty to forty-five minutes, was cut short due to the emergency broadcast.

The next day, as Congress declared war, patriotic fervor swept the country; in the first week after Pearl Harbor, twenty-five thousand recruits joined the American armed forces. On December 22, Roosevelt signed into law an expansion of the draft, requiring the induction of men aged twenty to forty-four. Nearly 17 percent of the film industry would serve—including thirty-four-year-old Gene Autry.

Gene had many business details to put in order before he could set aside his career and join the service. Less than a week after Pearl Harbor, he returned to the studio to record a series of "farewell numbers": "I Hang My Head and Cry" ("I know not how to ease my mind"), "You'll Be Sorry," and "Sweethearts or Strangers." In February he cut back-to-back hits: the folk standard "Deep in the Heart of Texas," a polished version of the Carter Family's "I'm Thinkin' Tonight of My Blue Eyes," and his and Fred Rose's upbeat "Tweedle-O-Twill." Rose had continuously collaborated with Gene on a string of best sellers: their "Tears on My Pillow," "Be Honest With Me," and "You'll Be Sorry" were all top sellers in April and May, followed that summer by "Tweedle-O-Twill," "Take Me Back Into Your Heart," and "There's a Rainbow on the Rio Colorado."[2]

Fred Rose's tenure with Gene would soon draw to a close, however. His wife, Lorene, had become extremely fearful of living on the Pacific Coast during wartime, exacerbated by air-raid sirens and bomb-threat measures. Fearing Los Angeles would be the next target, she insisted they return to Nashville. To fund the trip, Fred asked Gene for help. "Freddie . . . wanted $250," recalled Jimmy Wakely. "He said to Gene, 'I'll give you ten songs [in exchange],' and he wrote them overnight. . . . [Later] somebody asked Freddie, 'Don't you feel pretty bad that you gave up your rights on those? People think Gene wrote them, and he had nothing to do with writing the numbers,' and Freddie said, 'Well, *you* know I wrote 'em! Everybody else knows in the trade that I wrote 'em, and so it's a good recommendation that I wrote those hits. . . . What's important is not yesterday, but the fact that you know I wrote those hits, you know I can write some more, and you'll also record my numbers."[3] "Rose did not seem to resent Autry's purchase of material this way," Rose scholar John Rumble agrees. "He once refused the star's offer of several thousand dollars in repayment for one tune."[4] Gene would coauthor only three more songs with Rose after his departure for Nashville. There, to Gene's chagrin, Rose became partners with hillbilly star Roy Acuff, forming the powerful country music publishing company, Acuff-Rose—a formidable competitor with Gene's Western Music.

Gene was about to wrap *Cowboy Serenade* when the Japanese bombed Pearl Harbor, and his next scheduled production, *Heart of the Rio Grande*, continued as scheduled in January. This would be the sole Autry picture to feature the Jimmy Wakely Trio. The ever-observant Johnny Bond took note of his boss on the set in the midst of wartime. "He worked before the camera with the same ease that he did before the radio microphone," he remembered. "He . . . took it all in stride, reading his lines in a semi-amateurish way, donning a boyish-bashful approach to the leading lady, Fay McKenzie, while working the horses and fight scenes with much authority."[5] Thanks to her string of Autry pictures, the sizzling McKenzie was becoming known as Republic's "oomph girl" in the trades; some exhibitors, labeling her "The Camera Appeal Girl" "considered her, both in face and figure, the most photogenic of our younger crop," according to Hedda

Hopper.[6] Some observers whispered that her on-screen romance with Gene continued off-screen as well. But the pair only made one more film together: *Home in Wyomin'*. That picture introduced a new juvenile actor, Joseph Strauch Jr., playing "Tadpole," a miniature version of Smiley's Frog Millhouse. The eleven-year-old, 120-pound veteran of Hal Roach's "Our Gang" series was contracted by Republic to retain his weight for the role.

Between *Rio Grande* and *Wyomin'*, Gene kicked off his Flying A Ranch Rodeo at the high-profile Houston Fat Stock Show on February 6, 1942. Gene had spent more than one hundred thousand dollars establishing the Flying A, and Houston, Texas, was the first of several spring bookings. The timing could not have been worse. With wartime rationing of tires and gasoline, rodeos struggled to survive. For security reasons, most West Coast rodeos had been cancelled, and Rodeo Association of America (RAA) officials encouraged East Coast promoters to make patriotism a part of the pageantry. Gene's Flying A Ranch Stampede included a spectacular homage to the Wild West show, with actors (cast from *Rio Grande*) masquerading as such heroic American horsemen as Buffalo Bill, Teddy Roosevelt, Davy Crockett, and Kit Carson. "It brought the house down . . . and was one of the most colorful additions to a rodeo we'd ever seen," Bond recalled. "Unfortunately . . . it was never again duplicated. . . . Perhaps . . . because the use of the Hollywood actors proved to be much too expensive an act to sustain."[7] The Stampede's program booklet reported that "much of the fortune Gene has made in films and radio has been invested in the Flying A. . . . His Hollywood friends, when they heard of his enthusiastic plans to present his production in this most critical of years, shook their heads and recalled other film cowboys who went broke after they bought and presented a road show, but Gene . . . has no such misgivings."[8]

The Stampede featured such RAA-certified competitions as calf roping and bronc and bull riding, in which cowboys could win cash prizes. Unlike previous rodeos, cowgirls were excluded from bronc-riding competition and limited to trick-riding exhibitions, which would gradually become an RAA rodeo standard—to the dismay of women rodeo professionals. Whether such measures were intended to protect women from injury or to prevent their competition against men is uncertain, but the end result was the elimination of women from competitive events. Their presence as "ranch girls"—glamorous equestriennes—was enhanced. Other entertainment included a square-dancing sequence (harkening back to Gene's WLS touring days) complete with fluorescent costumes, as well as an exhibition of Texas longhorns and a segment with Gene putting Champion through his paces. Gene's musical segment, similar to that at his 1940–41 rodeo performances, was also becoming the industry standard; today all major rodeos feature country stars as part of the entertainment.

Gene had ten more cities booked for the Flying A following the completion of another film, *Stardust on the Sage*. His future schedule, though, revolved around sudden news he had received during a recent phone conversation: "I had a friend who worked at the local draft board," Gene later related.

> He called me and said, "We're going to have to draft you, Gene. It looks like you're going to have to go in in April." I said, "I have dates booked in April, May, June—all the way up into July." And he said, "There's no hurry about that—after July, though, you shouldn't book any dates because we'll draft you." So I went to Herb Yates, and I said, "The draft board told me that they were going to draft me. I've got an extension until the end of July, so if you're going to make some pictures, you'd better think about when you're going to do it, because I've got some [rodeo] dates that I have to make." And Yates said, "Don't worry about it, hell, they'll never draft you. We'll ask for a deferment on you." And I said, "I don't think that would be a good thing, either. There's a lot of other people going in the service—Jimmy Stewart's in, Clark Gable's going in, Ty Powers—a lot of them. For me to ask for a deferment, it would reflect very badly on my behalf, and on yours, too. There's a lot of kids out there on the farm and working in the coal mine, and they're drafting them, and a lot of those parents are going to say, 'How does Gene Autry stay out when my boy is going in?'"—I didn't want that.[9]

In addition, Gene's *Melody Ranch* program had evolved from promoting Americanism and war-bond pitches to dramas meant to inspire listeners to join the service: A dramatization of an historic military campaign was included in the mix, following a Western story and music. On some programs, Gene or the announcer conveyed "propaganda" about the powerful U.S. armed forces, even issuing warnings to "any enemies who might be listening." Wrigley's gum pitches now were slanted toward enlisted men and women, and civilians working hard for the war effort. Many of the shows (minus the commercials) were transcribed and provided to servicemen.

After Yates realized Gene's determination to enlist, he immediately began putting wheels in motion to prevent the departure of his cash cow. Gene had continued to top the Western stars survey in 1941, and he was still in the top ten (at number six) of overall box-office draws. Yates contacted the Army Air Corps head of public relations, a Colonel Ennis and his assistant Captain Howard Nussbaum, about Gene's enlistment and what it would mean for Republic. "I visited Colonel Ennis . . . to find out whether or not Autry would be able to appear in pictures," according to Yates. "Colonel Ennis said yes under certain conditions and provided Autry would consent to turning over all of his earnings to the Army Relief Fund, which is a strict Army regulation."[10] An inter-office memo from Yates to Republic's E. H. Goldstein stated: "Nussbaum will be in Hollywood next Monday morning. . . . I suggest u phone him early Monday morning and say at my request U would like to send a car for him to lunch and take a quick peek at the studio. . . . Ask him if we can put a car and chauffeur at his service while he is in Hollywood. . . . Very important U do everything U can in addition to the foregoing for Capt. Nussbaum during his short stay in Hollywood as he has been of great assistance to me in the Autry situation and I believe will so continue."[11]

Gene meanwhile proceeded to make his own plans. Realizing it would be impossible to operate the Flying A while in the service, he made a deal with Everett Colborn to merge their rodeo outfits: he would sell his stock to Colborn's Lightning C Ranch in Texas, and for one-quarter ownership of the outfit, he would provide the star power of his name. "Gene Autry and Associates World's Championship Rodeo" would be managed and produced by Colborn, debuting at Madison Square Garden in October. Gene hoped to obtain the military's permission to headline the New York and Boston run. "If it hadn't been for the war, [Gene] would have been the world's greatest rodeo producer," his foreman Lonnie Rooney said. "We didn't even have the ranch complete when Gene sold it. Everything just happened at the wrong time." After Colborn purchased the stock, Gene gradually liquidated his Flying A ranch, eventually selling the land at a loss in 1946.

He also contacted Columbia Records president Ted Wallerstein to encourage him to reissue his old ARC recordings: "Since I will not have any income than that accrueing [*sic*] from royalties on phonograph records that have been made in the past, and my tieups, I would appreciate very much if you could see your way to reissue my entire catalog again on the OKeh label, or if it cannot be done on the OKeh label put them on the Columbia label."[12]

As the deadline for his service approached, Gene set up meetings with military officials to arrange his enlistment around his professional commitments. He had been taking flying lessons for some time, recently earning his pilot's license, and hoped to parlay that into a commission. "I went to Hap Arnold, who was head of the Air Force, and told him that I'd like to enlist in the [Army Air Corps]," Gene said.

> I didn't want to be drafted and wind up in the infantry, or something like that. . . . So we had several talks, and I was a pilot at that time on small aircraft, . . . so he said, "Yeah, we can use you. What kind of airplanes have you flown?" and I told him. He said, "Well, I'll tell you what I think . . . we could use you in the special services in public relations, and then you can go to school and get some . . . time in heavier military aircraft. . . . We'll give you a commission." But about that time, there had been a couple of personalities in Hollywood who had gotten some big commissions, and there was quite an investigation on it, and the [military] came out then with a ruling that no more stars from Hollywood or no more sports figures could get a commission, so he called me and said, "I'm sorry, Gene, we can't give you a commission, so you're just going to have to go in and take it."[13]

Soon after his enlistment, Gene told a reporter that the military thought he could best serve in the Army Air Corps, to help recruit young men needed as pilots.

On May 8, Gene passed his military physical, conducted at the General Dispensary in Washington, D.C., where he was in town with his rodeo. Six weeks later, on June 17, a memo was sent by command of Lieutenant General

Somervell that "the enlistment in the grade of Technical Sergeant of Mr. Orvon Gene Autry is authorized for the Army Air Corps. . . . This authority expires July 17, 1942."[14] Time was indeed running out.

Gene had to squeeze in a recording session (he'd completed another one in April), some Flying A performances, plus two more pictures before his induction. He had parted ways with agent Harry Wurtzel and replaced him with Mitch Hamilburg, who handled his growing list of licensed and endorsed goods, earning Gene nearly thirty thousand dollars in 1941. He also hired as his attorney the brilliant and ambitious John O'Melveny of the respected O'Melveny and Myers law firm, which represented Paramount Pictures among other clients. In May they had negotiated a more lucrative contract with Republic, which planned to make two "specials" before Gene's tour of duty began. Each with six-figure budgets, *Call of the Canyon* and *Bells of Capistrano* were made back to back. *Bells* ended with a patriotic flourish, its finale a lavish production number featuring Gene singing the World War I number, "Don't Bite the Hand That's Feeding You."

A Chicago paper noted the "busy days for Gene Autry," who was "notified yesterday in Hollywood to report for induction at Chicago Wednesday. Autry planned to complete a picture Monday and leave Tuesday by air; on Thursday, he had been scheduled to lead rodeo stars in the Flying A Ranch Stampede show at Soldier Field through July 29."[15] On July 9, Gene officially enlisted in the Army Air Corps at the newly constructed Air Recruiting Station at Chicago's Merchandise Mart. His military service was set for the duration of the war, plus six months. Then on July 26, during an emotional final broadcast of *Melody Ranch*, with Ina in the audience, Gene was sworn in over the air by Lt. Col. Edward Shaifer.

The closing *Melody Ranch* drama found Gene riding the trail, where he met "Uncle Sam," who applauded his decision to enlist. When co-star Virginia Vass asked, "Why didn't you wait til they [drafted] you?" Gene explained the virtues of serving his country. Cast members showered him with fond words and a farewell stopwatch; Gene sang "Tears on My Pillow," and following Shaifer's first command—"Sing, Sgt. Autry!"—"Private Buckaroo" and "God Must Have Loved America." Shaifer announced the program would continue as *Sergeant Gene Autry*, with Wrigley donating the CBS time and Gene's participation as part of his military duties. The *Chicago Herald-American*'s report of Gene's induction, though, read more like an obituary: "Thus will close his career for the duration in the city where he began it twelve years ago as a radio singer."[16]

In August Gene reported for basic training in Santa Ana, California, about thirty miles from Los Angeles. There, Gene began fighting the war—with Herb Yates. "Satisfactory arrangements were made with Colonel Ennis to put two pictures into production," Yates angrily related,

> and I notified the studio to prepare the scripts. During the latter part of July, I saw Autry in Chicago and asked him whether or not he wanted to make pictures under

the Army ruling of turning all of his earnings over to the Army Relief Fund—he said yes he wanted to make pictures. He thereupon told me, with others present, that Wrigley, the sponsor of his radio program, was turning the program over to the Air Corps but was not paying Autry any salary, instead Wrigley was placing his salary each week in a trust fund which would be turned over to Autry, or to Mrs. Autry in case of Autry's death, at the end of the war. In this connection, it was also stated from a reliable source that before the date of Autry's induction into the air corps, Wrigley had paid an advance of fifty thousand dollars to Mrs. Autry. I told Autry our contract with him called for the payment of his earnings direct to him upon the completion of each picture, and unless I had Colonel Ennis's approval to handle these payments in a different manner I would not consider a change in plan. Even then Autry stated he was willing to make the pictures, and with full permission of Colonel Ennis we notified Autry to appear on August 15 to start production of *Starlight on the Trail*, which we had already prepared, and we intended to follow closely with *Sergeant Autry of the Air Corps*.[17]

Autry sent word through Captain Nussbaum that he would not make a picture until certain aspects of his contract were "clarified." Yates responded by wiring:

I SHALL CERTAINLY BE GLAD TO GIVE IT TO YOU, BUT THIS SHOULD HAVE NOTHING TO DO WITH STARTING THIS PICTURE ON SCHEDULE AND I HOPE YOU WILL SEE MY POINT AND AVOID UNNECESSARY COMPLICATIONS AND CONTROVERSIES.[18]

Yates was already enraged that earlier in the year Gene had "organized his own rodeo and without consultation with studio officials . . . booked this rodeo . . . which of course is in violation of his contract because the only time off he can claim without our permission is the month of December each year."[19]

When Gene refused to report to the set, Yates drew his most potent weapon: Republic's King of the Cowboys, Roy Rogers. In early September, Yates wrote his UK distributor British Lion:

> You can well understand our desire to push Rogers to the front, which we believe we can do much easier than we did Autry because Rogers' personal appearance is far superior to Autry's, his loyalty and interest in Republic is unquestionable, and his ability as an actor, cowboy, and singer surpasses Autry at his very best. I am looking to you for unstinted cooperation to quickly push Rogers to the front and in that way at least take up some of the slack because of the shortage or perhaps the entire elimination of Autry pictures for the duration of the war. We will spend liberally on Rogers' first picture in the 1942–43 program . . . and in my opinion it will top any Western picture we have made to date with any of our Western stars. We will also spend liberally on Rogers' next picture, the title of which will be *King of the Cowboys*.[20]

SINCE GENE'S RETURN TO REPUBLIC following his 1938 strike, the studio had continued to produce Roy Rogers pictures, but they lagged behind Gene's in production values and popularity. Gene had never shown any particular ill will toward Rogers for stepping in during his strike, stating that if he had been in Roy's place he would have done the same thing. He knew that if not Roy, the vengeful Yates simply would have found another cowboy to fill Gene's boots. Yet Republic officials, including Yates, tried to paint a different picture. "During the past two weeks," Yates wrote British Lion, "Autry has been moving heaven and earth to make the rodeos in Madison Square Garden . . . and the Boston Garden, which are the biggest events of the year. Previously, Colonel Ennis had given him permission but just as soon as Major General Surles, Colonel Ennis's superior officer, found out about it, he requested Colonel Ennis withdraw his permission. . . . Autry, in his real character, again moved Heaven and Earth to keep Rogers out of these rodeo engagements [as his replacement]."[21]

As the Madison Square Garden rodeo approached and Rogers, indeed, replaced Autry as headliner, Gene accused Republic's publicity department of attempting to discredit him by planting negative stories in the press, and a flurry of correspondence between Yates and Gene ensued. An October 20 letter from Gene to Yates illuminates his concern over the public's perception of him, his thinking in regard to his career, and his tendency toward diplomacy even when infuriated:

> I assure you that my calling attention to this is not because I am upset by going into the army and losing a certain amount of income, as you suggest. Naturally I anticipated this and was prepared for it. I have worked hard during the last ten years and have made close to a million dollars, and since I have never been a spendthrift, I have taken care of it to the place where I feel that my financial status is assured. I have also worked hard for the past several years to build up a reputation which could do us both credit, and my being in the Service is a stand which I am sure cannot be regarded as other than commendable. . . . I had hoped Republic studios would back me and take advantage of the situation for good publicity. . . . But ever since I entered the Army I have had nothing but bad remarks and stories from your publicity department. . . . It seems that the whole thing started because I didn't feel that I should make a picture for Republic after going into the Service. My attorney advised me definitely against making a picture while in the Army unless some of the other stars who were in ahead of me also made one—in other words he couldn't see why I should be the guinea pig and stand a chance of getting a lot of bad publicity . . . just in order to fill Republic's schedule.
>
> As far as [Republic PR man] Bill Saal . . . he was calling all the columnists in town, telling them I owned nothing of the rodeo. . . . Furthermore, I can see no reason for such hullabaloo over the show because if the publicity had been handled right, Roy would have benefited far more from it and it would have been much nicer for him and me too than the way it turned out. I do own the show, and Bill Saal and the publicity department's interference in publicity concerning it has been a detriment, and I want him to keep his damned nose out of my private affairs.
>
> As you know, I was originally assigned to appear in person at the Garden show, and at a very good salary, more than three times as much as Roy is getting, and it was to have been donated to Army relief. The Army had held up on giving

me authority to appear there until it was decided whether or not Joe Louis [also an inductee] could fight. . . . Therefore, I held off and the Garden held off as long as possible before making any other arrangements but when it became definite I wouldn't be able to go, [the Garden's] Major Dibblee called me and asked who I would suggest in my place. I suggested either Smiley Burnette or Roy Rogers, preferably Smiley because he had been with me over twelve years, and if I could give him a recommendation I certainly would do it. . . . The Major called me and told me he had decided to take Roy, and I said that was alright. But when the publicity started to break, it as much as said the Gardens didn't want me and had hired Roy Rogers in preference. The publicity would have been much nicer for Roy if it had read that I couldn't appear and that he was pinch-hitting for his friend. This happened a few years ago when a fellow with a pretty big reputation by the name of Will Rogers did some pinch-hitting for Fred Stone.

Your entire publicity staff . . . acting as if I was poison ivy and were so afraid my name would be mentioned at the rodeo or that I would be announced there . . . was really funny. After all, as long as I own the show, I will be announced at every performance that I attend; that is my privilege the same as it is yours to have your trademark on every picture you produce. I realize this letter has been lengthy, but there were a few things I wanted to get off my chest. . . . However, I want you to know there are no hard feelings as far as I am concerned, and when you are on the coast I will be very happy to see you.[22]

After sitting down to dictate this missive, Gene began to stake out his future. Over the next eighteen months, while traveling the country promoting war bonds, appearing at recruitment drives, and entertaining the troops, he began to formulate a plan. He determined to finally break from Republic, sign with a different studio, and also find investment opportunities to protect himself financially. More battles with Yates would follow; soon after he received Gene's letter, Yates touched a nerve by casting Smiley as Roy's new sidekick for the first time since the 1938 strike. Republic continued its campaign to elevate Rogers's status, spending lavishly on advertising and production. Yates even contacted Wrigley's advertising agency to suggest Gene be replaced by Roy Rogers as star of the radio show sponsored by the gum company.

AFTER BASIC TRAINING, Gene was remanded to the Sixty-sixth Squadron at Luke Field, in Phoenix, Arizona. Ina moved into the city's luxurious Adams Hotel, where Gene spent most nights. On occasional furloughs, the couple traveled to the Chatsworth house, which Gene had named Melody Ranch. Also during time off, Gene took private flying lessons to qualify for a transfer to the ferrying command (he was beyond the age limit to be a cadet flyer). Every Sunday, he broadcast *Sergeant Gene Autry*, now written and produced by the U.S. Army. The Jimmy Wakely trio had resigned, so his new group included B-Western actor Eddie Dean and his harmonizing brother Jimmy, whom Gene had known at WLS. After a few months, Johnny Bond rejoined Gene's backing group. In Phoenix they usually broadcast from station KOY, where young pianist Steve Allen frequently joined them, reading lines in the military dramas.

This marked the beginning of Allen's long career in show business; two decades later Gene would be a guest on his television program.

In December, Mitch Hamilburg again met with Republic's Moe Siegel to negotiate changes in Gene's contract: allowing him to make outside pictures, increasing his salary to twenty thousand dollars per picture, and limiting his one-year option to four months. He also requested the studio handle Gene's fan mail, which cost $130 a week. In addition, Siegel reported to Yates, Gene requested "that we will agree not to use Smiley Burnette in the Roy Rogers pictures. Autry would not have any objection to our starting a new series featuring Smiley Burnette. Hamilburg made another point, which he did not insist on . . . and that involved the small matter of buying Autry an airplane at a cost of about $6,000 or $7,000."[23]

Following the meeting, Siegel advised Yates to refuse Autry's demands but admitted he could not predict what the loss of Autry pictures would mean for Republic:

> Between you and me . . . the Rogers boom, in spite of all our efforts, might not accomplish what we are after, because John Q. Public still makes and breaks stars, as is indicated by the fact there was no good, earthly reason why Autry should have ever become a star and no good reason, if it would be based on ability, why Rogers during the four years or more that we have had him, did not top Autry by several city blocks. . . . I personally would like nothing better than to have Autry become a nonentity in this business and that Rogers become his successor."[24]

On December 16, John O'Melveny wrote Yates "entirely on my own accord without any consultation with either Mr. Hamilburg or Gene Autry." What precipitated his letter was another meeting with Siegel in which the Republic producer "stated that he wanted a long-term contract for at least five years in order to make those other concessions that Autry wanted." Gene capitulated, saying he "wanted the deal the way we had discussed it and that he was willing to make a long-term contract and be a good boy and go back into the arms of Republic." When his answer was delivered to Siegel, the word came back that Republic's previous offer had been withdrawn. Hamilburg then asked O'Melveny to start proceedings to break Gene's Republic contract—thus O'Melveny's letter to Yates. Worried that in a previous meeting, he had offended Yates and caused him to rescind his offer, O'Melveny asked that the long-term Autry contract be approved: "I do not wish [Autry] to suffer in the least for anything that I have done," O'Melveny wrote.

> Since I have been handling Mr. Autry's affairs I feel that I have tried in every way that I possibly could to get him to cooperate with the studio. I have told Autry again and again that he should be just as happy at Republic as any place else, that I didn't feel that he was or ever would be any great actor, and that you people had worked out a formula in pictures which was just suitable to him and his personality and that he ought to stick with you and that type of picture. When others were

telling Mr. Autry he should become a great actor and work for Paramount or MGM or others, I have stuck by my guns and told him repeatedly to stay with Republic and the type of pictures he is doing.[25]

Yates replied that his decision was not due to O'Melveny's actions, but that "the demands made by [Hamilburg] . . . we consider unreasonable. . . . Our position will not be affected by Mr. Autry's threat to start a lawsuit to break our contracts with him. This is just one more instance of his attitude toward his contracts with Republic for some years."[26] Negotiations ceased between Gene and Republic, and the studio announced it would begin re-releasing old Autry movies.

By December's end, Gene's popularity was as great as ever. He'd drawn massive crowds to bond drives, including a ten-day rally in Houston, in which more than $50 million in war bonds were sold. Numerous magazine and newspaper profiles applauded the sacrifice he was making for his country. The day after Christmas, the *New York Times* reported that Gene was still among the top ten box-office draws (at number seven), and "among Western stars Gene Autry is again the leader for the sixth consecutive year."[27]

The number two spot, however, was taken for the first time by Roy Rogers. The following year, the King of the Cowboys would move into first place—with Gene Autry never again making his way to the top.

29

SERGEANT GENE AUTRY

GENE USHERED IN 1943 IN THE SAME WAY that he had the previous four years—by participating in the annual "Salute to the President's Birthday." But this time he took part far from the glamorous fund-raising balls of past Januarys. Included in the January 30 NBC radio broadcast featuring such stars as Frank Sinatra and Danny Kaye, Gene's segment was transmitted from Luke Field: "With the *Melody Ranch* band and seven hundred cadets and enlisted men and myself," he informed Roosevelt and a national audience. "We'd like to sing a little ditty that we know is one of your favorites," Gene added, before launching into "Yellow Rose of Texas." He shared the mic with a few enlisted men, including—to Gene's obvious delight—the son of a New York Giants pitcher, as well as a Chinese cadet, among a group from Mainland China receiving pilot training in Phoenix.

Gene's fan club had organized a fund-raising drive, too, with proceeds donated by Gene to FDR's March of Dimes infantile paralysis fund, which elicited a letter of appreciation from Roosevelt. Soon after Gene's enlistment, fan club members actively worked on their idol's behalf, with 300 of the 1,300 members organizing a "postcard patrol." The well-executed plan involved a card-writing campaign to various publications requesting articles on Sergeant Autry. Their constant stream of correspondence to key editors helped to keep Gene in the public eye. They also mailed cards to such radio programs as *The Hit Parade* requesting Gene Autry music. Although Gene made no movies or recordings in 1943, the club's "fanzine," *Autry's Aces*, informed the predominantly female members of his bond-drive appearances, and also included a letter to the club from Gene. "Strange as it may seem, I don't miss Hollywood one bit, "he wrote in a 1943 issue. "You see, I could always adapt myself to most anything if I made up my mind to and that is just what I have done in the Army."[1] Another of the year's issues noted that "recently Gene made a speech to the Arizona State Legislature. . . . He is the first motion picture star to ever be invited to make a speech to such a body. In doing so, he gave his famous impression of President Roosevelt, and they say that nearly brought down the house. Many of us have seen and heard this, and he is just tops."[2]

In April, Gene secured a furlough to appear in Hollywood Superior Court on behalf of Private George Goodale: his old PR man was suing Gene's former agent Harry Wurtzel for $25,000—" 'a fair and reasonable percentage' of the agent fees he'd received through his association with Autry during the last two years," according to the *Los Angeles Times*. Goodale claimed that bringing together the client and agent entitled him to a percentage of Wurtzel's commissions from Gene's movie income. The singing cowboy's early contract struggles came to light when Wurtzel testified that he first met Gene in 1935: "At that meeting Autry told me he was getting a raw deal from his studio and said he was about to quit. I told him I couldn't handle him under those conditions. My relations with Autry ended then until February 1936, when he and Goodale came to my office." Gene then signed a five-year contract with Wurtzel, though Goodale was never rewarded for serving as liaison. Gene gave testimony that Goodale planned to sue Wurtzel for compensation in 1938 but at his request had not. "Mitchell J. Hamilburg, Autry's present agent, testified that it is a general rule among Hollywood agents to split commissions received from clients with the person making the introduction," the *Times* reported.[3] Goodale won the suit.

Over the course of the two-week hearing, Gene's thoughts turned to his current financial situation. The previous year, he had grossed more than $432,000; now, he received standard army pay of $114 a month. He accumulated some income from his publishing company and recording royalties: Western Music actually brought in nearly $18,000 in 1943, compared to less than $11,000 the year before. His shrewd purchase of song copyrights had paid off. Ironically, Gene would be sued in January by songwriter Jack Baxley for *not* adding "Gene Autry" to the composer credits of a collaborative effort, "I Wish All My Children Were Babies Again." "Baxley asserts the song did not sell well but would have if Autry's name had appeared on the cover," a news report noted.[4]

With fewer records being pressed due to shellac shortages and no new recordings released, including the reissues he had requested, Gene's Columbia earnings plummeted from $29,332 in 1942 to $16,662 in 1943. Royalties from tie-ups also had been negatively affected by rationing of raw materials, with some items being discontinued, including the Gene Autry cap pistols. His investments improved his bottom line, however, with his share of the Championship Rodeo bringing in a hefty $22,457 by year's end. He also bought into the Automatic Phonograph Company, an Arizona-based jukebox concern, which he staffed with employees from his prewar businesses. What better investment for a man who wanted to keep his own discs playing in roadhouses and diners? His connection to Columbia also assured enough platters to stock jukeboxes during a time when new records were quite scarce.

Gene received no payment for his broadcasts, but he still earned $14,700 from Wrigley (presumably part of the trust arrangement), compared with $71,000 the previous year. His only income came from partnerships, including a liquor distributor that he acquired, the All-American Distributing Company. He also invested in two Arizona radio stations, in Phoenix and Tucson.

In the spring of 1943 Gene bought his first airplane—a secondhand monoplane for three thousand dollars. He purchased the Phoenix-based Pacific Air School, where he took private flying lessons to qualify for Air Corps planes with greater horsepower. The military soon moved him into special services, where he toured U.S. bases to entertain the troops. Private Carl Cotner was also stationed at Luke Field, and joined Gene as violinist on the tours. His civilian trio, comprising the Dean brothers and Johnny Bond, accompanied them. They broadcast the radio show from where ever they happened to be on a Sunday. Not sounding as relaxed as he did on *Melody Ranch*, Gene often stumbled over his lines, while explaining a military tactic or introducing a guest army official. Presumably, rehearsal time was short. Gene was becoming more frustrated with "soft duty," telling the *Chicago Daily News* in May, "I don't want to stay here all the time. I think everyone would like to go over[seas]." He wanted to be a pilot like Jimmy Stewart, or see action like the men he entertained in General Patton's army camp in the California desert. Finally, on August 1, after one year of radio programs, he broadcast his last episode of *Sergeant Gene Autry*, sounding relieved as he said his on-air farewells. He later admitted, on *The Steve Allen Show*, "I wanted out of it . . . but I couldn't do anything about it. When you're in a uniform, they tell you what to do."

Republic continued to rerelease his old films, which were sometimes shown on double bills with the newer, high-production-value Roy Rogers pictures—and not faring well in comparison. This infuriated Gene's fans, who wrote letters complaining to *Autry's Aces*. When *Life* magazine ran a July 12 cover story on Roy Rogers, titled "King of the Cowboys," the postcard patrol became incensed. One loyal Boston member, Gladys Green, who groused to the editors about the article's inaccuracies, received a reply from *Life* editor A. E. Eggleston: "Gene Autry's public is evidently not forgetting him, judging from the mail *Life* has received. And if a poll were taken, it looks as if he would still be voted 'King of the Cowboys,' although he has given up making pictures for the duration."[5]

Gene frequently visited Washington, DC, meeting with members of Congress and nearly every president from Franklin Roosevelt to Bill Clinton.

Smiley Burnette's mini-me Joseph Strauch, Jr., played Tadpole in several Autry features, including 1942's *Heart of the Rio Grande*.

Ina loved flowers and prided herself in her gardening abilities; here, she and Gene take in the beauty of their San Fernando Valley ranch property.

The shell of Gene and Ina's home in North Hollywood, which was ruined by fire in 1941. (Stanley Rojo Collection)

Gene hired Mitchell Hamilburg (at left) to represent his licensing deals beginning in 1938, but by 1942 Hamilburg had become his theatrical agent as well.

Gene is sworn into the Army Air Corps before a studio audience, which was broadcast live on his *Melody Ranch* radio program in July 1942.

Gene Autry hangs up his spurs and fancy Western duds for a set of wings in the Army Air Corps during World War II.

In 1942, Gene was based at Luke Field in Phoenix, Arizona, where the Army Air Corps trained Chinese cadets, pictured here on a cola break with Sgt. Autry.

Gene's longtime musical collaborator, Carl Cotner (with violin), enlisted and served with him in the Army Air Corps, where the two performed on the *Sgt. Gene Autry Show* and entertained at numerous bases, along with Eddie Dean, Johnny Bond, and Jimmy Dean (from left).

After serving from 1942 to 1945 in the Army Air Corps, Gene traveled with a small USO troupe to the South Pacific to entertain the troops before returning to private life.

At a New York City fan club convention, Gene is flanked by the founder of the Gene Autry
Friendship Club, Dorothy Pinnick Crouse, and the president of his U.K. fan club, Alex Gordon.

Gene's very first picture for Columbia, *The Last Round-Up*, was filmed in Arizona in 1947 and featured
Russ Vincent (left) and Jay Silverheels, who later played Tonto in television's *The Lone Ranger*.

Gene, here with Little Champ and Champion, scouts out their next personal appearance tour.

A staged embrace for a fan magazine spread on Gene's return home from a long national tour. In 1948, *Life* reported that Ina had "always managed to keep [Gene's] feet on the ground."

Gene's brother, Dudley Autry, struggled unsuccessfully to follow in Gene's footsteps as an entertainer.

Gene and Ina relax at home with their beloved boxer, Mike.

Texans the Cass County Boys—bassist Bert Dodson, accordionist Fred Martin, and guitarist Jerry Scoggins—on the road with Gene.

Gene and Bing Crosby co-hosted a 1948 Christmas special on CBS radio, where they were joined by the Andrews Sisters (also pictured here) and numerous A-list celebrities.

A publicity stunt had Elena Verdugo and Gene pose for this kiss; the embrace was never actually filmed as part of 1949's *The Big Sombrero*, the second and final Gene Autry color feature.

New Orleans native Gloria Henry was not a fan of horses nor of co-star Gene Autry, with whom she appeared in two films, *The Strawberry Roan* and this one, *Riders in the Sky*.

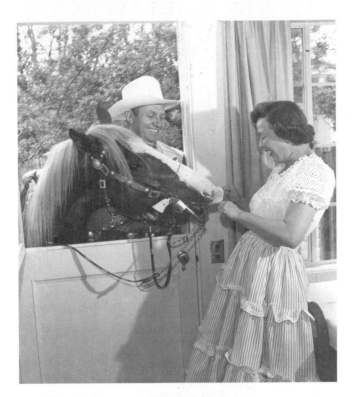

Fan magazines frequently depicted Gene and Ina as the perfect couple; here, visiting with Champion at their San Fernando Valley ranch.

Gene and boxer Jack Dempsey became very close friends and at one time co-owned some Texas oil wells.

Frankie Marvin, Gene's buddy since 1928, dressed in the Rudolph costume, complete with flashing nose, beginning with Gene's appearance at the 1949 World's Championship Rodeo at Madison Square Garden. Songwriter Johnny Marks supplied the costume.

Seasonal songs reinvigorated Gene's recording career, beginning with 1947's "Here Comes Santa Claus (Right Down Santa Claus Lane)"; its 1949 follow-up, "Rudolph, the Red-Nosed Reindeer," for years held the record as the second biggest-selling single after Bing Crosby's "White Christmas."

Champion gets the star treatment with Gene's help leaving his hoof prints at Graumann's Chinese Theatre in Hollywood; ace horse trainer Johnny Agee (in white hat) looks on.

The Autrys occasionally invited Gene's fan club members to their home; here, Friendship Club president Dot Crouse (left) with Ina (right) and Gene's longtime secretary, Louise Heising, who also played violin and viola in the *Melody Ranch* orchestra. (Stanley Rojo Collection)

Gene Autry's very close friend and second sidekick, Pat Buttram, met his future wife, Sheila Ryan, on the set of *Mule Train*, 1950.

Gene Autry and cowgirls in New York City for the World's Championship Rodeo held at Madison Square Garden, 1950.

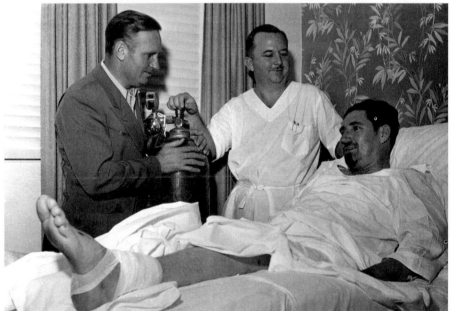

Gene Autry Friendship Club members, on location with Gene and Pat Buttram at Pioneertown, 1950. (Stanley Rojo Collection)

Gene Autry visiting Pat Buttram in the hospital after Pat was injured performing a stunt while filming an episode of *The Gene Autry Show*, 1950.

Though Republic Pictures head Herb Yates tried to promote a fierce competition between Gene and Roy Rogers, the pair were friendly rivals rather than enemies. In 1950, *Movie Life* magazine staged a "truce" over a game of golf at Lakeside Country Club, a favorite hangout for Gene until the 1980s.

Gail Davis starred with Gene in numerous movies and television shows in the 1950s. Here, the pair appear in 1951's *Whirlwind*, based on the title song by Stan Jones, who also played a bit part in the picture.

Gene also wrote a perturbed letter to *Life*, published in a subsequent issue:

> You state: "Roy and Arlene have an adopted daughter named Cheryl Darlene. Although she is not yet 4, she has her talents. Whenever she hears the name 'Gene Autry' she purses her lips, delivers a gentle Bronx cheer. Autry himself taught her this trick."
>
> I have never met Mr. Rogers' little adopted daughter, Cheryl Darlene. Furthermore, if I had, I have been taught better than to go around teaching the youth of our country such vulgar mannerisms. With times as they are today, I feel there are many things more important to teach them than the Bronx cheer.[6]

The Rogers feature was just one of Gene's frustrations. On July 20, he applied for his transfer to the Ferrying Division, having built up the required 284 hours and 45 minutes of flying time. Army headquarters turned down his request, with the caveat that if he built up an additional 15 hours and 15 minutes of flying time, he could apply for the Service Pilot Training Command. This he did, and finally on October 20 his application was accepted—only to be withdrawn on January 17, with the reason given that the Training Command was not using service pilots at the time.

Infuriated, Gene contacted his old friend Texas Governor James V. Allred and explained the situation. Allred in turn called Major General C. R. Smith about Gene's problems, following up with a letter stating:

> Autry has built up a total of 342 hours and 30 minutes of flying time. The Air Transport Command has, I understand, put in an order for him to be transferred to them, but the Adjutant at Luke Field, Arizona, where Autry is stationed, stated that they would not release him for ATC.
>
> As I told you over the telephone, Autry had an income of $360,000 a year when he enlisted as a Sergeant. He gave up this and asks for nothing except an opportunity to serve as an ATC pilot in the Ferrying Service, for which he seems to have more than qualified himself. He is not engaged in anything of importance at Luke Field, and it seems to me they are hiding his light under a basket.[7]

Gov. Allred's next call was to Congressman Lyndon Baines Johnson, to whom he later wrote

> In connection with [Gene's] difficulty about being tied down at Luke Field . . . [Gene] tells me that it may be due to the following: When he enlisted in July 1942, a Col. Ennis was in charge of public relations in Washington and asked him to do a radio program for the Air Forces. Gene was unfamiliar with army etiquette, etc., and Col. Ennis evidently did not consult with the personnel office in Washington, headed by General Bevans. It has been suggested to Gene that the General did not appreciate this, and [Gene] would like in some way to let General Bevans know that he certainly was not familiar with the appropriate course and simply acquiesced in Col. Ennis' request that he do this radio show. [8]

LBJ took care of the situation immediately, wiring Governor Allred:

HAVE HAD THE CONFERENCE WITH THE GENERAL CONCERNING GENE AS I
PROMISED. STRICTLY CONFIDENTIAL, BUT GENERAL IS WRITING PERSONAL
NOTE TO THE GENERAL IN TEXAS WHO IS IN CHARGE OF THE COMMAND IN
WHICH GENE IS STATIONED. HE IS PERSONALLY REQUESTING THAT TEXAS
GENERAL APPROVES OUR GENERAL'S REQUEST THAT GENE IS TRANSFERRED TO
AIR TRANSPORT. HE THINKS CHANCES ARE AT LEAST 90 PERCENT AND WILL
LET YOU KNOW. YOU MAY COMMUNICATE THIS TO GENE IN STRICT CONFI-
DENCE. WILL KEEP ON THE JOB. [9]

A wire to Gene from LBJ followed on March 6:

HAPPY TO TELL YOU GENERAL INFORMS ME YOUR MATTER WAS HANDLED
SATISFACTORILY. EXPECT YOU WILL RECEIVE OFFICIAL NOTIFICATION RIGHT
SOON. [10]

On March 9 Gene wrote a thank you letter to Congressman Johnson,

After receiving your telegram it was only a matter of hours until I received official
notification that I was being transferred to the 3rd Ferrying Division of the Air
Transport Command at Romulus, Michigan. . . . As far as I am concerned, the
Field at Phoenix was ideal. Everyone was very nice to me including officers and
men, but I did not feel I was doing a job that I was qualified to do. Therefore I
thought it best to get a transfer to the Ferrying Division where my abilities could
be better used. Again, I want to thank you for everything you did."[11]

Gene's transfer to Michigan initially landed him in the Air Transport
Command WAC recruitment program. His first orders were to fly to Cincinnati to make several radio appearances to recruit WACs. Gene was not particularly fond of the Women's Army Corps, which had been organized in May
1942. The previous spring, his secretary Vera Wooters (Mary Lee's sister) had
abruptly left Gene's employ to join the WACs. In his memoir, Gene spoke dis-
paragingly of the "fine ladies" among WACs, describing a run-in with a bossy
female lieutenant in Michigan, and according to Johnny Bond, he refused to
salute female officers. The "Petticoat Army" had proven a successful addition
to the armed forces, with women being trained, among other positions, as pilots for the Women's Auxiliary Ferrying Squadron—the job Gene desired.

On April 5 he notified Lyndon Johnson:

I am putting in my papers again for pilot's rating. . . . I believe if no hitch comes up
I will be able to get my rating as that is what I have wanted for quite some time.
However, I understand there are quite a number of pilots out of work and not getting their rating as they had hoped to. You probably know of this story as there has
been so much controversy about it in Congress. It really does seem quite a shame

to spend all the money training girls in this kind of work when there are so many pilots already qualified to do the same type work as they are being trained for.

Again I want to express my appreciation for everything you did. . . . If there is anything I can do to reciprocate, please do not hesitate to call on me.[12]

Johnson responded five days later:

My thought is that since General Smith and General George have both evidenced an interest in you and have been so helpful thus far your rating will come through in due course. However, if you feel the matter is not receiving attention and want me to contact General George, I will do so. I note the last paragraph of your letter and assure you that it is greatly appreciated. I may take you up on that some summer if the going looks tough.[13]

GENE AND JOHNSON WOULD, INDEED, RECIPROCATE FAVORS several times over the years. In July 1946, Gene would campaign for Johnson, as he had a decade earlier. Twice, however, Gene had to remain neutral and sit out a Johnson political bid: in 1948 during LBJ's senatorial race against Gene's friend, former Texas governor Coke Stevenson, and again in 1964 during the presidential election when Johnson's opponent was Gene's Luke Field squadron leader— Barry Goldwater (Gene donated money to both candidates).

Finally, on June 21, Technical Sergeant Gene Autry was promoted to Flight Officer and assigned to the Ninety-first Ferrying Squadron, at Love Field, in Dallas. "Among fliers, the ATC wasn't where the glamour was," Gene later related. "You were in the cargo business. The fellows who flew the fighters and the bombers sometimes compared us to truck drivers. . . . [But] I flew some beauties in the Air Corps—the Douglas dive bomber, P-51s, the C-47, but for the thrill that lasts a lifetime, nothing could beat the C-109. It had been converted into a tanker to haul fuel over the Hump [the Himalayas] and into Kumming, China. . . . This was the China-Burma-India Theater, the air zone with the highest fatality rate in the war. . . . I only flew the Hump once and that was enough." In September, Gene experienced another close call when "to avoid a typhoon over the Azores, a plane I was copiloting had to turn back and fly for five hours with an engine missing, low on fuel, back to Gander Bay, in Newfoundland. Then a fog bank moved in and we were stuck there for two weeks."[14] Other dangers included the possibility of sabotage: planes had to be guarded from terrorists who attempted to damage the planes by putting sand into their gas tanks.

On November 9 Gene proudly wrote to *Autry's Aces* about his adventures:

Have been practically around the world . . . and in so many countries [including Egypt and India] that if I had to have a passport for each of them it would fill a book. I wish I could share the experiences I have had with you but at the present time the War Department says "no telling" where I have been or what is going on. . . . Saw several of the boys overseas that I knew. Also met and entertained a lot of the fellows. In fact, almost every place I went, from some place they pulled out

a guitar and we had a show; which of course I was very happy to do. Since returning home have been ferrying all over the country all of the time. Usually make two
or three trips a week. I happened to get a trip to New York and so saw the Rodeo
and also several of you members there. I am always very happy to see you.[15]

Gene had one other matter to resolve, and that was his contract with Republic. He had hired attorney Martin Gang to initiate proceedings in June 1944
to terminate his contract with the studio. The *New York Times* reported that

movie producers are watching with interest the suit filed recently in Superior
Court in Los Angeles by Gene Autry . . . asking declaratory relief from his contract with Republic Pictures. At the time he entered the Army in August 1942,
Autry's contract had two years to run. . . . [He] maintains he no longer is employed
by reason of his entering the armed services. The interest of movie producers generally in the outcome of the suit is understandable, since a decision favoring Autry
would set a precedent and possibly lead to a flood of similar actions on the part of
other actors who have been called into service.[16]

And a Chicago paper noted that

barring the [contract] suspension, the contract would expire Sept. 22, 1945, but
every day in the army adds another day to the contract. The thought of this gives the
37-year-old visions of riding the range in a girdle and skull rug when he would rather
be managing his radio stations and other assorted enterprises as an unashamedly
solid and substantial businessman. So far, he needn't worry. He's lithe and harder
than when he went into the army, and is definitely neither round in the middle nor
shiny on top. But a long war might change a lot of things, he opined.[17]

This was the first public inkling that Gene desired anything more than to return
to his entertainment career, and he vehemently denied the implication in a note
to *Autry's Aces*: "There have been several articles in different papers insinuating
that I may retire when the war is over, and I want to straighten this out once and
for all—I will definitely be back on the screen and on the radio. I am not certain
what company I will be connected with, and intend to make bigger and better
pictures than I have ever made before. In fact I might produce them myself."

On December 1 Gene appeared in court in Los Angeles and testified that
Republic had no right to exercise an option on his contract after he entered the
armed services. He also contended that the studio had attempted to replace
him with Roy Rogers. "Autry stated on the stand," the *Los Angeles Times* reported, "that he and Herbert J. Yates . . . had discussed Rogers' participation in
a rodeo at Madison Square Garden. . . . Yates, he said, asked him which had
been his dressing room there the year before, saying he wanted Rogers to have
it. 'Well,' he quoted Yates as saying, 'you wouldn't cooperate, and I'll break you
if it's the last thing I ever do, and I'll make Roy Rogers the biggest thing that
ever happened in this business.'"

December also brought Gene some very bad news. His great friend, collaborator, and early mentor Johnny Marvin had contracted malaria while traveling overseas to entertain troops. He refused medical treatment, due to his Christian Science beliefs, and died at age forty-seven on the twentieth. In addition, Gene's twenty-five-year-old brother, Dudley, was not doing well. He had enlisted in the Marines in 1942, gotten married, then was shipped off to Guadalcanal, where he endured the devastating battles with the Japanese in August of '42. Upon his return to the States, he began drinking heavily. On December 16 the *Los Angeles Times* reported that "while he was AWOL from the Marines he was also AWOL from home,"[18] and a divorce had been granted to his wife, Patricia Autry.[19]

The bad news continued for Gene into 1945. On February 10 he lost his case against Republic, with the judge ruling that he was still "bound by paid contract to carry out the terms of the agreement" and that he was not "free to render services for himself or others as an actor, pending release by the studio."[20] According to his contract, Gene was required to make twenty-one pictures for Republic over the next three years; his attorney appealed the decision. In March he filed suit against Dave Gordon, a former partner with Gene and Johnny Marvin in Western Music. They had dissolved the partnership the previous year, but Gordon had continued to sell Autry songbooks, pocketing the profits.

Tragedy occurred, when later that month, two children were killed and eleven injured when the Gene Autry playsuits they were wearing ignited after being in close proximity to an open flame. When notified of the incidents, Gene was horrified and told one newspaper he "would get in touch with the manufacturer immediately to find out what the score was."[21] Legal ramifications from the accidents—and more that followed—would continue into the early 1950s.

On April 12 President Franklin D. Roosevelt died suddenly of a cerebral hemorrhage, just over three weeks shy of the Axis surrender to Allied Forces on May 7. Gene had already put in a request for his discharge. As before, he discovered that what he wanted conflicted with military plans. Instead of being discharged, he was reassigned from Air Transport Command back to Special Services. Following an early May meeting with Gene in Washington, Lyndon Johnson came to the rescue. "I arrived in California a few days ago and am now preparing to go on a USO tour for eight weeks," Gene wrote the congressman on June 11. "I have not yet received my final papers on the discharge but they have been approved in Washington. . . . It certainly was a pleasure to see you again . . . I enjoyed very much being with you at Mr. Rayburn's party and having lunch with you in the Speaker's dining room. I certainly appreciate everything you did concerning my army discharge."[22]

On June 17 Gene received his honorable discharge, and ten days later, his USO troupe flew to the South Pacific. After performing eighty-five shows at numerous bases, for nearly a million GIs, Gene and company arrived in Saipan on August 1. "We stayed [there] four days, while the activity and the tension grew visibly," he later wrote. "No one really knew what was going on at Tinian, another of the Mariana Islands a few miles away. . . . There was a great deal of talk about planes and people coming and going." Gene and his revue were invited to perform on Tinian by General Roger Ramey, whom he knew from Texas. "I had a highball with Ramey on the night of the fourth," said Gene, "two days before a plane called the Enola Gay took off from Tinian.' "[23] On August 6 it dropped the first atomic bomb over Hiroshima. Gene was back on Saipan when a second, plutonium bomb devastated Nagasaki three days later.

President Harry S. Truman made the announcement of the Japanese surrender on August 14, while Gene was on Iwo Jima. Two weeks later, he was en route to the States and to a new, postwar life.

30

DON'T FENCE ME IN

UPON HIS RETURN TO CIVILIAN LIFE, having just traveled thirty-five thousand miles in two months throughout the South Pacific, Gene seemed unable to stand still. He briefly spent time with Ina at their San Fernando ranch while plotting his course. With movie making on hold pending the outcome of his appeal, he traveled to Texas and Arizona, to deal with rodeo, broadcasting, and other business investments, then to Chicago for meetings with Wrigley.

On September 23 his radio program resumed, again sponsored by Wrigley, even though chewing gum was still unavailable due to sugar shortages. The newly titled *Gene Autry Show* ran for fifteen minutes on CBS and featured a revised format: a few songs by Gene, a chat between Gene and announcer Lou Crosby, and a spot by California natives, The Pinafores, an Andrews Sisters–type group composed of the three Kettle sisters, Ione, Beulah, and Eunice. The Glendale-based trio came to Gene upon the recommendation of an old pal from Chicago's WJJD, Les Paul, who had moved to Hollywood and made a name for himself as an innovative guitarist and brilliant recording engineer.

On November 25 Gene added another harmonizing group that would become an important part of his sound. The Cass County Kids (soon changed to Boys) were an accomplished vocal/instrumental trio he'd met while stationed at Love Field in Dallas. "We were on the radio down there," said accordionist Fred Martin, "and Gene heard us. 'When I get back . . . I'll send for you,' he said. Had anyone else said it, we'd never have expected to hear of it again. But Gene's word is his bond. A year later to the day, he long-distanced that he had a place for us." Also featuring Jerry Scoggins on guitar and Bert Dodson on upright bass, the trio would remain with Gene until his retirement from show business. Both the Cass County Boys and the Kettle Sisters added their harmonies to Gene's recordings in addition to the radio show.

Johnny Bond, now recording for OKeh and appearing on the *Hollywood Barn Dance* radio show, initially took on a smaller role on the Wrigley program—although it would grow the following year. He had been Gene's comedic sidekick during the military tours and a major part of *Melody Ranch*, but Gene apparently wanted some new elements for the revised show. At the beginning of each program, Bond, standing next to Gene, played a catchy acoustic guitar riff kicking off a revamped arrangement of "Back in the Saddle Again." Since buying the publishing rights in 1941 from Ray Whitley (who originally had placed the song with Warner Chappell) and adding it to his Western Music stable, Gene had made it his signature song.

Among the numbers featured on the program were Gene's recent hits, as well as a traditional folksong and a "cowboy classic." A musician's union strike that had lasted from July 1942 until November 1944 had prevented any commercial recordings during that period. But as soon as the strike ended, Gene had entered Columbia's Hollywood studio with Johnny Bond and a band featuring clarinet, sax, trumpets, violins, accordion, and bass. The two sessions yielded several 78s released early in 1945: the biggest was the two-sided smash, "Gonna Build a Big Fence Around Texas" and Cole Porter's "Don't Fence Me In." Roy Rogers had crooned the latter in the 1944 film *Hollywood Canteen*, but Gene's version made radio's *Western Hit Parade*—a spin-off of the pop music program. After years of being kept at a minimum on radio by the strong arm of James Petrillo's Musician's Union, 78s and performance transcriptions were now replacing studio musicians at a growing number of stations. In 1944, Gene's records "I Hang My Head and Cry" and "I'm Thinking Tonight of My Blue Eyes" had entered the top five of the brand-new "Most Played Jukebox Folk Records" chart, listed in *Billboard* magazine.

Gene's releases would climb into the chart's top ten seven times in 1945, with the massive "At Mail Call Today" lodged in the number one spot for eight weeks beginning in April. Gene came up with the song idea while stationed at Love Field. Perusing the servicemen's newspaper one day, he read a letter in the Mail Call Today column from a soldier whose gal had dumped him. Gene wrote a verse, then had Fred Rose join him in Dallas, where the song doctor turned it into a lilting waltz. Its flipside, "I'll Be Back," which Gene wrote with Eddie Dean and others, also struck a chord with listeners.

Gene added to his recorded output with three more sessions in 1945. Having lost Johnny Marvin, and with Fred Rose's contributions diminishing, he sought new writers to provide him with material. Johnny Bond offered "Don't Live a Lie," which hit the chart by year's end. Its flipside, "I Want to Be Sure," came from Kentucky native Merle Travis, who would redefine country music guitar playing. In the studio, Merle replaced Eddie Tudor, Gene's guitarist, who was tragically killed in action in France. Having first met Carl Cotner at WHAS, while they were both members of Clayton McMichen's Georgia Wildcats, Travis moved to California after wartime service in the marines. The talented songwriter—responsible for "Smoke! Smoke! Smoke! (That Cigarette)," "Dark as a Dungeon," and "Sixteen Tons"—would provide his distinctive electric guitar licks to numerous Autry sessions and performances over the next decade.

Gene also found success with "Don't Hang Around Me Anymore" ("I saw you jivin' in that juke joint") backed with "Address Unknown," two sides by Smiley Burnette's old WDZ radio partner, Denver Darling, now a successful New York–based country singer and songwriter. Gene's sessions maintained Frankie Marvin's Western-style steel guitar and the piano accordion of Paul Sells, who sometimes switched to keyboards. The lyrics Gene crooned were increasingly in the vein of the popular honky-tonk genre introduced by such country artists as Ernest Tubb: jilted lovers, backstreet affairs, and vengeful rebounders, epitomized by Fred Rose's "Don't Take Your Spite Out on Me."

As a side-effect of the war, moral standards had loosened: when soldiers knew they could be shipped out tomorrow, possibly never to return, booze-fueled one-night stands didn't seem so wrong. Getting drunk and carousing proliferated among servicemen, including Flight Officer Autry. "Drinking was and is part of the Air Force mystique," he later said. "When . . . not flying, there was little to do except hang around the non-com clubs and the officers' clubs, play poker, unwind, and raise your glass. . . . Without realizing it, I had grown dependent on liquor to relax. It is a hard habit to resist and, after a while, you really don't want to resist."[1] Although Gene had never been a teetotaler prior to the war, he'd kept his alcohol consumption in check. Now, he reached for a stiff scotch and soda at more frequent intervals, particularly on the road. At home, since Ina abstained from drinking, Gene repaired with such pals as Bing Crosby and Bob Hope to the Lakeside Country Club for a round of golf—and a few rounds of cocktails.

As Gene's material veered more toward a pop treatment and a honky-tonk lyrical content, his Western-themed recordings began to dwindle. He explained to songwriter Jack Howard, who pitched him a song called "Blue Ranger," "I have made it a practice not to fool with cowboy songs unless they are on the type of a standard number or have been popular in the past, simply because they do not sell on phonograph recordings. I have tried many of them but find that a good hillbilly song sells about ten to one the number of recordings and copies as a cowboy song." As had been his wont throughout his music career, Gene recorded what he or Art Satherley thought would sell.

Truer to Gene's old-style romantic numbers, "Have I Told You Lately That I Love You" was written by another WLS pal, Scott Wiseman. The song fell into Gene's hands by nefarious means, a circumstance that he righted once it was revealed to him. "Scott wrote that song in the hospital," Wiseman's wife, Lulu Belle, related. "A fellow who was supposed to get it copyrighted [for him while he was hospitalized] . . . copyrighted it in his own name. The first thing he did . . . was go to Hollywood and sell it to Gene Autry. Gene wouldn't record it unless he owned it. . . . When Scott got out of the hospital, [he] got in touch with Gene and told him what the fellow had done. So Gene made a trip to Chicago and signed that song back to Scott . . . Scott didn't have to give him anything [for it]."[2] Gene didn't issue his recording until after he had relinquished ownership to Wiseman in 1946, at which time it became a best seller, as did pop versions by Bing Crosby, the Andrews Sisters, and Perry Como. Gene had the first country hit with the song, after which came versions by Tex Ritter, Foy Willing, Red Foley, and a duet by Foley and Kitty Wells.

In November, Gene's appeal against the Republic verdict was heard in court. This time, Martin Gang argued that according to state labor law, a contract could last no longer than seven consecutive years: Gene's Republic agreement, dating to 1938, should expire in 1945 regardless of its suspension during his enlistment. Gang earlier had used this same argument to successfully win a case for Olivia de Havilland. Republic's attorneys rebutted with the fact that Gene's agent had signed an extension to the contract in May 1942. The same week Gene's court case made the papers, the *New York Times* published a glowing feature on Roy Rogers, in which the author, Lucy Greenbaum, favorably contrasted him with Gene. Noting that Rogers stayed out of the service due to "a wrenched back and chronic arthritis," Greenbaum declared that "Autry was chiefly a man's cowboy, [while] Rogers appeals to the women. His voice is more romantic, his smile warmer, his charm far more boyish."[3]

Four years older than Roy, Gene had put on weight in the service, which made him look older as well as heavier. He claimed to have dropped twenty of twenty-five extra pounds during his South Pacific tour—from sweating it off in the heat and a diet of Spam. Over the next few years, Gene's battle of the bulge would consistently pop up in media coverage of the star; newspaper columnist Sheilah Graham reported in 1946 his special weight-loss diet consisting of grapefruit and tea. She deemed it a success, exclaiming, "He looks better than I've ever seen him, and I mean it!" The military had allowed him to occasionally wear his cowboy boots while in uniform—which added an inch and a half to his 5' 9" frame. Now that he was back in his boots and Stetson when appearing in public, he looked taller. And returning to his civilian Western garb improved his physique, giving him a slimmer silhouette. Still, compared to the lanky, chiseled, and youthful-looking Roy, Gene looked stocky—with a softer jaw line, emerging double chin, and noticeable paunch. In December, Rogers sailed into the top ten box-office poll for the first time, with Bing Crosby at number one for the second year in a row (a position he would retain for several years). It appeared that—contrary to Gene's original assumption—staying out of military service actually boosted one's career, with

Rogers, Crosby, and John Wayne all receiving deferments yet ascending as major stars.

Gene's staff, too, had been affected by the war. Both of his Oklahoma-born publicists, George Goodale and Bev Barnett, had enlisted. When Vera Wooters departed, Gene hired Jack Long's ex-wife, Virginia MacPhail, to help out, particularly at Western Music. His longtime secretary, Dorothy Phillips, left his employ after marrying a career navy man whom she met through Gene's cousin Callie Jane. Dorothy later recalled Gene being quite upset over her marriage. Also to Gene's dismay, Mary Lee had eloped with a serviceman in 1943, ending her career; to help the struggling Wooters family (who'd just lost their breadwinner), Gene hired her father as his groundskeeper. Decades later, after his mother's death, Mary Lee's son wrote Gene to tell him that on her deathbed she'd expressed regret that she'd never shown Gene enough gratitude for his generosity toward her family.

While stationed at Luke Field in June 1943, however, Gene had found a new, loyal addition to his staff. Minneapolis native Louise Heising was a young musician in the orchestra at Phoenix's Arizona Biltmore hotel. She was hired to play viola for *Sergeant Gene Autry* when it broadcast from the Air Corps radio station KOY. "One day I overheard Gene grumbling that his secretary was leaving him to get married and that he didn't know what he'd do about handling his private mail," the tall, thin Heising later recalled. "Get a new secretary!" she remembered telling him.

"What about you?" he asked her.

When she explained that she "knew neither stenography nor bookkeeping," Gene told her such skills easily could be learned. Which she did: "Stenography from a book I bought and bookkeeping in night school," she reported. "A few weeks later I was Gene's private sec." By war's end, Heising had relocated to Los Angeles, where she worked in his office. After his discharge, as his "Girl Friday," she "never knew where [she] was going to land. My hard-ridin' boss is forever hopscotching about the country. It's my job to hopscotch with him, or after him." In addition, she played violin and viola in the *Melody Ranch* orchestra and on some of his recordings. In 1950 she told *Motion Picture* magazine, "You can judge what sort of boss he is by the fact that I'm almost the newest employee on the Autry payroll—after six years!"[4]

Finally, in January 1946, the judge in Gene's Republic case handed down a split decision, ruling that his original contract had indeed expired, but that the 1942 amendment, committing him to an additional one year and eight pictures, was still in effect. Republic filed an appeal with the California Supreme Court. Rather than await another decision, Gene sat down with Herb Yates to hammer out a compromise: Beginning in February, Gene would make four high-budget "photoplays" over a year's time. Then, pending the outcome of the Supreme Court decision, Gene would either stay with Republic—if the studio won—and make four more pictures, or if the decision were upheld, have no further obligation to the studio. In the new contract Gene got approval over his films' songs and the right to supervise the recording of his music, as well as the freedom to perform in rodeos and radio shows around his shooting schedule. Clauses were added that Armand Schaefer would produce the four pictures and that the promotion budget for Gene's movies would be the same as Rogers's. Republic also agreed to give Gene 10 percent of the gross profits of the final two. Plans got under way for his return via the upbeat *Sioux City Sue*, to begin production in July.

Although the mix of music, light drama, and comedy was akin to his early 1940s fare, changes were in the offing. After being cast as Rogers's sidekick, Smiley Burnette had starred in a few Republic pictures, then signed with Columbia, where he had been teamed with Charles Starrett for a series of "Durango Kid" Westerns. With Smiley unavailable (and Gene possibly resenting his working with Roy), Gene decided to forgo a sidekick. Instead, as comic relief, he suggested the effete red-haired Sterling Holloway, also a former serviceman. Gene had told Johnny Bond he preferred to work with fellow veterans as much as possible. Holloway was not a "Western" actor, but he had appeared in pictures with the late Will Rogers, who Gene continued to emulate. Gene's leading lady would be Lynne Roberts, originally billed as Mary Hart in a few early Roy Rogers films. After those pictures, she had been a player at 20th Century Fox and Columbia before returning to Republic. Gene invited the Cass County Boys to participate in the film, as well, and Republic signed them to contracts.

In *Sioux City Sue*, after a Bing Crosby hit song for which Republic bought the rights, Gene plays a trusting cowboy tricked by a pretty talent scout (Roberts) into providing the singing voice for the animated Ding Dong donkey. All the while, he believes he is being filmed as a gallant buckaroo. When he arrives dressed to the nines at the Hollywood premiere, he shows deep humiliation when he discovers the truth: his voice is coming from a cartoon jackass. Contrary to critics' past appraisals, this time Gene's face and voice convey painful emotion—perhaps he drew from past experiences, exposing his usually hidden reaction to those who'd ridiculed his abilities.

Before making the picture, Gene spent much of the spring organizing a new Flying A Ranch Rodeo. Still a partner with Colborn, while in the service he also had bought a one-third share in a 175,000-acre ranch that raised rodeo livestock in Florence, Arizona, owned by the Clemans Brothers. Gene's holdings had grown to include four Texas movie theaters and a percentage in an Arizona newspaper and in Phoenix Broadcasting, which operated radio station KPHO. He booked dates for his new rodeo to appear in Los Angeles as well as several other cities, just after his film wrapped. He planned a triumphal return as headliner to the World's Championship Rodeo in New York and Boston in the fall. Gene's various guest rodeo appearances were among his most lucrative ventures, grossing almost $84,000 in 1946. One newspaper reported that he had signed a two-year contract with the Garden at "the highest price ever paid a cowboy entertainer there—a hot $75,000 [total] for a twenty-six day stretch each year."[5]

When Philip Wrigley suggested Gene broadcast two fifteen-minute radio programs a week, he begged off: "In traveling around the country, there are many times that it is hard to get [transmission] lines and also musicians in some of the places that we will be playing," he wrote Wrigley. "I am planning on going down to Fort Worth . . . for the broadcast on March 10 and March 17 as I will be appearing at their annual Fort Worth Livestock show. . . . However, I am primarily interested in doing a good job for you and selling chewing gum as soon as it can be produced again. Naturally, I would like a thirty-minute spot, preferably on a Sunday."

ON THE ROAD WITH THE RODEO once again brought Gene into contact with ardent female fans. Decades later known to rock-and-rollers as groupies, some young women gladly agreed to spend the night with their idol. One such paramour later corresponded with Gene about their occasional trysts, which began when Gene was on furlough from the Air Corp in mid-December 1944:

> At the time we met, I was in Chicago with your fan club. You were appearing at Soldiers Field [as part of the Chicago Horse Show]. I happened to meet a girl from Chicago named Jean and she asked me if I wanted to meet you and get to know you. She was a friend of Abe [Lefton, Gene's rodeo announcer], who was with you. Jean and I went to your dressing room and somehow you took a liking to me, and we all went to your hotel room, where I did get a chance to know you. . . . After this meeting . . . you called me from New York and advised me that you were going to be in Chicago the next day and was wondering if I could come in [from Indiana] and meet you, and I told you I certainly would be happy to. This I did, and we had a wonderful time. . . . You were staying at the Ambassador East Hotel. Later on, you sent me a telegram stating you would be in Chicago, and I came in and met you once again. We had a wonderful time again even though you were quite busy.

By the paramours' third rendezvous, Gene was out of the service, constantly working to reclaim his position as Public Cowboy No. 1. Not only was he competing with the Rogers films, but Republic had also added a popular series of Red Ryder pictures starring "Wild" Bill Elliott, who had played the lead heavy in Gene's *Boots and Saddles*. When Phil Wrigley mentioned that his company was considering sponsoring a radio program starring Oklahoma-born Spade Cooley, a musical competitor who had played fiddle on prewar Autry recordings, Gene tried to convince him otherwise:

> On my [radio] program, I always have three different types of numbers, one of the real standard cowboy numbers, then a hillbilly type of song, and then of course the folk-lore ballad. In this way I always felt I was reaching the three types

of audience that like our particular kind of entertainment. Naturally enough, there are only so many of these numbers that are good enough to use on the air every week, and although Spade Cooley is known as strictly a swing band (as I believe he calls himself "King of Western Swing"), he has to have a vocalist with his band who I believe would be doing exactly the same songs that we do on our present program.

Something like this has been my chief complaint at Republic Studios, that because of the success that my pictures made at the studio they started making others of a similar nature but with other artists and I might point out that they never attained the success that my pictures had. . . . Sooner or later you are bound to run into each other's formulas, songs or ideas and still it is unintentional. . . . I do think [a Cooley program] would run into conflicting songs and programming because of the fact that I am doing the same type of numbers and material that Cooley is doing.

You might also want to consider whether another show of this type would be giving your audience too much of the same thing. It has been my experience that if an audience likes what you are doing, it is a better policy to leave them wanting more than to give them too much. . . .

I believe also that a radio program is much different from phonograph recordings as there are certain numbers that you can do on a phonograph record and they will sell, and at the same time they would not be good numbers for radio. . . . As far as Spade's recordings are concerned, it is hard to judge who his audience really is because he has only two records on the market. . . .

I do not for one minute want you to think that I am trying to stand in anyone's way or that I disapprove of a show of this type . . . because I feel that it is your program and that you are entitled to use whomever you think fit.[6]

Cooley, who had also performed with Roy Rogers and Jimmy Wakely (who'd moved into making Autry-style films for Monogram), had become a hugely popular bandleader during the war. Signed by Uncle Art, he began scoring hits in 1945. Apparently, Wrigley did not pursue him for the radio program.

Fortunately, Gene's old PR man Bev Barnett returned after his Navy discharge and helped put Gene back in the spotlight. He also hired New York City publicist and writer Dave Whalen to pitch Autry stories to national magazines. Gene must have been thrilled in June when he made it into a new nationwide poll conducted by George Gallup of the most admired men in the country. Although he wasn't among the top ten, which included military and political figures, he was the only Western star selected in the "Actors, Singers, Musicians" category, in the company of Bing Crosby, Orson Welles, Frank Sinatra, Betty Grable, Kate Smith, Bob Hope, Clark Gable, Paul Robeson, Marian Anderson, and Arturo Toscanini. In addition, Gene's "first-ever indoor rodeo" at Los Angeles' Pan Pacific Auditorium garnered reams of press, and he returned to the front page of the *New York Times* with his three-week stand at the Madison Square Garden rodeo. Barnett brokered a publicity deal with the paper, in which Gene guest-starred at a *Times*-sponsored children's book event, as well as the annual media-soaked Bellevue benefit performance.

Although his return to the screen, *Sioux City Sue*, drew well at theaters, it did not draw particularly positive reviews. One trade publication remarked, "Actor needs to quicken his pace . . . if he is to compete with present-day crop of singing cowboy stars. *Sioux City Sue* . . . is handicapped with unimaginative dialog and familiar situations, but Gene's voice is good and he shows his old flair for capturing interest."[7] The film, radio shows, recordings, rodeos, and other public appearances were not enough to propel Gene back into the box-office top ten. The annual exhibitors poll showed his rival, Roy Rogers, still firmly positioned among those in the coveted general category (yet again topped by Crosby) and for the fourth consecutive year holding down the top spot in the Western survey. To his great dismay, Gene even trailed Bill Elliott, landing in a discouraging third place.

31

BACK IN THE SADDLE

WHY DO I TRY TO KEEP ON MAKIN' MONEY? Well, I've seen what happens to old Western actors when the rain starts to fall. They get wet, sir. Gene's gonna stay dry."[1] These words attributed to Gene appeared in "Cowboy Capitalist," one of several 1947–48 features on Gene's business acumen in such magazines as *Time* and *Life*.

Among his new ventures, Gene Autry Productions, Inc., was announced in late 1946 as a partnership with Columbia Studios. Under a two-year contract, Gene would produce and star in four high-budget pictures a year. On January 3, 1947, the *New York Times* reported that Armand Schaefer had resigned from Republic to serve as president of the company, joining Gene as chairman of the board, Mitchell Hamilburg as vice president, and attorney Martin Gang as secretary-treasurer. "Autry disclosed that he will own a controlling interest in the corporation and that the profits from his pictures will be shared equally between the production company and the distributing company," according to the *Times*.[2] Gene announced in *Autry's Aces* that "we fully intend to make the best pictures possible," with "at least three of them in color this year. . . . I am about to start on my third picture at Republic . . . *Twilight on the Rio Grande* . . . and after this new picture is made I will have only one more picture to make at Republic Studios."[3]

Responding combatively to the news, Herb Yates stated that Autry owed Republic *four* more "photoplays" before he could join Columbia. But in March, following Gene's completion of Republic's *Twilight* and *Saddle Pals*, the *Los Angeles Times* reported another truce, with Gene agreeing to make the studio's

Robin Hood of Texas and one final film before moving on. Two months later, when the State Supreme Court ruled against Republic and in favor of the actor, Gene walked away from the studio forever. Having just completed *Robin Hood* in late April, he relinquished his rights to 10 percent of its gross to extricate himself for good. Newspaper commentators waxed nostalgic over his departure from Republic as though it were the end of an era, but Gene surely celebrated his newfound freedom.

Gene's last four Republic pictures, released throughout 1947, are breezy and light. They feature equal doses of comedy, provided by Sterling Holloway, and music, with songs split between the Cass County Boys and Gene. Following his five-picture tenure with Gene, the Cedartown, Georgia-born Holloway never acted in a Western again—though his voice remained well-known to children via Disney animated features like *Dumbo* and *Winnie-the-Pooh*. The Cass County Boys, at times, nearly attained sidekick status, serving as Gene's troublemaking traveling companions. Second-billed to Gene was Champion, the Wonder Horse of the West.[4] The original Champ, retired since 1942's *Bells of Capistrano*, had died in his sleep at age seventeen in 1946. His death was not made public until January 1947, when Champion's obituary ran in the *New York Times* and other national papers.[5] Later, an ugly rumor circulated that when notified of Champ's death by ranch foreman Johnny Brousseau, Gene callously told him to bury the animal as cheaply as possible rather than spend the money to have his famous horse's body preserved by a taxidermist.[6] In reality, Gene loved his first Champion more than any of his subsequent equine partners. In his autobiography, he addressed the gossip, saying, "I do not mind so much being made to appear thrifty, which is a staple of Hollywood humor. I do object to being made to appear insensitive . . . I had a feeling close to love for Champion, for each of them."[7]

Gene's newest Champion, a spirited stallion (later gelded), had been trained to do such spectacular tricks as jumping onto and standing atop a grand piano—a hit during rodeos, beginning with the feat's debut at Madison Square Garden in 1946. Originally named Boots, and sometimes referred to as Champion Jr., he had four high white stockings, a flaxen mane and tail, and—like his predecessor—a white spot on his belly. Gene bought him in 1945 for five hundred dollars from an Ada, Oklahoma, rancher who transported Boots to the Fort Worth Fat Stock Show for the cowboy star's perusal. Champ Jr., who could perform complicated dance steps, sometimes misbehaved on movie sets, however, and occasionally refused to follow direction, causing delays and an occasional script rewrite. (Champ doubles continued to be used for chase scenes, while Champ Jr. always appeared in close-ups and during Gene's running mounts.) In July 1946 Gene paid seven hundred dollars for another Champ look-alike, which he would take on the road for rodeos and personal appearances. This horse would appear with Gene at the 1947 Madison Square Garden rodeo and have his hoofprints preserved for posterity alongside Gene's handprints at Grauman's Chinese Theater in Hollywood. He also purchased a pony that closely resembled Champion—originally billed as the "Son of Champion" and later called "Little Champion." This mini-Champ would first appear with Gene at a Los Angeles rodeo in March 1947, and co-star with Champ Jr. in *The Strawberry Roan*, Gene's first color movie for Columbia.

Although Republic had started using "Trucolor" for Roy Rogers pictures, Gene's last four releases for the studio were shot in black and white. The spunky Dale Evans had become Roy's consistent costar in 1944 (and, in 1947, his third wife), while several female leads played alongside Gene: Lynne Roberts (*Saddle Pals, Robin Hood of Texas*), Peggy Stewart (*Trail to San Antone*), and Adele Mara (as a brunette in *Twilight on the Rio Grande* and a blonde in *Robin Hood of Texas*). A sultry former singer with bandleader Xavier Cugat, Mara portrayed a fiery Mexican chanteuse in *Twilight* and a conniving gun moll as well as Roberts's rival for Gene in *Robin Hood*. The latter film prominently featured the Cass County Boys, who spoke nearly as many lines as Gene. Guitarist Jerry Scoggins, who played Roberts's brother in *Robin Hood*, later recalled Gene's fondness for "beautiful girls" such as his co-star Mara. Likewise, Johnny Western, Gene's accompanist in 1956–57, remembered a discussion with the singing cowboy about his trysts with Mara and other costars: "Gene was the most charming guy in the world—he was a man's man," said Western.

> Guys liked him, but women just adored him. I knew that he was always a virile young man—men [like to] talk about [their] conquests. I said to him, "Some of the boys in the show told me that you made love to all your leading ladies at Republic," and he just looked at me with a smile and said, "Well, hell yes, kid, I felt I owed it to them!" It just broke me up that he would be that blunt about it.
>
> Adele Mara later married Roy Huggins, who was the producer of *The Rockford Files* with James Garner. Gene told me that he was riding on American Airlines going coast to coast for a business meeting and Roy Huggins was in the next seat. He introduced himself and told Gene, "I'm married to Adele Mara, who you made a couple of pictures with." So Gene very casually asked how she was and so forth . . . and Huggins turned to him and said, "You know, Gene, my wife told me that you made love to her when you were making *Twilight on the Rio Grande*." And Gene said to me, "Boy, I started thinking on my feet. I said to Roy, 'Oh hell, you know how these young actresses are. They like to chalk those kinds of things up—it sounds good when they tell their girlfriends. But I never touched her—she's a wonderful girl and very talented, and I loved being around her, and it worked great in the picture.'" Gene said that he lied through his teeth! He said, "I'm sitting next to the man, and I was not going to offend him in any way." Well, you know, Gene could be very convincing. He had that smile.[8]

According to Jerry Scoggins, Gene had dalliances with some of his female co-stars, and Ina "knew all about it" but chose to look the other way.[9] She continued to immerse herself in Christian Science and, following the religion's teachings, tried to focus on the positive, rather than become troubled by the negative aspects of her marriage to a rich and famous movie star. Still receiving one-half of Gene's earnings, she donated money each year to the church ($1,430 in 1947) and spent time with her fellow adherent, Gloria Marvin, Johnny's widow. She wrote "Glorie" about how much she admired her and her beliefs: "I thank you so much dear for being such an example of what we are trying to show Gene—and everyone for that matter. You have helped me more than anyone to show Gene that Science really does help us—make us more sincere and loving. Not fanatics. I don't think I tell you enough how much your friendship means to me. . . . What a wonderful friend I feel that you are. I love you so for your sincerity, courage, and good sense. I've never had a friend before like you so that's why it means a lot to me. I don't think I tell you enough how much our friendship means to me. How very much you help and set an example for me and how much I love you."[10] Ina's intelligence and beauty were remarked upon often by journalists and friends alike, and as Gene added to their growing list of assets, she remained her husband's behind-the-scenes business advisor. Gene often said that the key to their long marriage was the fact that Ina never took up a career but instead put all her energy into helping him succeed at his. She adeptly kept Gene's resplendent wardrobe organized and ready for his many public appearances, planned their annual Christmas party and other gatherings, and designed the interiors of their homes and eventually the hotels and office buildings Gene acquired.

After living with her husband in hotels in Phoenix and Dallas during the war, Ina was ready to establish a new home. Their own Melody Ranch, forty miles from Hollywood, had been their California base, but Ina had tired of living at the rustic spread, and complained that the adjoining indoor arena made her home smell like horses. With Gene's discharge, the Autrys intended to build an eleven-room Colonial in town but found that Federal Housing Administration (FHA) regulations restricted new construction costing more than ten thousand dollars. Gene again asked for help from Senator Lyndon Johnson, elected to Congress in July 1946. Just prior to the election, Gene had returned to Texas for his campaign, singing cowboy classics and urging voters to "put my friend Lyndon back in the saddle again, because that's where he belongs." This time, instead of BBQ and beer, LBJ's rallies featured ice-cold watermelon.[11]

On July 29, 1946, Johnson had wired Gene:

WE WON BY 25,000 VOTES. WILL NEVER FORGET YOU FOR THE HELP YOU GAVE ME.

A week later, the congressman's secretary Mary Rather was appealing to the FHA on Gene's behalf—to no avail. When his request to build an expensive house was denied by the FHA, Gene angrily responded to FHA Administrator Wilson Wyatt:

I am not requesting veterans' financing or asking for a priority . . . I am not requesting any new housing, but am merely asking that I be allowed to replace my home which was destroyed by fire in 1941. . . . In the past few weeks I have seen many homes being built where the cost obviously far exceeds the $10,000 limit. . . . For a number of years I have supported and backed the present administration, and several of the top people around President Truman can vouch for my loyalty and help in various campaigns in recent years. However, the decision on this application of mine is a little more than I can take. To replace my home . . . would take something like ninety or a hundred thousand dollars. . . . It simply does not make sense that a $10,000 cracker-box house should be put on a $40,000 piece of property. My home burned to the ground in November 1941. In 1942 I could have replaced the building but felt that during the war all materials should be used in the war effort. I also enlisted in the service and spent three and one half years in the army while others were staying at home and cashing in.

I realize that most veterans do not and cannot put as much into a home as my application requires but on the other hand, I feel that since I had that amount of money invested in the place that burned down, I am entitled to replace it now. . . . I am not asking for priority on materials. I am merely asking that the building permit be approved; then it is up to me to secure the materials.[12]

Gene sent a copy of his letter to Johnson colleague Walter Jenkins, who had also approached the FHA on his behalf, with a note to Jenkins saying, "I too was very much disappointed because I know that houses are being built and many other projects are going up that are not essential, and they are simply going up under the black market or through the pay-off routine. That is why I am so dead set against this sort of thing. I want to build a place but I want it legitimate. . . . If it were a standard procedure that no one could build a house or building for more than $10,000, I would have no kick coming, but as stated before, it is being done and we all know it, and that is why I feel as I do about it."[13]

Gene and Ina purchased four secluded acres on Brookdale, a quiet street off wooded, mountainous Laurel Canyon in Studio City, but it was 1949 before their new home was finally constructed. In the meantime, the Autrys would spend Christmas and other holidays at the Clearcreek Ranch, another Florence, Arizona, property they had recently bought. In 1947 Gene made other acquisitions, including a share in Santa Monica radio station KOWL and in Arizona KOPO and KOLD, a stake in some Texas oil wells, and three used airplanes: a Cessna twin-engine, a five-seater Beechcraft, and a military Beechcraft C-45—the latter kept at his Phoenix air field, where his flying school had expanded to include a crop-dusting service. Gene stayed in frequent touch with pilots he'd met during the war—several of whom had gone to work for Pan Am and American Airlines. He truly loved flying, and in her June 11, 1947, column, Hedda Hopper announced, "Gene flew his whole radio troupe back to Oklahoma City for the benefit show for victims of the Woodward tornado. After piloting the craft all night, he reached Hollywood at 8:30 Monday morning, and reported for work on his picture, *The Last Round-Up*, one half-hour later."[14]

Joining Gene on the picture were several of his old Republic colleagues: Schaefer, director of photography Bill Bradford, and director John English. In his memoir, Gene pointed out that his motivation for starting Gene Autry Productions was primarily financial. "I wanted to form my own company, frankly, because of the tax angles. If you earned over $100,000 in those days, 85 percent of it was taxable. The only way to hang on to your money was to form a corporation. . . . [The] contract with Columbia . . . was as good a deal as anyone in Hollywood had at that time. I had complete say over my films and I could take home half the profits."

Gene had hoped to shoot in color, but "the demands on the new Technicolor Corporation had already plunged it a year behind schedule," he said, so *The Last Round-Up* was filmed in black and white. Perhaps more to the point, Columbia could provide stock footage from its 1940 film *Arizona* that could be seamlessly edited into the new picture. Primarily shot in Old Tucson and nearby Rattlesnake Park, from May 19 to 24, the film was completed in June at the Columbia lot.

Although Gene and Mandy Schaefer had learned penny-pinching lessons from Herb Yates, the team sought to distance its new product from the traditional B, or series, Western. Columbia executive Hal Hody told Autry fan club members at their September 1947 New York City convention, "Unlike the features [Gene] has made before, each picture as it goes out will be a story unto itself. It won't be part of a series. We are not making or selling the new Autry pictures as a series. Each one will have the hero in another role. He won't have the same role all the time. . . . Quantity and quality just don't go together. For the current season, there will be four Autry pictures. In the year after that, there will be four more. These aren't hot dogs we're turning out. They are quality pictures."[15] The main character, however, would continue to be called Gene Autry.

Gene and Mandy knew from their Republic efforts that regardless of a film's quality, it was a hit song, like "South of the Border," Gene's top-grossing Republic release, that propelled a movie title into the public's consciousness. They bought a story from writer Jack Townley, who then helped to craft the screenplay with the title of Billy Hill's classic song, "The Last Round-Up"— one of Gene's favorites and his first big cowboy hit, in 1933. The movie's topical plot concerns the repercussions of urban sprawl on Native Americans living in the Arizona desert, treated with scorn by Anglos more concerned with their own water rights (and inspired by the growth of Phoenix and its effect on local tribes). That spring, in Hollywood, Gene had pledged his support of the American Indian Citizens League campaign to fight discrimination against Indians. He had attended a March meeting that included other Western stars as well as Native American war hero Ira Hayes. One of the Marines who famously raised the flag on Mount Suribachi at Iwo Jima, Hayes would die a penniless alcoholic, the subject of a 1964 song, "The Ballad of Ira Hayes," written by Peter LaFarge and made famous by Johnny Cash.

The Last Round-Up is a departure from Gene's previous films, and he often cited it as one of his favorites. Nearly eighty minutes long, its tone is somber, with no comedy except a lighthearted scene or two. During one of these lighter moments, Gene pitches a baseball through a window when it's missed by Mike, a young Native played by Robert "Bobby" Blake. The youthful veteran of "Our Gang," Blake had played Little Beaver in Republic's *Red Ryder* series. (Blake later starred in *In Cold Blood* and TV's *Baretta*, and would become tabloid fodder five decades later when charged with his wife's murder.) Playing Mike's father is Jay Silverheels, who, as Tonto on *The Lone Ranger*, would become an early television star. In *The Last Round-Up*, Gene earnestly approaches his role as Indian advocate, lobbying for the tribe to be given more fertile land. A rancher, he serves as diplomat between the various factions, including the municipal water director who wants to relocate desert residents so an aqueduct can be built. One prescient scene features Gene and his Native American friends being broadcast on a newfangled television (only just starting to appear in some American households), its TV "anchor" depicted by his radio announcer Lou Crosby.

GENE'S POSTWAR REPUBLIC OUTINGS had been criticized by reviewers for a dearth of such Western rudiments as horseback chases, cattle drives, fistfights, and gunplay. *The Last Round-Up* brought back such elements, placed in a modern context (although in the stock footage, the modern-day Indians suddenly "go native" when they attack a cattle drive). There were no big musical production numbers here, just a simple version of the title song (used during the opening sequence and a funeral scene) and some folk tunes performed by Gene backed by the Texas Rangers (a Sons of Pioneers–type group), and school children (accompanied by Gene and his love interest, a teacher/Native rights advocate played by Jean Heather).

"It is evident that the film was not intended as competition for [B-Western stars] Johnny Mack Brown or Tim Holt," points out Western film scholar Jonathan Guyot Smith.

> It is probably more accurate to see it as an attempt to place Gene in the John Wayne or Randolph Scott range, without losing sight of his vast legion of fans and their wishes. . . . We may perhaps safely generalize in viewing the setting and somber storyline as being stylistically closer to the supposed "A" westerns of the period, while not drastically removing Gene from the well-loved traditions he'd established on the screen twelve years before. Gene Autry Productions succeeded in having it both ways. Gene was still *Gene*, but the seventy-seven-minute film had the look of a non-series western.[16]

Although Gene had no sidekicks in *The Last Round-Up*, he surrounded himself with comedic pals on his *Melody Ranch* radio program, which had returned to its thirty-minute format "of music, chatter, and cowboy stories" on June 16, 1946.[17] The next month, Gene introduced his new female vocalist on the show—Colleen Summers, who as Mary Ford would become a star in the

1950s with Les Paul. *Melody Ranch* stalwarts Johnny Bond and Lou Crosby provided amusing repartees with Gene, as did Smiley Burnette who sporadically appeared as a guest between July 1946 and March 1947. Autry's *Aces* correspondent June Siegers reported on a September 1946 rehearsal where Smiley interacted with fans in attendance:

> Most of the cast was out to lunch and Gene and Smiley had just returned . . . Smiley sat down at the piano and started to play some old, old songs. . . . We grouped around the piano and started to request songs and Smiley would play one right after the other, switching one tune into the other. He's really terrific. We were standing there listening and enjoying ourselves very much and didn't notice anyone coming up behind us. Yes, you guessed it, it was Gene. He looked wonderful in a light blue cowboy business suit. My sister took the opportunity to wish him a successful and happy rodeo tour, but the rest of us just stood there with our mouths open. Smiley Burnette got a kick out of us, as did Gene.[18]

Melody Ranch's weekly "cowboy classic" segment became the theme of one of Columbia Records' first Western "albums," released in late 1947. Gene's sustained success as a hit-maker helped to make such a financial gamble possible: Gene would gross close to $56,000 from Columbia that year. His eight 1946 recording sessions had yielded a half-dozen top ten best-sellers in 1947. Some of his best new songs were penned by women songwriters—including Dale Evans ("I Wish I Had Never Met Sunshine"), Rosalie Allen ("You're Not My Darlin' Anymore"), and Cindy Walker ("Over and Over Again," "The Cowboy Blues," "Here's to the Ladies"). The Texas-born Walker, who appeared in Gene's 1940 picture *Ride, Tenderfoot, Ride*, became the greatest woman songwriter in country music, composing numerous hits for Bob Wills, Ray Price, and Willie Nelson, among others.

Anticipating *The Last Round-Up*, Gene had rerecorded its title song, along with polished remakes of his earlier Western hits, including "Mexicali Rose," "Tumbling Tumbleweeds," "South of the Border," and "Back in the Saddle Again." Traditionally, labels issued 78 rpm discs in blank paper sleeves; Columbia, on the other hand, had started experimenting with colorful, illustrated cardboard "albums" that enclosed four sleeves, each of which held a disc. (Prior to this, Sears, Roebuck had marketed illustrated, empty Gene Autry "albums" that could be filled with discs from one's record collection.) Photography or artwork graced the album cover, while text about the set's recordings and artist—the precursor to liner notes—was printed on the inside cover. Much more expensive than single-disc releases, Columbia albums were employed at first for classical music. *Gene Autry's Western Classics* became one of the label's first nonclassical releases in this more lavish format.

Another Autry recording marked a turning point for the singer in 1947. That summer Art Satherley had suggested Gene record a new Christmas song he had discovered, "An Old Fashioned Tree." For its flipside, Gene remembered a song idea he'd gotten while participating in the annual Hollywood "Santa Claus Lane" parade the previous November. Astride Champion Jr., ahead of St. Nick on his sleigh, he'd heard a child on the sidewalk shout, "Here comes Santa Claus!" Satherley took Gene's idea to Oakley Haldeman, the composer who operated Gene's music publishing division, and he came up with the melody. Johnny Bond recorded a demo version of the song at his home studio, where Art, cocktail in hand, stood next to the mic (as he usually did during recordings). The tingling of ice cubes was captured on the recording, inspiring the use of jingle bells on the August 28 Columbia session. After initial sales of two million following its December release, "Here Comes Santa Claus (Right Down Santa Claus Lane)" became a perennial top-ten hit every Yuletide season for years to come. More important, it opened up a whole new market for Gene—holiday discs aimed at children. Easter and Thanksgiving recordings would follow, as would one of the biggest-selling Christmas discs of all time.

Gene's second full year back in show business had yielded lucrative—and satisfying—returns. Back in the spotlight via radio, recordings, movies, and high-profile rodeo appearances, his licensing deals proliferated, bringing in more than fifty thousand dollars. His fortieth birthday was celebrated with his ever-growing fan club convening in New York during his annual rodeo appearance. Guest speakers also included Uncle Art, Columbia's Hal Hody, and Bill Burch, producer of *Melody Ranch*. One magazine reported about Gene's month-long sojourn in Manhattan that fall: "The kids are still with him—at Gimbel's Department Store in New York City, in one hour he signed 1,351 autographs, shook 5,439 young hands, as clerks sold 4,297 pairs of Gene Autry jeans. . . . His thirty-day rodeo engagement at Madison Square Garden drew 550,000 fans."[19] Yet box-office poll results were published in December, and Gene ran a close second to Roy Rogers.

Regardless, the *Chicago Sun-Times* feted him with a profile titled "Gold Plated Cowboy," followed a week later by a syndicated feature, "Gene Autry Popularity Goes on Up," courtesy of longtime ally Hedda Hopper. Published in time for *The Last Round-Up*'s November release, Hopper's lengthy "inside" story prophetically reported: "He will continue in pictures as long as he is wanted by the public, and if the day ever comes when he has no audience appeal, he will move into some other phase of the business."[20]

The following week, the announcement came that Gene Autry had just purchased his fourth radio station, KOOL, in Phoenix, for close to a quarter of a million dollars.

32

GENE AUTRY, INC.

THE STAMINA THAT AUTRY HAS!" Pat Buttram, Gene's longtime film, radio, and television sidekick once exclaimed. "I swear, I'd have cracked up a long time ago, working day and night the way Gene does. . . . He works like a mule, and yet he's always pleasant and willing to help another guy."[1]

In the late 1940s, humorist Pat Buttram became yet another entertainer whose career was boosted by Gene Autry. The pair first met in Chicago, after the comic raconteur joined WLS in 1934. Buttram, like Gene and Smiley Burnette, came from a rural background with religion in the family. His father was an itinerant Methodist minister who traveled around Winston County, Alabama, including the tiny town of Addison, where Pat was born Maxwell Emmett Buttram on June 19, 1915. One of seven children, he got his nickname when his brother Johnny gave him a cap with the word "Rat" stitched on it; wear-and-tear turned the R into a P, and since he wore it constantly, people started calling him Pat. Buttram's daughter, Kerry Galgano, visited her father's childhood home in 1966 and remembered it as "a tiny unpainted shack that was very dark inside."[2]

After graduating from high school in 1933, Pat won a scholarship to attend Birmingham Southern College, where he won a role in the student theatrical production *The Heathers at Home*. In January 1934 his humorous portrayal of "Oscar" grabbed the attention of former WLS staffer Steve Cisler, manager of radio station WSGN in Birmingham. He offered Buttram a spot five days a week, mornings and evenings, for a salary of six dollars. "There was a Depression on and that six dollars looked mighty good," Pat later recalled. "I told jokes . . . also got in a fair amount of philosophy."[3] Soon, Cisler took him to

Chicago, where Pat landed a fifteen-minute show sponsored by the Murphy Feed Company "doing the same type of humor and country boy stuff." After settling in, he wrote home, telling his family about his program: "I have to write, direct and play the leading part in it. It is a 15 minute phone call to Winston County . . . I have some big ideas on it and it may turn into something big."[4] His trademark crackled voice ("sounding like a handful of gravel thrown in a Mix-Master"[5]) and hillbilly aphorisms attracted attention: "They liked my country poems, the homespun gags, and philosophy of a sort of corn-fed kind," he remembered. Pat also announced the *Smile-a-While* program from 6 to 7 AM. Every Saturday night he told jokes on the *Barn Dance*, which is where he became acquainted with Gene, just before he left for Hollywood. When the Singing Cowboy returned to the Midwest to make personal appearances, he called on Buttram to join him. "I'd . . . go out with him and he kind of saved my job," Pat recalled in 1990. "In comedy, George Burns summed it up. He said, 'Nowadays there's no place to be lousy anymore until you learn your trade.' Gene would take me around to the county fairs and all the theaters with him, and you learned your trade that way. You learned jokes, learned timing. . . . It was good training ground, the greatest one in the world."[6]

In 1944 Pat got his own taste of Hollywood when he appeared in the Paramount picture, *The National Barn Dance*, featuring his WLS colleagues Lulu Belle and Scotty, the Hoosier Hot Shots, and the Arkansas Woodchopper, along with actors Robert Benchley and Jean Heather (Gene's leading lady in *The Last Round-Up*). Although he continued to write for WLS, Buttram stayed on in California, eventually finding work on the Phil Harris–Alice Faye radio show. "Jack Benny used to check the program," Pat later remarked, "and what I didn't learn about timing from him—*wow!*" In 1946 Buttram appeared on Roy Rogers's NBC radio show, with Gabby Hayes, Dale Evans, and the Sons of the Pioneers. Sponsored by Alka Seltzer, *The Roy Rogers Show* took over the Saturday night time slot originally held by the *National Barn Dance*. The following year, Gene approached Pat about working with him. He had recently performed with Pat's colleagues Phil Harris and Alice Faye at a benefit show in Texas, which may have resulted in his reacquaintance with Pat. Or perhaps he laughed at the quick-witted Buttram's wheezy banter on Roy's program.

Regardless, Pat was cast in a bit part in *The Strawberry Roan*, Gene's second film for Columbia, which got underway in June of '47. The cow-eyed, chunky funnyman played a ranch hand, alongside another cutup, Rufe Davis, renowned for his animal imitations and vocal sound effects. After a stint with "hayseed vaudevillians" the Weaver Brothers and Elviry, the Oklahoma-born Davis ventured to Hollywood in 1937, eventually joining the cast of Republic's Three Mesquiteers series. Both Rufe and Pat would work with Gene on the road and in future projects, but it was Pat who became his radio sidekick—and lifelong best buddy—beginning in 1948.

Pat strongly disliked horseback riding, but that didn't stop him from taking a buckaroo role in *The Strawberry Roan*. The film centers on a stallion that seriously injures the teenage son (Dick Jones) of a ranch owner (Jack Holt), who wants to destroy the strawberry roan (Champion), which is saved by Gene. The picture was inspired equally by the Curley Fletcher song (for which Ken Maynard bought the rights for his 1933 film) and Roy Rogers's 1946 film hit, *My Pal Trigger*, which had been produced by Mandy Schaefer and featured veteran Western star Holt. "I didn't get along too well with horses," Pat liked to joke. "I always say that horses are hard in the middle and dangerous at both ends."[7]

Gene's leading lady in *The Strawberry Roan* was not keen on horses either. New Orleans–born Gloria Henry plays the ranch owner's daughter and Gene's love interest; during a couple of scenes in then-unspoiled Sedona, Arizona, she discovered that Champ didn't particularly care for her either. "Champ tried to kill me twice!" she remembered.

> He was jealous of leading ladies. We were standing up on top of this mountain, and Gene's on one side, I'm on the other, and he's singing a love song . . . Champ looked over at me—a very intelligent horse—then looked back and suddenly leaned the other way and went *whomp!* against me with his head, like he was trying to knock me off the hill. It was on purpose . . . as hard as he could, he "whomped" me and I slipped a few feet down and the guys caught me, and I said, "That damn horse is trying to kill me!" And then another time, we were standing on fairly flat ground, and luckily I was wearing boots, because he took his hoof and looked over at me and went "stomp!" right on my foot. And so I kept my distance from him after that.[8]

Ironically, the film's press book published an item about Gene letting Gloria ride Champion to overcome her fear of horses—a story termed by Henry "a complete fiction!" Twenty-year-old Texan Dick Jones, who'd been a professional trick rider since he was five, did indeed mount Champ in the film, a crucial part of the script. Gene had probably heard of the young man's superb horsemanship through their mutual friend Hoot Gibson, who discovered Jones and brought him to Hollywood in 1935. In addition to acting in numerous Westerns, including *Destry Rides Again*, "Dickie" Jones provided the voice of Pinocchio in the 1940 animated Disney feature. "The story going around was that Gene said, 'Nobody is going to ride my horse, Champion, except Dickie Jones,'" Dick recalled, which led to his successful audition for the part. His and Champ's brief partnership was uneventful, but he impressed Gene to the extent that he would appear in several more Autry pictures. Eventually Gene would make him a television star.

The Strawberry Roan was directed by the well-liked Jack English, who would handle eighteen of Gene's Columbia features; his assistant director was Earl Bellamy. Of the three Autry films Bellamy participated in, he recalled,

"Gene was fun to work with. He was first class as far as a person goes. He was very funny—had a lot of humor. One particular afternoon, while it was getting dark, Gloria Henry was the girl, he was in her room, he was a little loaded and he was throwing all the furniture out of her room, and we had to [replace] it all. . . . The next day he felt a little bad."[9]

When asked about the episode sixty years later, Henry doesn't remember it, but she does recall that Gene's reputation as a ladies man caused her to keep him at arm's length off-camera. "I stayed out of his way so he wouldn't make any passes at me," she said. "That's what he was famous for. He's not a shy man about trying to get a girl in bed, but he didn't get me. He was pretty mad because the very first night in Sedona a couple of the guys—it could have been the assistant director and the camera man—and [I] were going to go to [nearby mining town] Jerome where they had dancing and great music and fun, and we had a ball. Well, when Gene found we had taken the only jeep to do that, he was quite furious, and he was sort of mad at me the rest of the time. . . . He would get very snippy with me and wasn't particularly nice to me after that, which was fine."[10]

During musical scenes together, said Henry, "he never really sings directly at you. He *is* shy in so far as actually singing a love song to a woman. He has a hard time looking into your eyes. But not at all shy if he's off camera! There was always a script girl on the set working on lines with him. He was no actor. He said his lines and that was that. I think he was terribly self-conscious in front of the camera, unless he was riding—he'd ride like hell. But he was afraid of the camera."[11]

Dick Jones has a different assessment of Gene's approach: "Actually, as an actor, he wasn't one . . . he was a *reactor*. He was *reacting* to what 'Gene Autry' would do." Dick recalled Gene looking at the pages in the script girl's hand as if he hadn't seen them before—but it became clear he had previously studied it. If lines seemed out of character for "Gene Autry," then he'd change them. According to Jones:

> He just got the story line and he would not read the dialogue word for word because the writer didn't write it like "Gene Autry" would say it. . . . If something wasn't right, Gene would change [it]. . . . He wouldn't change anything enough to change the whole story line, but if it didn't flow right . . . if "Gene Autry" wouldn't say it . . . if it was something that was foreign to what Gene would do as a person as "Gene Autry," he'd discuss it with the director, and the director would convey that information to the other actors working with Gene and they'd rehearse it and then they'd shoot it.[12]

Either to defray costs or because it was more readily available, Gene's first color film was shot using the Cinecolor process, rather than Technicolor. Henry remembered "Cinecolor is an awful thing to work with because you have to wear make-up that is bright orange. I couldn't stand to look at anybody because of the make-up. It was just beet red—orange—like you were on fire. And the funny thing is, when they shot these beautiful backgrounds up in the mountains, they looked like backdrops. It didn't even look real."[13]

Cinecolor would be used for only one more Autry picture, *The Big Sombrero*, which soon went before cameras. A lavish musical co-starring beautiful Elena Verdugo, the film more closely resembled Gene's final Republic outings than his first two Columbias. As a publicity stunt, a staged kiss between Elena and Gene was arranged for press invited to photograph the smooch; the published pictures ran with such headlines as GENE AUTRY FINALLY KISSES THE GIRL! Further hype stating that an overwhelmingly negative reaction poured in from fans, kept the so-called "scene" out of the movie. (A similar stunt with Ann Miller had spurred much publicity for Gene's 1940 picture *Melody Ranch*.) "Well, [the scene] never got in the picture, and it wasn't supposed to," Verdugo recalled of the *Sombrero* stunt. "I had a very pretty, soft pink negligee on. We went on a sound stage and it was full of photographers, and they put us inside this ring—and the photographers shot and shot and shot, and it did hit *Look* Magazine." Recently married to a good friend of Hamilburg's, Elena was impressed by her co-star: "He was a cutie, an attractive person. His shyness also had an attraction, because the man was smart, and most young people love a man who's successful. And he was wealthy and he was world-renowned and that, in itself, is attractive to people."[14]

Between takes, Gene tended to his business affairs with his secretary Louise Heising. Director Frank McDonald remembered "a quiet and unassuming" Gene, who one day on set had to break for a phone call, saying, "Excuse me, I've got to sell a radio station." McDonald never knew the budget for *The Big Sombrero* or what the film, released in March 1949, grossed. "Mandy never told anybody what the [budget was]. The studios would rather a director didn't know the budget because then he would know how much he could spend and would be tempted to go overboard. Mandy Schaefer was a darned good producer. He could get more out of a dollar than most producers could get out of a hundred dollars." As for discovering the gross, "they didn't want you to know because then you might ask for a raise."[15] After *Sombrero*, Mandy (who, according to McDonald, was partially deaf) and Gene—ever the astute businessmen—determined that color was financially unfeasible for the Autry pictures, so they switched to the cheaper Monochrome process, producing a sepia film with a reddish brown hue.

The traditional outlets for Autry pictures—small-town exhibitors—were balking at the higher price of Columbia's more expensive production, causing delays in the distribution of *The Last Round-Up*. Although the picture was officially released in November 1947, it didn't screen in some areas until mid-1948. Republic had flooded the market with Gene's final four films, as well as re-releases of his older prewar pictures. Londoner and UK fan club president Alex Gordon, who relocated to the States in January and would eventually work for the Autry organization, wrote the *Aces*: "I was glad to catch up on some of Gene's early pictures. . . . However, it is a pity that these dated pictures are still being shown, as they cannot stand comparison with the polished production and technical quality of up-to-date Western pictures."[16] This problem would plague the release of Gene's first Columbia films. The Republics rented at a much cheaper rate than the Columbias, so rural theaters—the bread-and-butter business for Autry pictures—resisted the new, pricier outings. At the same time, many metropolitan first-run theaters still considered Autry films as second-rate fare, so didn't book them either. Consequently, the release of *The Strawberry Roan*, the sole new Autry issue of 1948, was delayed until August. By then a brand-new competition for Gene's theatrical releases was becoming pervasive—television.

Gene tried to boost business for *The Last Round-Up* by embarking on two weeks of personal appearances throughout the South and Southwest in January. Backed by the Cass County Boys, Johnny Bond, and the Pinafores, he performed at theaters prior to the movie screening. This set the stage for the formation of a larger touring ensemble that would embark in late March for the Midwest and South. The entertainers for these one-night stands included his *Melody Ranch* performers, as well as Rufe Davis, and Pat Buttram, who soon became a regular radio cast member. The touring company, eventually named the Gene Autry Hit Show, would take to the road every year—with an expanding and ever-changing cast—for more than a decade. In 1948 Gene would spend 223 days out of Los Angeles, including sixty-four one-nighters and eighty-eight rodeo dates (grossing $358,000 in fees). Throughout the traveling, he maintained his weekly radio program and that summer made two more films, *Loaded Pistols* (in May) and *Riders of the Whistling Pines* (both released in 1949). In June-July, *Riders* featured the only screen appearance of *Melody Ranch*'s Pinafores.

For the most part, audiences flocked to see the Autry touring revue, with Gene in the public eye thanks to the high-profile *Melody Ranch* show and a stream of flattering magazine articles. Unlike most stories, however, the eight-page *Life* feature (June 28), "Gene Autry Inc.," cast a rather cynical eye on the dichotomy between Gene's public image as a "simple cowhand" and his behind-the-scenes role as a shrewd business tycoon with "an empire estimated anywhere between $4 million and $7 million in paying properties." Among the photos illustrating the lengthy piece were a full-page portrait of a content Gene astride Champ on a knoll overlooking his home, and "Gene Autry's U.S.A.," a map detailing his "multifarious business interests . . . from coast to coast." The influential article, which shaved a year off Gene's age, would paint a portrait downplaying his artistic talents and emphasizing his business acumen, an analysis widely accepted by pundits and critics for decades to come. Thirty years later, in his own memoir, a self-deprecating Gene perpetuated it: "It has always surprised me when people seem surprised by my success in business," he wrote in a chapter titled "Corporate Cowboy." "Actually, working with numbers was what I did best. What I did less well was sing, act, and play the guitar." He told those closest to him, too, that he considered himself a "personality" rather than an actor or singer.[17]

Life journalist Percy Knauth described Gene as "a chunky, slim-hipped smiling man" whose voice is "a somnolent tenor with a light twang, limited in range and volume." By always playing himself in his movies, it "obviates the tiresome necessity of trying to act like somebody else and also cuts down the range of possible criticism quite considerably." According to Knauth, Gene "did not like to see indications of his income, in whole or in part, publicly displayed" because "his fans prefer to think of him as a . . . homespun character whose primary interest is in horses and the great outdoors." In reality, he pointed out, the shrewd star serves "as his own business manager and delegates authority only in matters of detail to a few men whom he trusts implicitly": Schaefer, Hamilburg, press agents Whalen and Barnett, and his pilot Herb Green. Knauth also reported that "a good deal of the care and caution with which Autry manages his affairs is attributable to Mrs. Autry, a chic and charming, round cheeked woman [who] . . . has always managed to keep his feet on the ground. . . . She is a devout Christian Scientist, an avid follower of current affairs, and inclines to view Hollywood and all its works, including her husband, with the practical eye of an Oklahoma housewife, tempered by a touch of slight amusement." After observing a recent Autry business meeting, Knauth explained that Gene's "decisions . . . are usually based on a combination of hard sense, a native but not extreme caution, and the profit motive." Said Knauth, "In his public life as a screen cowboy, Autry can exhibit none of the qualities which have made him a successful businessman. It is not an easy life to live, being circumscribed by a strict 'cowboy's code,' any violation of which is likely to draw protesting screams from the 80,000 fans who write to Autry every month."[18]

Indeed, earlier in the year, Gene candidly told a teenaged reporter for *Pilgrim Life* magazine that being a role model to kids is "a tough job sometimes. There are times when you feel like doing something, but you can't because you feel you must live up to your reputation." He quickly added, "And the reputation I have for being a pretty square-shootin' guy, I wouldn't trade for anything. It gives me a lot of pleasure to know that young Americans look up to me as an example for their own lives."[19]

GENE'S DRINKING HAD CONTINUED TO ESCALATE and although he no longer tried to keep it a secret from journalists—Knauth noted his scotch and soda before a Richmond, Virginia, performance—he still carefully hid it from children. Gloria Henry remembered an occasion when a busload of young boys appeared on location in Sedona while Gene was relaxing with a beer. After a momentary exclamation of dismay, he quickly hid the beer, then turned on the charm to greet them. On the road doing his one-night stands and rodeos, Gene always wanted a drink before show time. As time passed, he stopped limiting his cocktail to just one. "I was always on the go," he later wrote, "fighting another deadline, racing to a studio or a business meeting, skipping meals. The more tired one gets, the easier it is to look for energy in a bottle. You just keep refueling."[20]

As usual, Gene spent the fall of 1948 in the Northeast, appearing at the Madison Square Garden and Boston Garden rodeos. That year, with Little Champ along, he devised a new publicity stunt: taking the horse with him in a Checker Cab to his Bellevue Hospital appearance. "I been hackin' for over twenty years," the taxi driver told the *New York Times*, "and I never carried no passenger like this before. I hope the hack bureau don't get after me. This is a violation even if I did for the kids."[21] Little Champ also accompanied Gene to appear on Arthur Godfrey's hit program on CBS, broadcast before a studio audience. After the diminutive horse performed tricks, Gene chatted with the host and crooned "Cool Water." The two men would remain friendly, and Gene later sent him a gift of a wristwatch with its own alarm. Gene had received one as a present from Lyndon Johnson earlier that year. It once disrupted his *Melody Ranch* show when the alarm went off on-air, but Gene liked the gadget so much he bought several of them to present to business associates.

In just two months time Godfrey's radio show would be televised, as the new medium continued to make inroads into American homes. Radio still predominated by the end of 1948, however, and one of the most highly touted programs of the season was CBS's two-hour afternoon broadcast, "Wrigley Christmas Special." Airing on December 25, it was co-hosted by Gene and Bing Crosby, who each confessed their "real" names: Harry Lillis Crosby and Orvon Eugene [*sic*] Autry.[22] The program featured comedy, music, and recitations from guests including George Burns and Gracie Allen, the "Park Avenue Hillbilly" Dorothy Shay, the Andrews Sisters, Rochester (of the Jack Benny program), Hedda Hopper, and Lionel Barrymore, among others. Gene and Bing each sang their massive hits—"Here Comes Santa Claus" and "White Christmas"—and other Yuletide songs. One humorous bit with Pat Buttram explained that *Melody Ranch* was shifting to Saturday nights, due to Jack Benny's move from NBC to CBS on Sunday evenings into the Autry time slot. Gene would later say he agreed to the new schedule in exchange for getting the Benny program on his Phoenix station KOOL. (The FCC had given approval for the purchase on the condition that Gene sell Phoenix station KPHO, which he did in November 1948.)

In January the *Melody Ranch* program began in its new slot on Saturday nights, with the broadcasts sometimes complicated by Gene's heavy touring schedule. Pat Buttram now wrote part of the show, as well as having taken over a prominent position as "Mr. Artery's" wheedling sidekick. A sort of Rochester-meets-Aunt Jemima character—a ranch cook named Raindrop played by Ruby Dandridge (mother of Dorothy Dandridge)—was added as well. Gene and company would sometimes perform the program live on the road, but occasionally—when there were no actors available to play the parts—the dramatic portion was prerecorded. For a time that summer, Gene and the cast would transcribe the entire show in advance, but radio listeners and Wrigley executives greatly preferred the spontaneity of the live broadcasts.

With a sixty-member company, Gene's Western variety show hit the road from January 4 to February 26, 1949. To reach forty-six venues in twenty-seven states, scattered between Amarillo, Texas, and Rochester, New York, Gene had purchased a larger Beechcraft D-18 twin-engine for $55,000 in December. Most of the cast and crew traveled by bus, while trucks and trailers hauled horses and equipment, and a station wagon served as a backup if flights were cancelled. Indeed, bad weather plagued the grueling trek, with Gene getting snowed in at some small airports. Performing twice daily was only part of Gene's touring routine; in each town, he usually visited sick children in hospitals, met with local officials, made appearances at movie theaters and department stores carrying Gene Autry merchandise, and gave numerous radio and newspaper interviews. Along the way, he was always on the lookout for new talent—particularly young female vocalists—to add to the show, which featured musicians, singers, comedians, trick ropers, acrobats, Western-clad dancers and chorus girls, and eventually a group of Jemez Indian dancers from a New Mexico pueblo led by Tony White Cloud.

These much-publicized appearances helped sell tickets to the new Autry films, beginning with *Loaded Pistols* in January, *The Big Sombrero* in March, *Riders of the Whistling Pines* in May, and *Rim of the Canyon* in July. Columbia had renewed its contract with Gene Autry Productions, requiring the release of six pictures a year. Budgets were cut and locations moved closer to home than Arizona, Gene's favorite place to shoot. Ten days after returning from the winter tour, Gene flew the 120 miles to Pioneertown, an Old West set recently developed in the high desert near Palm Springs. There, he started work on *The Cowboy and the Indians*, another picture focused on the plight of Native Americans (which also featured, rather implausibly, "Here Comes Santa Claus"). On March 14, from rustic Room #10 at the on-location Pioneertown Motel, he dictated two letters to business associates documenting a complete change in heart toward his entrepreneurial endeavors. The first was to his staff bookkeeper, to whom he gave a month's notice, explaining he was planning to sell his radio stations, streamline his publishing companies, and close his Hollywood business office:

> I have given considerable thought to my present set-up and have decided that it simply is not worthwhile to keep working as I have been doing for the past two or three years trying to establish a business. I am hardly ever at home and never have time to really take it easy so have definitely decided that I am going to dispose of every business enterprise that I have and devote my full time to my radio program, making movies, and recording.[23]

The other note went to an associate who had inquired if Gene had purchased a Las Vegas newspaper, as was erroneously reported in Louella Parsons's column:

> I'm working entirely too hard and have just about decided that I might cut loose from most everything I have and take a trip someplace for about six months so I could forget about it. It seems that if you do make an extra dollar, the income tax gets it anyway so there's not much sense in killing yourself.[24]

Whatever the reason that precipitated Gene's change of heart, his vow to slow down did not last for long. He continued to keep up the heavy pace, touring again in the spring throughout the South and Southwest, followed by such headlines as SINGING STAR MOBBED BY CHILDREN (San Antonio). A new generation was discovering Gene Autry, so there would be no time for rest.

33

FROM HORSES TO REINDEER, FROM BIG SCREEN TO SMALL

AMID THE FAST-PACED WHIRL OF BUSINESS MEETINGS, touring, movie making, and radio performances, Gene had spent little time since 1947 in the recording studio. He had scored only one other hit since "Here Comes Santa Claus" (a top-five smash in both '47 and '48): "Buttons and Bows" in October 1948, after it was featured in Bob Hope's Western parody, *The Paleface*. Gene had managed to cut "Buttons," along with the theme song to *Loaded Pistols* (originally a recitation-style hit for Phil Harris) and a couple of other numbers in December 1947. Then, a year-long strike by the American Federation of Musicians put an end to most recording in 1948, since all instrumentalists were barred from sessions until its resolution. In Chicago, on April 25, Gene had gotten around the strike by recording two sides with the Pinafores and Cass County Boys—their lush vocals backed by harmonicas, the latter of which were not classified by the AFC as musical instruments.

Finally, on New Year's Eve 1948—with the strike ended—Gene waxed the patriotic "The Bible on the Table and the Flag Upon the Wall" and "I Lost My Little Darlin'" with full instrumental backing. The former documented Gene's sustained fervor for "Americanism," which culminated with his spearheading a Loyalty Day parade in Hollywood to counter communists' annual May Day activities. The two-hour patriotic procession by six thousand paraders (including the newly chosen "Miss Loyalty"[1]) attracted twenty thousand spectators. Gene's first recording session of 1949 came on March 21, during which he cut a pair of lovelorn ballads (prominently featuring muted trumpet, violin, and piano) and two up-tempo numbers—three of which were co-credited to him (including

"Ellie Mae" about a "rootin' tootin' cutie"). But it was Gene's second session—on June 27, 1949—that yielded the most enduring hit of his entire career.

"Here Comes Santa Claus" had begged a follow-up: submissions arrived over the transom from numerous eager songwriters, including one tuneful narrative based on a 1939 poem popularized by Montgomery Ward. The story of an outcast reindeer whose "difference" ultimately helped him save Santa's threatened sleigh ride, "Rudolph, the Red-Nosed Reindeer" was written by veteran composer Johnny Marks. His brother-in-law, copywriter Robert L. May, originally had penned the verse for the department store's annual holiday booklet giveaway, a practice discontinued in 1947. The copyright became May's, who got the poem published as an illustrated children's book that sold one hundred thousand copies. May then permitted Marks to use the story for a composition. "I thought about it for a while and sat down to write a song about it," Marks related. "That song was easily one of the worst songs ever written. Then about a year later I was walking down the street when a new melody came to me. It's the only time that ever happened, and I have to admit, it's a great melody."[2] Marks sent a demonstration recording to RCA Victor recording artist Perry Como, but the pop singer turned it down when the composer wouldn't allow him to change any lyrics. Marks later confessed to Gene it had been rejected by Bing Crosby and Dinah Shore as well.

Over the years, Gene always told the story that he didn't care for the song either, but that Ina heard Marks's demo acetate and, "enchanted" by its "Ugly Duckling" theme, encouraged him to record it. It became widely acknowledged that if not for Ina, there would be no "Rudolph" by Gene Autry. According to Carl Cotner's widow, Juanita, Marks originally contacted Gene's musical director and "wanted Carl to talk Gene into [recording it] . . . Johnny Marks had . . . said, 'I'll give you a piece of the action if you will do it,' and Carl said, 'Well, I don't want that,' . . . which was not a good business [decision], but that was Carl. Carl had told Gene, 'I think it's a good song for you,' and Carl did the arrangement. When working out the material for the session, Gene said, 'How about that song that you're so crazy about?' They threw it up on the stands, and did it in one take. . . . [Later] a publicity man put it out that it was Ina that talked Gene into it."[3]

"Rudolph" eventually would be recorded by more than five hundred artists, but Marks always preferred Gene's version: "The great success of the Rudolph record," Marks wrote him the following year, "was your perfect rendition of the song. . . . Two bar intro, ad lib verse, solo chorus in tempo, thirty-two bar instrumental, and the last chorus with the Pinafores."[4] In 1961 he told Gene, "What I sent you in 1949 were ink dots on a piece of paper. You had to translate this into a sound, lyrically and musically, that people would like. How many great songs have been lost because of the wrong rendition? Many people have said: 'Any one could have made a hit with Rudolph.' My answer has always been: 'We'll never know. I only know that Gene Autry did do it, and that all the others followed.'"[5]

The same day as "Rudolph," Gene also recorded Oakley Haldeman's "He's a Chubby Little Fellow" (co-credited to Gene)—the obvious but not as catchy sequel to their "Here Comes Santa Claus." Apparently, perhaps because they did not own a copyright on "Rudolph," Haldeman felt Gene's recording it was a mistake, according to Marks: "I met Oakley Haldeman for the first time the other night," he wrote Gene just after the record's September release. "I was completely amazed and stunned at his attitude on the Rudolph song. He repeated to me a conversation which he told me he had with you. It strikes me that he has a very narrow and selfish viewpoint. Actually, as I tried to point out to him, your success with the song from the overall picture will help your other songs."[6]

Five weeks later, on August 4, Gene cut two more Christmas numbers, "Santa, Santa, Santa" (credited to Haldeman and Autry) and "If It Doesn't Snow on Christmas," the latter of which became the flipside to "Rudolph." As Columbia previously had packaged "Here Comes Santa Claus," "Rudolph" was issued in a colorful picture sleeve. "[This] marketing innovation . . . emerged in the late forties with Gene Autry's 'Here Comes Santa Claus' and 'Rudolph,'" according to music historian Dave Marsh. "This was little more than a sales technique based on the theory that if a youngster or his mother were shopping for records, and the kid spotted a colorful cartoon picture of Santa on the sleeve of 'Here Comes Santa Claus,' junior would pester mom until she put some cash into the pocket of the shrewd record marketer. Picture sleeves soon became a prestige part of any single release."[7]

"Rudolph" became a favorite on *The Hit Parade* and soared to the top of the *Billboard* country & western *and* pop charts—a first for Gene. (In 1947 "Here Comes Santa Claus" had been Gene's initial entry on the prestigious *Billboard* pop chart.) Marks later recalled how Gene helped to promote the song: "I recall my struggle of 1949 and how you went out of your way to help. Among the many, many things you did, I particularly remember asking you to sing the song at Madison Square Garden. You were reluctant and rightly so, but said you would try it out and you did. . . . I asked you to do it on your radio show. You told me the producer and sponsor were adamant against doing a Christmas song so early, but you did it anyway."[8] For the rodeo Marks even supplied Gene with a Rudolph costume with flashing red nose, donned by Frankie Marvin, who pranced around the arena. (After the Boston Garden stint, he somehow lost the pants, which Marks replaced for the 1950 rodeos.) During its first year of release, "Rudolph" sold two million copies, selling an estimated twenty-five million more over the next forty years. For decades it remained the best-selling single of all time after Bing Crosby's "White Christmas."

"Rudolph" also anticipated a new trend for Gene: recording discs specifically geared to the children's market. Two days later, he returned to the studio to make the spoken-word "Stampede," which included only snippets of Gene singing "Night Herding Song" and "Cowboy's Dream." A more child-friendly version of the *Melody Ranch* dramatizations, the action-packed Western tale co-starred Gene, his range-riding partner Chin Music (Wally Maher), "Indian lad" Katoma (Johnny McGovern), "ornery" bad guy Murdock (Gerald Mohr), and Champ (represented by very fake-sounding whinnies). In December, Gene and Maher recorded another story disc, "Champion (The Horse No Man Could Ride)," which gave an adventurous account of how Gene came together with his loyal steed (the sound effects had improved). Rather than Art Satherley, Hecky Krasnow, Columbia's executive in charge of special markets, began handling Gene's holiday and children's recordings—soon to monopolize his sessions.

By 1949 the recording industry was undergoing changes once again. The year before, Columbia had introduced the first LP, or long-player, a ten-inch (later twelve-inch) 33 1/3 rpm platter of vinyl—developed during the wartime shellac shortage. The LP's "microgrooves" permitted better aural quality and could hold more songs than a 78. RCA Victor countered this innovation in 1949 with an inexpensive seven-inch 45 rpm vinyl disc, which came to be known as a 45 (and later, singles). Eventually, all labels began issuing LPs (soon to be called albums) and 45s, with 78s gradually being phased out. Taking advantage of both new types of discs was the newly burgeoning children's music market. Later in the year, the *New York Times* announced the release of "Stampede" and also reported that "Victor has hit upon a new and useful idea for its children's albums, which it now issues in what it calls its 'Little Nipper' series. The small 45 rpm albums are easy for the youngster to handle and the text of the story is bound into the volume in book form."[9]

The sudden interest shown by Gene (and record labels) in appealing to children was motivated by the lucrative postwar baby-boom market. Young children were clamoring for cowboys, and by 1949 one of their favorites was Hopalong Cassidy, due to his frequent appearance on television. William Boyd had bought the rights to his old movies (produced between 1935 and 1943), and in 1948 he licensed edited-down versions to TV programmers desperately in need of ready-made material. Television could broadcast Hopalong Cassidy movies into homes across the nation. Hoppy's black cowboy outfit, gleaming white hair, and booming, fatherly laugh won over a whole new generation of little cowpoke wannabes (who had no idea that the buckaroo in reality loathed horses). Soon the "has-been" movie star was rivaling Roy and Gene in popularity polls, with the press issuing reports of a Cassidy-Rogers-Autry feud (just as fan magazines had capitalized on the Rogers-Autry rivalry). According to Jimmy Wakely, who appeared in Hopalong Cassidy pictures while on *Melody Ranch*, Boyd had held a grudge against Gene since 1940. Wakely recalled a revealing conversation with Boyd on set:

> I said, "Bill, I understand there's a little animosity between you and Gene, but Gene told me you were the greatest actor in the business, you're a fine person, and that I was very lucky to be working for you." And he said, "So he admits it—that

I'm a better actor!" And I said, "Of course, he does . . . Gene's not an actor, and he'll be the first to tell you!" I said, "What's your hang-up about Autry?" He said, "Well, we went to the President's birthday ball . . . and I was standing in the lobby of the Mayflower signing autographs, and Gene Autry walked in that lobby with a solid white cowboy suit on, and it was just a mass exodus—right there I stood with the pen in my hand."[10]

Now it was Gene's turn to feel the burn, indicated by an uncharacteristically snippy response when asked about a feud: "As far as I'm concerned," he snapped at a reporter, "there was never any kind of feud at all, because I don't consider Bill Boyd competition. I consider him just another third-rater. That's what the polls say and that's what I go by."[11] Gene later opined, "You can't make me believe that old films which were made for motion picture theaters can be cut and trimmed to satisfy the requirements of television for first-class entertainment."

Indeed, behind closed doors, Gene and Mandy Schaefer were beginning to investigate how they, too, could enter the television game. At the time, TV programming was shunned by Hollywood studios and actors, who viewed it an inferior novelty that threatened their monopoly of the movie business. Only poverty-row studios were licensing old serials and B-Westerns to the networks. Still, in 1949, half-hour versions of long-running radio programs were being produced for TV. One such television show, *The Lone Ranger*, starring Clayton Moore and Jay Silverheels (both of whom appeared in *The Cowboy and the Indians*, among other Autry pictures), became immediately popular. Not wanting to lose their radio star, Wrigley offered to add five hundred dollars a week to Gene's *Melody Ranch* salary if he would stay off TV.

Melody Ranch producer Bill Burch was questioned by Hedda Hopper about Gene's unceasing drive and ambition. "Why does he work so hard?" she asked him. "He loves it," Bill replied. "It's not for money. After a certain amount, the government gets practically everything anyway." An unidentified source told Hopper, "At heart, Gene's a horse trader. He gets a tremendous kick from out-witting sharpies on business deals. That's why he'll never quit working. It's like a tonic to him."[12]

The mention of Delbert Autry's former "occupation" must have been a thorn in Gene's side when he read the quote in Hopper's column. Delbert, his wife Ruby, and their daughters now lived in near-poverty northeast of Los Angeles in Bakersfield. Declaring his shiftless father as a dependent on his annual income tax returns, Gene sent Delbert a monthly check and frequently paid the family's overdue bills. Gene's brother Dudley also had become dependent on Gene's support. After the war, he had unsuccessfully tried to make it as a singing cowboy, under the name Doug Autry. Unable to hold down a job, he drank heavily and was jailed several times for brawls and bounced checks. Gene frequently came to his rescue, and at one point arranged for his brother to accompany his old friend Pee Wee King on a tour. In 1949 Gene became incensed when his brother joined a traveling circus that misleadingly advertised the name Autry. In April, newspapers reported that Gene "brought suit complaining the circus billing of Doug with 'Autry' in larger letters and 'Doug' in small ones, created the impression Gene Autry was being featured."[13] Regardless, Gene eventually offered Dudley/Doug a gopher job in his own touring revue.

"Autry Can't Get Around to Resting," Hedda Hopper's July feature in the *Los Angeles Times*, also implied a growing distance between Gene and Ina, when the columnist and her subject stopped by the Autry home:

"After greeting me, Mrs. Autry turned to her husband and said, 'Hello, dear.'

" 'Oh, hello, honey,' was the absent-minded reply.

" 'I haven't seen him for two days,' said the wife with a shrug and a smile.

"As if suddenly remembering, Gene grinned. 'She's right. I've been over in Arizona checking on our other ranch.'

" 'And he leaves tomorrow for Dallas, New York, Chicago, Minneapolis, and a few other points east,' said his wife." She would later joke to Hopper that Gene made himself scarce when moving day arrived: The Autrys' new home in Studio City had finally been completed, and that summer Ina would supervise its décor and their move from the San Fernando Valley. The couple and the interior of their Colonial style abode would soon appear in numerous fan magazines in pictorials with titles like "Design for Living."

When Hopper pushed Gene to explain his relentless workload, he told her, "Hedda, I don't suppose a man in my spot can slow down. You get so involved that you can't afford to take even a month off. So many people depend upon me for work. I feel obligated to those who've been loyal to me. There's Johnny Bond my guitar player, for instance. He's been with me 20 [*sic*] years. When I work, he works.' "[14] (In reality, Bond, who had joined Gene nine years earlier, had recorded six C&W hits for Columbia over the past two years and continued to perform on the *Hollywood Barn Dance* radio program when not working for Gene.) It is true, though, that Gene felt a responsibility for his longtime employees. As his horse trainer of twelve years, John Agee, became infirm that summer, Gene put out feelers for his replacement, writing one candidate: "Right now the old man is pretty sick and, quite frankly, at his age I don't know whether or not he will be able to train horses again. . . . I want you to understand that we are not letting him go as he will be more or less on a pension with me as long as he lives, but I do have some new horses that need to be broken and trained."[15]

In August, Gene forged a relationship with songwriter Stan Jones, a former Death Valley forest ranger whose composition "Riders in the Sky" had become a massive pop and C&W hit that year for Vaughn Monroe. Numerous production companies wanted the film rights to the vivid narrative song about ghostly range-riders chasing red-eyed steers. But Gene clinched the deal with Jones when the two happened to meet at a radio station. According to the *New*

York Times, Gene paid the songwriter fifteen thousand dollars and promised him a part in the film. (He would also purchase the rights to Jones's song "Whirlwind," which Gene recorded during the same session as "Riders in the Sky" and made into a 1951 movie; that film also featured Jones in a bit part but did not garner much commercial success.)

An Autry picture titled *Beyond the Purple Hills* was nearly complete, so they changed the title to *Riders in the Sky* and shot and tacked on a few scenes including a ghostly stampede chased by cowboy specters. A new opening was filmed featuring Gene and Stan Jones (uncredited) riding along singing the title song. The picture featured Gloria Henry and Pat Buttram, who had not made an Autry film since *Strawberry Roan.* This would be Henry's last Autry picture; she accidentally fell from her horse during filming, plus she had another altercation with Gene when he uttered nasty comments about Rita Hayworth's recent marriage to Ali Khan: "I told the head of talent at Columbia," she later related, " 'You can put me on suspension or whatever, but I don't want to work with that man again.' "[16]

Riders was the beginning of Pat Buttram's longtime screen collaboration with Gene, however. With this picture, he took the reins as Gene's first bona fide sidekick since Smiley Burnette, costarring in an eventual fifteen more Autry films (as well as eighty-three made for television). Pat's signature look became a plaid shirt, vest, baggy khakis, and a hat with a high peaked crown. His flat boots and slump prevented him from looking three inches taller than Gene, and he eventually grew a scraggly beard to disguise the fact he was eight years younger than the leading man. Buttram's antics often had Gene in stitches, and the singing cowboy delighted in imitating Pat's wheezy voice on *Melody Ranch* broadcasts.

Pat told one reporter he provided yet another role in the Autry pictures: "I have an unofficial job with Artery & Co. I'm sort of liaison man between Gene, who's overworked, and the . . . producers. Often, an assistant director will say, 'Gene hasn't had time to read that long speech and I have to ask him to stop and go over it. My cue here is to say, 'Hey Gene, I could use a little help with this bit here, would you run through it with me? Being a swell guy, he'll always take time out to help me, so the assistant director can breathe freely again."[17] Indeed, according to Pat's daughter, Kerry, he memorized Gene's lines as well as his own: "He learned all the dialogue for his scene, not just cues for his own lines. He said one of the most important things in acting was really listening to the other actor performing in the scene with him. He said if you're just waiting for a cue, that becomes obvious and destroys the authenticity of the scene. Staying alert and listening to each line of dialogue keeps the timing flowing. Gene and Dad were very much in sync."[18]

Gene's films had continued to evolve, with fewer songs and more action, usually including several fistfights. A regular cast of character actors appeared, including heavies played by House Peters Jr., Harry Lauter, Gregg Barton, and

Alan Hale Jr. (sometimes as a misguided lawman); Tom London as a grizzled old-timer; and occasionally Republic's former leading men, such as Three Mesquiteers Bob Steele and Bob Livingston. Often the films would center around a troubled adolescent boy or young man (frequently played by Dick Jones) with whom Gene intercedes, preventing him from "going wrong."

Gene's Ten Cowboy Commandments began to evolve from such Autry-related publicity as the item "Nine Cardinal Rules Govern Production of All Autry Films," which ran in the 1949 press book for *Riders in the Sky*. As early as August 1947, Gene had pronounced cowboy-code mandates during his *Melody Ranch* radio show dramas. Gene's PR team promoted his Cowboy Code, which was referred to in the 1948 *Life* magazine feature, and fan magazines began to publicize the rules as they evolved. Tenets promoting an ethical, moral, and patriotic lifestyle had an affinity to those of such youth organizations as the Boy Scouts, which developed similar doctrines. The rules were a natural progression of Gene's philosophies going back to his first *Melody Ranch* programs—and early pictures. But as the years progressed, some of the standards of conduct he established became harder for him to follow in his own personal life. And setting himself up as a role model for children meant he was held to much higher standards of behavior than was the typical movie star.

In his new films, Gene gradually stopped wearing his eye-catching, decorative wardrobe in favor of denim shirts and pants. A reporter, Bob Thomas, in his article "The New Autry's Tough," noted "The once easy-going cowpoke is becoming a rugged son of the West" and quoted Gene as saying, "I'm a tough cowboy now and I wear simple clothes that take a lot of wear. The only time I wear flashy getups is when I'm doing a personal appearance." Gene's grooming was always fastidious, and in 1950 he was voted one of America's top ten best-dressed men.

Riders in the Sky was rushed for release in November, but it failed to make the mark Gene had hoped. It was becoming clear that as television reached more households, budget Westerns were selling fewer tickets. Even hit songs could not motivate theater-goers. Gene cut his own version of another recent smash, "Mule Train," a chart-topper for both Frankie Laine and Vaughn Monroe, and paid a reported twenty thousand dollars for the film rights.[19] His final production of 1949, *Mule Train* did only mediocre business upon release in February of 1950 but was later selected by New York's Museum of Modern Art for its film collection.

Gene had started the new decade in serious discussion with his partners Mandy Shaefer and Mitch Hamilburg about their options in television. Celebrating the tenth anniversary of *Melody Ranch* in January, Gene had maintained a warm relationship with his sponsor Wrigley and his radio network CBS. Broadcasting from Chicago on January 24, Gene read aloud congratulatory telegrams from CBS executives William S. Paley and Frank Stanton. He profusely thanked them and Wrigley for their support. He would soon parlay these relationships into a television deal.

On April 18 the *New York Times* reported:

> Gene Autry will be the first motion picture star to produce and appear in films for television transmission, it was learned today from the cowboy actor's business manager Mitchell Hamilburg. Autry, Hamilburg, and Armand Schaefer, producer, have formed Flying A Pictures Inc., and have negotiated a sponsorship deal with the William Wrigley company for a series of half-hour Westerns, the first of which will go before cameras in three weeks. It is . . . understood that the deal will follow the previously established pattern for television subjects, whereby the sponsor pays a flat sum, usually from 30 to 50 percent of the cost of production for first transmission rights, while subsequent rights are retained by the producer and may be sold later to other sponsors."[20]

A week later, a follow-up column reported that Gene's move

> indicated that the production of films for television is here to stay. . . . It is believed that a major reason for Autry's entry into the television field is its importance as a means of recruiting new admirers. The popular renaissance of William Boyd (Hopalong Cassidy) since his old pictures have been regularly telecast is evidence of the importance of the medium to actors whose audience is drawn from the rising generation, and consequently there is speculation that other cowboy actors may follow Autry into the video corral."[21]

The same week, CBS president Frank Stanton wrote Gene a personal note: "CBS is mighty proud to have the Gene Autry Show. . . . Today the Columbia Broadcasting System has the largest nationwide coverage—day and night—of any network [NBC and ABC]. . . . During the first quarter of 1950, CBS averaged: 15 out of the top 20 night-time programs; 10 out of the top 15 daytime shows."[22] Initially, *The Gene Autry Show* was slated to debut on July 23 on CBS's "Eastern network," which included New York, Chicago, Baltimore, Boston, Philadelphia, and Washington. That fall Los Angeles, San Francisco, Dallas, and Atlanta, among other cities totaling 28 stations, also broadcast the weekly program, some on different networks. At the time of the program's debut, New York led the nation in the number of television sets, with 1,325,000, followed by Los Angeles with 563,406, and Chicago with 500,000.[23] By October 8 million TVs had been purchased in America, and producers had spent more than $100 million a year creating programming, according to a GE television set advertisement intended to prove that TV was no passing fad but rather "the world's greatest entertainment—available night after night, day after day in an every-growing cavalcade including drama, variety, comedy, music, news, sports, service, and children's shows."[24]

To produce Flying A Pictures' first six programs, Gene and his regular movie-production cast and crew began working twelve-hours days in May and June in Pioneertown. Each twenty-seven minute film cost an average of $17,500. To save time and money, the team simultaneously shot a pair of shows a week, originally with director Frank McDonald. "In shooting two video pictures at once, the director always looks for the possibilities of switching a location shot so it can be utilized in two films," reported the *New York Times* on Flying A's strategy. "If for instance the camera films a rider coming down the side of a mountain, it may also reshoot him going up the mountain for another picture." The article also pointed out "the camera always works at fairly close range, avoiding long shots, as a concession to relatively small television screens," necessitating Gene to do "some jobs in front of the camera which normally would be handled by a double."[25] In addition to more close-ups and medium shots, the series would feature chase scenes in which the action goes across the screen, rather than from background to foreground. Although there were a few exceptions, most programs would include Gene doing just one song, but Carl Cotner composed incidental music (a first for television). Using union musicians to perform the score, Gene negotiated a precedent-setting agreement with the AFM.

The making of Gene's television series did not prevent him from shooting movies. In March came *Indian Territory* in Pioneertown, followed by *The Blazing Sun* in Lone Pine. After completing the first six "video pictures," he made *Gene Autry and the Mounties* in the mountains at Big Bear. John English continued to direct the films, and *The Blazing Sun* was written by Jack Townley, who also contributed scripts to the TV shows (as did other frequent Autry film screenwriters). "Each is an original story written especially for television," Gene said as guest TV columnist in the *Chicago Sun-Times*.

> We've cut out distant shots because figures in them are apt to be blurred on most TV screens. . . . Strictly on the technical side, our photographers have found ways to cut down on the sharp contrasting shades that are so hard on the viewers' eyes. I've been asked if I intended giving up making movies in favor of TV. . . . As a matter of fact I am scheduled to make six pictures this year, and I will keep on making them just as long as people will come to see them. I can't see any conflict between television and the movies. They each will create a demand for the other. The thing I like most about television is the much shorter shooting schedule for TV pictures. I like this better than the longer drawn out shooting schedule of regular length movies.[26]

On July 23, when the big day arrived for the debut of Gene's first television picture, titled *Head for Texas*, even the critics who normally dismissed his films seemed impressed. Airing at 7 PM, "the snappy horse opera" was a tautly condensed version of an Autry film featuring Gene versus cattle rustlers, a ranch-owning love interest, and the humor of Pat Buttram.[27] Even though there were no commercial breaks, the first few shows opened with a relaxed

Gene, leaning against a corral, expounding the virtues of Wrigley's gum, which he popped in his mouth. (This personalized hard sale was soon eliminated.)

All the hard work had paid off again. Gene would later recall:

> I think my biggest thrill, as far as TV is concerned, was the reception my first TV film received from the public and the critics. I was one of the first movie people to make a film especially for television, but if I had listened to many of my friends, I never would have ventured into TV films. They told me I was making a big mistake by going into a new field and that I had better stick to regular feature-length movies. I must confess I wasn't sure myself just what reception my first TV picture would have.[28]

IN AUGUST, GENE WOULD RETURN to Pioneertown for a month to make the second set of television programs to air in the fall. With him was a petite auburn-haired actress who, after already co-starring in three of his movies, was becoming his favorite leading lady: Her name was Gail Davis.

34

LAST OF THE PONY RIDERS

MEET GAIL DAVIS, A LEADING LADY IN AUTRY TV FILMS, exclaimed the headline of an August 16, 1950, press release from the Columbia Broadcasting System: "Gail was such a hit in the four Columbia Pictures releases she has made with Autry that Gene found it natural to think of Gail when he was seeking leading ladies for his new series of TV films for CBS." Davis would eventually costar in fourteen Autry movies and numerous episodes of *The Gene Autry Show*, and, in 1953, play the lead in her own Flying A Pictures program, *Annie Oakley*—becoming the first woman to star in a Western television series.

Gail had been in Hollywood for three years when she first played opposite Gene in *Cow Town* during the summer of 1949. She was born Betty Jeanne Grayson in Little Rock, Arkansas, on October 5, 1925, the daughter of a physician. While a student at the University of Texas in Austin, she met and married Lt. Robert "Bob" Davis, a pilot stationed at the army air base there. After his discharge from the service, the newlyweds moved to Los Angeles, both hoping to get into show business. Bob found work in a theatrical agent's office, then a car dealership. Soon after their arrival Betty Jeanne had better luck. Sunbathing one day on the roof of the Hollywood Plaza hotel, the fetching twenty-one-year-old redhead was spotted by an agent. He arranged for her to get an MGM screen test, which led to a contract. She became Gail Davis—to avoid confusion with other similarly named young starlets signed to MGM.

While studying with various coaches, the 5'2" ingénue was cast in bit parts until the studio sold her contract to RKO. A few inconsequential roles later,

Gail found herself without a contract. She began acting in Republic and Columbia B-Westerns, in which she would play opposite Charles Starrett (the Durango Kid), Rocky Lane, and Monte Hale. In 1948 she landed the female lead in Roy Rogers's *The Far Frontier*. Also around this time she acted in *Brand of Fear* (Monogram) with Jimmy Wakely, who thought Davis showed "the most promise" of all his female co-stars. Wakely recommended Gail to Gene and Mandy Schaefer, who screened *The Far Frontier* and liked what they saw. Her natural, fresh-faced good looks fit the bill Gene described when asked over the years what kind of leading lady he favored. Gail, with her honey-coated voice and southern accent, had a down-to-earth, girl-next-door quality. Gene told the press she was "the perfect Western heroine."

Gail's first role with Gene was the stubborn ranch owner Ginger Kirby in *Cow Town*. Shot in 1949, the film was held for release until May 1950. When it screened in New York City, the *Daily News* called it "one of the better-class Westerns. . . . Gene is very astute in getting cute Gail Davis for his leading lady, a would-be spitfire who gradually mellows as the reels go by, and Autry has rustled up a couple of serenades for her benefit."[1] Indeed, Gene and Gail showed the kind of chemistry he once had with June Storey, and often Gail's roles were similar to the parts June had played. The *Hollywood Reporter* noted in its review that "Gene is looking slimmer and younger and he has seldom played a more strenuous role or give a better performance," while "Gail Davis is a cute little gal and gives a performance full of pep and punch."[2]

Davis next co-starred in *Sons of New Mexico* (released prior to *Cow Town*) as the concerned cousin of a troubled youth played by Dick Jones, with whom she would work in several films and TV shows. "A very lovely lady," is how Jones later remembered his co-star. "I thought she was just fantastic. I loved working with her. She was a very good actress."[3] Songwriter and *New York Mirror* columnist Nick Kenny wrote Gene, "That gal in *Sons of New Mexico* was something!"[4] After Gail's appearance in *Indian Territory*, filmed in June, the press book made much of the fact that "she was the first actress to be cast three times" as Gene's leading lady at Columbia. The item went on to say "Miss Davis admits to being an Autry fan from way back, and she thoroughly enjoys being 'sung at,' during rehearsals and filming of the Autry songs, no matter how many 'takes' are required." (Gene did only two songs in *Indian Territory*.) His roles were becoming more often the kindly, though fistfighting, uncle type, while the love interest of Gail's character was usually, as in *Indian Territory*, a younger protégé (or rival) of Gene's.

Gail rejoined Gene in Pioneertown while he was there for eight weeks between July and September. Fan club members Ginny Siegers and Myrla McDougall traveled to the scorching desert to observe television picture production, and filed a report for *Autry's Aces*:

> We found that making TV films [is] . . . plenty of hard work. . . . Met cute little
> Gail Davis too, and felt so sorry for her as she was wearing such a heavy ankle

length dress for her role in the picture and it was so warm. Gene and the whole crew had been working since 7:30 AM and were scheduled to quit about 6 that night. About the middle of the afternoon, everyone's nerves were a little jumpy. Gail, Gene and Pat . . . were going through a rehearsal for a scene prior to the actual shooting and Gail just couldn't get through her lines without "muffing" them. Poor kid was just plain tired out and of course with each slip of the tongue she became more upset. To top it all off, she was supposed to be bawling Gene out, with him sitting across the table from her, grinning for all he was worth. After about the fourth try, Gene looked at the director, winked at Gail and drawled, "Take it easy, I'm nervous." That was the pat on the back [she] needed and after that it was a take.[5]

It is uncertain exactly when, but at some point while working together at Pioneertown, Gene and Gail became lovers. The on-again off-again relationship would continue over the next eight years. "He kept after her, and from what I understand he finally did get her," according to Gloria Henry. "A couple of assistant directors told me that you could see the day it started [at Pioneertown]. They both nonchalantly came out of his room in the morning, and from then on they made no effort to hide it."[6] Cass County Boy Jerry Scoggins, on location at Pioneertown that summer, called Gail Gene's all-time favorite leading lady. "She was a beautiful girl and very friendly and very nice," Scoggins related, "and everybody liked her. Gene and she were very, very close."[7]

In his letter to the *Aces*, dated August 30, Gene wrote from Pioneertown, "Looks like a busy season ahead, but when you're doing things you like, it's fun to be working. . . . All of us working on these films are really enthused about them."[8]

Not everyone shared Gene's enthusiasm, however. Since the press announced his television series, a heated protest arose from movie exhibitors whom Gene had courted so arduously since the mid-1930s. Just after the program's July debut, P. J. Wood, secretary of the Independent Theater Owners of Ohio, called for a boycott of Autry films: "In view of his detrimental action, we are suggesting to theater owners that they urge Autry to have his pictures shown exclusively on TV, thus relieving exhibitors of showing old and new Autry films in the 10,000 American motion picture theaters." One theater owner, who cancelled his contract for Autry pictures, stated, "I cannot compete, charging admission for Gene Autry pictures, with free home television showing Autry in new pictures. It's a sin to think Autry would betray theater owners who made possible his popularity and financial success in years past by switching his talents to television when theaters are in such critical times as at present."[9]

Gene responded by writing an impassioned letter to the Ohio chain: "I am not an enemy or traitor to the exhibitor . . . but let's look it square in the face—television is going to stay here and the sooner we all start figuring how to benefit from it rather than run from it, the better off we all will be." According to the *Film Daily*, which reported on the squabble, Gene "cited the failure of metropolitan exhibitors to give his [Columbia] pictures 'a break.' 'If they did run one in a downtown house it was always at the bottom of a dual bill, with major company product given first position.' He said his pictures have always played small towns where, at present TV generally is not available. 'So how could TV hurt my pictures at the box office when they have not been given fair exhibition in the large cities?'" He expressed his dismay, too, that many theaters ran the old Republic pictures rather than his new ones "simply because they are a little cheaper." Gene added that each of his TV shows ended with a voice-over recommending viewers to "be sure and see Gene Autry and Champion in their latest full-length feature at your local theater." The announcement ran beginning with the first program and was most likely developed to appease Columbia Pictures, which like other studios, was opposed to television's encroachment on its territory.

As *The Gene Autry Show* continued airing September through November of 1950, Gene, in fact, became more convinced that television was his career's salvation. TV had so elevated Bill Boyd's stature by then that Hoppymania was the cover story of both *Time* and *Life*. The country had gone cowboy crazy, with merchandise deals exploding for Gene, Roy, and Boyd. *Life* predicted that Boyd would rack in an estimated $800,000 from his share of the $70 million worth of Hoppy merchandise sold in 1950. *Fortune* magazine named Gene "Hollywood's #1 Businessman," and "Gene Autry: Millionaire Cowboy" was the title of a splashy feature in *Look*, which focused on Gene's "mercantile empire" of "forty-five licensees" "giving livelihood to close to a million people."[10]

In addition to the menagerie of more than a hundred children's products that carried Gene's name, he also had invested in George Delacorte Jr.'s Dell Publishing Company to produce a line of Gene Autry comic books, for which he would receive a hefty percentage of the profits. (Gene had originally licensed his name to Fawcett, which published a series of Autry comics from 1941 to 1943.) Delacorte optimistically wrote Gene of the positive effect his weekly series would likely have on sales: "Comparing the October issue, which was the first issue affected by your television show, with the September issue, we find that sales were 5.2 percent better than in a similar area where the television show was not seen. . . . My circulation department feels that these results are favorable indeed, and they also point out that the effects of such a show should be cumulative. . . . We did not sell out of our entire distribution in the television area but, to the contrary, took a fair return. This, however, was part of the plan to keep this television area well saturated with the comic magazine so that we could reap the full effect of the television show."[11]

The Autry saturation of the market had been in affect all year: From January to March, a ten-thousand-mile tour of sixty-five cities brought him before an estimated half-million people during eighty-four performances. On March 21 Columbia Records issued a press release stating he had renewed his contract with the label for another five years. Gene's brand-new Easter hit,

"Peter Cottontail,"[12] had just sold 175,000 copies during its first week of release. Its composers, Steve Nelson and Jack Rollins, would provide Gene with Rudolph's follow-up, 1950's crossover Yuletide smash "Frosty the Snowman." Telling the story of another memorable children's character, with a catchy tune vocalized by Gene and the Cass County Boys, the song, also, became a perennial.

Hecky Krasnow oversaw the recording of several more Autry sessions that year, including the Thanksgiving numbers "Guffy the Goofy Gobbler" and "Little Johnny Pilgrim," which did not make much of an impact. Neither did Gene's country-pop offerings or his gospel duets with Dinah Shore ("The Old Rugged Cross" and "In the Garden"). Those sessions were produced by Art Satherley, with assistance from British-born Don Law, being groomed as his successor. As Uncle Art was nearing his required retirement (at age sixty-five) from Columbia in 1952, Don Law focused on the new artists on his roster, and Gene's country-pop sessions—termed "folk" by the label—were beginning to suffer for it.

Still, by year's end, Gene was listed in the ninth spot in a Gallup poll of the nation's favorite male singers—the only Western vocalist to make a survey list topped by Bing Crosby (followed by Perry Como). In July 1951, a year after America had become embroiled in the Korean War, Gene would score his final *Billboard* top tenner, the patriotic "Old Soldiers Never Die, They Just Fade Away"—with spoken verses and sung choruses, filled out by Pinafores and Cass County Boys. Inspired by Gen. Douglas MacArthur's impassioned speech to the joint session of Congress on April 19, Gene had rushed into the studio the following day to record the song that, like MacArthur's speech, quoted an old army ballad. Because of his aggressive strategy in Korea, MacArthur had been suddenly dismissed as commander in chief of U.N. forces due to fear that his approach would escalate into war with China and the Soviet Union. His forced retirement caused a national outcry, with Gene strongly supporting MacArthur. That fall, Gene arranged a meeting with the general, afterwards writing him, "I, as well as Mrs. Autry, am for you and your ideas one hundred percent . . . I would especially like for Mrs. Autry to meet you personally, as we both have always admired you for what you stand for."[13]

ALTHOUGH GENE'S WARM, INTIMATE VOICE remained perfect for children's narratives, he had lost some of the higher range required for the "countrypolitan" sound he enjoyed. Gene favored the material of smooth country tenors Eddy Arnold, Jim Reeves, and Red Foley, but simply didn't have the vocal chops to do such songs; ironically, all three men often said how much they admired Gene's work. For his TV program soundtracks, he rerecorded in a lower key numerous old songs from his twenty-year repertoire—the new versions retaining his pleasant, intimate tone.

Gene's PR writers managed to fill fan magazines with Gene Autry features, but he needed an additional new "advance man" to work on specific tours. Gene and his longtime New York promotion man, Dave Whalen, had decided to part company, following terse meetings and correspondence. During his Madison Square Garden residency that fall, Gene hired Alex Gordon, the British-born former president of England's Autry fan club. Since relocating to New York in 1947, the talented cineaste had written favorable Autry articles in various trade magazines, while working as an assistant booker for the Walter Reade theater chain and as a producer's rep. Gene had noticed his eloquent and knowledgeable essays in the *Aces*, including a recent lengthy defense of Gene's entrance into television: "Gene is absolutely right when he says that a new picture, if good, will always bring business to a theater if properly promoted," Gordon had written, "and that the more favorable publicity a star receives, in whatever field of entertainment, the greater the box-office receipts will be." An inveterate movie-goer (he saw forty-four films his first month in New York), Gordon commented that *Mule Train* had rated three stars in the *Daily News* and successfully played a Broadway theater. "I am always at the New York Theatre when one of Gene's pictures plays here, and there is always a good house and an appreciative audience . . . yet his movies have . . . a restricted showing in metropolitan situations."[14] As was his knack, Gene once again chose a talented and loyal employee. Gordon would pursue his other film interests intermittently over the years, but he would become a lifelong associate of Gene's—his most articulate and scholarly champion. His first salaried position would be promoting the winter tour of 1951, which kicked off in Sioux City, Iowa.

In the middle of his rodeo stint, Gene flew to Pittsburgh to appear at the Allied Convention of Exhibitors. Still determined to win back the allegiance of theater owners, he made an impromptu yet inspired speech to "200 exhibs who've been squawking," according to *Variety*. Comparing radio to TV, he pointed out that he, Bing Crosby, and Bob Hope had moved from radio to film and that "television will develop other stars that will make money for exhibs." Gene again reiterated his frustration that due to his new films' minimal bookings, "'kids don't even know who Gene Autry is except through radio and TV' . . . He asserted, for instance, that although he paid $10,000 for rights to 'Mule Train' song and it sold millions of records, theater-men made no effort to capitalize on that, and his film of that title wasn't booked in Los Angeles until a year after it hit its peak. He also revealed his first Republic picture cost $18,000 and his latest Columbia release cost $175,000."[15] He vowed to do all in his power to help promote movie-going to the American public.

Gene's dramatic appearance, which was highly publicized, seemed to do the trick: In its October 23 *Service Bulletin*, the Ohio exhibitors who had previously waged war stated:

As evidence that Gene is going to keep the promise he made at the recent Allied Convention . . . we have received from him the following telegram:

ON MY RADIO PROGRAM TODAY, OCTOBER 21, HEARD BY APPROXIMATELY 15 MILLION PEOPLE OVER 165 LEADING CBS STATIONS EIGHT PM . . . MR. PHIL WRIGLEY HAS CONSENTED TO MY INSERTING INTO THE CLOSING ANNOUNCE-MENT THE FOLLOWING PARAGRAPH: "HAVE YOU BEEN TO A MOVIE LATELY, IF YOU HAVEN'T YOU ARE MISSING SOME OF THE BEST ENTERTAINMENT THERE IS; NATURALLY WE HOPE YOU WILL SEE ONE OF OUR NEW PICTURES, THE LAT-EST ARE COW TOWN AND INDIAN TERRITORY, BUT THE IMPORTANT THING IS TO SEE A MOVIE." THIS COINCIDES WITH OUR POLICY OF COOPERATION IN EVERY WAY POSSIBLE WITH THE EXHIBITOR IN HIS PRESENT DAY PROBLEMS.[16]

Missing from Gene's *Melody Ranch* programs that fall was Pat Buttram. On September 11, while working at Pioneertown on the TV film, *The Rainmaker*, a prop cannon exploded, nearly killing Pat with a barrage of shrapnel. He suffered a twelve-inch-long gash in his chest, exposing a punctured lung, a severed artery in his leg, and his chin was nearly blown off. (Just a week earlier, he'd gotten stitches in his head when clocked by co-star Sheila Ryan, whom he'd met on *Mule Train* and would marry the following year.) Gene's plane was used to fly in a doctor to the remote area—via a makeshift runway lit with car headlights—to work on him until the ambulance arrived. Dr. William Ince (son of Thomas Ince, who pioneered Western movie making) saved Pat's life, but he spent the rest of the year in the hospital. For decades afterward, Pat carried in his wallet a *New York Times* clipping: "Autry Escapes Blast Injury," which taught him "humility," he used to joke. The article, reporting Pat's critical condition, went on to say "Mr. Autry was blown out of a small cabin, which was destroyed, but he escaped injury."[17] "Gene has been really swell about everything," Pat wrote a friend back in Alabama. "He has kept me on full salary during my illness, and of course the insurance company is taking care of the hospital bills."[18] A soundman who was also injured later sued Flying A for negligence.

The television programs resumed filming with character actors Chill Wills, Fuzzy Knight, and Alan Hale Jr. filling in for Pat, who would return for the next four seasons. In late October CBS announced that the final two programs of Gene's first season would be filmed in color. It noted that the FCC had authorized color television transmission beginning November 20. Unfortunately, the films actually aired in black and white due to transmission limitations, and in October 1951, the government temporarily halted color TV-set production due to Korean War needs. In 1954 the episodes finally would be broadcast in color, to much acclaim.

The script for the feature *Whirlwind* called for a sidekick, so Smiley Burnette stepped in to replace Pat. Although Gene and Smiley had worked together in 1946–47 on some *Melody Ranch* programs, it was their first film together in seven years. "There was no special emotion about it," Gene later wrote. "Events and timing had caused us to split, and the same conditions brought us back. But Smiley and I had come to Hollywood together and there was always that bond between us."[19] Rumors had surfaced over the years that Smiley begrudged Gene their early financial dealings, but neither man ever publicly hinted at any disagreement. Smiley also joined the cast of Gene's 1951 winter tour, as he did several subsequent Autry excursions.

While touring with his revue, which also included a recovered Buttram, Gene continued to woo theater owners, but his films' distribution still suffered. In May 1951, Roy Rogers's second seven-year contract at Republic expired and was not renewed after he came to loggerheads with Herb Yates, who refused to grant him contractual rights to produce his own TV show. Yates made a deal to sell Rogers's old pictures, edited down to fifty-three minutes each, to television, and Rogers filed an injunction to stop him.

In the meantime, Gene, in a desperate attempt to improve his new films' distribution, arranged a meeting with Herb Yates in October to discuss possibly working together again. The plan never materialized, though, after Gene's lawyers filed suit to prevent Republic from selling his fifty-six old movies to TV. Yates wired Gene,

AT YOUR REQUEST, I HAD DINNER WITH YOU. . . . YOU STATED YOU WANTED TO RETURN TO REPUBLIC TO MAKE PICTURES FOR THE THEATRE AND FOR REPUBLIC TO JOIN YOU IN SUPPLYING PICTURES TO TELEVISION. YOU STATED THAT COLUMBIA DID NOT KNOW HOW TO SELL YOUR TYPE PICTURE BUT REPUBLIC DID. ALSO THAT YOU HAD STARTED AT REPUBLIC AND YOU WANTED TO FINISH YOUR CAREER WITH REPUBLIC. . . . IN LIGHT OF ALL THE FOREGOING YOU CAN IMAGINE MY SURPRISE WHEN I WAS INFORMED BY THE STUDIO THAT YOU HAD AUTHORIZED MARTIN GANG TO START SUIT AGAINST REPUBLIC. . . . THE QUESTION NOW ARISES WHETHER YOU WERE SINCERE.[20]

Gene wired a response the next day:

TALKS AND CONVERSATION WITH YOU REGARDING FUTURE PICTURES WERE SINCERE AND IN GOOD FAITH BUT THE MATTER OF TELEVISION AND TELEVISION CONTRACTS ARE ENTIRELY SEPARATE BECAUSE OF THE FACT THAT NBC HAS ADVERTISED THAT THEY ARE TO TELEVISE "THE PHANTOM EMPIRE," AN EIGHTEEN-YEAR-OLD SERIAL BY A SPONSOR DIRECTLY OPPOSITE TO MY OWN SPONSOR, THE WRIGLEY CO., WHO SPONSORED MY RADIO PROGRAM FOR TWELVE YEARS AND MY TELEVISION PROGRAM FOR TWO YEARS. SINCE THE MASCOT CONTRACT IS TIED TOGETHER WITH THE REPUBLIC CONTRACT, MY

ATTORNEY ADVISED ME THEY BOTH MUST BE FILED TOGETHER. . . . I ASSURE
YOU THERE IS NO DIFFERENCE OF OPINION FROM OUR TALK AS TO WHERE FU-
TURE PICTURES ARE CONCERNED.[21]

Both Roy and Gene argued that the selling of their old films to TV would connect their name and image to advertisements over which they had no control. In October 1951 a federal judge ruled in Roy's favor, determining that his Republic films could be shown on TV only if there were no advertising tie-ins. A different federal judge ruled against Gene and in Republic's favor, however, in May 1952, stating "Autry's position was 'untenable' and 'unfair' in seeking to prevent the company from enjoying the full share of the profits to be derived from said photoplays." This outcome, reported the *New York Times*, "tended to deepen the confusion over the issue as to whether a movie company has the right to tie-in the showing of movies on television with commercial advertising without consent of the performers involved."[22] Appeals in both cases dragged into 1954, but the writing was on the wall: With the proliferation of TV's Western programming, including *The Roy Rogers Show*, which debuted on NBC on December 30, 1951, the audiences for Gene's feature-length movies continued to shrink. Republic finally won the right to present the edited-down Rogers and Autry films on television, where they played in syndication for years. "Many people think that we've made a fortune off those pictures, but we've never gotten a cent," Rogers later told author David Rothel. "They've made millions off them."[23] In 1972 Gene would buy all rights to his films from Republic.

With television obviously the wave of the future, Gene decided to invest more in that direction. He bought a building that housed a Safeway grocery on Sunset Boulevard and spent an estimated $500,000 converting it into Flying A offices and interior sound stages. According to Hedda Hopper, it was Hollywood's first sound stage built specifically for TV. By early 1951 plans were underway to start production on a second series of television Westerns: *The Range Rider*, starring 6'5" fringed-buckskin-clad Jock Mahoney. As Jacques O'Mahoney, he had been a favored stuntman in Autry pictures, then promoted to actor. His co-star was the adorable Dick Jones, self-described "oldest teenager in Hollywood," who played his sidekick Dick West. The action-packed *Range Rider* showcased Mahoney and Jones's expert riding and stunts, guided by the Frenchman George Archainbaud, who had directed many of the Autry programs. The youthful-looking Jones eventually starred in his own Flying A series, the similarly themed *Buffalo Bill, Jr.* To be cast in the lead roles, Jones and Mahoney were both required to sign Flying A's Mitch Hamilburg as their agent—conflict of interest be damned.

Jones and company had no complaints, though, about the quality of Flying A's production standards. On location in Pioneertown, "Flying A had a specially built camera car," Jones recalled. "They had their own sound truck for all the sound equipment—it was state of the art sound. It was 'uptown' compared to other TV shows! It was first class—Gene never did things second class."[24] Gene began shooting his second season of twenty-six programs in 1951, with each show costing an approximate $20,000. He described the setup to a reporter: "We have seventy-five or eighty on the TV staff, we live in motels [around Pioneertown], and make up the films in batches of thirteen. It's hard work—there isn't the money there is in pictures, and you have to shoot fast. From the TV location, I fly into L.A. on Saturday afternoons for the radio program, which goes on at 5 PM. I get in there by 1. We rehearse until about an hour before show time, knock off for a little rest and then go on."

In 1952 Flying A also produced the first season of the television program *Death Valley Days*, based on the popular long-running radio series. Other companies later produced the program, which ran until 1975 and featured at various times Ronald Reagan, Robert Taylor, Fess Parker, Dale Robertson, and Merle Haggard. Outside the Western genre, Gene toyed with the idea of producing a jungle series, featuring Tarzan star Johnny Weismuller, and a detective series starring blackface veteran Step'in Fetchit playing an undercover taxi driver. Neither program got off the ground, however.

Gene's own series had evolved by 1952, with many scripts written by women, including Betty Burbridge, Polly James, and Elizabeth Beecher. In addition to young female leads—frequently Sheila Ryan playing a conniving deputy, ranch owner, or crook—the show also cast older actresses, such as the matronly Mira McKinney, in strong roles, including mayor and sheriff. By the end of 1952 seventy-eight programs had been completed, enough for consecutive seasons into 1954. "In our first TV films we tried to tell too much story," Gene told reporter Lee Lane about the program's development. "Now we use simple, straight-line stories with . . . accent on character and characterizations. . . . You might say that TV film production for our line of Westerns boils down to this: Keep it simple, keep it moving, keep it close, and make it fast." He added another thought that pointed to his future. "I think that eventually the major studios will make the big, long expensive films for theater distribution and that smaller companies—or possibly subsidiaries of the major studios—will make the shorter half hour films for TV."

By 1952 budgets for Gene's feature films were slashed to an average $150,000: they ran no longer than an hour, and the use of stock footage was increased. Beginning with *The Old West*, Archainbaud took over as director, replacing John English. Missing for a while from the group of cast regulars was Gail Davis. A few months after acting in *The Old West*, she gave birth on December 31, 1951, to a daughter, Terrie Jeanne Davis. Bob and Gail had managed to stay together for seven years, but divorced not long after their child's birth. By early April, Gail was back working on an Autry feature, *Wagon Team*, and Terrie spent much of her early life with Gail's parents in Arkansas.

While on maternity leave, Gail had heard about a new Flying A series in development called *Annie Oakley*, for which a teenage girl would play the lead. "They ran a contest throughout the United Stages looking for someone who could ride and shoot *and* act," Davis later related. "I got very upset because this was right down my alley, really a part I wanted. I felt it was me." When she asked Mandy if she could audition for the part, he told her she was too well-known as Gene's leading lady. "So I went home, put on my blue jeans, a gingham shirt, put freckles on my nose, and put my hair in pigtails, and I walked back into Mandy's office and said, 'I think I should play the part.' "[25] On April 7 Hedda Hopper announced in her column that: "Gene Autry, after looking at hundreds of photographers and testing a score of girls for the 'Annie Oakley' television series, decided the property was too valuable to star a newcomer in it. So he's signed Gail Davis for the part. . . . She'll be the screen's first out-and-out Western heroine."[26] The first of two pilots would be shot that summer between Gail's appearances in a couple of *Range Rider* episodes and three Autry films. Then, in October, she would play the female lead in *Pack Train*, opposite Gene and costarring, once again, Smiley Burnette.

Smiley had been called back to appear in what were to be Gene's last six pictures, four shot in 1952 and the final pair in early 1953. "We had gone in together and we would go out together," Gene later said. "Fair is fair."[27] Playing "himself"—since Republic owned the name "Frog Millhouse"—Smiley still showed his old charisma, although his antics had become more subdued. He would struggle to earn a living after his last few Autry movies, until his career rebounded in the early 1960s when he became a cast member of the TV show *Petticoat Junction*.

Gene's movies weren't the only budget Westerns to cease production; such stalwarts as Charles Starrett, Rocky Lane, and Roy Rogers no longer made pictures. Republic's last gasp was to be former WLS *Barn Dance* star Rex Allen, who became known as the last of the Singing Cowboys and made his final picture for the studio in 1954. With a glut of Western programming available for free on TV and with more small-town theaters closing down, B-Western movie production simply ceased to exist.

Gene was exhausted, just off the road, in the spring of 1953, when his final feature went before cameras. His ninety-first picture since 1935, the aptly named period piece *Last of the Pony Riders* features Dick Jones, who gets more screen time than Gene. Jones plays a vigorous and dedicated Pony Express hero determined to complete his mission of delivering mail—a job on the verge of extinction due to encroaching stagecoaches and telegraph lines. Gene is the kindly former Pony Express rider about to start his own stagecoach line. Wearing a toupee, he looks heavy, moves rather sluggishly, and doesn't do much fighting. A *Hollywood Reporter* critic had just panned Gene for his role in the recently released *On Top of Old Smoky*: "Age or weight seems to have slowed Autry [who] fails to generate much excitement with what little activity he has."[28] The bad reviews would continue for *Pack Train*—"The faltering cowboy moves through the script in seemingly lackadaisical fashion"— and *Saginaw Trail*: "Autry plods through his role ... with some tepid brawling." After a week or so of filming, Gene's eighteen-year reign as motion pictures' Public Cowboy No. 1 was over. Five decades later, Dick Jones emotionally recalled, "When the director said, 'That's a wrap!' that was it. There were a lot of tears shed that day."

35

ON THE ROAD AGAIN—AND AGAIN

NINETEEN FIFTY-THREE MARKED the last year for new Gene Autry features to arrive on motion picture screens, yet Gene's touring continued unabated. His television program exposed a new generation of children to his derring-do, and families packed arenas for "The Gene Autry Hit Show of 1953." "Regardless of what else he does, a cowboy star has to get out and meet the people in their own hometowns," Gene said at the time. "Especially the kids—they need to know that you're real and not just something they see on Saturdays at the movies or at home on their TV set."[1]

"Gene toured more than any other star," according to Alex Gordon, who publicized his appearances from 1950 to 1953.

> He did up to eighty-five different towns or cities—two shows a day, seven days a week—with a troupe of about forty people. It was hectic. He played arenas that would hold fifteen to thirty thousand people—never anything less than five thousand people in a school gym. The promoter never had to put up any guarantees, like they did with other shows. It was a straight percentage deal, so if Gene made money, they'd make money. After the last show at night, which would finish about 11:00, Gene would get a few hours sleep and he'd start out real early and arrive at 8:00 in the morning, flying his own twin engine Beechcraft into the next town, which might be up to a hundred miles away. And the first thing I had set up for him was a visit to a children's hospital, an orphanage, or some kind of charitable thing— and he would make that every time, no matter how tired he might be. He never said a word or complained about anything like that. And then there would be the matinee at 2:30 and the evening show at 8:30 and then onto the next place—or a few hours of sleep, and early morning to the next place. So it was quite a schedule.[2]

The January/February tour broke records, according to a March 13, 1953, edition of *Daily Variety*: "Tour grossed an astronomical $585,548 from a 329,218 attendance figure for 46 matinees and 43 evening performances. Never in the six years Autry annually has been touring one-niters had he done such biz. His previous record, set in the January-February tour of last year, was topped by 14 percent."[3] The show was a combination Western variety show—somewhat like his old National Barn Dance revue—and traveling version of the popular Ed Sullivan TV program *Toast of the Town*.

Since 1950, the tour had featured Barbara Bardo, a comely Illinois-born rope trick artist who favored skimpy costumes. During her first year with the revue, she had met Dudley Autry, and after a stormy few weeks on the tour bus—at one point, she accused him of molesting her—the two married. Their relationship remained tempestuous, and the severely troubled Dudley's heavy drinking, erratic behavior, petty crimes, and increasingly bad health kept him perpetually unemployed. The couple would eventually divorce. In 1956 Dudley was diagnosed with tuberculosis, the same illness that had killed Jimmie Rodgers. According to Bardo, he contracted the disease from his stepmother Ruby's sister, with whom he'd been romantically involved in the late 1940s.[4] Dudley remained a constant source of emotional pain for Gene, as well as Veda and Wilma—all of whom tried in vain to help him.[5] Dudley died, at age forty-two, in a California veteran's hospital in June 1962. After divorcing Dudley, Bardo used her Autry surname to promote herself as a trick roper, angering Gene—who would contact newspapers and booking agents (who sometimes promoted her as Gene's daughter) to report they were not related. In response, Bardo would threaten Gene that she planned to expose his drinking and womanizing to the tabloids. This conflict would endure for decades, even after Gene retired as an entertainer.

On Gene's 1953 tour for the first time was Gail Davis, who'd gained recognition and good reviews for her work in Gene Autry films and TV shows. The first episode of *Annie Oakley* had not yet aired on television, as noted by Hedda Hopper (with a sly bit of innuendo): "What's been holding up production is the fact that Gail hasn't had time to make the TV films, because of her work as Gene's leading lady."[6] In reality, the original, rather weak pilot for *Annie Oakley*, "Bull's Eye," filmed the previous summer, had been unsuccessfully pitched to advertisers.

For pilot number two, "Annie Gets Her Man," Flying A commissioned a better script from one of Gene's best screenwriters, Norman S. Hall, and cast ten-year-old Jimmy Hawkins to play her brother, Tagg Oakley. Already a veteran (as Tommy Bailey) of *It's a Wonderful Life* and the successful series *The Ruggles*, the talented Hawkins replaced Billy Gray, who'd shown no chemistry with Davis in the first pilot. "I had a crush on her when I first met her," Hawkins said of his co-star fifty-some years later. "She was cute and—*wow*—what a nice lady."[7] Teamed with tall, dashing Brad Johnson as Deputy Lofty

Craig, the ensemble clicked when the greatly improved pilot was filmed just after the Autry winter tour. Sporting blond braided pigtails, Gail played the
town of Diablo's sharp-shooting, fast-riding cowgirl heroine—her expertise
with firearms about the only thing the TV character shared with the real Annie
Oakley. By summer's end, Flying A had sold the pilot to national sponsors—
Canada Dry and a snack-food company—and filming could go forward, with
the series' debut in January on CBS.

Word of the deal came in August while Davis was on tour with the Gene
Autry Show in London. Alex Gordon set up the four-week return engagement
to the country where, in 1939, Alex had been part of the hoards attending
Gene's appearances. This time, the show consisted of his touring revue, and
was booked twice daily for its full run at the eight-thousand-seat Empress
Hall. While his film career was ebbing in the States, Gene hoped to keep it go-
ing in England, and although his TV show had not made it to the BBC, he
wanted to promote his comic books and other merchandise as well. Along with
Gail, the performance included Gene backed by the Cass County Boys, and
Pat Buttram, Barbara Bardo, acrobat acts, Carl Cotner, and the Tony White
Cloud Indian troupe. As in the States, the finale featured Gene doing tricks
with Champion and Little Champ.

Gene's *Melody Ranch* producer, Bill Burch, also went along, and three radio
shows were broadcast from London. The program had undergone several
changes earlier in the year, primarily due to television's overriding popularity.
CBS had turned its spacious Hollywood radio studios, with room for a large
audience, into television studios. Thus, *Melody Ranch* was no longer performed
before a studio audience. To save money, scripts for the weekly Western drama
were recycled, with Pat Buttram acting the roles previously played by Johnny
Bond. Due to lack of space and as a cost-cutting measure, Carl Cotner's orchestra, which had provided stirring music for the program's dramatizations,
had been eliminated. Organist Buddy Cole now provided the sole dramatic
backing, and Gene's accompaniment consisted of the scaled-down ensemble of
Cotner, the Cass County Boys, steel guitarist (and popular bandleader) Alvino
Rey, trumpeter Andy Secrest, and Johnny Bond. That summer, Bond, disappointed that he wasn't included on the UK tour, left Gene's employ to take a
position at a Dallas radio station; he returned as Gene's guitarist in 1954. The
Kettle Sisters had departed in late 1951, and since then the Pinafores had been
made up of various female vocalists. Soon to be renamed the Gene Autry Blue-
jeans, the trio would include members of the King Sisters, one of whom was
married to Burch (and who would find fame on *The Lawrence Welk Show*).

Since 1950, when Gene began filming his TV series, his radio program had
gone on a month-long hiatus every summer (replaced by a fill-in program), and
gradually, as Gene's one-nighters had increased, more and more of the programs had been transcribed. "Gene's fans and the sponsor—and presumably the
network—relished the idea of doing live, spontaneous broadcasts," according to

the music historian Jonathan Guyot Smith. "There is a certain intimacy associated with a live radio broadcast. Not only do we 'witness' entertainment which is going on 'right now,' but we also hear the human errors which cannot be eradicated by re-takes. . . . Hearing a live broadcast gave fans the feeling that Gene was singing and talking to them 'in person,' which, in a very real sense, he was. . . . [When he transcribed] full programs for a later broadcast, the sponsor and the fans squawked." As Beverly Kimball put it in *Autry's Aces*, "We hope that the Wrigley Company will continue to present the show 'live' as it has a certain warmth that none of the transcribed programs have. Now if the show would have an audience to react to Pat's comedy and Gene's songs, it would be complete."[8]

Broadcasting from England that summer, *Melody Ranch* featured Gene, Pat Buttram, an English choir and actors, and instead of announcer Charlie Lyon, a BBC "presenter." The program won high praise from the *Boston Herald*: "Through the medium of his radio show, [Autry] is doing a great deal to help Great Britain and the United States understand each other. . . . Broadcasting in London, he let our common love of horses bring rodeo lovers and horseshow addicts together. . . . Perhaps Gene Autry, with a guitar and a horse, can do more than pacts and treaties to bring two peoples together."[9]

Following the London run, Gene met Ina in Paris for a rare, one-week European vacation. Although she never went on Gene's tours of one-nighters, she had spent part of the month with her husband at the luxurious Savoy Hotel, in London, where she "took the opportunity to see all the famous sights . . . museums, gardens, palaces, and several shows," Alex Gordon reported. Just before the trip, Ina had written Gene's New York press agent Pat Murphy that she was displeased when fan magazines called her "Ina Mae" (Gene's pet name for her): "I have asked that that name not be used . . . I very much dislike double names, and want only the name 'Ina' used. . . . At first I didn't pay any attention to it, because I thought that it would just cease to be used; but, now there are no stories in which it isn't used, and I find perfect strangers calling me Ina Mae. . . . You know the Southern clinging vine type has never appealed to me, and that's just what 'Ina Mae' sounds like—just like a little Southern gal who couldn't make up her mind about anything."[10] From Paris, Ina wrote Virginia MacPhail at the Autry office a cheery note about their travel plans: "We are going to take a short 'European' trip. Sounds real silly as we only have a week—But we will fly into the towns [in Spain, Italy, Belgium, and Switzerland] and get a car each day to show us the main places of interest. Gene seems to really be looking forward to it also."[11]

The couple returned to the States on September 4, then soon went their separate ways: Ina to visit family in Oklahoma and Gene to New York for the annual Madison Square Garden rodeo. As partial owner of the World's Championship Rodeo, Gene attended every year, but this was his first time to perform at the Garden since 1950. (The Lone Ranger and Vaughn Monroe headlined in '51, with Roy Rogers/Dale Evans/Pat Brady the following year.) This would be Gene's last Madison Square Garden performance.

For both the Boston and New York rodeos, Gene presented "The Range Rider and Dick West" (Jock Mahoney and Dick Jones) as his special guest performers. In Boston, Gene did not perform, but "The Range Rider" duo was such a huge draw that attendance broke the previous year's record. In New York, however, *The Range Rider* series had recently gone off the air, so the duo did not bring in the crowds. During his first few performances, Gene—who celebrated his forty-sixth birthday in the Big Apple—was so hoarse with laryngitis he could barely get through his numbers. He had lost his voice by the end of the winter tour, too, which was remarked upon in newspaper reviews, and recurrent laryngitis, hoarseness, and severe colds would increasingly plague him. The combination of continuous air travel, lack of sleep, back-to-back performances, and heavy drinking was taking its toll on Gene, who had previously enjoyed remarkably robust health.

Still, he managed to do a benefit performance for invalid children at Bellevue Hospital, a tradition that had started in 1940. "Gene was a stickler about visiting the hospitals," Dick Jones remembered. "Everybody was in awe that he would do it. The kids' hospitals and the orphanages would just tear me apart, because after you get in there and you're mingling with them, and then you start to leave and you've got ten kids and they're hanging on. It really got to me." When Dick asked Gene how he handled it, "he said, 'You've got to overlook the fact that it hurts you and makes you feel sad. You've got to be cheerful because all they need is somebody who's cheerful that recognizes the fact that they're there, that they're human beings, that they're alive and you've got to cheer them up—that's your job.' He was very adamant about that, but man, it sure tore me apart inside."[12]

In the early 1950s, Gene visited as many as a hundred hospitals per tour. Afterward, he received emotional letters from grateful parents whose now-deceased child Gene had visited. "I wonder if you realize how much this visit meant to him and to us," wrote one mother whose young son died of leukemia a few days after Gene's surprise visit.[13] Alex Gordon notified Gene of special requests from injured or critically ill children, and he would go out of his way to see them. Some of these visits made the papers, but others were behind the scenes.

Even though Gene had started the practice early in his career, his hospital visits may have increased to a near-daily occurrence in the wake of lawsuits filed over the flammable Gene Autry playsuit. Approximately twenty lawsuits resulted from the injuries—and in two cases, death—sustained by children wearing the outfit when it was ignited by fire. The suits charged the manufacturer M. A. Henry "with carelessly and negligently putting on the market an inflammable cowboy suit that they asserted was fire proof." Gene was charged with "permitting the use of his name and authorizing the sale and distribution of the outfit."[14] These were among the first lawsuits questioning a celebrity's liability for injuries caused by a product he had endorsed. When the first accidents occurred, in 1945, Gene told reporters that "the suits were of good quality when they . . . came out five years ago."[15] He and Hamilburg notified Henry that they wanted the outfits—with combustible chaps made of "high-pile" rayon—taken off the market without delay. Apparently, the manufacturer did not comply, additional outfits were sold, and more children were injured. In a 1949 deposition, Gene stated that "right after learning [in April 1945] of a fire said to involve Gene Autry Cowboy Pants, I notified Henry to stop making such articles and to make only holster sets . . . I personally and also my representative Hamilburg . . . told him to immediately withdraw the suits from the market, cease manufacturing them, and to notify stores, and Henry's reply was that he would do so at once."

Some of the plaintiffs eventually won their cases, while others settled out of court. Initially, Hamilburg had set up the licensing agreement with Henry, but Gene felt responsibility for the tragedies and visited some of the injured children while they were hospitalized. "That was a terrible thing," Virginia MacPhail recalled. "He was upset, but he didn't talk too much about that kind of thing. He was not a down person—of course, that was partly Ina's doing, too. Christian Scientists believe in keeping everything positive."

A positive event for Gene while in New York in September was a special Autry tribute presented by Ed Sullivan on his *Toast of the Town*. Opening with a dramatic retelling of Gene's "discovery" by Will Rogers, Sullivan welcomed Gene who, arriving onstage astride Champion, sang in good voice "Rancho Grande" accompanied by the Cass County Boys. No mention was made of Gene's final film, which had just hit theaters, and clips from his first feature (*Tumbling Tumbleweeds*) and 1940's *Melody Ranch* (which showed more of Jimmy Durante than it did Gene) were featured, as was newsreel footage of the day the town of Berwyn's name was changed to Gene Autry. After joking about his and his host's common Irish heritage, Gene enlisted the audience to sing along on "Rudolph," which would soon enter the charts for the fifth year in a row.

Gene's record royalties, however, had fallen to $38,708, from $96,826 in 1951. His income from licensing agreements still brought in hefty rewards: $135,238 in 1953, but significantly less than the $226,262 he'd earned in 1950. In addition to his broadcasting shares, he had continued to expand his business holdings. He now owned three music publishing companies—Western Music, Golden West Melodies (a BMI-affiliated company formed in 1945), and Caravan Music. He had established Gene Autry Tours Inc. to handle his traveling shows, and Gene Autry Realty Company Inc. to oversee his real-estate and rental properties. Gene had continued to make investments, including a one-third ownership of twenty-five Texas oil wells.

Near the end of 1952, he made his most spectacular purchase yet: Los Angeles radio station KMPC, "the Southland's most powerful independent broadcasting outlet," according to the *Los Angeles Times*.[16] He had been discussing the possibility of such an investment since he received a letter in 1951 from the station's general manager, Bob Reynolds. A former star football player at Stanford in the 1930s, the Oklahoma native had played pro ball in Detroit for a team owned by self-made millionaire G. A. Richards; Reynolds later started as a salesman at KMPC, which Richards had owned until his death in May of 1951. Reynolds informed Gene that he had the inside track to purchase the station and its substantial real estate from Richards's widow.[17] Reynolds and Autry did just that, forming a corporation and purchasing KMPC for $800,000. The partnership was just the beginning of a series of the pair's investments that would eventually transform Gene's life: the establishment of the multistation Golden West Broadcasters corporation and the formation of a new American League baseball team. In March Gene told a reporter, "I know that, like a baseball player, the time will come when I'll have to hang up my spikes . . . when instead of working in front of the microphones, I'll work behind them from a desk."[18]

Gene purchased yet another important California property in 1953: the 125-acre Monogram movie ranch in Newhall, where numerous early Westerns had been shot. Everything from his San Fernando Valley ranch on Balboa was moved to the sprawling property, including his horses. The deed to his old ranch was transferred to the St. Vincent De Paul Society, which turned the site into a summer camp for underprivileged boys. Hedda Hoper commended her friend on his generosity, "Gene Autry, who always wanted a son, will soon have a house full of them. . . . He's turned down an enormous offer from a syndicate that wanted to turn the place into a dude ranch."[19] His new Melody Ranch, formerly known as Placeritos Ranch, would soon become the location for the filming of his own and other Flying A series. Eventually, it would be rented to various television-production companies for the making of the "adult Westerns" that would supplant in popularity Gene's own series; these included *Maverick*, starring James Garner, and most successfully, *Gunsmoke*, with James Arness and Amanda Blake. (Fifty years later, the movie ranch would be the location of the über-adult Western, HBO's *Deadwood*.)

ANNIE OAKLEY BECAME A HIT soon after it began airing on January 5, 1954. Filming the previous fall had been delayed slightly after Gail was rushed to the hospital for emergency abdominal surgery, according to the *Los Angeles Times*, for an undisclosed ailment. She recovered in time to begin an arduous shooting schedule in Pioneertown in October. During its first season, *Annie Oakley* was nominated for an Emmy (the only Flying A series to receive the honor). Cowgirl mania swept the country, with a line of Annie Oakley merchandise produced by a sundry of licensees. Tie-Ups Company, a partnership between Gene, Schaefer, and Hamilburg, owned and marketed these rights, as it did for *The Range Rider*. A new craze for braided pigtails, festooned with ribbons, was

As Annie Oakley in the first television Western to star a woman, Gail Davis started a fashion craze in 1954 for braided pigtails. (Holly George-Warren Collection)

Mounted on Champion, Gene Autry looks over his script for *The Gene Autry Show*, ca. 1950.

Gene's original sidekick, Smiley Burnette, returned to the screen with Gene for the first time in a decade for *Whirlwind*, filling in for the seriously injured Pat Buttram, who had nearly lost his life due to an accident on the set of Gene's TV show in 1950.

In 1950, at the World's Championship Rodeo at Madison Square Garden, cowgirls from Northeastern dude ranches competed to be crowned "Queen of the Ranch Girls," with Gene among the judges who critiqued the gals on their beauty, equestrienne skills, and poise.

Several of Gene's films prominently featured Native Americans; in 1952's *Apache Country*, Tony White Cloud and his Jemez Indians demonstrated traditional Native dances, the origins of which were explained in the film.

Wagon Team, released in September 1952, featured Gene's most frequent backing group, the Cass County Boys, who joined him on his recordings, tours, television shows, and movies. From left: bassist Bert Dodson, accordionist Fred Martin, and guitarist Jerry Scoggins, with Gene.

Thanksgiving 1952 at the Autry house. Left to right: Herb Green's wife, Kitty; Carl Cotner; Herb Green's daughter; niece Nora Coppola; Gene Autry; Ina Autry; Ina's mother, Lilly Spivey; Alex Gordon; niece Giovanna Coppola; Benny Coppola; Gene's sister Veda Coppola.

Gene Autry and Pat Buttram promote both the radio and television versions of *The Gene Autry Show*, ca. 1953.

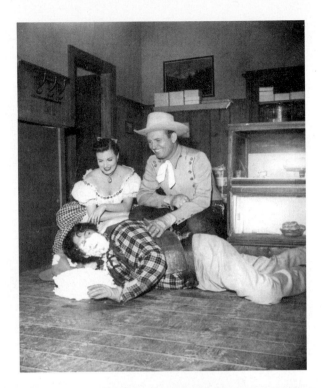

Sheila Ryan, Gene Autry, and Pat Buttram from the *Gene Autry Show* episode "Border Justice," 1953.

Gene Autry and Carl Cotner, his music arranger and friend; they worked together for nearly forty years on a handshake.

Gene Autry hosts a barbecue at his house in Studio City, ca. 1952. Left to right: Gene Autry, Pat Buttram, Ina Autry, Maggie Field (Jock Mahoney's fiancée and the mother of future star Sally Field), Dick Jones, Betty Jones, Sheila Ryan, and Jock Mahoney.

Gene and Ina built this new Studio City home in 1949 on four-plus acres after their North Hollywood house burned eight years earlier.

Gene took his troupe with him on a return engagement to London in July 1953. Mobbed by throngs, he rides Champion down the city's famed Oxford Street.

London's 8,500-seater, the Empress Theater, features Gene and Champ, here accompanied by some tap-dancing cowgirls; others on the show were Pat Buttram, Gail Davis, and Tony White Cloud and his Jemez Indians, July 1953.

Gene purchased the former Monogram movie ranch in 1953, renamed it Melody Ranch, and
there began filming his television program, among other productions. It would be the last home
of Champion (#3), here with Gene, ca. 1955.

Gene's final feature-length film, *The Last of the Pony Riders*, 1953, co-starred the excellent young
horseman Dick Jones, who would also star in two Flying A television programs, *The Range Rider*
and *Buffalo Bill, Jr.*

Gene and Champ jump through a ring of fire, one of the stunts they performed at numerous
rodeos and on personal appearance tours.

Kids loved cowboys in the 1950s, and Gene's numerous tour stops were packed with youngsters
dressed the part. Here, he visits with diminutive contest winners sponsored by a local organization in Burlington, Vermont, ca. 1951.

Gene first performed with Tony White Cloud and his Jemez Indian dancers, who hailed from a New Mexico pueblo, at Madison Square Garden in 1949. He consistently took the group on the road until the mid-1950s. (Alex Gordon Collection)

Gene with Canadian children at a CKX radio appearance. (Jerretts Photo-Art Studio, Brandon, Manitoba)

Gene, seen here on February 16, 1955, shared piloting duties with Herb Green in his twin-engined Beechcraft on his personal appearance tours throughout the United States and Canada. (Beech Aircraft Corp. Public Relations Dept., Wichita, Kansas)

Gene frequently participated in Boy Scout events, including this appearance with Scouts while on tour in Columbus, Ohio. (*Ohio State Journal*, Photo by Fred Shannon)

On Gene's last major tour, the Hit Show of 1960, he was accompanied by fellow road warriors Johnny Bond and Rufe Davis. Here, Public Cowboy No. 1 and Champ perform the show's grand finale.

Gene Autry and Johnny Western, who accompanied him on the road in 1956 and 1957, in Phoenix, Arizona, 1968. (Courtesy of Johnny Western)

Gene Autry joins his Los Angeles Angels for a bicycle ride during spring training, 1962, in Palm Springs.

Rex Allen, Nudie Cohn, Gene Autry, Eddie Dean, Roy Rogers, and Smokey Rogers at Nudie's Rodeo Tailors, ca. 1960. Nudie supplied highly decorative Western wear to movie cowboys and liked to pose with his favorite customers.

On the occasion of Gene's fiftieth anniversary in show business, in 1980, the singing cowboy was honored with a TV special on his Los Angeles station KTLA, as well as a feature in *People* magazine. Noted photographer Harry Benson captured Gene and Ina at their home at the Gene Autry Hotel, in Palm Springs, shortly before Ina succumbed to cancer on May 19, one month after her sixty-ninth birthday. (Courtesy of Harry Benson)

In July 1981, Gene, 73, married Jacqueline Ellam, 39, in Los Angeles, with his longtime buddies Pat Buttram and Johnny Grant as their attendants; here, the newlyweds attend a gala a few months after their wedding.

Dale Evans, Roy Rogers, Gene Autry, and Pat Buttram on the set of TNN's *Happy Trails Theatre*, 1987. Gene and Pat hosted TNN's *Melody Ranch Theatre*.

Two of Gene Autry's biggest fans, Johnny Cash and Willie Nelson, join him for the 1988 opening gala of the Gene Autry Western Heritage Museum. In 2005, it was renamed the Autry National Center, encompassing the Southwest Museum of the American Indian, the Museum of the American West, and the Institute for the Study of the American West.

Two of Gene's closest friends, Pat Buttram and Johnny Grant (both at left) with Gene and Jackie (standing behind Gene) during the unveiling of Gene's fifth star for "Live Performance/Theater," on the Hollywood Walk of Fame, 1987.

In 1994, Gene visited the Highwaymen in the recording studio. Johnny Cash, whom he first met in '57, was particularly close to Gene, writing an homage to him for a 1977 album. Gene's autograph emblazoned Cash's black Martin guitar in his last-ever video, "Hurt."

inspired by Gail's hairstyle—she was contractually required to wear the 'do, she told one reporter. In character as Annie, Gail would prove a popular addition to Gene's subsequent rodeos and tours, up through 1958. Riding her horse Target, her act would include a sharp-shooting exhibition, followed by a few vocal numbers, including "You Can't Get a Man with a Gun," from the musical, *Annie Get Your Gun*. "Colonel" Eddie Hogan, Gene's burly Boston-born driver and valet, was smitten with Davis, telling one reporter, "She's got the temperament of a kitten. Everybody's crazy about her." Gail would eventually tour on her own as a headliner, including the final run of the World's Championship Rodeo at Madison Square Garden in 1959.

The Gene Autry Hit Show of 1954 did not include Gail, however. It opened in snowy Minnesota in January and featured Patty Dunn, a high-school senior who had been singing with the Light Crust Doughboys and other acts in Dallas. Gene knew her parents, who owned a liquor store there, and the previous year Gail and Gene had stopped in, "palsy-walsy-ing around," as Patty recalled. She was hired as the "girl singer" for the fifty-two-day trek, for $150 a week. Thrilled to be on the tour, she found everyone in the troupe very hospitable toward a wide-eyed greenhorn. Patty became friends with Barbara Bardo, who confided to her that Ina had insisted Gail Davis not be included on the trek. Patty usually rode in the tour's customized Cadillac station wagon or in the Beechcraft with Gene. "He'd kid around," she remembered. "He was forty-seven—and I asked him if he had kids. He said he couldn't have any cause he'd had mumps. I said, 'Why would you be telling me that?' I caught on later—because it meant he didn't have to worry about a girl getting pregnant. During the show, he used to ask me to bring Little Champion [onstage] after he did his thing with Big Champ, and he'd just slap me on the rear—and it hurt. The next time I took Little Champ up there, I *backed* off the stage. Then the next show, I started to hand [the reins] to him, and he wouldn't take [them], and he walked around and popped me on the rear." Patty recalled one crazy night when the Ely Sisters, a tap-dancing act, "got in trouble. They came onstage and they had been drinking and they had these bicycles and they started giggling, and one of them stopped, the others crashed into her, and then they all fell over. Gene read them the riot act—that they were going back to L.A. if that ever happened again and that they better not be drinking."[20] Following the tour, Patty wrote "the most wonderful man I've ever met" a thank you letter for including her, with Gene responding "we, too, enjoyed having you on the show, and want you to know that you did a swell job."[21]

In May, Gene traveled to Nashville to record with Don Law. This was to be a full-blown attempt to cut the kind of honky-tonkers then riding the C&W charts. Live, Gene had been performing "Your Cheatin' Heart," by the late Hank Williams, a discovery of his old friend Fred Rose. But Gene's previous two years of recordings had focused on children's and seasonal music—including a pair of catchy Rosemary Clooney duets, "The Night

Before Christmas Song" (by Johnny Marks) and "Look Out the Window." In late 1951, he had cut a few C&W weepers, including Cindy Walker's terrific "I Was Just Walking Out the Door" and "Am I Just a Pastime," penned by his brother Dudley with Johnny Bond. Gene was in excellent voice on 1952's "Don't Believe a Word They Say," a dramatic duet with Phyllis Lynne, and the novelty "Diesel Smoke, Dangerous Curves," which predated the trucker-song craze. In 1954 Law intended to "get Gene to myself in Nashville for a few days, [to] make records every bit as good, or better, than the ones he made some years ago that were such fabulous sellers," he reported to the *Aces*:

> This was the culmination of over a year's effort on my part to get Gene away from Hollywood and into Nashville to make records. In Hollywood he always has sixteen guys following him around and the phone is always ringing constantly. Consequently it was very difficult to get him to devote his undivided attention to the serious business of making phonograph records. . . . [In Nashville] we spent the whole day quietly in a hotel room going over material. He considered, literally, hundreds of songs and finally selected eight which we felt had good commercial possibilities. That night Gene and Johnny Bond carefully learned and rehearsed them. In the meantime, I had lined up a band consisted of the best *country* musicians in Nashville [including guitarist Grady Martin]. In no time at all, they worked out good simple commercial arrangements and both sessions went like clockwork. Gene was completely relaxed and has never sung better in his life. On these records you will hear the old Autry at his best. The songs are first rate, the arrangements simple and commercial, and Gene is Gene as his fans want to hear him.[22]

Law was right about how good the session sounded, but unfortunately his prediction of a hit did not come to pass. (Not long after Gene's C&W records flopped, Webb Pierce released the Number One country song of 1955—his version of Jimmie Rodgers's "In the Jailhouse Now," which Gene had covered in 1930.)

Six of the eight were released, with the standout "20/20 Vision (and Walkin' Around Blind)" finding Gene emoting as he hadn't in years. Assisting Don Law in the studio was twenty-six-year-old Joe Johnson, new to Columbia via Vanderbilt Law School and military service. Johnson, who'd shaken Gene's hand during his 1939 appearance in Cookeville, Tennessee, was awestruck to work with his childhood idol. "He was a very professional singer," Johnson remembered of the sessions. "He learned the songs well and he did a good job in the studio—he would get it on an early take. He still loved that music—he did more of the kiddie stuff because of the success of it. And success by any name is sweet."

After the sessions, Joe accompanied Gene and Johnny Bond to the Tennessee State Penitentiary for a benefit performance. There, they discovered the Prisonaires, whose "Just Walking in the Rain" impressed them enough to offer a publishing deal for the song with Gene's Golden West Melodies. The song would later bring a windfall for Gene when it became a massive hit for pop stylist Johnnie Ray. The Prisonaires originally recorded the number for the Memphis label, Sun, which in July would issue the debut by a newcomer named Elvis Presley.

After the prison visit, Gene dashed back to California to start filming his TV show. The first two seasons had each comprised twenty-six programs, but season three (which started in July of 1953) had consisted of only thirteen shows. The second batch of thirteen, which he'd shot back in 1952, had been held for season four, which kicked off in July 1954. A new batch of thirteen were needed for season five. In the meantime, CBS had been broadcasting reruns of old episodes to fill out each season. The *Aces* complained, "Repeating a series once or twice may be a good idea, but when it runs into the set being shown four and five times, it is stretching a good thing too far."[23]

By 1954, with the transmission of technology to the home catching up with filming techniques, one of the episodes he'd shot in color in 1950 received notice from the *New York Times*'s TV critic, when it aired in color during reruns:

> The gentleman leading the cowhand invasion of color TV has been none other than Gene Autry. . . . If [Autry's] caliber of tinted image can be attained with a film made over two [*sic*] years ago, as Mr. Autry's was, the future success of 16 mm color picture can hardly be questioned. . . . In the "Double Barrelled Vengeance," the gleaming brown coats of the horses were a sight on home TV. Just a little puzzling, however, were the amazing recuperative powers of the cast. Mr. Autry and the evil-doers could "slug" each other madly but when it was all over there was not a hint of a discolored cheek. Possibly Champion also will not be too happy over color TV. In one household the loudest whistles were heard for a honey blonde [Nan Leslie]. It's going to be the ladies, not men and horses, who will benefit most from color TV.[24]

Gene's final thirteen shows would all be filmed in color. For fans missing his features, the well-crafted programs often recycled plot lines from the Columbia films, compacted into twenty-seven exciting minutes. Some episodes included no songs, but the Cass County Boys participated in shows filmed in the fall, providing musical accompaniment for Gene. Scenes were shot at Gene's new Melody Ranch, as well as at Lone Pine, and his studio on Sunset. (Interestingly, the program that kicked off season four in September was called "Civil War at Deadwood"—nothing like the HBO hit filmed at Melody Ranch in the twenty-first century!)

Interspersed between Gene's summer and fall TV shoots were one-off rodeo appearances beginning in June and running into early September. In January Gene had bought half interest in the rodeo that belonged to an old friend, Leo Cremer, a former Montana congressman who had been killed in a tractor accident. Gene stepped into the partnership with stockman Harry Knight and the Cremer family to fulfill Cremer's bookings at big Western rodeos and state fairs. For these shows Gene traveled solely with the Cass County Boys and, of course, Champion and Little Champ. (Gene and Harry Knight eventually would purchase a Colorado ranch together.)

AT THE CASPER, WYOMING, RODEO IN MID-AUGUST, a longtime member of the Gene Autry Friendship Club discovered that her idol's drinking had gotten out of hand. Twenty-eight-year-old Lucille Beckstead, raised a Mormon in Salt Lake City, had attended the fan club's various conventions and Gene's performances since the 1940s, which she sometimes described for the *Aces*. "He was good looking—that famous smile and those pretty blue eyes and the sound of his voice, which was completely different from anyone else's" is how she thought of him. But she knew he had a penchant for certain young women who belonged to the club, including her roommate at the 1948 convention. "She's the one he picked," she recalled, "and she went with him every night, and they even went dancing at a nightclub. Gene was making love to her, and she said, 'Have you ever did this with Dot [the club president], and then he said, 'Her husband's always around.' He'd always give everybody that ever went with him [an autographed] one dollar bill—he said it was for cab fare to go home on. They'd say they were never going to spend it. If he liked you real well, he asked you to come and work for him, so many girls went out [to Hollywood] and worked for him."

When Lucille traveled to Casper that summer of 1954, "Gene asked me if I was married, and I said no. And he said, 'Well then, how about you and me getting together tonight then?' . . . Gene [was] telling me what a beautiful suntan I had because I was standing there wearing a sun dress." She turned down his offer "to come up to my room so I can really get to know you," and instead went to the rodeo every night with her friend Velma. The first night, "the Cass County Boys went over with a bang," Velma remembered:

> and proved to be a bigger hit than Gene [who had fallen off his horse during the grand entrance]. . . . Beside us sat a character who booed at Gene's singing, and the audience all started agreeing with him, and laughing and making fun of Gene's singing, which sounded like he was really off key at the end of each line. It was really that he didn't have the breath to finish his words. The wind was howling like mad and blowing right at his face. Well, being a loyal Gene Autry fan, I knew we had to do something right away, so Velma and I stood up and we hollered to that character, "*Shut up!*" as loud as we could. We were asked if it was really true that Gene Autry was such a heavy drinker that they had to walk him all over the fairgrounds every night trying to sober him up before he could sing. Of course, we denied everything and told them to quit listening to all those stupid rumors. Velma noticed that the elevator boy [from Gene's hotel] was sitting ahead of us, so we started talking to him. He remembered us, and he said, "Gee, that Gene Autry is sure a heavy drinker, isn't he?" "Well no, not that we know of," we said. He told us that he had delivered four pints at a time up to Gene, and that everybody in the hotel was saying he sure was a heavy drinker. Of course, Velma and I had to disagree with him.

The second night, though, Gene arrived to the rodeo in the condition the gossips had alluded to, according to Lucille:

> We walked back to the dressing room and just in time to see Gene arrive in a cab. It stopped right in front of the door. Gene could hardly make it out of the back seat. He took ahold of the front seat and he tried to pull himself forward, as if it were really an effort—very slowly he just kept taking hold of the front seat and he'd raise himself up a little bit from the back and he'd just fall back in the seat, and he just kept trying and trying, and he just couldn't make it. Very slowly, he kept hold of the front seat and he managed to pull himself forward. I glanced at Velma and she glanced at me and we didn't say anything, because what could we do? Finally he started to step out through the door just as slow as he could, and he saw me standing there. He got out and he started staggering toward the dressing room door. He walked real slow and his eyes were glassy and his tongue was too thick to speak. Velma and I just kept exchanging glances, and sadly shook our heads. I walked over and put my hand on Gene's shoulder and wondered if he remembered his promise to me that afternoon [to autograph a photo for Velma's son]. He said, "Lucille, I stood you up and I really am sorry that I stood you up." He could hardly talk and he was certainly in no condition to even try, but he managed to tell me that anyway. He's pretty smart—he never forgets anything. I couldn't help but like Gene, no matter what had happened, and I knew he would always be my favorite cowboy.

Gene also managed to pull himself together enough to perform that night, but again got a bad reaction from the crowd:

> The show started and we really felt sorry for poor Gene, with all that wind in his face and the way it kept taking his breath away. The mic kept blowing over—it kept falling to the ground and Jerry [Scoggins] kept picking it up for Gene, and Gene's voice sounded so heavy and his tone so thick. He couldn't sing the words too well, and it sounded as though he hardly had a tune at all. The crowd just roared with booing. And when he sang "I'm heading for the last round-up," they all hollered that he was heading there, alright—"*That's* exactly where you're heading!"

36

THE LAST ROUND-UP

EMBARRASSING INCIDENTS SUCH AS THOSE IN CASPER, WYOMING, began to occur with more frequency during Gene's rodeo appearances in the second half of the 1950s. Staying in one place for more than a day afforded him enough free time to overindulge in alcohol. The negative reactions didn't seem to faze him, however. He just kept moving. In September, soon after the Cremer rodeo dates, the "Gene Autry Hit Show of 1954" took off for forty-two one-nighters. Joe Johnson helped to publicize the tour as Gene's new advance man. Johnson had lost his Columbia job due to budget cutbacks and filled the spot left by Alex Gordon, who had by then become a Hollywood movie producer. Johnson became an Autry employee during the waning days of his singing-cowboy career. By the early 1960s, Gene's live performances would mark his last stand as an entertainer.

"I did the last really extensive tours that he did," related Johnson, "up through the Houston Fat Stock Show in Houston in early 1955."[1] A new tour had been set for February and this one would include Gail Davis, as noted in the *Los Angeles Times*: "[Autry's] Flying A gang is really rolling this semester. Besides the Autry pictures, he's also producing Jock Mahoney's *Range Riders*, Dick Jones's *Buffalo Bill, Jr.* series, and the highly successful Gail Davis starrer, *Annie Oakley*. Gene is particularly high on Annie and, because of the large number of requests to see her in action, is taking her with him on his tour of one-nighters next month."

Gene made no attempt to disguise his affection for Davis on the road, Johnson recalled:

He called her "Bootsy"—she always wore her little Western outfit and those white boots. I think he had a real love affair with her. They were sweethearts. They were very loving and he didn't hide her from me or from any of the band or anybody that went on tour—because Ina never went on tour with him. So he had a wife on the road and one at home. The times that I was with them, we'd either go to dinner or in the dressing room area in the back, we'd have a few drinks and that sort of thing, and then after that they'd go off on their own. He and Gail drank a lot together. They drank vodka like it was water. He never got belligerent when he was drinking—he was a happy drunk. It was crazy—she was cute and perky and I never saw her sloppy. Gene stayed pretty much in control in most of the shows. The first time I ever saw him too drunk to perform was in Houston.

When he came in the ring on the horse, he almost fell off. . . . Then after the show, he did an outdoor show at an orphanage and he'd had too much to drink—but he had the ability to perform even under the influence. About the time he was ready to finish, Carl Cotner and I saw that he was a little unstable and we both got onstage and helped him off-stage. Back at the hotel, Gene went in the restroom, and I'm sitting in the living room of the suite, and he said, "Joe, tell me—how did I do?" And I said, "Gene, do you want me to tell you what you want to hear, or do you want me to tell you the truth?" He said, "Tell me the truth." And I said, "Well, you were too drunk to entertain those kids and you shouldn't have done it." He was silent for what felt like thirty minutes to me, and then he came out of the bathroom and said, "Look, I want you to come to work for me—consider yourself part owner of the company." And he gave me 25 percent of the [music publishing] company at that point and asked me to move to California. I think he respected the fact that I had the guts to tell him the truth. I guess it's the reason he wanted to hire me.

AFTER THE RODEO, the tour soldiered on to New England, where one newspaper reported, "Autry denied that he was thinking of retiring (he recently received . . . bad press during a rodeo in Texas). Gene said, 'I'll be going at 100 if the public still wants me.'" Gene had burned his bridges, though, at the prestigious Houston Fat Stock Show, at which he'd previously appeared three times, most recently in 1948. Gene's drinking buddy Pat Buttram told friends it had become necessary "to wire Gene to the saddle to keep him aloft"—and no one knew if he were joking or not. "Dad used to say Gene needed two drinks to go on in front of any audience," Kerry Buttram Galgano recalled, "but if he took three, it was one too many and he lost his timing. More than three and he was in noticeable difficulty."[2]

Gene had bookings lined up for rodeo appearances with Gail from July through October. Lucille Beckstead attended the July dates in her hometown of Salt Lake. "I saw him out on the grounds walking around a little tipsy," she recalled. "He come over there to me and said, 'Lucille, do you want to come in the trailer and have a drink with me?,' and I said yes, and so I went in the trailer and there sits Gail Davis. He got us each a drink, and as we were drinking it, he joked, 'I'm going to join those polygamists down in Short Creek, and I'm going to get me a bunch of wives just like they do—the first two I'm going to pick are you, Lucille, and Gail, here, too!'"[3]

Some of Gene's old pals were beginning to worry about his drinking. WLS writer and announcer Joe Kelly had visited Los Angeles the previous winter and been disturbed by Gene's behavior, writing him, "I couldn't help but notice that you seem to be using 'old red eye' too much as a crutch as though you've got personal troubles! If that is the case, Gene, get rid of those troubles before you end up like the poor guy who decided to drink 'Canada Dry.' He went up to Canada to try it and found out it couldn't be done."[4] Gene responded, "As to your paragraph about the red eye, perhaps sometimes you are right. I guess we all at some time or another have too many drinks, but you can rest assured it hasn't gotten the best of me and I will definitely watch it in the future if I partied too much with you or anyone else."

Joe had traveled to Hollywood with the misconception he could work on Gene's TV shows and returned to Chicago disappointed. In the same letter, Gene explained why things hadn't worked out. "In making a [television picture] it requires a lot of thought, a lot of the inside workings of unions and a lot of shortcuts with budgets because you can sink all the way from $25,000 to $30,000 in a television film and have nothing on the screen unless you have experienced personnel to do this type of work. Some of our top assistant directors now make around $400 or $500 a week, but they have had a lot of years of experience and they know every shortcut there is in order to save our money. If we have a cast of, say, forty people, sometimes one little scene can save several thousands of dollars by just getting it right."[5]

Flying A's assembly-line approach had expanded, and that summer Gene's studio planned to put two more shows into production. *The Adventures of Champion* starred the latest of Gene's performing sorrels; Champion number three would retire to Melody Ranch the following year. Gene offered the "human lead" to Monte Hale, a Texan who'd been one of Republic's last singing cowboys and went on to land a part in 1956's *Giant* (with James Dean, Rock Hudson, and Elizabeth Taylor). Hale—later one of Gene's closest friends—turned *Champion* down: "I didn't want to play second bill to a horse," he joked. "I just didn't feel it was right for me." (The part of Sandy North went to Jim Bannon, who'd been a stunt double at Columbia for Charles Starrett, while Barry Curtis played twelve-year-old Ricky North, owner of Champion, the Wonder Horse.)

The other planned series was based on the Red Ryder comic strip by another old buddy, Fred Harman, whom Gene met during his first year in Hollywood: "Many moons have risen over many tipis," Harman, now a Colorado rancher, wrote Gene, "since I had the pleasure of visiting with you so often [in 1935] when [*Strawberry Roan* author] Curley Fletcher and I were producing our magazine and I was drawing another western comic. I have followed your progress these many years with pride and it appears that our trails are coming together again. This is just a quick note to tell you that with you, Mandy and

Mitch, maybe we have gotten together on something which I hope will be very beneficial to all of us."[6]

But heavy competition was on the horizon in 1955. Republic had been legally cleared to sell Gene's fifty-six films to television, as well as Roy Rogers's, both of which began flooding TV channels. That summer Davy Crockett became the latest children's fad, thanks to the hugely popular Disney movie starring Fess Parker, with its theme song riding *The Hit Parade*.[7] There was a new sensation taking over the airways, too—rock and roll. Sun artist Elvis Presley, who had been touring with such country stars as Hank Snow, was causing pandemonium among teenage fans everywhere he went. That year Elvis would have his first number one country hit, followed by a new manager, Colonel Tom Parker—who had previously worked with Gene Austin and thereby was friendly with Gene Autry. By 1956 Elvis would move to RCA and monopolize the C&W and pop charts. Artists whose honky-tonk or "Nashville sound" had prevented Gene's "old-school" records from reaching the C&W surveys would be pushed aside by Memphis-born rockabilly. But back in September of 1955 Gene had responded to a music publisher pushing a cowboy number: "Right now, the toughest type of song to submit to the recording companies is a Western. Most of the good songs that they are accepting are coming of out Nashville."[8] Four years later, he would write Dudley, "If you are thinking about trying to do any type of entertainment, I believe you're wasting your time. In the first place, right now practically every standard entertainer, such as Ernie Tubbs [*sic*], Pee Wee King, and many others, are having a very rough time. It seems that the teenagers go strictly for rock and roll. Knowing your ability as an entertainer as I do, and from past experience, I don't think you will ever be able to make a living in this field."

Family-friendly cowboys were beginning to get lost in the shuffle. Among the casualties, *Red Ryder* never went farther than a pilot, and although *The Adventures of Champion* knocked *My Friend Flicka* off the CBS schedule in September, the new program ran for only one season. *Annie Oakley* endured until 1957, while *The Range Rider* ended production after seventy-eight episodes. *Buffalo Bill, Jr.*, with forty-two episodes, continued until September of 1956. With the youthful-looking Jones playing a teenaged Texas marshal and Nancy Gilbert as his little sister Calamity, who's a whiz with telegraph keys, the program's lead characters were reminiscent of the heroic, fast-riding Baxter siblings of Gene's first serial, *The Phantom Empire*. "[Sponsor] Mars Candy liked the show," remembered Dick Jones, "and they renewed for another thirty-odd episodes . . . but they wanted it to be in the same across-the-board, nationwide slot on CBS, and CBS wanted 25 percent and Gene said, 'There isn't 25 percent to give you.' You don't push Gene Autry—he could buy and sell you. So when they got uppity, he said 'Nope!' and that was it!"

Competition for viewers of Westerns in the new fall season included

Cheyenne, *Gunsmoke*, and *Wyatt Earp*, whose lead, Hugh O'Brian, got his start in Gene's 1950 picture *Beyond the Purple Hills*. A reporter asked Gene, "What about all the talk about the new shows being 'adult' Westerns?" Gene claimed not to see much difference between those shows and a "regular" Western and answered, "The kids of today are the adults of tomorrow. You have to satisfy them, too. They're just as important. Actually, we try to aim all our shows to satisfy kids and adults too. . . . There's room for all of us. If you look at the number of TV stations in every town, what the heck, there are hours and hours to fill up." Gene went on to applaud O'Brian's performance and admitted that he checked out TV newcomers "like the manager of a ball club likes to see what rookies show promise."[9]

TV programming and rock and roll were both impacting radio by early 1956. Variety programs and shows like *Melody Ranch* were giving way to jive-talking disc jockeys spinning the latest hits. Gene continued to transcribe many of his shows, but his drinking was beginning to affect these as well. Johnny Bond remembered that throughout the last half of 1955 once a month or so Gene would show up too inebriated to perform. His "voice had always been straight, crisp, and clear," Bond said, but on these occasions, "it was wavering somewhat with a noticeable tremolo. . . . He was having difficulty reading his lines and singing his songs." When this happened, an old tape had to be re-broadcast. "After that situation had taken place several times," Bond reported, "the sponsors came out from Chicago to see first-hand what was the matter. They had private meetings with Autry and Burch, but we soon got the message; this sort of thing could go on just so long and that would be it. Still the situation did not improve. We began to get the impression that the Boss had lost interest in the radio show. . . . Listeners to the show were beginning to notice the change in the voice. A small amount of unfavorable publicity . . . show[ed] up as the result of this and some of his recent tour capers."[10]

The Gene Autry Tour of 1956 covered twenty-seven cities in January and February, ending on February 20 in North Carolina, where "Gene Autry gave every indication of being . . . thoroughly exhausted," according to the *Charlotte Observer*. "His voice was hoarse and husky. His singing lacked his usual feeling for rhythm. He spoke as if half choked by the fog of fatigue." The reporter went on to rave about performances by Gail (who "stole the show") and Merle Travis (who "came close to stealing the show"); the pioneering electric guitarist had been appearing on *Melody Ranch* and wowed audiences with his show-stopping "Sixteen Tons," which Tennessee Ernie Ford had turned into a crossover smash in 1955. On March 7 TV newscasters and newspapers reported that Gene had been "ordered to bed rest," with papers alternately noting he suffered from exhaustion or laryngitis; on March 9 the *New York Times* reported that "a musical series titled 'Entertainment with Burgess Meredith'" was temporarily replacing Gene's radio show, and according to CBS, Gene "would be off radio indefinitely."[11]

For a month, Gene laid low at home, presumably going cold turkey. "Ina was a very devout Christian Scientist," said Virginia MacPhail, "and whenever he was 'still,' she had somebody stay with him at the house—she didn't send him to the hospital. I can't remember him ever being in the hospital." On April 6, the *Los Angeles Times* reported Gene was suffering from "extreme fatigue and nervous exhaustion," and therefore could not appear as a witness at a pre-divorce hearing between Georgia and Carl Cotner, who would marry his third wife, Juanita Crafton, once the divorce became final. Gene assured his close friend Howard Ketting, formerly of Wrigley's Chicago ad agency Rauthruff and Ryan, responsible for the radio show, "I am coming along all right now. Was just sort of pooped out after the thirty-one one-night stands. You know what they are." Tom Hargis, his radio producer, had been sidelined by illness when the show went on hiatus in March, and Gene wrote Tom's wife, Florence, "I knew there was a discussion of a change, but since it has been necessary for me to take this time off for myself and be quiet, I had decided to stay completely out of it since I didn't feel the decision was mine to make. I thought it had all blown over and didn't think they would make a change especially while Tom was ill . . . I want Tom to know how much I appreciate the effort he has given our show. I have always enjoyed working with him."[12]

Finally, in mid-April, Gene appeared ready to get back to work and return to radio. He told a reporter, "I took a whole month's vacation—my first ever. . . . As a result, I've never felt better in my life. I have always enjoyed my work so much that it never occurred to me that taking time away from it could be enjoyable. Matter of fact I always wondered why anyone would want to take a vacation if he honestly liked what he was doing. Now I know that a little let-up once in a while does a man a lot of good. I hope I'll be able to get another vacation—in, say, ten years or so." On April 13 Ina wrote the *Aces*, "Know you are just as happy as I am to have Gene go back on the air next Sunday. It is just wonderful to see him looking so well and feeling fine again. I for one have been grateful that he finally took such a nice long vacation, which he has really needed for many years but simply didn't take. This one has been great for him. In fact, after he got to feeling better we both had a good time, just being home, quiet. . . . We have our new little boxer puppy to keep us company . . . [you may have seen pictures of] our older boxer, Mike, and Pat is his little son. . . . The ranch is not far from town and we have gone up there a few times, so you can see it has been a very happy vacation while Gene was recouping."

A couple of radio shows went fine, but on Sunday, May 6, "the Boss was not able to go on," Johnny Bond reported. "His voice was shaky and so were his hands. An old tape was run at broadcast time. On Monday morning, Bud Offield of the Wrigley Company was in town and we all got the news. The *Melody Ranch* radio broadcast . . . was finished."[13] The news made headlines, with CBS, Wrigley, and the Autry office all covering up the real reason for the show's demise.

On May 11 it was announced Gene was retiring from radio, with Arthur Hull Hayes, president of CBS radio, quoted as saying "Autry's decision was a surprise to both the network and the sponsor, William Wrigley Jr. Co." The *New York Times* reported, "Although no reason was given, it was recalled that not too long ago his physicians had prescribed a rest of several weeks from the live broadcast. He has been with the same sponsor since January 1940"—which the *Chicago Tribune* called, "the longest sponsor-star relationship in radio history."[14] The Autry camp put out the word that the difference over transcribing shows resulted in Gene's departure. On May 13 the final *Melody Ranch* program was broadcast without the Boss. Pat Buttram and announcer Charlie Lyon pretended to look for the absentee Gene, when a "letter" arrived from the singing cowboy, which said he'd decided to take a rest. Wrigley was so impressed by the way Pat rose to the occasion that the sponsor offered him his own radio show, which got under way in ensuing weeks. (Buttram would continue acting in films, and in the 1960s he became a TV star on *Green Acres*.) Alex Gordon wired Gene and Ina:

MY CONSTANT THOUGHTS AND PRAYERS ARE WITH YOU AND I HOPE AND PRAY THAT EVERYTHING WILL WORK OUT ALL RIGHT FOR YOU. ALWAYS YOUR LOYAL FRIEND.[15]

In the meantime, speculation began that Gene's days were numbered on TV as well. "The question has arisen whether the William Wrigley Jr. Company will continue to sponsor Gene Autry's filmed television programs," reported the *New York Times*. "Wrigley's present contract expires next month, but it has not notified CBS of future plans. . . . When Wrigley's contract with CBS expires, all Mr. Autry's half-hour films produced so far will have been shown at least once. The western program is televised by a small number of CBS network stations on Saturdays at 7 PM and syndicated to other stations throughout the country."[16] Prognosticators proved correct and *The Gene Autry Show* ceased production of new films for television, and by year's end the reruns, too, had vanished from many stations.

Gene wasn't ready to give up yet. He told a reporter "if I can find a good format for a radio show, I'd like to do it on tape." Gene wrote *Autry's Aces* that "in all probability I will be back on the air . . . this fall, and I might even do a live television program in connection with the radio show. . . . After all of these years on the radio, our personal appearances, making television films and all other obligations . . . I have decided to just take it easy and rest up for a while."[17] With *Annie Oakley* ceasing production of new shows by year's end, Gene and Mandy began looking into Flying A producing color features. They hired Republic's former head of distribution J. R. "Jim" Grainger to test the waters by contacting major theater chains to see if there was interest in a wide-screen, Technicolor Gene Autry picture. Although he did receive a few positive replies, Grainger got nearly fifty letters stating that Gene's "overexposure" on a "kiddy show" on TV, as well as the public's association of his films with the old series Westerns, had ruined his box-office appeal. One theater owner from Bangor, Maine, wrote about Gene's recent personal appearance there: "According to all reports Autry did not increase his popularity here. His singing voice was very poor, the children who have seen his old features on TV were very disappointed with his appearance, as he is now on the stout side and does not have the youthful appearance of his old films. . . . They were very disappointed with the complete performance."[18]

Undaunted by the negative reviews, Gene prepared for a string of rodeo dates sprinkled throughout the summer and into fall. Just before he left in July, it was announced that Golden West Broadcasters had added another jewel to its crown: San Francisco station KSFO, at a price of one million dollars. Ironically, none of Gene's stations played his music; most featured pop, news, and sports.

Johnny Bond had quit the road but recommended in his place a talented young guitarist and vocalist, Johnny Western. The twenty-one-year-old Autry fan had first met Gene in 1949 in his home state of Minnesota; then in 1952 he had interviewed him for a local radio show. The boyishly handsome entertainer had made his way to California a few years later (and would eventually appear in TV's *Have Gun Will Travel*, and write and record its hit theme song).

"My very first date with Gene was the Pueblo, Colorado, State Fair and rodeo," Western recalled. "There were 12,000 people a day, then we had two days to get to Toronto, and we played fourteen days to three million people at the Canadian National Exhibition. It was just incredible." The revue included the Cass County Boys, Gail Davis, Barbara Bardo, Merle Travis, and Carl Cotner. "It was scaled down to that size for those last few years," said Western. "The Indians were gone, Frankie Marvin (who had retired) was gone, the piano player and the horn player were gone. I was the kid on the show." Western started on a six-week trial basis, but Gail Davis intervened on his behalf, he related. "Gail went to Gene, she had his ear, and she said, 'Gene, tell Johnny right now you're going to keep him—don't keep him in suspense for six weeks.' So the next day, he called me in and said, 'I've been thinking it over and it all looks like it's working real good, so how'd you like to just stay on the show?' Of course, it was the biggest thrill in the world." He stayed on for two years. But things got bumpy at the Ak-Sar-Ben Rodeo, in Nebraska, on September 21.

"When we got to the show that night, my heart just stopped," Johnny recalled,

> because when I saw Gene and started talking to him, he was slurring his words and I thought, "Oh, man, don't let this happen, please." We had a packed house— opening night at the biggest arena in Omaha, and it was going to be a ten-day stand. Well, it turned out to be a nightmare because Gene was on his horse, and they couldn't get him off. When he left to do the songs, he'd ride the horse out and [the trainer] would take the horse and walk him away while Gene did the song. Well, he almost fell off doing that, and then they did the songs, but it was kind of

like us working our way through the songs to get to the end. Somebody physically tried to put Gene back on the horse after the songs, and he couldn't get on. He just didn't realize where he was. So [the trainer] started putting the horse through the act where Champ does a hula routine. When it was supposed to be over, Gene wouldn't leave the arena. He just sat there. It was one of the most terrible, terrible things. I just died a thousand deaths, because Gene was just my hero, my idol, my everything, and there he was just dying out there in front of the crowd. Then the rodeo committee just landed on him with both feet. The newspaper came out the next day with a big headline [GENE AUTRY ILL; WILL MISS RODEO]. But my understanding was there was some money that [exchanged hands] because the Omaha paper was just going to crucify him but instead, they modified the headline.

While Gene was sent back to California, the troupe stayed behind to carry out the commitment. Western recounted:

I did a medley of Gene's songs with the Cass County Boys backing me up. They did a little extra of their stuff, [the trainer] put on one of Gene's fancy shirts and worked the horse act with Champ and Little Champ, and Gail was absolutely wonderful. She was the closer as Annie Oakley, because by that time she was doing the trick holding the gun over her shoulder like the real Annie Oakley—with the mirror mounted on the gun stock and she'd shoot the balloons over her shoulder. And actually, I wrote Gene a letter and told him what a great job Gail was doing, and that everyone was waiting for him to get back. And Gene sent me the sweetest note that said "Congratulations—I'm sure things are going good. I'm feeling much better and I'll see you on the next date."

GENE APPARENTLY WENT ON THE WAGON and arrived in good shape on October 5 for a nine-day stand at the rodeo in Chicago, followed by five days in Kansas City. "When he came back for those next shows," according to Western, "he was as straight as a string and Mr. Professional all the way, and it was just like night and day." Most of those close to the Autrys credited Ina with trying to stabilize Gene, although some said she had looked the other way too long. She traveled with Gene on his final shows of the year—keeping him away from Gail and booze. "Bert Dodson and I discussed the situation once," said Western, "and he said I'm sure Ina knows about Gail, but Ina's a Christian Scientist and the Christian Scientists have this belief that it's not happening. They kind of steel themselves up to the fact that they can look away and say, 'Well, this is just either a passing fancy or it's not even happening at all.' "[19]

While Gene was touring that fall, *Billboard* ran an item that Gene had left yet another longtime association—Columbia Records—and had started recording for the independent label Dot. When Johnny Marks wrote him about the news, he replied, "I am still under contract with Columbia, and expect to remain there. As you know, I have been with them for twenty-five years. I do have the privilege of recording outside numbers, and on this basis I did two sides for Dot, which looked like they might turn out to be good numbers."[20] Apparently, Columbia executives requested Gene not to release the Dot recordings, which have never surfaced. Still, Gene had cut very few tracks for his longtime label and would only do a few more before the label unceremoniously dropped him in July 1957.

Gene's old A&R man, Art Satherley, had fallen on hard times since his retirement, frequently asking Gene for loans. Earlier in the year, Uncle Art had written Gene that he'd abandoned him. Gene responded:

> Your letter seems to indicate you feel I was not grateful and have not repaid you for our friendship in the beginning. I feel I have fully repaid you. For many years I gave you part of my royalties even though I knew this was not ordinarily done in a recording company, but I was willing to do it to show you my gratitude. I have never discussed this with anyone and never will because I agreed to it at the time. And, in many cases I had bought and paid for the songs myself. I know you have always felt you were the benefactor of the "country boy" and "country music," but I know most all of them repaid you in the same way I did. When you built your lodge you asked to borrow several thousand dollars. To this day it has never been mentioned. . . . Years ago when Freddie Rose first came to Hollywood, I helped to keep him going for about three years. I made my pictures' scripts available so he could write the songs for which I never received a cent. I bought his songs, recorded them with Columbia, and you took one-half the royalties. . . . You took him to Nashville to go in with Acuff and then threw all of your songs in that company and never gave our firm a break."[21]

Eventually, Art and Gene would patch things up and see each other from time to time. He would continue to send money up until Art's death at age ninety-six on February 10, 1986, after which Gene wrote his widow, Harriet, "He and I had been so close for so many years and I always respected him so highly. Of course, in later years we had some differences between us but I still admired and loved him."[22]

Gene's father, Delbert, like brother Dudley, continuously asked for financial assistance in addition to what Gene sent on a regular basis. At one point, when Ruby Autry wrote requesting money to have their young daughter's rotten teeth pulled and replaced with dentures, Gene complied but was obviously upset at the condition of their lives. He wrote, "Ruby, I do not want you to think for one minute that I blame you for any condition in your family. I think I know the situation as well as anyone in the world, as I have had to go through this most of my life. Guess that's why I feel the way I do. I know you have a very tough job on your hands to make ends meet, and that is why I have always tried to tell my Dad that I thought it was just terrible to bring kids into the world and bring them up by the hair of the head, not giving any consideration to how they were going to be raised, and to what their future would be."[23] As much as Gene disliked Delbert—he never possessed a photo of himself with his father—with his livestock businesses, constant traveling, and weaknesses for alcohol and women, he and Delbert were more alike than he would ever care to admit. Perhaps Gene's urgent need to take financial responsibility for an extended family of friends and business associates helped reassure him that he was the provider his father never was.

Gene's generosity extended to several of his early mentors. He helped Frankie Marvin establish a fast-food business once he left show business in 1955, and would occasionally send him a "bonus" check. Johnny Western recalled meeting Ken Maynard one day in 1956 when he'd tried to sell Gene his Stetson for a hundred dollars. Instead, Gene told him to keep the hat, gave him five hundred dollars, and began sending him a monthly check. Gene's accountant since 1949, Bernie Solomon, related, "I'd want to write it off and Gene would say 'no, no,' because it could have been written off as a loan, but he wouldn't let me."[24] Other moneys were given freely as well. "He was fair with everybody," said former DJ, TV personality, and friend Johnny Grant. "He constantly wanted to lend a helping hand. He was a very compassionate fellow."[25] According to Johnny Western:

> In his right-hand pocket, he had a money clip that was given to him by Lone Wolf Gonzaullas, the head of the Texas Rangers, and it was a Texas Ranger badge with a big diamond in the center of it. And in that money clip he carried brand new hundred dollar bills. In his left-hand pocket, he carried fifty dollar bills, and when these old-timers who were really hurting came up to him—depending on who they were and what their story was—he either reached in his right-hand pocket and peeled off some hundreds, or [chose] fifty dollar bills for old rodeo riders or busted up guys or stuntmen that he'd known along the line that came and hit him up. They always knew he was a soft touch. And depending on what the story was, it was either the left-hand pocket or the right-hand pocket. And I thought that was a heck of a deal![26]

When Gene got his own windfall the following year with the success of Johnnie Ray's hit, he gave about $48,000 to Joe Johnson to start a record label. Gene planned to call it Champion, even printing up labels with the name, but Johnson discovered Decca still owned the rights to the old Champion label— originally an imprint of Gennett. Gene settled for Challenge instead, and Johnson's first discovery for the label propelled Challenge into the rock and roll stratosphere. Chuck Rio, who played in an Orange County bar band, had written a catchy instrumental called "Tequila." Johnson put him together with session musicians and called the group the Champs. The combo's first 45, "Tequila," stayed on the charts for nineteen weeks, rocketing to number one, and eventually selling six million copies. (Glen Campbell later became a member of the Champs before embarking on his stellar solo career.) Not as impressive sales-wise, the Challenge album *Christmastime with Gene Autry* still sold quite well when it was released during the 1957 holiday season. With their profits, Gene and Joe would buy the Four-Star label and its publishing catalogue, but in a rare misstep and much to Johnson's chagrin, Gene passed up the chance to re-sign the label's top female artist, Patsy Cline.[27]

Gene spent much of 1957 back on the road with one-night stands and rodeos. He and Gail continued their romance while out of town, but things had grown more turbulent. Tired of being "the other woman," she pressured Gene to leave Ina for her. "He was quite in love with her," according to Juanita Cotner, who traveled on the thirty-eight-date winter tour.

> I was with them in a car driving from Pennsylvania to New York, and you get to know people when you're in close quarters with them. But I do know from a woman's instinct—though I could be all wrong about this—but I got the feeling that it wasn't nearly as much with her towards him, as he towards her. When we were in New York, she was tired of him not being up to have dinner, and instead of staying and going home the next day on the airplane with all of us, she left early. In fact, she stayed one night and then she left, whereas we stayed another day in order for Gene to get [in] a little bit better [condition] to go home.[28]

The drinking "seemed like it was something that was not ever going to go away," recalled the Autrys' niece Ina Leffler, "but Ina said 'I will never give up,' and that was the way she looked at it. She cared for him to a point where she would never, ever stop trying to make things better. She saw a lot of good qualities there and thought those were worth furthering and protecting and nurturing and so forth. There were so many times that—without her there to hold things together and protect him somewhat—who knows what would have happened?"[29] (Eventually, Gene would lose his driver's license following two drunk driving arrests in Los Angeles in 1961.) More frequently, Ina accompanied Gene on his rodeo dates to keep him in line. Joe Johnson remembered, "She was a strong lady and determined to hold their relationship together, and I give her a lot of credit for Gene's survival, actually, and for his many successes, because she was right there in every area of his business life. She was always the guardian, and I never met a finer lady than Ina Autry."[30]

Finally, from February 7 to 16, 1958, Gene and Gail did their last performances together, appearing at the San Antonio rodeo. As they spent less time together, the relationship cooled. Gail began dating an RCA executive, Dick Peirce, who asked her to marry him. When she told Gene, he desperately tried to talk her out of it. "I don't know whether Gail thought maybe it would shake him up enough to leave Ina," Virginia MacPhail said, "but there was no way that was going to happen. He wasn't about to break that up."[31] Gene wrote in his autobiography that when he once joked to Ina that he was going to trade her in for a younger model, she told him "very coolly, very sweetly, . . . 'I have always said you could do that, dear, any time you wanted. Of course you'd wind up right where you started, with a guitar and a saddle.'"[32] In reality, Ina gave Gene the ultimatum regarding his relationship with Gail after she happened to pick up the upstairs phone extension while he was on the downstairs line having a romantic conversation with his lover. Furious, Ina confronted her husband and told him to end the affair or she was leaving him and taking everything he owned with her. Gail's marriage to Peirce in June 1959 was short lived and unhappy.

Just after the San Antonio rodeo, Gene took Ina, along with Juanita and Carl Cotner, to a date that turned out to be quite dangerous. He was booked to headline a rodeo in Havana, Cuba, from February 28 to March 10. The country was in turmoil with Fidel Castro's revolutionaries on the brink of ousting president Fulgencio Batista. "They had already kidnapped [celebrities] down there in Cuba," according to Juanita, "and . . . one who had been kidnapped told Gene, 'They put me in a hotel room, fed me really good, gave me stuff to drink, and gave me girls.' So Gene said, in front of Ina, 'Hell, I don't think I'd mind very much getting kidnapped!'" The Americans were given bodyguards to protect them. "I was going to go see the show," said Juanita, " but there were too many guys with machine guns around and Carl told me to go back to the hotel and stay there. At nighttime, there were bombings. We were probably the last bunch of American entertainers in Havana. Castro came in after that."[33] It was fortunate that Gene did not take Champ on the trip, because in the company's haste to flee the country, the rodeo's livestock had to be left behind for good.

Gene's other big tour of 1958 featured Gail's former co-star, fifteen-year-old Jimmy Hawkins, whose mother, Betty, went along as well. She spent time with Ina, shopping and attending the theater. Gene had turned fifty—the age at which Tom Mix predicted he might have to hang up his spurs. In an attempt to win back the younger crowd, Gene had Jimmy sing the novelty hit "Purple People Eater" (as Gail Davis had covered Haley's "Rock Around the Clock"). Hula hoops, then all the rage, were also part of the act. The tour traveled to small outdoor stadiums over ten weeks with generally good turnouts except for Hurley, Wisconsin, where the troupe played to an audience of five. It didn't seem to bother Gene, who remained even-tempered until the night he had a run-in with an anti-Semite. "Gene was sitting at the counter eating roast beef and mashed potatoes and gravy," Hawkins remembered. When Gene began sharing his dinner with the teenager, the man next to them at the counter acted huffy. "Gene said, 'Don't worry about it, just keep eating,' and then Herb Green came up and said 'we should take off in ten minutes,' and the guy looked at Herb talking to Gene Autry, and he said something derogatory about him being a Jew and Gene said, 'What did you say?,' and I'm thinking 'oh, jeez,' and I put the spoon down and Gene said, 'Just keep eating.' And he got into it. He said, 'I don't like what you called that man, and I don't like the way you're treating this kid . . . How'd you like to step outside?' Now, just about that time, Herb Green came back, and it was starting to get into a heated conversation, and Herb got the gist of it right away. And he just hustled us off."[34]

Gene had occasionally lost his temper on the road, once pulling his gun (with fake bullets) on a union official who threatened to shut down the show if the company didn't employ unnecessary local musicians. Another time, he pummeled an unlicensed vendor trying to sell merchandise not endorsed by Gene. In Los Angeles, in 1953, Gene had been sued for assault and battery by a man whom he punched in an altercation. Gene testified that he had stopped his car to buy a newspaper at a sidewalk stand and "this man stuck his head out the window and said, 'What are you trying to do, you son of a bitch?'" In response, Gene belted him on the chin. The judge dismissed the case.

As THE FINAL DAYS OF TOURING WANED, Gene called Johnny Bond back into service, to finish out the roadwork, just as Smiley had joined him for the last movies and Pat Buttram had handled *Melody Ranch*'s swan song. By 1959 the tour limped along to county fairs where Gene and Johnny attempted to sing over noisy amusement park rides. Sometimes, when audiences were particularly skimpy, the entertainers were happy if the show was rained out. Why did he keep doing it? "It was absolutely a family kind of thing," opined Joe Johnson. "Gene was very loyal and so were his employees. Herb [Green] was like a brother to him . . . or a son . . . and so was Carl Cotner, who led the band. The acts that were regularly on the show were all close with Gene and he treated them very royally. He was very compassionate with his crew and very close with them, and they supported him 100 percent. And any entertainer is going to tell you that the biggest thrill they get is when the audience responds to them, and I think Gene missed that so much, that he hated to give it up." Alex Gordon pointed out that "he loved the live interaction with an audience, and performing live was the part of his career he liked the most." In 1956 Gene had told a *Chicago Tribune* reporter, "I never get tired of traveling—it gets in your blood."[35] When he appeared as a guest with Merle Travis on an episode of the C&W television program *Town Hall Party*, starring Johnny Bond, he told the audience after being lovingly introduced by Johnny: "This kinda reminds me of back where I came from—Oklahoma, Texas. Ole 'Trav' and I appeared in practically every town and city in the United States and Canada."

Johnny, along with Rufe Davis, accompanied him on his last multicity trek in 1960. Bond later recounted how after playing a triumphal sold-out show at the Tournament of Thrills in Philadelphia, the pair were jeered at by former fans in the airport when it was discovered they were sloshed. Gene just shrugged it off. On the plane, Johnny asked him why he drank so much vodka instead of "taking the short Scotch in the tall glass." "That was when I was making the pictures and the tours," Gene told him. "I couldn't afford to let down. Now I can. You ask me why I take vodka. . . . It makes me feel good. I think I can afford it. . . . A man ought to be entitled to one little vice, don't you think?"[36] "I think one of the greatest compliments you can pay a man is how long people stay with him," Johnny Grant has remarked about the longevity of Gene's professional relationships. "Of the folks who worked for him, some spent their whole career—or a great portion of their entertainment life—with him."[37]

By then, Bond had scored a hit record on Gene's newest label, Republic, with "Hot Rod Lincoln" making the pop and C&W charts. Gene also had released a rock and roll-inflected Christmas song on the label, 1959's "Santa's Comin' in a Whirlybird"—a criminally overlooked Yuletide number revered by holiday-music collectors. Old pals Gene and Johnny traveled to their final date together in Shreveport, Louisiana, after visiting Governor Jimmie Davis, whose career had started with Gene's in the late 1920s. On October 30, at the Louisiana State Fair, Bond backed Gene for the last time on the road.[38]

On his own, Gene made a handful of appearances at county fairs in 1961, and finally in 1962, he played his last live performances, earning some $13,000. It is unknown where he appeared because his shows no longer made the papers and such records were no longer kept by his staff. Still, Gene made the news. His beloved Melody Ranch, which he'd hoped to turn into a museum, burned to the ground in August 1962, destroying most of the buildings as well as his vast collection of Western artifacts and personal memorabilia. Fortunately, Champion was unharmed, and Gene held onto the ruined property until the horse died of old age. (Gene then sold the property. Melody Ranch was later restored and has been in use ever since as a set for numerous productions.)

Gene's other activities were frequently covered in newspapers' business and sports pages: Golden West Broadcasters continued to acquire lucrative properties, including Los Angeles television station KTLA, and over the decades more radio stations in Seattle, Portland, and Detroit. Gene also began operating a number of luxury hotels in Los Angeles (the Continental on the Sunset Strip), Palm Springs, San Francisco, and Chicago. When these ventures proved less than profitable, he downsized, holding onto the Gene Autry Hotel (at one point named the Melody Ranch Hotel) in Palm Springs, where he and Ina built a second home on the premises. (Through all the ups and downs, the couple remained devoted to one another until Ina's death in 1980.)

Most newsworthy, the California Angels, the American League team Gene founded with Bob Reynolds in 1960, garnered plenty of ink. Beginning in 1961, Gene's team unsuccessfully pursued a pennant, but he became a beloved figure among his players—including such legendary figures as Reggie Jackson and Nolan Ryan. Gene rarely missed a game, to which he invited old friends, entertainers, business associates, and several U.S. presidents to join him. "Gene says the only difference in baseball and show business is that in the many films and television shows he portrayed the character of a cowboy wearing the big sombrero and boots," commented one reporter, "and now, while baseball is still a form of show business, you wear a baseball cap and spikes."

Alex Gordon disagreed: "In 1962 Gene retired from public performance and also made his last full-length recording [an album of Western classics appropriately released on RCA Victor, the label for which he first recorded in 1929.][39] And then he went into baseball completely. And that's where I step out. I've never been to a baseball game."

Gene's loyalty to friends and colleagues usually did not make the papers, however. In October 1965, when Johnny Cash was arrested in El Paso, Texas, for illegally transporting amphetamines across the border, he contacted Gene. The troubled performer had met his singing cowboy idol in the late 1950s, and the two had stayed in touch. With his myriad political connections in Texas, Gene knew who to contact there to help Cash with his legal problems. Sure enough, Cash was simply required by an El Paso judge to pay a fine. The following year, the Man in Black wrote Gene, "It's a hell of a long time to wait to thank you for the letter to El Paso for me, but my life has been in quite a turmoil these last few months. . . . Anyway, your letter was *the* #1 most important in getting me out of the trouble there, and I will always be grateful to you for going to such a trouble for me."[40]

GENE STOPPED PERFORMING IN THE EARLY 1960s, but he did not stay seated behind a desk. He often said that he traveled with his ball club as much as he had as a performer. Just as the American cowboy never stopped blazing trails in our imagination, Gene Autry never tired of the road. He ended his thirty-plus-year career as an entertainer much as he had started it—before the innovations in recording and radio, before sound came to motion pictures, and long before television arrived in living rooms. Traveling the byways of America, Gene Autry kept singing to anyone who would listen. His songs are with us still.

EPILOGUE

Studio City, California, March 18, 1997

Seated behind a massive oak desk in his roomy, memorabilia-filled office, Gene Autry, age eighty-nine, is thumbing through *Western Classics*, his 1947 bound volume of 78 rpm recordings. Gene is dressed in a tailored Western suit, with his white, ten-gallon Stetson hanging on a nearby hat rack.

"I'll be doggone," Gene says to me in a warm, very familiar-sounding voice as he inspects my vintage set, before awarding me a rare interview to be published in the *New York Times*. " 'Red River Valley,' 'Mexicali Rose,' 'South of the Border,' what a great song—that was a dandy." When the next title catches his eye, America's original singing cowboy suddenly begins to softly croon: "I'm back in the saddle again . . ." He stops mid-verse with a laugh, explaining, "I've done 'Back in the Saddle Again' so darn long, I could go to sleep and sing it."

The song is among the eighty-four tracks on Gene's very first CD box set, *Gene Autry: Sing Cowboy Sing*, released by Warner Brothers' hip Rhino label. Its three discs include original transcriptions of the *Melody Ranch* radio show. Four years earlier, Gene's signature song had been featured on the 1993 multi-platinum soundtrack, *Sleepless in Seattle*, for which a plaque hangs on his office wall, among numerous other awards, Western art, and cowboy knickknacks. And at the February 1997 Grammy Awards, the song was inducted into the Recording Academy Hall of Fame. "If you stay out there long enough," Gene tells me with his still-ravishing smile, "it'll come back in style."

Eleven years earlier, Gene had earned his fifth star on the Hollywood Walk of Fame, for radio, recording, motion pictures, television, and live theater performance—the only entertainer to accomplish such a feat. Also in the late 1980s he was seen on TV again, cohosting TNN's *Melody Ranch Theater*, with his old sidekick Pat Buttram, swapping tales as they introduced screenings of his feature films. A decade later, he still occasionally comes into the offices of Gene Autry Entertainment, on the corner of Moorpark and Colfax, to catch up with his attentive employees: Karla Buhlman, co-producer of the new box set, who oversees the restoration of his past work; Maxine Hansen, longtime executive secretary to Mr. and Mrs. Autry; and the inimitable Alex Gordon, who holds the title of vice-president of Flying A Pictures. Gene is usually accompanied by his second wife, Jacqueline Ellam Autry, a highly astute businesswoman and former bank vice-president whom he married in July 1981. She has taken the reins of most of his business holdings, divesting many of them at a hefty profit. A knowledgeable sports enthusiast, she has become quite involved in the baseball club as well, and she eventually would be named Honorary American League President of Major League Baseball.

"My squaw, here," Gene points to the tall redhead, "she manages my business. She was born in New Jersey and I roped her and brought her out here." "He's lying," Jackie, fifty-five, fires back, "because if he'd roped me, I would have been in diapers!" In fact, she first met Gene in 1961 as his Palm Springs banker. In 1984 Jackie spearheaded, with Joanne and Monte Hale, the effort to establish Los Angeles's Gene Autry Western Heritage Museum. Gene's stated goal was to "exhibit and interpret the heritage of the West and show how it has influenced America and the world." Opening in 1988, the spacious facility presents a detailed, multiethnic history of the American West, as well as a rich overview of the mythical West. (In 2005 the museum's scope would broaden to encompass the Southwestern Museum of the American Indian as well as the newly named Museum of the American West and the Institute for the Study of the American West. The new, larger entity would be called the Autry National Center.)

"Gene was a great believer in our Western history," Jackie would later tell the couple's close friend Johny Grant, honorary mayor of Hollywood. "We wanted to make sure it was perpetuated for generations to come. I think the museum, which he's now invested about $100 million in, is certainly a testament to Gene Autry's generosity. Over his lifetime, he's probably given about $180 million to charity"—with several hospitals and schools among the beneficiaries. In 1998 he was listed as one of "America's hundred most generous" by *American Benefactor* magazine. He appeared ten times on the Forbes 400 between 1983 and 1994.

"If the people like it," gene tells me on this spring day about "Back in the Saddle," "you better stick with it." Which is certainly what he did—as long as he could find an audience. He discerns that I'm a fan, and with a flirtatious grin he asks, "Did you bring your Kodak, so we can take a picture together?"

I didn't know it at the time, but Gene had been diagnosed the previous year with lymphoma, and this is to be my only opportunity to meet him in person. That morning, I read in the newspaper that his co-star Gail Davis had just died of cancer. But I don't bring this up—not wanting to spoil the elderly buckaroo's cheery mood. Tragically, many of those closest to Gene would succumb to cancer, including Smiley Burnette, Pat Buttram, Carl Cotner, and in May 1980, Ina Autry. Not long after the couple celebrated their forty-eighth wedding anniversary, she passed away at their Palm Springs home. He renewed his acquaintance with then thirty-nine-year-old Jackie at a New Year's Eve party, and after a whirlwind romance convinced her to marry him. "I think perhaps he was originally attracted to me because I did, in some ways, resemble Ina," according to Jackie. "Between Gene and myself, there was a thirty-four-year age difference, but I don't think age has anything to do with a relationship. I've known people who were the same age and could not get along after a few years, so it's really what's in the heart and how you relate to each other."

Near the end of our visit, I get a little tour of the office. Western artifacts abound, including a lifelike, headdress-wearing Indian, mounted six-shooters originally owned by Wyatt Earp and Wild Bill Hickok, and numerous portraits of Gene, from a hand-tooled leather likeness and a bronze sculpture to vintage movie posters and photographs. As he makes his way around the homey space, aided by a sturdy walking stick (crafted from a petrified bull penis—a gift from Monte Hale), Gene stops again to check out my fancy cowboy boots and embroidered cowgirl ensemble. "I'll tell you the truth, you did real good putting that outfit together," he declares with a twinkle in his eye. "Those are pretty nice boots you got there." Ever the role model, wearing perfectly buffed, ornately decorated red and black boots topped with a harlequin pattern and steer heads, Gene also dispenses a final piece of advice. "Boots are bound to get a little scuffed up," he says, "so you must really work on them."

ON JACKIE AUTRY'S FIFTY-SEVENTH BIRTHDAY, October 2, 1998, Gene died peacefully in his sleep at the couple's Studio City home. At age ninety-one, he succumbed to cardiopulmonary arrest and respiratory failure resulting from the lymphoma. "He used to say, 'I'm going to live forever, but if I go, I'm going to take all my money with me,'" Jackie would tell me with a wistful smile. "Which is why, before he was buried, I put a check in his pocket for 320 million dollars—what Forbes thought he was worth on the date of his death." Four years later, in 2002, the Angels would win the World Series "for the Cowboy."

For me, long after my Gene Autry profile ran in the New York Times, the Singing Cowboy's presence lingered. And after spending nearly a decade poring over the details of his life, I have tried to take the same care in his story's telling that he encouraged me to use on my boots.

NOTES

Note: Abbreviations for frequently cited sources may be found on page 330.

Chapter 1

1. R. A. Brooks and V. M. Bundy, *Descendants of Cornelius Autry, Immigrant*, 307 [log quoted from Samuel A. Courte Ashe, *History of North Carolina*, vol. 1 (North Carolina: Charles L. Van Noppen, 1908, 4]).

2. Ibid. Elijah Henry was born Aug. 15, 1813. He married Polly Parish on Nov. 4, 1832. She was born in 1814, the daughter of Sion Parish, in Granville County, North Carolina.

3. Carroll County Historical Society booklet.

4. *A History of the Baptist Association in Nashville, Tennessee*, with quotes from the records of Carroll County's historic Baptist churches.

5. *History of the Baptist Association*.

6. Ibid.

7. Ibid.

8. Polly Autry died on Oct. 24, 1860.

9. Brooks and Bundy, *Descendants of Cornelius Autry, Immigrant*. Betty was born Jan. 14, 1849 in Carroll County.

10. Dr. Terry G. Jordan, chairman of the department of geography at North Texas State University, quoted in Estes, *I Remember Things*.

11. Information derived from genealogical research conducted by Willeen Ozment Davis.

12. Malinda was born in July 1850, the daughter of Margaret and Wesley Pierce.

13. 1870 Cooke County Federal Census.

14. Elnora's eldest sister Lulu Ozment married John T. Quaid; this line of the family produced actors Randy and Dennis Quaid, who grew up in Texas.

15. 1880 Cooke County Federal Census.

16. Parker and Smallwood, *History Of Cooke County*.

17. Kirsten Gleissner (Gene Autry's niece), interview with the author, June 2006.

18. Some Ozment relatives contend this reunion took place much earlier in Nora's life; others say she was raised by an older sister.

19. Phyllis Engstrom, interview with Maxine Hansen, 2002.

Chapter 2

1. To this day, Autry kinfolk and other church members meet at Indian Creek Cemetery the first Saturday in May, originally to tend to the ground with rakes and hoes, followed by a "dinner on the grounds," in which everyone shares food and swaps stories. Gene Autry's grandparents and mother, along with aunts, uncles, and cousins, are buried there.

2. Estes, *I Remember Things*. E. W. Autry officiated over the March 1907 marriage of author Ross Estes to Annie McBride, who, according to Estes, "helped [Nora] slip her clothes out to marry [her first husband]."

3. Gerald Autry, interviews with the author, Sept. 2001, Sept. 2005.

4. Ibid. Adopted by his maternal grandparents, Roy Patterson grew up to become a jockey and never met his half-brother, Gene Autry. Roy did reunite with Delbert Autry and died in Bakersfield, California, where they both lived at the time.

5. Ibid. Later a rancher's wife in Wyoming, Bessie met her half-brother, Gene Autry, in the 1940s when he performed near her home. In 1982 the clerk of court in Natrona County, Wyoming, contacted Gene Autry to notify him that a Jacqueline F. Carter was to be appointed the legal guardian of his half sister, Bessie A. Middaugh, who apparently suffered from senility. Autry wrote back, "Mrs. Middaugh is my half-sister, however, she was my father's daughter by his first wife [*sic*] and she and I never really knew each other. I believe I only met her one time and therefore am not in a position to express any opinions in this matter. I have noted that she does appear to have a substantial estate and I trust the judgment of the Court to act in her best interests." Gene Autry to Natrona County clerk of court, Aug. 28, 1982.

6. The original birth certificate for Orvon Grover Autry either never existed or was lost. In 1939 a replacement certificate was prepared for Gene Autry by Cooke County registrar Mrs. Maud Hendrix. The name on the certificate was given as Orvon Gene Autry, born Sept. 29, 1907; physician E. E. Ledbetter, MD, of Tioga, Texas, signed the statement that the child was born at 4:30 AM. The certificate included a medical attendant's affidavit, in which Dr. Ledbetter stated that he was "the attendant at this birth, and that he is filing on this date this certificate of birth of Orvon Gene Autry, who was born on the 29 day of Sept., 1907, in lieu of a certificate that cannot now be found, or was not filed at the time." The Notary Public was S. P. Anderson, presumably Sam Anderson, a Tioga barber who employed young Orvon in the early 1920s. (Various other legal documents, including Orvon Autry's school enrollment form to the Achille, Oklahoma, school in 1922, list his birth date as September 29, 1908. Some early newspaper articles from the late 1930s on Gene Autry give this date

as well.) Accompanying the birth certificate mailed to Gene Autry on Feb. 25, 1939, was a letter addressed to him at his office, 6305 Yucca Street, Hollywood, CA, from Mrs. Maud Hendrix, which advised him: "This paper means much to you, in more ways than one. . . . I am due for my part in helping you get what I or we call the most valuable paper you can ever pocess [*sic*] in your life. It will carry you anywhere you want to go. The sum or small fee of $1.00 . . . . please send . . . Gene, I sent your sister a certificate just like I am sending you. I never have heard from her. I wish you would be good enough to write me if she got it, I sure would appreciate it. I'd like to have my pay for it."

7. Apr. 28, 1910, Federal Census report for Cooke County, TX, lists "Delbert Autry, farmer, 26 [*sic*], married 4 years to Nora Ozment, wife, 26 [*sic*], with son Orvon, 2, and Boarder Thomas Aden, 26."

8. Gerald Autry, interview with the author, Sept. 2005.

9. Gene Autry, interview with Mike Oatman, Feb. 14, 1983.

10. Winifred Ozment Johnson, interview with Maxine Hansen, 2002.

11. Autry and Herskowitz, *Back in the Saddle Again*, 3.

12. E. W. Autry died on Apr. 28, 1913, according to his headstone in Indian Creek Cemetery.

13. Gene Autry, interview with Mike Oatman, Feb. 14, 1983.

14. Ellen Kitchen Keene, interview with the author, March 2003.

15. Gene Autry, "I Have Always Tried to Keep My Line of Supplies Open," in *How to Stop Worrying and Start Living* by Dale Carnegie (New York: Simon and Schuster, 1944).

16. Autry and Herskowitz, *Back in the Saddle Again*, 5.

17. Gene Autry, "The Greatest Cowboy of Them All," *American Legion Magazine*, June 1951.

18. Autry and Herskowitz, *Back in the Saddle Again*, 3.

19. Ibid.

20. Gerald Autry, interview with the author.

21. Autry and Herskowitz, *Back in the Saddle Again*, 4. Raymond Priddy would later work for Gene Autry as the driver of his horse trailer.

22. 1920 Federal Census report for town of Achille, in Bryan County, Oklahoma, lists Delbert Autry, 36, laborer, wife Nora, 24 [*sic*], and children Orvan [*sic*], 11; Veda, 8; Willma [*sic*], 6, all born in Texas; and son Dudley, 2 mos. [*sic*], born in Oklahoma. The January 1920 enumeration list for Achille's school district listed among the enrolled "Orvan Autrey [*sic*], age 11, born 9/27/08 [*sic*]; Vada Autrey [*sic*], 9 [*sic*], born 12/15/10 [*sic*], and Wilma Autrey [*sic*], 6, born 4/14/13."

23. *Achille Press*, July 15, 1921.

24. Ibid., Sept. 16, 1921.

25. Vesta Gleissner (Gene Autry's niece), interview with the author, June 2006.

26. *Achille Press*, June 9, 1922; also the Jan. 1922 enumeration list for Achille's school district listed among the enrolled "Orvon Autry, age 13, born 9/27/08 [*sic*]; Veda Autry, 11 [*sic*], born 12/15/10 [*sic*], and Wilma Autry, 8, born 4/14/13." Contradicting this record, though, is Orvon Autry's employment application for the Frisco Railroad (in June, 1925): Listing his education and employment background, he stated that he was a student in school at Achille, OK (age 12) until May 1921 (age 13); in September 1921 he transferred to school in Tioga. The Achille Supt. of Schools confirmed GA "he was in school here don't remember the date."

Chapter 3

1. Estes, *I Remember Things*.
2. Ibid., 17.
3. Autry and Herskowitz, *Back in the Saddle Again*, 7.
4. Bernice Gordon Noah, *Tioga, Texas, Residents Remembering Gene Autry* (TTR-RGA), videotape by Laura Johnson, undated.
5. Velma Chaffin Willett, TTRRGA.
6. Nellie Gordon was born July 2, 1909. Charlene Gordon Brown, interview with the author, Sept. 2001.
7. Bernice Gordon Noah, TTRRGA.
8. Kate Anderson, interview with Jonathan Guyot Smith, 1971.
9. Jim Cook, TTRRGA.
10. Ibid.
11. J. W. "Skeet" Smotherman, to Arvella McKnight (Tioga Historical Society), June 24, 1986.
12. Cook, TTRRGA.
13. Mae Gary Richards, TTRRGA.
14. Unpublished manuscript by Carol Kemp, Dec. 17, 1957.
15. Autry and Herskowitz, *Back in the Saddle Again*, 6.
16. Bessie Patterson, "Hereford Man's Medicine Show Paid Gene Autry First Dollar," *Amarillo Daily News*, Dec. 12., 1951.
17. Ibid.
18. *Tioga Herald*, Sept. 21, 1923.
19. Ibid., Sept. 28, 1923.
20. Charlene Gordon Brown, interview with the author, 2005.
21. Gene Autry, interview with Maxine Hansen, 1994.
22. *High Flyer*, 1925.

Chapter 4

1. Gene may have lived briefly in Ravia in 1915 with his father, around the time the Autrys left Indian Creek for Oklahoma; Johnston County records show a school admittance form filled out on Jan. 24, 1915, by Delbert Autry, of Ravia, for Orvon Autry, whose date of birth was given as 1906 and age as seven; possibly, while Nora and baby daughters stayed with her brother in Achille, Delbert took Orvon with him for a time to Ravia. (Achille school records begin for the Autry children in 1920.)
2. *Daily Oklahoman*, "Fame Hasn't Spoiled Autry Says 'Key Punching' Tutor," Sept. 9, 1941.
3. Helen Conn to Gene Autry, June 28, 1971; *Oklahoman*, "Gene Autry Visits Vinita, Home Town," Mar. 28, 1937: "Autrey [*sic*], a former Frisco station agent at Vinita, stops to visit a while with old friends every time he passes through Vinita."
4. In June 1931 Gene Autry wrote a friend about the Weleetka depot: "That place is high jacked so dam [*sic*] much I don't care about it anyway." Gene Autry to Homer Shurley, June 7, 1931.

5. *Tulsa World-Tribune*, "KVOO History, Like World-Tribune Tied Closely to Tulsa's Development," Nov. 7, 1949.

6. *Tulsa World*, "KVOO to Note Anniversary" Jan. 23, 1955; Wayne Mason, "When Radio Was Young," *Tulsa Sunday World*, Sept. 19, 1971.

7. Wilson went on to become a state legislator and started his own radio station in Sapulpa in 1938. *Oklahoman*, "Station KOME," Dec. 11, 1938.

8. Gene Autry to Mrs. C. W. Webster, Dec. 15, 1959. Gene signed his letter "With Love Always" and wrote to the Websters on Dec. 30, 1954, "love and kisses to you and Ella," terms of affection he rarely used in correspondence.

9. Gene Autry, interview with Ronald L. Davis, director of the Southern Methodist University Oral History programs (SMU-OH), July 24, 1984.

10. Will Rogers, "Daily Telegram," Claremore, June 5, 1927.

11. Eric Estrin, "Gene Autry," *Ultra*, Apr. 1982.

12. Jonathan Guyot Smith, interview with the author, Feb. 2006.

13. Throughout his life, Gene Autry would receive letters from co-workers and relatives of co-workers who remembered his days on the railroad, with details about his singing and entertaining his fellow workers.

14. Autry and Herskowitz, *Back in the Saddle Again*, 11. Years later, Gene would become a close friend of Jack Dempsey.

15. Virginia MacPhail, interview with the author, Feb. 2006.

16. Doug Lemmon, interview with author, 2005.

17. Mary Bryant, "He'd Rather Play Guitar Than Baseball," *Star-Times* (St. Louis), 1950 (day and month unknown).

18. Jack Hurst, "Gene Autry: the Apprenticeship of One Smart Singing Cowboy," *Chicago Tribune*, Aug. 7, 1983.

Chapter 5

1. Gene Autry, *TV Picture Life*, 1955.

2. Beverly Long Moss, interview with the author, 2006.

3. Autry, *TV Picture Life*.

4. Gene Autry, interview with the author, March 1997.

5. Archie Green, *Variety*, Nov. 2, 1955 (reported in "Hillbilly Music: Source and Symbol," *Journal of American Folklore* (July–Sept. 1965); Peer also took credit for naming race and hillbilly music, according to Green, in a Nov. 4, 1957, letter to Green: "I originated the terms 'Hillbilly' and 'Race' as applied to the record business."

6. Whitburn, *Joel Whitburn Presents A Century of Pop Music*.

7. Jon Guyot Smith, "The Role of Johnny Marvin in the Developing Career of Gene Autry," in, *Gene Autry's Friends* (Winter 2005–2006).

8. Frankie Marvin, interview with Douglas B. Green, Apr. 1, 1971, Frist Library and Archive, Country Music Hall of Fame and Museum (FLA-CMHOFAM).

9. Autry and Hershowitz, *Back in the Saddle Again*, 12.

10. Rogers, *Writings of Will Rogers*. The May 1 telegram read:

CHELSEA, OKLA., MAY 1. I GOT THE REAL KICK OF MY LIFE OUT OF AVIATION TODAY. LEFT WESTERN KANSAS AND FLEW DOWN TO OKLAHOMA AND LANDED RIGHT ON THE OLD

RANCH I WAS BORN ON. FIRST MACHINE WAS EVER IN THERE. WHEN I WAS RAISED
THERE, I NEVER THOUGHT THERE WOULD EVER BE ANYTHING FASTER THAN A HORSE
GET IN THERE. I ASK AND PLEAD WITH YOU AGAIN, YOU LUNCHEON CLUBBERS, WILL YOU
PLEASE PAINT THE NAME OF YOUR TOWN ON TOP OF YOUR BUILDING? I WILL PAY FOR
THE PAINT IF YOU WILL DO IT. WE WERE LOST TODAY, AND ALL THE TOWNS IN KANSAS
HAD NO NAMES WE COULD MAKE OUT TILL WE GOT TO BARTLESVILLE, OKLA., WHO HAD
THEIR NAME OUT. ARE YOU ASHAMED OF YOUR TOWN? YOURS, WILL ROGERS.

11. Jim Tully, "Kids Vote Him Tops," *Chicago Daily News*, May 28, 1938.

12. Alva Johnston, "Tenor on Horseback," *Saturday Evening Post*, Sept. 2, 1939.

13. Stan Hayes, "Gene Autry talks about 'My Biggest Break," *National Enquirer*, June 20, 1971: "My biggest break came on a July night in 1925," says multimillionaire singing cowboy Gene Autry. "I was only 17 at the time and working as an Oklahoma railroad telegrapher. . . . I was getting nowhere fast until that night Will Rogers walked into my life. . . . He gave me the encouragement I needed, and I knew I'd never turn back." Autry repeated the story in interviews with Ronald L. Davis (July 24, 1984): "I was working what they called 'second trick,' that's four in the afternoon until midnight . . . [Rogers] came in to send a telegram one night. . . . I did two or three songs, and he said, 'You ought to get yourself a job on the radio or make some records.' " Autry, interview, with Bob Birchard, Apr. 12, 1974: "I'd met Will Rogers during that time, and he had heard me playing and singing, and so he said, 'You know, son, you ought to get yourself a job on the radio.' At first I thought he was just trying to make me feel good, but later on, why, when things got tough on the railroad and it didn't look like I was going to have a job, I thought: Well, if Will Rogers thought I was good enough to be on the radio, maybe I should try it." Ben Yagoda's Will Rogers biography repeats the story: "On one of these trips, [Rogers] walked into the Chelsea telegraph office to file his daily column and found the operator strumming a guitar and singing a tune. . . . When he finished, Will told him he had talent—he should think about going to New York and getting a job on radio. Gene Autry went west instead of east and into movies instead of radio [*sic*]—but he has always considered Will Rogers responsible for his show-business career" (278). Rogers himself never acknowledged his "discovery" of Autry in print or published interviews. Autry eventually met Rogers in Hollywood and received an autographed photo that said "To my friend Gene Autry." In 1949, Will Rogers's family gave permission to Autry to use the story of the Will Rogers telegraph office meeting in Autry's *Melody Ranch* radio show script of November 26.

14. Autry and Hershowitz, *Back in the Saddle Again*, 2.

15. Barbara Barry, "Comin' Round That Mountain," *Screen & Radio Weekly*, 1936 (n.d.).

16. Bond, "Gene Autry, Champion" (courtesy Sherry Bond); Virginia MacPhail, interview with the author, Apr. 2006.

Chapter 6

1. Tommy Overstreet, interview with Barry Mazor, Aug. 10, 2003.

2. Original manuscript written in 1981 by Gene Autry as the foreword to the book, *The Gene Austin Story*.

3. Local Tioga lore has it that many residents named their children after the man who brought them into the world—including Gene Autry. When Gene was a boy, though, he was known as Orvon, and it's unlikely that an affinity for the good doctor would have inspired the name change later on. Regardless, that's the story many of the townsfolk told the press when their hometown boy became a star in the 1930s, and the story has stuck.

4. Autry and Herskowitz, *Back in the Saddle Again*, 12.

5. Gene Autry, interview with Bob Birchard, 1977.

6. Gene Autry, interview with Mike Oatman, Feb. 14, 1983, Los Angeles.

7. Frankie Marvin, interview with Douglas B. Green, Apr. 1, 1975, FLA-CMHOFAM.

8. Ibid.

9. Gene Autry, interview with Ronald L. Davis, July 24, 1984, SMU-OH.

10. Gene Autry, "The First Round-Up," *Guideposts*, Sept. 1949.

11. *Tulsa World*, "Former Tulsa 'Brass Pounder' Sings Way to Fame Via Records," June 21, 1931.

12. Beverly Long Moss, interview with author, Mar. 2006.

13. Autry, "I Have Always Tried to Keep My Line of Supplies Open."

14. Gene Autry, interview with Ronald L. Davis, July 24, 1984, SMU-OH.

15. Frankie and Johnny Marvin, in a conversation with Johnny Bond in Bond, *Gene Autry, Champion* (courtesy Sherry Bond).

16. Frankie Marvin, interview with Douglas B. Green, Apr. 1, 1975, FLA-CMHOFAM.

Chapter 7

1. Autry and Herskowitz, *Back in the Saddle Again*, 14.

2. *Tulsa Daily World*, "Tulsa Show Man Claimed by Death," Aug. 23, 1941; Ashton Stevens, "Now Speaking of Gene Autry," *Chicago Sun-Times*, Nov. 24, 1941; *Tulsa Daily World*, "Robert Ridley, Autry's Guitar Instructor, Dies," undated clip; untitled item, *Radio News*, Oct. 21, 1933.

3. William B. Way, Gustav K. Brandborg, and Ted Walters of KVOO to Gene Autry, January 13, 1949; Gene Autry to William B. Way, January 24, 1949.

4. Frisco railroad records.

5. Helen Paul, interview with author, 2005.

6. Catoosa Historical Society, *History of Catoosa*, 2004.

7. Frankie Marvin, interview with Douglas B. Green, Apr. 1, 1974.

8. Autry, interview with Mike Oatman, Feb. 14, 1983.

9. Autry and Herskowitz, *Back in the Saddle Again*, 15.

10. Giddins, *Bing Crosby*, 117–18.

Chapter 8

1. Gene Autry, interview with Johnny Grant, Nov. 1991, at National Cowboy Museum and Hall of Fame, Oklahoma City.

2. Eddy Arnold, interview with Barry Mazor, 2003.

3. Gene Autry, interview with Mike Oatman, Feb. 14, 1983. Throughout his life,

in correspondence, oral histories, and interviews, Autry recalled his acquaintance with Rodgers, including an interview with this author in March 1997 when he was eighty-nine years old: "I knew Jimmie Rodgers very well," he told me. "I guess I tried to yo-del when I was younger, after Jimmie started. I was a good friend of his, and we got along good together, and I learned a lot from Jimmie Rodgers. He was a very good singer. He was from Mississippi to start with, he worked on the railroad in the South—and that kind of grew on me too—but then his home later was close to San Antonio, Texas."

4. Ibid.

5. Bond, "Gene Autry, Champion" (courtesy Sherry Bond).

6. Time/Life Books, *Time Capsule 1929.*

7. Frankie Marvin, interview with Douglas B. Green, Apr. 1, 1975, FLA-CMHOFAM.

8. *Frisco Employes Magazine*, "He Makes Records: Gene Autry of Sapulpa Scores as Recording Artist," Feb. 1930, 21.

Chapter 9

1. Whitewater Valley Gorge Park Committee, *History of the Whitewater Gorge* (Richmond, IN: Richmond Area Chamber of Commerce, 1983).

2. Grover T. O'Dell, of the Union Pacific Railroad Company, to Gene Autry, Nov. 8, 1971.

3. Kennedy, *Jelly Roll, Bix and Hoagy*, 1.

4. Ibid.

5. Packy Smith, liner notes, "Gene Autry: That Silver Haired Daddy of Mine."

6. According to the U.S. Census Bureau, 50–63.4 percent of families in Illinois, New York, and California owned radio sets.

7. David Kapp, "Reminiscences," (1959), reported in Barnouw, *Tower in Babel: A History of Broadcasting in the United States to 1933.*

8. Betty Barr, "Autry Leaves Friends, Memories in Aurora," *Beacon-News*, Nov. 15, 1991.

9. Amy Kolzow, "Stylish Auroran Was Dashing Haberdasher," *Beacon-News*, Aug. 27, 1995.

10. Barr, "Autry Leaves Friends."

11. Gene Autry to George Biggar, July 26, 1968.

Chapter 10

1. Kingsbury, *Encyclopedia of Country Music.*

2. David Ferrell, "Autry Goes on the Record: Uncle Art Got It All Started," *Santa Ana Register*, Aug. 9, 1983.

3. Arthur Satherley, interviews with Ed Kahn, June and July 1969; John Edward's Memorial Foundation, University of North Carolina at Chapel Hill.

4. Arthur Satherley, interview with Douglas B. Green, June 27, 1974, FLA-CMHOFAM.

5. Gene Autry, interview with Ronald L. Davis, July 24, 1984, SMU-OH.

6. Sutton and Nauck, *American Record Labels and Companies*.

7. Author, interview with Jonathan Guyot Smith, Feb. 2006. Gene's perfect rendition of "TB Blues" resulted in it accidentally being used by RCA on its 1978 compilation *Jimmie Rodgers: A Legendary Performer*.

8. Gene Autry to Homer Shurley, June 7, 1931.

Chapter 11

1. One of Gene's correspondents, H. L. "Homer" Shurley, wrote Gene in 1970, saying, "I just happened to run across one of the letters you wrote to me in 1931. . . . And I was just thinking how much things have changed since then especially in the music world. . . . I shall never forget the days when you were in Weleetka, and the good times we use [*sic*] to have." Gene responded on Sept. 30, 1970, "I do remember you and your sister very well. . . . I also remember the agent and yardmaster for the Fort Smith & Western Railway that was a partner, I believe, with your sister at that time."

2. Gene Autry to Callie Jane Autry, October 20, 1931.

3. Arthur Satherley, interview with Douglas B. Green, June 27, 1974, FLA-CMHOFAM.

4. In 1983 Gene told *Chicago Tribune* columnist Jack Hurst, "The idea of 'That Silver Haired Daddy of Mine' came from a song I heard as a kid called 'Dear Old Daddy, You've Been More Than a Mother to Me.' Another guy and I . . . got together and wrote 'That Silver Haired Daddy of Mine.'" Jack Hurst, "Gene Autry: The Apprenticeship of One Smart Singing Cowboy," *Chicago Tribune*, Aug, 7, 1983.

5. Author interview, with veteran record executive Jerry Wexler, June 2006.

6. Arthur Satherley, interview with Douglas B. Green, June 27, 1974, FLA-CMHOFAM.

7. Gene Autry, interview with Mike Oatman, Feb. 14, 1983.

8. Ibid.

9. Benjamin F. "Whitey" Ford, interview with John W. Rumble, July 13, 1984, FLA-CMHOFAM.

10. Autry to Shurley, July 17, 1931.

Chapter 12

1. Autry and Herskowitz, *Back in the Saddle Again*, 16.

2. "Radio Station WLS," from Sears, Roebuck and Company, one-hundredth anniversary book, 1986.

3. "Bring Home the Bacon" was vaudevillian Grace Wilson's first big pop hit, hence the nickname.

4. Karl Davis, "Gene Autry at WLS," Feb. 19, 1976.

5. *WLS Family Album, Prairie Farmer*, 1931.

6. Arthur Satherley, interview with Douglas B. Green, June 27, 1974, FLA-CMHOFAM.

7. Eleanor Lang Chapin to Maxine Hansen, June 7, 2004.

8. "3 Pals" by Gene Autry, *Country Song Roundup*, n.d.

9. Gruhn and Carter, *Acoustic Guitars and Other Fretted Instruments* (San Francisco: GPI Books, 1993).

10. Gene Autry, interview with Ronald L. Davis, July 24, 1984, SMU-OH.

11. Jack Hurst, "One Smart Singing Cowboy," *Chicago Tribune*, Aug. 7, 1983.

12. Nora Autry to Beulah Ozment, February 4, 1932.

13. Beverly Long Moss, interview with the author, February 2006.

14. Ina Kay Karns Leffler, interview with the author, August 2005.

15. *Duncan High School Yearbook* (courtesy of Stephens County Historical Society, Duncan, OK).

16. Judy Proctor, Southwest Missouri State University records assistant, to Autry researcher Wayne Glenn, Aug. 19, 1988.

17. Mrs. Gene Autry, "Open Letter to Gene Autry," *Movie Stars Parade*, Apr. 1949.

18. *Movie Thrills*, "Gene Autry's Love Story," Sept. 1950.

19. Ina Autry, "Private Life of Gene" (fan magazine clipping, ca. 1950).

Chapter 13

1. Gene Autry to Martin, January 2, 1932, Martin Guitar archives, Nazareth, PA.

2. Gene Autry, interview with Kenneth E. Baughman, July 5, 1990; Gene Autry, interview with Mike Oatman, Feb. 14, 1983.

3. Violet Petranoff to Gene Autry, July 16, 1986.

4. Orvon Autry to Bob Ozment, Feb. 16, 1932.

5. Gene Autry, interview with Kenneth E. Baughman, July 5, 1990.

6. Ibid.

7. Bob Greene, "His Barn Dance Ended . . . Melody Doesn't Linger," *Chicago Tribune*, Mar. 4, 1973.

8. Helen M. Patton to Gene Autry, May 30, 1984; Elsie Harms, "Autry Letter Makes Birthday Special," *Clipper-Journal*, May 31, 1984; Gene Autry to Helen M. Patton, May 16, 1984.

9. Arthur Satherley, interview with Douglas B. Green, June 27, 1974, FLA-CMIIOFAM.

10. Gene Autry, "Confessions of a Cowboy," undated/uncredited clipping from scrapbook; Alva Johnston, "Tenor on Horseback," *Saturday Evening Post*, Sept. 2, 1939.

11. Ina Autry, "Marry Your Man for Keeps," undated, uncredited clipping from scrapbook.

12. Anita Spivey Karns, interview with Don and Ina Karns Leffler.

13. Autry and Herskowitz, *Back in the Saddle Again*, 16.

14. Gene Autry," *TV Picture Life*, ca. 1955 (untitled clipping from a scrapbook); Orvon Autry and Ina Mae Spivey marriage license, St. Louis, Missouri, Apr. 1, 1932.

15. Ina Autry, "Gene Autry, My Hero," undated, uncredited clipping from scrapbook.

16. Ina Autry, "Marry Your Man for Keeps," undated/uncredited clipping from scrapbook.

17. Ina Karns Leffler, interview with the author, August 2005.

Chapter 14

1. Autry and Herskowitz, *Back in the Saddle Again*, 7.

2. Gene Autry. interview with Ronald L. Davis, July 24, 1984, SMU-OH.

3. James F. Evans, *Prairie Farmer and WLS*; Wayne W. Daniel, "WLS National Barn Dance," *Old Time Country* (Spring): 1992; Jack Hurst, "Barn Dance Days," *Bluegrass Unlimited*, Apr. 1986.

4. Stephen Cisler, interview with John Rumble, Feb. 20, 1984, FLA-CMHOFAM.

5. Nora Autry to Orvon Autry, May 8, 1932.

6. Winifred Ozment, interview with Maxine Hansen, June 14, 2000.

7. Sears, Roebuck catalogue, Fall 1932.

Chapter 15

1. Arthur Satherley, interview with Douglas B. Green, June 27, 1974, FLA-CMHOFAM.

2. Frankie Marvin, interview with Douglas B. Green, Apr. 1, 1975, FLA-CMHOFAM.

3. *Frisco Employes' Magazine*, "Frisco in Receivership Nov. First," Dec. 1932. The railroad's magazine reported: "Frisco employes throughout the nine-state territory served by the railroad read the newspapers on the morning of November 2 with feelings of deep regret. Therein they saw that the St. Louis-San Francisco Railway Company had entered receivership the day before in Federal Court at St. Louis, and they realized that the Depression and unregulated competition had at last, despite a gallant fight, forced a fine railroad system to temporarily accept receivership."

4. Beverly Long Moss, interview with the author, Mar. 2006.

5. Edwin Darby, "Gene Autry Riding Range in High Style," *Chicago Sun-Times*, July 4, 1963.

6. Virginia MacPhail, interview with the author, January 2006.

7. Kirsten Gleissner, interview with the author, July 5, 2006.

8. Joseph Kaye, "Gene Autry Tells His Own Story," uncredited magazine clipping from scrapbook, ca. 1949.

9. Undated handbill (courtesy Dick Hill).

10. Eleanor Lang Chapin to Maxine Hansen, June 7, 2004.

11. Gene Autry to Eleanor Lang Chapin, June 27, 1995.

12. *Frets Magazine*, "The Dreadnought Story," May 1988; C. F. Martin website; Gruhn and Carter, *Acoustic Guitars*.

13. Allen St. John, "That's One Big, Beautiful Guitar," *Wall Street Journal*, Jan. 21–22, 2006; Gene Autry's guitar is on exhibit at the Autry National Center Museum of the American West in Los Angeles; a letter he wrote to Fred Martin is on exhibit at the C. F. Martin Museum in Nazareth, Pennsylvania; Kurt Blumeran, "Martin's New Museum Gets in Tune with Visitors," *Morning Call*, Jan. 12, 2006.

14. Jon Guyot Smith, "Gene Autry on Victor Records: Elusive Collector's Items Throughout the Years," *Gene Autry Friends*, Spring/Summer 2005.

15. According to the Victor Recording Book ledger, the session immediately following Gene's that day was Louis Armstrong and his orchestra, which cut three "fox trots" between 1 and 5 PM.

Chapter 16

1. Green, *Singing in the Saddle*, 8.

2. Ibid., 15.

3. Gene Autry, interview with Mike Oatman, Feb. 14, 1983.

4. Eddie Brown to Gene Autry, July 23, 1986.

5. Gene Autry, *Art of Writing Songs*.

6. Jack Hurst, "Barn Dance Days," *Bluegrass Unlimited*, Apr. 1986.

7. Wade Hall, *Hell-Bent for Music*.

8. Undated handbill (courtesy Dick Hill).

9. Benjamin F. "Whitey" Ford, interview with John Rumble, July 13, 1984, FLA-CMHOFAM.

10. Pee Wee King, interview with Douglas B. Green, Mar. 8, 1974, FLA-CMHOFAM.

11. Ford, interview with John Rumble.

12. Ibid.; Ford, interview with Douglas Green, Jan. 22, 1975, both FLA-CMHOFAM.

13. Art Satherley, interview with Douglas Green, June 27, 1974.

14. The ARC ledgers and recording card for the session do not list the names of Gene's singing partner or accompanists.

15. The recording date of Gene's risqué numbers were not listed in the ARC log or any other log. Circulated for years among collectors, the tracks possibly originated from Roy Smeck's private collection. They were released for the first time on CD in 2006 on the nine-CD Bear Family box set, *That Silver Haired Daddy of Mine*, documenting Gene's every recording from 1929–33. The two tracks came as a shock to most longtime Gene Autry fans. A different version, titled "Bye Bye Cherry," was released in the 1970s on *Copulatin' Blues*, a vinyl compilation of hokum songs; this one opened with four lines about deflowering a virgin.

16. Gene Autry correspondence to Raymond Hall, Sept. 9, 1933; the letter was found in the Huntsville State Prison files by Rodgers biographer Nolan Porterfield. It is unknown if Gene ever recorded any of Hall's songs except for "Moonlight and Skies," which was credited to and recorded by Jimmie Rodgers and which Hall later contended he wrote. Hall told journalist Tom Miller, "Clayton McMichen . . . had discovered Gene Autry at a Chicago theater, and Gene, he came down to see Jimmie and asked him, 'Man, where you gettin' them kind of songs like "The Gamblin' Polka Dot Blues"?' Well, Jimmie, he told him, 'I got a man in the penitentiary down there, all you gotta do is give him a title and he'll send you a complete song by return mail.'" When Hall was finally released from prison in the mid-'70s, he wrote to "my admired friend Gene Autry" on July 25, 1981, asking for the help he had promised in the 1933 letter. He also wrote that Gene had referred Jimmie Davis to him in the 1930s, that Davis had recorded two of Hall's songs but never paid him royalties or given him credit for the songs. There is no record that Gene ever again contacted Hall, who died Jan. 27, 1983.

17. *Radio News*, Oct. 21, 1933.

Chapter 17

1. Gene Autry, interview with HFI-OHP, July 22, 1971, Columbia University collection.

2. Stephen Burnette, interview with the author, June 6, 2006.

3. Smiley's own account of this initial phone conversation, which he said occurred on Dec. 19, 1933, varied only slightly from Gene's. He related that his response when the well-known WLS star first gave him his name was, "Sure, and I'm General Grant." He also gave his WDZ income as $12.50 and $18 in various tellings: Undated Smiley Burnette publicity biography (Mitchell Hamilberg Agency); Jon Guyot Smith, interview with the author, Feb. 2006.

4. Gene Autry, interview with Len Morris, for the AMC documentary, *Melody of the West*, ca. 1991–94.

5. Gene Autry. interview with the HFI-OHP, July 22, 1971.

6. Patsy Montana, interview with John W. Rumble, Aug. 30, 1985, FLA-CMHOFAM.

7. Arthur Satherley, interview with Douglas Green, June 27, 1974, FLA-CMHOFAM.

8. Jimmie Dale and the Oklahoma Cowboys may have accompanied Gene on May 17, 1933 as "his Trio" and again on June 22, 1933, on "In the Valley of the Moon"; listed as Ray Weston in Gene's ledger, he was probably guitarist Don Weston, who played on Gene's recordings and occasional personal appearances.

9. Gene Autry, interview with Mike Oatman, Feb. 14, 1983.

10. Tex Atchison to Johnny Bond in 1972, quoted in Bond, "Johnny Bond—My 30 Years With Gene Autry" (courtesy Stanley Rojo).

11. *Tulsa World*, "WLS Roundup Played to Prison Audience," Mar. 24, 1934.

12. As told to Douglas Green by an unnamed source, and repeated to Wesley Rose in an interview on Mar. 12, 1975, FLA-CMHOFAM.

13. Atchison, "Johnny Bond—My 30 Years With Gene Autry" (courtesy Stanley Rojo).

14. Autry and Herskowitz, *Back in the Saddle Again*, 19.

15. Wade Hall, *Hell-Bent for Music*, 30–31.

16. In 1971, King and Autry became business partners when Gene bought King's publishing company Ridgeway Music.

17. Arthur Satherley, interview with Ed Kahn, John Edwards Memorial Foundation, May 21, 1977, University of North Carolina–Chapel Hill collection.

18. Autry, interview with Oatman, Feb. 14, 1983; Gene Autry, interview with Len Morris, ca. 1991.

Chapter 18

1. Gene Autry, "The Greatest Cowboy of Them All," magazine clipping from a scrapbook, ca. 1951.

2. Pee Wee King, interview with Douglas Green, Mar. 8, 1974, FLA-CMHOFAM.

3. Johnny Brousseau reminiscence, "A Fabulous Man," sent to Gene Autry, Apr. 1971. (Whether Maynard had actually mentioned Gene to the movie boss is unknown.)

Gene's correspondence to Brousseau in response, Apr. 8, 1971, read: " I was so happy to have your letter and your review of the different situations that came up over the years that you brought to my mind, many of which I had completely forgotten. I shall always treasure them and also your loyalty and integrity when you were associated with me."

4. This item marks Gene's first-ever mention in the *Los Angeles Times*.

5. Smiley Burnette reminiscence on *Melody Ranch*, 1963.

6. Autry and Herskowitz, *Back in the Saddle Again*, 37.

7. Gene Autry, interview with Mike Oatman, Feb. 14, 1983.

8. Jon Tuska, *The Winning of the West* (New York: Doubleday, 1976), 294.

9. Initially formed as the Pioneer Trio in 1933, the group originally included Nolan, Tim Spencer, and Leonard Slye (who later changed his name to Roy Rogers). Hugh and Karl Farr had joined the group by 1935.

10. Brousseau, "A Fabulous Man," April 1971.

11. Autry and Herskowitz, *Back in the Saddle Again*, 38.

12. Jack Hurst, "One Smart Singing Cowboy," *Chicago Tribune*, Aug. 7, 1983.

13. Len Morris, interview with Gene Autry, ca. 1991.

14. Tuska, *Winning of the West*, 300.

15. Ibid., 303.

16. Mascot Productions interoffice correspondence from B. Benjamin to Nat Levine, Sept. 4, 1934, and copy of Mascot contract; Gene is listed as "actor-writer-collaborator-composer."

17. Autry, "Greatest Cowboy of Them All."

Chapter 19

1. Sammie Jackson, Jackson Theatre, Flomaton, Alabama: "What the Picture Did for Me" column, *Motion Picture Herald*, Jan. 5, 1935, 60.

2. Cole Porter wrote "Don't Fence Me In" in 1934 for an unproduced film (possibly *Adios Argentina*), but it wasn't recorded until 1944: Roy Rogers sang it first in the film *Hollywood Canteen*, and Gene recorded it that same year.

3. Tuska, *Winning of the West*, 294.

4. Gene's letter to Molson, referred to by Fier, has not surfaced.

5. Gene Autry to Joe Kelly, Feb. 26, 1955, in response to a Feb. 14, 1955, letter from Kelly to Autry that stated: "Have watched you climb the ladder of success ever since Art Satherly [*sic*] and myself advised you to leave WLS and strike out for Hollywood and picture work."

6. In the mid-1930s, Burnette's first name in correspondence, on recordings, and on some documents was frequently spelled "Smilie"; "Smiley" became the standard spelling and was the one used in movie titling.

7. Tex Atchison, interview with Johnny Bond, reported in Bond, *Gene Autry, Champion*.

8. "Whitey" Ford, interview with John Rumble, July 13, 1984, FLA-CMHOFAM.

Chapter 20

1. "Tumbling Tumbleweeds" was released on Columbia and other ARC labels in Feb. 1935 and was designated a hit by *Billboard*.

2. According to Gene's 1934 tax return, he also spent $165.75 that year for his horse's trainer and their feed. He gave various accounts of where he bought the first of several similar-looking sorrels. Equestrian authority Petrine Mitchum, in her thorough and well-researched study of film horses (Mitchum and Pavia, *Hollywood Hoofbeats*), hypothesizes that the original Champ was acquired by Gene from the Hudkins Brothers Stables, a company that provided horses for Republic, and that the horse may have originated from Oklahoma, which is where Gene frequently said he came from.

3. As many as four Champion doubles were used for distant shots of a galloping horse and for scenes where a stuntman replaces Gene.

4. Fitzgerald and Magers, *Ladies of the Western*, 243–44.

5. Jon Guyot Smith, "The Wonderful Ann Rutherford," *Gene Autry Friends*, Spring/Summer 1997.

6. Fitzgerald and Magers, *Ladies of the Western*, 244.

7. Smith, "The Wonderful Ann Rutherford."

8. Ibid.

9. Princess Theatre ad, Tishomingo, OK, Sept. 26, 1935 (courtesy Glenn White).

10. *Hollywood Reporter*, Sept. 5 and 19, 1935.

11. *Los Angeles Times*, "Film Groups Consolidate," Oct. 15, 1935.

12. *Los Angeles Times*, "Popularity of Western Stars Enable Outdoor Productions to Continue," Dec. 4, 1935.

Chapter 21

1. Art Davis, interview with Douglas B. Green, Feb. 26, 1976, FLA-CMHOFAM.

2. Alva Johnston, "Tenor on Horseback," *Saturday Evening Post*, Sept. 2, 1939.

3. Gene Autry, interview with the author, Mar. 1997.

4. Autry and Herskowitz, *Back in the Saddle Again*, 18–19.

5. Gene Autry, interview with the Hollywood Film Institute Oral History Program (HFI-OHP), July 22, 1971.

6. Frankie Marvin, interview with Douglas B. Green and Johnny Bond, Apr. 1, 1975, FLA-CMHOFAM.

7. Johnny Ferguson, "Goodale's Been Angel to Autry," *Tulsa World*, Dec. 27, 1979. Gene never forgot Goodale's loyalty; after the publicist's retirement from the Angels, Gene paid for his living expenses until Goodale's death.

8. Gene Autry to Nat Levine, Feb. 24, 1936.

9. Nat Levine telegram to Gene Autry, May 9, 1936.

10. Trem Carr had left Republic in 1935, followed the next year by Way Ray Johnston.

Chapter 22

1. Virginia Long MacPhail, interview with the author, Jan. 2006.

2. Read Kendall, "Around and About Hollywood," *Los Angeles Times*, May 28, 1936.

3. Dorothy Phillips Bowman, interview with the author, 2001.

4. Virginia Long MacPhail, interview with the author, Mar. 2006.

5. Whitney Williams, "Singing Cowboy," *Screen Book*, Aug. 1937.

6. Barbara Barry, "Comin' 'Round That Mountain: Gene Autry, the Singing Cowboy, Helps to Bring the Westerns Up to Date by Warbling Some Fancy Notes," *Screen & Radio Weekly*, 1936.

7. Green, *Singing in the Saddle*, 152.

8. Gene told this story, as did Jimmy Wakely (to Doug Green, June 25, 1974) and Johnny Bond, related in his unpublished manuscript, "Champion" (courtesy Sherry Bond).

9. Ibid., 156.

10. Dallas MacDonnell, "Roamin' Around in Hollywood with Dallas MacDonnell," *Hollywood Citizen News*, Dec. 4, 1935.

11. Gene Autry, interview with Ronald L. Davis, July 24, 1984, SMU-OH.

12. Bowman, interview with the author, 2001.

Chapter 23

1. Bob Myers, "Autry One Man Conglomerate," *Columbus Dispatch*, Aug. 16, 1970.

2. For Gene's first White House visit in late 1937, he wore a "cowboy suit of snow white chamois," according to the Republic press book for *Boots and Saddles*.

3. Rosalind Shaffer, "Singing Cowboy Corrals Fans," *Chicago Sunday Tribune*, Nov. 21, 1937.

4. Jonathan Guyot Smith, "The Wonderful Ann Rutherford," *Gene Autry's Friends* (Spring/Summer 1997).

5. "High Salaries Paid in Nation in 1937 as Listed by Treasury," *New York Times*, Apr. 8, 1939. According to the survey, "the biggest corporation salary" paid in 1937 was $1,161,753, earned by movie mogul Louis B. Mayer, vice president of MGM and production executive of Loew's Inc. Nearly 50,000 people were included on the list compiled by the Treasury Department of those Americans earning $15,000 or more from corporations. The 1,132-page report was submitted to Congress on Apr. 7, 1939, and afterwards, Congress "revised the law requiring the report" so that 1938's list would "be limited to salaries of $75,000 and up."

6. *Chicago Sunday Tribune*, Nov. 21, 1937.

7. E. V. Durling, "On the Side with E. V. Durling, *Los Angeles Times*, Dec. 31, 1937.

8. Smith, "The Wonderful Ann Rutherford."

9. Soon to be a pop standard, "Blue Hawaii" later formed the basis for the 1961 Elvis Presley movie of the same name.

10. Art Davis, interview with Douglas B. Green, Feb. 26, 1976, FLA-CMHOFAM.

11. Wanda Hale, "Autry at Best in His Latest Central Film," *New York Daily News*, Aug. 17, 1938.

12. David Rothel, *Singing Cowboys*, 28.

13. Edwin Schallert, "Gleanings from Studio Citadel," *Los Angeles Times*, Dec. 30, 1937.

14. "News of the Screen," *New York Times*, Dec. 21, 1937. Shirley Temple and William Powell won first and second place in the general category. According to Edwin Schallert's Dec. 27, 1937, column in the *Los Angeles Times*, the Western category was led by Gene Autry, followed by William Boyd (as Hopalong Cassidy), with Buck Jones, Dick Foran, George O'Brien, and Tex Ritter trailing behind.

Chapter 24

1. Rothel, *Singing Cowboys*, 28.

2. Edwin Schallert, "Gene Autry Battles Studio," *Los Angeles Times*, Jan. 27, 1938.

3. R. B. C. Howell to Gene Autry, Dec. 19, 1952: "It has been a long time since that day you appeared in the Chancery Court here while I was Chancellor and I enjoyed the dinner with you at the Belle Meade Country Club."

4. Autry and Herskowitz, *Back in the Saddle Again*, 62.

5. "Gene Rides Again," *New York Times*, Apr. 3, 1938.

6. Frederick C. Othman, "Cowboy Gene Autry Goes on Strike for More Money," *Chicago Daily News*, Feb. 16, 1938.

7. Rogers and Evans, *Happy Trails*, 69.

8. Roy Rogers, in a conversation with Gene Autry, televised on TNN's *Melody Ranch Theater*, 1987.

9. In Rogers's memoir, he wrote that Yates wanted him to use the first name "Leroy," which Rogers hated and shortened to Roy—Yates approved of the alliteration, and Siegel liked it, according to Rogers, because *roi* was French for king.

10. Roy did sing "Dust" in the film, thus Gene never got to perform this evocative song in a picture, although his recording of it sold well on various labels. Republic paid Gene and Johnny Marvin fifty dollars for the use of "Dust," which received an Academy Award nomination for its use in *Under Western Stars*.

11. Rothel, *Singing Cowboys*, 28.

12. Gene Autry to Sue Allison, Aug. 29, 1980.

13. Jacobs, *Kenton Cast Iron Toys*, 8, 126.

14. Carl Drumm, "Down on the Farm, *Kenton News Republican*, Aug. 5, 1938.

15. Ibid.

16. "Kenton Theater Sets Attendance Record Monday," *Kenton News Republican*, Aug. 9, 1938.

17. Evans and Middlebrook, *Cowboy Guitars*, 22, 26.

18. Jim Tully, "Kids Vote Him Tops," *Los Angeles Times*, May 29, 1938.

19. Jonathan Guyot Smith, "An Informal History of the Gene Autry Friendship Club," *Gene Autry Friends*, Spring/Summer 1997.

20. Autry and Herskowitz, *Back in the Saddle Again*, 63.

21. In 1946 the Department of Justice banned block booking, determining it was a restraint-of-trade practice.

22. Hall, *Hell-Bent for Music*, 34.

23. Ibid.

24. "Hedda Hopper's Hollywood," *Los Angeles Times*, June 21, 1938.

Chapter 25

1. Dorothy Phillips Bowman, interview with the author, 2001.

2. *Los Angeles Times*, "Hedda Hopper's Hollywood," Dec. 6, 1939.

3. *Los Angeles Times*, "Autrys Dedicate Pool with Party," June 16, 1940.

4. John Woodruff Rumble, "Fred Rose and the Development of the Nashville Music Industry, 1942–1954" (PhD diss., Vanderbilt University, 1980).

5. Gene Autry to Lorene H. Rose, Nov. 11, 1968.

6. The publishing company's original spelling was West'rn Music.

7. Ray Whitley, interview with Douglas B. Green, July 1, 1974, FLA-CMHOFAM.

8. Stephen Burnette, interview with author, June 6, 2006.

9. A lifelong Mason, Gene went through both the Scottish Rite and the York Rite, and eventually received the Grand Cross—a top honor among Masons. According to his second wife, Jackie Autry, Gene was more proud of this than any of his other achievements.

10. *Los Angeles Times*, "Shrine Charity Ball Tonight Will Draw Crowd of 12,000," Nov. 23, 1938.

11. *New York Times*, "Film Folk Entertain Dust Bowl Children," Dec. 25, 1938.

12. *Los Angeles Times*, "On the Side with E. V. Durling," Nov. 15, 1938.

13. Autry and Herskowitz, *Back in the Saddle Again*, 67.

14. June Storey to Gene Autry, undated.

15. John L. Scott, "Horse Opera Vogue Revived," *Los Angeles Times*, Mar. 5, 1939; Frances S. Nugent, "A Horse of Another Color," *New York Times*, Mar. 12, 1939.

16. Douglas W. Churchill, "We'll Head 'Em Off at Eagle Pass," *New York Times*, Apr. 23, 1939.

17. *Oklahoman*, "Autry Tour Off! Europe Is Restless," Apr. 16, 1939.

18. Montana, *Cowboy's Sweetheart*, 82–83.

19. Bosley Crowther, "A Cowboy Without a Lament," *New York Times*, Aug. 6, 1939.

20. Gene would attend Mix's star-studded funeral in 1940, and when a monument was erected in Mix's honor in Florence, Arizona (the site of his fatal accident), Gene would be guest speaker at the ceremony.

21. Douglas W. Churchill, "Transformations in Hollywood," *New York Times*, Mar. 26, 1939.

22. Gene Autry, conversation with Pat Buttram, televised on *Melody Ranch Theater*, TNN, 1987.

23. *Glasgow Herald*, "Actor Mobbed in Glasgow," Aug. 21, 1939; *Daily Record*, "50,000 Welcome Cowboy Gene," Aug. 21, 1939; *Belfast News-Letter*, "Cowboy Star Mobbed," Aug. 15, 1939.

24. Gene Autry, interview with the author, Mar. 18, 1997.

25. *Evening Dispatch*, "Singing Cowboy Star Admires our Golf Links," Aug. 17, 1939.

26. *Los Angeles Times*, "Studios Call Stars Back from War-Menaced Europe," Aug. 26, 1939.

Chapter 26

1. Alva Johnston, "Tenor on Horseback," *Saturday Evening Post*, Sept. 2, 1939, 18–19, 74, 76.

2. David Cantwell, "Pennies From Heaven," *No Depression*, Nov.–Dec. 2006.

3. Autry and Herskowitz, *Back in the Saddle Again*, 20.

4. Doug Davis, "Now There Was a Song," *Texarkana Gazette*, Apr. 21, 2006.

5. *Daily Variety*, "In Old Monterey," July 22, 1939.

6. Mary Lee Wooters, "Me," autobiographical profile written for Republic Pictures, May 10, 1940.

7. *Los Angeles Times*, "Jimmie Fidler in Hollywood," Sept. 16, 1939.

8. Gene Autry to the CMA, undated.

9. *New York Times*, "Studio News and Notes," Jan. 7, 1940.

10. Gene Autry to Walter Winchell, Feb. 7, 1940.

11. Cheshire would eventually appear on Los Angeles radio station KMPC (a station later owned by Gene Autry) with his singing group, the Plainsmen, featuring Red Rowe and Carolina Cotton (a future Autry co-star), as well as being featured in the movies, including Gene's 1946 picture, *Sioux City Sue*.

12. Philip K. Scheuer, "Town Called Hollywood," *Los Angeles Times*, Aug. 4, 1940.

13. Boyd Magers, "From Rocky to Audie: An Interview with Producer Gordon Kay," *Western Clippings*, Fall 2005.

14. *Los Angeles Times*, "Jimmie Fidler in Hollywood," Aug. 13, 1940.

15. Rothel, *Singing Cowboys*, 24.

16. Bond, *Gene Autry, Champion*, 46–47 (courtesy Sherry Bond).

17. Ibid., 54–55.

18. Columbia Broadcasting System press release, Sept. 1940.

19. Autry and Herskowitz, *Back in the Saddle Again*, 145.

20. George A. Mooney, "Youth's Model 1940," *New York Times*, Oct. 27, 1939.

21. *New York Times*, "Rooney Tops Stars as Money Maker," Dec. 27, 1939.

Chapter 27

1. The majority of Gene's 1940 income: $67,450 from Republic, $65,000 from Wrigley, a reported $42,000 in personal appearance fees (although it may have been higher), and $29,941 in royalties.

2. Ray Whitley, interview with Douglas B. Green, 1974, FLA-CMHOFAM.

3. Les Gilliam, interview with the author, 2001.

4. Ibid.

5. *Tioga Herald*, editorial, Dec. 20, 1936; Sam Blair, *Dallas Morning News*, "Tall Tales from Tioga," Oct. 20, 1993, 1C; A. C. Greene, "Autry's Hometown Clung to Its Identity," *Dallas Morning News*, Feb. 19, 1995, 48A; James Hilliard, interview with the author, 2001. In 1961 an attorney interested in purchasing a section of Tioga contacted Gene with the proposition of changing the town's name, to which he responded: "I think this has been discussed pro and con in the past, and I would rather just let it stay the way it is rather than get into any more controversies" (Gene Autry to James R. Wiley, October 27, 1961).

6. Bond, "Gene Autry, Champion," 71–72.

7. Bond, interview with Douglas B. Green, July 1, 1974, FLA-CMHOFAM.

8. Michael Duchemin, "South of the Border: Gene Autry and U.S. Foreign Policy," unpublished manuscript, Museum of the American West, 2006.

9. Frederick G. Othman, "No Mexican Bandits, Says Hays Office," *Chicago Daily News*, Sept. 3, 1941.

10. John Chapman, "Gene Autry: One Man Industry," *Chicago Sunday Tribune*, Mar. 2, 1941.

11. Tom Treanor, "The Home Front," *Los Angeles Times*, July 30, 1941.

12. *Los Angeles Times*, "Fire Ruins Home of Gene Autry," Nov. 9, 1931.

13. Les Gilliam, interview with the author, 2001; Gene Dodson, "Berwyn Bows Out to Autry," *Daily Oklahoman*, Nov. 17, 1941; *Daily Ardmorite*, Nov. 16, 1941.

14. Gene Autry to Frank Brown, Dec. 17, 1971.

Chapter 28

1. Hedda Hopper, "Eventful Hollywood Year Ends," *Los Angeles Times*, Dec. 27, 1942.

2. Before *Billboard* initiated its "Juke Box Folk Records" chart in 1944, top-selling country discs were singled out in the publication's folk-music jukebox column, which listed all of these Autry records in 1942.

3. Jimmy Wakely, interview with Douglas B. Green, June 25, 1974, FLA-CMHOFAM.

4. Rumble, "Fred Rose" (PhD diss., Vanderbilt University, 1980), 73.

5. Bond, "Gene Autry, Champion," 80 (courtesy Sherry Bond).

6. *Los Angeles Times*, "Hedda Hopper's Hollywood," Dec. 14, 1942; Edwin Schellert, "News Clips from Studio Town," *Los Angeles Times*, Nov. 13, 1941.

7. Bond, "Gene Autry, Champion," 83.

8. Kathleen Lamb, *A Dream Comes True* (Gene Autry's Flying A Ranch Stampede program, Soldiers Field, Chicago, 1942), 13.

9. Gene Autry, interview with Mike Oatman, Feb. 14, 1983.

10. Herb Yates to S. W. Smith, British Lion Film Corp., Sept. 11, 1942.

11. Herb Yates interoffice memo to E. H. Goldstein, Aug. 6, 1942.

12. Gene Autry to Ted Wallerstein, July 13, 1942.

13. Autry, interview with Oatman, Feb. 14, 1983.

14. War Department memo to Army Recruiting and Induction Officer, Los Angeles, June 17, 1942.

15. *Chicago Daily News*, July 19, 1942.

16. *Chicago Herald-American*, July 22, 1942.

17. Yates to Smith, Sept. 11, 1942. Yates's financial accusations regarding Wrigley have not been substantiated, although Gene's tax return shows that he did receive payments from Wrigley in 1943, during which time his sole broadcasting was *The Sgt. Gene Autry Show*.

18. Yates telegram to Gene Autry, Aug. 12, 1942.

19. Yates to Smith, Sept. 11, 1942.

20. Ibid.

21. Ibid.

22. Gene Autry to Yates, Oct. 20, 1942.

23. M. J. Siegel to Yates, Dec. 9, 1942.

24. Ibid.

25. O'Melveny to Yates, Dec. 16, 1942.

26. Yates to O'Melveny, Dec. 22, 1942.

27. *New York Times*, "Abbott, Costello Top at Box Office," Dec. 26, 1942.

Chapter 29

1. *Autry's Aces* (Spring 1943).

2. Jean Shepard, "Gene's Town—Hollywood," *Autry's Aces* (Fall 1943).

3. *Los Angeles Times*, "Autry Testifies in Film Agent Deal," Apr. 1, 1943; *Los Angeles Times*, "Autry Says Agent Boasted of His Honesty," Apr. 2, 1943; *Los Angeles Times*, "Autry Agent Testifies in Own Defense in Suit," Apr. 7, 1943.

4. *Los Angeles Times*, "Autry Sued Over Song," Jan. 14, 1944.

5. A. E. Eggleston to Gladys Green, Aug. 11, 1943.

6. Autry to *Life* (n.d.); *Life*, July 19, 1943.

7. James V. Allred to Maj. General C. R. Smith, Jan. 26, 1944; LBJA FN, LBJL.

8. Allred to Hon. Lyndon B. Johnson, Feb. 14, 1944, LBJA FN, LBJL.

9. LBJ telegram to Allred, Jan, 31, 1944, LBJA FN, LBJL.

10. LBJ telegram to T/S Orvon G. Autry, Mar. 6, 1944, LBJA FN, LBJL.

11. Gene Autry to LBJ, Mar. 9, 1944, LBJA FN, LBJL.

12. Ibid., Apr. 5, 1944.

13. LBJ to T/Sgt. Gene Autry, Apr. 10, 1944, LBJA FN, LBJL.

14. Autry and Herskowitz, *Back in the Saddle Again*, 86–87.

15. Gene Autry to *Autry's Aces*, Nov. 9, 1944, printed in *Autry's Aces*.

16. Thomas M. Pryor, "By Way of Report," *New York Times*, July 9, 1944.

17. *Chicago Sun*, June 18, 1944.

18. *Los Angeles Times*, "Brothers of Two Stars Divorced," Dec. 15, 1944.

19. Dudley's absence from duty was eventually resolved, and he received an honorable discharge in 1945.

20. *Los Angeles Times*, "Autry Loses Court Contest," Feb. 11, 1945.

21. *Chicago Sun*, "Napped Rayon in Clothing Assailed as a Fire Menace," Apr. 10, 1945.

22. Gene Autry to Rep. Lyndon Johnson, June 11, 1945, LBJA FN, LBJL.

23. Autry and Herskowitz, *Back in the Saddle Again*, 92.

Chapter 30

1. Autry and Herskowitz, *Back in the Saddle Again*, 173.

2. Lulu Belle Wiseman, interview with William Lightfoot, ca. 1980, FLA-CMHOFAM.

3. Lucy Greenbaum, "A Sinatra in a Sombrero," *New York Times*, Nov. 4, 1945.

4. Louise Heising, "Life in a Ten Gallon Hat," *Motion Picture*, 1950.

5. Unidentified newspaper clipping from a Gene Autry scrapbook; according to Gene's income tax return, he grossed $33,000 per year in 1946–47 from his Madison Square Garden appearances.

6. Gene Autry to Philip K. Wrigley, March 1947.

7. *Daily Variety*, date unavailable (review came from a scrapbook). *Hollywood Reporter* said of the film: "It's standard Autry fare slated for his regular fans who have been fed on almost two dozen Autry reissues since his induction into the Army. . . . Following the fixed formula, pic combines a dash of action seasoned with romance, with the story acting as a peg for an arm-long musical score of pleasant oatunes" (Nov. 27, 1946).

Chapter 31

1. Charles Dexter, "Cowboy Capitalist," *Reader's Scope*, Feb. 1948.
2. Thomas F. Brady, "Lilli Palmer Is Set Opposite Garfield," *New York Times*, Jan. 3, 1947.
3. Gene Autry to *Autry's Aces*, Dec. 31, 1946.
4. In Gene's first two postwar Republic pictures, the horse was billed as Champion, with the Jr. added for his final three. The Jr. vanished on the Columbia title credits.
5. According to Gene's tax return for 1946, Champion, listed on his schedule of depreciation, died that year; his value as of his 1934 purchase was $425.Gene bought a new horse in July, perhaps the pony he named Little Champ, for $700; *New York Times*, "Autry's Horse of Films Dies," Jan. 26, 1947: "Champion, Gene Autry's sorrel horse and equine hero of dozens of Western films, is dead at the age of 17."
6. Conversely, after the death of Roy Rogers's famous horse Trigger, the animal was "mounted" and placed on display in the Roy Rogers and Dale Evans Museum, later joined by mounted versions of Trigger Jr., Dale's horse Buttermilk, and the German shepherd Bullet.
7. Autry and Herskowitz, *Back in the Saddle Again*, 126.
8. Johnny Western, interview with the author, 2006.
9. Jerry Scoggins, interview with the author, 2001.
10. Ina Autry to Glorie (Gloria Marvin), undated.
11. Congressman J. J. "Jake" Pickle oral history, May 31, 1970, courtesy of General Services Administration, National Archives and Records Service, LBJ Library, Austin, Texas, 47–49.
12. Mary Rather to Joe Maguire, FHA, Aug. 5, 1946; Gene Autry to Wilson Wyatt, FHA, Sept. 3, 1946, courtesy of LBJ Library, Austin, Texas.
13. Gene Autry to Walter Jenkins, Sept. 4, 1936. Courtesy of LBJ Library, Austin, Texas.
14. Hedda Hopper, "Looking at Hollywood," *Los Angeles Times*, June 11, 1947.
15. Jonathan Guyot Smith, "The Transition to Columbia Pictures and the Resulting Metamorphosis of the Singing Cowboy," *Gene Autry's Friends* (Winter 2005–2006).
16. Ibid.
17. From Lou Crosby's introduction to the June 16, 1946, *Melody Ranch* program; Crosby made much of the show's increase in time from fifteen to thirty minutes; on the previous program (June 9), Gene thanked the fans for their support, resulting in giving the show a thirty-minute format.
18. *Autry's Aces* (Dec./Jan./Feb. 1946–47).
19. Charles Dexter, "Cowboy Capitalist," *Reader's Scope*, Feb. 1948.
20. Hedda Hopper, "Gene Autry Popularity Goes On Up," *Los Angeles Times*, Nov. 9, 1947.

Chapter 32

1. William Lynch Vallée, "Prattlin' Partner," *Movie Thrills*, July 1950.
2. Kerry Galgano, interview with the author, April 2006.
3. Vallée, "Prattlin' Partner."

4. Pat Buttram to "Peggy [Buttram] & All"; envelope dated Oct. 27, 1934, courtesy of John Buttram and Zella Fuller.

5. Rothel, *Great Cowboy Sidekicks*, 108.

6. Pat Buttram and Gene Autry interview, with Kenneth E. Baughman, July 5, 1990.

7. Rothel, *Great Cowboy Sidekicks*, 112.

8. Gloria Henry, interview with the author July. 2006.

9. Earl Bellamy, interview with Maxine Hansen, Aug. 2002.

10. Henry, interview with the author, July 2006.

11. Ibid.

12. Dick Jones, interview with Maxine Hansen, 2002.

13. Henry, interview with the author, July 2006.

14. Elena Verdugo, interview with the author, Aug. 2006.

15. Rothel, *Singing Cowboys*, 31–33.

16. Alex Gordon, "An Englishman Discovers America!" *Autry's Aces* (March–May 1948).

17. Jackie Autry, interview with the author, 2006.

18. Percy Knauth, "Gene Autry, Inc.," *Life*, June 28, 1948.

19. Charles Tenny, "Hi-Yo, Autry," *Pilgrim Youth* (May 1948).

20. Autry and Herskovitz, *Back in the Saddle Again*, 173.

21. *New York Times*, "Taxicab Carries Colt to Bellevue," Oct. 12, 1948.

22. On the same day, December 25, 1948, Gene's *Melody Ranch* radio show also aired on CBS at its regular time slot.

23. Gene Autry to E. G. Moreton, Mar. 14, 1949.

24. Gene Autry to Colonel Tod Bates, Mar. 14, 1949.

Chapter 33

1. Gene loved beauty pageants. That year, he judged the Eastern Rodeo Queen competition held prior to the Madison Square Garden rodeo: contestants were judged on their beauty, equestrienne abilities, showmanship, and personal charm (for the latter category, "each contestant was required to step onto a wooden pedestal in front of the stand and pirouette slowly in the manner of a fashion model," according to "Queens Girl Wins Rodeo Queen Title," *New York Times*, Sept. 27, 1949). The previous year, while filming in Tucson, Gene judged a beauty pageant at a local hotel, with the winner getting a bit part in *The Big Sombrero*. It is unknown if he helped choose Miss Loyalty.

2. *La Crosse Tribune*, "Rewritten 'Rudolph' Makes Music History," Dec. 11, 1979.

3. Juanita Cotner, interview with the author, 2006.

4. Johnny Marks to Gene Autry, May 17, 1950.

5. Ibid., Dec. 18, 1961.

6. Ibid., Oct. 28, 1949.

7. Marsh and Propes, *Merry Christmas, Baby*, 16.

8. Johnny Marks to Gene Autry, Dec. 18, 1961. The previous year, 1960, Marks had another hit with a Christmas song: "Rockin' Around the Christmas Tree" by Brenda Lee. Among his other notable Yuletide numbers are "I Heard the Bells on Christmas Day" (1956) and 1964's "A Holly, Jolly Christmas," sung by Burl Ives in the animated television special *Rudolph the Red-Nosed Reindeer*.

9. Howard Taubman, "Records: Mazurkas," *New York Times*, Nov. 20, 1949.

10. Jimmy Wakely, interview with Douglas B. Green, June 25, 1974, FLA-CMHOFAM.

11. Charles Tenny, "Hi-Yo, Autry," *Pilgrim Youth* (May 1948).

12. Hedda Hopper, "Autry Can't Get Around to Resting," *Los Angeles Times*, July 31, 1949.

13. "Suit," *San Antonio Light*, Apr. 17, 1949.

14. Hopper, "Autry Can't Get Around to Resting."

15. Gene Autry to Johnny Cline, Clyde Beatty Circus, Aug. 29, 1949.

16. Gloria Henry, interview with the author, Sept. 2006.

17. William Lynch Vallée, "Prattling Partner," *Movie Thrills*, July 1950.

18. Kerry Galgano, interview with Maxine Hansen, Apr. 2001.

19. Though at the time, the trade papers reported Gene paid twenty thousand dollars for the rights, in 1951 *Variety* reported Autry telling those at the Allied Convention of Exhibitors that he paid ten thousand dollars for the rights.

20. Thomas F. Brady, "Gene Autry Signs for Video Movies," *New York Times*, Apr. 18, 1950.

21. Thomas F. Brady, "Autry's TV Movies," *New York Times*, Apr. 23, 1950.

22. Frank Stanton to Gene Autry, Apr. 24, 1950.

23. *Los Angeles Times*, "Hollywood Set to Become Television Capitol of U.S.," June 11, 1950.

24. GE display advertisement, *New York Times*, Oct. 25, 1950.

25. Val Adams, "Give a Horse a Man Who Can Ride," *New York Times*, Oct. 8, 1950.

26. *Chicago Sun-Times*, "Gene Autry Writes Radio-TV Column," Aug. 22, 1950.

27. Jack Gould, "Radio and TV in Review: Gene Autry Rides for Devotees of the Western in New Film Series Over CBS Video," *New York Times*, July 24, 1950.

28. Undated clipping from a fan's scrapbook.

Chapter 34

1. Dorothy Masters, review of *Cow Town*, *New York Daily News*, June 31, 1950.

2. *Hollywood Reporter*, "Unusual Plot Line Proves Interesting," May 10, 1950.

3. Dick Jones, interview with the author, Aug. 2005.

4. Kenny to Autry, Dec. 22, 1949.

5. *Autry's Aces* (Fall 1950).

6. Gloria Henry, interview with the author, Sept. 2006,

7. Jerry Scoggins, interview with the author, 2002,

8. *Autry's Aces* (Fall 1950).

9. *Film Daily*, "Let's Face It, TV Here to Stay—Autry," Aug. 8, 1950.

10. Jack Hamilton, "Gene Autry: Millionaire Cowboy," *Look*, Aug. 1, 1950.

11. Delacorte to Autry, Jan. 4, 1951.

12. Gene wrote its flipside, "The Funny Little Bunny," with Johnny Bond after Johnny Marks turned down Gene's request to co-write an Easter song with him.

13. Gene Autry to Gen. Douglas MacArthur, Nov. 21, 1951.

14. Alex Gordon, "Gene Autry on Television," *Autry's Aces* (Fall 1950).

15. *Variety*, "Autry Gallops Thru Allied's Ambuscade with Well-Aimed Shots," Oct. 3, 1950; earlier reports in the trades stated that Gene paid twenty thousand dollars for the rights to *Mule Train*.

16. *Service Bulletin*, Independent Theatre Owners of Ohio, Oct. 23, 1950.

17. *New York Times*, "Autry Escapes Blast Injury," Sept. 13, 1950.

18. Henry Vance, "How Buttram Got Bammed," Dec. 13, 1950

19. Autry and Herskowitz, *Back in the Saddle Again*, 101.

20. Yates to Autry, Oct. 31, 1951.

21. Autry to Yates, Nov. 1, 1951.

22. Thomas M. Pryon, "TV-Movie Tie-Ins Remain Confused," *New York Times*, May 15, 1952.

23. David Rothel, *Singing Cowboys*, 134.

24. Jones, interview with the author, Aug. 2005.

25. Magers and Fitzgerald, *Westerns Women*, 70.

26. Hedda Hopper, "Experience Pays," *Los Angeles Times*, Apr. 7, 1952.

27. Autry and Herskowitz, *Back in the Saddle Again*, 103.

28. *Hollywood Reporter* reviews: "'Old Smoky' Tame Gene Autry Oater," Mar. 4, 1953; "Gene Autry Oater Lacking in Action," Aug. 28, 1953; "Autry 'Train' Fails to Excite Action," June 16, 1953.

Chapter 35

1. Hedda Hopper, "Genial Gene," *Los Angeles Times*, July 13, 1952.

2. Alex Gordon, interview with the author, 2002.

3. *Daily Variety*, "Gene Autry Lassos 585G, New Record, On One-Niter Tour," Mar. 13, 1953.

4. Barbara Bardo Autry wrote Johnny Western on Sept. 18, 1999: "Gene raised Dudley after the death of their mother. Their father's fifth wife Ruby—a very beautiful and charming woman many years younger than him—had a young sister. Dudley dated the young sister before he met me, and she died of tuberculosis at the age of 21. It was Dudley's luck that he contracted tuberculosis from Ruby's sister. Dudley eventually died of TB. It had spread to every vital organ in his body."

5. On Jan. 12, 1960, following one of Dudley's drunken rampages in Phoenix, Gene, fed up by his behavior, had written his brother: "During the last two years I have spent over $3,000 on hospitals and doctor bills on you which were caused by just such capers as this last one, and for your information this is only a drop in the bucket of what you have cost me for 40 years. The money is important of course, but I also think it is a terrible crime for a man like you to throw your life away and put your sisters, family and my friends through such embarrassment with the shenanigans you have pulled. Now the doctors have advised me that any more drinking or one more drunk such as the last one and you will wind up in an insane institution or dead. As you know, you have had every opportunity since you were a kid to go to school as Veda and Wilma did, to work in an honorable manner and earn yourself a living. . . . But you were always on the bottle, writing bad checks, playing the slot machines, and trying to duck away from work. . . . I have given you several thousand times as much assistance as I have ever given all of the others in our family combined and not received one word of thanks. . . . You, as well as some of the family, have always thought I was rough on you, but ever since I can remember you were in trouble, and I haven't always told them what you cost me not only in dollars and cents, but the mental turmoil, agony, and embarrassment you have caused."

6. Hedda Hopper, "Linda Darnell to Do Two Films in Italy," *Los Angeles Times*, Apr. 8, 1953.

7. Jimmy Hawkins, interview with the author, Aug. 2005.

8. Jonathan Guyot Smith, "A Brief Review of Out Favorite Radio Program, Gene Autry's Melody Ranch," *Gene Autry's Friends* (Spring/Summer 1997); Beverly Kimball, "News Roundup on Gene," *Autry's Aces* (Summer 1954).

9. *Boston Herald*, "Ambassador on Horseback," Aug. 23, 1953.

10. Ina Autry to Pat Murphy, May 7, 1953.

11. Ina Autry to Virginia MacPhail, undated.

12. Dick Jones, interview with the author, Aug. 2005.

13. Mrs. Laban Smith to Gene Autry, Mar. 7, 1954.

14. *Chicago Tribune*, "Autry Cowboy Suit Catches Fire: Award Boy, Parents $40,000," Dec. 8, 1948.

15. *Chicago Sun*, "Napped Rayon in Clothing Assailed as a Fire Menace," Apr. 10, 1945.

16. *Los Angeles Times*, "Gene Autry Heads Station KMPC Deal," Nov. 21, 1952.

17. Bob Reynolds to Gene Autry, undated (but annotated as received by Autry on Nov. 11, 1951).

18. *Los Angeles Times*, "Autry's Many-Faceted Life Piles Up Holdings," Mar. 29, 1953.

19. Hedda Hopper, "Autry Converts Ranch for Underprivileged," *Los Angeles Times*, Feb. 28, 1950.

20. Patty Dunn (Mayes), interview with the author, Sept. 2001.

21. Patty Dunn to Gene Autry, Mar. 29, 1954; Gene Autry to Patty Dunn, Apr. 16, 1954.

22. Don Law, "Gene Autry Rides Again," *Autry's Aces* (Summer 1954).

23. Beverly Kimball, "News Roundup on Gene," *Autry's Aces* (Summer 1954).

24. Jack Gould, "Television: Color Goes Thataway," *New York Times*, July 7, 1954.

Chapter 36

1. Joe Johnson, interview with the author, 2006.

2. Kerry Buttram Galgano to the author, May 5, 2006.

3. Lucille Beckstead Major, interview with the author, 2006.

4. Joe Kelly to Gene Autry, Feb. 14, 1955.

5. Gene Autry to Joe Kelly, Feb. 26, 1955.

6. Fred Harman to Gene Autry, June 16, 1955.

7. In 1954 Parker had just signed with Flying A and appeared in *Death Valley Days* twice when tapped by Disney for the Crockett film. When he asked Gene for a release from his contract to pursue his big break, Gene gave him his blessing.

8. Gene Autry to Frederick Fox, Sam Fox Publishing, Sept. 9, 1955; Gene Autry to Dudley Autry, Sept. 1, 1959.

9. Harry Harris, "Autry Unworried By Competition," *Philadelphia Inquirer*, Feb. 10, 1956.

10. Bond, "Gene Autry: Champion" (courtesy Sherry Bond), 245–47.

11. Val Adams, "1952 TV Program Gets Promotion," *New York Times*, Mar. 9, 1956.

12. Gene Autry to Florence Hargis, Mar. 27, 1956. Tom Hargis was apparently fired by Wrigley.

13. Bond, *Gene Autry* 248–49.

14. Richard F. Shepard, "Autry to Turn In His Radio Spurs," *New York Times*, May 12, 1956.

15. Alex Gordon telegram to Mr. and Mrs. Gene Autry, May 16, 1956.

16. *New York Times*, "*Baseball Hall of Fame* Television Series Will Make Debut on Channel 5 Saturday," June 11, 1956.

17. Gene Autry to *Autry's Aces*, May 31, 1956.

18. Arthur S. Allaire (Opera House Theatre, Bangor, Maine) to M. J. Mullin (New England Theatres, Inc., Boston), June 20, 1956, sent to J. R. Grainger.

19. Johnny Western, interviews with the author, 2005, 2006.

20. Gene Autry to Johnny Marks, Sept. 12, 1956.

21. Gene Autry to Art Satherley, Mar. 14, 1956.

22. Gene Autry to Harriet Satherley, Feb. 10, 1986. Along with a check Gene sent Art on his ninety-fifth birthday, he wrote, "We can both look forward to the big 100."

23. Gene Autry to Ruby Autry, Dec. 14, 1956.

24. Bernie Solomon, interview with the author, Aug. 2005.

25. Johnny Grant, interview with the author, Aug. 2005.

26. In 1988 Gene's widow, Jackie Autry, found a total of $8,900 in the pockets of her husband's old show clothes while she was gathering them as a donation to the Gene Autry Western Heritage Museum.

27. Gene sold Four Star Music and Challenge Records to Johnson in 1963–64.

28. Juanita Cotner, interview with the author, 2006.

29. Ina Kay Leffler, interview with the author, Aug. 2005.

30. Joe Johnson, interview with the author, 2006.

31. Virginia MacPhail, interview with the author, 2006.

32. Autry and Herskowitz, *Back in the Saddle Again*, 190.

33. Juanita Cotner, interview; on Feb. 23, 1958, Cuban rebels kidnapped an Argentine racecar champion, and in March the Cuban cabinet resigned. After a two-year insurgency, Castro took control of Cuba in Jan. 1959.

34. Jimmy Hawkins, interview with the author, Aug. 2005.

35. Gordon Gould, "Gene Slowing Down to a Trot," *Chicago Tribune*, Aug. 24, 1956.

36. Bond, *Gene Autry, Champion* (courtesy of Sherry Bond).

37. Johnny Grant, interview with the author, Aug. 2005.

38. Bond would continue his association with Gene; from 1965 to 1970, on his own Los Angeles station KTLA, Gene broadcast the *Melody Ranch* television program, for which Johnny wrote scripts and performed along with Carl Cotner and the Cass County Boys. (Gail Davis's ex-husband, Bob Davis, directed the program.) Gene appeared only twice on the country music show, which sometimes featured Jimmy Wakely's daughter Linda, as well as other old friends.

39. Gene actually made one more recording—a recitation (backed by a full orchestra) titled "One Solitary Life"/ "A Cowboy's Prayer."

40. Johnny Cash to Gene Autry, Nov. 11, 1966.

SOURCES

Space does not permit a complete listing of the thousands of articles from newspapers, periodicals, music journals, and fan magazines I pored over during the course of my research. Numerous primary sources are cited in the endnotes. Most helpful were fifty years' worth of Gene Autry's personal and business correspondence, various paperwork, and contractual agreements made available to me by Gene Autry Entertainment and the Museum of the American West archives. Among the collections of the Autry National Center, the Gene Autry, Oklahoma Museum, and the Country Music Hall of Fame and Museum Frist Archive and Library, Gene Autry scrapbooks created by fans preserved hundreds of documents, some annotated, others not—including ticket stubs, show programs, and clippings from newspapers and magazines: these were a godsend to me. The personal correspondence between Gene Autry and Lyndon B. Johnson, as well as oral histories conducted by the General Services Administration/National Archives and Records Service, are housed at the Lyndon Baines Johnson Library in Austin, Texas. Among the papers of record I consulted were the *New York Times*, *Los Angeles Times*, *Chicago Tribune*, *Chicago Daily News*, *Chicago Sun-Times*, *Tulsa World*, and *Oklahoman*; archival copies of small-town papers in Tioga, Texas, and Achille, Oklahoma, also helped. The texts found in the Gene Autry songbooks, albums, and box sets from 1932 to 2006, were also beneficial.

The following abbreviations for frequently used citations have been used:

Frist Library and Archive, Country Music Hall of Fame and Museum
    FLA-CMHOFAM

Southern Methodist University Oral History programs   SMU-OH

Hollywood Film Institute Oral History program   HFI-OH

Lyndon Baines Johnson Archives Famous Names file (correspondence with
    national figures)   LBJ FN

Lyndon Baines Johnson Library, Austin, Texas   LBJL

Please note that the sources for some newspaper and magazine articles were scrapbooks created by Gene Autry fans and are currently housed at such museums as the Autry National Center's Museum of the American West, the Gene Autry Oklahoma Museum, and the FLA-CHMOFAM. Occasionally I quoted from clippings from which there were no full citation materials available. Such missing information is annotated within the notes.

Books

Autry, Gene. *The Art of Writing Songs and How to Play a Guitar*. Chicago: Frontier Publishing, 1933.

Autry, Gene, with Mickey Herskowitz. *Back in the Saddle Again*. Garden City, NY: Doubleday, 1978.

Barbour, Alan. *The Thrill of It All: A Pictorial History of the B Western form the Great Train Robbery and Other Silent Classics to the Color Films of the Genre's Last Days of Glory in the 50s*. New York: Macmillan, 1971.

Barnouw, Erik. *A Tower in Babel: A History of Broadcasting in the United States to 1933*. New York: Oxford University Press, 1966.

Beard, Tyler. *100 Years of Western Wear*. Salt Lake City, UT: 1998. Rev. ed., Gibbs Smith, 2003.

Black, Bill. *Roy Rogers and the Silver-Screen Cowboys: An Illustrated History of the Matinee Western Movie Star and His Comic Book Counterpart*. Longwood, FL: AC Comics, 1997.

Bond, Johnny. *Gene Autry, Champion*. Unpublished manuscript, ca. 1977.

———. *Reflections: The Autobiography of Johnny Bond*. Los Angeles: John Edwards Memorial Foundation, 1976.

Bridges, Dwayne A. *Lyndon Baines Johnson 1908–1973: Reflections in History, a Personal Collection*. Dallas: Brown Books Publishing Group, 2006.

Brooks, Robert Autry, and V. Mayo Bundy. *The Descendents of Cornelius Autry, Immigrant, of Edgecomb County, and Neil Culbreth of Sampson County, North Carolina, and Allied Families*. Vol. 3. Raleigh, NC: Richard Hadluyt Publisher, 1996.

Brown, Garrett, ed. *Classic Country: The Golden Age of Country Music—The 20s Through the 70s*. San Diego, CA: Tehabi Books/Time-Life Books, 2001.

Bufwack, Mary A., and Robert K. Oermann. *Finding Her Voice: Women in Country Music 1800–2000*. Nashville, TN: Country Music Foundation Press and Vanderbilt University Press, 2003.

Bunch, Bryan, and Alexander Hellemans. *The Timetables of Technology: A Chronology of the Most Important People and Events in the History of Technology*. New York: Simon and Schuster, 1993.

Buscombe, Edward. *The BFI Companion to the Western*. New York: Atheneum, 1988.

Cantwell, David, and Bill Friskics-Warren. *Heartaches by the Number: Country Music's Greatest 500 Singles*. Nashville, TN: Vanderbilt University Press/Country Music Foundation Press, 2003.

Caro, Robert A. *The Years of Lyndon Johnson*. Vol. 1, *The Path to Power*. New York: Random House, 1981.

Cary, Diana Serra. *The Hollywood Posse: The Story of a Gallant Band of Horsemen Who Made Movie History*. Norman, OK: University of Oklahoma Press, 1996.

———. *The Years of Lyndon Johnson.* Vol. 2, *The Means of Ascent.* New York: Random House, 1990.

Chambers, Stan. *News at Ten.* Santa Barbara, CA: Capra Press, 1994.

Cusic, Don. *Cowboys and the Wild West: An A-Z Guide From the Chisholm Trail to the Silver Screen.* New York: Facts on File, 1995.

Copeland, Bobby J. *Roy Barcroft: King of the Badmen.* Madison, NC: Empire Publishing, 2000.

Daniel, Wayne W. *Pickin' on Peachtree.* Urbana: University of Illinois Press, 2001.

Day, Donald, ed., *The Autobiography of Will Rogers.* Boston: Houghton Mifflin,1949.

Dillman, Bruce. *The Cow Boy Handbook.* Kansas City: Lone Prairie Publishing, 1994.

Estes, Ross. *I Remember Things: An Informal History of Tioga, Texas.* Compiled and edited by Robert Duncan. Mt. Pleasant, TX: Nortex Press, 1977.

Evans, James F. *Prairie Farmer and WLS.* Champaign, IL: University of Illinois Press, 1969.

Evans, Steve, and Ron Middlebrook. *Cowboy Guitars.* Fullerton, CA: Centerstream Publishing, 2002.

Everson, William K. *A Pictorial History of the Western Film.* Secaucus, NJ: Citadel Press, 1969.

Fenin, George N., and William K. Everson. *The Western: From Silents to the Seventies.* New York: Grossman, 1973.

Fitzgerald, Michael G., and Boyd Magers. *Ladies of the Western.* Jefferson, NC: McFarland, 2002.

Francke, Lizzie. *Script Girls: Women Screenwriters in Hollywood.* London: BFI Publishing, 1994.

George-Warren, Holly. *Cowboy! How Hollywood Invented the Wild West.* Pleasantville, NY: Readers Digest Books, 2002.

George-Warren, Holly, and Michelle Freedman. *How the West Was Worn.* New York: Abrams, 2001.

George-Warren, Holly, and Patricia Romanowski, eds. *The Rolling Stone Encyclopedia of Rock & Roll.* New York: Fireside/Simon and Schuster, 2001.

Giddins, Gary. *Bing Crosby: A Pocketful of Dreams, the Early Years 1903–1940.* New York: Little, Brown, 2001.

Gilbert, Douglas. *American Vaudeville: Its Life and Times.* New York: Whittlesey House, 1940.

Ginnell, Cary. *Milton Brown and the Founding of Western Swing.* Urbana: University of Illinois Press, 1994.

Grabman, Sandra. *Pat Buttram: The Rocking Chair Humorist.* Boalsburg, PA: Bear Manor Media, 2006.

Green, Douglas B. *Singing in the Saddle: The History of the Singing Cowboy.* Nashville: Vanderbilt University Press/Country Music Foundation Press, 2002.

Gruhn, George, and Walter Carter. *Acoustic Guitars and Other Fretted Instruments.* San Francisco: GPI Books, 1993.

Hake, Theodore L., and Robert D. Cauler. *Sixgun Heroes: A Price Guide to Movie Cowboy Collectibles.* Des Moines, IA: Wallace-Homestead, 1976.

Hall, Wade. *Hell-Bent for Music: The Life of Pee Wee King.* Lexington, KY: University Press of Kentucky, 1996.

Haslam, Gerald W. *Workin' Man Blues: Country Music in California*. Berkeley: University of California Press, 1999.

Heide, Robert, and John Gilman. *Box Office Buckaroos: The Cowboy Hero from the Wild West Show to the Silver Screen*. New York: Abbeville Press, 1989.

History of Catoosa. Catoosa, OK: Catoosa Historical Society, 2004.

Hurst, Richard Maurice. *Republic Studios: Between Poverty Row and the Majors*. Metuchen, NJ: Scarecrow Press, 1979.

Indian Creek Baptist Church: Dinner on the Ground. Kearney, NE.: Morris Press, 2000.

Jacobs, Charles M. *Kenton Cast Iron Toys: The Real Thing in Everything but Size*. Schiffer Publishing, 1996.

Katz, Ephraim. *The Film Encyclopedia*. New York: HarperCollins, 1979.

Kennedy, Rick. *Jelly Roll, Bix, and Hoagy: Gennett Studios and the Birth of Recorded Jazz*. Bloomington, IN: Indiana University Press, 1999.

Kennedy, Rick, and Randy McNutt. *Little Labels—Big Sound*. Bloomington, IN: Indiana University Press, 1999.

Kingsbury, Paul, ed. *Country: The Music and the Musicians—Pickers, Slicers, Cheatin' Hearts & Superstars*. New York: Abbeville Press, 1988.

———. *The Encyclopedia of Country Music: The Ultimate Guide to the Music*. New York: Oxford University Press, 1998.

Kingsbury, Paul, and Alanna Nash, eds. *Will the Circle Be Unbroken: Country Music in America*. New York: DK Publishing, 2006.

Lahue, Kalton C. *Riders of the Range: The Sagebrush Heroes of the Sound and Screen*. New York: Castle Books, 1973.

Lissauer, Robert. *Lissauer's Encyclopedia of Popular Music in America: 1888 to the Present*. New York: Paragon House, 1991.

Logsdon, Guy. *"The Whorehouse Bells Were Ringing" and Other Songs Cowboys Sing*. Urbana: University of Illinois Press, 1989.

Logsdon, Guy, William Jacobson, and Mary Rogers. *Saddle Serenaders*. Salt Lake City, UT: Gibbs Smith, 1995.

Lomax, John A. *Cowboy Songs and Other Frontier Ballads*. New York: Sturgis and Walton, 1910.

Lomax, John A., and Alan Lomax. *American Ballads and Folk Songs*. New York: Dover, 1994.

Loy, R. Philip. *Westerns and American Culture 1930–1955*. Jefferson, NC: McFarland, 2001.

Mackey, Albert Gallatin. *The History of Freemasonry*. New York: Masonic History Co., 1898.

Magers, Boyd. *So You Wanna See Cowboy Stuff? The Western Movie/TV Tour Guide*. Madison, NC: Empire Publishing, 2003.

Magers, Boyd, and Michael G. Fitzgerald. *Westerns Women*. Jefferson, NC: McFarland, 1999.

Malone, Bill C. *Country Music U.S.A.: A Fifty-Year History*. Austin: University of Texas Press, 1969.

———. *Singing Cowboys and Musical Moutaineers: Southern Culture and the Roots of Country Music*. Athens: University of Georgia Press, 1993.

Malone, Bill C., and Judith McCulloch, eds. *Stars of Country Music: From Uncle Dave Macon to Johnny Rodriguez*. Urbana: University of Illinois Press, 1975.

Marsh, Dave, and Steve Propes. *Merry Christmas, Baby: Holiday Music from Bing to Sting*. New York: Little Brown, 1993.

Mathis, Jack. *Republic Confidential:* Vol. 1, *The Studio*. Barrington, IL: Jack Mathis Advertising, 1999.

———. *Republic Confidential*. Vol. 2, *The Players*. Barrington, IL: Jack Mathis Advertising, 1992.

Mauldin, Bill. Foreword to *A Sentimental Journey: America in the '40s*. Pleasantville, NY: Reader's Digest Association, 1998.

McCloud, Barry. *Definitive Country: The Ultimate Encyclopedia of Country Music and Its Performers*. New York: Belfly Publishing Group, 1994.

McNamara, Brooks. *Step Right Up*. Oxford, MS: University Press of Mississippi, 1975, 1995.

Mitchum, Petrine, and Audry Pavia. *Hollywood Hoofbeats*. San Diego, CA.: Bowtie Press, 2005.

Montana, Patsy, and Jane Frost. *The Cowboy's Sweetheart: Patsy Montana*. Jefferson, NC: McFarland, 2002.

Nasaw, David. *Going Out: The Rise & Fall of Public Amusements*. New York: Basic Books/HarperCollins, 1993.

Newhan, Ross. *The Anaheim Angels*. New York: Hyperion, 2000.

O'Brien, P. J. *Will Rogers: Ambassador of Good Will, Prince of Wit and Wisdom*. London: Winston, 1935.

Oermann, Robert K. *A Century of Country*. New York: TV Books, 1999.

Parker, Frank, and James Smallwood, eds. *History Of Cooke County: A Pictorial Essay*. Gainesville: TX: Gainesville American Revolution Bicentennial Committee, 1975.

Parkinson, Michael, and Clyde Jeavons. *A Pictorial History of Westerns*. London: Hamlyn, 1973.

Porterfield, Nolan. *Jimmie Rodgers: The Life and Times of America's Blue Yodeler*. Urbana: University of Illinois Press, 1979.

Plantenga, Bart. *Yodel-Ay-Ee-OOoo: The Secret History of Yodeling Around the World*. New York: Routledge, 2004.

Rainey, Buck. *Sweethearts of the Sage: Biographies and Filmographies of 258 Actresses Appearing in Western Movies*. Jefferson, NC: McFarland, 1992.

Ridley, Jasper. *The Freemasons: A History of the World's Most Powerful Secret Society*. New York: Arcade, 2001.

Rogers, Roy, and Dale Evans, with Jane and Michael Stern. *Happy Trails: Our Life Story*. New York: Simon and Schuster, 1994.

Rogers, Roy Jr., with Karen Ann Wojahn. *Growing Up with Roy and Dale*. Ventura, CA: Regal Books, 1986.

Rogers, Will. *The Writings of Will Rogers*. Stillwater, OK: Oklahoma State University Press, 1983.

Rogers-Barnett, Cheryl, and Frank Thompson. *Cowboy Princess*. Lanham, MD: Taylor, 2003.

Rothel, David. *The Gene Autry Book*. Madison, NC: Empire Publishing, 1988.

———. *The Great Cowboy Sidekicks*. Lanham, MD: Scarecrow Press, 1984.

———. *The Singing Cowboys*. South Brunswick, NJ: A. S. Barnes, 1978.

Russell, Tony. *Country Music Records: A Discography, 1921–1942*. Editorial research by Bob Pinson, assisted by the staff of the Country Music Hall of Fame and Museum. New York: Oxford University Press, 2004.

Ryan, Jim. *The Rodeo and Hollywood*. Jefferson, NC: McFarland, 2006.

Savage, William W., Jr. *Singing Cowboys and All That Jazz: A Short History of Popular Music in Oklahoma*. Norman, OK: University of Oklahoma Press, 1983.

Schlesinger, Arthur M., Jr. Foreword to *Chronicle of the 20th Century: The Ultimate Record of Our Times*. New York: Dorling Kindersley, 1995.

Shaughnessy, Mary Alice. *Les Paul: An American Original*. New York: Morrow, 1993.

Shelton, Robert, and Burt Goldblatt. *The Country Music Story: A Picture History of Country & Western Music*. New York: Bobbs Merrill, 1966.

Sherman, Michael W., and Kurt R. Nauck III. *Note the Notes: An Illustrated History of the Columbia 78 rpm Record Label 1901–1958*. New Orleans: Monarch Record Enterprises, 1998.

Slaughter, John Robert. Foreword to *Decade of Triumph: The '40s*. Alexandria, VA: Time-Life Books, 1999.

Smith, Packy. *Gene Autry: That Silver Haired Daddy of Mine*. Liner notes to box set of CDs. Vollersode, Germany: Bear Family, 2006.

Snow, Hank. *The Hank Snow Story*. With Jack Ownbey and Bob Burris. Urbana: University of Illinois Press, 1994.

Stambler, Irwin, and Grelun Landon. *Encyclopedia of Folk, Country, and Western Music*. New York: St. Martin's Press, 1969.

Stanfield, Peter. *Hollywood, Westerns and the 1930s: The Lost Trail*. Exeter: University of Exeter Press, 2001.

———. *Horse Opera: The Strange History of the 1930s Singing Cowboy*. Urbana: University of Illinois Press, 2002.

Sterling, Bryan B., ed. *The Will Rogers Scrapbook*. New York: Bonanza, 1976.

Streissguth, Michael. *Eddy Arnold: Pioneer of the Nashville Sound*. New York: Schirmer, 1997.

———. *Johnny Cash: The Biography*. New York: Da Capo, 2006.

Sutton, Allan, and Kurt Nauck. *American Record Labels and Companies: An Encyclopedia (1891–1943)*. Denver, CO: Mainspring Press, 2000.

Thorp, Jack. *Songs of the Cowboys*. Bedford, MA: Applewood Books, 1908.

Time Capsule 1929: A History of the Year Condensed from the Pages of Time. New York: Time/Life Books, 1967.

Tosches, Nick. *Where Dead Voices Gather*. New York: Little, Brown, 2001.

Townsend, Charles. *San Antonio Rose: The Life and Music of Bob Wills*. Urbana: University of Illinois Press, 1976.

Tuska, Jon. *The Filming of the West: The Definitive Behind-the-Scenes History of the Great Western Movies*. Garden City, NY: Doubleday, 1976.

———. *The Vanishing Legion: A History of Mascot Pictures, 1927–1935*. Jefferson, NC: McFarland, 1982.

Whitburn, Joel. *The Billboard Book of Top 40 Hits*. New York: Billboard Books, 1996.

———. *Joel Whitburn Presents A Century of Pop Music*. Menomonee Falls, WI: Record Research Inc., 1999.

———. *Joel Whitburn's Top Country Singles, 1944–1988*. Menomonee Falls, WI: Record Research, 1989.

———. *Joel Whitburn's Top Country Singles, 1944–1997*. Menomonee Falls, WI: Record Research, 1998.

Williams, Hank. *Crusaders of the Sagebrush*. Melbourne, FL: Sweet-Water Press, 2005.

Willman, Chris. *Rednecks and Bluenecks: The Politics of Country Music*. New York: New Press, 2005.

Wolfe, Charles K. *Classic Country: Legends of Country Music*. New York: Routledge, 2001.

Yagoda, Ben. *Will Rogers*. New York: Knopf, 1993.

GENE AUTRY RECORDING SESSIONS

This listing of Gene Autry's recording sessions has been compiled with help from Tom Tierney at the Sony/BMG Archives, Karla Buhlman at Gene Autry Entertainment, Marva Felchlin at the Museum of the American West research library, independent scholar Kevin Coffey, Arthur Satherley's recording log (housed at the Frist Archive and Library at the Country Music Hall of Fame and Museum), longtime Autry discographer Jonathan Guyot Smith, Tony Russell and Frank Mare's research published in *That Silver Haired Daddy of Mine* box set, released by Bear Family Records, and the masterful volume, *Country Music Records: A Discography: 1921–1942*, by Tony Russell with editorial research by Bob Pinson, assisted by the staff of the Country Music Hall of Fame and Museum, published by Oxford University Press. Even with all these efforts, there is much missing information, and some of the musicians listed on the sessions are a matter of conjecture. Unfortunately, complete studio records were not kept by labels until recent times. (Should any readers be willing to share such missing information or suggest corrections, please contact the author at www .hollygeorgewarren.com or write to me c/o the publisher, and I will happily incorporate revisions in future printings of the book.) In addition, there is a variance of spellings of song titles and musicians; in order to remain consistent with the titles listed in this book's text, in most cases I have used the copyrighted song title. I have used the accepted spelling of musicians as well (Smiley, rather than Smilie, regardless of how it was listed on the original recording log). I have not included matrix or recording numbers (collectors can find these up to 1942 in the Russell volume), and I have listed the record companies that released the recording in its original format (78 rpm, etc.), rather than include later reissues on CD. The following key is for the abbreviations used for record labels and instrumentation.

Record Labels

Al	Allegro (Britain)	MR	Melody Ranch
Ang	Angelus	MW	Montgomery Ward
Apex	Apex	OK	OKeh
ARC	American Record	Or	Oriole
	Corporation	PaAu	Parlophone (Australia)
Au	Aurora	Pan	Panachord
Ba	Banner	Pe	Perfect
Ch	Champion	Pic	Piccadilly
Chg	Challenge	Rad	Radiex
Cl	Clarion	Re	Regal
Cli	Clifford	ReE	Regal (Britain)
Co	Columbia	ReE	Regal (England)
CoC	Columbia (Canada)	Rep	Republic
CoE	Columbia (England)	Rex	Rex
CoSs	Columbia (Swiss)	Ro	Romeo
Cq	Conqueror	RZ	Regal-Zonophone
CrC/	Crown (Canada), Melotone	RZAu	Regal-Zonophone
MeC/	(Canada), Royale, Sterling		(Australia)
Roy/Stg		RZIn	Regal Zonophone (India)
De	Decca	RZIr	Regal Zonophone
DeAu	Decca (Australia)		(Ireland)
Di	Diva	Sp	Spartan (Canada)
EBW	Edison Bell Winner	Spr	Superior
Eld	Electradisk	Spt	Supertone
Emb	Embassy	Sr	Sunrise
Ge	Gennett	Sta	Starday
GG	Grey Gull	TT	Timely Tunes
Ha	Harmony	VD	Van Dyke
Hil	Hilltop	V-D	V-Disc
Je	Jewel	Ve	Velvet Tone
Lyric	Lyric	Vi	Victor
Me	Melotone	Vo	Vocalion
MeC	Melotone (Canada)	ZoSA	Zonophone (South Africa)
Min	Minerva		

Instruments and Frequently Used Terms

In the case of an instrument or vocal appearing on a specific track, that track number follows the instrumentation citation (for example, sg: 77)

ac	accordion	eff	sound effects
acc.	accompaniment	eg	electric guitar
b	bass	esg	electric steel guitar
bj	banjo	f	fiddle
cel	celesta	fl	flute
cl	clarinet	g	guitar
h	harmonica	sb	string bass

jh	jaw harp (also known as Jew's harp)	sg	steel guitar
		t	trumpet
k	kazoo	tb	trombone
md	mandolin	unkn	unknown
orch	orchestra	v	vocals
p	piano	v eff	vocal sound effects
pac	piano accordion	vb	vibraphone
P.D.	public domain	vla	viola
per	percussion	vn	violin
poss.	possibly	wb	washboard
prob.	probably	y	yodeling
s	saxophone		

*denotes a gold record

\# denotes a platinum record

1929

October 9, 1929   New York
Gene Autry & Jimmy Long, v duet: Frankie Marvin, sg/y; Johnny Marvin, sg

1. "My Dreaming of You" (Frankie Marvin)
   Vi
2. "My Alabama Home" (Jimmy Long)
   Vi

Mid-October 1929   Long Island City, NY
Gene Autry, v/y; acc. Frankie Marvin, sg: 3, own g.

3. "Stay Away from My Chicken House" (Marvin)
   GG, VD, Rad
4. "My Oklahoma Home" (Gene Autry)
   Rad, VD, GG
5. "I'll Be Thinking of You, Little Gal" (Gene Autry)
   Sr
6. "I'll Be Thinking of You, Little Gal" (Gene Autry)
   QRS
7. "Cowboy Yodel" (Gene Autry)
   GG, VD, Rad
8. "Why Don't You Come Back to Me" (Gene Autry)
   VD, Sr
9. "No One to Call Me Darling" (Gene Autry)
   GG, Rad, VD
10. "Living in the Mountains" (Frankie Marvin)
    QRS
11. "Blue Yodel No. 6" (Jimmie Rodgers)
    QRS
12. "Oh for the Wild and Wooly West" (Frankie Marvin)
    QRS

13. "That's Why I Left the Mountain" (Arthur Fields)
    QRS
14. "Yodelin' Gene" (Arthur Fields)
    QRS

October 24, 1929   *New York*
Gene Autry (Yodelin' Cowboy), v/y; acc. own g

15. "Blue Yodel No. 5" (Jimmie Rodgers)
    Ha, Ve, Di, ReE/RZ, RZAu
16. "Left My Gal in the Mountains" (Carson Robison)
    Ha, Ve, Di, Cl

December 3, 1929   *New York*
Gene Autry, v/y; acc. own g

17. "Why Don't You Come Back to Me" (Gene Autry)
    Cl, OK (as by Johnny Dodds)
18. "Hobo Yodel" (Gene Autry–Jimmy Long)
    Ve, Di, Cl
19. "Dust Pan Blues" (Frankie Marvin)
    Cl, Ve, Di
20. "No One to Call Me Darling" (Gene Autry)
    Cl, Ve, Di, OK (as by Johnny Dodds)
21. "Yodeling Them Blues Away" (Frankie Marvin)
    Co unissued
22. "Frankie and Johnny" (Rodgers/Leighton Bros–Shields)
    Cl, Ve, Di, OK, PaAU (as by Johnny Dodds)

December 5, 1929   *New York*
Gene Autry, v/y; acc. own g. Frankie Marvin, v. eff: 27, 28

23. "My Dreaming of You" (Frankie Marvin)
    Co unissued
24. "The Railroad Boomer" (Carson Robison)
    OK
25. "My Alabama Home" (Gene Autry–Jimmy Long)
    Cl, Ve, Di
26. "Slue-Foot Lue" (Frankie Marvin)
    Cl, Di, Ve, OK
27. "Stay Away from My Chicken House" (Frankie Marvin)
    Cl, Di, Ve, OK
28. "Waiting for a Train" (Jimmie Rodgers)
    Cl, Di, Ve
29. "Lullaby Yodel" (Jimmie Rodgers–Elsie McWilliams)
    Cl, Di, Ve

December 6, 1929   *New York*
Gene Autry, v/y; acc. own g

30. "California Blues (Blue Yodel No. 4)" (Jimmie Rodgers)
    Ve, Di

31. "I'm Sorry We Met" (Jimmie Rodgers)
    Co unissued
32. "Daddy and Home" (Jimmie Rodgers)
    Ve, Di, Cl

1930

March 3, 1930   New York
Gene Autry v/y; acc. own g; Frankie Marvin sg: 33

33. "That's Why I Left the Mountains" (Fields–Hall)
    Cl, Di, Ve
34. "Cowboy Yodel" (Gene Autry)
    Cl, Di, Ve

March 5, 1930   New York
Gene Autry, v; acc. own g

35. "I'll Be Thinking Of You, Little Gal" (Gene Autry)
    Cl, Di, Ve
36. "My Rough and Rowdy Ways" (Jimmie Rodgers–Elsie McWilliams)
    Di, Ve.

March 5, 1930   Long Island City, NY
Gene Autry, v/y; acc. own g

37. "I'll Be Thinking of You, Little Gal" (Gene Autry)
    Ge rejected
38. "Cowboy Yodel" (Gene Autry)
    Ge rejected

March 8, 1930   New York
Gene Autry, v/y; acc. own g

39. "I'll Be Thinking of You, Little Gal" (Gene Autry)
    OK (as by Johnny Dodds)
40. "Cowboy Yodel" (Gene Autry)
    OK (as by Johnny Dodds)

June 5, 1930   Richmond, IN
Gene Autry, v; acc. own g

41. "Whisper Your Mother's Name" (Jimmie Rodgers)
    Ge, Spt, Ch, De, MW, MeC, Rex
42. "The Girl I Left Behind" (Johnny Marvin)
    Spr
43. "I'll Be Thinking of You, Little Gal" (Gene Autry)
    Ch, Spt
44. "Cowboy Yodel" (Gene Autry)
    Ge, Ch, Spt, MW, MeC
45. "Why Don't You Come Back to Me" (Gene Autry)
    Ge rejected

46. "Dust Pan Blues" (Frankie Marvin)
Ge rejected

June 6, 1930   Richmond, IN
Gene Autry, v/y; acc. own g

47. "In the Shadow of the Pine" (Hattie Lummis–G. O. Long)
Ge, MeC, Ch, Spt, MW, De, DeAu, Rex
48. "Hobo Yodel" (Gene Autry–Jimmy Long)
Ge, Ch, Spt, MW
49. "They Cut Down the Old Pine Tree" (Willie Raskin–George Brown–Edward Eliscu)
Ch, Ge, MeC, Spt, MW, De, DeAu, MeC, Rex, Ang, Lyric, Clifford, Embassy
50. "The Tie That Binds" (P.D.)
Ge rejected

August 4, 1930   Richmond, IN
Gene Autry–v/y; acc. own g

51. "Texas Blues" (Jimmie Rodgers)
Ch, Spt, MW
52. "Hobo Bill's Last Ride" (Waldo—Lafayette—O'Neal–Autry)
Ge, Ch, Spr, Spt
53. "Dust Pan Blues" (Frankie Marvin)
Ge, Ch, Spt, Spr, MeC
54. "I'm Sorry We Met" (Jimmie Rodgers)
Ge rejected
55. "My Carolina Sunshine Girl" (Jimmie Rodgers)
Ge, Spr, Spt, De, MW, Rex
56. "Train Whistle Blues" (Jimmie Rodgers)
Ge, Ch, Spt, MW, MeC
57. "I'm Lonely and Blue" (Jimmie Rodgers–Elsie McWilliams)
Ge rejected
58. "That's Why I'm Blue" (Jimmie Rodgers–Elsie McWilliams)
Ge rejected

November 6, 1930   Richmond, IN
Gene Autry: v/y; acc. own g

59. "Anniversary Blue Yodel (Blue Yodel No. 7)" (Jimmie Rodgers)
Ch
60. "In the Jailhouse Now No. 2" (Jimmie Rodgers)
Ch, MW
61. "Any Old Time" (Jimmie Rodgers)
Ge rejected
62. "I'm Sorry We Met" (Jimmie Rodgers)
Ge rejected
63. "That's Why I'm Blue" (Jimmie Rodgers–Elsie McWilliams)
Ge rejected

November 18, 1930   *New York*
Gene Autry, v/y; acc. own g
> 64. "The Yodeling Hobo" (Gene Autry)
>   Ba, Je, Or, Pe, Re, Ro, Cq, CrC/MeC/Roy/Stg, Pic
> 65. "Pictures of My Mother" (Gene Autry)
>   Cq, Bwy (as by Bob Clayton), CrC/MeC/Roy/Stg
> 66. "Blue Days" (Gene Autry)
>   Ba, Je, Or, Pe, Re, Ro, Cq

November 20, 1930   *New York*
Gene Autry, v/y; acc. own g
> 67. "He's in the Jailhouse No. 2" (Jimmie Rodgers)
>   Ba, Je, Or, Pe, Re, Ro, Cq, Bwy (as by Bob Clayton), Pic (as by Gene Autry, the Yodeling Hobo)
> 68. "Cowboy's Yodel" (Gene Autry)
>   Ba, Je, Or, Pe, Re, Ro, Cq, Bwy (as by Bob Clayton), Min, Pan
> 69. "Dad in the Hills" (Gene Autry)
>   Ba, Je, Or, Pe, Re, Ro, Cq, Bwy (as by Bob Clayton)

November 24, 1930   *New York*
Gene Autry, v/y; acc. own g
> 70. "High Powered Mama" (Jimmie Rodgers)
>   Ch, De, MW, MeC
> 71. "Whisper Your Mother's Name" (Jimmie Rodgers)
>   Ge rejected
> 72. "I'll Be Thinking of You, Little Gal" (Gene Autry)
>   Ge rejected
> 73. "The Yodeling Hobo" (Gene Autry)
>   Ch, MW, De, MeC

1931

January 29, 1931   *Richmond, IN*
Gene Autry, v/y; acc. own g; unkn md: all but 77
> 74. "Mean Mama Blues" (Jimmie Rodgers)
>   Ch, Spr, MW, MeC
> 75. "Blue Yodel No. 8" (Jimmie Rodgers)
>   Ch, Spr, MW
> 76. "Pistol Packin' Papa" (Jimmie Rodgers)
>   Ch, Spr, MW, De, MeC, Rex
> 77. "Dad in the Hills" (Gene Autry)
>   Ch, Spr, MeC, Rex, DeAu
> 78. "Pictures of My Mother" (Gene Autry)
>   Ch, Spr, MW, MeC, Rex
> 79. "Texas Blues" (Jimmie Rodgers)
>   Ge rejected

February 9, 1931 *Richmond, IN*
Gene Autry: v/y; acc. own g

  80. "Any Old Time" (Jimmie Rodgers)
      Ch, Spr, De, DeAu, MeC, Rex
  81. "Money Ain't No Use Anyway" (Gene Autry)
      Ch, Spr, MW, De, DeAu, MeC, Rex
  82. "Blue Days" (Gene Autry)
      Ch, Spr, MW, De, DeAu, MeC, Rex
  83. "Call Me Back Pal of Mine" (Johnny Roberts–Jimmie Davis)
      Ge rejected

February 17, 1931 *New York*
Gene Autry: v/y; acc. own g

  84. "The Gangster's Warning" (Gene Autry–George Rainey)
      Co (as by Overton Hatfield), Ve, Cl
  85. "Pictures of My Mother" (Gene Autry)
      Ve, Cl, Diamond
  86. "That's How I Got My Start" (Gene Autry–George Rainey)
      Ve, Cl
  87. "True Blue Bill" (Gene Autry–Frankie Marvin–George Rainey)
      Ve, Cl, Diamond

February 18, 1931 *New York*
Gene Autry, v/y; acc. own g; Frankie Marvin, h: 90, 91; sg: 88, 92, 93

  88. "Do Right Daddy Blues" (Gene Autry)
      Vi, MW
  89. "Money Ain't No Use Anyway" (Gene Autry)
      Vi unissued, Vi, MW
  90. "That's How I Got My Start" (Gene Autry)
      Vi unissued
  91. "That's How I Got My Start" (Gene Autry)
      Vi, ZoSA, HMVIn
  92. "Bear Cat Papa Blues" (Gene Autry–Frankie Marvin)
      Vi unissued
  93. "Bear Cat Papa Blues" (Gene Autry–Frankie Marvin)
      Vi

February 25, 1931 *New York*
Gene Autry, v/y. own g; Frankie Marvin, h: 94, sg: 95–97, g: 98

  94. "True Blue Bill" (Gene Autry–George Rainey–Frankie Marvin)
      Ba, Je, Or, Pe, Re, Ro, Cq, Apex, CrC/MeC, Stg, Roy, Min, Pan, EBW
  95. "The Gangster's Warning" (Gene Autry–George Rainey)
      Ba, Je, Or, Re, Ro, Cq, Apex, CrC/MeC, Stg, Roy, EBW (as by Hank Bennett),
      Pan, Pe
  96. "I'll Always Be a Rambler" (Gene Autry)
      Ba, Or, Pe, Ro, Cq, Bwy (as by Bob Clayton)

97. "The Death of Mother Jones" (W. C. Callaway)
    Ba, Je, Or, Pe, Re, Ro
98. "Bear Cat Papa Blues" (Gene Autry–Frankie Marvin)
    Ba, Me, Or, Pe, Re, Ro, Cq, RZ, RZIn, RZIr
99. "The Old Woman and the Cow" (P.D./Gene Autry)
    ARC unissued

March 31, 1931   *New York*
Gene Autry, v/y; acc. own g
100. "High-Steppin' Mama" (Gene Autry)
    TT unissued
101. "High-Steppin' Mama Blues" (Gene Autry)
    Vi, MW, ZoSA
102. "She Wouldn't Do It" (Gene Autry)
    Vi, ZoSA
103. "Don't Do Me That Way" (Gene Autry)
    Au, Vi, MW, ZoSA
104. "High-Steppin' Mama Blues" (Gene Autry)
    TT, Au (as by Gene Johnson)
105. "She Wouldn't Do It" (Gene Autry)
    TT, MW, Au (as by Gene Johnson)
106. "Do Right Daddy Blues No. 2" (Gene Autry)
    TT
107. "TB Blues" (Jimmie Rodgers)
    TT, Au (as by Gene Johnson)
108. "Jimmie the Kid" (Jimmie Rodgers)
    TT, Au (as by Gene Johnson)
109. "Travellin' Blues" (Jimmie Rodgers–Shelley Lee Alley)
    TT, Au (as by Gene Johnson)

April 1, 1931   *New York*
Gene Autry: v/y; acc. own g; Frankie Marvin, h: 114, 115; sg: 116, 117; jh: 114, 115
110. "There's a Good Gal in the Mountains" (Gene Autry)
    Vi, MW
111. "There's a Good Gal in the Mountains" (Gene Autry)
    TT, Au (as by Jimmie Smith)
112. "She's a Low Down Mamma" (Gene Autry)
    Vi, MW, ZoSA
113. "She's a Low Down Mama [*sic*]"
    TT, Au (as by Jimmie Smith)
114. "The Old Woman and the Cow" (P.D./Gene Autry)
    Vi unissued
115. "The Old Woman and the Cow" (P.D./Gene Autry)
    MW (as by Jimmie Smith)
116. "Bear Cat Mama from Horner's Corner" (Jimmie Davis)
    TT, Au (as by Jimmie Smith)

117. "She's a Hum Dum Dinger" (Jimmie Davis)
     TT, Au (as by Jimmie Smith)

April 1, 1931   *New York*
Frankie Marvin & Jimmie Smith (aka Gene Autry); Frankie Marvin, v/y: 118–120; sg:
118–122; Gene Autry, v/y, g: 121, 122

118. "Valley in the Hills" (P.D.)
     TT, Au (as by Jimmie Smith)
119. "Valley in the Hills" (P.D.)
     Vi unissued
120. "Valley in the Hills" (P.D.)
     Vi unissued
121. "She's Always on My Mind" (Fleming–Townsend)
     TT, Eld 1932 (as by Jimmie Smith)
122. "I'm Blue and Lonesome" (Fleming–Townsend)
     TT, Eld, Au (as by Jimmie Smith)

April 10, 1931   *New York*
Gene Autry, v/y, acc. own g

123. "Pistol Packin' Papa" (Jimmie Rodgers–Waldo O'Neal)
     Ba, Me, Or, Pe, Re, Ro, Cq, Bwy (as by Bob Clayton), Pan, RZ, RZIn, RZIr
124. "Jail House Blues" (Gene Autry)
     Ba, Me, Or, Pe, Ro, Cq, Bwy (as by Bob Clayton), CrC/MeC/Stg/Roy, Pan, R,
     RZIn, RZIr
125. "That's How I Got My Start" (Gene Autry)
     Ba, Or, Pe, Ro, Cq, Bwy (as by Bob Clayton), Mel-O-Dee, Apex, CrC/MeC/Roy,
     Stg
126. "Methodist Pie" (P.D.)
     Ba, Or, Pe, Ro

April 13, 1931   *New York*
Gene Autry, v/y; acc. own g; Frankie Marvin, h: 128, sg: 129, g: 127

127. "Do Right Daddy Blues" (Gene Autry)
     Pe, Ba, Or, Ro, Cq, Re
128. "Money Ain't No Use Anyway" (Gene Autry)
     Pe, Ba, Or, Ro, Cq
129. "I'll Be Thinking of You, Little Gal" (Gene Autry)
     Pe, Ba, Or, Ro, Cq

April 14, 1931   *New York*
Gene Autry, v/y, acc. own g; Frankie Marvin, sg: all

130. "Dallas County Jail Blues" (Gene Autry–W. R. Callaway)
     Ba, Or, Pe, Re, Ro, Cq, Bwy (as by Bob Clayton)
131. "She Wouldn't Do It" (Gene Autry)
     Ba, Or, Pe, Ro, Cq
132. "TB Blues" (Jimmie Rodgers–Hall)
     Ba, Or, Pe, Ro, Cq, Bwy

April 16, 1931   Richmond, IN
Gene Autry: v/y; acc. own g

133. "T.B. Blues" (Jimmie Rodgers–Hall)
     Ch, Spr, MW, De, DeAu, MeC
134. "True Blue Bill" (Gene Autry–Frankie Marvin–George Rainey)
     Ch, Spr, MW
135. "That's How I Got My Start" (Gene Autry–George Rainey)
     Ch, Spr, De, DeAu, MeC
136. "I'll Always Be a Rambler" (Gene Autry)
     Ch, MW, MeC, Rex
137. "Bear Cat Papa Blues" (Gene Autry)
     Ch, De, MeC
138. "I've Got the Jail House Blues" (Gene Autry)
     Ch, Spr, MW, De, MeC, Rex

October 29, 1931   New York
Gene Autry & Jimmy Long, v duet: 142–144; Frankie Marvin, v eff: 143, sg: 144, Roy
Smeck, sg: 142, 143, b: 140, 142, 144

139. "Rheumatism Blues" (Gene Autry)
     Pe, Me, Ba, Or, Ro, Cq
140. "I'm Atlanta Bound" (Gene Autry)
     Pe, Me, Ba, Or, Ro, Cq, CrC/MeC/Roy/Stg, Pan
141. "High-Steppin' Mama Blues" (Gene Autry)
     Pe, Me, Ba, Or, Ro, Cq
142. "That Silver Haired Daddy of Mine" (Gene Autry–Jimmy Long)
     OK/Vo, Pe, Ba, Or, Ro, Vo, Cq, Bwy (as by Clayton & Green), CrC/MeC/Roy/Stg
143. "Missouri I'm Calling" (Jimmy Long)
     Cq, Pe, Me, Ba, Or, Ro, Bwy (as by Bob Clayton)
144. "My Alabama Home" (Gene Autry–Jimmy Long)
     Ba, Me, Or, Pe, Ro, Cq

October 30, 1931   New York
Long Brothers (Jimmy Long & Gene Autry), v duet; acc. own g; Jimmy Long, sg

145. "Mississippi Valley" (Gene Autry–Jimmy Long)
     Vi
146. "My Old Pal of Yesterday" (Jimmy Long)
     Vi, ZoSA
147. "Missouri Is Calling" (Jimmy Long)
     Vi
148. "Cross-Eyed Gal that Lived Upon the Hill" (Jimmy Long–Gene Autry)
     Vi
149. "I'm Always Dreaming of You" (Jimmy Long)
     Vi, MW, RZ, RZIr
150. "Why Don't You Come Back to Me" (Gene Autry)
     Vi, MW, RZ, RZIr

October 30, 1931   New York

Gene Autry, v/y; acc. own g; Frankie Marvin. k: 154

151. "Jailhouse Blues" (Gene Autry)
     Vi, MW, Zo, RZ, Twin
152. "Rheumatism Blues" (Gene Autry)
     Vi, MW
153. "I'm Atlanta Bound" (Gene Autry)
     Vi
·154. "Wild Cat Mama" (Gene Autry)
     Vi, MW, Zo, Twin

October 30, 1931   New York

Jimmy Long & Gene Autry, v/y duet; acc. own g; Frankie Marvin, h: 157, sg: 155–156; Roy Smeck, sg: 155, 156

155. "Mississippi Valley Blues" (Gene Autry–Jimmy Long)
     Ba, Or, Pe, Ro, Vo/OK, Cq, CrC/MeC/Stg/Roy, Pan
156. "My Old Pal of Yesterday" (Jimmy Long)
     Ba, Me, Or, Pe, Ro, Vo, Vo/OK, Cq, CrC/MeC/Stg/Roy, RZAu
157. "My Cross-Eyed Girl"
     Ba, Me, Or, Pe, Ro, Cq, CrC/MeC/Stg/Roy

November 11, 1931   New York

Gene Autry, v/y; acc. own g; Frankie Marvin, sg: 159, g: 160; Roy Smeck, sg: 159, bj: 158

158. "Birmingham Daddy" (Gene Autry)
     Pe, Or, Ro, Ba, Me, Cq
159. "Why Don't You Come Back to Me" (Gene Autry)
     Ro, Or, Pe, Ba, Me, Cq, Vo/Ok, CrC/MeC/Roy/Stg
160. "She's A Low Down Mama" (Gene Autry)
     Cq

November 16, 1931   New York

Gene Autry, v/y; acc. own g; Roy Smeck, sg: 161, 162; bj: 163, 164

161. "I'm A Railroad Man (Waitin' on a Weary Train)"
     Cq
162. "Under the Old Apple Tree" (Gene Autry)
     Cq
163. "Wild Cat Mama Blues" (Gene Autry)
     Pe, Me, BA, Or, Ro, Cq, RZ, RZIn
164. "There's a Good Girl in the Mountains" (Gene Autry)
     Pe, Ba, Or, Ro, Cq

Unknown Date

Gene Autry v; acc. poss. Roy Smeck, g

"Bye Bye Boyfriend" (trad.)

unissued ARC
"Frankie and Johnnie" (trad.)
unissued ARC

1932

June 24, 1932   *New York*
Gene Autry, v; acc. own g, Jimmy Long, v: l66 poss. Roy Smeck, g
  165. "That Ramshackle Shack" (Gene Autry–Hugh Cross)
       Pe, Me, Ba, Or, Ro, Cq, Bwy (as by Bob Clayton)
  166. "Back to Old Smoky Mountain" (Gene Autry–Hugh Cross)
       Ba, Me, Or, Pe, Ro, Cq, Bwy (as by Bob Clayton)

June 27, 1932   *New York*
Gene Autry v/y; acc. own g; Roy Smeck, sg
  167. "Back Home in the Blue Ridge Mountains" (Gene Autry–Thomas Burton)
       Cq, Bwy (as by Bob Clayton)

June 28, 1932   *New York*
Gene Autry & Jimmy Long, v duet: 168, 170; Autry v/y; acc. own g; Roy Smeck, sg
  168. "The Crime I Didn't Do" (Gene Autry)
       Cq, Pe, Me, Ba, Or, Ro, Bwy (as by Clayton & Green), CrC/MeC/Roy/Stg
  169. "Kentucky Lullaby" (Gene Autry)
       Cq
  170. "Alone with My Sorrows" (Gene Autry–Jimmy Long)
       Cq, Pe, Me, Ba, Or, Ro, Bwy (as by Clayton & Green), CrC/MeC/Roy/Stg

June 29, 1932   *New York*
Gene Autry, v/y; acc. own g; Jimmy Long, v: 171; Roy Smeck, bj: 173, sg: 171, 172, 174
  171. "I'm Always Dreaming of You" (Jimmy Long)
       Ba, Me, Or, Pe, Ro, Cq, CrC/MeC/Stg/Roy, Pan
  172. "Moonlight and Skies" (Raymond Hall–Jimmie Rodgers)
       Vo, Pe, Me, Ba, Or, Ro, Cq, CrC/MeC/Roy/Stg
  173. "Returning to My Cabin Home" (Autry–Burton)
       Cq, CrC/MeC/Roy/Stg
  174. "In The Cradle of My Dreams" (Jimmy Long)
       Cq

June 30, 1932   *New York*
Gene Autry, v/y; acc. own g; Jimmy Long, v: 175, 176; Roy Smeck, bj: 177, sg: 175, 176
  175. "My Carolina Mountain Rose" (Gene Autry)
       Cq, Pe, Me, Ba, Or, Ro
  176. "Have You Found Someone Else" (Jimmy Long)
       Cq, Pe, Me, Ba, Or, Ro, CrC/MeC, Bwy
  177. "In the Hills of Carolina" (Autry–Burton)
       Cq, Bwy (as by Bob Clayton)

June 30, 1932   *New York*
Gene Autry, v/y; acc. own g

178. "The Gangster's Warning" (Gene Autry–George Rainey)
     Vi, MW
179. "Back to Old Smoky Mountain" (Hugh Cross–Gene Autry)
     Vi
180. "Back Home in the Blue Ridge Mountains" (Gene Autry–Thomas Burton)
     Vi
181. "That Ramshackle Shack" (Gene Autry–Hugh Cross)
     Vi, MW
182. "Black Bottom Blues" (Gene Autry)
     Vi
183. "Kentucky Lullaby" (Gene Autry)
     Vi

1933

January 27, 1933   *Chicago*
Gene Autry, v/y; acc. own g; unkn f: 187, 188

184. "Cowboy's Heaven" (Frankie Marvin–Gene Autry)
     Vi
185. "The Little Ranch House on the Old Circle B" (Gene Autry–Volney Blanchard)
     Vi
186. "The Yellow Rose of Texas" (P.D.)
     Vi
187. "Your Voice Is Ringing" (Percy Wenrich–arr. Gene Autry)
     Vi
188. "Louisiana Moon" (Gene Autry)
     Vi

March 1, 1933   *New York*
Gene Autry with Jimmy Long, v duet; acc. unkn f; poss. Bob Miller, p: 194, 195; unkn cel: 189, 190, 192, 193

189. "Louisiana Moon" (Keithley)
     OK/Vo, Pe, Me, Ba, Or, Ro, Cq
190. "Cowboy's Heaven" (Frankie Marvin–Gene Autry)
     Vo, Pe, Me, Ba, Or, Ro, Cq, CrC/MeC/Roy/Stg
191. "The Little Ranch House on the Old Circle B" (Gene Autry–Volney Blanchard)
     OK, Vo, Ro, Or, Pe, Me, Ba, Cq, CrC/MeC/Roy/Stg
192. "If I Could Bring Back My Buddy" (Gene Autry)
     Ba, Me, Or, Pe, Ro, Vo, OK, Cq, CrC/MeC/Roy/Stg
193. "The Old Folks Back Home" (Jimmy Long)
     Cq, Pe, Me, Ba, Or, Ro, CrC/MeC/Roy/Stg
194. "The Yellow Rose of Texas" (P.D.)
     ARC unissued
195. "The Yellow Rose of Texas" (P.D.)
     OK, Vo, Cq, Pe, Me, Ba, Or, Ro, CrC/MeC/Roy/Stg, RZAu

March 2, 1933   *New York*
Gene Autry & Jimmy Long, v duet; acc. unkn f

196. "Gosh! I Miss You All the Time" (Jimmy Long)
Ba, Me, Or, Pe, Ro, Cq, CrC/MeC/Stg/Roy

197. "The Answer to 21 Years" (Bob Miller)
Cq, Pe, Me, Ba, Or, Ro, Vo, CrC/MeC/Roy/Stg

198. "When It's Lamplightin' Time in the Valley" (Goodman–Lyons–Hart–Upson–Poulton)
Cq

199. "Watching the Clouds Roll By" (Jimmy Long)
Cq, Pe, Me, Ba, Or, Ro

March 2, 1933   *New York*
Gene Autry, v, own g; unkn f

200. "Don't Take Me Back to the Chain Gang" (Gene Autry–Ed Condon)
Cq, Pe, Me, Ba, Or, Ro, CrC/MeC/Roy/Stg

April 17, 1933   *Chicago*
Gene Autry & His Trio, personnel unkn, poss. Pete Canova, f; Don Weston, g; Bob Miller, cel

201. "In the Valley of the Moon" (Burke–Tobias)
Cq, CoC

202. "When the Mailman Says No Mail Today"
ARC unissued

April 17, 1933   *Chicago*
Gene Autry, v/y; acc. own g; unkn sg

203. "When the Humming Birds Are Humming" (Gene Autry)
Cq, CoC

204. "When the Humming Birds Are Humming" (Gene Autry)
ARC unissued

June 20, 1933   *New York*
Gene Autry, v/y; acc. own g; Roy Smeck, sg

205. "Roll Along Kentucky Moon" (Bill Halley)
Cq

206. "That Mother and Daddy of Mine" (Gene Autry)
Cq

June 22, 1933   *New York*
Gene Autry, v/y; acc. own g; Roy Smeck, sg

207. "Way Out West in Texas" (Gene Autry)
Cq, Pe, Me, Ba, Or, Ro, Vo/OK

208. "The Dying Cowgirl" (Gene Autry)
Cq

June 22, 1933   *New York*
Gene Autry, v; acc. own g; Roy Smeck, sg

  209. "When the Humming Birds Are Humming" (Gene Autry)
      Cq
  210. "The Death of Jimmie Rodgers" (Bob Miller)
      Pe, Me, Ba, Or, Ro, Vo, Cq, RZAu, CrC/MeC/Roy/Stg

June 22, 1933   *New York*
Gene Autry, v; acc. Jimmy Dale's Oklahoma Cowboys (cel, g, f)

  211. "In the Valley of the Moon" (Burke–Tobias)
      Cq

June 22, 1933   *New York*
Gene Autry, v/y; acc. unkn, poss. Perry Botkin, g

  212. "The Life of Jimmie Rodgers" (Bob Miller)
      Ba, Me, Or, Pe, Vo, Cq, CrC/MeC/Roy/Stg
  213. "If You'll Let Me Be Your Little Sweetheart" (Gene Autry)
      Ba, Pe, Me, Or, Ro,Cq, CrC/MeC/Roy/Stg

June 23, 1933   *New York*
Gene Autry, v; acc. Frankie Marvin, sg: 215; poss. Bob Miller, p

  214. "That Old Feather Bed on the Farm" (Gene Autry–Louis O'Connell)
      Pe, Me, Ba, Or, Ro, Cq, CrC/MeC/Roy/Stg
  215. "There's An Empty Cot in the Bunkhouse Tonight" (Gene Autry)
      Pe, Me, Ba, Or, Ro, Vo/OK, Cq, CrC/MeC/Roy/Stg

October 4, 1933   *Chicago*
Gene Autry, v; acc. Don Weston, g; Pete Canova, f; Benny Ford, bj; Frankie Marvin, sb

  216. "A Hill-Billy Wedding in June" (Freddie Owen–Frankie Moore)
      Cq, Pe, Me, Ba, Or, Ro, CrC/MeC/Roy/Stg

October 9, 1933   *Chicago*
Gene Autry, v/y; acc. unkn, poss. own g; Pete Canova, f; Don Weston, g

  217. "Moonlight Down in Lover's Lane" (Pitman–Costello–Kortlander)
      Cq
  218. "The Last Round-Up" (Billy Hill)
      Ba, Me, Or, Pe, Ro, Vo/OK, Cq

November 1, 1933   *Chicago*
Gene Autry, v/y; acc. poss. Pete Canova, f: 217; own g or Don Weston, g

  219. "When Jimmie Rodgers Said Good-bye" (Dwight Butcher–Lou Herscher)
      Cq, Pe, Me, Ba, Or, Ro
  220. "Good Luck Old Pal ('Til We Meet Bye and Bye)" (Gene Autry)
      Ro, Ba, Cq, Me, Or, Pe

1934

March 26, 1934   *Chicago*
Gene Autry, v/y; acc. poss Salty Holmes, g; Tex Atchison, f; Jack Taylor, sb
  221. "The Round-Up in Cheyenne" (Smiley Burnette)
       Pe, Me, Ba, Or, Ro, Cq, CrC/MeC/Roy/Stg, Min

March 26, 1934   *Chicago*
Gene Autry & Jimmy Long, v duet; acc. unkn, poss. Tex Atchison, f; Salty Holmes, g;
Frankie Marvin, sb: 224
  222. "Memories of That Silver Haired Daddy of Mine" (Gene Autry)
       Cq, Ba, Me, Pe, Ro, Or, CrC/MeC/Roy/Stg, Min
  223. "After Twenty-one Years" (Bob Miller)
       Cq, Pe, Ba, Me, Or, Ro, CrC/MeC/Roy/Stg, Min
  224. "Eleven Months in Leavenworth" (Gene Autry)
       Cq, Pe, Ba, Me, Or, Ro, CrC/MeC/Roy/Stg

March 27, 1934   *Chicago*
Gene Autry, v duet with Jimmy Long: 226, 228; Gene Autry, v: 227; acc. poss. Chick
Hurt, md; Tex Atchison, f; Salty Holmes, g; Jack Taylor, sb
  225. "Little Farm Home" (Smiley Burnette–Jimmy Long–Gene Autry)
       Ba, Pe, Mel, Or, R, MeC
  226. "There's a Little Old Lady Waiting" (Smiley Burnette–Gene Autry–Jimmy Long)
       Me
  227. "Dear Old Western Skies" (Smiley Burnette–Gene Autry)
       Cq, CrC/MeC/Roy/Stg

March 31, 1934   *Chicago*
Gene Autry & Jimmy Long, v duet; acc. poss. Tex Atchison, f; Chick Hurt, md; Salty
Holmes, g
  228. "Beautiful Texas" (W. Lee O'Daniel)
       OK/Vo, Pe, Me, Ba, Or, Ro, CrC/MeC/Roy/Stg

April 28, 1934   *Chicago*
Gene Autry, v duet with Jimmy Long; acc. Tex Atchison, f; Chick Hurt, md; Salty
Holmes, g
  229. "There's a Little Old Lady Waiting" (Smiley Burnette–Gene Autry–Jimmy Long)
       Ba, Or, Pe, Ro, Vo/OK, CrC/MeC/Roy/Stg

May 24, 1934   *Chicago*
Gene Autry, v; acc. Tex Atchison, f; Chick Hurt, md; Salty Holmes, g
  230. "Beautiful Texas" (W. Lee O'Daniel)
       ARC unissued

May 28, 1934   *New York*
Gene Autry, v duet with Jimmy Long; acc. Roy Smeck, bj; poss. Perry Botkin, g
  231. "Memories of That Silver Haired Daddy of Mine" (Gene Autry)
       ARC unissued

232. "When the Moon Shines on the Mississippi Valley" (Smiley Burnette)
      Cq, Ba, Pe, Me, Or, Ro, CrC/MeC/Roy/Stg, Min

May 29, 1934   New York
Gene Autry, v; acc. unkn

133. "Shine On, Pale Moon" (Jimmy Long)
      ARC unissued.
234. "The Stump of the Old Pine Tree" (Bob Miller)
      Cq, Ba, Pe, Me, Or, Ro, MeC
235. "Seven More Days" (Jimmy Long)
      Cq, Ba, Pe, Me, Or, Ro, MeC

May 31, 1934   New York
Gene Autry, v; acc. unkn

236. "My Shy Little Bluebonnet Girl" (Jimmy Long)
      ARC unissued

June 11, 1934   New York
Gene Autry, v; acc unkn, sg: 238, 240; Bob Miller, cel: 238; unkn, md: 239, 240; unkn g,
poss. Perry Botkin

237. "Memories of That Silver Haired Daddy of Mine"
      ARC unissued
238. "The Stump of the Old Pine Tree" (Bob Miller)
      Ba, Me, Or, Pe, Ro, Cq, CrC/Me/Stg/Roy
239. "Seven More Days" (Jimmy Long)
      Ba, Me, Or, Pe, Roy, Cq, CrC/MeC/Stg/Roy
240. "My Shy Little Bluebonnet Girl" (Jimmy Long)
      Ba, Me, Or, Pe, Ro, Cq, XL Radio Productions, CrC/MeC/Stg/Roy

June 25, 1934   New York
Gene Autry, v; acc. unkn

241. "Shine On, Pale Moon" (Jimmy Long)
      ARC unissued

1935

January 11, 1935   New York
Gene Autry Trio: Gene Autry, Jimmy Long, Smiley Burnette, v trio; acc. Tex Atchison,
f; Chick Hurt, md; Salty Holmes, g; Jack Taylor, sb

242. "Tumbling Tumbleweeds" (Bob Nolan)
      Ba, Me, Or, Pe, Ro, Vo/OK, Cq, Co, CrC/MeC/Stg/Roy
Gene Autry, v/y; acc. Tex Atchison, f; Chick Hurt, md; Salty Holmes, g; Jack Taylor, sb
243. "Texas Plains" (Stuart Hamblen)
      Ba, Me, Or, Pe, Ro, Cq, CrC/Me/Stg/Roy, Lucky
Gene Autry & Smiley Burnette, v duet; acc. Tex Atchison, f; Chick Hurt, md; Salty
      Holmes, g; Jack Taylor, sb; poss. Smiley Burnette and others, animal imitations
244. "Uncle Noah's Ark" (Smiley Burnette)
      Ba, Me, Or, Pe, Ro, Cq, CrC/MeC/Stg/Roy

January 14, 1935   *New York*
Gene Autry & Jimmy Long, v duet/y duet: 247; acc. Tex Atchison, f; Salty Holmes, g, h:
247; Chick Hurt, md; Jack Taylor, sb
  245. "Angel Boy" (J. Long–Paul Dennis)
       Cq, CrC/MeC/Stg/Roy
  246. "Red River Lullaby" (Jimmy Long–Gene Autry)
       Cq, CrC/MeC/Stg/Roy
  247. "Some Day in Wyomin'" (Smiley Burnette–Gene Autry)
       Ba, Me, Or, Pe, Ro, Vo/OK, Cq, CrC/MeC/Stg/Roy

January 15, 1935   *New York*
Gene Autry, v; Gene Autry & Smiley Burnette, v duet: 249; acc. unkn, sg; Salty
Holmes, g; Jack Taylor, sb
  248. "Dear Old Western Skies" (Smiley Burnette–Gene Autry)
       Cq, CrC/MeC/Stg/Roy
  249. "The Old Covered Wagon" (Smiley Burnette)
       Cq, CrC/MeC/Stg/Roy

January 16, 1935   *New York*
Gene Autry Trio: Gene Autry, Jimmy Long, Smiley Burnette, v trio; acc. Tex Atchison,
f; Salty Holmes, h/g; Chick Hurt, md; Jack Taylor, sb
  250. "Hold On, Little Dogies, Hold On" (Smiley Burnette–Gene Autry)
       Ba, Me, Or, Pe, Or, Cq, CrC/MeC/Stg/Roy, Lucky

January 16, 1935   *New York*
Gene Autry & Jimmy Long, v duet; acc. Tex Atchison, f; Salty Holmes, g, h: 251; Chick
Hurt, md; Jack Taylor, sb
  251. "Answer to Red River Valley" (Smiley Burnette–Gene Autry)
       ARC, Vo/OK, Cq, CrC/MeC/Stg/Roy, MeC/Min
  252. "That Silver Haired Mother of Mine" (Jimmy Long)
       Cq, CrC/MeC/Stg/Roy

January 16, 1935   *New York*
Gene Autry & Smiley Burnette, v duet; acc. Tex Atchison, f; Chick Hurt, md; Salty
Holmes, g; Jack Taylor, sb
  253. "Ridin' Down the Canyon" (Smiley Burnette)
       ARC, Cq, CrC/MeC/Stg/Roy

January 17, 1935   *New York*
Gene Autry, v; acc. Tex Atchison, f; Chick Hurt, md; Salty Holmes, g; Jack Taylor, sb
  254. "Wagon Train" (Smiley Burnette)
       Cq, CrC/MeC/Stg/Roy

January 17, 1935   *New York*
Gene Autry & Jimmy Long, v duet; acc. Tex Atchison, f; Chick Hurt, md; Salty
Holmes, g; Jack Taylor, sb
  255. "Old Missouri Moon" (Jimmy Long–Paul Dennis)
       Ba, Me, Or, Pe, Ro, Vo/OK, Cq, Co, CrC/MeC/Stg/Roy, RZAu

January 17, 1935   *New York*
Gene Autry Trio: Gene Autry, Jimmy Long, Smiley Burnette, v trio; acc. Tex Atchison, f; Chick Hurt, md; Salty Holmes, g; Jack Taylor, sb

256. "Ole Faithful" (Michael Carr–Joseph Hamilton Kennedy)
    Ba, Me, Or, Pe, Ro, Vo/OK, Cq, CrC/Me/Stg/Roy, Lucky

September 22, 1935   *Dallas*
Gene Autry & Jimmy Long, v duet; acc. Art Davis, f; Jim Boyd, g

257. "Vine Covered Cabin in the Valley" (Smiley Burnette)
    Cq
258. "Rainbow Valley" (Smiley Burnette–Gene Autry)
    Cq
259. "I'd Love a Home in the Mountains" (Smiley Burnette–Gene Autry)
    Cq

September 22, 1935   *Dallas*
Gene Autry, v; acc. Frankie Marvin, sg

260. "Nobody's Darling but Mine" (Jimmie Davis)
    Vo/OK, Cq, Co, CoC, RZAu, Lucky

September 23, 1935   *Dallas, TX*
Gene Autry & Jimmy Long, v duet; acc. Art Davis, f; Jim Boyd, g

261. "Just Come On In" (e.D.)
    ARC unissued

December 5, 1935   *Chicago*
Gene Autry, v/y; acc. Art Davis, f: all but 265; Frankie Marvin, sg: 4/v: 5; unkn, md: 6; Charles Sargent, g; Smiley Burnette, ac

262. "My Old Saddle Pal" (Gene Autry–Odie Thompson)
    Vo/OK, Cq
263. "Ridin' the Range" (Fleming Allen–Gene Autry–Nelson Shawn)
    Cq, CrC/MeC/Stg/Roy, Min
264. "The End of the Trail" (Smiley Burnette–Gene Autry)
    Cq, CrC/MeC/Stg/Roy, Min
265. "Don't Waste Your Tears on Me" (Gene Autry)
    Vo/OK, Cq, Co, CoC, RZAu
266. "You're the Only Star (In My Blue Heaven)" (Gene Autry)
    Vo, Cq, CoC

December 24, 1935   *Chicago*
Gene Autry, v; acc. Art Davis, f; Charles Sargent, g; Frankie Marvin, sb

267. "Mexicali Rose" (Helen Stone–Jack Tenney)
    Vo/OK, Cq, Co, CoC

1936

May 12, 1936   *Los Angeles*
Gene Autry, v; acc. Art Davis, f; unkn, cel: 269; poss. Aleth Hansen, md: 260, 270; Charles Sargent, g

268. "The Answer to Nobody's Darling" (Jimmie Davis)
     Vo/OK, Cq
269. "Mother, Here's a Bouquet for You" (Smiley Burnette–Gene Autry)
     ARC unissued
270. "Ridin' All Day" (Smiley Burnette)
     Cq

August 26, 1936   Los Angeles
Gene Autry, v/y: 271; acc. Art Davis, f; Frankie Marvin, sg: 272, 273/wb: 271/v: 271/y: 271; Charles Sargent, g

271. "The Old Gray Mare" (Frankie Marvin)
     Cq (as by Gene Autry with Frankie Marvin)
272. "Guns and Guitars" (Oliver Drake–Gene Autry)
     Cq
273. "I'll Go Ridin' Down That Old Texas Trail" (Smiley Burnette)
     Vo/OK, Cq

1937

March 22, 1937   Los Angeles
Gene Autry, v; acc. Art Davis, f; poss. Frankie Marvin, sg, esg: 274; Charles Sargent, g

274. "The Convict's Dream" (Gene Autry–Hadley Hooper)
     Vo/OK, Cq
275. "That's Why I'm Nobody's Darling" (Jimmie Davis)
     Vo/OK, Cq

May 29, 1937   Chicago
Gene Autry, v; or Gene Autry & Jimmy Long, v: 279, 281, duet; acc. Art Davis, f: 276; poss. Frankie Marvin, esg; poss. Curly Hoag, g

276. "The One Rose (That's Left In My Heart)" (Lani McIntire–Del Lyon)
     ARC unissued
277. "End of My Round-Up Days" (Pee Wee King–J. L. Frank-Estes)
     ARC unissued
278. "Sing Me a Song of the Saddle" (Gene Autry–Frank Harford)
     Cq
279. "With a Song in My Heart"
     Cq
280. "My Star of the Sky" (Gene Autry)
     ARC unissued
281. " I Hate to Say Goodbye to the Prairie" (Gene Autry–Odie Thompson)
     Vo/OK, Cq, Co, CoC
282. "My Rose of the Prairie"
     ARC unissued
283. "When the Tumbleweeds Come Tumbling Down Again" (Gene Autry)
     ARC unissued

June 2, 1937   Chicago
Gene Autry & Jimmy Long, v duet; acc. Frankie Marvin, esg; Curly Hoag, g

   284. "Down a Mountain Trail" (Gene Autry–Odie Thompson)
       ARC unissued
   285. "When the Golden Leaves Are Falling" (C. A. Havens)
       Cq

October 11, 1937   Los Angeles
Gene Autry, v; or Gene Autry, poss. Johnny Marvin, poss. Smiley Burnette, v trio: 288; acc. Carl Cotner, f; Frankie Marvin, esg/v; Curly Hoag, g; Rudy Sooter, sb

   286. "The One Rose (That's Left in My Heart)" (Lani McIntire–Del Lyon)
       Vo/OK, Cq
   287. "Blue Heaven" (Leo Robin–Ralph Rainger)
       OK, RZ, RzIr
   288. "Dust" (Johnny Marvin–Gene Autry)
       Vo/OK, Cq, Co, CoC, RZ

October 11, 1937   Los Angeles
Gene Autry & His String Band: Gene Autry, v; acc. Carl Cotner, f; Frankie Marvin, esg; Curly Hoag, g; Rudy Sooter, sb

   289. "Rhythm of the Range" (Johnny Marvin–Gene Autry)
       Vo/OK, Cq
   290. "Eyes to the Sky" (Gene Autry)
       Vo/OK, Cq

October 15, 1937   Los Angeles
Gene Autry, v; acc. Carl Cotner, f; Heinie Gunkler, cl; Frankie Marvin, esg; Curly Hoag, g; Rudy Sooter, sb

   291. "Old Buckaroo Goodbye" (Johnny Marvin–Gene Autry)
       Vo/OK, Cq
   292. "In the Land of Zulu" (Johnny Marvin–Gene Autry)
       Vo/OK, Cq.
   293. "It's Round-Up Time in Reno" (Owens–Lawrence–Gene Autry)
       Vo/OK, Cq
   294. "Were You Sincere?" (Gene Autry–Mark Halliday)
       OK, Cq, RZ, RzIn

October 15, 1937   Los Angeles
Gene Autry, v; acc. Carl Cotner, f; Frankie Marvin, esg; Curly Hoag, g; Rudy Sooter, sb

   295. "End of My Round-Up Days" (Pee Wee King–J. L. Frank–Milton Estes)
       Vo/OK, Cq, Co, CoC, RZAu

October 18, 1937   Los Angeles
Gene Autry, v; poss. Johnny Marvin, v; poss. Smiley Burnette, v trio: 298, 299, 301, 302; acc. Art Davis, f; Frankie Marvin, sg/v; Curly Hoag, g; Rudy Sooter, sb

   296. "My Star of the Sky" (Gene Autry)
       Vo/OK, Cq, RZAu

297. "When the Tumbleweeds Come Tumbling Down Again" (Gene Autry)
Cq, Vo/OK, Co

298. "When It's Springtime in the Rockies" (Mary Hale Woolsey–Milton Taggart–Robert Sauer)
Vo

299. "When It's Springtime in the Rockies" (Mary Hale Woolsey–Milton Taggart–Robert Sauer)
Cq, Vo/OK, Co

300. "I Want a Pardon for Daddy" (Charles Roat)
Vo/OK, Cq, Co, CoC

301. "Take Me Back to My Boots and Saddle" (Powell–Leonard Whitcup–Walter G. Samuels)
ARC unissued

302. "Take Me Back to My Boots and Saddle" (Powell–Leonard Whitcup–Walter G. Samuels)
Vo/OK, Cq, Co, CoC

November 24, 1937   Los Angeles
Gene Autry & His String Band (same as October 18, 1932)

303. "The One Rose (That's Left in My Heart)" (Lani McIntire–Del Lyon)
Co, CoC

304. "There's a Gold Mine in the Sky" (Charles Kenny–Nick Kenny)
Cq, Vo/OK, Co, CoC

305. "Sail Along, Silv'ry Moon" (Harry Tobias–Perry Wenrich)
Cq, Vo/OK, Co, CoC

306. "At the Old Barn Dance" (Peter Tinturin–Jack Lawrence)
Cq, Vo/OK, CoC

1938

June 22, 1938   Los Angeles
Gene Autry, v/y; acc. Curly Hoag, g; Frankie Marvin, esg; Karl Farr, g; Hugh Farr, f; Rudy Sooter, sb

307. "I Don't Belong in Your World (And You Don't Belong in Mine)" (Autry–Rose)
Vo unissued

308. "Ride Tenderfoot Ride" (Johnny Mercer–Richard A. Whiting)
Vo/OK, Cq, CoC, RZAu

309. "Good-Bye Pinto" (Johnny Marvin–Fred Rose–Gene Autry)
Vo/OK, Cq, RZAu

310. "As Long as I Have My Horse" (Johnny Marvin–Fred Rose–Gene Autry)
Vo/OK, Cq

June 23, 1938   Los Angeles
Gene Autry, v; acc. Hugh Farr, f; poss. Frankie Marvin, esg; Curly Hoag, g; Karl Farr, g; Rudy Sooter, sb

311. "I'm Beginning to Care" (Gene Autry–Fred Rose–Johnny Marvin)
Vo unissued

312. "If Today Were the End of the World" (Thomas Oatman Jr.)
Co, CoC

313. "The Dude Ranch Cowhands" (Gene Autry–Fred Rose–Johnny Marvin)
     Vo/OK, Cq
314. "Panhandle Pete" (Gene Autry–Fred Rose–Johnny Marvin)
     Vo/OK, Cq, CoC, RZ, RZAu
315. "The Old Trail" (Gene Autry–Fred Rose–Johnny Marvin)
     Cq, Vo, CoC, RZ

1939

April 13, 1939   Los Angeles
Gene Autry, v; acc. Sam Koki, esg; unkn, g; unkn, 2nd g: 319, 320, 321; Rudy Sooter, sb; unkn, vb: 316, 317, 318

316. "Paradise in the Moonlight" (Gene Autry–Fred Rose)
     Vo/OK, Cq, RZ, MR, RZAu, RzIn, RzIr
317. "Old November Moon" (Johnny Marvin–Gene Autry)
     Vo/OK, Cq, CoC, CoSs
318. "You're the Only Star (In My Blue Heaven)" (Gene Autry)
     Vo/OK, Cq, Co
319. "I Just Want You" (Gene Autry–Fred Rose–Johnny Marvin)
     Vo/OK, Cq, RZAu
320. "I Don't Belong in Your World (And You Don't Belong in Mine)" (Gene Autry–Fred Rose)
     Vo/OK, Cq
321. " 'the Blue Montana Skies" (Gene Autry–Fred Rose–Johnny Marvin)
     Vo/OK, Cq, RZ, RzIn, Twin

April 14, 1939   Los Angeles
Gene Autry, v, acc. Carl Cotner, f; unkn, f; prob. Sam Koki, esg; unkn, g; Rudy Sooter, sb

322. "When I First Laid Eyes on You" (Gene Autry–Marshall)
     Vo/OK, Cq, RZAu
323. "If It Wasn't for the Rain" (Ed E. Nelson–Fred Rose)
     Vo/OK, Cq
324. "Little Old Band of Gold" (Gene Autry–Charles Newman–F. Glickman)
     Vo/OK, Cq, Co, CoC, RZ, RZAu, RzIn, RzIr
325. "Rhythm of the Hoof Beats" (Gene Autry–Fred Rose–Johnny Marvin)
     Vo/OK, Cq, CoC, CoSs
326. "Little Sir Echo" (Smith–Fearis)
     Vo/OK, Cq

April 18, 1939   Los Angeles
Gene Autry, v, acc. Carl Cotner, f; unkn, f; unkn, ac; prob. Frankie Marvin, esg; unkn, g; unkn, sb

327. "I Wonder if You Feel the Way I Do" (Bob Wills)
     Vo/OK, Cq
#328. "Back in the Saddle Again" (Gene Autry–Ray Whitley)
     Vo, OK, Cq, Co, CoC, Min, RZ, RZAu, RzIn

329. "I'm Gonna Round Up My Blues" (Gene Autry–Johnny Marvin)
Vo/OK, Cq
330. "We've Come a Long Way Together" (Sam H. Stept–Ted Koehler)
Vo/OK, Cq, RZ, RZIn

September 11, 1939   Chicago
Gene Autry, v, acc. Alan Crockett, f: 332, 333; unkn, ac; poss. Frankie Marvin, esg;
Chick Hurt, eg; Salty Holmes, g; Jack Taylor, sb
331. "South of the Border (Down Mexico Way)" (Michael Carr–Jimmy Kennedy)
Vo/OK, Cq, Co, CoC, M-595, Co-Philco, RZ, MR6, RzIn
332. "Little Pardner" (Gene Autry–Fred Rose–Johnny Marvin)
Vo/OK, Cq, RZ, RzIn
333. "The Merry-Go-Roundup" (Gene Autry–Fred Rose–Johnny Marvin)
Vo/OK

September 12, 1939   Chicago
Gene Autry, v, acc. Alan Crockett, f; Augie Klein, ac; Chick Hurt, eg; Salty Holmes, g;
Jack Taylor, sb
334. "A Gold Mine in Your Heart" (Gene Autry–Fred Rose–Johnny Marvin)
Vo/OK, Cq, Co, C, RZ, RZIn
335. "I'm Beginning to Care" (Gene Autry–Fred Rose–Johnny Marvin)
Vo/OK, Cq
336. "Darling How Can You Forget So Soon" (Gene Autry–P. W. King–J. L. Frank)
Vo/OK, Cq, RZ, MR, RZAu, RZIn, RZIr

1940

March 12, 1940   Los Angeles
Gene Autry, v, acc. Carl Cotner, f; Spade Cooley, f; Paul Sells, pac; Frankie Marvin, esg;
Oliver E. (Eddie) Tudor, g; Walter Jecker, sb; band, v eff: 339
337. "The Singing Hills" (Mack David–Dick Sanford–Sammy Mysels)
Vo/OK, Cq
338. "Goodbye, Little Darlin', Goodbye" (Gene Autry–Johnny Marvin)
339. "El Rancho Grande (My Ranch)" (Bartley Costello–Silvano R. Ramos)
Vo/OK, Cq, RZ, MR, RZIn, RZIr
340. "Mary Dear" (P.D.) (Arr. Gene Autry–Cactus Mac)
Vo/OK, Cq, CoC, RZ, MR, RZIn, RZIr
341. "There's Only One Love in a Lifetime" (Gene Autry–Johnny Marvin–Tobias)
Vo/OK, Cq, CoC, RZ, RZIn
342. "When I'm Gone You'll Soon Forget" (Keith)
Vo/OK, Cq, Co, CoC, RZ, RZAu, RZIn

August 20, 1940   Los Angeles
Same lineup as March 12, 1940
343. "Blueberry Hill" (Al Lewis–Larry Stock–Vincent Rose)
OK, Cq, Co, CoC, RZ, RZAu, RZIn, RZIr
344. "A Face I See at Evening" (Gene Autry–Fred Rose)
OK, Cq, Co, CoC, CoSs, RZAu

345. "Be Honest with Me" (Gene Autry–Fred Rose)
     OK, Cq, Co, CoC, RZ, RZAu, RZIn, RZIr
346. "Call of the Canyon" (Billy Hill)
     OK, Cq, Co, CoC, RZAu
347. "Call of the Canyon" (Billy Hill)
     OK unissued

August 21, 1940   Los Angeles
Same lineup as March 12, 1940

348. "There'll Never Be Another Pal Like You" (Gene Autry–Johnny Marvin–Tobias)
     OK, Cq, Co, CoC
349. "Broomstick Buckaroo" (Gene Autry–Frank Harford–Johnny Marvin)
     OK, Cq, Co, CoC, RZAu
350. "Sycamore Lane" (Gene Autry–Fred Rose)
     OK, Cq, Co, CoC, RZAu
351. "There Ain't No Use in Crying Now" (Gene Autry–Johnny Marvin)
     OK, Cq, Co, CoC, CoSs, RZAu

August 22, 1940   Los Angeles
Same lineup as March 12, 1940

352. "You Waited Too Long" (Gene Autry–Ray Whitley–Fred Rose)
     OK, Cq, Co, CoC, RZ, RZAu, RZIn, RZIr
353. "That Little Kid Sister of Mine" (Gene Autry–Fred Rose)
     OK, Cq, Co, CoC, RZ, RZAu, RZIn, RZIr
354. "What's Gonna Happen to Me" (Gene Autry–Fred Rose)
     OK, Cq, Co, CoC, RZ, RZIn, RzIr
355. "Tears on My Pillow" (Gene Autry–Fred Rose)
     OK, Cq, Co, CoC, RZAu, RZIn, RZIr
356. "Sierra Sue" (Joseph B. Carey)
     OK, Cq, RZ, Rzln, RZAu

August 27, 1940   Los Angeles
Same lineup as March 12, 1940

357. "There's Nothing Like a Good Old Fashioned Hoedown" (Gene Autry)
     Cq, Co, CoC, RZ, RZIr
358. "When the Swallows Come Back to Capistrano" (Leon Rene)
     OK, Cq, RZ, RZAu, RZIr
359. "We Never Dream the Same Dream Twice" (Gene Autry–Fred Rose)
     OK, Cq
360. "The Cowboy's Trademarks" (arr. Gene Autry)
     Cq, Co
361. "The Last Letter" (Rex Griffin)
     Cq, Co, CoC
362. "I'll Never Smile Again" (Lowe)
     OK, Cq

1941

June 18, 1941   Hollywood

Gene Autry, v, acc. Carl Cotner, f; Mischa Russell, f; Paul Sells, pac; Frankie Marvin,
   esg; Johnny Bond, g; Dick Reinhart, sb

363. "You Are My Sunshine" (Jimmie Davis–Charley Mitchell)
      OK, Cq, Co, RZ, RZAu, RZIr
364. "It Makes No Difference Now" (Jimmie Davis–Floyd Tillman)
      OK, Cq, Co, V-D 240, RZAu
365. "After Tomorrow" (Gene Autry–Fred Rose)
      OK unissued
366. "A Year Ago Tonight" (Gene Autry–Fred Rose)
      OK, CoC, RZ, RZIr

July 28, 1941   Hollywood

Gene Autry, v, acc. Carl Cotner, f; Don Linder, t; Paul Sells, pac; Frankie Marvin, esg;
Eddie Tudor, g; W. Fred Whiting, sb

367. "I'll Never Let You Go (Little Darlin')" (Jimmy Wakely)
      OK, CoC, RZ, RZAu, RZIr
368. "I'll Be True While You're Gone" (Gene Autry–Fred Rose)
      OK, Cq, Co, CoC, Colr, RZ, RZAu, RZIr
369. "Under Fiesta Stars" (Gene Autry–Fred Rose)
      OK, Cq, CoC, RZ, RZAu
370. "Spend a Night in Argentina" (Gene Autry–Fred Rose)
      OK, Cq, CoC, RZAu
371. "I'll Wait for You" (Gene Autry–Fred Rose)
      OK, Cq, CoC, RZAu

July 30, 1941   Hollywood

Same lineup as July 28, 1941

372. "I'll Wait for You" (Gene Autry–Fred Rose)
      OK, Cq, Co, CoC, RZ, Me, MR, RZAu, RZIr
373. "Too Late" (Jimmy Wakely)
      OK, Cq, Co, CoC, RZAu
374. "Don't Bite the Hand That's Feeding You" (Thomas Hoier–Jimmie Morgan)
      OK, Co
375. "After Tomorrow" (Gene Autry–Fred Rose)
      OK, Cq, V-D 240, VD Navy 20, CoC, RZ, MR, RZAu, RZIr

August 1, 1941   Hollywood

Same lineup as July 28, 1941

376. "God Must Have Loved America" (Gene Autry–Fred Rose)
      OK, Co
377. "You Are the Light of My Life" (Gene Autry–Fred Rose)
      OK, Cq, Co, CoC, RZAu
378. "Lonely River" (Gene Autry–Fred Rose–Ray Whitley)
      OK, Cq, Co, CoC, RZ, Me, RZ, MR, RZAu, RZIr

379. "Dear Little Dream Girl of Mine" (Gene Autry–Fred Rose)
     Cq

August 11, 1941   Hollywood
Gene Autry, v, acc. Carl Cotner, f; Mischa Russell or Tex Atchison, f; Ted Bacon, vla;
Andy Iona Long, esg; Eddie Tudor, g; Fred Whiting, sb
  380. "Purple Sage in the Twilight" (Gene Autry–Jule Styne–Sol Meyer)
       OK, Cq, Co
  381. "I Wish All My Children Were Babies Again" (Jack Baxley)
       OK unissued
  382. "Dear Old Dad of Mine" (Gene Autry–Johnny Marvin)
       Cq
  383. "I'm Comin' Home Darlin'" (Gene Autry–Eddie Dean–Hoefle)
       OK, Cq, Co, CoC

August 27, 1941   Hollywood
Gene Autry, v, acc. Carl Cotner, f; Spade Cooley, f: Frankie Marvin, esg; Eddie Tudor,
g; Fred Whiting, sb
  384. "If You Only Believed in Me" (Gene Autry–Fred Rose)
       OK, Cq, Co
  385. "Keep Rollin' Lazy Longhorns" (Gene Autry–Johnny Marvin)
       OK, Co
  386. "Blue-Eyed Elaine" (Ernest Tubb)
       OK, Cq, Co, CoC

September 26, 1941   Hollywood
Gene Autry, v, acc. Carl Cotner, f; Tex Atchison or Spade Cooley, f; Don Linder,
t; Thurman Ratraff, cl; Paul Sells, pac; Karl Farr, g; Fred Whiting, sb; unkn, v trio
  387. "I Wish All My Children Were Babies Again" (Jack Baxley)
       OK, Cq, Co, CoC, RZ MR, RZAu, RZIr
  388. "Amapola (Pretty Little Poppy)" (Albert Gamse–Joseph Lacalle)
       OK, Cq
  389. "Maria Elena" (Lorenzo Barcelata)
       OK, Cq
  390. "I Don't Want to See the World on Fire" (Eddie Seiler–Sol Marcus–Benny
       Benjamin–Eddie Durham)
       OK, Cq, Co, CoC

December 13, 1941   Hollywood
Gene Autry, v, acc. Carl Cotner, f; Mischa Russell, f; Jack Mayhew, cl: 392, 393; Paul
Sells, pac; Frankie Marvin, esg; Johnny Bond, g; Fred Whiting, sb
  391. "Take Me Back into Your Heart" (Gene Autry–Fred Rose)
       OK, Co, CoC, RZAu
  392. "Sweethearts Or Strangers" (Jimmie Davis)
       OK, Co, CoC, RZAu
  393. "I Hang My Head and Cry" (Gene Autry–Fred Rose–Ray Whitley)
       OK, Co, CoC, RZAu

394. "You'll Be Sorry" (Gene Autry–Fred Rose)
   OK, Co, CoC, V-D 20, RZAu

1942

February 24, 1942   Hollywood
Gene Autry, v, acc. Carl Cotner, f; Don Linder, t; Joe Krechter, cl; Paul Sells, pac; Frankie
Marvin, esg; Johnny Bond, g, v: 396; Fred Whiting, sb; poss. Eddie Dean, Jimmy Dean v:
396/clapping: 396

   395. "Tweedle-O-Twill" (Gene Autry–Fred Rose)
      OK, Co, CoC, RZAu
   396. "Deep in the Heart of Texas" (June Hershey–Don Swander)
      OK, Co, RZAu
   397. "I'm Thinking Tonight of My Blue Eyes" (A. P. Carter)
      OK, Co, CoC, Colr, RZ MR, RZAu, RZIr
   398. "Rainbow on the Rio Grande" (Gene Autry–Fred Rose)
      OK, Co, CoC, RZAu

March 26, 1942   Hollywood
Gene Autry, v, acc. Carl Cotner, f; Mischa Russell, f; Paul Sells, pac; Frankie Marvin,
esg; Johnny Bond, g; Fred Whiting, sb

   399. "Private Buckaroo" (Allie Wrubel–Bob Newman)
      OK, Co, CoC
   400. "Call For Me and I'll Be There" (Gene Autry–Fred Rose)
      OK, Co, RZAu
   401. "Yesterday's Roses" (Gene Autry–Fred Rose)
      OK, Co, RZAu

June 10, 1942   Hollywood
Gene Autry, v, acc. Carl Cotner, f; Don Linder, t; Jack Mayhew, cl; Paul Sells, pac; Frankie
Marvin, esg; Johnny Bond, g, v: 403; Fred Whiting, sb; unkn, poss. Eddie Dean, Jimmie
Dean, v; unkn woman, v: 403

   402. "(I've Got Spurs That) Jingle Jangle Jingle" (Frank Loesser–Joseph Lilley)
      OK, Co, CoC, RZ MR, RZAu, RZIr
   403. "I'm a Cow Poke Pokin' Along" (Gene Autry–Fred Rose)
      OK, Co, CoC, RZX MR, RZIr

1944

November 29, 1944   Hollywood
Gene Autry, v, acc. Johnny Bond, g; Frankie Marvin, esg; Carl Cotner, vn; Louise Heising, vn; unkn t, b, v, cl, s

   404. "Don't Fence Me In" (Cole Porter)
      OK, Co
   405. "I'll Be Back" (Gene Autry–Eddie Dean–Rex Preis–Bill Bryan)
      OK, Co
   406. "Gonna Build a Big Fence Around Texas" (Cliff Friend–Katherine Phillips–
      George Olsen)
      OK, Co

407. "Darlin' What More Can I Do?" (Gene Autry–Jenny Lou Carson)
OK, Co

December 6, 1944   Hollywood
Same as November 29, 1944

408. "I Guess I've Been Asleep for All These Years" (Gene Autry–Fred Rose)
OK, Co
409. "The Same Old Fashioned Girl" (Gene Autry)
Col unissued
410. "At Mail Call Today" (Gene Autry–Fred Rose)
OK, Co

1945

June 13, 1945   Hollywood
Gene Autry, v, acc. Johnny Bond, g; Frankie Marvin, esg; unkn p, eg, vn, pac, b

411. "Don't Hang Around Me Anymore (Gene Autry–Denver Darling–Vaughn Horton)
Co, RZ, MeAu
412. "Address Unknown" (Gene Autry–Denver Darling–Vaughn Horton)
Co, RZ
413. "I Want to Be Sure" (Gene Autry–Merle Travis)
Co, RZAu, Me
414. "Don't Live a Lie" (Gene Autry–Johnny Bond)
Co

June 15, 1945   Hollywood
Gene Autry, v, acc. Johnny Bond, g; poss. Frankie Marvin, esg; Carl Cotner, vn; poss.
Tex Atchison, vn; unkn t, ac, b

415. "Was Yesterday a Dream" (Gene Autry–Jenny Lou Carson)
Co unissued
416. "There's a New Moon Over My Shoulder" (Jimmy Davis–Ekko Whelan–Lee
Blastic)
Co unissued
417. "Don't Take Your Spite Out on Me" (Gene Autry–Fred Rose)
Co unissued

November 1, 1945   Hollywood
Gene Autry, v, acc. Johnny Bond, g/v: 419; Carl Cotner, vn; unkn vn, pac, b, cl, t, male v

418. "Don't Take Your Spite Out on Me" (Gene Autry–Fred Rose)
Co, CoC
419. "Silver Spurs" (Gene Autry–Cindy Walker)
Co, RZ, MR, Me
420. "I'm Learning to Live Without You" (Gene Autry–Johnny Bond–Billy Folger)
Co
421. "Have I Told You Lately That I Love You" (Scott Wiseman)
Co, RZ, RZAu

1946

January 11, 1946 *Hollywood*

Gene Autry, v, acc. Johnny Bond, g; Frankie Marvin, esg; unkn pac, p, b, t, cl

422. "I Wish I Had Never Met Sunshine" (Gene Autry–Dale Evans–Oakley Haldeman)
Co, RZ

423. "You Only Want Me When You're Lonely" (Gene Autry–Steve Nelson)
Co, RZ

424. "You're Not My Darlin'" (Rosalie Allen–Fred Rose–Sam Martin)
Co

425. "Ages and Ages Ago" (Gene Autry–Fred Rose–Ray Whitley)
Co

February 13, 1946 *Hollywood*

Gene Autry, v; acc. Johnny Bond, g; Frankie Marvin, esg; Carl Cotner, vn; Bert Dodson, b; Fred Martin, pac; Jerry Scoggins, g; unkn vn, t

426. "The Last Round-Up" (Billy Hill)
Co

427. "Take Me Back to My Boots and Saddle" (Walter G. Samuels–Leonard Whitcup–Teddy Powell)
Co

428. "There's a Gold Mine in the Sky" (Nick Kenny–Charles Kenny)
Co

429. "Back in the Saddle Again" (Gene Autry–Ray Whitley)
Co

430. "Mexicali Rose" (Stone–Tenney)
Co

April 8, 1946 *Hollywood*

Same lineup as February 13, 1946

431. "You Laughed and I Cried" (Ray Whitley–Milton Leads–Billy Hayes)
Co, RZ, MeAu

432. "Over and Over Again" (Gene Autry–Cindy Walker)
Co, RZ, CoAu

433. "Sioux City Sue" (Dick Thomas–R. Freedman)
Co, CS

434. "Oklahoma Hills" (Jack Guthrie–Woody Guthrie)
Co unissued

435. "It's a Shame We Didn't Talk it Over" (Gene Autry–Cindy Walker)
Co unissued

436. "Wave to Me My Lady" (Frank Loesser–Jule Stein)
Co, CoAu

June 4, 1946 *Hollywood*

Same lineup as February 13, 1946

437. "South of the Border (Down Mexico Way)" (Michael Carr–Jimmy Kennedy)

438. "Ridin' Down the Canyon" (Smiley Burnette)
Co, RZAu

439. "Rounded Up in Glory" (P.D.)
     Co, Ha
440. "When it's Round-Up Time in Heaven" (Jimmie Davis)
     Co, Ha, RZ, Me, IZ

June 5, 1946   Hollywood
Same lineup as February 13, 1946
441. "Ole Faithful" (Michael Carr–Jimmy Kennedy)
     Co, RZ
442. "Home on the Range" (P.D.)
     Co, Ha, RZAu
443. "Tumbling Tumbleweeds" (Bob Nolan)
     Co
444. "There's an Empty Cot in the Bunkhouse Tonight" (Gene Autry–Frankie
     Marvin)
     Co, Ha, RZ, Me

July 2, 1946   Hollywood
Gene Autry, v; acc. Johnny Bond, g; poss. Fred Martin, pac; Frankie Marvin, g; Carl
Cotner, vn; unkn p, b
445. "Cowboy Blues" (Gene Autry–Cindy Walker)
     Co, Ha
446. "Gallivantin' Galveston Gal" (Steve Nelson–Milton Leeds–Wise)
     Co
447. "Someday" (Jimmy Hodges)
     Co, RZ, MRAu.

August 30, 1946   Hollywood
Same lineup as February 13, 1946
448. "Can't Shake the Sands of Texas from My Shoes" (Gene Autry–Pitts–Johnson)
     Co, DoAu, RZ, Me
449. "Twilight on the Trail" (Sidney D. Mitchell–Louis Alter)
     Co, Ha
450. "Red River Valley" (P.D.)
     Co
451. "Cowboy's Heaven" (Frankie Marvin–Gene Autry)
     Co

September 9, 1946   Hollywood
Gene Autry, v; acc. Johnny Bond, g; Merle Travis, eg; poss. Fred Martin, pac, Carl
Cotner, vn; Tex Atchison, vn; unkn vn, b, t
452. "Here's to the Ladies" (Gene Autry–Cindy Walker)
     Co
453. "The Last Mile" (Gene Autry–Oakley Haldeman–Fred Rose)
     Co
454. "Dixie Cannonball" (Gene Autry–Red Foley–Vaughn Horton)
     Co

1947

March 5, 1947   Hollywood
Gene Autry, v, acc. Johnny Bond, g; Frankie Marvin, esg; Carl Cotner, vn; Louise Heising, vn; Bert Dodson, hb; Fred Martin, pac; unkn vibes

455. "When the Snowbirds Cross the Rockies" (Gene Autry–Leonard Joy–Dick Howard)
Co

456. "A Broken Promise Means a Broken Heart" (Gene Autry–Rex Allen–Dave Bohm)
Co, CoC, RZ, MR

457. "The Leaf of Love" (Tex Williams–Bob Newman)
Co

458. "The Angel Song" (Curt Massey–Mary Millard–Gene Autry)
Co

August 28, 1947   Hollywood
Gene Autry, v; acc. Johnny Bond, g; Bert Dodson, v/b; Carl Cotner, vn; Fred Martin, v/pac; Jerry Scoggins, v; unkn horns, vn, jingle bells.

459. "An Old Fashioned Tree" (Becker–Williams)
Co, CL, RZ

*460. "Here Comes Santa Claus (Right Down Santa Claus Lane)" (Gene Autry–Oakley Haldeman)
CO, RZ, MR, CoAu

461. "Pretty Mary" (Gene Autry–Oakley Haldeman–Mitchell–MacDonald)
Co, CoAu, RZ

December 5, 1947   Hollywood
Gene Autry, v; acc. Johnny Bond, g; Merle Travis, eg; Bert Dodson, b; Carl Cotner, vn; Louise Heising, vn; Jerry Scoggins, g; Frankie Marvin, esg; Fred Martin, pac; unkn t, p

462. "I'm a Fool to Care" (Ted Daffan)
Co, RZ, MR

463. "I've Lived a Lifetime for You" (Ray Whitley–Bob Newman)
Co

464. "Little Big Dry" (Billy Weber)
Co, unissued

465. "They Warned Me About You" (Gene Autry–Johnny Bond)
Co

December 6, 1947   Hollywood
Same lineup as December 5, 1947

466. "Kentucky Babe" (Buck–Geibel)
Co, Ha, RZ

467. "Missouri Waltz" (James Shannon–John Eppel–Frederick Logan)
Co, Ha, RZ

468. "Rolling Along" (Martin Kotel–Rose Cooper)
Co, CoE, Ha

469. "Play Fair" (Ray Whitley–Milton Leeds–Billy Hayes)
Co, RZ

December 26, 1947   *Hollywood*
Same lineup as December 5, 1947

470. "Serenade of the Bells" (Kay Twomey–Al Goodhart–Urbano)
     Co
471. "Lone Star Moon" (Friend–Franklin)
     Co
472. "Loaded Pistols and Loaded Dice" (Johnny Lange–Hy Heath)
     Co, RZ, Me
473. "Buttons and Bows" (Jay Livingston–Raymond Evans)
     Co, RZ, Me, ReE, RZIr, Co

1948

April 25, 1948   *Chicago, IL*
Gene Autry, v; Bert Dodson, v; Jerry Scoggins, v; Fred Martin, v; The Pinafores, v; acc.
unkn, h

474. "A Boy from Texas, a Girl from Tennessee" (McCarthy, Jr.–Segal–Brooks)
     Co, RZ
475. "Blue Shadows on the Trail" (Johnny Lange–Elliot Daniel)

December 31, 1948   *Hollywood*
Gene Autry, v; acc. Johnny Bond, g; Fred Martin, pac/v; Bert Dodson, b/v; Jerry Scoggins, v; Carl Cotner, vn; Louise Heising, vn; Frankie Marvin, esg; The Pinafores, v

476. "The Bible on the Table" (Paul Cunningham–Leonard Whitcup–George Bennett)
     Co, RZ, Me, RZIr
477. "I Lost My Little Darlin'" (Oakley Haldeman–Kraus-Coburn)
     Co, RZ, MR, Ha, RZIr

1949

March 21, 1949   *Hollywood*
Gene Autry, v; acc. Johnny Bond, g; Carl Cotner, vn; Louise Heising, vn; Frankie Marvin, esg; Bert Dodson, b; unkn p, t

478. "My Empty Heart" (Gene Autry–Porter–Mitchell)
     Co, CoC
479. "I Wish I Had Stayed over Yonder" (Gene Autry–West)
     Co, CoC
480. "Sunflower" (Mack David)
     Co
481. "Ellie Mae" (Gene Autry–Favilla)
     Co

June 27, 1949   *Hollywood*
Gene Autry, v; acc. Johnny Bond, g; Bert Dodson, b; Carl Cotner, vn, Louise Heising,
vn; The Pinafores, v; unkn cl, t

#482. "Rudolph the Red-Nosed Reindeer" (Johnny Marks)
     Co, Ha, CoE, CoAu

483. "He's a Chubby Little Fellow" (Gene Autry–Oakley Haldeman)
Co, Ha, CoC

June 29, 1949   Hollywood
Narration: Gene Autry, Wally Maher, Gerald Mohr, Johnny McGovern

484. "Stampede" (Story: Henry Walsh–Peter Steele)
Co, Ha
485. "Stampede" Part 2
Co
486. "Stampede" Part 3
Co
487. "Stampede" Part 4
Co

August 4, 1949   Hollywood
Gene Autry, v; acc. Bert Dodson, b/v; Carl Cotner, vn; Louise Heising, vn; Fred Martin, pac/v; Jerry Scoggins, g/v; Johnny Bond, g; The Pinafores, v; unkn cl, t

488. "Santa, Santa, Santa" (Gene Autry–Oakley Haldeman)
Co, CoE, CoC
*489. "If It Doesn't Snow on Christmas" (Pascal–Marks)
Co, CoAu
490. "Story Book of Love" (Eaton)
Co, CoC

August 16, 1949   Hollywood
Same lineup as August 4, 1949

491. "Whirlwind" (Stan Jones)
Co, CoC
492. "Riders in the Sky" (Stan Jones)
Co
493. "When the Silver Colorado Turns to Gold" (Paul Herrick–T. Mitchell)
Co, CoC, CoE
494. "Texans Never Cry" (Oakley Haldeman–Gene Autry–Hank Fort)
Co, CoC

November 2, 1949   New York
Gene Autry, v; acc. Johnny Bond, g; Bert Dodson, b/v duet: 497; Carl Cotner, vn; Louise Heising, vla; Frankie Marvin, esg: 497; unkn cl, per, vn, s, poss. Merle Travis, eg

495. "Mule Train" (Johnny Lange–Hy Heath–Glickman)
Co, CoC
496. "A Cowboy's Serenade" (Nick Kenny–Charles Kenny–Fina)
Co, CoC
*497. "That Silver Haired Daddy of Mine" (Jimmy Long–Gene Autry)
Co, CoC

December 3, 1949   Hollywood
Narration: Gene Autry, Wally Maher, Pat McGeehan, Gil Stratton

498. "Champion (The Horse No Man Could Ride)" Parts 1–4 (Story: Walsh & Steele)
Co, Cl

December 8, 1949   Hollywood
Gene Autry, v; acc. Johnny Bond, g; poss. Merle Travis, eg; Bert Dodson, b; Carl Cotner, vn; Louise Heising, vla; unkn, p, vn

  499. "Poison Ivy" (George Wyle–Eddie Pola)
        Co, CoC
  500. "The Roses I Picked for Our Wedding" (Peter Tinturin–Gene Autry)
        Co, CoC
  501. "Love Is So Misleadin' " (Gene Autry–A. Simms)
        Co, CoC
  502. "A New Star Is Shining in Heaven" (Peter Tinturin)
        Co, CoC

1950

March 2, 1950   New York
Gene Autry, v; acc. Johnny Bond, g; Carl Cotner, vn; unkn vn, b, per, eg, fife

*503. "Peter Cottontail" (Steve Nelson–Jack Rollins)
        Co, CoC
  504. "The Funny Little Bunny" (Gene Autry–Johnny Bond)
        Co, CoC

April 12, 1950   Hollywood
Gene Autry, v; acc. Johnny Bond, g; Fred Martin/Bert Dodson, b/v duet: 507; Frankie
Marvin, esg; Carl Cotner, vn; unkn vn

  505. "Don't Send Your Love (to Me by Mail)" (Oakley Haldeman–R. Wright)
        Co, CoC
  506. "Roses" (Tim Spencer–Glen Spencer)
        Co, CoC
*507. "Mississippi Valley Blues" (Gene Autry–Jimmy Long)
        Co, CoC

April 20, 1950   Hollywood
Gene Autry, v duet with Dinah Shore; acc. full orchestra with strings and choir
backing

  508. "The Old Rugged Cross" (Rev. George Bennard)
        Co, CoC
  509. "In the Garden" (Miles)
        Co, CoC

April 24, 1950   Hollywood
Gene Autry, v; acc. Johnny Bond, g; Fred Martin, pac/v; Bert Dodson, b/v; Carl Cotner,
vn; The Pinafores, v; Jerry Scoggins, v; unkn p: 513; unkn vn

  510. "Broomstick Buckaroo" (Gene Autry–Frank Hartford–Johnny Marvin)
        Co
  511. "Blue Canadian Rockies" (Cindy Walker)
        Co, CoC, CoE
  512. "I Love You Because" (Leon Payne)
        Co, CoC, CoE

513. "The Last Straw" (Floyd Tillman)
     Co, CoC

June 12, 1950   Hollywood
Gene Autry, v; acc. Johnny Bond, g/v; Bert Dodson, b/v; Carl Cotner, vn; Jerry Scoggins, v; Fred Martin, v; The Pinafores, v; unkn v, horn, chimes

514. "When Santa Claus Gets Your Letter" (Johnny Marks)
     Co, CoC
*515. "Frosty the Snowman" (Steve Nelson–Jack Rollins)
     Co, CoC
516. "Onteora (Great Land in the Sky)" (Anderson–Andrea)
     Co, CoC

July 17, 1950   Hollywood
Narration: Gene Autry, Joan Rae, Jeff Silver, Tim Graham; orchestra and chorus directed by Carl Cotner. Released in England as "A Cowboy's Christmas"

517. "The Story of the Nativity" (Story: Bill Burch)
     Co, CoE
518. "The Story of the Nativity" Part 2
     Co, CoE
519. "The Story of the Nativity" Part 3
     Co, CoE
520. "The Story of the Nativity" Part 4
     Co, CoE

July 18, 1950   Hollywood
Narration: Gene Autry, Gil Stratton Jr., Leo T. Cleary, Jeff Silver, Tyler McVey, Robert G. Bruce Jr., Bert Dodson, Fred Martin, Jerry Scoggins, David Light, Eugene Twombley, eff

521. "Gene Autry at the Rodeo" (Story by H. Walsh)
     Co, CoE
522. "Gene Autry at the Rodeo" Part 2
     Co, CoE
523. "Gene Autry at the Rodeo" Part 3
     Co, CoE
524. "Gene Autry at the Rodeo" Part 4
     Co, CoE

July 26, 1950   Hollywood
Narration: Gene Autry with supporting cast. Producer: Hecky Krasnow

525. "The Story of Little Champ" (Story by Walsh and Steele)
     Co, CoE
526. "The Story of Little Champ" Part 2
     Co, CoE
527. "The Story of Little Champ" Part 3
     Co, CoE
528. "The Story of Little Champ" Part 4
     Co, CoE

July 28, 1950   Hollywood
Gene Autry, v; acc. Johnny Bond, g; Bert Dodson, b; Carl Cotner, vn; unkn vn, t, p

  529. "Bucky the Bucking Bronco" (Gerald Marks–Milton Pascal)
       Co
  530. "Rusty the Rocking Horse" (John Jacob Loeb)
       Co
  531. "Little Johnny Pilgrim" (Kane–Fidler)
       Co
  532. "Guffy the Goofy Gobbler" (Gerald Marks–Milton Pascal)

August 1950   Hollywood
Gene Autry, v; acc. Johnny Bond, v; Carl Cotner, vn; Bert Dodson, b/v; Jerry Scoggins, v; Fred Martin, v; The Pinafores, v; unkn vn, t, p

  533. "Goodnight Irene" (Huddie Ledbetter–John Lomax)
       Co, CoC, Ha

September 18, 1950   Hollywood
Gene Autry, v; acc. Johnny Bond, g/v: 534; Bert Dodson, b/v: 534; Jerry Scoggins, v: 534; Fred Martin, v: 534; The Pinafores, v: 534; Carl Cotner, vn; unkn cl, v

  534. "The Statue in the Bay" (Monte Hale–Billie Wagner–Jimmie Carlyle)
       Co, CoC
  535. "Let Me Cry on Your Shoulder" (Hershey–Swander)
       Co
  536. "Rose Colored Memories" (Gene Autry–Oakley Haldeman–Wright)
       Co

December 1, 1950   Hollywood
Gene Autry, v; v duet with Jo Stafford: 537, 538; unkn choral group: 539; acc. unkn g, b, per, esg, vn, t, p

  537. "Teardrops from My Eyes" (Rudolph Toombs)
       Co
  538. "My Heart Cries for You" (Percy Faith–Carl Sigman)
       Co
  539. "The Place Where I Worship" (Tarr–Foster–Goodhart)
       Co, CoC

1951

January 31, 1951   Chicago, IL
Gene Autry, v; acc. The Pinafores, v; acc. unkn b, per, fl, vn, brass, bells

  540. "Bunny Round-Up Time" (Stephen Gale–Leo Israel)
       Co, CoC
  541. "Sonny the Bunny" (Tommy Johnston)
       Co, CoC

March 21, 1951   Hollywood
Gene Autry, v; acc. The Pinafores, v; unkn bj, b, per, p, eg, vns, t

  542. "Mister and Mississippi" (Irving Gordon)
       Co, CoC

543. "Stop Your Gambling" (Robison–Pepper)
     Co, CoC

March 26, 1951   Hollywood
Gene Autry, v; acc. Johnny Bond, g; The Pinafores, v: 545, 546; unkn b, per, esg, vn, brass

544. "How Long Is Forever" (Johnny Marks)
     Co, CoC

545. "Gold Can Buy Anything but Love" (B. Sherman–D. Sherman)
     Co, CoC

546. "Crime Will Never Pay" (Willard Robinson–Jack Pepper)
     Co, CoC

April 20, 1951   Hollywood
Gene Autry, v; acc. The Pinafores, v; Jerry Scoggins, v/g; Fred Martin, v; Bert Dodson, b/v; unkn vn, t, per

547. "Old Soldiers Never Die, They Just Fade Away" (arr. by Gene Autry)
     Co

548. "God Bless America" (Irving Berlin)
     Co

July 11, 1951   Hollywood
Gene Autry, v; acc. Johnny Bond, g/v; Fred Martin, v; Bert Dodson, b/v; Jerry Scoggins, v; Carl Cotner, vn; The Pinafores, v; unkn per, vn, cl, t, chimes

549. "He'll Be Coming Down the Chimney" (J. Fred Coots–Al J. Neilburg)
     Co, CoC

550. "Thirty-Two Feet, Eight Little Tails" (John Redmond–James Cavanaugh–Frank Weldon)
     Co, CoC

551. "The Three Little Dwarfs" (Stuart Hamblen)
     Co, CoC

552. "Poppy the Puppy" (Tommy Johnston)
     Co, CoC

July 13, 1951   Hollywood
Gene Autry, v/narration; acc. Johnny Bond, g; unkn bj: 554

553. "Buffalo Bill" (Jay Glass–Steve Nelson–Fred Wise)
     Co

554. "Kit Carson" (Jay Glass–Steve Nelson–Fred Wise)
     Co

December 27, 1951   Hollywood
Gene Autry, v; acc. Johnny Bond, g; Fred Martin, pac/v; Bert Dodson, b/v; Jerry Scoggins, v; Frankie Marvin, esg: 559, 560, 561

555. "On Top of Old Smoky" (P.D.)
     Co (Playtime)

556. "The Old Chisholm Trail" (P.D.)
     Co (Playtime)

557. "Clementine" (P.D.)
     Co (Playtime)

558. "The Big Corral" (P.D.)
    Co (Playtime)
559. "I Was Just Walking Out the Door" (Cindy Walker)
    Co, CoC
560. "A Heartsick Soldier on Heartbreak Ridge" (Fidler–Kane)
    Co
561. "Am I Just a Pastime" (Johnny Bond–Doug Autry)
    Co, CoC

1952

March 25, 1952   Hollywood
Gene Autry, v; v duet with Phyllis Lynne: 562; acc. Johnny Bond, g; Carl Cotner, vn;
Fred Martin, pac: 563; unkn bj, esg, per, organ, strings

562. "Don't Believe a Word They Say" (Leo Manners)
    Co, CoC
563. "Diesel Smoke, Dangerous Curves" (Martin)
    Co, CoC

June 19, 1952   Hollywood
Gene Autry, v; acc. Johnny Bond, g/v; Frankie Marvin, esg; Bert Dodson, b/v; Fred
Martin, pac/v; Jerry Scoggins, v; Carl Cotner, vn; unkn vn

564. "Smokey the Bear" (Steve Nelson–Jack Rollins)
    Co
565. "Back in the Saddle Again" (Gene Autry–Ray Whitley)
    Co
566. "God's Little Candles" (Jimmy Kennedy)
    Co, CoC

June 20, 1952   Hollywood
Gene Autry, v; v duet with Rosemary Clooney; acc. Johnny Bond, g; Carl Cotner, vn;
unkn orch

567. "The Night Before Christmas" (Johnny Marks)
    Co
568. "Look Out the Window" (Lew Porter–TeePee Mitchell)
    Co CoC

July 20, 1952   Hollywood
Gene Autry, narration/v: 569, 570; v: 571, 572; acc Johnny Bond, g/v:571, 572; Bert
Dodson, b/v: 571, 572; Fred Martin, pac/v: 571, 572; Jerry Scoggins, v: 571, 572; unkn
strings, per, esg

569. "Johnny Appleseed" (Story: Henry Harvey Walsh; Music: Stephen Gale; Prod.
    & Dir.: Hecky Krasnow)
    Co
570. "Johnny Appleseed" (Part 2)
    Co
571. "The Night Before Christmas in Texas" (Leon A. Harris, Jr.–Bob Miller)
    Co, CoC

572. "Merry Texas Christmas You All" (Leon A. Harris Jr.–Bob Miller)
     Co, CoC

1953

June 24, 1953   Hollywood
Gene Autry, v; acc. Mitchell Choirboys, v; unkn g; b, per, t, strings

   573. "Where Did My Snowman Go?" (Venis–S. Mann–Poser)
        Co
   574. "Freddie, the Little Fir Tree" (Merle Travis–Fairchild)
        Co

June 25, 1953   Hollywood
Gene Autry, v; acc. King Sisters, v: 575; Jerry Scoggins, v: 577; Bert Dodson, b/v: 577;
Fred Martin, pac/v: 577; unkn g, per, brass, woodwinds, strings

   575. "Santa Claus Is Comin' to Town" (Haven Gillespie–J. Fred Coots)
        Co
   576. "Here Comes Santa Claus (Right Down Santa Claus Lane)" (Gene Autry–Oakley Haldeman)
        Co
   577. "There's a Big Candy Round-Up" (Dick Manning–Joe Estells–Louis Robino)
        Co

June 26, 1953   Hollywood
Gene Autry, v; acc. King Sisters, v: 575; Jerry Scoggins, v: 577; Bert Dodson, b/v: 577;
Fred Martin, pac/v: 577; unkn g, per, brass, woodwinds, strings

   578. "Up on the Housetop" (Jane Whitman)
        Co
   579. "Happy Little Island" (Stephen Gale–Hector Marchese)
        Co

October 29, 1953   Hollywood
Gene Autry, v; acc. Johnny Bond, g: 582; The Pinafores, v; Jerry Scoggins, v; Bert
Dodson, v; Fred Martin, v; unkn g, b, per, strings, brass, woodwinds

   580. "I Wish My Mom Would Marry Santa Claus" (Gene Autry–Michael Carr)
        Co, CoE
   581. "Sleigh Bells" (Gene Autry–Michael Carr)
        Co, CoE
   582. "A Voice in the Choir" (Gene Autry–Michael Carr)
        Co

December 13, 1953   Hollywood
Gene Autry, v; acc. Johnny Bond, g; Merle Travis, eg; Fred Martin, pac/v: 584; Jerry
Scoggins, v: 584; Bert Dodson, b/v: 584; unkn per, possibly Andy Secrest, t; Buddy
Cole, organ

   583. "Bimbo" (Rodney Morris)
        Co, CoC, Phillips (British)
   584. "Angels in the Sky" (Glasser)
        Co

585. "Roly Poly" (Fred Rose–Gene Autry)
     Co, CoC

1954

January 4, 1954   Hollywood
Gene Autry, v; acc. Johnny Bond, g/v; Fred Martin, pac/v; Jerry Scoggins, v; Bert Dodson, b/v; unkn per, strings

   586. "Easter Mornin' " (June Winters–Mary Alice Ruffin)
        Co, CoC, Phillips (British)
   587. "The Horse With the Easter Bonnet" (Al Hoffman–Dick Manning)
        Co, CoC

January 4, 1954   Hollywood
Gene Autry, v; acc. Johnny Bond, g; Merle Travis, eg; Frankie Marvin, esg; Carl Cotner, vn; unkn b, per

   588. "Closing the Book" (Smiley Burnette)
        Co
   589. "It's My Lazy Day" (Smiley Burnette)
        Co

May 18, 1954   Nashville, TN
Gene Autry, v; acc. Johnny Bond, g; Jack Shook, eg; Marvin Hughes, p; Grady Martin, f, g; Bob Foster, esg; Frank Vaden, f; Ernie Newton, b; Murray Harman, per

   590. "When He Grows Tired of You" (Aldrich)
        Co
   591. "You're the Only Good Thing" (Jack Toombs)
        Co
   592. "It Just Don't Seem Like Home When You're Gone" (Tex Atchison)
        Co
   593. "I'm Innocent" (Pee Wee King–Redd Stewart)
        Co

May 19, 1954   Nashville
Same lineup as May 18, 1954

   594. "You're an Angel" (Byrum)
        Co
   595. "20/20 Vision (and Walking around Blind)" (Allison–Estes)
        Co

July 19, 1954   Hollywood
Gene Autry, v; acc. Johnny Bond, g; Jerry Scoggins, v: 596; Bert Dodson, v: 596; Fred Martin, v: 596; unkn b, brass, per, strings, eff

   596. "God's in the Saddle" (J. Hope–Moraine)
        Co
   597. "Barney the Bashful Bullfrog" (Gene Evans)
        Co, Ha, Philips (British)

598. "Little Peter Punkin Eater" (Emmett Langeston–Ace Hampton–Carl 'Deacon' Moore–Malcolm Underwood)
Co, Phillips (British)

1955

September 30, 1955   Hollywood
Gene Autry, v; acc. Johnny Bond, g; Bert Dodson, b/v duet: 601; Fred Martin, pac; unkn per, brass, vn

599. "Round, Round the Christmas Tree" (Fred Stryker)
Co

600. "Merry Christmas Waltz" (Inez Loewer–Bot Batson)
Co

601. "You've Got to Take the Bitter With the Sweet" (Fotine–Miles)
Co

October 4, 1955   Hollywood
Gene Autry, v; acc. Johnny Bond, g/v: 603; Fred Martin, ac/v: 603; Bert Dodson, b/v: 603; Jerry Scoggins, v: 603; poss. Frankie Marvin, esg; unkn per

602. "Two Cheaters in Love" (Jack Toombs)
Co

603. "If Today Were the End of the World" (Gene Autry)
Co

1956

February 27, 1956   Hollywood
Gene Autry, v; acc. Johnny Bond, g; Carl Smith, v; Rosemary Clooney, v; Don Cherry, v; Collins Kids, v; unkn b, per, esg, vn. (For LP: *Country Spectacular*)

604. "You Are My Sunshine" (Jimmie Davis)
Co

April 23, 1956   Hollywood
Gene Autry, v; acc. Johnny Bond, g; Merle Travis, eg; unkn b, per, esg

605. "I Hang My Head and Cry" (Gene Autry–Fred Rose–Ray Whitley)
CL

606. "Be Honest With Me" (Gene Autry–Fred Rose)
CL.

October 17, 1956   Hollywood
Gene Autry, v; acc. Johnny Bond, g; unkn b, per, brass, strings, chorus

607. "Everyone's a Child at Christmas" (Johnny Marks)
Co

608. "You Can See Old Santa Claus" (Joe Johnson–Lefty Frizzell–Bob Adams)
Co

1957

May 3, 1957   New York
Gene Autry, v; acc. The Riders of the Purple Sage, v; unkn per, ac, b, g

609. "Johnny Reb and Billy Yank" (Charles Tobias)
     Co

June 6, 1957   Hollywood
Gene Autry, v; acc. Johnny Bond, g; unkn b, per, p, electric md, chorus

610. "Darlin', What More Can I Do" (Jenny Lou Carson–Gene Autry)
     Co
611. "Half Your Heart" (Blair–Duhig)
     Co

Summer 1957   Hollywood
Gene Autry, v; acc. Johnny Bond, g; unkn b, per, p, g, electric md, choral group, conducted by Carl Cotner

612. "No Back Door to Heaven" (Dave Burgess)
     Chg, Sp, MRC
613. "You're the Only Good Thing" (Jack Toombs)
     Chg, Sp

Autumn 1957   Hollywood
Gene Autry, v; acc. full orchestra and chorus conducted by Carl Cotner. Originally released in 1957 as *Christmastime with Gene Autry* on Chg

614. "Jingle Bells" (arranged by Carl Cotner)
     Chg, Rep, Sp, Al
615. "Silver Bells" (Livingston–Evans)
     Chg, Rep
616. "Here Comes Santa Claus" (Gene Autry–Oakley Haldeman)
     Chg, Rep, Sp, Al
617. "Up on the House Top" (Arr: Cotner)
     Chg, Rep, Sp, Al
618. "Rudolph the Red Nosed Reindeer" (Johnny Marks)
     Chg, Rep
619. "Santa Claus is Coming to Town" (Haven–Gillespie–Coots)
     Chg, Sp
620. "O Little Town of Bethlehem"
     "Silent Night"
     "Joy to the World"
     Chg, Rep, Sp, Al

1959

Autumn 1959   Hollywood
Gene Autry, v; acc. orchestra and chorus conducted by Carl Cotner

621. "Buon Natale" (Bob Saffer–Frank Linale)
     Rep, Lon

622. "Nine Little Reindeer" (Gene Autry–Johnny Marks–Merle Travis)
    Rep, Lon, Al
623. "Santa's Comin' in a Whirlybird" (Ashley Dees)
    Rep

1961–1962

Winter 1961–1962   Hollywood (International Sound Studios)
Gene Autry, v; acc. Johnny Bond, g; unkn b, per, esg, sl, t, Carl Cotner and his Rainbow
Strings

624. "You're the Only Star (in My Blue Heaven)" (Gene Autry)
    RCA Victor
625. "Tweedle-O-Twill" (Gene Autry–Fred Rose)
    RCA Victor
626. "I'll Wait for You" (Gene Autry–Fred Rose)
    Unissued
627. "You Are My Sunshine" (Jimmie Davis–Charley Mitchell)
    RCA Victor
628. "Lonely River" (Gene Autry–Ray Whitley–Fred Rose)
    RCA Victor
629. "San Antonio Rose" (Bob Wills)
    RCA Victor
630. "Trouble in Mind" (Richard M. Jones)
    RCA Victor
631. "Hang Your Head in Shame" (Fred Rose–Ed Nelson–Steve Nelson)
    RCA Victor
632. "Be Honest With Me" (Gene Autry–Fred Rose)
    RCA Victor
633. "Blues Stay Away from Me" (Delmore–Raney–Glover)
    RCA Victor
634. "Tears on My Pillow" (Gene Autry–Fred Rose)
    RCA Victor
635. "I Hang My Head and Cry" (Gene Autry–Fred Rose–Ray Whitley)
    RCA Victor
636. "Ages and Ages Ago" (Gene Autry–Fred Rose–Ray Whitley)
    RCA unissued
637. "Darlin' What More Can I Do" (Gene Autry–Jenny Lou Carson)
    RCA unissued
638. "Goodbye, Little Darlin', Goodbye" (Gene Autry–Johnny Marvin)
    RCA Victor

1964

Hollywood
Gene Autry, narration; acc. orchestra with full strings
639. "One Solitary Life"
    Hil
640. "A Cowboy's Prayer"
    Hil, Sta

GENE AUTRY FILMOGRAPHY

Detailed synopses, cast lineups, and other information about each film, as well as every Gene Autry television program, can be found at www.geneautry.com. Films are listed in order of release; if film was made in a year prior to its release date, the year is listed in parentheses.

1934
In Old Santa Fe   Mascot (starring Ken Maynard)
Mystery Mountain   Mascot serial (starring Ken Maynard)

1935
The Phantom Empire (1934)   Mascot serial
Tumbling Tumbleweeds   Republic (all films are Republic unless noted otherwise)
Melody Trail
The Sagebrush Troubadour
The Singing Vagabond

1936
Red River Valley
Comin' 'Round the Mountain
The Singing Cowboy
Guns and Guitars
Oh, Susanna!
Ride, Ranger, Ride
The Big Show
The Old Corral

1937
Round-Up Time in Texas (1936)
Git Along, Little Dogies
Rootin' Tootin' Rhythm
Yodelin' Kid from Pine Ridge
Public Cowboy No. 1
Boots and Saddles
Manhattan Merry-Go-Round
Springtime in the Rockies

1938
The Old Barn Dance (1937)
Gold Mine in the Sky
Man from Music Mountain
Prairie Moon
Rhythm of the Saddle
Western Jamboree

1939
Home on the Prairie (1938)
Mexicali Rose
Blue Montana Skies
Mountain Rhythm
Colorado Sunset
In Old Monterey
Rovin' Tumbleweeds
South of the Border

1940
Rancho Grande
Shooting High (20th Century Fox)
Gaucho Serenade
Carolina Moon
Ride, Tenderfoot, Ride
Melody Ranch

1941
Ridin' on a Rainbow (1940)
Back in the Saddle
The Singing Hill
Sunset in Wyoming
Under Fiesta Stars
Down Mexico Way
Sierra Sue

1942
Cowboy Serenade (1941)
Heart of the Rio Grande
Home in Wyomin'
Stardust on the Sage
Call of the Canyon
Bells of Capistrano

1946
Sioux City Sue

1947
Trail to San Antone
Twilight on the Rio Grande
Saddle Pals
Robin Hood of Texas
The Last Round-Up　　　Columbia (the following films were all released by Columbia)

1948
The Strawberry Roan (1947)

1949
Loaded Pistols (1948)
The Big Sombrero (1947)
Riders of the Whistling Pines (1948)
Rim of the Canyon (1948)
The Cowboy and the Indians
Riders in the Sky

1950
Sons of New Mexico (1949)
Mule Train (1949)
Cow Town (1949)
Beyond the Purple Hills (1949)
Indian Territory
The Blazing Sun

1951
Gene Autry and the Mounties (1950)
Texans Never Cry (1950)
Whirlwind (1950)
Silver Canyon
Hills of Utah
Valley of Fire

1952
The Old West (1951)
Night Stage to Galveston (1951)
Apache Country (1951)
Barbed Wire (1951)
Wagon Team
Blue Canadian Rockies

1953
Winning of the West (1952)
On Top of Old Smoky (1952)
Goldtown Ghost Riders (1952)
Pack Train (1952)
Saginaw Trail
Last of the Pony Riders

ACKNOWLEDGMENTS

The genesis of *Public Cowboy No. 1* goes back nearly a decade to 1997. Along the way, I've met a number of terrific people who have helped make this biography a reality. Just as Gene Autry had the good fortune to cross paths with mentors (some well known and others behind the scenes), so have I been fortunate to discover supporters who gave their all to assist me on my journey.

My heartfelt thanks go first and foremost to those closest to Gene Autry, particularly his wife, Jackie, and his very loyal staff: Karla Buhlman, Maxine Hansen, and the late Alex Gordon. I first made their acquaintance the day I met Gene Autry, on March 18, 1997, when I traveled to Los Angeles to interview Gene for the *New York Times*. The meeting itself was several months in the making: the Singing Cowboy rarely gave interviews anymore, and it took the utmost diplomacy and perseverance of my good friend James Austin, co-producer of the Grammy-nominated Autry box set, *Sing Cowboy Sing*, to convince them to let me meet with Gene. I am also grateful to then-editor of the *New York Times*'s Arts and Leisure section, Fletcher Roberts, for making the assignment that would change my life.

I cannot convey enough how trusting and supportive those closest to Gene have been in permitting me complete access to all of his personal papers and memorabilia, as well as contact with his closest friends and relatives—all without attempting to exert control over my discoveries, the conclusions I drew, or what I chose to include in the book. Researching a life as rich and complicated as Gene Autry's is bound to turn up some difficult material, and they trusted me with this information. I only wish this book could comprise two volumes, in order to include the last decades of Gene's life as businessman, ball club owner, and husband to Jackie Autry. It is my hope that another book eventually will document this equally fascinating period of Gene's long, very active life. The most energetic and enthusiastic women I have ever known, Karla Buhlman and

Maxine Hansen, and their indomitable staff and associates—Irynne Isip, Kim Mansfield, Bob Fischer, Howard and Jill Levine, and RPG Productions—jumped through hoops to provide me with everything they could to facilitate the researching and writing of this book. The legacy of Gene Autry is most precious to them, and I am honored they shared it so generously with me. A special note of remembrance of the late Alex Gordon, perhaps the world's foremost Autry authority and self-described biggest fan: I only wish he could have lived to read my manuscript and perhaps quibble over some of my conclusions and a fact or two.

My initial interview with Gene Autry also led me to the institution originally known as the Gene Autry Western Heritage Museum. Since then, some of the staff there who offered guidance and support have moved on to other places, but they were among my first benefactors: Joanne and Monte Hale, Suzanne Fox, James Nottage, Kevin Mulroy, and Susan Van De Veyvre. Having spent hundreds of hours at the Autry National Center since 1997, I have been blessed with the expertise and unflagging support from so many there: I particularly owe my deepest gratitude to the director of the Institute for the Study of the American West, Marva Felchlin, and her super associate Manola Madrid; Autry curator Michael Duchemin has graciously shared his research and knowledge with me, and the exceedingly helpful Sage Guyton was always there to lend a hand. Others who have assisted in various ways include John Gray, Steve Aron, Marlene Head, Bobbie Bell, LaLena Lewark, and Evelyn Davis.

Over the past seventeen years, my astute agent and dear friend Sarah Lazin has been my great advocate, and I offer her my thanks. I'm also grateful to Kim Robinson, who originally signed the book to Oxford University Press, and her successor, my very helpful editor Suzanne Ryan, along with equally supportive associate editor Norm Hirschy and editorial assistant Lora Dunn, senior production editor Joellyn M. Ausanka, copyeditor Mary Sutherland, publicity director Christian Purdy, publicist Claudia Dizenzo, Andrew Varhol, and others.

Fortunately, other Autry scholars—both professional and amateur—helped to fill the void left by Alex Gordon, entrusting me with their vast knowledge and their years worth of collecting, researching, and *enjoying* the work of Gene Autry: I will be forever grateful to Jonathan Guyot Smith, whose incisive writing and wealth of knowledge were unfailingly offered to me, including his complete set of original Gene Autry recordings, rare periodicals, his own in-depth writings, his meticulous discographical research, and his extraordinary wit and most enjoyable correspondence—the man uses more catchy metaphors than Carter has liver pills. Others who generously shared their research include Douglas B. Green, aka Riders in the Sky's Ranger Doug, whose masterful *Singing in the Saddle* is highly recommended to anyone wanting the complete history of Western music. Les Gilliam, songwriter and balladeer of Oklahoma, entrusted me with his rare collection of materials and detailed memories and knowledge of Gene's career. The always-cheerful Stanley Rojo went above and beyond to make available to me one of the largest private collections of Autryana, including photographs, artifacts, articles, and recordings—I am truly grateful for his support. Collector Dick Hill generously lent his impressive archive of radio shows and other rare recordings as well as articles from his collection, and Glenn White also provided singular recordings and information. Johnny Western not only delighted me with his detailed memories of working with Gene Autry but also passed along some crucial taped interviews with Gene. Sherry Bond trusted me with her father Johnny Bond's insightful and well-written unpublished manuscript, "Gene Autry, Champion," as well his fascinating scrapbooks. Billy Holcomb and Doug Altheizer also provided me with documents from their years of research and collecting. Wayne Glenn's detective work yielded Autry's Frisco records and other information. And Eleanor and Richard Eaton kindly transported and shared Eleanor's beautifully organized and annotated Autry scrapbooks dating back to the 1940s. The scrapbooks kept for decades by Gene's ardent fans, such as those in the Gene Autry Friendship Club, were absolutely invaluable. Former fan club president Rose Marie Addison and her husband, Ray Addison, helped in many ways. Other collectors who have helped tremendously include Jimmy Glover and Republic Pictures scholar, the late Jack Mathis. For this edition, Jack Duncan's sleuthing turned up info about Nora Autry's first marriage.

Elvin Sweeten, assisted by his late colleagues Bruce Dillman and Willie Johnston, gave me unlimited access to his treasure trove of research materials, scrapbooks, photos, recordings, and artifacts housed at the Gene Autry Oklahoma Museum. The sudden passing of Western scholar and writer Bruce Dillman leaves another void in the realm of Autry scholarship. Those in Tioga, Texas, who presciently documented the remembrances of Gene's schoolmates and celebrated their native son, particularly Char Gordon Brown and Laura Johnson, and Sue Harrison and the folks in Kenton, Ohio, at the Kenton Gene Autry Days Festival, Chamber of Commerce, and Kenton Historical Society also helped in many ways. These institutions and the hardworking folks there work tirelessly to keep Gene Autry's history alive, and they deserve not only my thanks but that of all Autry fans.

For several years, I became a near-fixture at the Country Music Hall of Fame and Museum Research Center and Library, in Nashville, whose senior historian John Rumble made available to me precious recordings and transcripts of interviews with numerous Autry colleagues. His own expertise on the life and career of Fred Rose was also a boon to the book. Former librarian Dawn Oberg went above and beyond to provide me with a myriad of research materials, and Jay Orr, Michael Gray, Alan Stoker, and former staffer Daniel Cooper also helped in many ways. *Tulsa World* researcher Keith Binning, through his tireless efforts, uncovered a missing piece of very important information, among other gems. Sony/BMG librarian Tom Tierney was also a godsend, as were the staffs at research centers located at the Lyndon B. Johnson Presidential Library and Archive, the National Cowgirl Museum and Hall of Fame, the National Cowboy Museum and Hall of Fame, and at public libraries in Chicago; Tulsa, Oklahoma; Columbus, Ohio; Rome, Georgia; and Phoenicia, New York. Music scholars Nolan Porterfield, Charles Wolfe, Robert K. Oermann, and Ronnie Pugh were all generous with their time and their research.

Those who gave their precious time and retrieved detailed memories—in a few cases, going back eighty years!—deserve to be named here (and sadly, some have passed on since our interviews): Veda Autry Coppola's daughters Nora Coppola and Giovanna Dal Ponte; Wilma Autry Gleissner's daughters Kirsten Gleissner and Vesta "Vicki" Gleissner; Ina Kay and Don Leffler, Pauline Autry, Gerald Autry, A. C. Lyles, the late Alex Gordon; Bernard Solomon, Jimmy Hawkins, Betty Hawkins, Beverly Long Moss, Bobbie "Nudie" Cohn, Bob Reynolds, Carol Adams, Charlene "Char" Renfro Brown, Cheryl Rogers-Barnett, Larry Barnett, Dale Evans, Dusty Rogers, Stephen Burnette, Dick Jones, Virginia MacPhail, Dorothy Phillips Bowman, Doug Green, Doug Lemmon, Dwight Yoakam, Marty Stuart, Willie Nelson, Johnny Cash, Waylon Jennings,

Kris Kristofferson, Manuel, Eddy Arnold and Tommy Overstreet (thanks to Barry Mazor!), Elena Verdugo, Laura Tipton, Ellen Keene, Elvin Sweeten, Bruce Dillman, Les Gilliam, Willie Johnston, Rose Marie and Ray Addison, Lucille Beckstead Major, Jim Ryan, Fred Martin, Jerry Scoggins, Terrie Davis, Kerry Buttram Galgano, John Buttram, Zella Fuller, Dick Hill, Glenn White, Gloria Henry, Les Paul, Russ Paul, Mrs. Joe Knight, Helen Paul, Hank Thompson, Maxine Hansen, Karla Buhlman, Stan Schneider, James Austin, Sue Veluzat, Lawrence Cohn, Jimmie Dale Gilmore, James Hilliard, Joanne Hale, Monte Hale, Bill Hale, James Nottage, Jim Shoulders, Joe Johnson, Johnny Western, John Rumble, Sherry Bond, Linda Wakely, Deanna Wakely, Jonathan Guyot Smith, Charles Wolfe, Nolan Porterfield, Boyd Magers, Juanita Cotner, Glen Campbell, Wanda Jackson, Johnny Grant, Iris Stout, Jerry Wexler, Seymour Stein, Patty Dunn Mayes, Sabina Marquez, Sky Corbin, Tommy Howard, Stanley Kemp, Mrs. Kemp, Billy Holcomb, Dale Berry, William "Flash" Gordon—and most important, Jackie Autry, who gave me hours of her time, and the Singing Cowboy himself—I will be forever grateful for having the opportunity to conduct one of Gene's final interviews.

Others who conducted precious interviews over the years with Gene and his associates generously made them available to me or to Gene Autry's office: Thanks go to Petrine Mitchum, Kenneth Baugham, Ronald L. Davis, Bob Birchard, and Barry Mazor. Ed Kahn and other members of the John Edwards Memorial Foundation collected wonderful interviews with Art Satherley and early Autry associates, which are now housed at the University of North Carolina, Chapel Hill—many thanks. John Rumble, Douglas Green, and the other oral historians associated with the Country Music Hall of Fame and Museum also got priceless interviews. A special thank you to ace detective Maxine Hansen, who helped to track down and interview numerous members of the Autry and Ozment families, including Winifred Johnson, Don Heflin, Vel McAllister, Phyllis Engstrom, and Linda Thornsberry, as well as conduct oral histories with many of Gene's colleagues and friends.

The following individuals also helped in various ways: Willie Nelson, Mark Rothbaum, Izzy Young, Mark Loete, Carolyn Aguayo at KTLA, Tim Mead of the California Angels, Sue and Renauld Veluzat, Vincent Guerriero, Rosalie Howard, Debra Mosner, Mrs. Joe Knight, Mary Alice Shaughnessy, Gregg Geller, Steve Berkowitz, Jim Eigo, Mick Oakleaf and Sue Lashley, Baker Rorick, Andy Schwartz, Ellen Nygaard, Shawn Dahl, Tyler Beard, Mary Bassel, Parke Puterbaugh, Tim Hamblin, Jim Marshall, Jo Rae Dimenno, Brenda Colliday, Nancy Breslow, Cary Mansfield, Flo Sweeten, Pat Riley, Dave Hoekstra, Amy Hoban, Bill Sellars, Anthony DeCurtis, Mike Buhlman, Mellon Tytell, Alanna Nash, Paul Kingsbury, Joe Specht, Kevin Coffey, Neila Brenke, Richard Weize, Sam Rayburn Archive, Starr Gennet Foundation's Elizabeth Surles, Aurora Historical Society's John Jaros, Brigham Young University Archives' James D'Arc; and all those who provided me with accommodations and hospitality during my many travels: Amy Hoban, Fats Kaplin and Kristi Rose, Trine Mitchum, Mary Bassel, John McCormick, Bob Oermann and Mary Bufwack, Katy K, John and Ann Buttram, Terrie Davis, Deb O'Nair, and Betsy and Bill Abel.

My always-helpful transcriber Judy Whitfield turned stacks and stacks of audiocassettes into hundreds of pages of transcripts. The talented members of my writers group—Laura Claridge, Richard Hoffman, John Milward, and former member Sue

Erikson Bloland—were the first to read this manuscript and provided their expert editorial suggestions, not to mention moral support, when I needed them most.

Finally, I could not have written this book without the love and support of my loved ones and friends. I only wish that some of my greatest supporters at the outset were here to hold this book in their hands: my parents Martha and Alvis George, my grandmother Brownie George, and my Aunt Frances Spratt. My loving husband, Robert Burke Warren, and our incredible son, Jack, made many sacrifices to help me accomplish this task. They were my greatest cheerleaders and gave me the encouragement to go on during the most difficult times. This book is as much theirs as it is mine.

INDEX